THE YALE LIBRARY OF MILITARY HISTORY

Donald Kagan and Dennis Showalter, *Series Editors*

THE
GRAND
STRATEGY OF
CLASSICAL
SPARTA

The Persian Challenge

Paul A. Rahe

Yale UNIVERSITY PRESS

New Haven and London

Published with assistance from the Kingsley Trust Association Publication Fund
established by the Scroll and Key Society of Yale College.

Published with assistance from the Mary Cady Tew Memorial Fund.

The prologue is adapted from *Republics Ancient and Modern:
Classical Republicanism and the American Revolution,* by Paul A. Rahe.
Copyright © 1992 by the University of North Carolina Press.
Used by permission of the publisher. www.uncpress.unc.edu.

Yale University Press books may be purchased in quantity for
educational, business, or promotional use. For information,
please e-mail sales.press@yale.edu (U.S. office) or
sales@yaleup.co.uk (U.K. office).

Designed by James J. Johnson.
Maps by Bill Nelson.

Set in Minion Roman and Trajan Pro types by
Integrated Publishing Solutions.
Printed in the United States of America.

Library of Congress Control Number: 2015940163
ISBN 978-0-300-11642-7 (cloth : alk. paper)

A catalogue record for this book is available from the British Library.

This paper meets the requirements of ANSI/NISO Z39.48–1992 (Permanence of Paper).

10 9 8 7 6 5 4 3 2 1

James Joseph Rahe

Battles are the principal milestones in secular history. Modern opinion resents this uninspiring truth, and historians often treat the decisions in the field as incidents in the dramas of politics and diplomacy. But great battles, won or lost, change the entire course of events, create new standards of values, new moods, new atmospheres, in armies and in nations, to which all must conform.

WINSTON S. CHURCHILL

Contents

Maps

Introduction

A Clash of Civilizations

I N 1846, shortly after the first two volumes of George Grote's monumental *History of Greece* appeared, John Stuart Mill penned for the *Edinburgh Review* an essay discussing them both. In it, he observed,

> The interest of Grecian history is unexhausted and inexhaustible. As a mere story, hardly any other portion of authentic history can compete with it. Its characters, its situations, the very march of its incidents, are epic. It is an heroic poem, of which the personages are peoples. It is also, of all histories of which we know so much, the most abounding in consequences to us who now live. The true ancestors of the European nations (it has been well said) are not those from whose blood they are sprung, but those from whom they derive the richest portion of their inheritance. The battle of Marathon, even as an event in English history, is more important than the battle of Hastings. If the issue of that day had been different, the Britons and the Saxons might still have been wandering in the woods.

There is only one thing that can be said in just criticism of Mill's remarks, and it is that he left out something altogether essential: to wit, that the engagement at Marathon, important though it may have been, was a mere skirmish in comparison to the series of battles that took place a decade or more thereafter—in places such as Thermopylae, Artemisium, Salamis, Plataea, and Mycale.

Two thousand five hundred years ago, the Greeks living in the Balkan peninsula and on the adjacent islands in the Aegean were puzzling over the danger that they had dodged a handful of years earlier when the Athenians had unexpectedly massacred the Persian footsoldiers at Marathon, and they were contemplating the future as well. For, as the more astute among them understood, it was perfectly possible that the barbarians might return—this time with a much larger force.

This was a possibility well worthy of contemplation. Achaemenid Persia was the largest empire hitherto known to man. Even by much later standards, it must be judged exceedingly grand. It encompassed the civilized world west of the Gobi desert almost in its entirety. It counted among its subjects something like two-fifths of the human race—a greater proportion than any empire before or since. From its Sumerian, Akkadian, Babylonian, Hittite, Assyrian, Elamite, Urartian, and Median predecessors in the Near East, it had inherited an apparatus of power projection and domination that these despotic polities had articulated gradually by a process of trial and error over a period almost as long as the two and a half millennia separating the era of its dominion from us. Moreover, the Great Kings of Persia had devised improvements of their own—collecting tribute on a scale hitherto unknown and spurring a maritime military revolution that enabled them to project power over great distances by land and sea as no previous ruler had ever done—and their morale was sustained by the conviction that the Wise Lord Ahura Mazda, greatest of gods and creator of the universe, had chosen them to bring order, beauty, prosperity, and happiness to a world in commotion, afflicted with every species of conflict, ugliness, and misery. For Achaemenid Persia, the attempt to conquer Hellas was no ordinary war. It was divinely ordained. It was what would later be called a *jīhad*.

Even after Marathon, no sane person would have supposed that the tiny cities of Hellas—only two of them capable of fielding more than ten thousand heavily armored men—had a chance in a contest with a monarch who, with considerable justice, styled himself the King of Kings. But, as it turned out, they won nonetheless. David not only defeated Goliath. He did so in a fashion that precluded the barbarian's return.

This book tells that story. It describes a clash of civilizations in which liberty successfully withstood the assault of despotism and a collection of diminutive and impoverished self-governing cities defeated one of the greatest empires the world has ever known. It describes that clash, moreover, as it has never before been described—from the perspective of Lacedaemon, the remarkable city around which the victorious coalition formed. In 480 and 479 B.C., had it not been for the Spartans, resistance to the Persian juggernaut would have been nonexistent or ineffective. They and they alone possessed the prestige required for instilling confidence in the Hellenes living in and outside the Peloponnesus. They and they alone could take the lead—and this, in magnificent fashion, they did, as we will have soon occasion to observe.

This volume, the first in a projected trilogy focused on the conduct of diplomacy and war by ancient Sparta, is part of a larger attempt to see the Lacedaemonians whole. In the Prologue—which restates in abbreviated form with minimal annotation the conclusions that I argue for at length in the companion volume, *The Spartan Regime*—I first describe their peculiar way of life, the mode of fighting they preferred, and their form of government, the first in human history to embody a system of balances and checks. Then, I trace their gradual articulation of an ingenious grand strategy designed to provide for the defense of Lacedaemon and the way of life that it fostered.

In the remainder of this book, I examine at length and in detail the manner in which the Lacedaemonians coped with Achaemenid Persia—a power that posed a challenge both military and moral in no way anticipated in the grand strategy the Spartans had initially devised. If, then, in the Prologue, I sketch the Lacedaemonian polity as a political regime at rest, in these later chapters I seek to show it in motion—prudently adjusting its grand strategy to unexpected developments thrown up by a larger geopolitical environment itself always in motion and never at rest. Throughout, I take as my subject the remarkable qualities of character and judgment fostered at Sparta that caused their fellow Hellenes and men of later times to regard them with wonder and awe.

This book is meant to throw light not only on ancient Lacedaemon; its first great adversary, Achaemenid Persia; and its chief ally, Athens. It is also intended as an invitation to re-envisage late archaic Greek history from a Spartan perspective, and I hope as well that it will turn out to be a contribution to the study of politics, diplomacy, and war as such. As I argue elsewhere, and try to demonstrate obliquely here by way of my narrative, one cannot hope to understand the diplomatic and martial interaction of polities if one focuses narrowly on their struggle for power. Every polity seeks to preserve itself, to be sure; and in this sense all polities really are akin. But there are also, I argue, moral imperatives peculiar to particular regimes; and, if one's aim is to understand what has happened in the past and is apt to take place in the future, these cannot be dismissed and ostentatiously swept aside or simply ignored. Indeed, if one abstracts entirely from these imperatives—if one treats

Sparta, Achaemenid Persia, and Athens or, for that matter, the United States, Russia, China, and Iran simply as "state actors," equivalent and interchangeable, in the manner advocated by the proponents of realpolitik—one will miss much of what is going on.

Wearing blinders of such a sort can, in fact, be quite dangerous. For, if policy makers were to operate in this fashion in analyzing politics among nations in their own time, they would all too often lack foresight—both with regard to the path likely to be taken by the country they serve and with regard to those likely to be followed by its rivals and allies. As I intimate time and again in this study, in thinking about foreign affairs and in pondering diplomacy, intelligence, military strength, and its economic foundations, one must always acknowledge the primacy of domestic policy.

The Grand Strategy of Classical Sparta

Map 1. Mainland Greece

Prologue

A Regime and Its Grand Strategy

The greatest inconvenience associated with my endeavor is that here one sees men who resemble us almost in nothing, who seem to us to be outside of nature—perhaps as much because we are in that state ourselves as because they are in fact there. Their crimes inspire in us horror. Sometimes their virtues themselves make us shiver. Because we are weak and pusillanimous in good times and in bad, everything that bears a certain character of force and vigor seems to us impossible. The incredulity that we parade is the work of our cowardice rather than that of our reason.

—JEAN-JACQUES ROUSSEAU

IF, in times of trouble, the Hellenes far and wide looked to Lacedaemon for leadership, there was a reason.[1] Sparta was a *pólıs,* but she was no ordinary *pólıs,* and everyone knew it. She possessed resources—moral, political, and military—that, in the late archaic period constituted by the sixth and early fifth centuries of the pre-Christian era which forms the focus of this book, no other Greek city could even hope to match. Herodotus of Halicarnassus, the earliest surviving writer to have described from an anthropological perspective the *nómoı*—the mores, manners, customs, and laws—of Lacedaemon, called her form of government and way of life a *kósmos:* a beautiful, elegantly ordered whole. This is what it was. For, although Sparta had once apparently been characterized by disorder and lawlessness [*kakonomía*], already in the seventh century she was celebrated for her orderliness and her embodiment of the rule of law [*eunomía*].[2] This *eunomía* was a consequence of Lacedaemon's acquisition of what the Greeks in and after Herodotus' time called a *polıteía*—which is to say, rules defining citizenship, the city's form of government, her constitution, ruling order [*políteuma*], regimen, and regime.

There was, to be sure, more to a *polıteía* or political regime than a set of rules. One acute ancient observer defined it broadly as "the one way of life of a whole *pólis*." Another in the same spirit dubbed it "the city's soul."[3] In one passage of *The Politics*, Aristotle suggests that it is the provision of a common education [*paideía*]—and nothing else—that turns a multitude into a unit and constitutes it as a *pólis*; in another, he indicates that it is the *politeía* which defines the *pólis* as such. Though apparently in contradiction, these two statements are in fact equivalent—for, as the peripatetic recognized, man is an imitative animal, the example we set is far more influential than what we say, and it is the "distribution and disposition of offices and honors [*táxis tôn archôn*]" constituting the *políteuma* of a given polity that is the most effective educator therein.[4] If Sparta differed from other cities, as she surely did, it was because her *politeía* possessed a coherence and a clear-cut orientation largely absent elsewhere. It was this coherence that made her a *kósmos* and endowed her with *eunomía*—and it was with an eye to safeguarding the *politeía* which constituted Lacedaemon's "soul" and gave rise to "the one way of life" of the whole *pólis* that the Spartans by a process of trial and error gradually articulated a grand strategy for the city's defense.[5]

The Spartan Regimen

Ancient Lacedaemon was a political community. It was not a state. With only trivial exceptions, the *póleis* of Hellas had no state apparatus: no bureaucracies, no magistrates blessed with long tenure, no professional armies. It was futile to try to distinguish the governors from the governed; the *pólis* itself depended on the identity of soldier and civilian; and the farmer had the right to own land solely by virtue of his status as a citizen. The differentiation of roles which the modern distinction between state and society presupposes simply did not exist.

Moreover, the ancient Hellenic republic was, as James Madison would later observe, "a pure democracy . . . consisting of a small number of citizens, who assemble and administer the government in person." The *pólis* really was, as the Greeks often remarked, the men. In one poem, Alcaeus of Mytilene contended that "warlike men are a city's tower of defense." In another, which survives only as paraphrased by later authors, he played variations on the same theme:

> Neither stone blocks
> Nor ships' timbers

> Nor even the carpenter's art
> Can make a *pólis.*
> But where there are men
> Who know how to preserve themselves
> There one finds walls and a city as well.[6]

Because they shared the poet's conviction, the Hellenes never spoke in an abstract way of the deeds of Athens, Corinth, Megara, and Lacedaemon. As the public inscriptions assert, the real actors were the Athenians, the Corinthians, the Megarians, and the Lacedaemonians. And when the Greeks did speak of the *polis* as such; when they alluded to Athens, Corinth, Megara, or Lacedaemon by name as a political community; and, strikingly, even when they spoke of one these *póleis* as their fatherland [*patrís*], they employed nouns feminine in gender, personifying the community as a woman to whom they were devoted (and so, to bring this home to my readers, I with some frequency use the feminine pronoun to refer to Sparta and other Greek cities here).

Of all of these ancient Hellenic political communities, Sparta came the closest to giving absolute primacy to the common good. She did this—as a number of ancient observers noted—by turning the city into a camp, the *pólis* into an army, and the citizen into a soldier. She did it by taking the institutions and practices embryonic in every *pólis* and developing them to an extreme only imagined elsewhere. Except with the express permission of the magistrates, her citizens were prohibited from traveling abroad and foreigners were forbidden to visit Lacedaemon. As a consequence, she was able to exert an almost absolute control over the circumstances which shaped her citizens' lives. Everything that she did in this virtually self-contained world was aimed at a single end: at nurturing what Lord Macaulay would later refer to as "that intense patriotism which is peculiar to members of societies congregated in a narrow space."[7] This radical fidelity to the principles particular to the *pólis* as a species of political community explains why a city so rarely imitated was so universally admired.[8]

With the danger of faction in mind, Sparta took great care to insulate the polity from the influence of the marketplace. Fearful that competition for wealth would set the members of her *políteuma* at odds, she coined no money and employed flat iron ingots instead. Eager to prevent a differentiation of interests, she barred her citizens from engaging in commerce and prohibited their practice of the mechanical arts. Nowhere were the latter held in less esteem. Lacedaemon even banned visits to the commercial *agorá* by citizens

under the age of thirty. The Spartans had but one purpose in life: to gain a reputation for valor. From childhood on, they trained to secure victory in battle
by land.

To eliminate those unfit for this endeavor, the city practiced infanticide,
subjecting the newborn to a careful scrutiny and exposing to the elements
those who were deformed or otherwise lacking in vigor. To enable those who
survived this initial test to pursue in due course the chief goal set by the regime, the city authorized a grant to every citizen of a *klêros*—an equal allotment of public land—and servants called helots to work it.[9] The labor of this
depressed class made it possible for the *Spartíatai*—the Spartiates or Spartans,
as we would now say—to devote their time and efforts to mastering the martial arts and to gaining that confidence which fortifies civil courage. While the
ordinary Greek city was a community of smallholders and gentleman farmers, Lacedaemon was a legion of men-at-arms.

She was also an aristocracy of masters, a city of seigneurs, a common-
wealth of leisured gentlemen—who could be described as *kaloì kagathoí*: men
both noble and good. The Spartans called themselves *hoi hómoioi*: "the equals,
the similars, the peers." In a sense, they were equal. By means of the land
grants, the *pólis* abolished the distinction, vitally important elsewhere, between those with land and those without. At Lacedaemon, some of the soil
did remain in private hands and there was an unequal distribution of property. But, in late archaic Sparta the gap between rich and poor was not profound. As men of property, the Spartans had the same interests.

To encourage *homónoia*—unanimity, solidarity, and likemindedness regarding the advantageous, the just, and the good—Lacedaemon exercised
close control over the education of children and the daily comportment of the
citizens. The rich and the poor grew up together, subject to the same regimen.
Thereafter, they took their meals together in squads of about fifteen at the
common mess [*sussitía*], partaking of the simple fare day after day; and it was
there, with their "tentmates [*súskēnoi*]," that the "young men of Sparta," the
néoi under forty-five, bunked at night.

At Lacedaemon, the giving of dowries was strictly forbidden. But, thanks
to the continued existence of private property, some women were able to inherit. In consequence, the magistrates were empowered to fine those who paid
more attention to opulence than to virtue in matters of love and marriage. To
the same end, there were severe sumptuary laws to deny the great families the
public display and use of their riches. An exception was made for the breed-

ing and racing of horses. But the ordinary citizen was allowed free use of the helots, horses, and hounds of his wealthier fellows-in-arms. As many ancient observers emphasized, the Spartiates shared a common way of life.

The Helots

Those with scanty resources apart from the civic allotment may still have felt envy, as human beings are apt to do. But, if so, it was a jealousy dampened by fear. The helots who tilled the soil were both a precondition for the Spartan way of life and a permanent threat to the city's survival. The "old helots," descended from the ancient Achaean stock ascendant in the Mycenaean age, resided near their masters within Laconia in the southeastern Peloponnesus and gave every appearance of being docile. In time of need, some from among them were even freed and recruited as heavy infantrymen into the army of Lacedaemon. To outsiders, they sometimes seemed broken in spirit. But— when the opportunity presented itself—many of these Laconian helots proved to be fully capable of rebellion. Aristotle rightly speaks of them as a hostile force "continuously lying in wait for misfortune" to strike.[10]

In this regard they were by no means alone: for, throughout much of the archaic and nearly all of the subsequent classical period, the Spartans controlled not just Laconia, but the neighboring province of Messenia in the southwestern Peloponnesus as well. The latter region was fertile and exceedingly well watered but extremely difficult of access, shut off as it was from Laconia's Eurotas valley by the rugged peaks of Mount Taygetus. There, where the Spartans themselves were few, the helots were numerous, conscious of their identity as a separate people, bitterly hostile to their masters, and prone to revolt.

The danger posed by the helots of Laconia and perhaps even that posed by those in Messenia would perhaps have been manageable had Lacedaemon lacked foes abroad, but unfortunately for her this was not the situation. Not far from Sparta's northeastern border, her ancient enemy Argos, a large and powerful city, stood poised, watching and waiting to take advantage of any disaster that might strike. To make matters worse, in the early archaic period, the Arcadians, just to the north of Messenia and Laconia, were allied with Lacedaemon's Argive foe and ever ready to lend a helping hand should the helots revolt.

Even in the best of times, the helots of Laconia and Messenia appear to have outnumbered their masters by a margin of, some say, four but quite possibly even seven to one; and in an emergency, the Spartans could never be fully confident that their allies within Laconia and Messenia would rally to their cause. If the "dwellers-about [*períoikoi*]"—the class of non-Spartiate Lacedaemonians who resided in the subject villages of these two provinces and retained in privilege a measure of local autonomy—were generally loyal, it was chiefly out of fear.

Piety, *Paideía,* and Pederasty

As a consequence of the community's strategic situation, fear was also the fundamental Spartan passion. It was fear that explained why Lacedaemon was notoriously slow to go to war; it was fear that accounted for the remarkable caution she displayed on the field of battle. This omnipresent fear lay behind her flagrant inability in matters of state to distinguish the dictates of interest from the biddings of honor, and it was fear that made the distrust and deceit that governed her relations with other communities pronounced and glaring. Fear, the great equalizer, rendered the Spartan regime conservative, stable, and —despite the presence of a wealthy, landed aristocracy—socially harmonious. The Spartans were well aware of this fact. As Plutarch remarks, they established a temple to *Phóbos*—not to ward off panic in battle, but because they recognized that fear held the polity together.[11] The Spartiates had to be friends: as members of a garrison community, they desperately needed one another.

This awareness of need the Spartans magnified by sentiment. Because piety was understood to be the foundation of patriotism, citizens were from an early age imbued with a fear of the gods so powerful that it distinguished them from their fellow Greeks. Reverence and dread came easily to a people living in fear. More effectively than any other Greek city, Sparta used superstition to reinforce that total obedience to the law which constituted civic virtue and that steadfastness in battle for which the Lacedaemonians were famous. It is by no means fortuitous that the most important unit in the Spartan army was called an *enōmatía*. As the word's etymology suggests, this platoon of forty or so men was a "sworn band" united by a solemn oath binding its members to remain in formation if they did not wish to bring down on their own heads the wrath of the gods.

Superstition was by no means the only force employed. At Lacedaemon, civic *paideía* reigned supreme. There, in keeping with the logic underpinning

the city's *polıteía,* the Spartiates instilled in future members of the city's *políteuma* the same opinions and fostered in them the same passions by means of
the *agōgé,* their much-celebrated system of education and moral formation.
When the son of a citizen reached the age of seven, he was taken from his
mother, classified as a *paîs,* and added to a herd of boys his own age. When he
returned home thereafter, he returned as a visitor: his true home was to be the
community of his contemporaries. In this new home, he would learn to think
of himself not as an individual, nor as a member of a particular household,
but as a part of the community. Apart from that community, he was nothing.

In the herd, the boys were subjected to a regimen of exercise interspersed
with sessions dedicated to learning the communal dances, the poetry, and
the songs of Sparta. Because physical stamina and an ability to march to the
cadence of the flute were required for victory in hoplite warfare, the boys were
encouraged to compete in athletics, in mock battles, in dancing, and musi-
cal contests. Because endurance and craft were necessary for success when
on campaign, they were inured to pain and hardship and kept on short rations; for additional sustenance, they were forced to steal, and those who were
caught were severely punished.

In the late archaic period, the young men who survived the *agōgé* and
became Spartiates were a highly select group. On their journey to manhood,
they had been subjected to a formal magisterial scrutiny at regular intervals:
initially, at birth; then, probably, as boys at seven and twelve; again, as youths
at eighteen; and finally, at twenty, when they joined the young warriors called
hoi néoi. As a boy approached adolescence and, then, the threshold of manhood, his physical training became more and more rigorous and the tests of
his strength and courage more and more severe. The final test, the period of
concealment [*krupteía*], appears to have taken place when he was a youth
approaching his twentieth birthday. For a full year, the young man withdrew
from the community and was thrown back entirely on his own resources.
Armed with a dagger, he hid in the wilds during the day, only to emerge at
night to secure provisions by theft and to kill any helots found roaming about
after curfew. The *krupteía* helped head off servile rebellion and functioned as
a rite of passage marking the boy's initiation into manhood.

His performance in this last ordeal might well determine the young man's
fate: he could become a full citizen and join the *hómoioi* constituting the Lacedaemonian *políteuma* if and only if he submitted to the Spartan regimen, successfully completed the *agōgé,* and was accepted into a *sussıtía.* It was, it appears,

only under these circumstances that he could actually take up possession of the allotment of land reserved for him shortly after his birth and begin to collect the rent intended for his support. Those judged to have fallen short in the *agōgḗ* were not just denied entrance into a *sussitía* and excluded thereby from the august ranks of "the equals, the similars, the peers." They were deprived of what was called "the ancient portion [*archaîa moîra*]," and they were pointedly singled out and referred to, ever after, as *hupomeíones* or "inferiors."

In general, when a boy became a man and joined the *néoi*, his *sussitía* supplanted the herd as his true home. His ties to his parents, his wife, and his children were intended to be weak: he had left his mother's care and had been removed from his father's authority when he was seven; and although he was expected to take a spouse while still a *néos* and was subjected to civic disabilities and to rituals of harassment and humiliation if he failed to do so, he would not as a husband then reside with his wife. During the initial period of their marriage, shame and dread governed the comportment of the couple. The *néos* visited his bride's bedroom in secret at night, and all their relations were conducted under the cover of darkness. The Spartan might beget a child. But at least until he had himself graduated from the ranks of the *néoi* and, at forty-five, joined the class of "older men [*presbúteroi*]," he would not live within his own household; and even then his sons would depart from that household at a tender age. As Plutarch remarked, the institution of marriage existed at Sparta solely for the procreation of children, and the practices associated with it presupposed on the part of the husband "a strong and unadulterated lack of passion [*apatheía*] with respect to his wife." It is easy to see why Josephus described the Spartan regime as unsociable and accused the Lacedaemonians of slighting matrimony.[12]

The tendency evident in these arrangements was exacerbated by the Spartan practice of pederasty. In Lacedaemon, the boys were neither shy nor coy. In fact, when a boy reached the age of twelve, he assumed the role of a beloved [*erṓmenos*], and he aggressively sought out from among the *néoi* and eagerly took as his lover a figure whom the Spartans dubbed an *eispnélas* or "breather-in." From this day on, the man with whom he had made this connection was to be far more than just his sexual partner. He was to be the boy's patron, his protector, and friend. The ultimate purpose of pederasty as an institution was that a young man's loyalty be fixed neither on the parents he had left, nor on the wife and son he so rarely saw, but rather on his *eispnélas* and *erṓmenos*. In normal circumstances, both were members of his *sussitía*; and as a consequence, the two would usually be stationed in his immediate vicinity, if not on either side of him in the battle formation. It is not fortuitous that the Spartans customarily sacrificed to Eros before drawing up their phalanx. They apparently thought that victory and their safety would depend on the love uniting the men about to be posted.

Music, Poetry, and War

Music was central to the *paideía* underpinning the Spartan *politeía*. This phenomenon deserves respectful attention, for it would be a mistake to underestimate the integrating force of the choral performances, the dancing, and the other public rituals that marked the Carneia, the Gymnopaidiai, the Hyacinthia, and the other great festivals of Sparta. The ancient commentators credited music with warding off *stásis* and with infusing into the city the *eunomía* that gave it its strength. It also played a role in preparing the Spartans for combat. Of the examples of Spartan poetry surviving in his own time, Plutarch remarked, "They were for the most part eulogies of those who had died on Sparta's behalf, celebrating their happiness; censure of those who had fled in battle, depicting their painful and unfortunate lives; and professions and boasts of virtue of a sort proper for the different age-groups."[13]

When on campaign, the Spartans would chant the verses of Tyrtaeus as they marched. In the evening after dinner, they would first raise the paean, and then each, in turn, would sing something by this poet—with the polemarch acting as judge and awarding extra meat to the victor. The poetry Tyrtaeus composed in the seventh century did much to reinforce the exaggerated piety that was the foundation of Spartan morale and to instill an ethos conducive to *eunomía*. His principal subject, however, was not peace, but war. In one of his hortatory elegies, he drew the attention of his compatriots to the manner in which their well-being depended on the fate of the city itself.

It is a noble thing for a brave man to die,
Falling in the front ranks, doing battle for the fatherland.
But for a man to forsake his city and his rich fields
And to go begging is of all things the most grievous
As he wanders with his dear mother and his aged father,
With his small children and his lawful, wedded wife.
For he is hated by those among whom he goes as a suppliant
Yielding to need and loathsome penury;
He disgraces his lineage; he refutes his splendid appearance,
And every dishonor and evil follows in his train.

> Now if no heed is paid to a wandering man
> And neither reverence nor regard nor pity is his,
> Let us then fight with spirit for our land and children
> And let us die, not sparing our lives.

In the young men posted in the formation's front ranks, the poet sought to instill what he called "a spiritedness great and firm." He encouraged them not to
hold life dear as they did battle with the foe; he exhorted them to stand closely
bunched; and he warned them never "to make a start of fear and shameful
flight." There is something splendid, he argued, about the death in battle of a
young man, blessed with the bloom of youth, admired by his fellows and beloved of women. But there is no sight quite as disgraceful and none as horrid
as that of a graybeard fallen in the front ranks, "sprawled on the earth before
the young men, breathing out his life in the dust, and clasping his hands to a
bloodied groin." The Spartan king Leonidas reportedly spoke of Tyrtaeus as "a
poet good for stirring up the young."[14] It is not difficult to see why.

Tyrtaeus' debt to Homer was immense. That much is obvious from his
diction alone. But despite all that he owed his great predecessor, the Spartan poet rejected Homeric precedent and radically altered the heroic ethic.
Tyrtaeus did not glorify that Achilles who had valued his own honor above
the interest of the Achaean host; nor did he celebrate the exploits of Odysseus, "the man of many ways" who wandered through "the cities of many men
and learned their minds." He heaped praise not on the great individual who
sought "to be the best and to excel all others," but on the citizen who never
traveled abroad except on campaign and who fought gamely alongside his
companions in the city's hoplite phalanx.[15]

To make his point in the boldest possible fashion, Tyrtaeus turned to the
mythological tradition. To bring home to his listeners the inadequacy of the
traditional understanding of human excellence, he provided them with a list
of legendary individuals who exhibited qualities and faculties universally admired but who nonetheless performed in a fashion that called into question
the esteem conventionally conferred on those very qualities and faculties. As
the poet indicated in the priamel of his most famous work, there was only
one trait truly worthy of celebration:

> I would not call to mind a man nor relate a tale of him
> Not for the speed of his feet nor for his wrestling skill
> Not if he possessed the stature and force of a Cyclops
> And could outpace Boreas, the North Wind of Thrace

Not if he were more graceful in form than Tithonos
And exceeded Midas and Cinyras in wealth
Not if he were more fully a king than Tantalid Pelops
And possessed the soft-voiced tongue of Adrastus
Not if he had reputation for all but prowess in battle.[16]

Figure 1. Hoplite poised for assault, figurine, formerly part of a bronze vessel, ca. 510–500, found at Dodona (Photograph: bkp Berlin/ Staatliche Museen zu Berlin—Preußischer Kulturbesitz/Johannes Laurentius/Art Resource, NY).

Quickness, agility, brute strength, physical beauty, the golden touch, regal bearing, and even the eloquence evidenced by the poet himself—though men longed for these, they were of little import when distinguished from and compared with the stamina, grit, endurance, and courage required of the Spartan hoplite in war.

As a warrior, the hoplite was distinguished not by the helmet on his head, nor by the greaves, cuirass, or corslet he may have worn—though these all formed part of the standard hoplite panoply. He was set apart, instead, solely by the peculiar shield that he bore. The long thrusting spears that hoplites carried and the short swords to which they resorted when these spears were broken or lost did little to distinguish them from infantrymen of other sorts. Their hallmark was the *aspís;* and, tellingly, the Greeks sometimes thought it sufficient to refer to this shield as the *hóplon,* using for this particular item the generic term for hoplite equipment. It was, after all, the *aspís* that made the hoplite a hoplite.[17] This shield was designed for phalanx warfare, and it was, as Aristotle points out, very nearly "useless" for anything else.[18]

It is easy to see why the *aspís* would be of little use and perhaps even burdensome to an infantryman fighting alone, out in front of the host, in the manner described by Homer in the *Iliad.* The hoplite shield was round and, as the Greeks put it, "hollow" (which is to say, from the perspective of the man bearing it, the *aspís* was concave). It was also roughly three feet in diameter; and, depending largely on whether its core, usually constructed of poplar or willow, was faced with bronze, it could weigh up to twenty pounds. For an isolated individual, a fifteen-pound shield (which was evidently the norm)—borne on his left arm and, when possible, supported at the lip on his left shoulder—was an encumbrance more unwieldy and awkward than we are apt to imagine. In ancient times, as we must with some frequency remind ourselves, human beings were considerably smaller in stature than they are today.

The *aspís* borne by the hoplite had a bronze armband in the center, called a *pórpax,* through which the warrior slipped his left arm, and a leather cord or handle on or near the shield's right rim, called an *antílabḗ,* for him to lay hold of with his left hand. This shield might provide adequate cover for a warrior temporarily stretched out sideways in the manner of a fencer with his left foot forward as he prepared to hurl a javelin or to put his weight behind a spear thrust. But this pose could not long be sustained, for it left him exceedingly vulnerable to being shoved to the right or the left and knocked off his feet. Moreover, the minute he pulled his left foot back for any reason

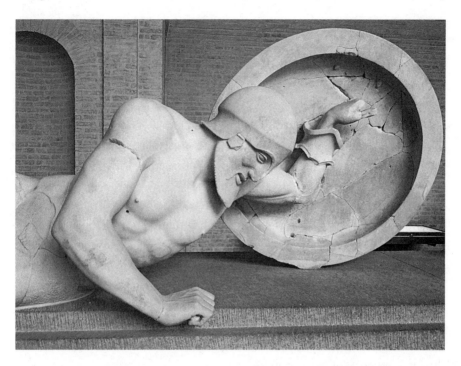

Figure 2. Fallen hoplite with hollow shield and *pórpax* (Trojan warrior), probably Laomedon, situated on the east pediment of the Aphaia temple at Aegina, ca. 505–500 (now in the Staatliche Antikensammlungen und Glyptothek in Munich; Photograph: Daderot, Wikimedia Commons, Published November 2015 under the following license: Creative Commons CCO 1.0 Universal Public Domain Dedication).

or brought his right foot forward while actually hurling the javelin or driving the thrusting spear home, he will have turned willy-nilly to face the enemy; and, when he was in this posture, the *aspís* left the right half of his body unprotected and exposed, and it extended beyond him to the left in a fashion of no use to him as a solo performer. Even if the hoplite ordinarily stood in an oblique position, braced with his legs wide apart and his left foot a bit in advance of his right so that he could rest his shield on his left shoulder, his right side will have been in some measure exposed. As this analysis should suggest, when infantrymen equipped in this fashion were operating on their own, cavalry, light-armed troops, and enemy hoplites in formation could easily make mincemeat of them; and the same was apt to happen when agile light-armed troops equipped with javelins caught hoplites in a situation unsuited to seeking a decision by way of phalanx warfare. The hoplite was, as Euripides contended, "a slave to the military equipment that he bore."[19]

When, however, men equipped with the *aspís* were deployed in a close order in ranks and files on suitable ground, this peculiar shield made each hoplite warrior a defender of the hoplite to his left—for, as Thucydides explains, the *aspís* failed to shield the hoplite's own right side and covered, instead, the right side of the man on his left. It is this fact that explains the logic underpinning a statement attributed by Plutarch to the Spartan king Demaratus to the effect that "men don helmets and breastplates for their own sake, but the *aspís* they take up for the sake of the formation which they and their fellows share."[20]

It is with the integrity of this formation in mind that Tyrtaeus writes, "Each man should treat life as something hateful and hold the black ruin of death as dear as the beams of the sun." It is in this context, with an eye to the soldiers protecting one another by "forming" what he elsewhere calls "a fence of hollow shields," that he emphasizes the need for Sparta's infantrymen "to stand by one another and to march into the van where the fighting is hand to hand." When they do so, he tells us, "Rather few die, and they safeguard the host behind." It is, moreover, with the phalanx in mind that the poet limns this striking portrait of the hoplite warrior:

> Let him take a wide stance and stand up strongly against them,
> digging both heels in the ground, biting his lip with his teeth,
> covering thighs and legs beneath, his chest and his shoulders
> under the hollowed-out protection of his broad shield,
> while in his right hand he brandishes the powerful war-spear,
> and shakes terribly the crest high above his helm.
> Our man should be disciplined in the work of the heavy fighter,
> and not stand out from the missiles when he carries a shield,
> but go right up and fight at close quarters and, with his long spear
> or short sword, thrust home and strike his enemy down.

"Placing foot next to foot," Tyrtaeus concludes, "pressing shield against shield, bringing crest near crest, helm near helm, and chest near chest, let him battle it out with the man [opposite], grasping the handle of his sword or the long spear."[21]

To support the revolutionary new morality required by a species of warfare itself relatively new in his own time, Tyrtaeus introduced a novel, fully political standard for measuring the merit of men. No longer would the Spartans assess a man's status by anything other than his contribution to the welfare of the *pólis* as a whole. After dismissing those qualities which were so widely thought to be virtues, the poet went on to explain,

Figure 3. Clash of phalanxes represented on the Protocorinthian olpe known as the Chigi Vase, ca. 640 (at Museo Nazionale Etrusco di Villa Giulia 22679; from Ernest Pfuhl, *Malerei und Zeichnung der Griechen* [Munich: Bruckmann, 1923], pl. 59).

> For no one ever becomes a man good in war
> Unless he has endured the sight of the blood and slaughter,
> Stood near, and lunged for the foe.
> This is virtue, the finest prize achieved among human kind,
> The fairest reward that a young man can carry off.
> This is a common good, shared by the entire city and people,
> When a man stands his ground, remains in the front ranks
> Relentlessly, altogether forgetful of disgraceful flight,
> Nurturing a steadfast, patient spirit and soul,
> And heartening with words the man posted alongside.
> This is a man become good in war:
> With a sudden attack, he turns the rugged phalanx
> Of the enemy host, sustaining with zeal the wave of assault.[22]

Tyrtaeus was the supreme poet of civil courage. To reinforce his celebration of bravery in the city's cause, Tyrtaeus added encouragement and an admonition —for, in the end, justice was to be done: the brave would be rewarded and the coward, punished. Even death would lose its sting.

What made this achievement possible was not the activity of the poet in calling to mind the feats of the heroes. Here, too, Tyrtaeus broke with Homer. If death was to rule no more, it was because public memory was guaranteed by the continued existence of the *pólis* itself. While ordinary Spartans were buried in a manner both simple and frugal, wrapped in the purple cloak worn in battle and crowned with olive leaves, the city's champions were treated like those honored in its hero cults. As Tyrtaeus puts it,

And he who falls in the front ranks and gives up his spirit
So bringing glory to the town, the host, and his father
With many a wound in his chest where the spear from in front
Has been thrust through the bossy shield and breastplate:
This man they will lament with a grievous sense of loss
The young and the old and the city entire.
His tomb and his children will be noted among human kind
And the children of his children and his lineage after them.
Never will his shining glory perish, and never his name,
For he will be an immortal though under the earth, the man
Who excels all others in standing his ground in the fight
For his children and land, he whom the raging Wargod destroys.[23]

Tyrtaeus then devoted the final ten lines of this remarkable poem to recounting the honors that were customarily showered on those brave men fortunate enough to survive. By the end, it has become evident that courage in battle confers on a man all of the advantages normally attributed to the qualities and faculties conventionally admired.

But if he eludes the doom of death, which lays bodies out,
And, conquering, seizes by spearpoint the shining object of prayer
All will honor him, the young together with the old,
And he will enter Hades after enjoying many delights
Having grown old in distinction among the men of the town.
Nor will any wish him harm, denying him reverence or right.
And all—the young, those his own age, and those
Older than he—will yield him place on the seats.
This virtue a man should attempt with whole heart to attain,
Straining for the heights and never ceasing from war.[24]

This was a communal poetry fit for the education of citizen-soldiers who would be expected to spend their lives at home in Laconia and to risk them abroad on the city's behalf.

The Spartans committed these and similar verses to memory and recited them about the campfire and while on the march for the same reason that they prepared for combat in ritual fashion by combing out their long hair and donning cloaks of royal purple in such a manner as to terrify and discomfit their foe. Like the wine which the Lacedaemonians customarily imbibed before battle; like the strains of the flute played by men occupying an hereditary office, which accompanied their steady march into combat; and like the paean which they chanted as they approached the enemy phalanx, the songs of Tyrtaeus were an intoxicant intended to reduce tension, dull pain, and make men—at least momentarily—forget the specter of death. With the city's poets in mind, Plutarch suggests, the Spartan king would sacrifice to the Muses at the onset of battle. His purpose was to remind Lacedaemon's warriors to accomplish feats worthy to be remembered by the city in song.[25]

The ancients wondered at this spectacle, and so should we. The first and most important step that anyone can take in attempting to understand it is the recognition that, of all the Greek cities, Sparta went the furthest in promoting civil courage. By giving to every citizen the same opinions, the same passions, and the same interests, her social and economic institutions were intended—as Isocrates, Demosthenes, and Polybius point out—to foster that sense of solidarity and likemindedness which the Greeks called *homónoia*.[26] The distribution of offices and honors stipulated in Lacedaemon's political constitution served precisely the same function.

Governance

Sparta was neither a monarchy nor a democracy. We hear little of court intrigue and even less of demagoguery. The most subtle of the ancient authors described her *politeía* as a mixed regime. According to Aristotle, the two kings [*basileîs*] represented the monarchical element; the council of elders [*gerousía*], the oligarchic element; and the ephorate, the democratic element.[27] In order to secure the consent of the governed, Sparta ensured the participation of every element of the citizen population in the administration of the city; in order to prevent the emergence of an overmighty subject, she employed an elaborate system of balances and checks to restrain her magistrates from excess. These safeguards were essential. The fostering of citizen virtue and the enforcement of the Spartan regimen necessitated the establishment and maintenance of a vigorous inquisitorial tribunal. This could not be accomplished without a concentration of extraordinary power in the hands of Sparta's officials.

The most dangerous element within the Spartan regime was the kingship. Even a cursory glance at the privileges and prerogatives associated with that office is adequate to demonstrate the truth of this proposition. Two Spartiates were not among "the equals." Two held office for life; two escaped the *agōgḗ;* two took their meals outside the barracks. Other Spartiates served in the *gerousía,* but only a king or his regent could serve in that venerable body before his sixtieth year. Other Spartiates sacrificed to the gods, but only a

king or regent could do so year after year on the city's behalf. Other Spartiates commanded troops, but only a king or his regent could normally lead
out the Spartan army and the forces supplied by her allies. Prior to the fifth
century and apparently, as we shall see, for a few years after its beginning, the
two *basileîs* ordinarily shared the command; and when acting in concert, they
could reportedly wage war against any territory they wished. It was a sacrilege
for a Spartiate to resist their authority to do so. As hereditary generals and
priests with life tenure, the Agiad and Eurypontid kings stood out from the
ranks.

In the strict sense, the two kings were not Spartiates at all. Envoys sent
on missions abroad could claim to represent two entities at the same time:
"the Lacedaemonians and the Heraclids from Sparta."[28] Tradition taught that
the Spartiates were Lacedaemonians precisely because they were adherents of
men who traced their ancestry back to Heracles, the son of Zeus. The Athenians and the Arcadians might think of themselves as autochthonous: "always
possessed of the same land," and even "born from the earth." But the Spartans
were acutely aware that they were interlopers in the Peloponnesus, that they
had invaded and seized Laconia by force, and that their servants—the "old
helots" of the province—were descended from the original Achaean stock,
which had ruled Lacedaemon in the epoch described by Homer. As Dorians,
the Spartans had no legitimate place in what was, in fact, an alien land. The
righteousness of their cause and its continued success were founded on the
quasi-feudal relationship binding the citizens to their two kings: for the first
Dorians to call themselves Spartans had purportedly been among the followers of the sons of the old Achaean prince Heracles, and the latter were thought
to have inherited from their illustrious father and to have passed on to their
descendants the right to rule Argos in particular and the Peloponnesus more
generally. As long as their *basileîs* were Heraclids, the Spartans of later times
could rest confident in the legitimacy of their tenure in Laconia and in the
support of the gods. But if they expelled their charismatic kings or counte-
nanced an illegitimate succession, they could expect to suffer the fate which
the gods had reserved for their Dorian neighbors in Messenia. The Spartans
justified their conquest of that province and their reduction of its inhabitants
to a servile condition on the grounds that the Dorians of Messenia had extin-
guished their own claim to the land when they drove out their Heraclid king.
The Spartan conquerors had merely reasserted Heraclid control.

In a community in which military concerns predominate and in which there is a popular element in the constitution, generals—even hereditary generals—are men of great power and influence. A soldier's opportunity to distinguish himself on the field of battle and gain the admiration and support of his comrades depends more often than not on the goodwill of his commander. This was particularly true among the Lacedaemonians. When on campaign, a Spartan king or regent conducted the sacrifices, and he exercised an almost absolute sway: he had the power to appoint his own officers, to issue orders to all and sundry, to send troops wherever he wished, to raise fresh forces, to execute cowards, and even to levy money. No matter what happened, until the army returned home, his word was law.

The two kings possessed other politically important prerogatives as well. One of these privileges was symptomatic of royal preeminence in the making of foreign policy. In antiquity, it was not the practice for a city to maintain resident ambassadors in the polities with which its citizens had frequent dealings. Instead, the Greeks adapted the traditional aristocratic institution of guest-friendship [*xenía*] to serve the needs of the political community as a whole. Ordinarily, the citizens of one community selected from among the citizens of another one or more vice-consuls called *próxenoi* to provide hospitality when they dispatched embassies and, in general, to look after their interests in that particular locality. Here, in typical fashion, Lacedaemonian practice diverged from the norm. The Spartans insisted on regulating and controlling all intercourse with outsiders. They were unwilling to allow foreigners to choose their own representatives from among the citizens of Lacedaemon, and theirs, tellingly, is said to have been the only city in Hellas in the time of Philip of Macedon that was never ruined by treachery on the part of its own citizens. There is evidence suggesting that the two kings also selected those who served as Sparta's *próxenoi* abroad.

In similar fashion, the *basileîs* appointed the four officials known as the *Púthioi*—each naming two to keep the records of the oracles for him and to share his mess. When the city itself wished an oracle from Delphi concerning a given matter, it chose its messenger from among these four men. This practice assured royal predominance in religious matters and made the manipulation of religion for political purposes almost the sole prerogative of the two dyarchs. In a community as traditional and as pious as ancient Lacedaemon, this could have extraordinary consequences. A wily king could use religion to control the city.

At Lacedaemon, two circumstances worked to prevent tyranny—the power of the ephors and the rivalry between the two kings. The Spartan ephors were magistrates of no mean importance. On two different occasions, Cicero compared them with the tribunes of the Roman plebs, suggesting that they were a check on the kings in much the same sense that the tribunes were a check on the consuls at Rome.[29] This does not, however, do them full justice—for the tribunes represented the plebs only; the ephors were chosen from the political community as a whole.

No one is known to have been ephor more than once, which suggests that iteration in office was prohibited; and the board of five held office for only a year. During that year, however, the ephors exercised by majority vote arbitrary, almost unchecked power. It was only at the end of their period in office that they were called to account for their deeds and subjected by their successors to a formal, judicial examination of the sort employed in other Greek cities to guarantee that magistrates remained responsible to the political community.

In the period before that day of reckoning, the ephors played a predominant role in the making and implementing of public policy. They were empowered to summon "the little assembly"—apparently constituted by the board of ephors and the city's *gerousía*—as well as the general assembly of the Spartiates. They could introduce laws, decrees, and declarations of war and peace to the latter through the former; and when the general assembly met— whether on an extraordinary occasion or at the regular monthly time—they decided who would present a particular proposal. One of their number then presided, put the question, and determined whether those shouting for the measure outnumbered those shouting against. It is an indication of their central importance that Xenophon—the ancient writer most intimately familiar with Spartan practice and parlance—thrice ascribes important decisions to "the ephors and assembly." It would not be an exaggeration to say that the ephors governed Sparta with the advice and consent of the *gerousía* and the assembly. Aristotle rightly observes that a magistracy empowered to convene a city's assembly, set its agenda, and preside over it is virtually "authoritative [*kúrios*] within the regime."[30]

The ephors were particularly influential in the sphere of foreign relations. It was within their prerogative to determine when and for how long a foreigner might visit Sparta and a Spartan might go abroad. They ordinarily received embassies, conducted negotiations with foreign powers, and decided when to bring matters before the *gerousía* and assembly. They had influence, if not control, over the appointment of the harmosts who administered communities under Sparta's dominion, and they were competent to issue these officials directives. In time of war or civic emergency, the ephors called up the army, and they determined which age groups were to march. In foreign affairs, there were few functions that these magistrates did not perform—other than serve as Sparta's commanders in the field.

At home, the ephors' chief task—as the title of their office suggests—was oversight. They enforced the sumptuary laws and determined which pieces of music and poetry would be tolerated within the community. They kept tabs on the *agōgḗ,* checking each day to see that the youth observed the regulations regarding clothing and bedding and subjecting them every tenth day to a physical examination. Ultimately, they appointed three outstanding young men who had reached their prime to select from among their fellow *néoi* and command the three hundred *hippeîs* that formed the royal bodyguard; and, when the *néoi* in a given age-class reached forty-five and became *presbúteroi,* they selected the five in their number who had most distinguished themselves as *hippeîs,* named them "doers of good [*agathoergoí*]," and employed them for a year on missions of special importance requiring discretion. Likewise, the ephors controlled the treasury, disbursing necessary funds, overseeing the collection of taxes, and receiving the proceeds from the sale of prisoners and other booty captured in war. They also manipulated the calendar, intercalating months when this was deemed necessary. At Sparta, the ephors controlled virtually every aspect of daily life.

Each year, when they took office, the ephors declared war on the helots, employing the young men of the *krupteía* to eliminate the obstreperous and those menacingly robust. At the same time, Aristotle tells us, they reissued the famous decree calling on each Spartiate to obey the law, to comply with the customs of the land, and to observe the ancient practice of shaving his upper lip. According to Plutarch, this last injunction was intended as a reminder to the young men that they were to obey the city even in the most trivial of matters.[31]

In overseeing the many aspects of Spartan life and public policy for which they were responsible, the ephors exercised broad judicial powers. At the time they took office, they apparently subjected all of the retiring magistrates to a judicial examination. Thereafter, they had the authority to suspend their fellow officials at any time. Individually, the ephors judged civil suits. As a board, they functioned as moral censors and criminal justices empowered to

impose fines on malefactors; and, in capital cases, they could hold preliminary, fact-finding hearings before joining the thirty members of the *gerousía*
to form a jury competent to banish or execute the accused.

The importance of the ephors is perhaps most obvious from their relationship with the two kings. Here, they had clearly defined prerogatives designed
to make manifest and enforce the sovereignty of the political community as a
whole. They alone remained seated in the presence of a king; they alone had
the power to summon the kings and even to fine them for misconduct; and
in and after the fifth century, if not before, when one of the kings led out the
army, two of their number ordinarily accompanied him to observe his every
action and to give advice when asked.

One Eurypontid king is said to have remarked that "the magistrate rules
truly and rightly only when he is ruled by the *nómoi* and ephors." His cou-
pling of the rule of law with the rule of the ephors is not an accident. At the
time of his institution, the Spartan *basileús* swore to maintain the *nómoi* of
the *pólis*. Each month thereafter, the ephors exchanged oaths with the kings,
the latter swearing to reign in accord with "the established laws of the city," the
former pledging to "keep the kingship unshaken" as long as the latter abided
by their "oath to the city."[32]

There was a threat implicit in the ephors' part of the bargain, and they had
the power to make good on it. If the ephors judged that a king or regent had
acted against the interests of the city, they could arrest him and bring him to
trial on a capital charge just like any other Spartan citizen. In the course of the
turbulent fifth century, they were to exercise this prerogative time and time
again.

It might, then, seem that the kings were virtual prisoners of the ephors.
Two sets of circumstances precluded this. In the first place, the kings were
kings for life, while the ephors held office but for a year and apparently could
never again serve. Equally important, the kingships were hereditary, while the
ephorate, which was a democratic office for which every *presbúteros* among the
Spartiates was eligible, seems to have been filled either by lot from an extremely
large elected pool or by some other similar procedure no less subject to the
vagaries of chance. Thus, as board after board of ephors served, then retired,
and as the *gérontes* slowly died off, a strong king endured, exercised his prerogatives, and worked the political and social system to benefit his friends
and impose a burden of gratitude on those judged politically prominent. In a
given year, a particular king might find himself in difficulties and might deem

it prudent to remain quiet, but he knew that the annual game of chance by which the ephors were chosen always offered the hope for a board more favorable to his cause or more easily influenced. The institution of the ephorate would not alone have staved off tyranny. The fact that the kingship was dual was essential for accomplishing that feat. When the two kings were united, the ephors may not have had the authority to withstand them.

It was almost inevitable that there be rivalry between the two *basileîs*. The aristocratic ethos virtually dictated the conflict between the two houses which came to be the norm. In general, where the two kings are not known to have been friends and allies or proponents of the same policy, it is reasonable to suspect that they were at odds—which left leeway not just for the ephors but for the *gérontes* as well.

The *gerousía* was the least dangerous branch within the Spartan *politeía*, but not the least important. In fact, Plutarch came very close to the mark when he described the Spartan regime as a mixture "of democracy and kingship, with an aristocracy to preside over it and adjudicate in the greatest affairs." In normal circumstances, when the ephors were nonentities and the two kings, rivals of no particular talent, the *gérontes* were in a position to exercise great influence, though not to initiate policy. One measure of their authority is the fact that Demosthenes speaks of this body of men as "the master of the many." Dionysius of Halicarnassus advances a similar claim, contending that, while Sparta retained her independence, "the kings of the Lacedaemonians were not autocrats able to do whatever they wished, for the *gerousía* possessed full power over public affairs."[33]

Even if we were to discount these assertions and suppose them hyperbolic —as we probably should—we would still have to acknowledge that the *gerousía* was a formidable instrument of government. Even if it had been effectively divorced from the exercise of power, the prestige of its members would have been sufficient to guarantee that its recommendations were generally heeded. Demosthenes and Aristotle both speak of election to membership in the *gerousía* as "the prize allotted to virtue."[34]

As the Spartan name suggests, the *gerousía* was a council of the aged. Twenty-eight of its thirty members—all but the two kings—were always men of experience and proven worth over the age of sixty. Drawn exclusively from the priestly caste that seems to have constituted the city's ancient aristocracy, directly elected by popular acclamation, and guaranteed the office for life, the *gérontes* performed three functions: the first, probouleutic; the second, judicial; and the third, sacerdotal. With the ephors presiding, the "old men" met to set the agenda for the assembly, and thereafter they could annul any action on its part that exceeded the authority which they thereby conferred. In capital cases, the *gérontes* joined the ephors in forming a jury. In circumstances left unclear, they also apparently functioned as augurs. No legislation could be enacted; no war, declared; and no treaty, ratified without their permission— and it was prudent for magistrates to consult the *gérontes* on all matters of administration entrusted to their care.

The kings and the ephors had particularly strong reasons for heeding the advice of these old men. Whether a king or former official was eventually indicted for malfeasance of office, because left to a board of ephors annually and more or less arbitrarily chosen, was in some measure a matter of chance. But whether the defendant would then be convicted, because entrusted to a tribunal dominated by *gérontes* elected for life, was a subject for calculation— even if, in capital cases, the verdict and sentence had to be confirmed by the public assembly, as one scholar contends.[35] It is no wonder that aging Spartan nobles openly canvassed for the office, and it is highly likely that the factions that tended to grow up around the two royal houses played an active role in promoting the election of their adherents.

There were, to be sure, limits to what the *gérontes* could accomplish: except perhaps in a period of general disarray, the "old men" could not have pushed legislation through the assembly releasing their fellow aristocrats from the egalitarian restrictions that so limited their wealth and its use. But, much of the time, albeit within clear confines, the *gerousía* was in a position to be the arbiter of events. If great seriousness was attached to the selection of the *gérontes,* Isocrates tells us, it was because this handful of elderly men "presided over the disposition of all public affairs."[36]

Like the Nocturnal Council of Plato's *Laws,* the *gerousía* was the guardian of the constitution. It served a function comparable to that which Alexander Hamilton would later attribute to Britain's House of Lords. The *gérontes* had a greater stake in stability than any other group at Sparta. As wealthy aristocrats, they had no pressing need to tamper with the system of land allotments; as recipients of the city's highest honor, they should generally have been satisfied with existing political arrangements; and as old men on the threshold of death, they had little for which to hope from revolution or reform. In short, like England's peers, they had "nothing to hope for by a change, and a sufficient interest by means of their property, in being faithful to the National interest." In consequence, they formed "a permanent barrier ag[ain]st every pernicious innovation" and endowed the government with "a permanent will." Their very "duration" in office was "the earnest of wisdom and stability."[37]

The predominance of the old served Sparta well. The very qualities which make it proper that young men serve in the front lines in time of battle render them unfit for rule, particularly in a *politeía* like that at Lacedaemon. Fighting and the actual conduct of war may favor the passionate and the bold, but diplomacy and statecraft generally require caution and precise calculation. The qualities which render old men less generous and more selfish than the young render them also shrewder, less trustful of foreigners, and far less apt to embark on grand but foolish ventures. In foreign affairs, where interest presides, pusillanimity is certainly not a virtue, but then neither is the excessive highmindedness of the young. Statesmen should not be bashful. They must, in fact, be prepared to be shameless on occasion. In particular, they must be ready to sacrifice the noble for the sake of advantage, for they must care more for the city's survival than for its reputation. Furthermore, in making peace and in preparing for war, the rulers of a community must neither love nor hate with any real vehemence. Instead, they must cherish the city's friends and allies in the full expectation that someday enmity will be required, and they must be hostile to her foes in the full knowledge that these may well become friends and allies at some point in the not too far distant future.

Similarly, the young are hardly fit for rule in any regime aimed at fostering *homónoia* and at achieving stability. Young men are in all places an unsettling element. Even where reared in accord with the spirit of the laws and encouraged to deem honorable precisely what convention prescribes, they rarely display that reverence for the past and that veneration for tradition which is the foundation of communal solidarity. In contrast, because the old are backward-looking and enslaved to memory, they tend naturally to assume that precedent should govern in all cases and that what has been done from time immemorial has an authority and a sanction almost religious in character.

It is not fortuitous that the Spartans rarely conferred political responsibilities on anyone young. Within any community, Aristotle observes, there are two functions—the martial and the deliberative—and both justice and good sense dictate that they be distributed to the young and to the old, respectively: for the young are generally strong, and the old are often prudent.[38] Nor is it an accident that the Spartans were famous throughout ancient times for the exaggerated respect which they paid to age.

Peloponnesian Hegemony

As a ruling order, the Spartiates of the late archaic period constituted a seigneurial class blessed with leisure and devoted to a common way of life centered on the fostering of certain manly virtues. They made music together, these Spartans. There was very little that they did alone. Together they sang and they danced, they worked out, they competed in sports, they boxed and wrestled, they hunted, they dined, they cracked jokes, and they took their repose. Theirs was a rough-and-tumble world. But it was not bereft of refinement, and it was not characterized by an ethos of grim austerity, as some suppose. The Spartans, in fact, lived a life of great privilege and pleasure enlivened by a spirit of rivalry as fierce as it was friendly. The manner in which they mixed music with gymnastic and fellowship with competition caused them to be credited with *eudaimonía*—the happiness and success that everyone craved—and it made them the envy of Hellas. This gentlemanly modus vivendi had, however, one precondition: Lacedaemon's continued dominion over Laconia and Messenia and its brutal subjection of the helots on both sides of Mount Taygetus.

The grand strategy the Lacedaemonians gradually articulated in defense of the way of life they so cherished was all-encompassing, as successful grand strategies often are. Of necessity, it had domestic consequences on a considerable scale. As we have seen, its dictates go a long way toward explaining the Spartans' aversion to commerce; their practice of infanticide; their provision for every citizen of an equal allotment of land and of servants to work it; the city's sumptuary laws; their sharing of slaves, horses, and hounds; their intense piety; the subjection of their male offspring to an elaborate system of education and indoctrination; their use of music and poetry to instill a civic spirit; their practice of pederasty; the rigors and discipline to which they habitually subjected themselves; and, of course, their constant preparation for war. It accounts as well for the articulation over time within Lacedaemon of a mixed regime graced with elaborate balances and checks. To sustain their dominion in Laconia and Messenia and to maintain the helots in bondage, the Spartans had to eschew faction; foster among themselves the same opinions, passions, and interests; and employ—above all, in times of strain—procedures, recognized as fair and just, by which to reach a stable political consensus consistent with the dictates of prudence. There was, in sum, an almost perfect match between the moral imperatives of the Lacedaemonian *políteía,* the way of life it fostered, and the prerequisites for its defense.

Not surprisingly, the grand strategy the Spartans embraced had serious consequences for Lacedaemon's posture in the international sphere as well. Their perch was precarious. In the fourth century, one Corinthian leader summed up Lacedaemon's strategic position elegantly by comparing her to a stream. "At their sources," he noted, "rivers are not great and they are easily forded, but the farther on they go, the greater they get—for other rivers empty into them and make the current stronger." So it is with the Spartans, he continued. "There, in the place where they emerge, they are alone; but as they continue and gather cities under their control, they become more numerous and harder to fight." The prudent general, he concluded, will seek battle with the Spartans in or near Lacedaemon where they are few in number and relatively weak.[39] Thanks to demographic decline, the structure of Sparta's defenses was at that time fragile in the extreme. But it had never been more than tenuous, and the Lacedaemonians understood from early on what history would eventually confirm: that it took but a single major defeat in warfare on land to endanger the city's very survival.

Even when their population was at its height, as it was in the late archaic period, there were never more than ten thousand Spartiates, if that; and the territory they ruled was comparatively vast. The underlings they exploited were astonishingly numerous and apt to be rebellious. In Messenia, if not also in Laconia, the helots saw themselves as a people in bondage, and geography did not favor the haughty men who kept them in that condition. The Spartans could look to the *períoikoi* for support, and this they did. But the latter were also few in number, and it was never entirely certain that they could be relied on. They, too, had to be overawed. In the long run, the Spartans could not sustain their way of life if they did not recruit allies outside their stronghold in the southern Peloponnesus.

It took the *políteuma* at Lacedaemon some time to sort out in full the implications of their position. From the outset, trial and error governed their approach to the formulation of policy. At first, they were preoccupied with the conquest of Messenia. In the latter half of the eighth century, it took them two decades of blood, toil, tears, and sweat to make the Stenyklaros plain tributary. Two generations thereafter, they had to devote eleven long years to the suppression of a rebellion, and it was not until the end of the seventh century that they fully consolidated their hold on the region.

At this point, the Spartiates turned north and tried to apply the same formula to Arcadia—but to no avail. By the middle of the sixth century, they had come to recognize that it was not within their power to make helots of the Tegeans and the other Arcadians, and they had also begun to suspect that, if they did not find some way to leverage the manpower of their neighbors, they would not long be able to sustain their dominion over Messenia. So, with great reluctance, they abandoned the dream of further expansion and embraced as their motto: "*Mēdèn ágan*—Nothing too much! Nothing in excess!"

Then, when the Argives flagged in their support for their traditional allies within Arcadia, the Spartans pounced, seized the opportunity this afforded them, and repositioned themselves to the satisfaction of their neighbors as the defenders of Arcadian autonomy. By this time, they had already begun presenting themselves to the larger Hellenic world as the scourge of tyranny, the champions of liberty, the friends of oligarchy, and the heirs of Agamemnon. It was under this banner that they rearranged the affairs of their fellow Peloponnesians to their liking and founded a regional alliance designed to keep their Argive enemies out, the helots down, and the Arcadians, above all others, in.

Taken as a whole the grand strategy of classical Lacedaemon was brilliantly designed for the purpose it was intended to serve. It had, however, one grave defect. It presupposed that for all practical purposes, under Sparta's hegemony, the Peloponnesus was a world unto itself—which, of course, it was . . . at the time that this strategy was first formulated. If, however, there ever came a moment when a power equal to or greater than Lacedaemon appeared—or even threatened to appear—in force at or near the entrance to that great peninsula, the Spartans would have to rethink this strategy and recast it to meet an unanticipated challenge.

It was in the mid-540s that such a prospect first loomed in the distance on the horizon. Although the Spartans were by no means slow to take note of the challenge they faced, they were exceedingly cautious in the mode of proceeding that they then adopted, as we shall soon see.

Part I

THE CRISIS OF SPARTA'S GRAND STRATEGY

By the fire you ought to say something of this sort in the season of winter, as you recline on your soft couch, your belly full, drinking sweet wine and munching on chickpeas: "Who among men are you and of what stock? How many years have you passed, brave fellow? And how old were you when the Mede first came?"

—XENOPHANES OF COLOPHON

IN the long stretch of years in which their political community first gradually took shape and they conquered the Stenyklaros plain, then reconquered that district, subjugated the remainder of Messenia, put together their alliance system, and seized from Argos hegemony within the Peloponnesus, the Spartans enjoyed great good fortune in one crucial particular. They were left alone—as were nearly all of their fellow Hellenes, apart from those living in Cyprus, in Cilicia, or along the coasts of Asia Minor.

Our information is limited, but the outlines can be discerned from what we are told in the Jewish Bible, in the chronicles kept by the neo-Assyrian and neo-Babylonian kings, and in other stray documents that happen to survive on stone, clay tablets, and papyrus. Early on in this span of years, in the ninth and eighth centuries, the Assyrians grew powerful and gradually became predominant in Mesopotamia and beyond. For a time, in the seventh century, they even ruled Egypt. The Babylonians staged a successful revolt in 625, joined with the Medes of northwestern Iran in capturing the capital of the Assyrians at Nineveh thirteen years later, and then destroyed Assyria's dominion once and for all. Thereafter, under Nebuchadrezzar, the Babylonians extended their sway into Syria and Palestine to the very borders of the Sinai peninsula, and they attacked and may even have overrun Egypt for a brief time.[1]

In these years, so full of drama for the Jews and the other peoples of the fertile crescent, no great power seriously bothered the islanders of the Aegean, the Greeks in the Balkans, or those who ventured forth to settle in Sic-

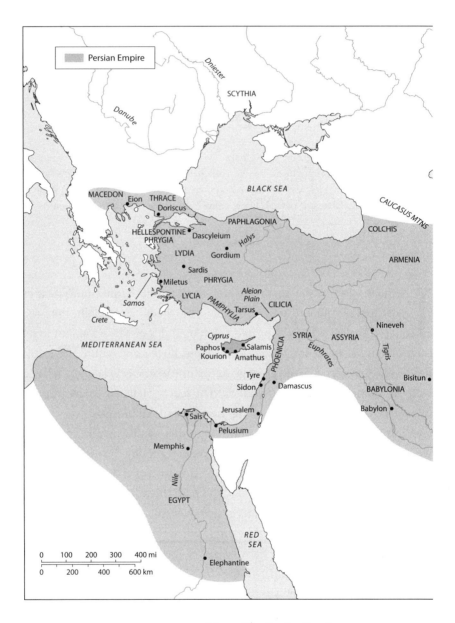

Map 2. The Persian Empire

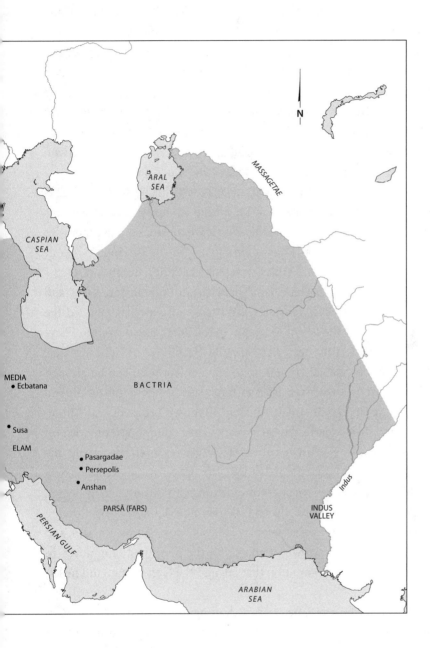

N

ARAL
SEA

MASSAGETAE

CASPIAN
SEA

MEDIA
• Ecbatana

BACTRIA

• Susa

ELAM

• Pasargadae
• Persepolis
• Anshan

Indus

PARSĀ (FARS)

INDUS
VALLEY

PERSIAN GULF

ARABIAN
SEA

ily, around the Black Sea, or along the coast in Libya, Italy, southern Gaul, or eastern Iberia. The Hellenes lived, as Plato's Socrates put it, "like ants and frogs around a pond between the Pillars of Heracles" at the western edge of the Mediterranean "and the river Phasis" on the eastern shore of the Euxine,[2] and they lived in comparative comfort and safety. For the majority of these communities, perched precariously along or not far inland from the seacoast between Gibraltar and the Caucasus, this early period was a golden age, and the Spartans were prominent—if not, in fact, preeminent—among those who profited from it. But, of course, it did not last. Few things do.

It was when the power of the Assyrians was at its height that the Greeks in Cilicia, Pamphylia, and Cyprus first for a time fell under a great empire's sway. Later—for some years in the sixth century, when Amasis, a usurper who had seized the Saite realm, was Pharaoh in Egypt—the quasi-Homeric monarchs who ruled the cities of Cyprus were subject to his dominion. Gyges established the power of the Mermnadae at Sardis in Lydia in about 678, and he and his successors Ardys, Sadyattes, Alyattes, and Croesus extended the Mermnad dominion to the Sea of Marmara in the north and deep into Phrygia to the Halys River in the east. According to Herodotus of Halicarnassus, whose testimony can now be brought in to supplement what can be gleaned from the Near Eastern evidence, Croesus' forebears also on occasion probed the defenses of the Greek settlements situated on the west coast of Asia Minor. For the most part, however, in the early years, these communities fended off the Mermnad assaults. But, in the time of Croesus himself, in the decade following 560, they succumbed one by one. The only notable exception was Miletus, which had reached an accommodation with Alyattes long before. Thereafter, we are told, toward the end of his reign, Croesus began giving thought to building a fleet for use against Lesbos, Chios, Samos, Rhodes, and the lesser islands off the Asia Minor coast. But the Mermnad king never, in fact, managed to extend his ambition that far, and the Greek mainland he left alone.[3]

The Spartans—who were, because of the fragility of their hold on Messenia, quite sensitive to threats both distant and near—kept a watchful eye on Croesus and maintained cordial relations with the Mermnad monarch. But from him, in truth, they had little to fear, and this they understood. The Greeks in the Balkans and the islanders were thoroughly familiar with the Lydian kingdom across the Aegean in western Anatolia. Croesus and his predecessors had generally been attentive to Greek religious concerns. As Herodotus emphasizes, they had built or rebuilt temples in the cities on the Asia Minor coast, and they had sent rich votive offerings to the oracle at Delphi and to other Hellenic cult sites in the eastern Mediterranean. Economically, as well as culturally, the wealthy kingdom in the interior of Asia Minor existed in a symbiotic relationship with the Hellenic cities on the coast. From the perspective of Greeks not, in fact, under its dominion, the barbarian kingdom based at Sardis was generally regarded as a benign buffer state and a bulwark against foes far more dangerous found further east and south—which helps explain why, when Croesus approached them near the end of his reign, the Lacedaemonians quickly agreed to form an alliance. As we have already had occasion to note, they had a stake in the status quo.[4]

The particular occasion deserves attention. Croesus' father Alyattes had extended Lydian power to the western bank of the Halys in the east. Somewhere nearby he reportedly encountered Cyaxares, king of the Medes, who, in the decades following his involvement in the sack of Nineveh in 612, is said to have gradually extended his dominion from the region about his capital at Ecbatana in the foothills of the Zagros mountains in northwestern Iran deep into Anatolia to the opposite bank of the same river.

There is reason to suspect that Cyaxares made a powerful impression on the Hellenes on the Asia Minor coast subject to or allied with Alyattes and that he had sought with some success to lure these Greeks into an alliance against the Lydian monarch. For, long after the Medes had ceased to be an independent force, the Greeks were wont to brand individuals and communities who sided with their Persian successors as Medizers, and, when commenting on the empire governed by the Great King of Persia, they and the Jews persistently referred to him as the Mede.[5] In this instance—because our information is so limited—we know of no particular cities or individuals that sided with Cyaxares. But that they existed seems nonetheless clear.

What we can assert with considerable confidence is that, on 28 May 585, the Lydians and their allies among the Carians and Greeks on the Asia Minor coast squared off against the army fielded by Cyaxares and that, soon after the fighting began, there was a solar eclipse. It is an open question whether Thales of Miletus, who is said to have been present on the occasion of the battle, actually predicted this startling astronomical occurrence, as is claimed. Even, however, if this report is true, no one appears to have profited from the knowledge —for we are told that the eclipse was interpreted as a religious portent by both kings, who out of superstitious fear quickly reached a truce. In the aftermath, if Herodotus' account is sound, the Babylonian king and a Cilician prince mediated negotiations between the two, and they made an alliance, which was sealed in time-honored fashion by the marriage of Alyattes' daughter to Cyaxares' son and heir Astyages.[6]

The event that later caused Alyattes' son Croesus to seek an alliance with the Spartans followed upon his brother-in-law Astyages' overthrow in 550. This revolution in the affairs of Iran was the consequence of a rebellion against the rule of the Medes instigated at least three years prior to that date by Cyrus, the king of a minor tributary principality, Elamite in origin and still in his time to a very considerable degree Elamite in culture, which had once been connected with the ancient Elamite kingdom based at Susa.[7] Long known to the Elamites, Babylonians, and Assyrians as Anshan; sometimes, in the seventh and sixth centuries, referred to by the Babylonians, Assyrians, and Elamites as Parsu or Parsumaš; called by at least some of its sixth-century Iranian inhabitants Parsā; and dubbed by the Greeks Persia, the little kingdom handed down by Teispes to the first Cyrus and by the latter's son Cambyses to the Cyrus responsible for Astyages' demise was located in a highland region now called Fars, many miles south of Ecbatana at some distance inland from the Persian Gulf well to the southeast of Susa.[8] If the Lydian monarch had not already made an alliance with Amasis of Egypt and Nabonidus of Babylon, he did so at this time in response to the unexpected turn of events that caused him to befriend Lacedaemon.

In the aftermath of Astyages' fall, Croesus watched in dismay as Cyrus consolidated his hold on the empire built up by the Medes.[9] In the mid-540s, probably not long after the Persian conquest of Urartu in the spring of 547, the Lydian monarch sought the advice of the Delphic oracle and was told that if he crossed the river Halys with an army he would destroy a great empire. Encouraged by this, he led the Lydian army and his Greek and Carian subject allies into Cappadocia, along with a contingent of Egyptians sent him by Amasis. There, Herodotus reports, in the heartland of Asia Minor, where the Hittites had once held sway, his forces and the much larger army brought northward by Cyrus fought to a standstill.[10]

It was already then fall. The campaigning season was coming to an end, and Cyrus did not renew the assault. In consequence, Croesus withdrew to winter quarters in Sardis, dismissed his mercenaries, and ordered his Greek and Carian allies to reassemble in the spring. He also sent emissaries to Amasis and Nabonidus, as well as to the Lacedaemonians, asking that they send as many soldiers as possible to Lydia in four months' time.[11] By this point, it was clear to all concerned that Cyrus and the Persians were a force to be reckoned with and a threat to the established balance of power not only in the Near East but further afield.

The alliance that Croesus' emissaries had negotiated with the Spartans was short-lived. Cyrus held back when Croesus withdrew from Cappadocia, and he waited. But he did not tarry long. As soon as Croesus' allies had dispersed and his ambassadors had departed, the Persian king crossed the Halys, marched on Sardis, defeated the cavalry of Lydia, and mounted a siege. At the end of two weeks, we are told, his men found a weak spot in the fortifications and made their way into the citadel. Months before the Egyptians, Babylonians, Spartans, and Croesus' more immediate Greek and Carian allies were due to reconnoiter at Sardis, the war between the Persians and the Lydians had come to an abrupt end, and Croesus was either a captive and client, as Herodotus and Ctesias suggest. Or, as the poet Bacchylides implies, he was already dead.[12]

Like Cyaxares before him, Cyrus had sought, presumably by offering generous terms, to induce the Greek cities on the coast to defect from their Lydian overlord. But—except, perhaps, at Miletus where Thales is said to have dissuaded his compatriots from actively supporting Croesus—he had found no takers. When, after the fall of Sardis, these same cities offered submission on condition that he renew the terms accorded them by Croesus, the Persian monarch refused, with an eye to making an example of these holdouts; and he left it to his minions to bring them to heel. The Milesians were allowed to retain their rich estates inland from the coast. Those in the other cities faced a grim prospect—almost certainly the demand that they cede to their new overlords much of the fertile farmland that they had hitherto tilled.[13]

After the Persian king's departure, his Lydian agent Pactyes turned on his new master and staged a rebellion, which all but one of the Greek cities vigorously supported. In response, Cyrus sent a Mede named Mazares and, after his death, Harpagus, his chief supporter among the Medes, to quell the rebellion in Lydia, capture Pactyes, and subjugate the Greeks. In brutal fashion over a period of four years, by the standard Near Eastern expedient of having their soldiers pile up siege mounds against the city walls of those who did not surrender, this they did. In the end, the only Hellenic city on the mainland of

Asia Minor that managed to retain even a shadow of independence was Miletus, whose citizens had stood aside, as they had done earlier in the time of Croesus, while yet another set of barbarians conquered their fellow Hellenes.[14]

In the years immediately following, Cyrus extended Persia's dominion eastward to the very edge of the Indian subcontinent. Upon his return, he conquered Babylon, which surrendered in 539. The conquest of Egypt, which had been part of his program, he was forced to leave to his son and designated heir Cambyses, who accomplished this in 525.[15] At the time of the latter's death in Syria from a self-inflicted wound three years thereafter, the Spartans were the only erstwhile allies of Croesus of any consequence who had not been subjugated. If they were still free, however, it was chiefly because of their apparent insignificance. Lydia, Babylonia, and Egypt were rich and powerful. Greece was comparatively poor; and, to the unsuspecting glance, it appeared to be weak and inconsequential.

Croesus had thought otherwise. When the army of Cyrus defeated the Lydians on the plain of Hermus to the north of Sardis and began preparing to conduct a siege, the Mermnad king is said to have dispatched emissaries to his allies, asking them to send a relief force immediately. His hopes were reportedly focused on the Spartans, who were less far away than the Egyptians and Babylonians; and he also is said to have sought to enlist mercenaries elsewhere in the Peloponnesus.[16]

The Lacedaemonians were, however, preoccupied. The Argives, as was on occasion their wont, had made a bid to regain from the Lacedaemonians the fertile plain of Thyrea in the district of Cynouria southwest of the Argolid. Instead of fighting a battle, however, the two communities had opted for a duel apt to be less costly in manpower. Each fielded a force of three hundred champions. To the victor would go the land. This was the plan. Unfortunately for all concerned, the scheme did not work—for there were survivors on both sides, and neither won an outright victory. In consequence, the battle that they had sought to avoid took place; and, as usual, the Lacedaemonians were victorious. From this time on, we are told, the Argives, who had always let their hair grow long, vowed to cut it short until they recovered the territory they had lost; and the Spartiates, who had always cut their hair short, began to let it grow long. If we know about this particular battle, it is probably because the event was commemorated and the memory kept green in this fashion.[17]

Of course, even had the Spartans not been distracted in this manner, it is highly unlikely that they would have been able to mount an overseas expedition in time to be of help to Croesus. Cyrus was not in any way behindhand. By the time that Lacedaemonians could have been ready to come to Croesus' aid, the Persian king was already the master in Sardis.[18]

When, in the aftermath, Cyrus spurned the offer put forward by Greek cities on the west coast of Asia Minor that they be subject to him on the terms previously extended to them by Croesus, these *póleis*—in anticipation of the onslaught to come—began building walls and fortifications, restoring those which had been partially dismantled, and reinforcing those intact. At the same time, they sent delegates to a gathering at the Panionium opposite Samos on the peninsula of Mount Mycale in the territory of Priene, where it was decided that they should petition the Dorians of Sparta for help.[19]

This decision should for two reasons give us pause. To begin with, it confirms what common sense would in any case suggest: that long before the Persian Wars—in part as a consequence of interaction with Lydia, Babylon, Assyria, and Egypt and in part as a consequence of the colonization movement that began in the mid-eighth century—the Greeks had come to regard themselves as a single people. They knew themselves, first and foremost, as citizens of particular *póleis,* to be sure; and they thought of themselves next as Dorians, Ionians, Arcadians, Thessalians, Boeotians, and the like. But they also recognized that they spoke dialects of a single language; that they shared certain cult sites and sacrifices; that they had Homer, the Delphic Oracle, and the Olympic Games in common; that their mores, manners, and ways were alike; and that they were a kinship community of sorts—situated precariously on the margins of a world populated by a host of potentially hostile barbarian nations.[20] The decision reached at the Panionium is also of interest because it indicates that the Spartans were at this time regarded as the natural leaders of Hellas. Such was the prestige already then possessed by Lacedaemon.

The Spartans were not at this time prepared to engage in such a venture on behalf of the Ionians. They may have been thunderstruck, as Herodotus reports, when Pythermos of Phocaea donned a cloak of royal purple before addressing their assembly. They may have regarded such a personage with amazement and even awe. But they turned down his request, nonetheless. What they did do, however, is telling. In the standard warship of that time—a penteconter powered, as the etymology of the word in Greek suggests, by fifty oars—they dispatched to Phocaea a team of observers. Herodotus called them spies. We would perhaps resort to euphemism and speak of this as a fact-finding mission. It was that, for sure, and it was much more—for the most distinguished member of the team, a Spartan named Lakrines, was sent on from there to Sardis to deliver to Cyrus a message from his compatriots, warning the Persian king that the Lacedaemonians "would not overlook his wantonly destroying any city on territory belonging to the Hellenes."

Cyrus is said to have questioned the Greeks within his entourage about the character of the people who had sent him this admonition, and he inquired as to the size of their population. Then, after having taken the measure of his foe, he reportedly responded to the Spartan herald with a contempt unconcealed: "I do not fear men of the sort that set aside in the middle of their city a place in which to assemble, swear oaths, and deceive one another, and if my health holds out, it is not the sufferings of the Ionians that these men will talk about but their own."[21]

If there is any truth in this tale told by Herodotus, as there is apt to be, there should be evidence that the Spartans took Cyrus' threat to heart—which, in fact, as we shall in due course see, they did. At this time, however, the Lacedaemonians stood idly by not only while Cyrus' agents quelled Pactyes' revolt and hunted him down but also afterward when they methodically subdued the Aeolic and Ionian cities on the west coast of Asia Minor. Nor did they intervene when Harpagus the Mede marched south to subdue the Carians and the Dorian Greek cities on Asia Minor's southwestern coast as well as the Caunians and the Lycians further east.[22] The masters of Laconia and Messenia were nothing if not cautious. They were not apt to go looking for trouble if they could avoid it. If they could do so, they would watch, wait, and ruminate. The grand strategy on which they had so recently settled had nothing to teach them concerning the Persian challenge. Of course, if they were going to have to fight the Persians, they would do so. But this they would do—or so they hoped—at a time and place of their own choosing when and where they thought it fit.[23]

CHAPTER 1

A Shadow Growing in the East

The nations are at his mercy. The kings are subdued by his coming, flying like dust before his sword, scattered like chaff in the wind at the threat of his bow. He routs them in battle, and passes through their country unmolested, leaving not a footprint behind. . . . The islands and the coasts have seen it, and trembled at the sight; the remotest parts of the world have been smitten with dismay; they draw near and his summons obey.

—ISAIAH

W E are not at all well-informed concerning the conduct of Lacedaemon in the second half of the sixth century. Herodotus is our main source of information. His approach was in certain respects akin to that of an epic poet. Longinus described him as "the most Homeric" of all writers. He wrote first and foremost, as he himself put it, to prevent "events" from becoming "evanescent" and "the great and wondrous deeds" of the Hellenes and the barbarians from being "deprived of fame." He preferred a "politics of public deliberation [*isēgoríē*]" to tyranny without a doubt.[1] But he was not a radical egalitarian. The republics that he admired, even the most democratic of the lot, were sharply distinguished from the liberal democracies of modern times by the holding of slaves. Alexis de Tocqueville rightly called these polities (Athens included) "aristocracies of masters"; and, in keeping with this fact, the tastes and instincts of Herodotus and those of his intended audience were thoroughly aristocratic.

In democratic ages, Tocqueville tells us, historians tend to be fatalists. "The better part of them attribute almost no influence to the individual over the destiny of the species or to citizens over the fate of the people. But, instead, they give great general causes for every little particular fact." In aristocratic ages, however, historians "ordinarily make all events depend on the particular will and humor of certain men, and they willingly derive from the least acci-

39

dents the most important revolutions. With sagacity they cause the smallest causes to spring forth, and often they do not perceive the greatest."[2]

The book which Herodotus called his *Inquiries* fits perfectly Tocqueville's description of aristocratic history.[3] The man from Halicarnassus was by no means averse to the investigation of causes. But, in their pursuit, he was more apt to spin out fanciful tales he had been told, focused on personal idiosyncrasies and intended to point up a moral, than to explore the dictates of necessity within a given strategic environment.

There is no reason to suppose that Herodotus was himself a fabricator of tales, as some scholars assert. But he was perfectly capable of retailing lies told him by others. He had aristocratic patrons in Macedonia, on Samos, in Athens, and in many other corners of the Greek world. He enjoyed hobbing with the nobs; he depended on audience engagement and approbation; and he very much wanted to please. It is not, however, terribly hard for the reader to pick out the most egregious of the fibs he was fed. In fact, it is striking just how often, when he echoes special pleading of this sort, Herodotus takes care to provide his readers with the evidence necessary to recognize that they are being gulled. It is as if, when he was about to retell a whopper, he was inclined to give his readers a wink and a knowing nod. One must read him with an eye to these asides. With regard to one story he passes on, he remarks, "I am obligated to report what is said, but I am not obligated to believe it in its entirety." Then, he adds a word of warning that his readers should take to heart, "Let this dictum of mine hold for the entire account I provide."[4]

There is one other difficulty. In his treatment of the period prior to the Persian Wars, Herodotus' focus was on the Persians as such and on the growth of their *imperium*. He mentions the Spartans, or so it seems, only as he mentions the other Greek cities—sparingly, with regard to their interchanges with the Persians, and in digressions on events pertinent to the growth of Persia's power in which they played a tangential role. It is all quite deftly done lest one notice that one of his purposes is to introduce early on the Hellenic cities that will later play a major role in confronting the Persian forces sent to conquer mainland Greece. Herodotus is, nonetheless, exceedingly terse. All that we get is an occasional glimpse of the Lacedaemonians. Tellingly, however, when we do get such a glimpse, the Spartans seem—sometimes, perhaps, unbeknownst to Herodotus himself—either to be making an attempt to block the approaches from Asia Minor to the Hellenic heartland at the bottom of the Balkan peninsula, or to be engaged in an endeavor to prevent Medizers from becoming dominant in Greek cities in the heartland as yet by Persia unsubdued.[5]

This last point needs emphasis. Like his predecessors among the Babylonians and Assyrians, Cyrus represented himself as "King of the universe," authorized to hold dominion over "all the kings, who sit on thrones, from all parts of the world"; and, in the Near East and around the shores of the Mediterranean and the Black Sea, he was for good reason widely regarded as such.[6] He ruled over nearly all of the civilized world—at least, insofar as that world was known to those who lived west of the Gobi desert—and what he did not already control this "King of the universe" evidenced a settled intention to seize. Universal empire was the raison d'être of the Persian monarchy. It was the imperative driving the regime.

In keeping with the aspirations evident in the documentary record, the Persians during and after Cyrus' reign were intent on expansion, and they were methodical in their approach. As we will have ample opportunity to note, before barging into a region, they ordinarily explored and studied with great care the geopolitical terrain.[7] Moreover, before mounting an invasion, the minions of the Great King carefully prepared the ground. For subversion, they had a knack.

We should not be surprised that, when the Medes and the Persians came to blows, Astyages' principal general Harpagus and a substantial part of his army defected to Cyrus. The Persian monarch had assiduously laid the groundwork. Herodotus may conceivably have interviewed descendants of Harpagus in Lycia, where, in a suggestive fashion, the Mede's name features prominently in the fifth century,[8] and he has an elaborate story to tell about the background to the defectors' abandonment of the Median king. Some of the details may be too outlandish for belief. But there can be no doubt that the abandonment took place, for the Babylonian chronicles confirm its historicity; and there is no reason to question whether there had been collusion between the general leading the Medes and his Persian counterpart. It is in light of Cyrus' deviousness on this occasion that we should read Herodotus' report that, before he came to blows with the Lydians, the Persian monarch made a concerted attempt to lure the Ionians into rebellion, and it is in this light that we should also consider the evidence suggesting that at some point he may actually have succeeded with the Milesians. Consonant with all of this is what we can infer from the Jewish Bible and the surviving Mesopotamian texts concerning Cyrus' conquest of Babylon—that he exploited to considerable advantage the disaffection with Nabonidus that existed among the Babylonians themselves as well as that which animated the Jews held in captivity there.[9]

Cambyses appears to have been no less interested in gathering intelligence than his father and to have been no less adept at the art of subversion. Herodotus makes much of the defection of Phanes of Halicarnassus who had served in Egypt among the Greek and Carian mercenaries of Amasis. He reportedly helped the Persians chart the path of their invasion and persuaded them to follow the example of their Assyrian predecessors and negotiate an alliance with the Bedouin inhabiting the Sinai to facilitate their passage through that forbidding, waterless land.[10] It is also revealing that Cambyses' invasion followed closely upon the accession of a new Pharaoh in Egypt. Amasis was a man of prestige—a wily and able monarch who had ruled Egypt for forty-four years. His son and heir Psammetichus III was inexperienced and untried; and in monarchies, as Cambyses had no doubt learned firsthand, transitions are apt to produce instability and to occasion on the part of the deceased king's surviving servants an inclination for a reassessment of their allegiance.

At Pelusium on the east bank at the mouth of the easternmost branch of the Nile, this Psammetichus mounted a fierce defense. When the city fell or later, when the Persians had already penetrated into the Delta, an Egyptian official, a eunuch named Combaphis, is said to have betrayed his new master by making it possible for the Persians to use the bridges over the Nile. If there really was a Combaphis and if he did this, he was probably not the only servant of Psammetichus to turn coat. We are not told in so many words that Udjahorresnet—the learned physician who was tasked with commanding the Egyptian navy under both Amasis and Psammetichus III—defected to the Persians. But it would not be surprising were this the case. For we do learn— from reading the autobiography that he had carved on the statuette of himself which he had erected in the temple of Osiris at Sais—that after the Persian conquest of Egypt this Udjahorresnet lived on and flourished as a collaborator: becoming a court physician, an advisor to Cambyses regarding Egyptian affairs, and a person of trust at the court of his successor before being sent back from Susa to Egypt to reform medical education in the old administrative center at Sais.[11]

The Spartans are unlikely to have known all of the details mentioned here, but they can hardly have escaped learning of the Persian modus operandi. What we can glean today from the scattered scraps of evidence that happen to survive is almost certainly the tip of a much larger iceberg—about which they were no doubt better informed than we can ever hope to be. From the Persians, they and everyone else who was at all attentive knew what to expect. "Divide and conquer" could have been the motto of the Mede. If, when the Lacedaemonians intervened in the affairs of other Greek cities, their motives are apt to have been many and complex, in this period their concern with the Persian threat was, as we shall see, paramount.

The expedition that the Spartans and their Corinthian allies mounted in 525 against Polycrates, the celebrated tyrant of Samos, is a case in point. The context within which it took place deserves close attention—for there was clearly much more to the thinking of the Lacedaemonians than Herodotus' narrative suggests, and we can guess at their thinking only if we pause to consider the larger strategic significance of political developments on that island and within the Aegean more generally. There was, as we shall soon see, a maritime military revolution under way.

A Pirate Prince

Of course, we need not reject outright Herodotus' testimony regarding the deliberations that took place when the citizens of Sparta and Corinth considered whether to accept the appeal for help made to them at this time by a group of Samians driven into exile by Polycrates. Everything we know about the conduct of Greek diplomacy is consistent with the notion that the dissident Samians would have made mention of the aid that their compatriots had given Sparta against the Messenians in the distant past, and everything we know about the sort of deliberations that ordinarily took place in public assemblies on occasions like this is consistent with the notion that old grievances would also have been revived and aired. Moreover, as both Herodotus and Xenophon testify, the Greeks were not averse to bringing what we would think of as legendary events into such discussions.

On such an occasion, had no Lacedaemonians renewed their city's complaint that pirates, sponsored by the government at Samos, had intercepted in the early 540s a Spartan embassy to Croesus and confiscated the massive bronze bowl designed for mixing wine that it was conveying to Lacedaemon's Lydian ally, it would have been exceedingly odd. The same could be said had they all been silent about the Samians' quite similar interception the year before of an Egyptian embassy on its way to Amasis' Spartan ally and their seizure of the magnificent linen breastplate embroidered with fibers made of cotton and of gold intended as a gift for the Lacedaemonians. It also stands to reason that the Corinthians would have recalled to mind the fact that, about 590, pirates from Samos had intercepted an embassy from Corinth dispatched to Alyattes of Lydia with a gift of three hundred Corcyraean boys fit for castration and service as eunuchs in his court and that the Samians had protected the boys, freed them, and arranged for their return to their families in Corcyra.[12]

It did not matter that, in the interim, the Corinthian regime had undergone a change—that the Cypselid tyrant Periander had sent the gift and that Corinth had long since become an oligarchy. The hostility between the Corinthians and their ungrateful colonists on Corcyra was very old. It ran deep and was an enduring feature of ancient Greek political life. In 525, when these deliberations took place, the Corinthians were as inimical to the Corcyraeans as Periander had been sixty-five years before, and the antipathy dividing the two communities was still a powerful force eighty years thereafter.[13]

Nor would the Corinthians or the Spartans have bothered to consider whether the government of Samos was in Polycrates' hands when these acts of piracy took place. For they knew what it has taken scholars in recent times considerable detective work to surmise: that a relative (perhaps a great-uncle)—a son of Calliteles bearing the rare but apt name (or nickname) Syloson, which means "Booty-Taker" or "Privateer"—had founded the tyranny after defeating the Mytilenians at sea back in Periander's day in the late 590s, not long after the island's aristocratic Landlords [*Geōmóroi*] had been overthrown and about the time in which the hoplites of Samos had been bested in battle on the mainland by the citizens of Priene. Moreover, they were aware that, upon the death of this Syloson, Polycrates' own father Aeaces son of Brychon, a princely privateer of whom his descendants were understandably proud, had taken charge—governing the island much of the time from then on down to the period of Polycrates' own rule, continuing his predecessor's policy of city-sponsored piracy, and advertising his connection with Syloson by giving the man's name to his third-born son. This Aeaces was no shrinking violet. He boasted of his family's prospects by calling the firstborn of his sons Polycrates or "Very Powerful" and the second-born Pantagnotos or "All-Knowing." He convinced the celebrated poet Anacreon to come to Samos to tutor his eldest son, and he persuaded the poet Ibycus to visit the island and write in praise of the surpassing beauty possessed by the young man.[14]

The grievances entertained by the Corinthians and the Spartans with regard to Polycrates and his swashbuckling forebears were real enough, and recalling them to mind may well have been galling. The long-standing ties of guest-friendship, stretching back to the era of the first two Messenian wars—which linked the leading families of Lacedaemon with those among the wealthy *Geōmóroi*, ascendant at Samos prior to the rise of the tyrant clan, whose offspring appealed in 525 for aid—may also have been exceedingly tight.[15] Moreover, settled Spartan policy dictated a hostility to tyranny as such. But had these motives really been sufficient in and of themselves to persuade the Spartans and their Corinthian allies to take action in 525, it would be hard to explain why the two communities waited so long before seeking revenge. To grasp what it was that induced Corinth and Sparta to mount an expedition at this particular time, one must review the history of Polycrates' relations with the Persians and ponder the changing military balance of power in 525 as it pertained to mastery over the sea.

An Ionian Thalassocracy

In the aftermath of the Persian conquest of Lydia, as Harpagus the Mede methodically subjugated the Ionian and Aeolic cities on the coast of Asia Minor, the *póleis* on the islands along that coast grew fearful and submitted to Cyrus' rule. So Herodotus tells us in one passage. In two others, however, he seems to imply the opposite, claiming that "the islanders had nothing to fear—for the Phoenicians were not then subjects of the Persians. Nor were the Persians seafarers."[16] Strictly speaking, of course, the two claims are compatible. One can easily enough fall prey to panic when, in fact, one has as yet nothing to fear—and this may well be what happened. In practice, however, the situation is likely to have been more complicated than Herodotus lets on, for the various *póleis* on the islands were independent of one another, and human beings thrust into similar situations frequently make different calculations.

The Mytilenians and the Chians appear, for example, to have chosen collaboration. Before Harpagus arrived on the scene, when Mazares the Mede had managed to quell the Lydian revolt, Pactyes, its instigator, fled to the Aeolian city of Cumae on the Asia Minor coast. When Mazares demanded that the Cumaeans surrender the fugitive, they balked. Pactyes was a suppliant and, as such, they believed, sacred to Zeus. So, instead of giving him up, the Cumaeans ferried him across the straits to Mytilene, an Aeolian city on the island of Les-

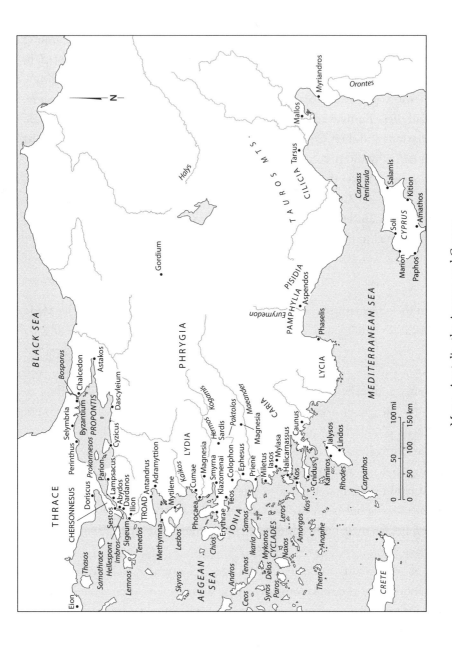

Map 3. Anatolia, the Aegean, and Cyprus

bos; and when they learned that the Mytilenians were about to sell the Lydian rebel to Mazares, they sent a contingent to take their suppliant from Lesbos to the Ionian *pólis* on Chios—only to have him dragged from the sanctuary of Athena Polias by the Chians and handed over in return for the fertile district of Atarneus on the continent. We do not know whether, after being rewarded, the Chians remained faithful to the Persians, but the Mytilenians appear to have done so. Otherwise, it would be hard to explain why two decades later, after Cambyses' initial victory at Pelusium, the Persian monarch conferred on the citizens of this city on the island of Lesbos the signal honor of conveying his herald up the Nile in a galley to negotiate the terms of surrender with Psammetichus III.[17]

We do not know whether Polycrates ever formally submitted to Cyrus by sending him earth and water, as appears to have been the custom. We cannot even be certain that he was in power on Samos in the first few years after the fall of Sardis. There seems to have been a republican interregnum between the period of his father's rule and that of his own—in which the sage Pythagoras, upon his return from Egypt and Babylon, briefly loomed large. It is clear, however, that, in the aftermath of Harpagus' conquest of the peoples along the western and southern coasts of Asia Minor, Samos chose a path different from the one followed by the Mytilenians and the Chians, for we are told by the geographer Pausanias that the Persians were responsible for the fire known to have destroyed the temple of Hera on that island in about 540. The decision to resist Persian pressure was almost certainly a consequence of Polycrates' seizure of the power that had once belonged to his father and, before him, to the elder Syloson—a coup d'état which he effected, at some point in the 540s, with the help of his two brothers, and which he then quickly consolidated with reinforcements provided by Lygdamis, the recently installed tyrant of Naxos.[18]

We are well-informed concerning Polycrates in part because, as a consequence of the Persian Wars, the Greeks came to be as keenly interested in the role played by sea power in history as Alfred Thayer Mahan at the U.S. Naval War College would be in the late nineteenth and early twentieth centuries of the modern era, and because someone in the early fifth century, whom we cannot now identify, apparently attempted to re-imagine the course of events in the eastern Mediterranean as a story of the rise and fall of a series of what he termed thalassocracies—dominions over the sea. With this schema in mind, Thucydides attributes to the Ionians a period of strength at sea in the time of

Cyrus and Cambyses, asserting that they exercised just such a thalassocracy while they were at war with Cyrus, and remarking that, in Cambyses' day, Polycrates, the tyrant at Samos, possessed a maritime supremacy enabling him to subject islands other than his own. Two late Roman sources provide additional details, specifying that it was the Samians who controlled the sea in the wake of Croesus' fall, that Cyrus launched a fleet against them, and that, on this occasion, Polycrates inflicted a great defeat on the Persians.[19]

If these reports are true, as I think they are, the Persian fleet defeated by Polycrates must have been supplied by the Great King's Greek allies—for, as we have seen, Cyrus had no other naval resources on which to call. There is, moreover, evidence suggesting that Polycrates attempted to lure the Milesians, the very first of the Ionians to have thrown in their lot with the Persians, away from the Mede and into an alliance with Samos. Herodotus may well be alluding to the consequences of the Samian tyrant's failure in this diplomatic endeavor and to his defeat of the fleet fielded on Cyrus' behalf by the latter's Hellenic allies when he reports Polycrates' decisive victory in a naval battle against the Mytilenians at a time when the latter came out in full force in support of the Milesians.[20]

In the aftermath of this struggle—when he is said to have possessed a fleet of one hundred galleys, a hoplite army of mercenary stock, and one thousand archers who could be deployed on both ship and shore—the Samian tyrant really would have been in a position to do what Herodotus claims he did: lay his hands on "a great many islands and many towns on the mainland" as well. It is no wonder that the author of the *Historíai* spoke of him as the first since Minos of Cnossus known without a doubt to have attempted the establishment of a thalassocracy, and it is no surprise that Thucydides thought his little empire in the eastern Aegean and his dedication of the island of Rheneia to Delian Apollo noteworthy. There is even reason to suspect that, towards the end of his tenure as tyrant, Polycrates deliberately trumpeted his hegemony over Ionia as a whole by instituting a festival for the Ionians on the isle of Delos.[21]

A Fleet of Penteconters

According to Herodotus, the galleys that Polycrates deployed in defying Cyrus, in defeating the Mytilenians, and establishing his maritime hegemony throughout Ionia were penteconters.[22] These were long, relatively narrow ships equipped with a single sail and rowed—in battle and when the sea was becalmed or the wind was an obstacle or simply inadequate—by fifty strong men, twenty-five on a side. The penteconter was an admirably flexible vessel —larger and more formidable than its thirty-oar counterpart the triaconter. In one form or another, by Polycrates' day, it had been in use for centuries. It had a roomy hold and could, if desired, support an ample deck—where, in time of war, archers and hoplites could be stationed. It could function quite easily as a troop carrier, and, especially if single-banked [*monókrotos*], it could also—and, early on, quite frequently did—double as a merchant ship.

In the eighth century, as commerce expanded and communities became more prosperous, specialization began to take hold, a maritime military revolution gradually unfolded, and it became much easier to deploy expeditionary forces by sea. Wealthy merchants persuaded shipwrights to produce bowl-shaped galleys with larger holds able to carry considerably more merchandise, and ambitious maritime polities pressed them to produce "long ships" better adapted for war. By the end of that century, the Phoenicians, the great seafarers of the age, had perfected a new species of penteconter. It was shorter by one third and, as a consequence, far less fragile than its predecessors. It was rowed by two banks of oarsmen, one stationed at the topwale and the other either in the hold or, conceivably, on outriggers situated on the topwale (we are not sure which); and eventually it came to be equipped with a bronze-sheathed ram with a single sharp spike mounted on a bow that had been powerfully reinforced. If deftly handled by an astute captain, an expert helmsman, and an experienced and highly disciplined crew, a double-banked [*díkrotos*] penteconter fitted out with a ram could outmaneuver an adversary, hole his vessel, and swamp or even sink the enemy ship. By the end of the sixth century, moreover, Phoenician merchants had also begun employing "round ships" or "bathtubs" [*gaúloi*]—sailing vessels manageable by relatively small crews, which were equipped with large holds capable of transporting anywhere from seventy to five hundred tons of cargo, depending on the size of the ship. Although the *gaúlos* did not replace the merchant galley, it existed alongside it and from this time on competed with it for cargo on runs where the prevailing winds were favorable.[23]

Herodotus does not tell us what sort of penteconters Polycrates had built. But it stands to reason that they must have been rowed by oarsmen in two banks and that they came to be equipped with rams. If the pirate prince of Samos was to establish and sustain his suzerainty over the eastern Aegean, his

Figure 4. Double-banked [*díkrotos*] penteconter on a piratical raid closing in on a
merchant *gaúlos,* painted on the outer surface of an Athenian black-figured cup, ca.
520–500, found at Vulci. Artist unknown (British Museum 1867,0508.963.
© The Trustees of the British Museum).

fleet had to be state of the art, and there is ample evidence that he displayed a
keen interest in maritime military technology—for we are told that he was the
first to have his shipwrights construct penteconters of the sort that came to be
known as "Samos craft" [*Sámaina naûs*]. These were double-banked vessels
fully decked; and they were, we are told, "quite hollow and pot-bellied, meant
for voyaging [under sail] in the open sea and for moving through the water
[under oars] with speed."[24] Polycrates' Samos craft were evidently designed
not only for armed conflict but also for transporting hoplites as well as booty
and other cargo of value over considerable distances.

It is no surprise, then, that, in the wake of Cyrus' conquest of Lydia and
Babylon, Amasis of Egypt should have sought a guest-friendship and an alliance with Polycrates. The Saite monarchs of Egypt had long relied for the
defense of their realm on mercenary hoplites drawn from Ionia and Caria;
and Amasis—who had long gone out of his way to be on good terms with
the Ionians, Aeolians, and Dorians who lived on or just off the coast of Asia
Minor—was no exception. After Mazares and Harpagus seized the coastal
regions of Asia Minor for Cyrus, the Egyptian Pharaoh may well have needed

a reliable agent in the region, willing and able to recruit and transport the men he required; and, given Egypt's vulnerability to invasion from the Mediterranean, he had good reason to seek an alliance with the man who had mastered the Aegean.[25]

The Saite monarch and the Samian tyrant had a formidable enemy in common. It was no doubt with this enemy in mind—and it was almost surely with ample financial assistance from his Egyptian ally—that Polycrates launched the ambitious campaign of construction for which he was later renowned. First, he built magnificent walls to protect the city of Samos and had his Mytilenian prisoners dig a deep trench around those walls. Then, he constructed the double-branched mole that provided the Samians with a closed harbor and had boat-sheds fashioned for the fleet he lodged therein; and, finally, he rebuilt the Heraeum and drove a tunnel six-tenths of a mile in length through Mount Ampelos to serve as an aqueduct, bring water into the city so that it could withstand a long siege, and provide in a pinch a route of escape.[26] In the absence of generous help from an exceedingly wealthy ally, it is hard to see how a Greek *pólis* in this period could have commanded the resources necessary for fielding so large a fleet and for building on so grand a scale.

A Maritime Military Revolution

At some point in the first half of the 520s, however, there was a breach between Polycrates and Amasis. As is his wont, in an attempt to explain the collapse of their alliance, Herodotus tells a colorful story. He attributes the decision not to Polycrates but to Amasis—who purportedly broke with his Samian guest-friend and ally out of fear that the latter's good fortune would attract nemesis.[27] It is, in fact, far more likely that Polycrates—as he watched from afar Cambyses' preparations for invading Egypt after the death of Cyrus in 530—recalculated the odds of his own survival in what was a rapidly changing strategic environment and tried to switch sides.

At some point, probably not long after Cyrus' capture of Babylon in 539, the Persians absorbed Phoenicia into their empire. The kings governing the cities on the island of Cyprus may have shifted their allegiance to Cyrus at the same time, as Xenophon's testimony suggests. But Xenophon, who falsely attributes the acquisition of Egypt to Cyrus, systematically exaggerates the man's achievements, and it makes more sense to suppose that, after the accession of Cambyses, the Persians leveraged the naval strength of the Phoenicians and persuaded the Cypriot monarchs to abandon Amasis. In any case, one thing is certain: shortly before embarking on the Egyptian expedition, Cyrus' son and heir put together a formidable navy with the help of his Phoenician and Cypriot subjects—and with this navy, as Herodotus tells us, he seized control of the sea.[28]

Powerful though he was, Polycrates was outmatched, and he must have known as much, which is why—probably right after the maritime balance of power shifted and Amasis' navy proved incapable of preventing a Persian takeover on Cyprus—he made a daring attempt to turn coat. It is not plausible to suppose that Amasis would jettison such an ally on the eve of a massive Persian invasion of Egypt. But Polycrates had a motive for doing the like, and he thought that he had the means by which to profit from such a diplomatic revolution. Diodorus Siculus tells us that for a time the Samian tyrant welcomed and harbored wealthy fugitives from Lydia unhappy with Oroites, the Persian satrap at Sardis, but that the day came when he suddenly turned on them, put them to the sword, and confiscated their possessions; and Herodotus reports that he dispatched a herald to Cambyses as the Persian king was mustering his forces against Egypt and offered, on his own initiative, to send a contingent of forty triremes to join the Persian monarch's expedition. These forty triremes—which Amasis, who had triremes of his own, may initially have financed or even placed at the disposal of his far less wealthy Samian ally—are the first ships of this new type that we hear of actually being deployed in Greece.[29]

Thucydides tells us three things once thought to cast light on the emergence of the weapons system then for the first time in Polycrates' possession: first, that "the Corinthians are said to have been the first to handle naval matters in a manner quite near to the way now prevailing"; second, that, "in Greece, triremes are said to have first been constructed at Corinth"; and, third, that a Corinthian shipwright named Ameinocles appears to have journeyed to Samos to make "four ships for the Samians." Thucydides' source dates this last event—not, as we might expect, a century before the outbreak of the Peloponnesian War to the time when Polycrates held sway, but some three hundred years prior to that war's final denouement in 404.[30]

In the past, scholars tended to suppose that all three of the items mentioned in Thucydides' report were indications of the proliferation of the trireme as a weapons system. It seems unlikely, however, that a triple-banked vessel decisively superior to the double-banked penteconter could have been

Figure 5. Section of Athenian trireme carved in stone; fragment of Lenormant relief, ca. 410–400 (Acropolis Museum, Athens; Photograph: Marsyas, Wikimedia Commons, Published November 2015 under the following license: Creative Commons: Attribution Share-Alike 2.5 Generic).

invented as early as the eighth century. Even if we were to reduce the very considerable span of time mentioned by Thucydides—and to do so on the presumption that his source had calculated its length on the basis of the number of generations known to have separated Ameinocles from his own time, using forty years per generation where thirty or even twenty-five was likely to be more accurate—it would still be exceedingly hard to account for the fact that at Samos early in Polycrates' reign, a half century or more after the Samians had acquired their first four triremes, the penteconter was still the warship preferred. Indeed, if the age of the trireme had begun many decades before, it would be impossible to explain how, in 535, a fleet of sixty penteconters rowed by Ionians could have managed to defeat a joint Etruscan-Carthaginian fleet twice that size—as, we are told, it did.[31]

It is likely, then, that Thucydides' reference to the production of triremes at Corinth is an aside, illustrative of his larger point concerning the pioneering efforts of the Corinthians. The first and third items on his list could nonetheless be quite closely linked. When he reports that the Corinthians are said to have been the first to handle naval matters in the manner prevailing in his own time, Thucydides may have meant to indicate that they were reportedly the first in Hellas to build a civic navy of dedicated warships; and, when he speaks of Ameinocles, his point may be that the Corinthian shipwright is thought to have built four of these then-newfangled vessels for the Samians and to have done so in the late eighth century or as late as a century thereafter.[32]

The trireme appears, in fact, to have been an invention of the sixth century, and it may have been Egyptian in origin. Herodotus first mentions triremes being built in a discussion of Nechos son of Psammetichus, who ruled Egypt from about 610 to 595. This report may be accurate, but scholars now have their doubts. Herodotus' Egyptian informants could easily have left him confused, for the Egyptians appear to have used the same term to refer to penteconters that they later employed for triremes. In Greece, we do not hear of triremes as such for more than a half-century after the reign of Nechos, when the poet Hipponax of Ephesus, thought to have flourished from about 540 to 520, first makes use of the word; and they did not fully replace the much smaller penteconter as the standard Hellenic man-of-war until the century's end.[33]

It is possible, of course, that the Greeks were slow on the uptake, but it might make sense to suppose that Nechos' son Psammis, his grandson Apries, or, more likely, their distinguished successor the usurper Amasis was the first to introduce the trireme and that in self-defense, after the last-mentioned Pharaoh's conquest of Cyprus, Egypt's maritime neighbors in Phoenicia and, in time, their Greek rivals in the Aegean followed suit. It is also conceivable that Clement of Alexandria, who wrote many centuries after Herodotus but relied heavily on the Hellenistic author Philostephanos of Cyrene, is correct in attributing the invention of the three-banked galley [*tríkrotos naûs*] to the citizens of Sidon in Phoenicia. We do not know precisely when the vessel first materialized and who first produced it, and to date underwater archaeology has failed to turn up even a single example—in part, perhaps, because, when disabled, triremes fairly often did not fully sink right away and could be recovered and repaired by one side in a battle or the other, and because those that actually made it to the bottom of the sea carried little cargo of a sort likely to get in the way of marine predators and retard the deterioration of the ship's hull.[34]

What we do know, however, is this: the trireme became to naval warfare in the last third of the sixth century what the Dreadnought was to be in the decade preceding World War I. It was powerful, fast, and impregnable to attack by lesser craft; it rendered all previous warships obsolete; and it revolutionized warfare at sea. This graceful vessel was shaped like a wineglass, and, in the manner of the *díkrotoi* penteconters that preceded it, it sported a prow equipped with a bronze-sheathed ram. Its ram, however, had not one, but three horizontal cutting blades capable of slicing through the hull of virtually

Figure 6. Warship ram on a relief showing naval trophies and priests' emblems from Rome (precise findspot unrecorded), Augustan period (Stanza dei Filosofi, Palazzo dei Conservatori, Rome; Photograph: Courtesy of William M. Murray © William M. Murray).

any vessel equal or smaller in mass that it struck amidships or in the stern. On the basis of what archaeologists have learned regarding the size of the ancient shipsheds in Athens' military harbor at Peiraeus, scholars generally suppose the triremes of the archaic and classical age to have varied in size from about one hundred seventeen to one hundred thirty feet in length and from about fifteen to eighteen feet in width, though some now think that those deployed in the third century were considerably smaller.

When fully manned, each of these early triremes was powered by one hundred seventy oarsmen facing the stern, each plying a single oar fourteen feet in length, using as a fulcrum a tholepin to which the oar was tied by a well-greased leather oarloop. These rowers, who slid back and forth on cushions of fleece so that they could leverage the muscles in their legs as they pulled the oars, were organized on three levels—with at least two-thirds of them enclosed within the hull and unable to see their own oars.

In Phoenician ships, which sported majestically high bulwarks lined with shields, the remainder were also situated inside the trireme—some think, at the topwale. In the ships later deployed by the Athenians, however, they were perched on outriggers mounted above and outboard from their colleagues on the topwale. We do not know whether the triremes built by or for Polycrates and those which came to be deployed by the other Ionian cities were constructed on the Phoenician model or not.

Within such a trireme, there were officers on deck to decide on and direct the ship's course, to dictate and sustain the tempo of the oarsmen's strokes,

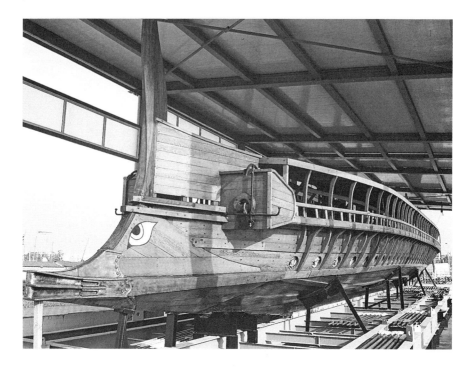

Figure 7. The Olympias, Naval Tradition Park, Palaio Paliro, Greece (Photograph: Χρήστης Templar52, Wikimedia Commons. Published November 2015 under the following license: "The copyright holder of this file allows anyone to use it for any purpose, provided that the copyright holder is properly attributed. Redistribution, derivative work, commercial use, and all other use is permitted.").[35]

and to convey to them the orders of the trierarch awarded command. There was also a shipwright on board and a purser, and there were specialists trained in handling the sails as well as archers and marines fully equipped for combat —enough to bring the boat's full complement to two hundred men at a minimum. Its weight, when loaded with all of the pertinent equipment and personnel, was, most scholars believe, something on the order of fifty tons.[35]

When fully manned—as it had to be if it was not to be underpowered, slow, hard to maneuver, and unlikely to survive a contest—this newfangled ship was a formidable fighting machine.[36] When supplemented by merchant galleys and *gaûloi* bearing grain, fresh water, and other provisions aplenty, it opened up—for the first time in human history—the possibility that a truly magnificent empire could be instituted over the briny deep and from there project power over the surrounding lands.

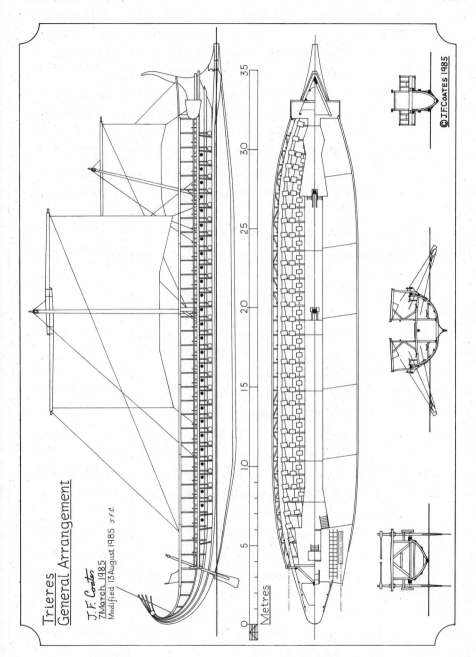

Trieres
General Arrangement

J. F. Coates
7 March 1985
Modified 13 August 1985 j.f.c.

Metres

©J.F.Coates 1985

Figure 8. J. F. Coates's sketch of a trireme (1985) (Courtesy of the Trireme Trust © Trireme Trust).

It says a great deal about Polycrates' acumen that, in the early 520s, he was in the process of substituting triremes for the pentecounters that had hitherto made up his fleet. It says even more that he recognized that the game was up when Cambyses began assembling a navy made up not only of pentecounters and triremes drawn from the Aeolian and Ionian cities on and along the coast of Asia Minor, but also of ships, almost certainly triremes, provided by the cities of Phoenicia and Cyprus.[37] When the Cypriot cities switched their allegiance to the Mede and the wily Samian tyrant adopted a posture of supreme ingratitude, jettisoned his alliance with Egypt's Saite monarch, and sought an accommodation with the Persian king whose father's embrace he had spurned, he was playing a game with high stakes, but he knew what he was about.

Persia, however, was not the only problem that Polycrates had to confront. There were Samians hostile to his tyranny. There no doubt had always been some in the city, descended from the ancient *Gēomóroi,* who grumbled against the Samian tyrant's rule. As his situation vis-à-vis the Persians grew more delicate, however, their numbers may have grown. Now, as a consequence of Polycrates' diplomatic reversal of course, they must have sensed his weakness. The poet Anacreon—who, after tutoring the young Polycrates, had stayed on as a retainer at his court to sing his patron's praises—dismissed the members of this faction as "big-talkers [*muthiētaí*]," but he acknowledges that their influence was pervasive throughout that "sacred town."[38]

Polycrates was certainly sensitive to the danger. Cambyses had responded to his offer with a request for warships. To alleviate the threat posed to him at home, the Samian tyrant reportedly manned the forty triremes he dispatched to the Persian ruler at least in part with these dissidents, and he asked that Cambyses not allow their return. If those from among his opponents who were dispatched on these ships did not divine his intentions from the start, they soon caught on. After their departure from Samos—when they put in for water and rest at Carpathos en route to their rendezvous or, later, after they reached Cambyses and he had them arrested—the dissidents took matters into their own hands, seized control of at least some of the ships, and sailed back to Samos. There, they surprised and vanquished the fleet of pentecounters that made up what was left of Polycrates' navy, landed on the island, and were themselves defeated in battle by the mercenaries the tyrant kept on hand. It was at this point that Anacreon's "big-talkers" sailed off to make their appeal to the Lacedaemonians and the Corinthians.[39]

A Venture Overseas

Although the Spartans had no doubt found Samian piracy an irritation, they must initially have welcomed Polycrates' defeat of the fleet fielded on Cyrus' behalf by his Aeolian and Ionian allies, and they must have regarded with favor the emergence of his little maritime empire in the eastern Aegean. They were always more than willing to let others do their fighting for them; and, as long as Polycrates' thalassocracy remained intact and he stood fast, they knew that the Persians would be unable to sail through the Cyclades to attack mainland Greece. When, however, Cyrus came to rule Phoenicia and Cambyses put together a fleet, acquired Cyprus, and made preparations for the conquest of Egypt—especially when Polycrates then responded by abandoning Amasis, switching sides, and putting his navy at the disposition of Persia's Great King—the Lacedaemonians became alarmed. In the circumstances, the arrival of the Samian dissidents must have seemed a godsend—especially since Cambyses was for the moment preoccupied in Egypt—and the Spartans seized on their appeal as an opportunity to install their guest-friends in power and to return Samos to its previous anti-Persian policy.

We should not underestimate the significance of what the Spartans and the Corinthians tried to accomplish in 525. Never before had the Dorians of Lacedaemon ventured so far from home. Never had they come anywhere near the coast of Asia Minor. They would not have taken so great a risk on this occasion had they not felt compelled to do so. The force they sent was, we are told, quite large. It had to be. To land an army on Samos, they had to defeat or overawe Polycrates' fleet. To initiate a siege, they had to defeat or overawe the mercenaries in his hoplite army. In the end, they accomplished both.[40] But the city they did not take.

When it came to sieges, the classical Greeks were amateurs. Almost never do we hear of them building a siege mound or digging mines under the walls of cities in the manner of the Assyrians and the Persians. In this pursuit, the Spartans were especially inept. They were homebodies—nervous about the possibility that, in their absence, the helots might rise—and they did not have the patience to maintain a siege long enough to starve the defenders out. Even in the fifth century, they were notorious for this particular incapacity.[41]

Regarding this particular siege—and, indeed, on Samian matters more generally—Herodotus was exceedingly well-informed. At one stage, relatively early in his adult life, he had been driven from his native Halicarnassus by a tyrant, and he had lived in exile on Samos for a time. He was acquainted with descendants of those who had been besieged, and he had imbibed a great deal of family lore from the Samian aristocrats with whom he had whiled away his time. Time and again this lore shows up in his narrative. Moreover, Herodotus had visited Sparta, and there among those whom he had interviewed was the grandson of a distinguished Lacedaemonian warrior who had demonstrated great valor and gained lasting glory in losing his life in the struggle on Samos. It was, the historian makes clear, the fortifications constructed by Polycrates that stymied the attackers' efforts. After a siege of forty days, the Spartans and the Corinthians returned home.[42]

At the end of his account of the siege, Herodotus mentions in passing a story in circulation that he describes as "quite groundless." According to this tale, Polycrates had managed to persuade the Spartans to call off the siege by way of a clever trick. He had supposedly struck a substantial number of Samian coins in gilded lead with an eye to passing them off as pure gold, and with these he had both gulled and bribed those among the Spartans who mattered. This story is not on its face implausible; it may well be true; and Herodotus may have mentioned it in order to encourage us to draw a conclusion that he, for reasons personal to him, chose not to draw. In reaction, it would seem, to the severity of the discipline to which they were subject, the Spartans were notoriously vulnerable to bribery when out from under the purview of their fellow *hómoioi;* and a number of Samian coins made of lead covered with a thin layer of electrum do, in fact, survive.[43]

The enterprise undertaken by the Spartans and the Corinthians failed. But the venture may not have been entirely without consequence. Like Polycrates, Lygdamis of Naxos was also at odds with some of the wealthier citizens of the island community he governed, and there is reason to suspect that he may have joined his friend and ally Polycrates in attempting to reach an accommodation with the Mede. With him, something was certainly amiss. According to Plutarch, the Spartans at some point sent an embassy to the island, and Lygdamis went very far out of his way to avoid a meeting; and Plutarch also reports that they later ousted the Naxian tyrant from power. The only time when the Lacedaemonians could have done so with ease was in the course of their expedition to Samos. They then had the means, and Lygdamis must somehow have supplied the motive. It is certainly telling that the regime that succeeded his tyranny proved to be a bulwark against Persia's advance. According to Herodotus, a quarter of a century after the Spartan expedition against Polycrates, when Cambyses' successor dispatched an armada of two hundred triremes to conquer Naxos, its citizens bravely resisted the assault and steadfastly withstood four months of siege.[44]

Polycrates did not long survive the attack launched by the Spartans and Corinthians, and Samos soon lost whatever independence it then still retained. For understandable reasons, Oroites—whom Cyrus had put in charge of the Persian satrapy at Sardis at some point after the collapse of the Lydian revolt—regarded the Samian tyrant with loathing and distrust. In his heyday, Polycrates had thrashed Persia's Aeolic and Ionian Greek allies. He had later made a mockery of Oroites himself by treating the satrap's emissaries with contempt,[45] and the force of triremes that he had promised Cambyses had either failed to join the expeditionary force attacking Egypt or had abandoned its post soon after arriving. Polycrates was fair game.

Two or three years after the Spartan siege at Samos was lifted—after Cambyses first fell ill, we are told, but while he was still alive—Oroites lured the Samian tyrant to Magnesia on the Maeander with a promise of gold. He professed to have learned that Cambyses had issued an order for his execution. He expressed a desire to flee from Asia with Polycrates' help, and he promised the tyrant ample compensation for his pains. Polycrates may not have been in a position to spurn Oroites' offer. He had lost his fleet of triremes, and the conflict with the Samian aristocrats and with Lacedaemon had cost him a pretty penny and left him weaker and more vulnerable than before. There is, moreover, reason to suppose that he had once been able to rely on Amasis' largess. But that day had passed, and he could not support his lavish establishment at Samos, pay the mercenaries who sustained his rule, and pursue his imperial ambitions within Ionia with the scanty resources available from that island alone—and so he walked into the trap. When Polycrates presented himself on the mainland at Magnesia, the satrap seized him and crucified him on the shores of the Mycale peninsula where he could be seen by Samians on the other side of the straits.[46]

When Polycrates traveled to Magnesia, he left his secretary Maeandrius son of Maeandrius in charge on Samos. In the aftermath, this man, who had served as an intermediary and may have been party to Oroites' plot, is said to have proposed to his fellow citizens the establishment of a republican government guaranteeing *isonomía*—equality in the distribution of booty and under the law. But, when those on the isle better-born than this upstart did not welcome his initiative, Maeandrius and his brothers had Polycrates' mercenaries arrest and execute the most outspoken of his opponents, and they then acted forcefully to consolidate their hold on the island.⁴⁷

As it turned out, however, neither Maeandrius nor Oroites lasted long. Both were soon overtaken by events beyond their control. Cambyses' unexpected demise while in Syria en route home from Egypt altered the political playing field—initially in a manner that no doubt encouraged them both, but ultimately in a fashion neither they nor the Spartans can have welcomed.

The Emergence of Darius

In 522, Persia's dominion very nearly collapsed. In this regard, a few things are clear. There was at that time widespread discontent within the realm. Cambyses died without issue and without a designated heir. His younger brother Bardiya (transliterated, variously, as Mardos or Smerdis in fifth-century Greek sources) or someone representing himself as such briefly occupied the throne; and a well-placed Persian noble named Darius managed—with the help of a number of prominent Persian families and with backing from the army that Cambyses had taken to Egypt—to assassinate and replace the man. The rest is surmise.⁴⁸

There was an official story. Darius soon had it carved in cuneiform, alongside an elaborate relief emblematic of the tale, into the cliffs at Bisitun above the Khorasan road leading from Babylon to Ecbatana—where it can still be found in the Old Persian script that, Darius tells us, he had his scribes devise, and also in the venerable scripts of Elam and Akkad. This text he had his minions post in prominent places throughout the realm. It was presumably his aim to have it proclaimed, as the book of Esther puts it, "in every polity according to its script and to every people according to its tongue." This propaganda effort appears to have been quite effective. Two generations later, when Herodotus inquired, he was told by his Persian informants a more elaborate, detailed, and, perhaps in some particulars, confused version of the same tale.⁴⁹

The account propagated by Darius and his associates was, to say the least, dramatic. According to it, Cambyses had become suspicious and jealous of his younger brother and had secretly had him killed. Later, as Cyrus' successor and only surviving male heir was making his way back from Egypt, a Magus of Median extraction, who had been left in charge of the royal household and was one of the few fully apprised of the murder, persuaded his brother to

VUE GÉOMÉTRALE
DES BAS-RELIEFS

Figure 9. Etching by Auguste-Alexandre Guillaumot after a drawing by Pascal Coste of the view from the Khorosan road of the cliff at Bisitun, featuring at a distance the relief that Darius had carved into that cliff ca. 519 (From Eugène Flandin and Pascal Coste, *Voyage en Perse de Mm. Eugène Flandin, Peintre, et Pascal Coste, Architecte, Entrepris par Ordre de M. le Ministre des Affaires Étrangères, d'après les Instructions Dressées par l'Institut* [Paris: Gide and Baudry, 1851], pl. 16; Photograph: General Research Division, The New York Public Library, Astor, Lenox and Tilden Foundations).

masquerade as Bardiya, and the two staged a rebellion against Cambyses and managed to rally support among the Persians, the Medes, and their subjects by announcing a three-year tax holiday and exemption from military service. Among the first to recognize the impostor as such, according to this story, was the Darius already mentioned, who traced his lineage to a shadowy figure named Achaemenes, whom he would in due course represent as having been a king and the father of Cyrus' great-grandfather Teispes.[50]

This Darius knew the court well. The lineage to which he belonged was exceedingly well-connected. A relative of his, a fellow Achaemenid named Cassandane daughter of Pharnaspes, had been the principal wife of Cyrus; and she it was who gave birth to the Great King's designated heir and to his younger brother Bardiya. Perhaps, in part, as a consequence of this connection, Darius' father Hystaspes son of Arsames was in due course made satrap of Parthia, and Darius himself became a close personal attendant of, first, Cyrus and, then, Cambyses. The former he reportedly served as "quiver-bearer"; and, in the court of the latter, he was the "spear-bearer."[51] According to the officially sanctioned account, this Darius had secured the aid of six co-conspirators no less distinguished—Intaphernes, Otanes, Gobryas, Hydarnes, Megabyzos, and Ardumanish—and together they had assassinated the impostor and set things to rights.

For understandable reasons, scholars have long regarded this story with suspicion.[52] The tale as told by Darius, even when fleshed out by Herodotus' sources among the descendants of his co-conspirators,[53] does not survive at all well the application of Ockham's razor. It is simply too convoluted, too complex, and improbable to be plausible; and it serves all too conveniently to justify and even glorify the conduct of those who spread it. It would, in fact, be simpler to suppose that the financial support and military service required by Cyrus and Cambyses to fund their endless wars had stirred discontent throughout the realm and that the latter's ambitious younger brother attempted to exploit this discontent for the purpose of seizing the throne. It would be simpler to suppose that Cambyses died unexpectedly while en route home to suppress his brother's rebellion and that a group of seven Persians of great prominence, who had occupied positions of high trust within Cambyses' army and court while in Egypt, suddenly and unexpectedly found themselves isolated and had to choose between eliminating Bardiya and the prospect of suffering disfavor, a loss of property, and perhaps even torture and death. It would be simpler to suppose that, when faced with this dilemma, the seven chose the more honorable and audacious course and that, in the aftermath, Darius emerged on top.[54]

This reconstruction of the story has three virtues. It fits the known facts. It is consistent with Xenophon's report that, after Cyrus' death, his sons fell into dissension. It gibes reasonably well with Aeschylus' treatment of Darius' immediate predecessor as a lawful monarch brought down and assassinated by a conspiracy spearheaded by a man bearing the name of Darius' brother Artaphernes.[55]

In the end, however, our efforts at making sense of the available evidence can be no more than guesswork, for the full truth is beyond recovery. Nonetheless, some parts of the official story told in the Bisitun inscription cannot be gainsaid—for there is independent evidence that, in the aftermath of the coup d'état carried out by the seven conspirators, rebellions really did erupt in virtually every corner of the realm—among the Elamites, the Babylonians, the Assyrians, the Armenians, the Medes, various peoples of the Iranian plateau, the Egyptians, and even, tellingly, the Persians in Parsā.

It is easy to see why these rebellions took place. To begin with, Darius' claim to the throne was tenuous in the extreme. His assertion that Cyrus was the great-great-grandson of his own great-great-grandfather Achaemenes and that he was, therefore, himself a member of a cadet branch of the royal family is unsubstantiated by any evidence prior to his own reign. Even, however, if one were to credit this self-serving assertion, Darius was a quite distant relative of Cyrus. His own grandfather and father—who were, as he boasts, still alive at the time of his accession—certainly had a better claim to the kingship than he did, and there must have been a great many Persians directly descended in the male line from Cyrus' more immediate predecessors on the Persian throne who had better claims than the members of Darius' family. The fact that two of the rebellions he had to put down originated in Parsā and that suppressing these revolts required multiple campaigns weighs heavily against Darius' legitimacy.[56]

That was one challenge that Darius had to face. There was another. The Persian empire was itself quite fragile. There may have been uprisings in various regions when Cyrus died. Those that took place outside Parsā after the assassination of Bardiya were numerous. It is, moreover, highly indicative that most of them appear to have been aimed at restoring local independence and autonomy under men claiming to be heirs to the kings overthrown by Cyrus and Cambyses.[57] Had Darius been less capable or had the rebels managed to cooperate effectively against the common foe, the assassination of Bardiya would have marked the end of a brief, anomalous period of Persian domination in the Near East. But, as it turned out, the notable of Achaemenid stock who had served as Cyrus' quiver-bearer and Cambyses' spear-bearer possessed all of the strategic acumen, courage, daring, and determination that had been displayed by the empire's founder. Methodically, over the course of a year, he deftly deployed elements of the army of veterans that had marched back from Egypt—in one theater after another—to crush the rebellions, using as subordinate commanders his own co-conspirators and those among Cambyses' satraps who rallied to his support.

Darius' venture appears to have had an ethnic dimension. Herodotus intimates that what was at stake in 522 was whether Cyrus' empire was to be ruled by the Medes or the Persians, and he tells us that Darius' coup d'état eventuated in a massacre of the Magi, who were all Medes. As if to confirm this claim, in the Bisitun inscription, Darius expressly and emphatically identifies each of his fellow conspirators one by one as Persians, and a silver plaque, owned by his co-conspirator Otanes, explicitly confirms in his own case the same claim. In other inscriptions, Darius repeatedly and emphatically identifies himself as a Persian, as does his son Xerxes on at least one occasion.[58]

Cyrus did nothing of the sort. In his inscriptions at Babylon, he identifies himself, his father, grandfather, and great-grandfather proudly as kings of Anshan, using the ancient Elamite name for his seat of power; and he does not identify himself or his forbearers as Persians or even as Iranians. His name, which he shares with his grandfather, is, moreover—unlike those borne by Darius and the members of his family—Elamite, rather than Iranian, in derivation; and the same can be said with regard to the name he gives for his great-grandfather. There is no reason to doubt the testimony of Herodotus, Ctesias, and Xenophon that he and his predecessors on the throne of Anshan thought of themselves as Persians, and it is telling that Cyrus chose as his principal wife a woman from the proudly Persian Achaemenid clan, but it seems highly likely that the royal descendants of Teispes had Elamite as well as Persian antecedents; and, in distributing office and honors, they may have made little or no distinction between the two peoples.[59]

The empire that Cyrus established and left to his son Cambyses seems, moreover, to have been as much a project of the Medes as it was of the Persians. According to Herodotus, its founder's mother was the daughter of Astyages the Mede; and Ctesias, although he denies this claim, nonetheless contends that the Bactrians in eastern Iran submitted to Cyrus because they regarded him as the rightful successor of the kings of the Medes. Xenophon confirms Herodotus' assertion, and he reports that Cyrus encouraged his associates, who may have been accustomed to Elamite garb, to dress henceforth in the manner of the Medes—which, Herodotus confirms, they did. There is, moreover, a passage in the Bisitun inscription in which Darius seems to acknowledge that the Medes (but strikingly, not the Elamites) were in some unspecified way legitimate players in the great drama described therein. Prior to his own intervention, he laments, "there was no man—neither a Persian, *nor a Mede,* nor anyone from our family—who could deprive that Magus Gaumata of the kingship."[60] If there was ever any ambiguity about the ethnic character of the empire, however, Darius' accession eliminated it.

There was a religious dimension to Darius' enterprise as well, and it may explain both the massacre of the Magi and his assertion in the Bisitun inscription that he had restored cult sites destroyed by Gaumata. We know next to nothing about the religious commitments of Cyrus and Cambyses. We know that, in dealing with the Babylonians, Jews, and Egyptians, they were accommodating. What we are told regarding Cyrus' tomb and the commemorative rites maintained there through subsequent reigns by the Magi is compatible with later Zoroastrian practice. But—if Cyrus and his sons really were followers of the prophet whom the Persians called Zarathustra and the Greeks, Zoroaster—they did not go to any great lengths to broadcast their allegiance; and there are scholars who suspect, with some reason, that Cyrus, Cambyses, Bardiya, and the Magi of the time, who rallied the Medes in their support and played a prominent role in the administration of their empire, gave their allegiance first and foremost to the god Mithra.[61]

By way of contrast, Darius—whose father bore the name of Zarathustra's princely patron and may well have been named after that figure—vigorously and ostentatiously trumpeted his faith. In the Bisitun inscription, he repeatedly acknowledges his debt to the Wise Lord Ahura Mazda—a divinity previously almost unheard of, except as the principal god in the *Gathas,* the oldest part of the Zoroastrian *Avesta.* This deity Darius mentions in the Bisitun inscription no fewer than seventy-six times; and, on the silver plaque instanced above, his co-conspirator Otanes expresses gratitude to Ahura Mazda in precisely the same fashion. In all of his other inscriptions of any length, moreover, Darius returns to this theme; and in these inscriptions, like the Zoroastrians known in later times, he depicts this Ahura Mazda as the creator of the world. Xerxes follows his father's lead in all of these particulars; and, in an inscription known to have existed in at least five different copies, he denounces "demon-worshipers" in a manner reminiscent of the *Avesta*.

Strikingly, neither Otanes nor either of these two kings ever mentions by name any god other than the Wise Lord Ahura Mazda, and the same can be said regarding Xerxes' legitimate son and heir Artaxerxes and the latter's bastard son and heir Darius II. If Ahura Mazda was, as these kings proclaim, "the greatest of all the gods," it was presumably because Mithra, Humban, and the other deities of Iranian and Elamite origin worshipped by the Persians at Persepolis and elsewhere resembled the angels of the Judeo-Christian tradition in one crucial particular: they were creatures summoned into being by the supreme god. In telltale fashion, Darius' Elamite scribe identifies Ahura Mazda in one of former's inscriptions as "*the god* of the Aryans"—which is to say, of the Iranians.[62]

This evidence is by no means dispositive, but it is suggestive in the extreme. For Zoroastrianism was clearly a force in early Achaemenid Iran. Its cosmology exercised a profound influence on the sixth-century Greek theologian Pherecydes of Syros and on the pre-Socratic philosophers Anaximander of Miletus and Heraclitus of Ephesus. In the army deployed by Darius' son shortly after that great man's death, there was at least one exceedingly learned, literate Zoroastrian who survived its invasion of Greece; and in the book that Xanthus of Lydia composed concerning the Magi in the mid-fifth century, he not only mentioned Zoroaster by name and depicted those belonging to that venerable religious order as his successors and disciples. He also located the prophet chronologically in a manner suggesting that his own sources among the Magi were inclined to situate the endeavors of the Achaemenid kings within a temporal framework provided by the account of salvation history and the eschatology articulated within the *Avesta*.[63]

Moreover, the terms in which Darius denounces Gaumata and those within the realm of Darius and Cambyses who rebelled in the wake of the conspirators' assassination of the man are akin to what we know regarding the cosmological imperatives of Zoroastrianism. Herodotus, writing in the mid-to-late fifth century, tells us that the Persians taught their sons "three things only: to ride, to shoot the bow, and to speak the truth," and he insists that their commitment to telling the truth was for them a matter of supreme importance. Plato—writing in the first half of the fourth century at a time when we have conclusive evidence for the presence at the Achaemenid court of self-styled "followers of Zarathustra"—reports that the sons of the Great King were taught, while quite young, to ride and hunt and were later instructed by the royal pedagogues in "the religious lore [*mageía*]" of "Zoro-aster son of Horomazes." From them, he observes, the sons of the king learned not only "the care due the gods" but also "kingly things," which include cour-age, self-mastery in the face of pleasure, and that which is "most just: to speak the truth through the entirety of one's life." It is for this reason quite striking that, in the Bisitun inscription, Darius indicts not only Gaumata, but also the *bandaka* or "bondsmen" who renounced their allegiance to Cambyses and those who desperately sought to free themselves from the Achaemenid yoke by rebellion after Gaumata's death for having committed the greatest of all crimes—by breaking their bond, betraying truth and trust, and thereby em-bracing what the Persians called *Drauga:* "the Lie." On the silver plaque be-longing to Otanes, Darius' co-conspirator similarly promises to punish "the liar."[64]

Within the *Avesta,* there is a strikingly similar, dramatic juxtaposition of adherence to the truth with adherence to the lie, and therein this juxtaposi-tion arises as a consequence of the radical dualism—attributed to the Magi of Persia by Aristotle, Plato's student the mathematician Eudoxus, and the historian Theopompus of Chios—which, to this day, forms the centerpiece of the religious doctrine of the Zoroastrians. That the early Achaemenids also embraced this theological dualism and articulated in its light a doctrine foreshadowing the sharp distinction that Muslim jurists would later draw be-tween the House of Submission [*Dar al-Islam*] and the House of War [*Dar al-Harb*] we can infer from a report in Plutarch indicating that Artaxerxes, Darius' grandson and Xerxes' son and heir, considered Hellas—which lay out-side the domain he governed on Ahura Mazda's behalf—a part of the realm controlled by the Evil Spirit Ahriman, whose name is an elision, found also in the later Zoroastrian writings, of Angra Mainyu: the title given the satanic figure depicted in the Gathas and elsewhere in the *Avesta* as the source of all opposition to the Wise Lord.[65]

It seems almost certain, then, that with Darius' accession we are witness-ing in the Near East the triumph of a distinctive strain of Zoroastrianism, which was militant and thoroughly politicized;[66] and it is clear that, within this creed, judgment in the afterlife and salvation of the sort outlined in the *Avesta* were thought to depend not only on the proper worship of Ahura Mazda but also on faithful service in this world to the chosen one of the Wise

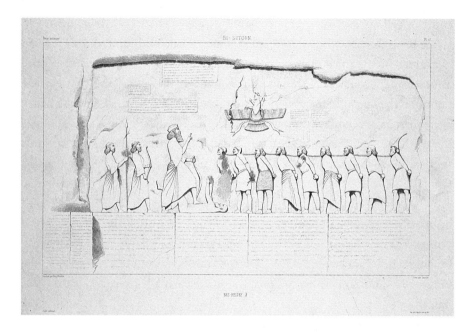

Figure 10. Etching by Nicolas-Auguste Leisnier after a drawing by Eugène Flandin
of the relief featuring Darius with the "liar kings" in captivity as well as the related
inscriptions in Elamite, Akkadian, and Old Persian that Darius had carved into the
cliffs at Bisitun, ca. 519 (From Flandin and Coste, *Voyage en Perse,* pl. 16; Photograph:
General Research Division, The New York Public Library, Astor, Lenox and Tilden
Foundations).

Lord as specified in divinely sanctioned law. It should come, then, as no surprise that a Persian at prayer was expected, as Herodotus tells us, to pray first
and foremost for the Great King and for the Persian nation—the people chosen for a sacred mission by the great god.[67] The religious fervor evident in the
inscriptions of Darius and Xerxes was one of the distinguishing features of
the nascent Achaemenid regime; and, as we shall in due course have occasion
to note, the imperatives attendant on the faith which these two Persian monarchs embraced and propagated powerfully informed the aspirations of each
and every Achaemenid Great King.[68]

In the aftermath of his coup d'état, Darius cannily moved to shore up the
legitimacy of his line. He took as wives the daughters of Cyrus and Bardiya.
He sired a firstborn son to succeed him and three more to spare with Atossa,
the elder of Cyrus' two daughters. And in the Old Persian, Elamite, and
Akkadian scripts, he had inscriptions carved into columns and above a relief
at Cyrus' palace in Parsā at Pasargadae—in which, in a fashion favorable to

the pretensions of the son of Hystaspes, the founder of the Persian empire is made to identify himself as "the Achaemenid."[69]

Under Cyrus and Cambyses, the administration of the empire may have been in some measure an *ad hoc,* ramshackle affair, but this was not the case under Darius, who is said to have reorganized Persia's domain in such a fashion as to consolidate royal control, guarantee himself and his successors a steady stream of income, and render uprisings less likely and much easier to suppress. As the tablets found in Darius' palaces at Susa and Persepolis confirm, the report provided by Polycleitus of Larissa in the late fourth century is accurate, if garbled and incomplete. "On high ground in Susa," he tells us, Darius built and his successors maintained "a palace, treasuries, and storerooms" where they kept "the tribute" they received from their subjects—and, though he does not mention it, they did the same at Persepolis and they presumably used the old palaces at Ecbatana and Babylon for much the same purpose. "From the coastal communities," Polycleitus then adds, "they extracted silver; and from those in the interior they took the things each territory produced." Among these things were to be found not only the beer, grain, horses, beautiful young women, and castrated boys highlighted in our other sources, but also the "dyes, drugs, hair or wool, other things of this sort, and livestock as well" mentioned by Polycleitus. The Persians thought of Cyrus as a father, Herodotus tells us. They considered Cambyses a slavemaster. But Darius they regarded as a shopkeeper.[70]

The administrative apparatus that Cyrus, Cambyses, and Darius in particular put in place and the system of surveillance that came with it were formidable. Within the Persian empire, no one traveled any real distance without authorization; virtually every transaction that took place was directly or indirectly taxed; the conduct of the satraps was closely monitored by subordinates who reported directly to the Great King; and the local militias, supplied by the military colonies and by individuals who were given fiefs in return for a promise of military service, were mustered for inspection annually. We know very little about the empire's administration in the days of Cyrus and Cambyses. In the aftermath of Darius' reorganization of the empire, however, the Achaemenid monarchs who, in emulation of Darius himself, called themselves Kings of Kings operated like spiders at the center of a great web. They were anything but sedentary. Within the core provinces of their great empire, they were frequently on the move. With a vast retinue, they summered at Ecbatana in the highlands of Media. In cooler weather, they sojourned at Susa and in Parsā at the great palace Darius had built at Persepolis; and, on occasion, they no doubt stayed in Babylon as well. From these strategic vantage points, Darius and his successors labored to keep close tabs on everything that was going on.[71]

The Reluctance of Cleomenes

When Darius and his fellow conspirators assassinated Bardiya and the various nations conquered by Cyrus and Cambyses erupted in revolt, Lydia had remained quiet. Oroites, who might have offered help to the conspirators in putting down these revolts and who may well have been called on to do so, stayed out of the fight. Instead, he seized on the time of disorder that followed Bardiya's death as an opportunity to kill his colleague Mitrobates, who administered another satrapy in Asia Minor from Dascyleion near the Sea of Marmara, and he murdered as well Mitrobates' son. Then, he proceeded to unite Phrygia, Lydia, and Ionia under his control. During this period, when Darius sent him a message by courier that displeased him, he had the courier killed and all trace of the man eliminated. In consequence, when he had quelled the various rebellions elsewhere, Darius arranged for the renegade satrap's execution.[72]

Soon thereafter, Darius dispatched Otanes, one of the seven conspirators, to seize Samos for Persia and install as tyrant an exile from the island—with whom, in his days in Egypt as spear-bearer to Cambyses, he had formed cordial relations. As it happens, this man—who was named Syloson after the first tyrant of Samos—was a younger brother of the Polycrates whom Oroites had crucified.[73]

When Otanes came to Samos, Maeandrius is said to have welcomed him at first with open arms. Then, while his brother Charilaos launched a surprise attack on Otanes' Persian entourage, using the mercenary force put together long before by Polycrates, Maeandrius fled the town by way of a tunnel, probably the one housing the city's aqueduct. Then, he took ship and made his way to Lacedaemon. There, he attempted to bribe the Agiad king, Cleomenes son of Anaxandridas, who is said to have witnessed the appeal made just a few years before by the Samian exiles hostile to Polycrates. Knowing his compatriots susceptible to bribes, and fearing that the man might use his considerable wealth to corrupt them, Cleomenes had the ephors expel him not just from Lacedaemon but from the Peloponnesus as well.[74] The Spartans were not a seafaring lot. They had blundered into trouble in the eastern Mediterranean once. They were not going to be quick to do so again—not if Cleomenes had anything to say about it.

And Cleomenes was, as it happens, a man with plenty to say, for he was adamant on the matter, and he was formidable in his role as king. He was young and energetic, he was exceedingly spirited and keenly intelligent, and he was a fierce proponent of the grand strategy finally worked out in his father's generation. We do not have the sort of evidence for Cleomenes' conduct at Lacedaemon within the domestic sphere that we have for Agesilaus in the fourth century. We are not in a position to watch him exploiting the prerogatives of kingship and the patronage associated with that office to maximum advantage. But there can be no doubt that he did so. In the three decades preceding the battle of Marathon, every time that we find Sparta taking the initiative or resolutely refusing to do so, Cleomenes is the figure in the lead.[75]

A few years after Maeandrius' visit to Lacedaemon, probably not long after 514 or 513—when, as we shall see, Darius undertook a disastrous expedition to the region north of the Black Sea and east of the Danube against the Scythians—that nomadic people reportedly sent a deputation to Sparta to propose that the Lacedaemonians join them in a grand expedition aimed at taking vengeance on the Achaemenid colossus. The Spartiates would later complain that these Scythians introduced Cleomenes to the consumption of wine unmixed with water and that he soon became addicted to this shocking practice. But they never breathed a word about an attempt on his part to persuade the Spartans to field an expeditionary force in support of the Persians' Scythian foe.[76]

Cleomenes had a third opportunity to reconsider his profound reluctance to involve his compatriots in an expedition overseas. In 499, as we shall see, the cities of Aeolis and Ionia—those on the mainland of Asia Minor and the *póleis* on the islands along the coast—staged a great revolt. Miletus, the largest and most prosperous of these communities, led the way. The story is complex and worthy of consideration, but, in this chapter, the details need not detain us long. Here, it is sufficient to mention that a man named Aristagoras son of Molpagoras, who was in charge at Miletus, recognized that the Ionians needed all the help that they could get. In consequence, like Pythermos of Phocaea, like the "big-talkers" of Samos, like Polycrates' erstwhile secretary Maeandrius, and the ambassadors of the Scythians, this Aristagoras soon followed the well-worn path to Lacedaemon in search of help. According to

Herodotus, the former tyrant of Miletus played down the difficulty of the venture he proposed, denying that the Persians were courageous; noting that in battle they bore inferior arms, which is to say bows and relatively short spears [*aichmè brachéa*]; and pointedly insisting that they were equipped neither with the sizable shield [*aspís*] nor with the long, heavy thrusting spear [*dóru*] that distinguished the Greek hoplite. With him, he brought a map of the world, perhaps a copy on bronze of the one known to have been devised by the pre-Socratic philosopher Anaximander of Miletus and to have been corrected by Aristagoras' friend, advisor, and fellow Milesian Hecataeus. His aim was to bring home to the Agiad monarch the vast empire that the Spartans could hope to gain; and, to this end, he reportedly exhorted Cleomenes, "It is requisite that you put aside your battles with the Messenians (with whom you are equally matched) over territory narrowly confined, which is neither especially extensive nor serviceable; and you must also put aside your battles with the Arcadians and the Argives, who possess none of the gold and silver for which men with eagerness fight to the death."

Aristagoras is said to have blundered in one particular only. When asked how many days it would take for the Spartans to march from the Aegean to the court of Persia's Great King, he told the truth—that the march would take three months. This was enough to cause Cleomenes to bring the conversation to an abrupt halt with the remark that the Lacedaemonians would never agree to be led on "a journey of three months' duration away from the sea." When the Milesian attempted to bribe him with the princely sum of fifty talents (which is to say, 1.425 tons) of silver, the Agiad king reportedly left the room, and Aristagoras soon departed.[77]

If, in the face of invitation after invitation, Cleomenes was skeptical and cautious, it was because he understood only too well the imperatives of the Lacedaemonian regime. His task as king was to protect and preserve the Spartan way of life. If he and his compatriots were to achieve this, they would have to be wary and canny. They might properly be inclined to shore up a polity, such as Samos, that stood in Persia's way, but they had to weigh the risks against the likelihood of success. Lacedaemon had tried such a ploy on the eve of Cleomenes' kingship in circumstances that seemed highly favorable —but to no avail. To attempt it again in the quite different circumstances that prevailed when Maeandrius, the Scythians, and Aristagoras made their approaches to Cleomenes, to intervene directly and forcefully in a conflict in which the Mede was already deeply engaged—such a maneuver might well be suicidal. It would almost certainly provoke and infuriate the Persian colossus, and it might bring on the very crisis that Cleomenes and his fellow Spartans devoutly wished to avoid. If, moreover, they did nothing at all, the Persian threat might recede. This had very nearly happened in 522. In the sphere of politics, diplomacy, and war, patience is an asset; and the Lacedaemonians possessed this virtue in abundance.

CHAPTER 2

Mainland Defense

They were free states; they were small ones; and the age being martial, all their neighbors were continually in arms. Freedom naturally begets public spirit, especially in small states; and this public spirit, this amor patriæ, must encrease when the public is almost in continual alarm, and men are obliged, every moment, to expose themselves to the greatest dangers for its defence. A continual succession of wars makes every citizen a soldier: He takes the field in his turn: And during his service he is chiefly maintained by himself. This service is indeed equivalent to a heavy tax; yet it is less felt by a people addicted to arms, who fight for honour and revenge more than pay, and are unacquainted with gain and industry as well as pleasure.

—DAVID HUME

WHEN word reached Lacedaemon of the rebellions that took place within the Persian empire in 522 and 521, the Spartans must initially have felt a measure of relief. These erstwhile allies of Croesus would no doubt have welcomed the dissolution of the great empire that Cyrus and Cambyses had built, and they were no doubt disappointed when Darius and those among his compatriots who were intent on restoring and bolstering Persian control emerged victorious. Of course, had the Great Kings of Persia been content to rule western Asia and Egypt, the Lacedaemonians would have had no need to depart from the grand strategy that they had gradually articulated in the century following their reconquest of the Stenyklaros plain in Messenia. When, however, Cambyses gathered a fleet and took control of the sea, as we have already seen; and again, even more emphatically, when Darius and his son Xerxes began to interest themselves in a serious way in the affairs of the Aegean islanders and in those of the Thracians and Macedonians to the east of Thessaly on the European mainland, as we shall soon see, the Spartans found themselves in a quandary.

Their numbers were limited, and their responsibilities at home, daunting.

If the Lacedaemonians sallied forth to confront the Persian threat, they would have to reduce the size of the garrisons that, we must assume, they maintained in Laconia and Messenia and leave the cities of the Peloponnesus, at least for a time, to their own devices. In doing so, they would risk giving the helots, who lay in wait for a sign of weakness on their part, an opening; and the same could be said with regard to those within the Peloponnesus unhappy with Sparta's hegemony. If, however, they failed to sally forth, there was every likelihood that, in time, the Argives and others unhappy with the status quo within the Peloponnesus would mount a successful appeal to the Persians for aid and challenge them nearer to home. In initially elaborating a grand strategy for the defense of their dominion and way of life, the Spartans had not anticipated such a challenge. They were caught on the horns of a dilemma, and they were to remain for decades in that profoundly uncomfortable and awkward position, confronting grave danger on every side.

The Lacedaemonians had an aversion to overseas ventures, as we have seen. But Cleomenes and his fellow Spartans were far less hesitant when it came to expeditions within the Greek heartland on the Balkan peninsula. We get a glimpse of them in 519—if Thucydides' chronology is to be trusted—not long before Maeandrius made his pitch to the Agiad king. Herodotus tells us that "Cleomenes son of Anaxandridas and the Lacedaemonians just happened to be in the vicinity" of Plataea; that the citizens of that *pólis* appealed to the Agiad king for help against the Thebans, who were, we are led to infer, trying to consolidate all of Boeotia under their control; and that the Spartans begged off, pleading that Lacedaemon was too far away for them to be relied on, and suggesting, instead, that the Plataeans turn to the Athenians, "who live nearby and are not bad at providing assistance." The advice proffered by the Lacedaemonians stemmed, Herodotus contends, not from "goodwill," but from a desire to burden the Athenians with "troubles vis-à-vis the Boeotians and bring the two communities into conflict." This is, in fact, precisely what happened when the Plataeans appeared in Athens as suppliants—for the Thebans then launched an assault on Plataea and the Athenians rallied to the defense of their newly acquired client.[1]

It is hard to know what to make of this report. We are not told why Cleomenes and the Lacedaemonians were so far afield. Some think that they made this expedition to bring Megara within the Spartan alliance. This certainly happened at some time, but we do not know when. The inclusion of Megara within the alliance was very much to the advantage of everyone within it—for there were mountain passes in the territory of Megara that could be used to control entrance into and exit from the Peloponnesus. If the Lacedaemonians feared that the Persians might someday come; if they wanted to be able to block their progress by land at the isthmus linking the Peloponnesus to the rest of the mainland; if they wished free access to Attica, Boeotia, and Thessaly with an eye to establishing a defensive perimeter further to the north, they would need the cooperation of the Megarians.

The Spartans almost certainly had an additional concern. Decades thereafter, when the Persians did come, there were Medizers in Thessaly and Thebes all too willing to be of help to Hellas' barbarian foe. If, in the wake of the debacle at Samos, the Spartans got wind of visits by Persian emissaries to Thessaly and Boeotia, they may have thought it prudent to make their presence felt. Herodotus treats their advice to the Plataeans as an act hostile to Athens. But, in a much more obvious way, it was an act aimed at checking the growth of Theban power within Boeotia.

The aftermath is telling. The Corinthians—who were among the most important and earliest of Lacedaemon's allies and who were, as a maritime power, even more attentive to developments in the Aegean than were the Spartans themselves—just "happened to be in the vicinity" when the Athenians and Thebans were about to come to blows. To prevent the battle, they intervened in force, imposed themselves on the two sides as arbitrators, and issued a judgment highly unfavorable to the Thebans, specifying the boundary between the territory of the Plataeans and that of the Thebans, and stipulating that the latter "leave alone those Boeotians unwilling to be enrolled as such" for the purpose of taxation and military service. It is no less revealing that the Thebans are said to have been unwilling to accept this settlement as final. As soon as the Corinthians withdrew, when the Athenians were about to do the same, the Thebans reportedly attacked them, lost the battle, and suffered an additional territorial loss.[2]

Of course, none of this means that Herodotus' suspicions with regard to the intentions of Cleomenes and the Lacedaemonians were wrong. Turning the Athenians into a check on the ambitions of the Thebans could easily have been a way of killing two birds with one stone—for it set two potential rivals of the Spartans at one another's throats and thereby weakened them both. Moreover, the Spartans had reason to view Athens with a measure of suspicion. There may well have been guest-friendships linking certain leading Spartans, such as the two kings, with the Peisistratid tyrants then governing

Athens, as Herodotus asserts.[3] But this cannot have been even remotely as significant as the other connections abroad maintained by this clan. At this time, within Hellas, as Cleomenes surely understood, the Peisistratids were a force to be reckoned with. The details, which bear on Lacedaemonian calculations, deserve close attention.

Peisistratus and His Sons

The father of the men who ruled Athens at the time of the Spartan expedition in 519 and the founder of the tyranny they sustained was a dynamo named Peisistratus son of Hippocrates.[4] This man belonged to the Eupatrids, Athens' ancient aristocracy, as did his rivals; and he hailed from Brauron in the deme of Philaidae, not far down the Attic coast from the plain of Marathon, which lay northeast of Athens in the backlands on the far side of Mount Hymettus and Mount Pentelicon.[5] At some point in the 560s, he led Athenian troops in a war with Megara, fought over the control of Salamis; and, by capturing Nisaea, the Megarian port on the Saronic Gulf, he forced the Megarians to concede Athens' claim. In the aftermath, he made two attempts to establish himself as tyrant at Athens, capitalizing on his accomplishments and drawing on his family's connections both in the region of Attica where his estates lay and elsewhere in and beyond the highlands outside the capital. Both attempts were short-lived.

On the first occasion, "the men of the plain" near Athens itself, led by a shadowy figure named Lycurgus (almost certainly a member of the Eteobutad clan), joined with "the men of the shore" from the coastal areas near Cape Sunium, led by Megacles, scion of the Alcmaeonid clan, to overwhelm Peisistratus' supporters—"the men from the hills"—and drive the bodyguards he had been voted by the Athenian assembly from their perch on the acropolis. In mounting his second attempt, Peisistratus took advantage of the strife that erupted thereafter between the faction of Lycurgus and that of Megacles. When the latter, in distress, turned to him for an alliance, he jumped at the chance and sealed the deal in time-honored fashion by taking Megacles' daughter as his bride. It was presumably in celebration of this match that Megacles gave his younger son the name of Peisistratus' father Hippocrates. But the marriage did not last, and the alliance soon came apart.[6]

The Alcmaeonids were extraordinarily well-connected. Alcmaeon, the father of this Megacles, had commanded the Athenian forces in the First Sa-

Map 4. Attica, Salamis, and the Border with the Megarid and Boeotia

cred War in or soon after 595. In the aftermath, according to Herodotus, he appears to have been of signal assistance to an embassy dispatched to Delphi by the king of Lydia, and this Mermnad monarch later rewarded him for his efforts by inviting him to carry from the treasury at Sardis as much gold dust as he could lug. If the story is true—and there is no reason to reject it—the king who rewarded Alcmaeon cannot have been Croesus, whom Herodotus names; he must have been Alcmaeon's contemporary Alyattes, who is also known to have been keenly interested in the oracle. A generation later, in a famous contest pitting the leading young men of Greece against one another, Megacles, son of this Alcmaeon, won the hand of Agariste, daughter of Cleisthenes, the Orthagorid tyrant of Sicyon.

Some, however, thought the Alcmaeonid family accursed as a consequence of the lengths to which they had gone in the generation before Alcmaeon when, in the course of putting down an attempt to establish a tyranny at Athens, they had purportedly incurred pollution by dragging suppliants from religious sanctuaries and executing them on the spot. Peisistratus, who had sons already from two previous marriages, was apparently reluctant to sire children who would inherit this curse; and when his new Alcmaeonid wife reported to her mother that her husband had disgraced her by being unwilling to have sexual relations with her "in the customary fashion," Megacles broke off the marriage and saw to the tyrant's expulsion and to the confiscation and sale of his estates.[7]

At this point, Peisistratus reportedly withdrew to the island of Euboea, across the straits from his political stronghold in northeastern Attica, where, among the horse-riding aristocrats [*Hippeîs*] of Eretria, he appears to have had powerful guest-friends. There he took counsel with his sons; and the eldest of these, a young man named Hippias, urged him to endeavor to recover the tyranny. This time, Peisistratus and his sons looked outside Athens for support. There is reason to suspect that the Macedonian king was among their guest-friends, and they appear to have turned first to him. For it was surely with his permission and support that they established a settlement named Rhaecelus on the Thermaic Gulf, then shifted eastward to the area around Mount Pangaeum and grew wealthy there, mining the gold and silver that were so plentiful in that district near the river Strymon.[8]

It took Peisistratus and his sons something like a decade to amass the necessary resources. Then, they hired mercenaries in Thrace and returned to Eretria to stage an invasion of Attica. It was at this point that their guest-friends from far and wide rallied to their support. According to Herodotus, the Peisistratids collected "donations from cities that were in any fashion obligated to them." Many of these reportedly came up with "large sums of money." Prominent among the donors, Aristotle tell us, were the *Hippeîs* of Eretria—among whom, in a luxury-loving woman named Koisyra, the once and future tyrant had apparently found for himself yet another well-connected wife. We should almost certainly also include on the list of Peisistratus' allies the horse-barons of Thessaly. But, "in the giving of money," Herodotus claims, "the Thebans surpassed" all others.[9]

Map 5. Euboea, Boeotia, Thessaly, Macedonia, the Chalcidice, and the River Strymon

Money was not the only form of support that the Peisistratids received. As we have already had occasion to note, Peisistratus was a much-married man. We do not know the name of his first wife, who was an Athenian and appears to have borne him three sons—Hippias, Hipparchus, and Thettalus. His second wife had, however, been a woman of some note. Her name was Timonassa. She was the daughter of an Argive notable named Gorgilos, and the alliance with Peisistratus was her second dynastic marriage. Earlier, she had been the wife of Archinos, the last Cypselid tyrant of Ambracia—whom the Spartans had ousted and perhaps killed not long before her father gave her in matrimony to Peisistratus. She bore her Athenian husband two sons, Iophon and Hegesistratus. By the time of Peisistratus' marriage to his fourth wife, Koisyra, and his return from exile, Timonassa had presumably long since passed from the scene, and her son Hegesistratus had come of age—for he is said to have brought one thousand men from Argos to participate in the invasion of Attica. We are also told that a wealthy adventurer named Lygdamis, already instanced, came as a volunteer from Naxos with both money and men.[10]

The precise dates of Peisistratus' first two attempts to establish himself as tyrant are in dispute,[11] but Herodotus makes it clear that his third attempt took place after Cyrus' defeat of the Mede Astyages in the early 540s, a short time before Croesus forged his alliance with Sparta. On this occasion, Peisistratus and his sons, mercenaries, and supporters crossed from Eretria to the plain of Marathon, mustered their troops there and rallied their supporters from within Attica, then marched on the city of Athens and defeated their opponents at Pallene—which controls the strategic pass where the main road leading from Marathon to the city of Athens runs between Mount Pentelicon to the northeast of the city and Mount Hymettus to the east. In the aftermath, he sent his sons on horseback to exhort those in flight to have no fear and return to their homes.[12]

Soon thereafter—when Lygdamis, who was a member of the oligarchy dominant on Naxos, returned home, established himself as a patron of the multitude, and began exploiting civil strife on the island with an eye to establishing himself as tyrant—Peisistratus returned the favor he had received by dispatching mercenaries to provide his friend with the military support required for the success of his venture. When his ally was firmly ensconced in power as tyrant on Naxos, Peisistratus then lodged with him the children of leading Athenian families, whom he had seized as hostages for the purpose of guaranteeing the subservience of their parents.[13]

The fact that this same Lygdamis was involved in helping Polycrates establish his tyranny on Samos soon after these events suggests the possibility that the Naxian tyrant's patron in Athens may, at least indirectly, have had a hand in the matter as well. Like Polycrates and at about the same time, Peisistratus found himself at odds with Mytilene on the island of Lesbos. From it he regained control of Sigeum in the Troad—a city that had been awarded to Athens after a much earlier struggle with Mytilene by Periander, the Cypselid tyrant of Corinth, whom the Athenians and the Mytilenians had chosen as arbitrator. Moreover, like Polycrates and in roughly the same years, Peisistratus was active, with an eye to asserting hegemony over the Ionians, in honoring the god Apollo on Delos, their holy island. As firmly established tyrants, these two were almost exact contemporaries. They had the same enemies, the same friends, and many of the same concerns. It is not likely to have been an accident that, after his friend and patron Polycrates' murder, the poet Anacreon fled Samos and joined Peisistratus' luxury-loving younger son Hipparchus in Athens. There seems to have been interchange between Polycrates' court and the establishment maintained by the Peisistratids. Otherwise, it would be hard to explain how, in one of the poems he is said to have composed while still on Samos, Anacreon came to celebrate the beauty of the son of one of Peisistratus' closest associates.[14] Given the circumstances, it would have been extremely odd had the two tyrants not at some point become guest-friends and allies.

Peisistratus ruled Athens with a firm hand for something like twenty years. It was in the period in which Polycrates controlled the sea that the Athenian wrested Sigeum from the Mytilenians, installed his son Hegesistratus as tyrant, and dominated the Troad—quite possibly, in defiance of the Persians.[15] By the time that Cambyses put together the fleet with which he conquered Egypt, and Persia came to dominate the sea, however, Peisistratus had passed from the scene. His sons and heirs at Athens—Hippias, Hipparchus, and Thettalus—must at that time have come to the same realization as Polycrates: that sooner or later they would have to come to terms with the Mede.

It should not, then, be surprising that Cleomenes, the Spartans, and their Corinthian allies should seek in 519 to embroil the Athenians with the Thebans. The Peisistratids were a real force, and they had long been quite intimately associated with Sparta's Argive foe. They were, moreover, closely linked with the Eretrians, the Thebans, the Thessalians, and the king of Macedon; and, if they had not done so already, it was obvious that they would sooner or later have to reach an accommodation regarding Sigeum with the Achaemenid potentate who styled himself the King of Kings. The fleet put together by Cambyses ruled the sea. The islands along the Asia Minor coast were now fully dominated by the Mede, and the Spartans were increasingly anxious.

Scythia and Thrace

They had good reason to be nervous. To an even greater degree than Cyrus, Darius fancied himself a universal monarch. The god Ahura Mazda, he tells us in one inscription, was a universal god who had created "this earth" and "the sky yonder." He had "created man," and for man he had created "happiness"; and to provide for human happiness he had "made Darius king." "Great King," he was, "King of Kings, King of lands, King on this great earth." In another inscription, Darius asserts that the god had "bestowed" on him a "kingship over this wide earth, in which there are many lands: Persia, Media, and the other lands of other tongues," lands constituted by "mountains and plains," stretching "from this side of the sea to that side of the sea, from this side of the desert to that side of the desert." He was, as he puts it in another such inscription, "King of this great earth far and wide." Darius was "the man in all the earth," which is to say, "King in all the earth." He was chosen by the Wise Lord Ahura Mazda, when the god "saw this earth in commotion" and one nation smiting another, to restore the order prerequisite for human happiness and "situate" everything "in its proper place." He took it for granted that those on this wide earth not already subject to the King of Kings as his *bandaka* or "bondsmen" would become such in due course; and it went without being expressly stated that the chosen one of Ahura Mazda would, in pursuing the mission he had been assigned by this god, do anything and everything that was required. The followers of "the Lie" could not expect at the hands of such a man any quarter, but those who cooperated with the imperial project and kept faith would be richly rewarded. This is how Darius presented himself to the world—as the supreme benefactor destined to bring joy to the world by restoring to the earth order, peace, and prosperity; and the spectacular program of imperial art and architecture that he initiated and his successors carried out—at Bisitun; at Naqsh-i Rustam, where the Achaemenid kings were to be buried in tombs cut into the cliffs; at Persepolis, where he built a palace all his own; and at Susa, which functioned as his principal capital—was aimed at conveying the good news to all mankind by way of inspiring texts and arresting visual images.[16]

By 520, Darius had consolidated his grip on the empire he had inherited from Cyrus and Cambyses, and he was beginning to consider how to round it out. To this end, he sent Democedes of Croton and fifteen Persians on a voyage of exploration through Greece as far as Magna Graecia in Italy. To this end, he dispatched Scylax of Caryanda in Caria and his crew down the Indus, out past the Persian Gulf, around the Arabian peninsula, and up the Red Sea to Egypt. To this end, he ordered his kinsman Ariaramnes, the satrap of Cappadocia, to sail across the Black Sea with a fleet of thirty penteconters and take prisoners from among the Scythians who lived along its northern and eastern shores.[17]

In 519–18, Darius marched through eastern Iran toward the Caucasus to subdue the Scythians [*Sakā*] ruled by Skunkha. It was arguably soon thereafter that he turned south to conquer the Indus valley (the Punjab and Sindh in what is now Pakistan) and add it to Persia's already vast domain. If Scylax' circumnavigation of the Arabian peninsula inspired on the part of Darius a larger project aimed at improving the transport of tribute and communications more generally within the empire and induced him, with this end in mind, to complete a canal, begun but not finished by the Egyptian Pharaoh Nechos, linking the Mediterranean via the Nile with the Red Sea—which is what the inscriptions set up by Darius along the canal certainly seem to suggest —the enterprise foundered solely because the difficulties posed by the winds prevailing, by the currents, and the dearth of fresh water to be found along the Arabian peninsula's unfriendly shores proved in the long run an obstacle insuperable.[18]

In 514 or 513, Darius turned west, then north to conquer eastern Thrace up to the Danube; to construct a string of eight large forts at intervals along a river marking the frontier of this new province; and to mount what Herodotus depicts as a punitive campaign aimed at the Scythians of the steppe nearby. To this end, initially, he had Mandrocles of Samos build a bridge of ships across the Bosporus at its narrowest point (between what the Turks today call Anadolu Hissar and Rumeli Hissar), and he led his troops across, instructing the tyrants of his Hellespontine, Ionian, and Aeolic Greek dependencies to sail on

Map 6. From the Danube on the Black Sea to the Thermaic Gulf in Macedonia

to the Danube—where, upriver at a suitable place above the delta, they were instructed to build another such bridge of ships for the Great King and his troops.[19]

Herodotus does not give us a full account of Darius' objectives in eastern Thrace and Scythia, and the latter's aims have long been a matter for scholarly dispute.[20] It is hardly likely that the Great King of Persia would amass so large and complex a force, accompany it himself, and go to the trouble of bridging the Bosporus solely for the purpose of punishing the Scythians for an incursion into Anatolia and Iran that had taken place more than a century before.[21] If this was the stated purpose for the expedition, it was a cover for something else. Among scholars in the late nineteenth century, there was speculation that one of the Persian monarch's aims might have been to secure control of the rich gold mines of the Siebenbürgen—for these were located, not far from the course of his march, west of the easternmost tributary of the Danube in the Apuseni mountains on the northwestern edge of Transylvania twenty to thirty miles north of the modern town of Deva, which lies in the valley of the Mureş River along which Herodotus' "gold-wearing" Agathyrsi resided.

In favor of such speculation, there is, in fact, a shred of concrete evidence. Almost eighty years ago, a brick inscribed in Old Persian purporting to come from a palace built by Darius the Achaemenid turned up in Gherla at a strategic river crossing deep in Romania some sixty miles north-northeast of the site of these western Carpathian mines. In their incredulity, scholars are inclined to dismiss the find as a forgery or to suppose that, in later times, the brick was borne there from somewhere in Thrace well to the south. It would be far simpler to suppose, however, that in or near Gherla, during or in the aftermath of the Scythian expedition, Darius or one of his agents began building a royal palace on the model of those, adorned with parks and gardens, scattered hither and yon throughout the Persian domain. It is also conceivable that Darius or one of his agents established a military settlement in the area of the sort commonplace elsewhere within the Great King's realm—for Herodotus reports that, in his time, there lived beyond the Danube a mysterious people called the Sigynnae, who dressed in the Median manner and claimed to be colonists drawn from among the Medes.[22]

There is also another possibility. Darius may have dreamed of turning the Black Sea into a Persian lake. Scholars have long wondered whether, in confusion about the vast distances involved and unaware of the difficulty of the terrain, he hoped to march from the Danube to modern Georgia on the eastern shores of the Pontus. He controlled Anatolia, and Herodotus tells us that every fourth year the people of Colchis in western Georgia were required to send, as "gifts" to the Great King, one hundred maidens and boys. Thanks to the efforts of archaeologists working in the region, we now have excellent reason to believe that the Persian administration extended deep into the Caucasus, for, in both

Georgia and Azerbaijan, they have uncovered sizable Achaemenid administrative structures almost certain to have been royal or satrapal palaces.[23]

Whatever his ultimate purpose may have been, when he reached the Danube, Darius proposed to cross and have the bridge of boats dismantled forthwith. This, however, he did not do. Before he and his army made their way across the river, Coës, one of the generals sent from Mytilene to command the contingents from that long-loyal city, sought out the Great King and advised him to have the Greeks keep the bridge intact—lest, upon his return, he should need to evacuate quickly. This Darius did, instructing them to break up the bridge and return home if he was not back within sixty days.[24]

Herodotus' description of the Scythians and of their customs and ways is for the most part borne out by the archaeological evidence. His account of Darius' foray across the Danube is, however, profoundly confused with regard to the terrain and the overall geography. Scythia is, he tells us initially, a land "flat, grassy, and well-watered" with no fewer rivers than there are canals in Egypt. Then, he consigns Darius and Scythia's Persian invaders to a long march through a land "dry and barren." He has the Persians make this difficult journey from the Danube as far east as the Don and even beyond it. The territory they would have had to traverse is vast, and, given the impossibility of transporting grain and other foodstuffs any considerable distance by land with animal transport, they would have died of starvation en route long before they had gotten half that far. Indeed, given the distance, the terrain, and the limited duration of the time allotted for their expedition, it is unlikely that the Persians made it past the Dniester. The brief account provided by the geographer Strabo, which had them journey in great thirst through the virtually waterless "Desert of the Getae" between the Danube and the Dniester, is far more plausible than the fable told by Herodotus, and it makes better sense of what Herodotus has to say regarding the suffering the Persians endured than does the historian's own tale.[25]

Although they are at odds with regard to the extent of territory traversed, all of our sources are in agreement on one fact. The trans-Danubian expedition turned out to be an unmitigated disaster. The Scythians Darius encountered were not a sedentary people. These horsemen could refuse battle, and they did so. They could easily afford a scorched-earth strategy, and such a policy they resolutely pursued. As the Persians approached, Herodotus tells us, the Scythians withdrew, leading their prey on and on through a desiccated landscape, and harassing them whenever, in desperation, they dispersed for the purpose of foraging—which, in the circumstances, they were frequently forced to do.[26]

At one point—when Darius' troops were exhausted, depleted in number, bereft of water, and desperately short of food—the Scythians are said to have sent a delegation to the Ionians and Aeolians awaiting the Great King at the Danube. Their aim was to persuade them to take apart the bridge and go home, leaving Darius and his men to starve in the steppes. The sixty days had, in fact, passed; and the Greeks were sorely tempted. If Herodotus can be believed, one of the tyrants even suggested that, in this fashion, the Greeks of the Hellespont, Aeolis, and Ionia could recover their lost liberty. His name was Miltiades son of Cimon, and he was a scion of the Philaid clan from Athens, which had maintained a little fiefdom among the Dolonci on the Thracian Chersonnesus for something like a half century.[27]

The odds are good that it was only when Darius crossed with his army over to Europe, where the Thracian Chersonnesus lay, that this Miltiades had been forced to pay fealty to the Great King. He owed Darius nothing. He was not one of the Persian king's creatures. Some, if not most, of the other Greek tyrants—men such as Hippoklos of Lampsacus, Strattis of Chios, and the younger Aeaces, who had by then succeeded his father the younger Syloson as ruler of Samos—were in a very different situation; and upon reflection, we are told, they chose to reject Miltiades' advice. Histiaeus, the tyrant of Miletus, the most prosperous and accommodating of these cities, probably did not have to remind the quislings of the Great King that their rule as tyrants in the cities they governed would not long survive their master's demise, but he did so anyway.[28]

The Scythian campaign was for the Persians more than a setback and an embarrassment. It severely damaged their prestige. It appears to have occasioned an immediate rebellion on the part of the citizens of Byzantium and Chalcedon, and a chronologically confused report in Herodotus suggests that the Scythians crossed the Danube in hot pursuit of Darius and followed him to the Hellespont, where from Sestos in the Thracian Chersonnesus—from which Miltiades had apparently already fled—he crossed over by ship to Asia Minor. That, in the late sixth century, the Scythians mounted a major foray into Thrace and burned the suburbs of Istria, a Milesian colony at the mouth of the Danube, the archaeological record confirms. Darius' legacy in the region immediately to the north and the east of the Black Sea was a time of troubles and widespread destruction.[29]

Darius took his disappointment in stride. When he abandoned Europe for Asia, he left behind a man of evident ability named Megabazos, whose patronymic Herodotus does not specify; and he instructed this Megabazos to subjugate those in the Hellespontine region who had not yet medized and to conquer Thrace—which is what he began to do, starting with Perinthus on the north shore of the Sea of Marmara, then turning to that city's Thracian neighbors to the west along the Aegean coast. While in Thrace, he also dispatched an embassy either to demand homage from Amyntas of Macedon and his son and heir Alexander and make them the *bandaka* of Darius or perhaps, as some scholars suspect, to accept earth and water already on offer from the two. It was almost certainly at this time—and not considerably later, as Herodotus seems to imply—that Boubares, one of the Persian general's sons, sealed the arrangement with the Macedonian king by contracting a marriage with his daughter. The money Herodotus mentions as having been given to Boubares was no doubt a "gift," as such contributions were called, or tribute intended for the Persian king. In return for paying homage, Amyntas of Macedon was made, as Herodotus' choice of words implies, a native satrap in the employ of the King of Kings.[30]

Along the way—presumably with an eye to securing for his royal master the rich gold and silver mines known to exist along the river Strymon near Mount Pangaeum—Megabazos uprooted from their ancestral homeland in that river valley the Paeonians, a people who claimed descent from the Teucrians of Troy. On Darius' instructions, he then deported them to Phrygia in Asia Minor, where a certain Oebares son of Megabazos—his own son, perhaps, or, conceivably, his father—was or soon would be satrap.[31] When he reached the Hellespont with the Paeonians in tow, Megabazos wrote ahead to ask for an interview with the Great King, who had remained in Sardis for a time after the Scythian expedition.

This Megabazos was a man of importance at the Achaemenid court. If, as we have reason to suspect, his patronymic was Oebares, he was, in all probability, the son or father of a man who, in his capacity as Darius' squire, was credited with having provided crucial assistance to the Achaemenid in his quest to secure for himself the Persian throne.[32] When such a personage sought an interview, the Great King was apt to grant his request and listen with care.

There was something that worried Megabazos. After the Scythian expedition, when Darius had first reached safety at Sardis, he had summoned Histiaeus—the tyrant of Miletus who had saved his life by insisting that the bridge across the Danube be maintained past the sixty-day limit stipulated—and he had offered him a reward, asking only that he name it. In response, Histiaeus had requested and been granted Myrcinus—a strategic site located in Thrace in the territory of the Edonians on the river Strymon, which was also known as Ennea Hodoi or "The Nine Ways" because there, where there was an island that divided the stream, the river could be bridged and a host of roads came together. By the time that Megabazos reached Sardis, he had become aware that Histiaeus was already busy building fortifications at Myrcinus. As he told the king, he was afraid that, if left in command of a district where there was not only timber for the construction of ships and oars but gold and silver in abundance as well, this Histiaeus might become a power in his own right and come to pose a threat to Persia's dominion not just in Thrace but on the sea as well. According to Herodotus, Megabazos then suggested that the Great King summon Histiaeus and see to it that he never returned to Hellas—which is what Darius did when he named his benefactor a counselor of the King of Kings and carted him off to Susa. It was in this fashion that Aristagoras son of Molpagoras, cousin and son-in-law of Histiaeus, became the steward and de facto ruler of Miletus, and there is reason to suspect that he bore responsibility for administering Histiaeus' stronghold at Myrcinus as well.[33]

Once Megabazos had pacified Thrace and secured Macedon, Darius appointed as his successor a notable named Otanes, this one the son of a judge named Sisamnes, and this Otanes then recovered Byzantium and Chalcedon on the Bosporus, captured Antandrus and Lamponia in the Troad, and—with the help of Persia's longtime allies the Mytilenians of Lesbos—secured Lemnos and Imbros, two islands in the Aegean which controlled the approaches to the Hellespont. By 509 or 508, as a consequence of the efforts of Megabazos and this Otanes, the Persians were in full control of the waterways leading from the Black Sea to the Mediterranean. They maintained at this time a fort in Thrace at Doriscus on the river Hebrus, capable of accommodating a garrison of ten thousand, and, one must suspect, another similar stronghold at Eion at the mouth of the river Strymon; and their dominion on land stretched to the borders of Thessaly, the northernmost region in the Greek heartland.[34]

Cleomenes and the Peisistratids

It may not be fortuitous that—while Megabazos and Otanes were extending Persian control to the northern Aegean—Cleomenes and the Lacedaemonians intervened at Athens to expel the Peisistratids. We do not know precisely when Hegesistratus, the Peisistratid tyrant of Sigeum, first gave earth and water to the Great King and became his bondsman. He may have done so in 526 or 525 when Polycrates switched allegiances. He may have waited until the son of Sisamnes came to the Troad to subjugate Antandrus and Lampsonia in 509 or 508. He could have done so at any time in between those events and probably did. We do know, however, something else to which the most astute of the Spartans, in their assessment, would surely have given even more weight.

As we have seen, one of the tyrants who accompanied Darius to the Danube was a man named Hippoklos, whom the Persians had sometime before placed in control of Lampsacus, a city situated on the Asian shore of the Hellespont which had often in both the distant and recent past found itself at war with the little fiefdom maintained by Athens' Philaid clan in the Thracian Chersonnesus.[35] Soon after 514, Hippias son of Peisistratus put aside the quarrels pursued by his compatriots and married his daughter Archedice to Hippoklos' son Aeantides. He sidled up to the ancient enemy of the Athenians in the region, we are expressly told, with an eye to the fact that the family of Hippoklos "was able to do great things with Darius."

Hippias knew what he was about. He and his brothers had almost certainly inherited from their father rich gold mines in the vicinity of Mount Pangaeum—an area that Megabazos had just brought under Persian control. If the Peisistratids had any desire to continue to profit from those mines or to reassert their right to do so, it was incumbent upon them to establish cordial relations with the Great King. Hippias had another motive as well. It is by no means an accident that, in 510, when he and his family were driven from Athens, they went first to his half-brother Hegesistratus at Sigeum, then to his son-in-law Aeantides at Lampsacus, and then, after an interval lasting a few years, to the court at Susa where Darius and his successors as Great King customarily received and entertained embassies and visitors from Hellas.[36] In 513 or 512, when he negotiated the terms of his daughter's marriage with the son of the tyrant of Lampsacus, there were storm clouds on Hippias' horizon.

In suppressing the tyranny at Athens, the Spartans almost certainly had more than one motive. Peisistratus died in 527, leaving his sons Hippias, Hipparchus, and Thettalus in charge. For something like two decades, he had ruled Athens with notable success. He operated in the manner of a political boss. He maintained the laws and institutions already in place and thought it sufficient to arrange for the election of magistrates willing to accept his guidance. Initially, of course, he did what he needed to do to cow the Eupatrids apt to resent his preeminence. But then he set out to co-opt and charm them, and he established circuit judges to subvert in an unobtrusive manner the influence that these great magnates had hitherto exercised in the localities where their estates lay. He almost certainly continued to draw considerable income from the mines along the river Strymon near Mount Pangaeum, and to this he added the revenues generated by a tax on produce which he had the city impose. With this income, like Polycrates of Samos, he maintained a sizable mercenary army sufficient to safeguard his rule; he instituted a program of public works, including the construction of the temple of Zeus Olympios; and he provided aid and employment for the poor. He also appears to have served as a patron and protector for the foreigners—many of them artisans—who flocked to Attica in these years of exceptional prosperity.[37]

Hippias, who took the lead after his father's death, pursued the same policy with similar success. He continued his father's building program—it was his son Peisistratus who was responsible for constructing the altar of the twelve gods—and Hippias himself appears to have coined the first of the tetradrachms which came to be known as Athens' Owls. His younger brother Hipparchus became a patron of the arts. The latter is said to have arranged for the recitation of Homer's epics by rhapsodes at the Panathenaea; to have sent a penteconter to Samos for the poet Anacreon of Teos, presumably after Polycrates was killed; and to have paid Anacreon's rival Simonides of Ceos a tidy sum to join him in Athens. To lure the dithyrambist Lasus of Hermione, he no doubt did something similar.[38]

We do not know whether Peisistratus reached an accommodation with the Alcmaeonids or his sons did, but that this was accomplished is clear. For the purpose of asserting his authority and consolidating control, Hippias became the archon eponymous in the year after his father's death. The archon eponymous for the next year was none other than Cleisthenes, the son of Megacles and the latter's Sicyonian bride Agariste; and at about this time, to seal the deal between the two families, his younger brother Hippocrates, the one named after Peisistratus' father, married Koisyra, the daughter of Peisistratus and his like-named Eretrian bride. Miltiades son of Cimon followed Cleisthenes as archon eponymous, and, two years thereafter, Peisistratus son of Hippias held the post.[39] For thirteen years, the sons of Peisistratus prospered.

In 514, however, things began to come apart. Many Athenians made homo-erotic connections when they were young. Most abandoned these when they grew older, then married and started a family. Hipparchus was an exception to the rule; and, as a member of the ruling family, he was no doubt used to getting what he wanted and sometimes apt to overreach—which is what he did in the case of an exceptionally good-looking adolescent named Harmodius. This young man was already the beloved of Aristogeiton, an older member of the same aristocratic clan—the Gephyraioi. When Hipparchus repeatedly pressed his attentions on Harmodius, it upset the two. When he took revenge on the unwilling young man by staging a public insult to his younger sister, Harmodius, Aristogeiton, and their friends banded together in a conspiracy to assassinate the Peisistratids.

In the event, as is usually the case in such matters, they lost their nerve. In consequence, their plans went awry, and only Hipparchus was killed. The Panathenaic procession was then under way, and Hippias moved quickly to disarm his fellow citizens and to arrest anyone found in the possession of a dagger. Harmodius was killed and Aristogeiton, captured. Under torture the latter listed as fellow conspirators many of those who had hitherto seemed friendliest to the tyranny, and Hippias and his mercenaries soon had a great deal of blood on their hands. Never again, while he remained at Athens, did he or those whom he ruled know peace of mind.[40]

Among those who escaped into exile at this time were Cleisthenes and his fellow Alcmaeonids. At some point soon thereafter, they crossed the bor-der from Boeotia and seized the fort at Leipsydrion on the slopes of Mount Parnes, hoping that the Athenian populace would rally to their standard. When this failed, they turned to Delphi, where they were well-connected— for, earlier, they had achieved renown by rebuilding the temple of Apollo not in tufa, as stipulated in the contract that they signed, but in Parian marble. There, on this occasion, by proffering a bribe, they are said to have persuaded the oracle to instruct all Spartans who came on business, public or private, to liberate Athens from the tyrants.[41]

It would be a mistake to reject out of hand the analysis put forward by Herodotus and Aristotle. The Spartans were, as we have had occasion to note, exceptionally god-fearing, and they looked to Delphi for guidance. Aristotle tells us that they were also swayed by concerns arising from the long-standing friendship linking the Peisistratids with the Argives—which was also no doubt true.[42] Some Spartans, however—and not the least of them—surely had their eye on the recent conquests made by the Persians in the Hellespont, in Thrace, and Macedon, and they will have paid attention to the relations linking the Peisistratid tyrant at Sigeum with the Persian court and to the surprising marriage alliance that Hippias had so recently forged with one of Darius' favorites.[43]

Initially, in 511, the Spartans dispatched by sea a notable named Anchimolios son of Aster with a small force. Hippias appears to have had ample warning—for, well before the Lacedaemonians attempted an amphibious landing at Phalerum on the coast near Athens, he had alerted his guest-friends the horse-barons of Thessaly, and they had dispatched to Attica a thousand cavalrymen. As a consequence, when Anchimolios and his men tried to come ashore, they met with an unpleasant surprise. The Thessalian commander Kineas unleashed his horsemen on them while they were disembarking and had not yet formed a phalanx, and the Thessalians ran the Spartan hoplites down.

Afterward, probably in the following year, the Lacedaemonians sent Cleomenes with a much larger force by land. He and his hoplites in phalanx quite easily routed the Thessalian horsemen. Then, they bottled up Hippias, his supporters, and mercenaries in the Pelargikon on the slopes of the acropolis. Had he not then tried to smuggle the Peisistratid progeny out of the country, Hippias would have outlasted the patience of the Spartans. So we are told, and the claim makes sense—for, as we have seen, the Lacedaemonians lacked the perseverance requisite for siege warfare. When these children were captured, however, Hippias agreed to withdraw, and he was given safe passage to Sigeum in the Troad on condition that he depart from the city within five days.[44]

Cleomenes Thwarted

In the aftermath, the Athenians re-enacted the statute declaring would-be tyrants, their supporters, and the descendants of both outside the protection of the law. It was presumably in this connection that they banned from the city the Peisistratids, listing them each by name. At about the same time, they set up statues honoring Harmodius and Aristogeiton as tyrannicides, and they scrubbed from the list of citizens those in Athens "not pure in descent"—a group, apparently sufficient in number to attract attention and resentment, which had long been sponsored, protected, and patronized by Peisistratus and his sons. Some of those "not pure in descent" were no doubt descended from artisans whom Solon's legislation had encouraged to immigrate to Attica.[45]

Also included among the foreigners who settled in Athens in these years were presumably the bodyguards and foreign supporters of the Peisistratids. In the course of the three and a half decades that the tyranny lasted, many of these immigrants will have started families with wives drawn from among the less well-born Athenians.

In 508, the Athenians held the first fully free elections that had taken place in more than thirty-six years. Initially, they reverted to the norm. The struggle that ensued pitted two aristocratic coalitions against one another. One of these was led by a shadowy figure named Isagoras son of Teisandros, whose patronymic suggests that his grandfather may perhaps have been related by marriage to the Philaids. His coalition is likely to have had as its core the old party of the plain. The other, undoubtedly based on the old party of the shore, was led by Cleisthenes the Alcmaeonid. Understandably missing and, in effect, excluded from the contest was the old party encompassing the hill-folk, the erstwhile Athenian supporters of Peisistratus and his sons, and the foreigners who had prospered at Athens under Peisistratid protection. We are told that both candidates carried out their campaigns in time-honored fashion through the *hetairíai*—the dining clubs or "companionships" to which men of the leisure class belonged—and that Isagoras emerged victorious as archon eponymous. This the Spartan king Cleomenes must have found gratifying, for Isagoras had become his guest-friend. On his visit to Athens, the Agiad king had resided with the man, and Isagoras was extraordinarily hospitable on that occasion—prepared, it was claimed, to share even his wife with his royal guest.[46]

When the election was over, Cleisthenes dramatically altered course. The language employed by Herodotus to describe what happened is quite revealing and must have been used at the time, for it constitutes an awkward attempt to understand a new democratic phenomenon within a framework inherited from Athens' aristocratic past. As Herodotus put it, "Having lost," Cleisthenes "added the *dêmos*"—which is to say, the common people, the people of the villages or demes—"to his *hetairía* [*prosetairizétai*]." What he did, in fact, was propose in the Athenian assembly a tribal reform, substituting for political purposes ten new tribes for the four ancient Ionian tribes to which his fellow citizens had hitherto belonged, mixing up the populace in such a way as to break up the ancestral kinship corporations, confine the influence of local magnates, and allow the foreigners who had flocked to Athens under the tyranny and had intermarried with ordinary Athenians to be registered as citizens within the demes and find a secure place within the polity. In effect, Cleisthenes had attracted into his coalition those in Athens who had been most comfortable with the rule of the Peisistratids, and they appear to have rewarded him with the election from his family of an archon eponymous for 507/6 bearing the telltale name Alcmaeon.[47]

The consequences of what Cleisthenes had done were revolutionary, and Isagoras recognized as much—which is why he turned to Cleomenes, inviting him to intervene once again in Athenian politics. The Agiad king, who was an adept at the use of religion for political ends, began by sending a herald to Athens, demanding that the Athenians cast out Cleisthenes and all of the accursed. In response, Cleisthenes and no doubt others (including Alcmaeon) withdrew from the city. Then, Cleomenes journeyed to Athens with a small force and drove out some seven hundred Athenian families identified as accursed by Isagoras. To underline the danger of pollution, he even had the bones of their ancestors dug up and cast beyond the limits of the civic territory. Finally, Cleomenes sought to dismiss the city's probouleutic Council, which was almost certainly by this time chosen by lot from an elected pool in accord with the procedures specified in Cleisthenes' tribal reform—for he hoped to place Athens' magistracies in the hands of three hundred of Isagoras' partisans.[48] His purpose, which had probably been his aim already at the time of his first visit to Athens, was the establishment of an oligarchy at Athens along lines familiar within the Peloponnesus. In effect, Athens was to become a satellite of Lacedaemon and a reliable adjunct to the larger Spartan alliance.

What Cleomenes did not fully comprehend was that the tribal reform had crystallized a profound sea-change in Athenian sentiment long in preparation. Much to the Agiad king's astonishment and chagrin, the new probouleutic Council refused his orders and organized resistance. Joined by Isagoras and his supporters, Cleomenes seized the acropolis; the Athenians then besieged them there; and, three days later, the Spartans negotiated a truce and, with Isagoras in tow, departed for Lacedaemon. The supporters of Isagoras left behind were bound and jailed to await execution, and the Athenians recalled Cleisthenes and the seven hundred households that had been expelled and made preparations to resist the Spartan onslaught that was bound to follow.[49]

Cleomenes, who was a man of choleric disposition, was not the sort to accept defeat, as the Athenians no doubt knew; and he took the rebuff personally, thinking that he had been "treated with insolence in both word and deed." The Lacedaemonians, once committed, could be expected to be of similar mettle. This time—the year was 506—Cleomenes returned with over-whelming force, bringing with him not only the Spartans and *períoikoi* of Lacedaemon but also contingents of hoplites from all of the members of the Spartan alliance. By prearrangement, the Thebans to the north seized Oenoe and Hysiae, districts on the slopes of Mount Cithaeron near Attica's Boeotian border; and the Chalcidians, with whom they appear to have allied them-selves, crossed over from Euboea to the east to plunder nearby areas of Attica. The nascent Athenian democracy appeared to be doomed.

Then, an astonishing event occurred. When the army from the Pelopon-nesus reached Eleusis, in Attica but not far from Athens' border with Megara, Sparta's Corinthian allies had second thoughts about the propriety of their intervening to install in power at Athens a narrow oligarchy constituted by Is-agoras and his fellow quislings, and they ostentatiously withdrew. After them went Cleomenes' colleague Demaratus, the Eurypontid king, who evidently shared their misgivings; and then, taking his departure as their cue, Sparta's other allies also withdrew.[50]

This event should give us pause. We do not know the precise terms of the various alliances binding Lacedaemon and her allies. In a later time, each of Sparta's allies was required to pledge to have the same friends and enemies as the Lacedaemonians. At this time, however, there is reason to suspect that they may have been bound to do as instructed by Sparta's two Heraclid kings—which seems to have been the situation of the Lacedaemonians themselves. When Herodotus discusses "the prerogatives" of the city's Agiad and Eurypon-tid *basileîs* as these pertain to war, he emphasizes the sacral character of these two magistrates. First, he mentions their status as priests—the one of Lacedae-monian Zeus, and the other of Heavenly Zeus. Then, in the same sentence, he tells us that these kings are authorized "to wage war against any territory they wish" and "that no Spartiate can be a hinderer or preventer of such a war." To this, he adds "that anyone who acts as such embroils himself in pollution." When Demaratus withdrew, he may, in effect, have broken a spell—that is, he may, by way of absenting himself, have released both the Lacedaemonians and their allies from their obligation to complete the mission that the two kings had initiated. It was in the aftermath of this embarrassment—precisely when, however, we are not told—that the Spartans decreed that, in the future, only one king would be sent out on any given expedition.[51]

When the Spartans had also withdrawn, the Athenians attacked and de-feated, first, the Thebans and, then, their Chalcidian allies, slaughtering many and capturing seven hundred of the former, whom they later ransomed for a sizable sum. Afterward, they crossed over to Euboea, seized rich landholdings on the Lelantine plain from the horse-breeding *Hippobótai* of Chalcis, and left behind four thousand Athenians as cleruchs to draw their livelihood from that land. In their euphoria, after these resounding victories, the Athenians built funeral pyres for those who had died in this campaign and buried their remains under a mound in Homeric fashion near the battlefields where they had fought alongside the Euripus, the narrows between the Greek mainland and Euboea. Then, they commissioned from the poet Simonides an epigram in celebration of the valor displayed by the deceased. "Under the folds of Diphrys," it read, "we were laid low, and a mound for us / Near Euripus was heaped up at public expense / Not without justice—for we laid waste youth much loved / when we embraced the savage cloud of war."[52]

Athens' Entanglement with the Mede

At the beginning of the crisis, the Athenians had in a panic dispatched an embassy, seeking aid, to Artaphernes, brother of the Great King Darius and his satrap at Sardis in west-central Asia Minor. The task assigned these ambassadors was, in all likelihood, a hard sell. Four years before, Hippias had fled to Sigeum and Lampsacus. In the interim, given the calculations that lay behind the marriage alliance that he had forged with the tyrant of Lampsacus, he must have approached Artaphernes himself. The way of the Athenian envoys may, however, have been smoothed by Alexander son of Amyntas of Macedon, who had not long before negotiated on his father's behalf the wedding of his sister to Megabazos' son Boubares and Macedon's adherence to the Persian empire. His father was almost certainly a guest-friend of Hippias. Alexander is himself, however, later represented as a "benefactor" of the Athenian people and as having been selected as their *próxenos*—which would make sense only if he had done something of considerable significance to earn their gratitude—and, tellingly, after the battle of Salamis, he was employed by the Persians vis-à-vis the Athenians as a go-between.[53]

Artaphernes received the Athenian delegation and listened to their plea, then informed them that giving earth and water was the price required for an alliance. We are told that the envoys were not authorized to give homage and make their compatriots *bandaka* of the Great King in this fashion but that, in desperation, they did so on their own responsibility. Given, however, what we can surmise with regard to the degree to which the Greeks had become familiar with Persian practices in the course of the previous four decades, it is hard to believe that the proponents of this diplomatic enterprise failed to anticipate Artaphernes' demand.

In the aftermath, however, they may have had reason to feign ignorance—for, when the ambassadors returned home, things had changed; and the diplomatic maneuver that had initially looked like a brilliant stroke soon came to be seen as a serious blunder. Miraculously, Athens had weathered the crisis. The Peloponnesians had withdrawn; the Thebans and Chalcidians had been defeated; and the envoys incurred "charges of a very serious sort."[54]

Whether this means that a trial was held, as Herodotus' language might seem to suggest, we do not know. Whether charges were lodged at this time or later we do not know. We do not even know who the envoys were. But it is striking that, after the recall of the accursed, we hear no more about Cleisthenes as a political actor, and it is no less striking that, in some quarters, the Alcmaeonids were regarded as Medizers for a considerable time thereafter. The fact that Cleisthenes was eventually given a public funeral suggests, however, that, if there was a trial, he escaped conviction.[55]

Cleomenes did not take well to being thwarted. The Athenians had humiliated the Agiad king but they had not seen the last of him. He was a man whom rage could deprive of all judgment. What he had attempted to do with Isagoras may have been folly. What he tried to do two years later in 504 was madness. At this point, he reversed course entirely; charged that the Spartans had been duped and that the Alcmaeonids had bribed the oracle at Delphi, which they almost certainly had; and called for the restoration of Hippias. He was partly moved, we are told, by what he had discovered about Athens' future relations with Sparta when he rummaged through the collection of oracles kept by the Peisistratids on the acropolis. He is also said to have been sensitive to the damage he had done a guest-friend and to have been disturbed at the noteworthy success of the Athenians on the field of battle against their Theban and Chalcidian neighbors.

When, however, delegations came from the cities belonging to the Spartan alliance, the Corinthians rose to the defense of the Athenians. We do not know what moved them, but we can guess. When it came to projecting power outside the Peloponnesus, the Corinthians were the most formidable ally that the Spartans possessed. They fielded the largest fleet in mainland Greece, and they controlled the narrow isthmus attaching the Peloponnesus to the rest of Hellas. Scholars have suggested that, in the estimation of the Corinthians, adding Athens to the Spartan alliance would weaken their independence. This makes good sense. They surely did not want to be surrounded on every side by Lacedaemonian lackeys. But they may have had an additional and weightier motive. The Corinthians were a sea-faring folk with a multitude of colonies to the west in the Adriatic and Sicily and one to the northeast in the Chalcidice in Thrace. Their city was the crossroads of the northeastern Mediterranean. The safest way to transport goods from the Black Sea, Asia Minor, and the Aegean to Italy and other points west or vice versa was to take them to Corinth and convey them by one means or another across the narrow isthmus separating the Saronic from the Corinthian Gulf. This could be done by carts, but there was also a slipway [díolkos] by which galleys and other small vessels could be shifted from one side to the other. In consequence of their position, the Corinthians generally knew more about developments abroad and sooner than any other community on the Greek mainland, and like modern merchant venturers, they were exceedingly alert to the drift of things. They maintained especially close ties to their colonists at Potidaea in Thrace,[56] and the citizens of that pólis would certainly have kept them fully informed as to everything that they divined regarding the intentions of their new Persian overlords. In a fit of rage, Cleomenes may have forgotten the Persian threat and turned back to Hippias, but no such charge could be lodged against the Corinthians.

In coming to the defense of the Athenians on this particular occasion, at least if Herodotus is to be trusted, the Corinthians made no mention of such fears. They knew their audience and its parochial character. The farmers of the Peloponnesus were not especially sensitive to a threat thought to be posed by a people far away of whom they knew little or nothing. In the circumstances, there was another, far more effective rhetorical theme that it behooved the Corinthians to sound. And so it was in this situation that Socleas of Corinth attacked the Spartans where they were most vulnerable, taking them to task for abandoning their vaunted antipathy to tyranny and for proposing to overturn a regime of equally shared power [isokratía]. And, as he expected, Sparta's other Peloponnesian allies quickly lined up behind the Corinthians.[57] The Lacedaemonians were trapped by their own policy. They could not abandon their crusade against tyranny without making the oligarchies that constituted their alliance restive and open to rebellion.

When Hippias left Sparta, we are told, his friends abroad lined up to provide him with a place of refuge. Amyntas of Macedon offered him the town of Anthemous in Mygdonia, and the Thessalians suggested Iolkos. Instead, however, he went to his half-brother Hegesistratus at Sigeum on the Troad; and from there, in all likelihood by way of Lampsacus, he journeyed to Sardis, where he reportedly missed no opportunity to cast aspersions on his compatriots with an eye to securing their submission to Darius and to himself. The Athenians, having heard of this, sent envoys—probably, the men who had given earth and water a short time before—to persuade Artaphernes to pay the exile no heed. In this mission, however, they did not succeed. The satrap ordered the Athenians, if they wished to be safe and secure, to take Hippias back. When the citizens of Athens refused to do so, Herodotus observes, it became manifest that they were enemies of the Mede.[58]

From the perspective of the Great King, the Athenians were, in fact, much worse than this. Like the nations that had revolted against Cambyses and had refused to give their allegiance to Darius when he overthrew Bardiya, they were *bandaka* who had rebelled, and they were guilty of the greatest of crimes, for they had embraced what the Persians called *Drauga:* "the Lie." When, after giving earth and water, the Athenians refused to take direction from Artaphernes, they made liars of themselves. They had pledged their troth as bondsmen. Then, when called upon to make good on their promise, they had broken their bond and they had refused to honor their pledge.[59] It was perhaps at this time—when Artaphernes made so unwelcome a demand—that those at Athens responsible in the first place for giving earth and water to the Great King were accused, tried, and acquitted.

Cleomenes can hardly have been satisfied. When his wrath abated and he regained a modicum of equanimity, he must have been rueful. He had much to regret. In attempting to apply to Athens something quite closely resembling the formula that had for some decades worked so well for the Lacedaemonians within the Peloponnesus, he had blundered; and, in doggedly persisting in his endeavor to turn Athens into a Spartan satellite, he had very nearly accomplished the very thing that he had most wanted to prevent.

Cleomenes' original aim had been sound and sensible. To stop Hippias from reaching a thorough-going accommodation with the Mede, he had exploited domestic dissent within Athens in such a manner as to oust the Peisistratids. In attempting to substitute for the tyrannical family a narrow oligarchy, however, he had overreached. The Athenians were not a diminutive community easily dominated. They were numerous, their territory was large, and they were no longer inclined to defer to the well-born. The citizens of Athens were perfectly capable of charting their own path; and, at least in the long run, there was no way that Sparta could stop them from doing so. In stubbornly and foolishly persevering in so ill-considered an enterprise, Cleomenes had very nearly driven the Athenians into the hands of the Mede. Thanks to his Corinthian allies, who repeatedly displayed in this matter a prudence he seems to have set aside, and thanks to the spiritedness of the Athenians, who defeated the Theban and Chalcidian invaders, the worst had been avoided, and the brief alliance of Athens with Persia had, in effect, been repudiated. But the eye of the Great King had nonetheless been directed to the Greek mainland, and against the Athenians he now had a grievance and a claim that he could assert.

CHAPTER 3

The Ionian Revolt

Our affairs, men of Ionia, are balanced on a razor's edge. Either we will be free or we will be slaves—and runaways at that. If you are now willing to embrace hardship, at the present time you will experience toil, and you will be able to overcome the enemy and remain free. If, however, you habituate yourselves to softness and disorder, I have no hope that you will escape paying the penalty reserved for rebellion against the King.

—DIONYSIUS OF PHOCAEA

IN 499—seven years after the Athenians had dispatched the embassy to Sardis that ended up giving earth and water to the Great King and two or three after Darius' brother Artaphernes, the satrap stationed at the former capital of Lydia, had ordered them in their capacity as bondsmen of the King of Kings to restore the Peisistratid tyrant Hippias to power—Aristagoras son of Molpagoros, whom Histiaeus had left in charge at Miletus, sailed to the Greek mainland in search of help against the Mede, journeying first to Lacedaemon, as we have already seen, and then to Athens.

In his capacity as ruler of Miletus, this Aristagoras had been approached not long before by a group of wealthy exiles from Naxos, eager to effect their return; and he had persuaded the Persians to send an expedition against the island, promising them an easy success, and suggesting that they would thereby secure Paros, Andros, and other islands within the Cyclades and gain a base from which to stage an assault on Euboea. In the event, he had quarreled with Megabates, the Achaemenid Persian in command of the fleet. The Naxians had been forewarned; the venture itself foundered; and Aristagoras had come to suspect that, when Megabates informed his kinsman Darius of the expedition's failure, his office and, perhaps, even his life would be forfeit. Aristagoras calculated his odds of survival; and, finding them slim, he broke with Persia, announced the establishment of *isonomía* at Miletus, and called for the other cities to follow suit. The tyrannies in the region then collapsed like a massive house of cards, and the revolt spread like wildfire. It was one thing to be subject to a tyrant of one's own choosing, as these cities often had been in the time before the Persians came. It was another thing to be subject to the nominee of a foreign power, who was more interested in raising tribute for his distant masters than in ingratiating himself with those whom he ruled.[1]

That Aristagoras found the Athenians more open to his pleas on behalf of the Greeks of the Hellespont, Aeolis, and Ionia than Cleomenes had been should in no way be surprising. The Spartans could entertain the possibility that the Persians might never come to the Greek mainland. The Athenians could not. Thanks to the blunders of Cleomenes, which they had in turn compounded, they were already embroiled with the Mede; and they knew it. When the Persians sent two hundred triremes—some of them fully manned for battle at sea, others functioning as troop transports—halfway across the Aegean to initiate a siege at Naxos, those Athenians not addicted to wishful thinking recognized that it would not be long before a Persian fleet appeared off their shores and they, too, came under assault. Moreover, thanks to the attacks on Athens by Thebes and Chalcis that Sparta's Agiad king had engineered in 506 in his abortive attempt to establish an oligarchy in that city, the Athenians now had an exalted sense of what they could accomplish on the field of battle.

Had the Athenians not already been entangled, they would nonetheless have been highly sympathetic to the revolt. The Ionians were their kin. They spoke a dialect of Greek similar to Attic. Most of the Ionian cities had religious calendars almost identical to the one possessed by Athens. And tradition taught that many of those who settled Ionia had first come there after an extended sojourn in Attica.[2] With some reason, the Athenians considered their *pólis* the mother city of Ionia. Moreover, the Athenians had particular reason to be alarmed when the Persians seized control of the waterways linking the Black Sea with the Mediterranean, and the island of Naxos, which the Persians had more recently attacked, was even closer to Attica than it was to Euboea.

There is considerable evidence suggesting that, in the sixth century, the Athenians could not grow enough grain in Attica to feed their population. Otherwise, it would be hard to explain their eagerness to seize Salamis from Megara, Sigeum from Mytilene, and the rich Lelantine lands of the "Horse-Breeders" from Chalcis, not to mention the fertile farmland of the Thracian Chersonnesus. These acquisitions may not, however, have been sufficient to make up their shortfall. At some point in the sixth century, the Athenians almost certainly began supplementing their domestic sources of cereals with grain imported from afar—as, we know, they later did on a very considerable scale. The natural source for the cereals they needed lay on the north coast of the Black Sea in the Crimea whence grain ships regularly passed through the Bosporus, the Sea of Marmara, and the Hellespont on their way to the cities scattered on both sides of the Aegean and in between.[3] The Athenian settlements at Sigeum in the Troad and on the Thracian Chersonnesus were designed in part to give Athens a foothold on both shores of what was for them a strategic waterway. The subjection to the Great King of Persia of the Greek settlements on both sides of this passage meant a serious deterioration in Athens' strategic environment.

And so, mindful of the unwelcome demands made by Artaphernes, of what they owed their kin, and of the dictates of geopolitics, the assembly at Athens dispatched a distinguished citizen named Melanthios with twenty of the fifty men-of-war that the city appears then to have possessed, and they instructed him to support the rebellion undertaken by the Greeks of Asia Minor. Whether the twenty ships sent with Melanthios were penteconters or triremes is disputed. Thucydides, whose authority is great, contends that, in Darius' lifetime, the Greeks, apart from the Ionians, were still reliant on penteconters. But Charon of Lampsacus, who was a contemporary of Herodotus, tells us flatly that the squadron dispatched on this occasion was made up of triremes. Herodotus speaks vaguely of "ships" being sent by the Athenians, and he does so in a context in which one might have expected him to specify triremes if that is what they were. This has caused scholars to suppose that he is implying that Melanthios' fleet was made up solely of penteconters. But it is far more likely that what he meant to convey was merely that it did not consist solely of triremes.

At the very beginning of the fifth century in Athens, these newfangled warships may well have been in short supply, but they did exist. Fifteen years earlier, Herodotus tells us, when the Peisistratids had dispatched Miltiades son of Cimon to the Thracian Chersonnesus, they displayed their magnificence by having him conveyed there in a trireme. It is hard to believe that this was the only such galley then in their possession. The sons of Peisistratus are not likely to have simply ignored the implications of the maritime military revolution then under way. The wealthy merchants of Aegina, the Athenians' neighbors in the Saronic Gulf, were certainly not behindhand in responding to this transformation. Six to seven years after Cambyses' conquest of Egypt, in a battle at sea, they managed to inflict on the squadron of triremes in the possession of the exiles from Polycrates' Samos a decisive defeat. Had the Aeginetans not then possessed thirty or more triremes themselves, this would have been impossible.

Hippias and his brothers certainly had the wherewithal with which to pay for the construction of a small fleet of these warships. Moreover, as we now know, Athens had the administrative capacity for their manning and maintenance; and there is evidence suggesting that, in the time of Hippias, trierarchs were named and triremes, built. But, at Athens, the latter cannot at this time have been numerous. As we have seen, in 511, Hippias anticipated the amphibious assault launched against the Peisistratid regime by the Lacedaemonians. Had he been able to deploy even fifteen triremes, the Spartan Anchimolios would not have been in a position even to attempt a landing at Phalerum. We could, of course, suppose that the construction of a sizable fleet of, say, fifty triremes followed closely upon the establishment of the democracy by Cleisthenes in 508. Arrangements do seem to have been made at this time for the provision of fifty warships. But there is no evidence that any of the ships contemplated were triremes; and, in light of what we know of the situation in which the Athenians found themselves two decades thereafter, it seems unlikely that many of them were.[4]

One fact, however, firmly insisted on by Herodotus, cannot be denied. The Eretrians, who joined the Athenians in the venture proposed by Aristagoras in 499, did send triremes—in number, five. Eretria's participation in the expedition and its willingness to dispatch on it something on the order of one thousand men should give us pause. This *pólis,* which was located on the island of Euboea just off the Attic coast, had a population considerably smaller than that of Athens; and, early on, it could reportedly field a hoplite force of no more than three thousand along with a cavalry force of no more than six hundred. In the archaic period, it was an important city nonetheless. It was one of the three Ionian members of the Delphic Amphictyony, and it had something that Athens at this time lacked: a distinguished seafaring tradition.[5]

Alongside its neighbor Chalcis, Eretria had played a leading role at the end of the Greek Dark Ages in the late tenth, ninth, and eighth centuries not only in opening up overseas trade—both with the peoples resident in Sicily and Italy and with Assyria via the Levant—but also in establishing colonies in the West. Toward the end of the eighth century, the Eretrians are said to have lost a struggle with their neighbors the Chalcidians for control of the Lelantine plain. But this setback, which appears to have put an end to the dispatch of colonies on their part, seems not to have dampened their ambitions overall. In the 540s, we find the *Hippeîs,* who then constituted the city's ruling order, sponsoring the tyrannical enterprise undertaken by Peisistratus with regard to Athens, and we must suspect that in the aftermath, when he set out to install his friend Lygdamis as tyrant at Naxos,[6] they with their navy helped him convey his troops to the island.

Epigraphical evidence suggests that, by the 520s, the Eretrians, as a political community, had made arrangements to guarantee a wage to rowers ordered to conduct ships of war past the Petalai islands in the north and Cape Kenaion in the south—which is to say, outside the long, narrow channel separating Euboea from the mainland. If, as some scholars suspect, the pertinent inscription is an indication that, at this time, the Eretrians were fielding a fleet sufficient for projecting power in the Cyclades, this effort may account for their sudden decision to mint coins in substantial numbers late in the sixth century. It was almost certainly in these years that they exercised the considerable leverage over Andros, Tenos, Ceos, and the other islands nearby that was later attributed to them; and it is, presumably, their projection of power in this fashion that explains the Eretrians' inclusion on the thalassocracy list put together early in the fifth century and the high praise later accorded their military prowess by Plato.[7]

Herodotus tells us that the Eretrians joined the Athenians on this expedition in order to pay back a debt of honor owed the Milesians, who had rallied to their support long ago, at the time of the Lelantine War, when the Samians had provided aid to the Chalcidians. This fact may well have figured in their deliberations, but the Eretrians no doubt had other reasons as well for joining in this undertaking. Even if we were to dismiss as implausible the evidence suggesting that the Persians made a landing of some sort on Euboea near Eretria when they launched their attack on Naxos, their attempt to seize the latter island must have left the Eretrians even more unsettled than their Athenian neighbors. Naxos was almost as near to the island on which the Eretrians lived as it was to Attica. If so close a neighbor fell to the Mede, it was obvious to all concerned, as Herodotus makes clear, that Euboea would be next.[8] The Eretrians are not to be underestimated. In the event, when Aristagoras of Miletus sought their aid, they proved far more resolute than the Athenians.

The Great Rebellion

Herodotus describes the Athenians' and Eretrians' dispatch of a fleet to support their Ionian kin as "the beginning of evils for both the Hellenes and the barbarians."[9] The support that Athens and Eretria gave the Ionian revolt arguably marked the beginning of the Persian wars as well. Up to this time, no power on or near the Greek mainland had actually crossed swords with the Mede. One could even argue that the intervention of Athens and Eretria provoked the Persian invasion. This was an opinion later voiced by the Lacedaemonians. Herodotus himself seems at times to have thought as much, and others since have followed his lead.

This is almost certainly an error. What the Athenians and the Eretrians did on this occasion was, indeed, a provocation. But the unfolding logic of Persian expansionism was evident years before the revolt. The Persians had gained control of the Hellespont, of Lemnos and Imbros, and of Thrace and Macedon in the first few years after the Scythian expedition. In 500, on the orders of the King of Kings himself, they made an attempt on Naxos with an eye to securing Paros, Andros, and other islands in the Cyclades, purportedly as a staging ground from which to launch an assault on Euboea just off the coast of Attica. There is every reason to suppose that Darius already intended to move on by land to Thessaly and Thebes and by sea to Chalcis, Eretria, and beyond. World conquest was, as we have seen, the raison d'être of the Achaemenid regime. Moreover, Darius' brother in Sardis had demanded and received earth and water from the Athenians, and subsequently—albeit to no avail—he had instructed them to restore the tyranny of Hippias. If the provocation staged by the Eretrians and the Athenians moved the King of Kings in any way, it was merely to increase his ardor for an enterprise long contemplated.

Herodotus may be accurate in describing the pitch that Aristagoras of Miletus made to Cleomenes in 499. As we have already had occasion to note, the way in which he tells the story suggests that he had interviewed Cleomenes' daughter Gorgo, who at the age of eight or nine overheard at least part of the conversation between the Milesian notable and the Spartan king, if not, in fact, the whole thing. If the historian had not been in a position to consult the daughter of Cleomenes and widow of Leonidas, then he had certainly spoken with someone who had heard her recount at length her experience as a child.

If Herodotus' account is, indeed, accurate, Aristagoras misjudged the Spartans. That they were greedy is a given. Most men are. But the helot threat was a drag on their capacity for audacity in this regard. They had already taken on about as much as they could handle, and the grand strategy that they had articulated in the first half of the sixth century was an acknowledgment of this fact. To persuade the Lacedaemonians to support the Ionians, Aristagoras would have had to convince them that what they already possessed was at stake. To be precise, he would have had to persuade them that the attack on Naxos was a harbinger of what was to come, that a conquest of the Greek mainland was high on the Persian agenda, that their own liberty and way of life was being weighed in the balance, and that the war being fought by the Ionians in a land far away of which they professed to know little or nothing was, in fact, their war, too. Aristagoras had a compelling argument to make, but he apparently did not make it, and Cleomenes and the Spartans were, for understandable reasons, risk-averse. Nonetheless, one thing is clear. Had the Ionian revolt succeeded, the Greek heartland would have been safe. Moreover, had the Lacedaemonians and their allies thrown their resources into the fray, the Ionians might very well have won their liberty. In the event, the Greeks of the East very nearly did so without much in the way of outside support.

The Ionian revolt had a propitious beginning. When the expedition against Naxos that the Great King's cousin Megabates had mounted on the advice and with the assistance of Aristagoras foundered and the Persian forces fell short of supplies, they built a fortified place on the island for the wealthy Naxian exiles who had first approached Aristagoras with an eye to effecting a change of regime in their native city, and then the various civic contingents sailed back to Myous in Asia Minor. The fleet did not then disperse, and the trierarchs did not take home the ships that their cities had been asked to provide. Megabates evidently intended to gather supplies, return to Naxos, and renew the siege. According to Herodotus, Aristagoras, who had quarreled with Megabates and knew that he would be blamed for the setback suffered by the expedition, took counsel with his friends and supporters at Miletus, which was nearby; and then and there he decided to raise Ionia in revolt. To this end, he sent an associate to spread the word within the fleet among those most apt to be sympathetic and to quietly arrest those of the tyrants known to be stalwarts of the Persian cause. Then, after having announced that he was resigning the tyranny and establishing at Miletus what the Athenians of that time and their kin in Ionia called *isonomía,* Aristagoras visited the chief cities of Aeolis and Ionia one by one, overturning the tyrants installed by Darius, establishing a republican arrangement in which booty would be shared equally and there would be equality under the law, and calling on the citizens of each to elect generals for the struggle ahead.[10]

In most of the cities, we are told, those who took control dismissed their former tyrants and, then, released them. Mytilene on Lesbos was a noteworthy exception to the rule. It was ruled by a man named Coës. Fifteen years before, as we have seen, in his capacity as general of the Mytilenian contingent accompanying Darius on the Scythian expedition, this man had suggested that the bridge of boats on the Danube be kept intact to give the Persian army an easy route by which to evacuate should that be necessary. When this expedient turned out to be the salvation of his army, Darius had urged his benefactor to name his reward, and Coës had asked that he be installed as tyrant over his native Mytilene. Now, however, when Aristagoras turned Coës over to the citizens of that community, they took him out to a field and stoned him to death.[11] For this particular act of savagery, they presumably had a motive. The Mytilenians appear to have long been faithful adherents of the King of Kings. The evidence suggests that they had reached an accommodation with Cyrus when Harpagus' soldiers first came to the coast of Asia Minor and that they had remained loyal to Persia ever after. One must suspect that, in return, they were left free and self-governing—until, of course, Darius thought it appropriate to confer a reward on one of Mytilene's generals, and the man expressed an interest in taking from his compatriots the liberty they treasured and had for decades so carefully maintained.

Scholars have criticized Herodotus' account of the origins of the Ionian revolt, arguing that there must have been a broader conspiracy and a great deal more planning.[12] But it is also possible that the time was right—that the level of discontent was universally high, that the Greeks in the fleet were all but openly grumbling, and that Aristagoras correctly calculated that a bold stroke on his part would be a spark sufficient to set off a great conflagration. In other places and times, when frustration and humiliation have reached a tipping point, rebellions have sprung up suddenly and unexpectedly and then spread like wildfire from one polity within a particular cultural sphere to another. The collapse of communism in eastern Europe was predictable, but it was not the consequence of a plan, and the same can be said of the Arab Spring of 2011. When Darius systematically installed tyrants of his own choosing in the Greek cities and imposed on them the collection of tribute, he sowed seeds of discontent that would yield as their fruit a fury immense, and the abject failure of his campaign against the Scythians must have set a-wandering not only the minds of those present but also the minds of those at home with whom they later talked. In the intervening years, some among them must have begun considering what it would take on their part to do to the Persians what the Scythians had done.

Aristagoras had certainly given thought to the question, and he had resources with which to work. Miletus was at this time a power of consequence. It sat on a peninsula extending from Asia Minor into the Aegean. It had easy access to the sea; the fortifications stretching across the peninsula linking it with the mainland were formidable. As its adversaries tended to learn, it was extremely hard to attack by land and almost impossible to take if one did not also control the sea. During the period of Lydian domination under Alyattes and Croesus, it had managed by a combination of military prowess and diplomatic skill to fend off Lydian attacks, then placate the Mermnad rulers while retaining its autonomy and the fertile farmlands that formed the foundation for its prosperity; and it had later adeptly accomplished the same feat vis-à-vis Cyrus and Cambyses.

In Darius' day, Herodotus tells us, Miletus reached its acme. Thanks to a period of rule under an enlightened oligarchy, it was, he said, "the very ornament of Ionia." This was the gem that Histiaeus had taken possession of in his capacity as Darius' nominee; and, as a consequence of Darius' gratitude and generosity after the Scythian campaign, he had increased the city's wealth and power by adding Myrcinus on the Strymon to its dominion. When the King of Kings took Histiaeus to Susa to serve as his counselor, the latter's son-in-law and cousin Aristagoras ruled over his possessions as a steward in his stead.[13]

This Aristagoras was nothing if not bold. Before the Athenians and the Eretrians arrived, he sent a messenger to Phrygia to summon the Paeonians, promising that, if they made their way to the coast, the Ionians would convey them by sea back to their ancestral home. The first leg of this proposed journey was easier to imagine than to accomplish, for the satrapies of the Persian empire were by no means without resources. There was undoubtedly a garrison of infantrymen and archers at Dascyleium, where the satrap held court; and, in addition, he was charged with maintaining, as part of his household, a substantial cavalry force. Even more to the point, dotted about the landscape of Anatolia (and, without a doubt, the other regions within the Great King's domain) were military colonies, made up of Persians and of others alien to the district, which were charged with providing infantrymen, archers, and a mounted militia for the defense and policing of the realm. Hated by the native peoples, whose most fertile land had been awarded them, these men were among the most loyal and enthusiastic adherents of the King of Kings.[14]

When the Paeonians took up Aristagoras' offer, they managed to reach the Aegean before the Persian cavalry, sent in pursuit, caught up with them. As promised, the Chians then ferried them from Asia Minor to Lesbos. From there, the people of the latter island bore them to Doriscus in Thrace, where the Persians maintained a stronghold; and, after overcoming its garrison and the one at Eion or bypassing them both, these exiles made their way on foot back to their fatherland along the river Strymon. Herodotus has nothing further to say about the Paeonians and the larger strategic purpose that Aristagoras had in mind when he liberated them. But we can be confident that, in deliberating concerning their welfare, Aristagoras had in mind what might be done with the timber and the gold and silver so abundant in their ancestral homeland. A few years later, when the prospects of the rebellion in Ionia dimmed and Aristagoras began thrashing about in a desperate search for resources to throw into the fray, it was to Myrcinus, Histiaeus' stronghold on the Strymon, that he would flee.[15]

In the summer of 498, when the Athenian long ships and the Eretrian triremes reached Ionia, Miletus was already under attack on the landward side. Aristagoras was, however, an enterprising fellow. To aggression, characteristically, he responded with aggression—by organizing a surprise attack on Sardis, the seat of Artaphernes' satrapy, designed not only to provide Miletus with relief but also to encourage rebellion on the part of Miletus' prospective allies. Most of the soldiers dispatched to Sardis came from the city that Histiaeus had entrusted to his cousin and son-in-law. The Athenians and the Eretrians lent a hand, and the Ephesians provided guides. The Milesians and their allies marched inland along the Cayster River, then crossed over Mount Tmolus on a path bypassing the normal route, and descended on the city—which they caught unawares and captured, there being no resistance. Artaphernes soon found himself bottled up in the acropolis with its garrison. Whether the Greeks put the city to the torch or the fire that engulfed it was an accident, as Herodotus reports, is hard to tell. But burn it did, as did the sanctuary of the goddess Kybele; and, rather than confront the desperate inhabitants who had fled from their homes to the open spaces in the city's agora, the Greek raiders withdrew back to Mount Tmolus and along the Cayster River in the direction of Ephesus. There, we are told, a Persian force—drawn from the military colonists who had been settled in the districts in Asia Minor to the west of the Halys River and no doubt entirely or almost entirely made up of the cavalry for which that nation had by then become famous—caught up with them, rode them down, and slaughtered a great many. It may have been at this time that the Ephesians came to terms with the Mede. They are not mentioned again as participants on the Ionian side; the temple of Artemis at Ephesus was not in revenge later burned as the other temples in Ionia were; and, when we next hear of the Ephesians, they are busy slaughtering the Chian survivors of an epic battle against the Mede.[16]

The Athenians had second thoughts as well. From the outset, they were no doubt deeply divided over the wisdom of their intervention in this war. The Alcmaeonids, who were almost certainly responsible for the envoys' giving earth and water in 506, seem to have preferred appeasement as a strategy to open defiance, and they were no doubt joined in this by the erstwhile supporters of the Peisistratid tyranny. These divisions—reflected in the charges later lodged against both factions—explain why the setback outside Ephesus caused the Athenians to withdraw their support from the Ionians, and their misgivings regarding the policy that had given rise to Melanthios' ill-fated expedition prompted them to elect as archon eponymous in 496 Hipparchus son of Charmos, a long-time supporter of the Peisistratid cause.[17]

As a boy, this man's father had reportedly once been the beloved of Peisistratus himself, and this Charmos is said later to have been the lover, then the father-in-law of Peisistratus' eldest son Hippias. Scholars have speculated that Charmos also became Peisistratus' son-in-law, which would explain why he named his own son Hipparchus after the son of Peisistratus eventually killed by the tyrannicides. Be this as it may be, Charmos' son Hipparchus was himself related to Hippias by marriage, if not also by blood—i.e., by Hippias' marriage to his sister after the death of the tyrant's first wife, by his own marriage to a daughter of Hippias, or, as some suspect, by both. For a time, moreover, this adherent of the Peisistratid clan was a figure of surpassing importance and influence in Athens. At one stage, the city even honored him with a bronze statue on the acropolis. If Hippias' son the younger Peisistratus ever returned from exile to Athens, as may have been the case, the year in which this Hipparchus was archon was the likely time.[18]

It is worth pausing to contemplate what a difference it might have made had the Spartans and the Peloponnesians joined the fray. For, as we shall see, subsequent events suggest that the cavalry of the Persians would not have

been able to defeat and slaughter the Milesians and their Athenian and Eretrian allies had the latter been willing to stand firm against them in a well-
placed phalanx. No horse will charge into a solid mass of men carrying spears
at the eye level of the beast. In open territory, a cavalry unit could play havoc
with the flanks of such an infantry force. If it managed to attack from behind,
it could disrupt the cohesion of a phalanx. But in a head-on confrontation
with a phalanx as disciplined as the one deployed by the Spartans and their
allies, even the best cavalry stood no chance. To be effective against disciplined hoplites, the Persians would have had to attack a force with no cavalry
of its own in broad plains where heavy infantry is at a marked disadvantage.[19]
There were patches of such terrain along the road that the Milesians, Eretrians, and Athenians followed in their march back to Ephesus from Sardis, but
they could have been traversed quickly and prudently, if not avoided in their
entirety.

From the Hellespont to Cyprus

The Ionians took in stride the defeat these hoplites had suffered outside
Ephesus. In its aftermath, they took to the sea, sailing up the Hellespont, the
Sea of Marmara, and the Bosporus and bringing over to their side all the cities along the coast, including Byzantium. Then, they turned to Caria, which
came over to them; and Caunus on the south coast, encouraged by the burning of Sardis, did so as well. All the Greek cities on Cyprus also lent them
their support.[20] There is no reason why this coalition could not have ruled the
sea—and for a time it did.

In Asia Minor, in 497, Darius followed up on the victory outside Ephesus
by deploying three armies under the command of his sons-in-law. One was
led by Daurises. It was sent initially to the Hellespont and recovered five cities along the Asian shore, including Abydos and Lampsacus, before turning
south in an attempt to cope with the Carians. A second was led by Hymaees.
It was sent to the Sea of Marmara and, when Daurises marched south, it took
up his charge in the Hellespont and pacified the Troad. The third was led
by Otanes son of Sisamnes. It operated in conjunction with the satrap Artaphernes and began recapturing the less well-defended cities on Asia Minor's
west coast. The only strategically important part of this struggle took place
between the troops of Daurises and those of the Carians. He defeated them in
one battle. Then, when they engaged him again with the help of the Milesians,

he defeated them again. Finally, however, under the command of Heracleides of Mylasa, they set an ambush on the road to Pidasa, a town in the hill
country near Mount Grion; and, in a battle at night, they annihilated Daurises' army and killed him and a number of other worthies—including, we are
told, Amorges, Sisimakes, and a notable, apparently descended from Lydia's
Mermnad monarchs, named Myrsos son of Gyges.[21]

Cyprus was the fulcrum of the war. It was no less important to the Ionians
than it had been to Amasis on the eve of Cambyses' conquest of Egypt. If the
Greeks could dominate the island, use it as a naval base, and control the seas
in its immediate vicinity, they could easily enough bar from the Aegean the
Phoenician fleet and any ships that the Persian satrap in Egypt could send in
their support; and, if and when they so desired, they could even carry war to
the Levant and possibly stir up a rebellion in Egypt itself.

Darius understood the importance of Cyprus. In 497 or 496, he sent a
massive expedition to retake the island under the leadership of Artybios. It
may well have been on this occasion that the Persians first built horse transports of the sort that are later mentioned with regard to the expedition they
sent against Marathon. By the time, however, that the Persian general's infantry and cavalry were prepared to cross over to the island from the base
they maintained on the plain of Aleion near Tarsus in Cilicia and the Phoenicians were ready to sail from that mustering point around the Carpass peninsula, the Ionian fleet had arrived. The struggle that followed was the first
of a series of contemporaneous naval and infantry confrontations between
the Greeks and the soldiers and oarsmen deployed by the King of Kings that
would take place over the course of the fifth century in the vicinity of Cyprus.
On this occasion, the Ionians—with the Samians in particular distinguishing themselves—won the battle at sea, but their Cypriot Greek counterparts
lost the struggle on land. As in the past, medizing proved decisive. Stesenor,
the tyrant of Kourion, had been persuaded to betray his own side, and the
war chariots of Cypriot Salamis followed his lead. Otherwise, we can surmise,
the Greeks of Cyprus might well have won. It is telling that the Persian commander lost his life in the course of the struggle.[22] Here, too, of course, had the
hoplites of the Peloponnesus been present in force, it might well have tipped
the balance.

It took the Persians considerable effort to pacify Cyprus after their victory. Herodotus tells us that Soloi held out for five months against a siege. At
Paphos, archaeologists have been able to study in detail the tactics employed

by both the Persians and their adversaries and to examine the siege mound built by the Persians, the mines driven by the defenders under the mound, the arrows used by the archers deployed by the Persians, the great stones hurled by their catapults, and the javelins cast from the walls of the city by its Greek defenders. Within a year, we are told, pacification was complete.[23]

The Battle of Lade

In 494, the Persians were in a position to turn to Asia Minor, where they had been less than fully successful in the preceding years. Miletus had been the source of the rebellion. Miletus had proved to be remarkably resilient and supportive of the efforts of others. So, it was against Miletus that they initially focused their efforts, investing the city from the landward side, and bringing up the combined naval forces of Phoenicia, Cyprus, and Egypt on the seaward side. All of this was made possible by the fact that, in the intervening period, the Persians had persuaded the Carians of Pidasa to switch sides.

We do not know who commanded the Persian navy at this time, but it is worth hazarding a guess. Ctesias, who served as a physician at the Persian court in the late fifth and early fourth centuries, tells us that on the Black Sea—presumably at the time of the Scythian invasion—a figure named Datis, whom Herodotus elsewhere identifies as a Mede, was in charge of the fleet. This Datis came from a family of very great importance. He had sons named Harmamithres and Tithaeus, who would in due course command the Great King's cavalry. He may himself have been a son of the Tithaeus [*Ziššawiš*] known from the Persepolis Fortification Tablets to have served as the deputy of Darius' uncle Pharnaces [*Parnaka*] from 507 to 494, when the latter was the treasurer of Persia. It is also a reasonable guess that the Ziššawiš known from the Persepolis Treasury Tablets to have served in the same high office from 471 to 468 was Datis' equestrian son.[24]

The tablets from Persepolis indicate that a certain Datis journeyed from Sardis to Susa in January and February of 494, and they show him to be a man of exceedingly high rank who was awarded rations inferior only to those known to have been reserved for the treasurer Pharnaces and for Gobryas, Darius' co-conspirator, spear-bearer, and brother-in-law. There can be no doubt as to this traveler's identity, and there is reason to suspect that this same Datis may have returned to the Mediterranean coast at winter's end to marshal the navies of Phoenicia, Cyprus, and Egypt in cooperation with Gobryas' son Mardonius, who had a few years before been awarded in marriage a daughter of the Great King—for, at Lindos on the island of Rhodes, there is an inscription mentioning an expedition against the Greeks in which the two were involved, which reports that Datis, its commander, paused there on route to bring that city under Persian control and leave a chariot and rich Persian robes as an offering to the goddess Athena.[25]

When they got wind of what was to come, the Ionians met in council at the Panionium and decided to leave the defense of Miletus by land to its inhabitants and to unite their forces at sea in an attempt once more to reassert their command over that element. They amassed, we are told, three hundred fifty-three triremes—twelve from Priene, three from Myous, seventeen from Teos, three from Phocaea, eight from Erythrae, eighty from Miletus, one hundred from Chios, seventy from Lesbos, and sixty from Samos. The numbers are testimony to the decline of the coastal cities, apart from Miletus, and to the continuing strength of the islands off the coast. The fact that there is mention neither of Halicarnassus nor of the three *póleis* on the island of Rhodes nor of Byzantium suggests that the Dorian cities in the south may never have joined the revolt or that they had already surrendered and that the cities along the waterway leading from the Black Sea to the Mediterranean that had not yet been subjugated were beleaguered or cowed.[26]

The force that Herodotus describes was formidable. If Herodotus' figures are right—and they are sufficiently precise when broken down to elicit confidence—the Ionians deployed a naval force at the island of Lade near the harbor of Miletus crewed by anywhere from seventy to eighty-three thousand men. Against this fleet, the Persians fielded—so we are told—an armada of six hundred triremes, manned by one hundred two thousand rowers, nine thousand six hundred officers and specialists, twenty-four hundred archers, and anywhere from six to twenty-four thousand marines.[27]

The number of ships attributed to the Persian fleet by Herodotus is large, round, and suspect. It no doubt represents a guess on the part of the Ionians, and some scholars think it an exaggeration. We can be confident, nonetheless, that the Greeks were badly outnumbered. The Persians commanded immense resources. They were not addicted to half-measures, and they did not take well to losing. In similar circumstances, far from their own homes, the Ionians and their Aeolian allies had come to the aid of the Cypriot Greeks and had won an earlier battle at sea against the Mede. There was no reason that they could not have done so again on this particular occasion, as the Persians

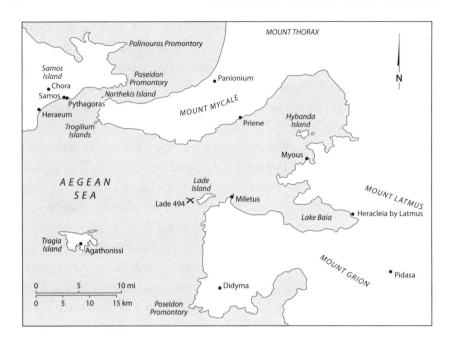

Map 7. The Battle of Lade

understood all too well; and, in the circumstances, the Ionians and Aeolians might well have eked out a victory—had there not been treachery.

The background to the betrayal of the Ionian cause deserves close attention, for it casts considerable light on the nature of trireme warfare and, more generally, on the sources of Persian strength and Hellenic weakness. When the Ionian fleet gathered in the bay separating Miletus from Lade, a number of assemblies were held in which those present deliberated concerning the struggle to come. Among the men who spoke, Herodotus tells us, was a commander named Dionysius who led the three triremes dispatched from Phocaea. Initially, the Ionians opted to follow his advice. They had reason to do so.

The Phocaeans were the most experienced seafarers in Ionia. They had opened up the Adriatic and the western Mediterranean and had grown rich from that region's trade. They had established close relations with Arganthonios of Tartessos on the Atlantic coast of Iberia; and, in gratitude for their support, he had helped fund the construction of the magnificent walls, nine miles in length and made up of rectangular stone blocks, that adorned and protected their city. The Carthaginians they had defeated at sea, and they had founded the city of Massilia in Gaul near where the Rhône river empties into the Mediterranean. In the first half of the sixth century, Phocaea reached its acme.[28]

When the Persians conquered Lydia in the mid-540s and set out to subjugate the Ionian cities on the Asia Minor coast the following year, the Phocaeans soberly sized up the odds of their fending off the onslaught, then resolutely evacuated their city, and relocated to Alalia on the coast of Corsica —whence, roughly a decade thereafter, they set out onto the Sardinian Sea with a fleet of sixty penteconters (the first such ships known to have been armed with rams) and won a dramatic, if Pyrrhic, victory in battle against a fleet twice that number deployed by the Etruscans and Carthaginians. This the Phocaeans could hardly have accomplished had they not possessed something that gave them a decisive and unexpected advantage—such as a new weapons system, unknown to their enemies, and tactical skills enabling them to use it to good effect. We are not told that the Phocaeans invented the ram, but there is reason to suspect as much.[29]

Dionysius represented the Phocaeans—many in number, we are told, but considerably less wealthy than those who persevered in the western migration —who had returned in desperation to repopulate their native city; and, as we have seen, he led a flotilla of exceedingly modest significance. But as a Phocaean, presumed to be familiar with the mode of warfare that had won his compatriots so impressive a victory in the western Mediterranean four decades before, he had earned a hearing, and at the assembly convened at Lade the words that he spoke commanded respect. "Our affairs, men of Ionia," he reportedly said,

> are balanced on a razor's edge. Either we will be free or we will be slaves—
> and runaways at that. If you are now willing to embrace hardship, at the
> present time you will experience toil, and you will be able to overcome the
> enemy and remain free. If, however, you habituate yourselves to softness
> and disorder, I have no hope that you will escape paying the penalty reserved for rebellion against the King. But be persuaded by me, and to me
> entrust yourself; and I promise—if the gods hand out equal treatment to
> both sides—that either the enemy will not mix it up with you or that, if
> they do, they will prove your inferior by far.[30]

Dionysius' point was simple, straightforward, and far wiser than we may be inclined fully to appreciate. If one is tempted, as one might be, to discount the significance of Herodotus' highlighting of the Phocaean commander's speech as yet another example of moralizing on the historian's part, one should firmly resist the temptation.

As Dionysius and Herodotus understood, it took extraordinary grit, determination, discernment, and discipline on the part of a great many men for a trireme to be operated in battle to advantage. The trierarch in command had to be a man of fine judgment—quick to sense danger, and no less quick in recognizing opportunity—and he had to have an intimate knowledge of the capacity of his ship and crew and of their limits. The helmsman [*kubernḗtēs*] stationed immediately below the trierarch's perch at the stern was in charge in the trierarch's absence and had to possess the same capacities. He also had to be skilled and precise in his use of the vessel's two steering oars. Everything depended on his ability to maneuver the galley into a position from which it could strike and not be struck in return, and an error or even a measure of imprecision on his part could easily be fatal to all concerned. When the trireme was in motion the archers and marines on deck had to remain seated lest they destabilize the vessel. In consequence they had to be able to shoot or hurl projectiles with great accuracy from an uncomfortable, sedentary position. With the help of a flutist [*aulḗtēs*] located amidships keeping time with his instrument, the exhorter [*keleustḗs*] situated on the gangway near the stern and his colleague, the bow-master [*prōrátēs*] stationed near the prow, had to drill the oarsmen in synchronizing their strokes and in rowing forward now at this pace, now at that. These two also had to teach them how to reverse themselves on the benches and back water without missing a beat, and they had to instruct them in the procedure of partially shipping their oars on command at a time when a few seconds' delay on their part could result in the oars on one side being sheared off, in some of the men wielding them being killed by whiplash, and in the galley itself being left entirely disabled. In time of battle, moreover, these two officers had to convey the helmsman's orders quickly and accurately, and throughout they somehow had to sustain the morale of men whom they were driving hard.

The oarsmen themselves had to learn endurance and close coordination. This was no small thing, as scholars first came fully to appreciate in the late 1980s and early 1990s—when, under the guidance of an intrepid group of British classicists and naval experts, a Greek shipyard built a replica of a trireme, and every other summer volunteers gathered from far and near to take the *Olympias,* as it was called, to sea and put it through a series of trials. There was, these scholars discovered, a great deal to endure, and everything depended on a precise synchronization of the rowers' strokes.

On journeys, for example—when the sea was becalmed, when the wind blew from the wrong quarter or was insufficient—it became clear that the oarsmen of ancient times had to row steadily for hours and hours. When the fleet was arranged for battle in line abreast, they had to row gently forward and then back water and do this again and again to maintain their galley's position in the formation. In the battle itself, when maneuvering for advantage, they had to be able to turn the vessel on a dime; and, when closing in for a kill or fleeing attack, they had to drive the vessel forward at maximum speed. If, at the end of such a sprint, their ship succeeded in ramming at high speed an enemy trireme, they had to back water at a moment's notice to prevent the two vessels from being locked together in such a manner that the footsoldiers seated on board the damaged ship could attempt to board and seize their own. Alternatively, if the trierarch's aim was to approach an enemy vessel head-on at full tilt, then narrowly dodge a collision and coast along the enemy boat's starboard or port side with an eye to shearing off half of its oars and rendering it defenseless and incapable of maneuver, the oarsmen on the vulnerable side of his own trireme had to be able to partially ship their oars at a moment's notice while their colleagues on the other side of the vessel simultaneously lifted theirs out of the water. For the rowers in a trireme to be able to do all of this with maximum effectiveness, those who conducted *Olympias'* sea trials discovered, they had to drill and drill and drill once more. Following orders and close coordination had to become second nature for each and every oarsman.

The crew of a trireme fully manned included one hundred seventy oarsmen organized in three banks along the beam on each side of the vessel. In the fourth century, at Athens, there were ordinarily sixty-two *thranítai* situated outboard on the outriggers. Slightly below and alongside them within the trireme itself, seated on the thwarts or cross-beams [*zúga*] running inside along the ship's hull, were fifty-four *zúgioi*; and, deep in the hold [*thálamos*], rowing through oarports situated a foot and a half above the waterline and sealed against leakage from the sea by a well-greased leather sleeve, were fifty-four *thalamioí*. At Lade, in 494, the arrangement may have been slightly different. There may have been sixty *thranítai*, fifty-eight *zúgioi*, and fifty-two *thalamioí*, and the *thranítai* may have been situated Phoenician-style within the hull. We do not know.

But whatever the arrangement and the distribution of men between the three banks may have been, the circumstances will have been similar. As the oarsmen in *Olympias* discovered, their ancient counterparts had been accorded next to no elbow room. Between the oarsmen in each bank the gap—

called by the Roman architect Vitruvius the *interscalmium*—was, at most, a
yard and an inch or two. When not at work, the rowers had no place in which
to stretch out—unless they were willing to descend to the hold, where the
spare oars were kept and the sweat, urine, feces, and vomit of the oarsmen
above gradually accumulated. On Athenian ships in the late fifth century, the
thranítai were in a position of advantage. They had the benefit of access to
fresh air, and they could see the blades of their own oars and those of their
colleagues nearby. In consequence, at this time, each *thranítēs* was almost certainly in charge of coordinating the efforts of a triad of rowers including the
zúgios beside and slightly below him and the *thalamiós* on a bench far below
in the hold. The situation of the *zúgioi* and *thalamioí* (and that of *thranítai* in
Phoenician-style triremes) was less desirable. In the heat of the summer, the
rowers situated on the *zúga* and in the hold below them must have suffered
grievously from a lack of ventilation, and, in all seasons, the stench from the
hold must have been overpowering.[31]

After listening to Dionysius, the Ionians entrusted themselves to his care,
and for a week he led them out each day in line ahead. On these occasions,
presumably after having had the triremes turn in unison and smartly redeploy
in line abreast, he had their crews repeatedly practice a complex maneuver
called the *diékplous*. This maneuver—which his fellow Phocaeans, rowing
penteconters in the West, may have been the first to employ some forty years
before—consisted, as the etymology of the Greek term suggests, in the galleys
belonging to one fleet "rowing through and out" between the ships of the rival
fleet. This each galley may have done, as one scholar supposes, with an eye to
shearing off the oars on one side of one of the two enemy ships as it passed
between. Alternatively, the crews may have "rowed through and out," as most
others presume, with the aim of repositioning their ships behind the enemy
fleet where each could then do a "swing around [*anastróphē*]" and at high
speed ram a hostile trireme in the stern, as the Phoenicians had apparently
become wont to do. Or they could have carried out this maneuver, as yet another scholar argues, in order to swing around and position themselves at the
stern of an enemy trireme, poised for boarding and seizing the vessel.[32] There
is also a fourth and, I think, more likely possibility, which to date no one has
canvassed: that the *diékplous* was a preliminary maneuver designed to open
up all three options, leaving it up to the trierarch to select which of the three
modes of attack best suited the occasion and the capacity of his crew.

Each day, when the Ionians were finished practicing this maneuver and the ships came to anchor, Dionysius kept the crews busy working, presumably for the purpose of building up their stamina. And so it went on, day after laborious day, until the eighth such day, when the Ionians—unused to such exertions, worn out by their toil, and enervated by the summer heat—dug in their heels, refused further effort, and pitched their tents on Lade, where they could luxuriate in the shade. In Herodotus' opinion, it was this display of softness and self-indulgence that induced the generals of one Ionian city to rethink their chances of success in the battle to come and that occasioned on their part the act of betrayal that enabled the Persians to engineer the Ionians' defeat.[33]

Herodotus' explanation is certainly instructive and apt, and it may also be true. The indiscipline displayed by the Ionians on the eve of the battle can hardly have been reassuring. But the historian's observation should perhaps also be taken with a grain of salt, for it serves to excuse in some measure the treachery of a people to whom he was himself personally indebted. The Ionians were all afraid of the consequences of losing. They had reason to be. But none were more afraid than the Samians, who had firsthand knowledge of what the Persians might well do. Back when Maeandrius and his brother Charilaos had tried to prevent the Persians from installing the younger Syloson as tyrant in Samos, Otanes had turned his troops loose on the people of Samos, authorizing them to kill everyone they met, whether in a sanctuary or not; and thereafter they had reportedly conducted a dragnet on the island, walking shoulder to shoulder across it and rounding up the survivors—a population much diminished—for a deportation that might well have been permanent. Thanks, one must suspect, to the entreaties of this same Syloson, their time in exile turned out to be blessedly brief, but the nightmare the Samians had been through cannot have been forgotten.[34]

On the eve of the battle of Lade, with this memory in mind, the Samians listened to the blandishments of their former tyrant the younger Aeaces, who had succeeded to his father Syloson's position on their island at some point prior to Darius' Scythian expedition; and when the day of decision came, all but eleven of the Samian ships abandoned their post and sailed directly home, leaving the rest of the Ionians to the mercy of the Mede. The Mytilenians and the others from Lesbos soon thereafter panicked and followed the Samian example.

The battle was reportedly hard fought, nonetheless. The Chians, in particular, distinguished themselves. Seated on the decks of their triremes, alongside the ordinary complement of ten marines and four archers, were another thirty marines, armed as hoplites with thrusting spears and swords and equipped no doubt with javelins as well. We are told that the Chian ships repeatedly performed the *diékplous* and that they captured a multitude of enemy ships. When the opportunity presented itself, they must have sidled up to triremes in the Persians fleet and hurled grappling irons onto them so that their marines could board and take control. But the heroic efforts of the Chians on this occasion fell short, nonetheless. In the absence of nearly all of the Samians and of the contingents from Lesbos, their defeat and that of the Milesians, of the Phocaeans, and of the contingents from Priene, Myous, Teos, and Erythrae was foreordained.[35]

Mopping Up

When the battle ended, Miletus was cut off from resupply by sea, and the siege began in earnest. Later in the year, the city fell. The majority of the men were killed; their women and children were made slaves; the sanctuary at Didyma was plundered and set on fire. Many of the Milesians who did manage to survive were deported to Mesopotamia, where they were settled in a small town near the mouth of the Tigris River within easy reach of the Persian Gulf. The fertile farmland near Miletus was handed over to individual Persians.[36]

The fleet of Phoenicians and Egyptians wintered at Miletus; and, in 493, the Persians used them to seize control of the cities along the coast and to capture Chios, Lesbos, and Tenedos. Then, they performed a dragnet on each of the islands. The most handsome of the boys they castrated, the most beautiful of the young girls they took from their parents. Both, in keeping with long-standing Persian practice, they shipped to the Great King's court. The cities they burned and their sanctuaries as well. Then they sailed into the Hellespont and the Sea of Marmara and did the same with the cities, as yet unconquered, along the European shore and with the Proconnesus and Artace as well. The Byzantines and Chalcedonians escaped the worst by fleeing north to Mesembria on the western coast of the Black Sea.[37]

The Samians, who were made to accept the younger Aeaces again as tyrant, the Persians spared. Immediately after the sack of Miletus, the latter subdued the Carians not then on their side; and the Carians of Pidasa, who had evidently turned coat, they rewarded with the hill-country around Miletus.

The King of Kings and his underlings had a better understanding of the un-written rules of prudence that guide the conduct of foreign policy than we do today. They were as good as their word. They had to be—if they were to lure others to medize as the Samians and the Carians of Pidasa had done. They knew it, and they carefully cultivated their image—both as men protective of the King's *bandaka,* profoundly hostile to "the Lie," and devoted to truth and trust, and as statesmen who knew better than anyone else how to help their friends and to harm their enemies in the manner thought by all at the time to distinguish real from effeminate men.[38]

When the killing was over—on the advice of his brother Artaphernes, to whom the Ionians in defeat had sent Hecataeus on an embassy to make a plea for lenient terms—Darius imposed a new settlement on Ionia. First, he had the satrap at Sardis summon envoys from the Ionian cities and make them swear to submit all disputes to arbitration and to refrain from raids on one another. Then, he had him do a survey of the land held by each city so that tribute could be assessed equitably, and he dispatched his nephew and son-in-law Mardonius son of Gobryas to establish democracies in some of the cities where there had hitherto been tyrannies, but apparently not in all.[39] We should not underestimate the intelligence of the men who governed the Persian empire. They learned from their mistakes, punished the rebels with exemplary severity, then moved to placate the survivors. Only then did they turn their minds once again to the Greeks on the mainland of Europe as yet unconquered.

Mardonius made straight the way. Late in the summer, when he had fin-ished making adjustments in the governance of the Greek cities under Persian control, he undertook the second task that he had been assigned. He made his way to the Hellespont, took in custody a large fleet and a large army that had gathered there. Then, he retraced the path followed by Megabazos more than a decade before. His first aim was to reassert and extend Persian control in Aegean Thrace and Macedon. Along the way, however, he paused briefly to subjugate Thasos—a Greek island community blessed with vast wealth drawn from gold mines long established on the mainland and scattered throughout the island itself, which had briefly come under siege toward the end of the Ionian revolt. In the aftermath, this city had begun using its riches both to strengthen the circuit, two-and-a-half miles in length, constituting the city's walls and to construct a sizable fleet of triremes for the city's defense. In the face of the Persian threat, however, the Thasians did not even bother to put

up a fight. A year later, when their neighbors accused them of plotting a revolt, they were called upon by the Great King himself to tear down a section
of their city walls and dispatch their fleet to Abdera in support of the Persian enterprise, and this they did without protest.[40] Such was their fear of the
Mede.

Mardonius did not have an entirely easy time. Herodotus reports that, as
his fleet rounded the Chalcidice, a powerful north wind drove three hundred
of his triremes against the twenty-mile-long shore at Mount Athos and that
twenty thousand men died in the process. The number of triremes and men
lost may seem inflated. But, given what we know of a disaster that took place
along this rugged lee shore eight decades thereafter, it is, in fact, surprising
that so many men survived. The waters about the Acte peninsula are treacherous and cold; and, late in the summer and in the autumn and winter, storms
are frequent and fearsome. Herodotus also tells us that Mardonius' army suffered severely at the hands of the Thracian Byrgoi and that Mardonius was
himself wounded, and he indicates that, toward the end of the year, the Persian commander and his forces withdrew to Asia Minor.[41]

Mardonius' visit to Macedon cannot have lasted long, but this probably
mattered not at all. We have no indication that Amyntas of Macedon ever
strayed from his pledge. We are told that, after marrying the Macedonian
king's daughter, Megabazos' son Boubares stayed on with his bride at her father's court through the remainder of the latter's reign,[42] and we can easily
imagine that he had been instructed by his father to keep an eye on things and
to provide the Macedonian king with sage advice of a sort acceptable to the
King of Kings. Moreover, Boubares' brother-in-law Alexander I, who came to
the throne in about 495, was a man of keen intelligence who could tell which
way the wind was blowing.

Cleomenes and the other leading Spartans, as they watched with interest
these developments from afar, cannot have been altogether pleased. They had
exercised caution, and they had played no role in these events. But their absence had nonetheless been felt, and their strategic situation had deteriorated.

Some at Lacedaemon and in Hellas more generally no doubt hoped that
the Persian advance would stop for good at the southern border of Macedon,
and they surely welcomed Mardonius' decision not to winter in Europe but,
instead, to lead his forces back to Anatolia. As, however, they must have recognized, it was by no means clear that the withdrawal he then staged was part
of that commander's original plan. Herodotus describes his return to Asia

Minor as a tactical retreat occasioned by the severe losses suffered by his fleet and the damage inflicted on his army, and Mardonius' absence from the lists in 490 suggests that he may for a time have been put out of commission by his wounds.[43] Though relieved, few of the Hellenes closely observing developments can have been fully sanguine as they watched and waited, wondering what would be Darius' next move.

CHAPTER 4

The First Round

I heard a man, a Mede, say that the Persians do not at all agree with the Greeks regarding these matters. They claim that Darius dispatched those about Datis and Artaphernes against Naxos and Eretria and that these men laid hold of these two cities and made their way back to the King. They report that, while the Persian fleet was moored in the vicinity of Euboea, a handful of ships, no more than twenty, were separated from the rest and drifted on to the Attic coast, where some sort of skirmish took place between the sailors and those who lived in those parts. Later on, they assert, Xerxes led an army against Greece, conquered the Lacedaemonians at Thermopylae, and killed their king Leonidas; then seized the city of the Athenians, razed it to the ground, and sold into slavery those who did not manage to flee; and imposed tribute on the Hellenes before withdrawing to Asia. That these tales fall short of the truth is clear enough, and it is apt to be the case—for it is by no means impossible—that the King had this account propagated among the peoples residing up country in Asia with an eye to preventing an uproar, tumults, and confusion.

—DIO CHRYSOSTOM

DARIUS son of Hystaspes was not a man to be trifled with. The Athenians had given earth and water. They had become his *bandaka*. Then they had broken their bond. They had not only refused to take direction from his satrap. They had supported the rebellion of the Ionians; and, with the Eretrians, they had also participated in an attack on the capital of one of his satrapies. They had ostentatiously embraced *Drauga*—"the Lie." If Darius was "the man in all the earth" and "King in all the earth," as he claimed to be, he could hardly let their insolence pass unpunished.

Darius prided himself on being "a friend to the right" and "no friend of the man who follows the Lie," and he knew how to be a friend to his friend and an enemy to his enemy: "The man who cooperates—him do I reward in proportion to his cooperation. He who does harm I punish according to the damage done. . . . What a man does or performs according to his abilities satisfies me . . . ; it gives me great pleasure and I give much to faithful men." Darius professed also to be steadfast in "intelligence" and "superior to panic," whether in the presence of "a rebel or not," and he claimed to be

> a good fighter of battles . . . furious in the strength of my revenge with my two hands and my two feet. As a horseman I am a good horseman. As a bowman I am a good bowman, both on foot and on the back of a horse. As a spearman I am a good spearman, both on foot and on the back of a horse. These are the skills which the Wise Lord Ahura Mazda has bestowed on me and I have the capacity for their use.[1]

There is no reason to dismiss these bold assertions as mere propaganda. As King of Kings, Darius had nearly always been as good as his word.

As one would then expect, in 491—after Mardonius had consolidated Persia's hold on Thrace and Macedon, and probably quite early in that year— Darius took the next logical step.[2] According to Herodotus, he sent out heralds to the free cities throughout Hellas, "ordering that they request earth and water for the King," and at the same time he sent out another set of heralds "to his tribute-paying cities along the coast, ordering that they produce not only long ships but horse transports," the first such of which we have any report. His aim, we are told, was to discover "whether the Greeks had it in mind to go to war with him or to hand themselves over."[3] The handwriting was now on the wall.

The Battle of Sepeia

In truth, it had been there for some time, and the Greeks within the ruling order in each of the various cities had frequently given it thought. In 494, the crucial year in which the battle of Lade took place, when Cleomenes led the Spartan army against the Argives, it was surely not Argos that he chiefly had in mind. Nearly two generations had passed since the Battle of the Champions in the mid-540s. If Argos' defeat on that occasion had been followed by a peace of specified duration—thirty or fifty years, as seems to have been the norm—it was no longer in effect. Moreover, whatever casualties the Argives had sustained at that time had long since been recouped. Another showdown over Thyrea was in the cards, and Cleomenes, who was no less vigorous than he had been a quarter of a century before, was intent on crushing the Argives well before the Persians could come.

We do not know how the trouble began. Cynouria, the long-disputed district wherein the fertile Thyreatis plain lay, was easier to get to from Argos than from Sparta. It is conceivable that there was a peace of fifty years' duration, that it ended in 496 or 495, and that the Argives then seized the territory. It is also possible that, in this regard, they issued a challenge, as appears to have happened fifty years before. What we are told is that Delphi supplied an oracle to Cleomenes, predicting that he would take Argos. It is a reasonable presumption that, in this exchange, Cleomenes took the initiative—that, in accord with ordinary protocol, he sent one or more of the four *Púthioi* to Delphi to pose the question. Given what is known regarding the Agiad king's proclivities for the use of religion as an instrument of political manipulation, it would not be surprising if he had made arrangements in advance to secure the answer he had in mind. He is known to have done just that on at least one other occasion. Cleomenes was not apt to be passive. Nearly always, he was a man with a plan.

On this occasion, Cleomenes led his army to the Erasinos River on the border of the Argolid. There, Herodotus reports, the omens were not favorable —which may be an indication that it had come to the attention of the Agiad king that the Argives had occupied the high ground on the other side of the stream, or it may simply indicate that this maneuver was a feint. In any case, undeterred, Cleomenes then retreated to the south and marched his army east to the plain of Thyrea, where he sacrificed a bull to the sea and made arrangements for the Aeginetans and Sicyonians to convey his army to the district of Tiryns and Nauplia on the coast of the Argolid.[4] If maritime transport was not, in fact, prearranged, as I suspect it was, this must have taken some time. Aegina was situated in the Saronic Gulf not far from Cynouria and the Argolid, but Sicyon was located on the Corinthian Gulf. To get from there to Thyrea on the Argolic Gulf, a ship must either circumnavigate the Peloponnesus or be conveyed across the *díolkos* at Corinth.

The Argives appear to have been caught off guard by Cleomenes' second approach. Herodotus tells us that they rushed to the coast and deployed their troops near Tiryns at a place called Sepeia, leaving very little space between themselves and the Lacedaemonians. They were nervous, we are told, because, in an oracle issued to the Argives, doom had been predicted both for the Milesians and for them. When Cleomenes learned that the Argives were paying close attention to the orders issued by the Spartan herald and acting accordingly, he instructed his men to ignore the herald's announcement of the mid-day meal and strike when, upon hearing this order, the Argives dispersed

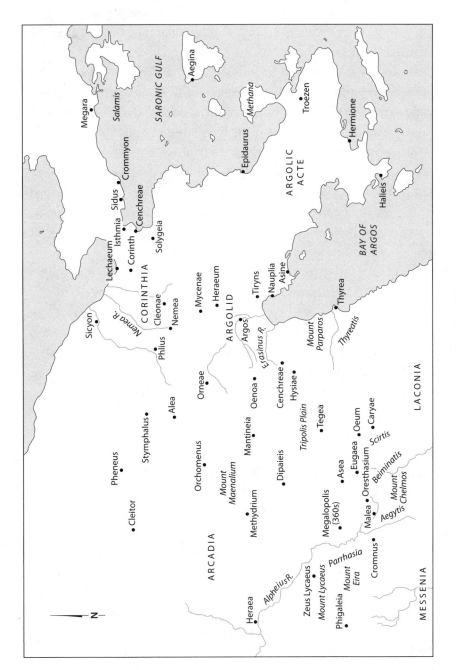

Map 8. The Argolid

to take their own meal. The stratagem worked. When the herald made his announcement, the Lacedaemonians paused briefly, then attacked and routed the Argives—who, in desperation, sought refuge and sanctuary in a nearby grove, sacred to Apollo.[5]

Cleomenes was nothing if not ruthless, and he was not put off by the thought of committing a sacrilege. By one means or another, the Spartans were able to secure the names of some of the survivors. On the Agiad king's order, they sent a herald to call these out from the grove one by one at intervals by name, announcing that they had been ransomed for the standard fee. When each of these came out, however, he was led away and executed. Some fifty lost their lives in this fashion. Eventually, however, one of those trapped inside the grove climbed a tree and discovered what was happening, and the Argives stopped responding—at which point, Cleomenes ordered the helots with his army to pile up brushwood around the grove and set it alight in order to roust or roast the rest. All in all, we are told, the Argives lost something like six thousand men in this encounter. This was the greatest loss of life known to have been suffered in a single battle by a Greek city in the entire classical period.[6]

This catastrophe appears to have had profound political consequences. Herodotus reports that, before heading home, Cleomenes visited the sanctuary of Hera near Mycenae, north of the city of Argos, where he insisted on conducting a sacrifice and had an attendant whipped who told him that for an outsider to do so was a sacrilege. He does not mention any attack on the city itself, and he implies that none took place. In other sources, thought to be derivative from local histories, however, there are reports suggesting that Cleomenes or a contingent from his army may at some stage, at least, have approached the walls; and, tellingly, Plutarch mentions the name of the Eurypontid king Demaratus son of Ariston in this connection. We are told, moreover, that, in the absence of the city's men, a woman named Telesilla organized the defense of the city's walls, rallying the old men, the young, her fellow women, and the underlings attached to their households [oιkétaι] to wield whatever weapons they could find and fend off an assault; and Herodotus appears to be aware of this tradition, for the oracle he cites associates Argos' defeat with a victory and achievement of glory on the part of that city's women.[7]

It is a reasonable guess that the oιkétaι mentioned by Plutarch were drawn from the city's substantial and downtrodden pre-Dorian population. In the aftermath of the battle, Herodotus tells us, there was a revolution at Argos, and the slaves [*doûloi*] seized power. Aristotle has a different tale to relate. According to his report, the Argives were forced, after their defeat, to accept some of their *períoikoi* into the ruling order. This may have been a matter of military necessity—for, in the aftermath of the battle, the Lacedaemonians apparently refused to agree to the peace of extended duration that the Argives sought. Plutarch confirms what we would in any case surmise: that those whom Herodotus' aristocratic Argive informants disdainfully called *doûloi* outsiders would be inclined to identify as *períoikoi;* and he mentions that, because of a shortage of male citizens, the widows and young girls of Argos married these men.[8]

At Sparta, Cleomenes had enemies. Men who throw their weight around, as he did, always do. And when he returned home, they tried to hoist him on his own petard. The oracle, at his prompting, had predicted that he would take Argos. It was presumably by announcing this that he had encouraged the Spartans to choose war. But he had not delivered as promised, and his enemies asserted that his failure to perform as the god had foretold was proof that the Agiad king must have been bribed. Cleomenes was a man of exceptionally quick wit—equal to almost any occasion—and at this time it did not fail him, for it was by a large margin that he was acquitted in the court constituted by the ephors and *gérontes*. As Cleomenes explained in court, the grove sacred to Apollo was called the grove of Argos. It must, he told them, have been this that the oracle had in mind—for when, as king, he had made his sacrifice at the Argive Heraeum, he had done so with an eye to obtaining an omen favorable to a full-scale assault on the town, and this boon he had been denied.[9]

Later, when the word came that the Ionians had gone down to defeat at Lade and that Miletus had fallen, those at Lacedaemon attentive to the power waxing in the east must have felt a measure of consolation and relief when they contemplated Cleomenes' accomplishment at Argos. The Agiad king may not have delivered on the oracle's promise, but, in slaughtering the Argives on a scale unprecedented, he had done what the situation required. When the crisis came, politically divided and crippled by a lack of manpower, the Argives would not march out—against the Medes or in their support—and their neighbors in the Argolid at Tiryns, near where Cleomenes had landed and fought the battle, and at Mycenae, near the Argive Heraeum where the Agiad king had ostentatiously made sacrifice, rallied to the Panhellenic cause, as he no doubt hoped they would.[10]

Earth and Water

At the time of Cleomenes' expedition against Argos, Athens remained divided with regard to the question of Persia. But, under the pressure of necessity, it advanced in the direction of a decision, nonetheless. In 493/92, after Miletus fell, the archon eponymous at Athens was a man not much more than thirty years in age named Themistocles son of Neocles. Of this figure, when he had occasion to record his death, the historian Thucydides wrote,

> Themistocles was a man who in a fashion quite reliable displayed strength of nature, and in this regard he was outstanding and worthy of greater admiration than anyone else. By his own native intelligence, without the help of study before or after, he was at once the best judge in matters, admitting of little deliberation, which require settlement on the spot, and the best predictor of things to come across the broadest expanse. What he had in hand he could also explain; what lay beyond his experience he did not lack the capacity adequately to judge. In a future as yet obscure he could in a preeminent fashion foresee both better and worse. In short, by the power of his nature, when there was little time to take thought, this man surpassed all others in the faculty of improvising what the situation required.[11]

Of no one else did Thucydides ever speak with comparable awe and respect. Themistocles was, in his estimation, the greatest of statesmen.

We know little about this man prior to 493, but in that year, when he presented himself on the political stage, he made it clear that he was deeply concerned at the turn events were taking in Ionia. Prior to this time, the Athenians had not had a proper harbor. The ships that they possessed and the merchantmen that visited from abroad simply pulled up on the beach at Phalerum, which was sheltered by a bay from the northern gales. This left the Athenians vulnerable to attack, as they had more than once recently learned. In his year as archon, Themistocles persuaded them to begin the construction of a proper harbor supplemented by fortifications at Peiraeus. There is reason to suspect that Themistocles may also have convinced his compatriots at this time to begin gradually building a substantial fleet of triremes. Already then, Thucydides intimates, this great man recognized that there was a future for his compatriots as a power on the sea. That he already then feared a maritime assault on the part of the navy that was victorious the year before at Lade we need not doubt. It was in the late 490s, as we have seen, that the citizens of Thasos, just off the coast of Thrace, began using the income from their mines to improve their fortifications and construct a proper fleet. After Lade, no one in Hellas of genuine discernment could suppose that pentaconters would any longer suffice.[12]

Themistocles appears also to have had an appreciation for Greek tragedy as a tool for political instruction. Years later, in 476, he undertook a public *leitourgía* as *chorēgós* and paid for the production of a series of plays entered in the tragic competition by a tragedian named Phrynichus. One of these, *The Phoenician Women,* was a reminder of the prescience of the *chorēgós,* for it touched directly on Xerxes' invasion of Greece four years before. It may not then be an accident that, shortly after the fall of Miletus, almost certainly when as archon Themistocles oversaw the competition, this same Phyrnichus was chosen to put on a series of tragedies, among which he included a play entitled *The Sack of Miletus.* Some later observers thought the play an argument for defeatism in the face of the Persian threat, but the late Roman historian Ammianus Marcellinus, who ranks alongside Thucydides in astuteness as a judge, tells us that the play was intended as a reproach to the Athenians for having abandoned their Ionian kin. This is certainly the way in which the play was perceived by the Athenian public. Herodotus, who makes explicit reference to the didactic dimension of the playwright's art, tells us that on this occasion the audience broke into tears; that, soon thereafter, the assembly fined the playwright for having reminded them of their kinship with the Milesians and of the "evils" which had just taken place "within their own household"; and that it ordered that his play never again be staged.[13] Even if Themistocles was not behind the production—as, some scholars suspect, he was—this minor political tempest is yet another sign that at Athens a struggle was still going on in the later 490s between those who thought it prudent to appease Persia and those intent on preparing for a war they judged a foregone conclusion.

It was not the last such indicator—for it was in 493 or very soon thereafter that Miltiades son of Cimon returned to Athens. After having accompanied Darius and his army to the Danube, when his advice that the Greeks take apart the bridge of boats over that river and leave the Great King to the mercy of the Scythians was rejected, he appears to have withdrawn to his stronghold in the Thracian Chersonnesus. When, soon thereafter, Darius made for Sestos with the Scythians in hot pursuit, Miltiades appears to have withdrawn once again—this time, perhaps, to the court of his father-in-law, the Thracian prince Olorus, and, almost certainly, to Athens for a time as well. At some point thereafter, he returned to his stronghold. Precisely when is unclear. The pertinent passage in Herodotus makes no sense and is clearly corrupt. But, as long as the Persians remained a real force in that corner of the Aegean, it would have been dangerous for a man known to have crossed the King of Kings to have returned to the Hellespont. It was, then, almost certainly in the early years of the Ionian revolt that Miltiades came back to the Chersonnesus, and it must have been at this time that he seized for Athens Lemnos and presumably Imbros as well—both of which Otanes son of Sisamnes had taken for the Persians a year or two after the Scythian expedition. Later, in the wake of Miletus' fall, when the Phoenician fleet approached Tenedos and the dragnet there was about to begin, Miltiades loaded five triremes with all of his wealth and sailed from Kardia via Imbros to Athens—where, in 493 or 492, he was indicted by his enemies, tried for having conducted himself as a tyrant in the Chersonnesus, and acquitted.[14]

It is not certain that this trial reflected in any way the divisions within Athens stirred up by the Persian question, but it would be surprising if this were not true. As a Philaid, Miltiades was a man of considerable stature, and he was also by this time a known quantity. At the Danube, he had crossed the Great King. He had expelled Persia from Lemnos and seized the island for Athens. And he had fled the Hellespont in the wake of the collapse of the Ionian revolt. Everyone knew where he stood. In 491, when Darius sent out heralds to demand earth and water from the free cities of Hellas, nearly all of the islanders complied and became his *bandaka* and many on the mainland reportedly did so as well. Eretria and Plataea were notable exceptions to the rule, as was Athens. There, the assembly voted to treat the Persian heralds as common criminals, to execute them, and toss them into a pit. The man who urged that they do so was none other than Miltiades, and he had firm backing from Themistocles, who persuaded them to execute as well the Ionian accompanying the heralds as interpreter.[15] Both Athenians were persuaded that the most effective way to unite Athens behind a policy of resistance was to rule out appeasement as an option once and for all.

The one other *pólis* known to have responded in the same manner was Lacedaemon—where, in 491, the authorities or perhaps the assembly of Spartiates chose to hurl the heralds into a deep well and leave them to starve, taunting them with the suggestion that it was from their place of confinement that they could best secure earth and water for the King. Soon thereafter, the Athenians called on the Spartans for help. For some time the former had been involved in an undeclared war with Aegina in which no heralds passed back and forth between the two communities. Now the Athenians learned that the oligarchs on that island had given earth and water to the King of Kings, and they turned to Lacedaemon. Herodotus' use of the imperfect in his report suggests that the Spartans may have been reluctant and that the Athenians may have had to send more than one embassy.[16]

In the end, however, Cleomenes decided to take matters into his own hands—and he did so with his accustomed dispatch, journeying to Aegina with the intention of arresting those responsible for that community's submission to the Great King. We do not know the terms of Lacedaemon's relations with Aegina at this time. Originally, the island had been a dependency of Epidaurus on the mainland nearby. In later times, it was independent but closely associated with Argos; and, in the 490s, some sort of obligation was still thought to pertain—for we are told that, in the wake of the catastrophe at Sepeia, the Aeginetans (and the Sicyonians) were asked to pay a fine to the Argives in recompense for having ferried the hoplites of Lacedaemon from Thyrea to the Argolid; and some years later, when Aegina asked Argos for aid against Athens, a thousand Argive hoplite volunteers put in an appearance. By 491, however, there must also have been some sort of arrangement with Sparta.[17] Otherwise, the Athenians would not have turned to Lacedaemon, and Cleomenes would not have made his trip.

It is telling that, when the foremost of the Aeginetans—a man named Crius son of Polycritus—confronted Cleomenes on this occasion and threatened him, warning that he would not fare well if he tried to lay hold of anyone at Aegina, he did not deny that Lacedaemon had the authority to act in such a fashion. Instead, he charged that Cleomenes was acting without authorization from "the community of the Spartiates," and he accused him of having been bribed by the Athenians—for otherwise, he argued, "the other king" would have accompanied him on this mission.[18] This last claim is especially revealing—for it suggests that the two kings acting in tandem still possessed an authority that neither king could properly exercise on his own. Indeed, like the passing reference in Plutarch to the Eurypontid king Demaratus' presence in the Argolid in 494, it suggests that the Lacedaemonians had not yet altered the law specifying collegial leadership on the part of the two kings in war and in foreign policy more generally, and it also suggests that the terms of Sparta's relations with her allies remained what they had been in 506 when Demaratus' withdrawal occasioned a similar withdrawal on the part of Lacedaemon's Peloponnesian allies and thereby torpedoed Cleomenes' attempt to impose on the Athenians the rule of Isagoras and his clique.

Crius was emboldened because he had in his possession a letter from Demaratus in support of his stance, and he let Cleomenes know it. The Agiad king was not, however, a man to be trifled with, and he left Aegina in high dudgeon, warning Crius, whose name meant "ram," that he would be well advised to have his horns coated with bronze—which was the normal preparation for such an animal's sacrifice—for "the evil" he was "about to encounter" was "great."[19]

Cleomenes was as good as his word. When he reached Lacedaemon, he challenged Demaratus' right to the Eurypontid kingship, raising questions about his paternity and charging that he was an impostor. There were apparently grounds for wondering whether he really was the son of Ariston, his Eurypontid predecessor. Demaratus was the offspring of Ariston's third wife. Of this there was no doubt. But she had previously been married to one of Ariston's friends, and Demaratus was born all too soon after Ariston had prevailed upon his friend to relinquish the woman. This, though it had been enough all along to cast suspicion on Demaratus' paternity, was not evidence sufficient to enable Cleomenes to have his way, and the matter was referred to the oracle at Delphi, as the Agiad king had expected. Having anticipated this eventuality, he had, by way of bribery, made sure that the priestess would pronounce against his colleague. Demaratus was demoted. Cleomenes and the new Eurypontid king Leotychidas son of Menares returned to Aegina to lay hold of Crius son of Polycritus and nine other leading Aeginetans whom they conveyed to Athens to be held as hostages. Thereafter, life at Lacedaemon was made sufficiently unpleasant for Demaratus that he fled to Elis, then to the island of Zacynthus off the Peloponnesian coast, and on to the court of Darius at Susa.[20] Whether the support Demaratus lent Crius at Aegina was indicative of the existence of a faction at Sparta favorable to a policy of appeasement vis-à-vis Persia we do not know. His conduct is the only evidence in our possession suggesting the existence of would-be Medizers at Lacedaemon, and it is an exceedingly slender reed on which to lean. But the possibility certainly cannot be ruled out.[21]

The Expeditionary Force

While all of this was going on, the cities under the control of the Great King were building "long ships" for the conveyance of men and horse transports, as he had ordered. In the spring of 490, his forces mustered at the plain of Aleion outside Tarsus in Cilicia. To lead them, Darius sent the like-named son of his brother Artaphernes, the satrap at Sardis, along with Datis the Mede, a man, as we have seen, of trust and considerable experience. The task assigned Datis and the younger Artaphernes was the subjugation not only of Athens but also of Eretria—which, according to Lysanias of Mallos in Cilicia, had continued to lend support with its triremes to the Ionian cause all the way through the Cyprus campaign. The expedition's commanders were instructed to bring great numbers of the citizens of these two communities in chains to the Great King at Susa.[22]

Datis and the younger Artaphernes are supposed to have had six hundred triremes under their command. Some scholars doubt that the Persian fleet can have been this large. The Greeks of the mainland and of the islands as yet unconquered did not have navies even remotely comparable to the fleets fielded at Lade by the Milesians, Samians, Chians, and Mytilenians. A force half the size mentioned by Herodotus—which is, as it happens, the precise number that Plato mentions[23]—would have been more than sufficient to control the seas; and the Persians, who were masters in collecting military and political intelligence, would have been well aware of this. The logistical difficulties presented by a force as large as the one mentioned by Herodotus would, moreover, have been considerable.

Had control of the sea been the Persians' only aim, these arguments would have great force. But, of course, Darius and his commanders had more than this in mind. Theirs was, in fact, the first great overseas expeditionary force known to history, and it required not only men of war but troop carriers and horse transports in considerable numbers as well. A great many archers, infantrymen, and cavalrymen were needed if Athens was to be overawed or defeated and subdued.

Initially, the warships, the horse transports, and the galleys dedicated to the transport of archers and infantrymen made their way to Samos. They were not in a great hurry, but they probably did not long tarry. From Samos, however, they did not head for the Hellespont and Thrace, as Mardonius had done the year before. His experience at Mount Athos was a warning and a deterrent. Instead, they chose to retrace the route followed by Megabates shortly before the Ionian revolt, sailing past Ikaros to Naxos and the Cyclades.[24]

This time, if Herodotus is to be trusted, the Persians caught the Naxians by surprise. As they approached, the citizens of Naxos are said to have abandoned their city and to have taken to the hills. The Persians captured a few

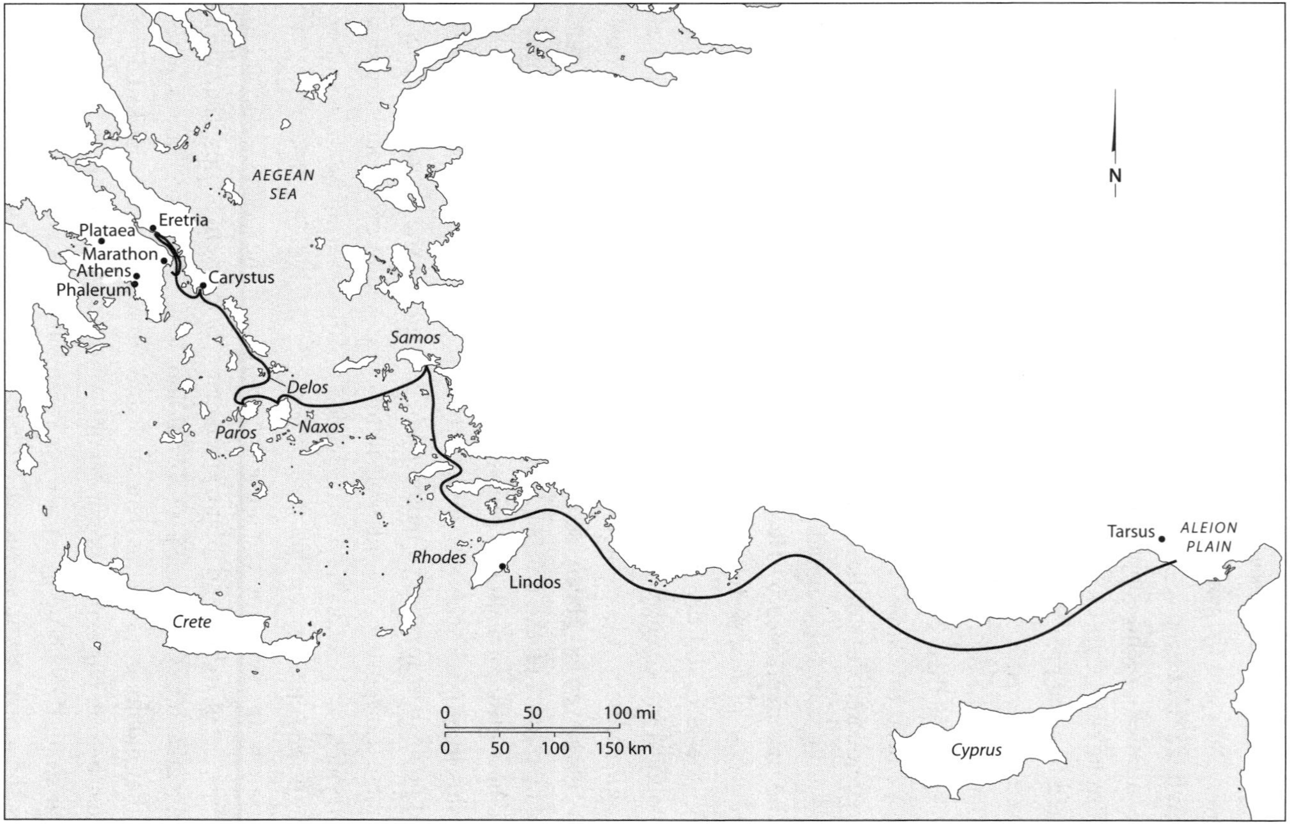

Map 9. From Tarsus to Marathon

of them, set fire to their sanctuaries and to the city, and moved on. The local chroniclers tell a story less plausible but more favorable to the Naxians. They acknowledge that Datis and his men burned the sanctuaries but claim that they were then driven off. On neither account did the forces led by Datis and Artaphernes stay long.[25]

At Delos, Datis, Artaphernes, and their men paused to honor the god. Upon the altar of Apollo, they are said to have burned three hundred talents (8.55 tons) of frankincense, and there, the inscriptions tell us, Datis acted much as he had four years before at the temple of Athena at Lindos on Rhodes, leaving behind a gold necklace as a votive offering. Theirs was a leisurely pace. The expedition the two were conducting on the Great King's behalf was, at first, more like a royal progress aimed at consolidating support than a bold venture in war and conquest. They toured the Cyclades to confirm the loyalty of those who had recently given earth and water, putting in here and there, adding to their forces, and taking the sons of leading figures as hostages. On the rare occasion when the Persians met fierce resistance, as they did at Carystus on the southern coast of Euboea, they mounted a siege and ravaged the land until the citizens acquiesced,[26] which is precisely what they would also have done at Naxos had they encountered opposition there.

When the Persians reached Eretria, their mode of operation changed. The Eretrians, anticipating the worst, had strengthened their fortifications with an eye to resistance. Initially, they had also turned to the Athenians for help, and the latter had offered them the assistance of the four thousand Athenian cleruchs who had been assigned the land of the Horse-Breeders of Chalcis on the Lelantine plain nearby. The Eretrians were, however, deeply divided with regard to policy, and the Medizers within their midst were men of influence. The city's principal leader, despairing, warned the cleruchs who showed up that the city was apt to be betrayed, and so the latter crossed over to Attica at Oropus and lent their compatriots a hand. There is reason to suspect that the Thebans may have seized upon the opportunity afforded by the withdrawal of these cleruchs from Euboea to slip across the Euripus, intervene at Chalcis, liberate their erstwhile ally from the Athenian yoke, and restore to that city's well-born *Hippobótai* the rich estates the latter had lost in 506.[27]

When Datis and the younger Artaphernes arrived with the Persians, the two commanders anticipated trouble. So they landed their men simultaneously at three different points and, when no one appeared to oppose their landing, the two had them disembark their horses, muster, and march on the city. For six days, the Eretrians defended their walls, and on the seventh two prominent citizens opened the gates to the Persians—who sacked the city, set fire to the sanctuaries, conducted a dragnet, and rounded up citizens to be shipped to Darius. In Asia, the King of Kings had ample resources with which handsomely to reward Medizers such as the two who betrayed this Euboean community.[28]

Datis, Artaphernes, and their men waited in Eretria a few days. The Persians had plenty of time, or so they must have presumed. When, finally, they were ready to leave Euboea and complete the task they had been assigned, they followed a suggestion proffered by Hippias, the aged son of Peisistratus. Mindful of the threat that the Eretrian prisoners might pose, they left them under guard on the little island of Aegilia in the Gulf of Euboea.[29] Then, at his bidding, they crossed the straits to Marathon, where Hippias and his father had landed with a sizable mercenary force fifty-six years before.

Marathon

We do not know the precise date of the Persians' arrival. In all likelihood, however, it was just before or quite soon after the beginning of September. Greek cities operated on a lunar calendar, and the new month customarily began when the brief span of moonless nights came to an abrupt end. At Athens, we have reason to believe, the month of Metageitnion had by this time passed, the moon had become visible again, and Boedromion was under way. In later years, the Athenians would commemorate the battle of Marathon at Agrae near Athens on the sixth day of the latter month at the festival of Artemis Agrotera. In consequence, as the centuries passed, they came to suppose that the battle itself had taken place on that day. If, however, Herodotus is to be trusted, the date of commemoration may have coincided with the arrival of the Persians in Attica—for, as he makes clear, the battle took place no earlier than eleven days subsequent to their arrival at Marathon and perhaps as much as two weeks thereafter, soon after the appearance of the full moon in the middle of the lunar month.[30]

Hippias' advice was sensible. Marathon was the obvious place to go. It was close by and suitable. The journey was brief, and the bay, broad. The beach was long; the plain, well-suited to cavalry, as Herodotus emphasizes; and, at its northwest end, there was a lake and ample marshland, where the horses could forage. Moreover, the city of Athens was sufficiently far away that Datis,

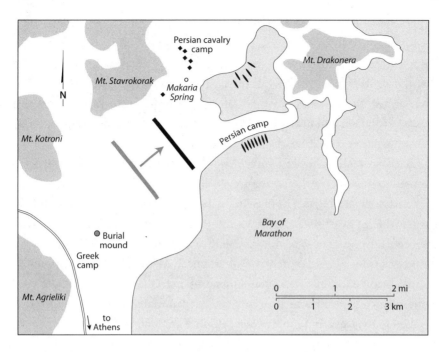

Map 10. The Plain of Marathon

Artaphernes, Hippias, and their associates could be confident that they could land unopposed, water their horses, and muster their men—which they did.[31]

It must have been quite a show. The poet Simonides, who was a contemporary, attributes to the Persians a force of ninety thousand men in all—which would have allowed them three hundred triremes fully manned by sixty thousand rowers, officers, specialists, archers, and marines as well as an additional twenty-five thousand infantrymen, archers, and cavalrymen. Nine thousand of those who doubled as archers and infantrymen could have been carried, in accord with what is likely by then to have become a Persian practice, as marine reinforcements on the decks of their men-of-war. The footsoldiers who could not be accommodated in this fashion may well have been relegated to penteconters or to older triremes fitted out as troop transports—each of the latter rowed, as was the Athenian custom in later years, by a skeleton crew of sixty *thranítai* and managed by the usual complement of officers and specialists.[32]

As we have had occasion to note, the Peisistratids hailed from Brauron in the deme of Philaidae, which was not far away, some miles down the coast.

Hippias presumably hoped that there would be an uprising in his favor in the hinterland, which had been a political stronghold of his family in earlier days—but we hear of none. Datis and Artaphernes may well have expected that those Athenians who had in the past sought for their community a Persian connection would betray their fatherland to the invaders, as others elsewhere so inclined had nearly always done when offered the chance—but these men were either unwilling or unable to do so.

Barring such an eventuality, the two Persian commanders no doubt planned to march on Athens after mustering their cavalry and their troops, as they had done at Eretria. Hippias knew the routes. The shorter, more difficult road—which ran westward over Mount Pentelicon to Cephisia or Acharnae, then south to Athens—was not especially well-suited to cavalry and may not have been fully cleared of debris at this time.[33] As we have seen, Hippias' father had won a famous victory at Pallene—where the easier but longer road, some twenty-five miles in length, proceeded initially along the coast, then climbed to the west, and ran between Mount Pentelicon and Mount Hymettus before descending to the city. Hippias and his Persian patrons no doubt hoped for a repeat. But they were in for a nasty surprise.

At Athens, the militia—for this is what it was—gathered quickly. The Athenians had known for some time what was coming. The ten generals elected that year—Miltiades among them—dispatched a runner of great talent named Philippides to Sparta to ask for help. Then, at the suggestion of Miltiades, the assembly passed a decree, famous in later times, authorizing the emancipation of slaves willing and able to fight, and directing the polemarch to lead the militia directly to Marathon to confront Athens' barbarian foe.[34]

Before departing, the militiamen, enrolled by tribes in the hoplite ranks, took a blood oath, which presupposed that the Lacedaemonians would subscribe to the same oath and soon come to their aid, and which seems to have been modeled on the pledge required of the *enōmatíai* at Sparta. The victims sacrificed they covered with their *aspídes*. First, they swore to punish the Thebans—who, perhaps because of the deep-seated hostility to Athens that had grown up in the wake of the Athenian alliance with Plataea, had been among the first in Greece to medize—and they promised to exercise restraint in any future conflict with the Spartans, the Plataeans, and anyone else who joined their alliance. Then, they pledged to obey the taxiarchs leading Athens' tribes and their counterparts, Sparta's enomotarchs; and they swore that they would bury those of their comrades killed in the war, not give up the fight on as long as they were alive, and not prefer life to liberty.

Initially, Athens' defenders took this oath. Then, at the sound of a trumpet, they called down upon themselves and the city in which they resided a curse if they failed to live up to their pledge. "If I keep true to what has been inscribed in the oath," they chanted, "may my city be free from disease; if not, may it suffer disease." If I keep true, they continued, may my city escape ravaging, may my land bear fruit, may our women bear children like their progenitors, and our animals, animals of the same kind. If not, may my city be ravaged and my land become barren and may our women and animals give birth to monsters. Such were the imprecations they cast on themselves.[35]

It must have required eight to ten hours to make the march if the militiamen of Athens took the easier, longer route with an eye to interdicting a Persian advance in the direction of the city, as they surely did. When they arrived, probably in the middle of the night, they took up a position in the precinct of Heracles—which, thanks to the discovery of two inscriptions, we can now confidently locate at the southeastern end of the plain at the foot of Mount Agrieliki quite near the narrow entrance leading from the Marathon plain to the road that ran down the coast, then west to Pallene, and on to Athens. In the latter of these inscriptions and in another at Athens, this place was referred to as "the gates" of Marathon. In this spot, tucked away in a corner of the plain that Pindar called "Marathon's nook," they were soon joined by the Plataeans, who arrived in full force. All in all, the Athenians and Plataeans did not number many more than ten thousand hoplites, if that—though there were presumably light-armed troops to support them in something like equal numbers, as there would be later when Athens' infantry next encountered the Mede.[36]

And there the Athenians and Plataeans sat. Initially, they were no doubt waiting for the Lacedaemonians. Philippides moved with astonishing alacrity. We are told that it took him only a day and a half to make the one-hundred-fifty-mile journey to Sparta; and, though some today are incredulous, there is no reason to doubt the claim. Modern endurance runners have duplicated the feat in the Spartathlon annually each and every year since 1982.[37]

At Lacedaemon, the Athenian runner was told that the Spartans were resolved to come in support of Athens but that *nómos*—custom or law—forbade their setting out until the full moon some days thereafter. It was, Herodotus reports, the ninth day of the lunar month, and scholars have long suspected that the Spartan month in question was Carneios and that the nine-day festival of the Carneia, which always came to an end at the time of the full moon, had begun two days before. If these scholars are correct (as, I think, they are), religious custom prohibited the Lacedaemonians in 490 from setting out for Attica until the morning of the tenth of September—for, in Carneios that year, the moon was not full until the night of September ninth.[38]

It could be an accident that the Persians arrived at Marathon at a time when the Spartans could not in a timely fashion come to Athens' defense. But there is another possibility. The Spartans had pointedly refused to become the Great King's bondsmen and to give earth and water when called upon to do so. Datis and Artaphernes must have known this; and if they had no idea who the Spartans were—which is highly unlikely, given that the two were chosen for this mission in part because of their familiarity with the Aegean and those who lived there—Hippias son of Peisistratus was in attendance to provide intelligence. The religious prohibition the Spartans appear to have been honoring was well known, and it applied not just to them but to Dorians in general—including those already subject to the Great King and well known to the likes of Datis and the Lydian satrap's son.[39] Moreover, if the erstwhile Athenian tyrant was unfamiliar with the Spartan religious calendar (which is almost inconceivable), there were, no doubt, other Greeks in the entourage of the two generals who were alert to the consequences. It was certainly convenient for the Persians that the Spartans were otherwise occupied at this particular moment, and it is perfectly possible that they timed their descent on Attica with this likelihood in mind.[40]

We do not know precisely when Athens' ten generals first became aware of the delay. If they knew of the prohibition affecting the Spartans, as they probably did, they must have anticipated the problem. Of course, they may have been unwitting. If so, however, they must have become aware of the difficulty within three or four days of Philippides himself receiving the news—and it goes without saying that this awareness must have shaped their calculations. At this point, if Cornelius Nepos is to be believed, a careful consideration of the Lacedaemonian timetable influenced Persians calculations as well. In the circumstances, if the Athenians had reasons for dragging their heels, the Persians had reasons for attempting to force a decision. On the ninth of September, the moon would be full; and, if all went well, the Spartans would soon thereafter set off. But, even if they hurried, it was apt to take them some days to march with all of their gear the requisite one hundred seventy-six miles separating Lacedaemon from Marathon.[41]

The Athenian generals at Marathon were not in accord. Five of the ten, including Miltiades, wanted to fight at Marathon. The other five favored withdrawal. According to Herodotus, Miltiades pulled aside Callimachus of Aphidna—who had been elected to the archonship, then chosen polemarch by lot—for the purpose of persuading him to break the tie in his favor. If the Athenians fail to confront the Persians at Marathon, he is said to have argued, the city will succumb to faction, the citizens' determination to resist will be shaken, and the Medizers in their midst will prevail. We can by no means be certain that Herodotus received an accurate report of this conversation, which took place in private between two men who died well before he came on the scene. But this we can say with confidence. If Miltiades did not issue such a warning, he should have—for what he is credited with saying was surely true.[42]

After deliberating, Callimachus broke the tie, and he did so in support of the strategy proposed by Miltiades. Each day a different general was in command. Each day thereafter, the commanding general ceded his responsibilities to Miltiades. But Miltiades persistently held back.[43] He had served with the Persians at the time of Darius' Scythian expedition. He knew how they were armed and how they customarily conducted themselves on the field of battle, and among the Athenian generals he was probably unique in this particular.

Miltiades also knew that time was on the side of the Athenians and the Plataeans. They were comparatively few in number, and the position they occupied was hard to attack—for there were, we are told, scattered trees nearby and perhaps also a grove. It is even conceivable that they built a stockade, for something of the sort had been done in the recent past by others similarly situated.[44] They also had water close by. Moreover, they were in their homeland, and the road back to Athens ran from their camp. It was easy for their compatriots to cart in provisions.

The Persians were in less good shape. They had something on the order of ninety thousand men to feed and no easy access to local supply on the scale required. They had no doubt brought provisions with them on their ships, but these may at this point late in the campaigning season have been in short supply; and the longer so large a body of men and horses stayed in the same place, the more likely it was that sanitation would become a serious problem. They could not, however, leave Marathon and march on Athens without first confronting the Athenian hoplites bivouacked in "the nook" athwart "the gates" of Marathon.

That was one set of problems. There was another. In the Middle Ages, it was proverbial that, in the Mediterranean, there are only four good ports for a fleet of galleys: June, July, August, and Port Mahon. The same was true in antiquity, and it mattered a great deal on this particular occasion. For mid-August had come and gone, and Port Mahon was far, far away in the western Mediterranean and of no use to anyone in the Aegean. It was well past the time when Hesiod thought it tolerably safe to take to the sea. At this season, Greece is often subject to high winds—Hellesponters from the northeast, above all else; and the Sirocco from Libya as well. Moreover, October was on the horizon. It is a month in which, early on, the weather in the Mediterranean shifts suddenly and dramatically as the jet stream changes its course, and it is often a time of violent storms.[45] For Datis and Artaphernes, the clock was running out.

Had the Athenians been less well-positioned, the Persians could have launched an attack on their camp. In the circumstances, however, the Persian cavalry could not get at them. Moreover, the Athenians could quite easily reposition themselves so that, if the Persian footsoldiers attacked, they would be at a serious disadvantage in having to make an assault uphill. The best that Datis and Artaphernes could do was to send contingents of their cavalry on ravaging expeditions into the Attic countryside to the north, away from the city of Athens toward Oropus and Rhamnous, which they apparently did.[46]

It was not until the day actually allotted to him as general commander that Miltiades made his move. Herodotus does not tell us what had changed, but we can easily guess. We know that the Persians had landed their cavalry at Marathon. Herodotus tells us as much. But, in his detailed description of the battle that eventually took place, although he takes care to specify that the Athenians had no cavalry of their own,[47] he makes no mention whatsoever of the Persian commanders' deployment of their own horsemen—which, in the circumstances, is decidedly odd.

We do not know the size of the cavalry unit that accompanied the armada led by Datis and the younger Artaphernes. It would, however, be a grave error to suppose that it was negligible. Three-quarters of a century later, after the Athenians began converting superannuated triremes into horse transports,

Figure 11. Persian *gerróphoroi* battling Greek hoplites, Side A of an Athenian red-figure cup by the Painter of the Oxford Brygos, ca. 490–480 (Ashmolean Museum, Oxford, 1911.615; drawing, in part a restoration, by N. Griffiths, © Margaret C. Miller).

they were able to cram thirty mounts onto a single vessel suited to being rowed from Athens to Sicily by a skeleton crew of sixty oarsmen. Even if, as is perfectly possible, the horse transports built in 491 were less capacious, it would have been within the power of the Persians to convey one or even two thousand mounts from Tarsus in Cilicia westward along the southern coast of Asia Minor, then across the Aegean to Marathon, and it would have been very much in their interest to do so.[48]

Indeed, if the cavalry were absent when the battle of Marathon took place, this circumstance would have been profoundly important. The Persian infantry was not the strongest branch of its forces. Ordinarily, the Persians employed archers on foot and on horseback as a species of primitive artillery to break up enemy formations; then, these same horsemen—equipped with javelins or thrusting spears, with iron clubs, and, one must suspect, short swords—as shock cavalry to rout and massacre the undisciplined ranks that remained; and, finally, their spearmen (most of whom doubled as archers) to clean up.[49]

In the absence of their cavalry, especially if the Athenians and the Plataeans could minimize the harm wrought by their archers, the forces brought to Marathon by Datis and Artaphernes would have been at a considerable disadvantage. In battle, the *sparabara* within the ranks of the Persian infantry —who were dubbed, in Greek, *gerrophóroi*—bore wicker shields faced with leather, which they called *spara,* using a term the Hellenes transliterated as *gérra.* With these shields, which were tall and rectangular in the manner of a pavise, they were in the habit of constructing a barricade. Behind this protective wall, those of their colleagues who were armed with bow and spear would then fire volleys of arrows into the enemy ranks. If, however, this artillery barrage failed and those attacking the Persian army managed to reach and push through the barricade of wicker shields, there was apt to be a battle royal. For the Persians, Medes, and Cissians armed with bow and spear, though they may well have been equipped with body armor as well, bore as individuals no shields at all. Even if, in addition, the army fielded by Datis and Artaphernes included a force of dedicated infantrymen, as is certainly possible, these spearmen had nothing with which to protect themselves apart from body armor and either small *aspídes,* offering them little in the way of coverage, or bucklers mounted on their left arms or held by a handle at arm's length. This is what Herodotus had in mind when he described the Persian footsoldiers engaged in a later battle as "naked [*gumnêtes*]" and spoke of them pointedly as "lacking the hoplite shield [*ánoploi*]." If, in a battle against such an army, each of those who punched through the protective barricade set up by its *gerrophóroi* bore a capacious shield and if the spears carried by these assailants were also longer and heavier than the spears borne by the infantrymen of the Great King, as would be the case if the latter were up against hoplites from Athens and Plataea (or anywhere else in mainland Greece), there was apt to be a massacre.[50]

Two conjectures have been advanced to explain the apparent absence of the Persian cavalry from the battlefield at Marathon. One recently proffered postulates that the Persians tethered and hobbled their horses in the Tricorynthos valley north of the lake and marsh at the northern end of the Marathon plain, as they may well have done; that it took their grooms some time to feed these horses, give them water, put on their saddlecloths and bridles, and conduct them single file down the narrow track between Mount Stavrokoraki and the Makaria spring, as seems reasonable; and that, as Xenophon observes, it was extremely difficult for the Persians to start this process before daybreak. Realizing this, we are told, Miltiades chose to attack the Persian footsoldiers at dawn at a run before the cavalry could be deployed.[51]

This hypothesis cannot be ruled out, and it has the very considerable virtue of simplicity. It presupposes nothing on the part of the Persians that is not, in fact, likely on other grounds. But if it were true, it would be extremely difficult to explain why none of our sources says anything about an intervention

Figure 12. Greek hoplite fighting a shieldless Persian depicted in the interior of an
Athenian red-figure cup by the Triptolemos Painter, ca. 490–480 (National Museums
of Scotland, Edinburgh, 1887.213; from Paul Hartwig, *Die Griechischen Meisterschalen
der Blüthezeit des Strengen Rothfigurigen Stiles* [Stuttgart: Spemann, 1893], pl. 56).

of the Great King's cavalry late in the battle in defense of the retreating Persian
infantry or mentions an Athenian capture of hundreds of magnificent steeds
of a quality hitherto unknown in Hellas, even among the proud horse-barons
of Thessaly. At a minimum, the Persians at Marathon had with them more
than a thousand horses. They may have had more. These animals are large,
skittish, and hard to handle. They do not like confinement, and they fear the sea.
It takes skill, patience, and time to load horse transports, a great deal of skill, patience, and time. Even if the Persians started the process soon after the battle
commenced and the battle took six hours or more, which is highly unlikely,

there was not enough time for them to make much progress; and it is, in fact, most unlikely that, if they had not completed the loading process before dawn, they decided to do so after the battle had begun—for one of the chief functions of cavalry on ancient battlefields was pursuing enemy soldiers in flight and harrying those pursuing one's own footsoldiers.[52] On both counts, at Marathon, the cavalry would have been of great use to the Persians.

The alternative hypothesis requires a presumption not necessary on other grounds. But, as presumptions go, it is not at all unlikely; and it has this advantage. It explains why only a handful of horses, barely worth mentioning, were captured. It starts from a late source, known to have made use of the fourth-century Atthidographer Demon, which asserts that Ionians in the Persian force approached the trees shielding the Athenian camp, apparently during the night, to alert the Athenians and their Plataean allies to the fact that the cavalry brought by Datis and Artaphernes were "away"—having staged "a withdrawal [*apochōrēsis*]," apparently under the leadership of the former—and would not that day appear in the enemy ranks.[53] According to this hypothesis, that night—by the light of the harvest moon or, more likely, at daybreak—Miltiades' look-outs must have confirmed the Ionian claim from their vantage point up the hill behind the Athenian camp. Moreover, they must also have reported that the Persians were in the process of withdrawing at least a part of the force that they had landed and that they had spent the night loading the horse transports, almost certainly with an eye to circumnavigating Cape Sunium, disembarking again at the Bay of Phalerum, and descending on the city of Athens—which was located fewer than three miles inland and was defended by a skeleton force, if even that. It is, we must add, perfectly possible that the timing of this maneuver—if, of course, there was such a maneuver—was dictated by the Persians' awareness of the significance of the Spartan calendar, for there had been a full moon on 9 September, reinforcements were soon thereafter on their way from Sparta to Attica, and things were brought to a head one day before the Lacedaemonians arrived.

One thing is clear, and it weighs heavily—if not, in fact, decisively—against the sufficiency of the first of the two hypotheses under consideration here. Had the Persians not been in the process of effecting a strategic withdrawal, it would have been foolhardy in the extreme for Miltiades to launch an assault when, in fact, he did. At this stage, time was even more emphatically on the side of the Athenians. They were still well situated. Supply remained easy. Additional hoplites were en route and would soon arrive. Their numbers and strength would grow, as would their confidence. Had the Persians not forced the issue, prudence would have dictated further delay.

If, however, we were to suppose the alternative hypothesis correct in whole or in part, we would have to conclude that the Athenians had no other option more viable than the one Miltiades chose. Datis and Artaphernes had put the Athenians and Plataeans on the spot. They could not sit idly while the forces of the Great King moved against the town of Athens. Moreover, as the Persian commanders may not have fully appreciated at the time, the withdrawal of much, if not all, of their cavalry afforded the Athenians and Plataeans a golden opportunity, for it left the footsoldiers of the Great King far more vulnerable than they had been before. The hoplites of Athens and Plataea were more than a match for the bowmen and spearmen of Iran. They could withstand an archery assault far better than the infantry that the Persians had come up against in Asia. They were relatively well protected against such primitive artillery by the helmet, cuirass or corslet, and greaves each wore; and the large, round *aspís* each bore provided them with ample additional cover. They would be even less vulnerable if, when they came within range of the barbarian bowmen, they advanced at a jog in order to minimize the period in which they could easily be targeted—which, recent studies have shown, they clearly could do, the weight of their equipment notwithstanding—and the spearmen they would encounter at the end of their jog were not even remotely as well equipped as they were and did not operate in phalanx with interlocking individual *aspídes*.

All of this Miltiades seems to have understood. The Lacedaemonians had not yet arrived; the Persians were regrouping in a way that threatened the city of Athens; and something had to be done . . . without delay. This he knew. Mindful, then, of the opening that the Persians had afforded him, he lined up his army in front of Marathon's "gates" shortly after dawn and posted the polemarch Kallimachus on the right, the Plataeans on the extreme left, and the tribes one by one in numerical order in between, stretching out the line to the same length as that of the soldiers in the Persian army, who gradually positioned themselves in defense of the ships beached along the shore to the northeast. To achieve this, given that he was outnumbered by a considerable margin, Miltiades weakened and extended the Athenian center while keeping the wings at full strength eight men deep. Knowing that his center was apt to give ground, he instructed those on the wings that, if they were victorious, they not pursue those whom they had defeated but wheel and seek to envelop the Persians likely to be trapped in a pocket between the two wings.

Miltiades' calculation paid off. The battle progressed in the manner in which he had anticipated. The Athenians got the jump on their opponents and charged at double-time for nine-tenths of a mile while the Persian *gerrophóroi,* those who doubled as archers and spearmen, and the dedicated infantrymen who accompanied them (if there were any) were still preparing for battle. In the center, the Athenians were forced back in the direction of "the gates." On the two wings, the Athenians were victorious, and those whom they routed fled into the marsh, where many of them lost their way and were eventually slaughtered. It was only after the center of the Persian line had been enveloped and annihilated that the Athenians could push forward to the ships on the beach.[54]

There, they were for the most part too late. They managed to capture a few horses, as was many centuries later reported. But they were not able to lay hold of more than seven ships, and they watched in frustration and fury as the rest—especially (if my reconstruction of developments is correct) the horse transports in which a host of terrified animals made a great racket—pulled away to pick up the Eretrian prisoners from Aegilia, round Cape Sunium, and complete the seventy-mile journey to Phalerum.[55]

In the aftermath—that very day, Herodotus implies and Plutarch asserts, though some modern scholars think that it must have been the next morning—the Athenians left one of the two tribes posted earlier in the center of the phalanx to guard the battlefield. Then, they marched back to Athens and positioned themselves at the Heracleum at Cynosarges near Phalerum in such a way as to be able to oppose a landing should the Persians attempt one. The Persian fleet, which arrived en masse no earlier than thirty to forty-five hours after the battle, paused for a time to allow Datis and Artaphernes to consider their options—which, given the season and the circumstances, were not promising—and then they sailed back in the direction of Asia.[56]

In due course, the Athenians made their way back to Marathon to collect their dead and those of the Plataeans, to burn the bodies on funeral pyres in the manner sanctioned by Homer, and bury the remains. They had lost one hundred ninety-two men, and these they interred not in the Ceramicus in Athens, as would later be the custom, but on the field of battle itself, piling up a commemorative mound that is still there today, just as they had done at the Euripus in 506 after defeating the Thebans and the Chalcidians. Nearby they did the same for the Plataeans and the emancipated slaves who had died; and near the first of the two mounds, they set up an inscription for each of Athens' ten tribes listing their dead under the tribe's name in the most egalitarian fashion possible—simply and solely by name. Two thousand four hundred ninety years later, one of these inscriptions, listing twenty-two or more of those belonging to the tribe Erechtheis who had died at Marathon that day, was discovered in Cynouria in the Peloponnesus on an estate owned by Herodes Atticus, a fabulously wealthy Athenian living in the time of Trajan and Hadrian who claimed descent from Miltiades. Preceding the list on the stone is this epigram: "Reputation, indeed, as it reaches ever to the ends of the sun-lit earth/The valor [*aretế*] of these men shall make manifest: How they died,/Doing battle with the Medes and crowning Athens/Very few, awaiting and welcoming war at the hands of a multitude."[57]

The soldiers of Persia the Athenians apparently interred in a great trench not far from the center of the plain, where they also set up an Ionic column as a trophy [*tropaîon*] commemorating the victory on the spot where the battle had turned. Herodotus tells us that something like six thousand four hundred of the Great King's soldiers had lost their lives. There is no reason to question the number he provides. It was imperative that the Athenians get as accurate a count as they could—for, before the battle, which took place some days after the festival of Artemis Agrotera, either Callimachus or Miltiades had vowed that the Athenians would sacrifice a goat at future festivals for every Persian killed. In later years, mindful of the limited number of goats available, they reduced the number sacrificed to five hundred.[58]

The booty captured was considerable. Plutarch mentions "silver and gold scattered about promiscuously, clothing of every sort, and wealth in the tents untold." Much of what they gained was soon thereafter spent on lavish dedications made in thanks to Zeus at Olympia and Apollo at Delphi and on the construction of sanctuaries for Artemis and Pan, who were thought to have been favorable to the Athenian cause.[59]

Cleomenes' Bitter Legacy

Before the Athenians managed to gather and bury the bodies of the men they had lost, two thousand Lacedaemonians appeared. The latter paused briefly to visit the battlefield and gawk at the Persian dead. They congratulated the victors. Then they set out for home. So we are told, and this we need not doubt. But that, on a forced march, the Spartans had made the long journey with their equipment from Lacedaemon to Marathon in fewer than three days, as Herodotus claims—this some scholars take with a grain of salt. For, if the Lacedaemonians did anything of the sort—as, most scholars still believe, they did—it was a truly astounding feat.[60]

One fact does need explanation. The Lacedaemonians were not only delayed in their departure. When they finally did appear, they showed up with a very small contingent. Ten years later they were able to field five times that number.[61] Moreover, on a mission that was arguably of vital importance to their own security and to that of all their neighbors, the Spartans did not bring with them any of their Peloponnesian allies.

There is reason to suspect that the Spartans had encountered difficulties that, inclined to secrecy as they were,[62] they were extremely loath to divulge. Cleomenes, the Agiad king who had dominated their counsels for at least twenty years and perhaps as many as thirty, had become a threat to the well-being of the people whom he had led.

We do not know the precise chronology. But it is clear that events moved at a rapid pace. Sometime, not long after Demaratus' flight in the direction of Susa, the Spartans discovered that, in pursuing the Eurypontid king's ouster, the royal son of Anaxandridas had bribed the oracle at Delphi. For once, when confronted with the evidence, the Agiad king did not have an apt rejoinder. Initially, he fled to Thessaly—in search of refuge, perhaps, or a species of aid that he did not secure—or, if, as some suppose, Herodotus' text is in need of emendation, to Sellasia on the northern border of Lacedaemon. Then, he made his way to Arcadia, and here he proved once again his grasp of the authority that sacral kingship of the sort wielded by the Heraclids of Sparta could confer. For Cleomenes tried to instigate a rebellion by uniting the Arcadians against Lacedaemon, and there is reason to suspect that the Tegeans, who were not then on friendly terms with the Spartans, gave him their support. Indeed, he was sufficiently successful in getting the Arcadians to swear that they would follow him wherever he might lead them that his compatriots capitulated, recalled him to Lacedaemon, and reinstated him as king on the terms that had hitherto pertained.[63]

The odds are good that the Spartans were caught up in this little drama at the very moment that Philippides arrived with his appeal that they march to the aid of the Athenians—and this may not have been the greatest of the difficulties they faced. In *The Laws,* Plato, who had taken care to learn as much as possible about Lacedaemon, intimates that the Spartans were unable to answer Athens' appeal because they were preoccupied at the time with a helot revolt.[64] Scholars often dismiss this report out of hand. It is late, they say. It looks like an excuse, and Herodotus, who interviewed the survivors from the pertinent generation, knew nothing of it. They are right on all counts, but their argument is not dispositive.

The Spartans were notoriously uncommunicative. Their relations with the helots were a matter of the greatest delicacy; and, as Thucydides intimates, it was difficult to get past their reluctance to reveal the fragility of their dominion. Moreover, the story told by Plato makes sense of Strabo's claim that there were four, not three, Messenian Wars and of Pausanias' assertion that a Spartan dedication at Olympia, dateable on the basis of the script and the statue base to the late archaic period, had to do with a war against the Messenians. It clarifies chronologically confused allusions in the same author to a conflict between the Spartans and the Messenians in the time of the Eurypontid king Leotychidas and the tyrant Anaxilaus of Rhegium. And, given what we know of Cleomenes' activities on the eve of Marathon, it makes excellent contextual sense.[65] The helots must have overheard their masters discussing the Persian armada wending its way through the Cyclades. Cleomenes was making trouble in nearby Arcadia, and there may well have been contact between his adherents in Arcadia and runaway helots holed up in the mountains of Messenia. The mountainous regions were contiguous, and there had frequently been contact in the past.

In assessing the Spartan plight, we should not underestimate the aura of sacral kingship. The Messenians looked back to a time when they had been led by a Heraclid of their own. Moreover, a Persian invasion that the Spartans viewed as a worrisome challenge they may well have regarded as an opportunity. If Plato's Athenian Stranger is right, if there really was a helot revolt, and if it coincided with Cleomenes' attempt to unite the Arcadians against Lacedaemon, it would not only explain why the Spartans were delayed in sending the Athenians help. It would also explain why a city that could field an army of ten thousand hoplites and rally at least twenty thousand more from its Peloponnesian allies delivered in 490 a paltry force of only two thousand men.

From the Persian perspective, the battle of Marathon was a skirmish and a rebuff, a disappointment but not a disaster—a bump on the road to the subjugation of the Greeks and an indication that a larger and better-equipped force would be required. From the Athenian—and perhaps also the Spartan—perspective, it was a magnificent victory and a harbinger of other victories to come. Up to this time, the Persians had presented their adversaries with a choice between the carrot and the stick. For those who medized, the rewards could be immense. For those who did not, horrors were in the offing. Psychologically, this prospect was a potent mix. But, as the Persians understood, its full effectiveness depended upon their inculcating in all of their potential adversaries the conviction that, if there were an armed conflict, a victory on the part of the King of Kings was inevitable—that resistance was vain and its cost, prohibitive. The Scythians had shaken this conviction, and for a brief span of years the Ionians and the other Greeks in the east had challenged it. But, of course, the latter had in time gone down to an exemplary defeat.

At Marathon, however, for the very first time, Greek footsoldiers, greatly outnumbered, had fought, withstood, and decisively defeated the Mede. If the Athenians can do it, the Lacedaemonians surely thought, we can do it as well—and they were right. Marathon may have been little more than a skirmish, but it marked the turning of a tide. Darius and his minions did not understand this fact. Many in Greece remained incredulous. But the Persian empire had reached its zenith. A century and a half would pass and the Greeks would give way to the Macedonians of Phillip and Alexander before the full consequences of what happened at Marathon on or soon after the twelfth of September 490 were fully worked out.

For the Athenians, their victory at Marathon must have been intoxicating. In the course of two decades, they had remodeled their polity; they had stood up to the Spartans; they had defeated the Thebans and subdued the Chalcidians. And now they had not only survived a confrontation with Achaemenid Persia. On the field of the sword, they had thrashed and massacred the Mede. It would be an error to suppose that they had little or no sense of themselves as a people in the time of Draco, Solon, and Peisistratus. But their sense of common identity and of collective importance was no doubt powerfully reinforced and enhanced by their achievements in these decades.[66]

That, however, which for the Athenians had been exhilarating must have been for their Spartan allies quite sobering. The troubles stirred up by Cleomenes in Arcadia and the helot rebellion, though they had both been weathered, were a terrifying reminder of the vulnerability of Lacedaemon's little empire in the southern Peloponnesus and of the fragility of the Spartan regime and way of life that depended on it. If the Persians were to come again and in greater force, as well they might, it was incumbent upon the leadership at Lacedaemon to see to it that the helots were not restive and that the city's allies within the Peloponnesus were thoroughly reliable. If Athens' victory relieved one source of anxiety, it reinforced another.

Part II

THE CRISIS COMES TO A HEAD

Xerxes the King proclaims: By the favor of the Wise Lord Ahura Mazda I am of such a kind that I am a friend to the right, I am no friend to wrong. . . . I am no friend of the man who follows the Lie. I am not hot-tempered. When I feel anger rising, I keep that under control by my intelligence. I control my impulses. . . . I am furious in the strength of my revenge with my two hands and my two feet. As a horseman I am a good horseman. As a bowman I am a good bowman, both on foot and on the back of a horse. As a spearman I am a good spearman, both on foot and on the back of a horse. These are the skills which the Wise Lord Ahura Mazda has bestowed on me, and I have the capacity for their use.

—XERXES OF PERSIA

T HE loss that they had suffered at Marathon no doubt frustrated the Persians, but it did not leave them disheartened. In most regards, the expedition had been a success—or so they presumably thought. They had managed to mount an overseas expeditionary force. The Eretrians had been punished. The Cyclades were now theirs,[1] and there was every prospect that the Greek mainland would in due course come under their sway. It was only a question of resources and time, and Achaemenid Persia was well supplied with both.

It was in keeping with this conviction that Datis the Mede handled himself. Having discovered, we are told, that someone in the expedition—presumably a stray cavalryman on a raid in the direction of Oropus—had taken a gilded statue of Apollo from the cult site at Delium in Boeotia just over the border from Attica, he paused ostentatiously at Delos to leave the votive offering at the sanctuary of Apollo, asking that the Delians see to its return to Delium. Then, he sailed on to Asia with Artaphernes, and the two made their way to Susa to deliver to Darius the Eretrians seized on Euboea and, one must suppose, the children taken hostage in the various cities within the Cyclades. Darius settled these Eretrians at a station on the royal road about twenty-five miles outside the ancient Elamite capital in a place where petroleum was apt to bubble up to the surface.[2] We are not told what he did with the hostages.

To make it easier for them to hold their vast empire together, the Persians maintained, patrolled, and closely controlled an extensive network of roads replete with guard posts, inns, stables, and courier stations; and along these highways they operated a pony express by which couriers could convey messages to and from the King of Kings. It was no doubt by this expedient that Darius first learned what had happened at Naxos and elsewhere in the Cyclades, at Eretria, and in Attica. Herodotus reports that the news concerning the battle of Marathon served only to intensify his desire to make war on the Greeks and that he ordered straightaway that steps be taken to prepare an expedition against Hellas on a much larger scale than the one conducted by Datis and Artaphernes. This he may well have done—but only, we must presume, after thoroughly interrogating the two commanders concerning the setback they had suffered on the plains of Marathon. Herodotus mentions him ordering ships and horses, food, and transports, and he tells us that all of Asia was agitated for three years as a consequence of the preparations. He does not say that Darius resolved never to leave his footsoldiers unprotected by cavalry, as Datis and Artaphernes appear to have done, but we can be confident that this is one of the conclusions that the Great King drew.[3]

Had Darius had his way, had he been able to stage an invasion of Greece in 486 or even 485, the odds are good that the endeavor would have been a success. But there was a rebellion in Egypt, and he had to turn his attention to that rich and vitally important satrapy and redirect his energies to quelling the revolt. Then, before he could set out to do what needed doing in the land along the Nile, he died, having ruled for more than thirty-five years.[4]

Herodotus tells us that it was the custom [*nómos*] for the Great King of Persia to name his heir before going off to war.[5] There is, however, no indication that Darius had chosen to abide by this custom when he put down the rebellions that occurred at the time of his coup d'état, when he crushed the Saka of Skunkha and conquered the Indus valley, or when he subdued eastern Thrace and conducted his ill-fated invasion of Scythia. This time, however, the situation was different. He was now an old man—in his mid-sixties, if not older—and he may have become noticeably frail, for he was reportedly pressed by his advisors to let his choice be known.

According to Herodotus, there were two plausible claimants—Artobazanes, the eldest son of the daughter of Gobryas, whom he had married well before becoming King of Kings, and Xerxes, his eldest son by Atossa, the daughter of Cyrus. In thinking through the choice he had to make, Darius is said to have

Figure 13. Great King (Darius or Xerxes) with crown prince (behind throne), relief found in the Treasury at Persepolis (Courtesy of the Oriental Institute of the University of Chicago).

listened politely to the advice of Demaratus, his Spartan guest, but to have been guided in the end by his wife Atossa.[6]

That Darius kept his options open is clear. It is even conceivable that Justin is correct in asserting that the succession was not settled until after the Great King's death and that his brother Artaphernes decided the question as the family judge. Men who have persistently overcome great vicissitudes are rarely willing to concede that the grim reaper is nigh. The grit and determination that once stood them in good stead then obstructs their judgment. If, perchance, Herodotus is mistaken and this is, in fact, how things transpired, Xerxes, who was in his early to mid-thirties when he came to the throne, made a point of concealing the fact. After his accession, he had multiple copies of a text inscribed in various languages at various places in the magnificent palace built by his father at Persepolis. It asserted in celebratory fashion that Darius had singled him out from among his brothers to be "the greatest after himself" while he was still alive and as his heir when he died.[7]

It is now fashionable to dismiss as a species of fanciful orientalism Greek reports of intrigue within the Great King's harem. But what Tacitus and Suetonius have to teach us concerning the role played by scheming women in the Julio-Claudian dynasty suggests that we should take quite seriously what Aeschylus, Herodotus, Plato, and others have to say with regard to the bizarre family dramas that are apt to take place in despotisms in which the ruler has the right to select his own successor. The degree to which the troubles that enveloped Tunisia, Egypt, and Jordan in the spring of 2011 arose out of resentment over the influence exercised by the rulers' wives is quite striking.[8]

When Darius died late in November 486, he left it to his successor to put down the revolt in Egypt, which Xerxes did with admirable alacrity, leaving his younger brother Achaemenes behind as satrap. In 484, the new king also had to deal with rebellions in Babylon of the sort apt to take place when an old king of great distinction dies and a new and untried successor replaces him.[9] As a consequence, he was not prepared to turn his undivided attention to the unfinished business in Greece until 483.

When the time came, however, Xerxes was anything but behindhand. He had, he knew, the example set by his grandfather Cyrus, his uncle Cambyses, and his father Darius to live up to, which was no small thing. From him, rebellious *bandaka,* such as the Athenians, could expect no mercy—for, repeating the very words used by his father, he represented himself in an inscription as "a friend to the right," as "no friend of the man who follows the Lie," and as a man who gives "much to faithful men." He professed also to be "good fighter of battles . . . furious in the strength of my revenge" in the very terms used by his progenitor.[10]

Like all three of his predecessors, Xerxes also fancied himself a universal monarch. He, too, styled himself "Great King, King of Kings, King of countries containing many peoples, King on this great earth far and wide," and he considered it his duty to promote "happiness," suppress "commotion," and put things in their "proper place." The words that Herodotus puts in his mouth on the eve of his invasion of Greece are certainly apt, and some such words may actually have been uttered when Xerxes turned his mind to the Athenians and the other Hellenes. One can easily imagine an Achaemenid king aspiring to have "the land of Persia border on the lofty realm of the great god" and trying to see to it that "the sun not look down on any territory bordering our own" so that there "remains no city of men and no nation of human beings capable of going into battle against us," and one can even imagine him supposing that, with his entry into Europe and conquest of Hellas, he could achieve this exalted aim.[11]

Universal empire was, after all, the aspiration of every Persian monarch. It was the raison d'être of the regime. It was a religious imperative. A campaign of conquest launched by an Achaemenid king was the holiest of all holy wars. For the followers of Ahura Mazda at this time, participation in such a campaign was the performance of a solemn religious obligation, and it was an expression of religious devotion far more compelling than the deep-seated piety that would later animate a Christian crusade or even an Islamic *jīhad.*

The chronological scheme within which Xanthus of Lydia would a few decades later situate Xerxes' crossing of the Hellespont and entry into Europe suggests that his informants among the Zoroastrian Magi in the Great King's entourage envisaged the struggle then about to ensue in eschatological terms as the final battle that would once and for all destroy the Lie, eviscerate the Evil Spirit Ahriman, and bring on the end times.[12]

The stories that Herodotus tells regarding the utterances of Darius' son and heir and the advice he was given—by Mardonius son of Gobryas, for example; by Greeks such as the Aleuads of Larissa in Thessaly, the Peisistratids from Athens, and Demaratus the Spartan; and by his uncle Artabanus son of Hystaspes—are laced with the fanciful.[13] But they may not be pure fiction and should not be dismissed out of hand.

Herodotus was gregarious. There is reason to suspect that he interviewed the descendants of Demaratus, who had large estates in western Asia Minor just to the east of Atarneus in the Troad in an area that the historian almost certainly visited. On a visit to the island of Chios, where some members of the Peisistratid clan seem to have ended up, he may have had access to the descendants of one or more of the five sons of Hippias son of Peisistratus, at least some of whom joined Xerxes in his expedition to Greece. He spoke with the Athenian Medizer Dikaios son of Theokydes, who was in Attica with the Persians at the time of Salamis and appears to have been a member of Xerxes' entourage. And he was almost certainly acquainted in Athens with the Persian refugee Zopyrus, great-grandson of Darius' co-conspirator Megabyzos and son of the like-named general who not only accompanied Xerxes to Greece but continued to play a major role in Achaemenid affairs long after the Persian Wars. Mindful of the degree to which Herodotus' identification of Persian personnel dovetails with what we learn from the tablets and inscriptions found at Persepolis, some scholars suspect that he must have had the assistance of a Greek who had served as a scribe or interpreter either at the court of the Great King or at one of the courts maintained by his satraps.[14] We do not know with any certainty how he learned what he knew. But for much of what he reports concerning the royal entourage, the author of the *Inquiries* had warrant. Of this, there can be no doubt.

Even if, as scholars tend to suppose, Herodotus invented the conversations between Xerxes and his *bandaka* that he reports, he clearly did so on the basis of a deep understanding of the imperatives animating the Achaemenid regime and the distinctive practices of the court. There is, for example, excellent and extensive Near Eastern precedent for the tallest and most implausible of the tales Herodotus tells with regard to the Achaemenid court: that, at Xerxes' command, Artabanus substituted himself for his nephew, assuming the garb of the Great King, occupying his throne, and sleeping in his bed—all with an eye to testing the validity of a dream, favorable to the invasion of Hellas, that Xerxes as Great King reported having had.[15]

Similarly, we may think it implausible that someone such as Mardonius son of Gobryas should, in attempting to persuade Xerxes to mount an invasion of Greece, have made much of Europe's extreme beauty, of its fertility, and of the variety of cultivated trees to be found scattered about its territory. But, in the Achaemenid context, this was, in fact, an argument with considerable purchase.

The Great Kings of Persia may have been martial, and world conquest was certainly their aim. But, in dramatic contrast with their Assyrian predecessors, they thought of themselves less as warriors who savored butchery and subjugation than as defenders of peace and harmonious order, as exponents of prosperity, and as gardeners. In every corner of their empire, they sought to improve communications, and they promoted irrigation and horticulture. Within every land, they and their satraps built magnificent palaces along with elaborate parks and gardens landscaped with care and replete with cultivated trees. When referring to a garden or park walled off, distinguished by beauty and order, and adorned with flowing water and a great variety of flora and fauna, the Achaemenids called it a *pairi·daiza* and their Greek subjects, by way of imitation, a *parádeisos*.

There is reason to believe that, in this period, the Great Kings of Persia thought it their mission to make the entire earth a paradise of breathtaking loveliness—which is, they believed, what it had been in its pristine form at the time of its creation by the Wise Lord Ahura Mazda before the appearance of the Evil Spirit Ahriman and the introduction of desiccation and disorder. Such a restoration would, they supposed, rightly earn them praise, devotion, exotic gifts, items of surpassing beauty, and generous material support from all the peoples of the earth.[16]

CHAPTER 5

The Formation of the Hellenic League

Leaving behind Susa, Ecbatana,
And the ancient Cissian walls,
These men journeyed,
Some on horse, some by ship, some on foot,
Regiments in close array, furnished for war.
Men such as Amistres and Artaphernes,
Megabates and Astaspes,
Chieftains over the Persians,
Kings, subjects of the Great King,
Guard as overseers a great host,
Subduers with the bow and horsemen,
Fearful to behold, in battle a terror
Famed for a spirit enduring much.

—AESCHYLUS

I T took four long years, we are told, for Xerxes and his minions to gather the provisions necessary for the expedition against Hellas—longer than had been required for Darius, who was not initially faced with distractions within the empire itself. It was in the fifth year of his reign that Xerxes finally collected his forces and set out with an enormous army in the direction of Greece, planning initially to retrace the steps taken by Megabazos after the Scythian expedition and Mardonius after the Ionian revolt.[1]

Herodotus' account of the expedition is modeled on Homer's *Iliad*, and at the outset he makes a point of telling his readers that the expeditionary forces of Xerxes far outnumbered those of Agamemnon.[2] That he should draw this comparison is, in fact, fitting—for, like his father and, for that matter, Cyrus and Cambyses as well, Xerxes had a keen appreciation for the significance of what foreign policy analysts now call "prestige," and he understood that dominion is largely founded on illusion and owes more to the presumption of a superiority in power than it does to its substance. In consequence, the chosen one of the Wise Lord Ahura Mazda was at least as interested in pageantry and a display of grandeur, in overawing his subjects and potential adversaries, as he was in bloody conquest on the field of the sword.

During three of the four years in which he was gathering provisions, Xerxes had Boubares, son of Megabazos and brother-in-law of the Macedonian king, busy co-directing a project in the Thracian Chalcidice, in which teams of Persia's subjects competed with one another to cut a shipping canal—wide enough for two triremes to pass and a mile and a third in length—through the sandy marl at the narrow point of the Acte peninsula stretching inland from Mount Athos. They completed this canal, which had a breakwater at each end to prevent the entrance from silting up, in time for Xerxes' fleet to pass through it on its way to Greece; and, though no efforts were made to maintain it after Persia's expulsion from Thrace, the canal continued to function for a considerable period of time thereafter.[3] In ordering its construction, Xerxes presumably had in mind the catastrophe suffered by Mardonius' fleet in 492. The canal would spare his own sailors and those who came thereafter the perils associated with rounding Mount Athos. But it was also, as Xerxes well knew, an engineering marvel—a wonder meant to serve as a permanent monument to the power and the grandeur of the Achaemenid monarch who called himself the King of Kings.

Much the same story can be told about the two bridges supported by six hundred seventy-four penteconters and triremes that Xerxes had Harpalus build across the Hellespont at the narrow point stretching from Abydos in Asia to the promontory on the European side between Sestos and Madytos. These narrows were almost twice the length of those in the Bosporus stretching from Anadolu Hissar to Roumeli Hissar, which Darius had Mandrocles of Samos span at the time of the Scythian expedition. Harpalus' two bridges were nonetheless built for the most part on similar principles. Like the bridge of Mandrocles, the two that Xerxes had Harpalus construct were pontoon bridges supported by a host of penteconters, supplemented by a handful of triremes—all of them firmly anchored against the ever oncoming flood. Harpalus' bridges were rendered distinctive by the fact that each of the two roadways supported by pontoons was attached to and rested on six immense cables—two of white flax and four of papyrus—each weighing something like eighty tons.[4] The bridges that Mandrocles and Harpalus built were no doubt magnificent structures and a tremendous convenience, but none of these bridges was absolutely necessary. When the armies of the two Great Kings

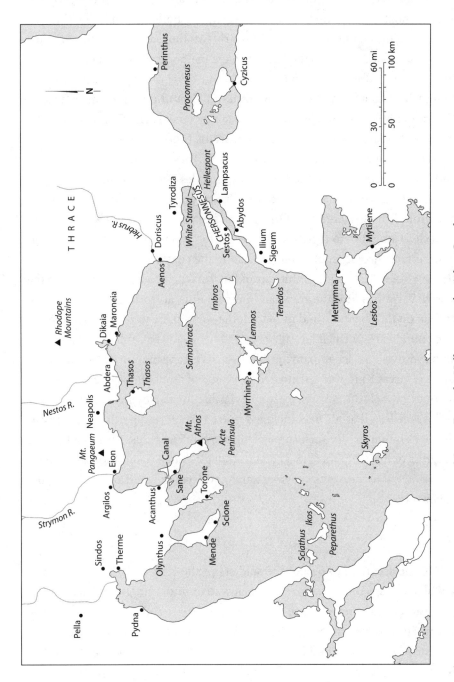

Map 11. From the Hellespont to the Athos Canal

made their return, they found the bridges gone and crossed from Europe to Asia by boat, and no one thought it worth the bother to bridge either the Hellespont or the Bosporus again for nearly two thousand five hundred years.

In the conduct of war, the Persians were methodical. We can be confident that Xerxes had good intelligence. He could draw on the reports made by those who had accompanied Democedes of Croton on a reconnaissance of Greece in his father's day, and there were surely other such missions. We know that the Peisistratids from Athens, Demaratus (once the Eurypontid king at Sparta), and the Aleuad clan from Larissa in Thessaly provided information and encouragement. That there were others no less well-informed concerning particulars, and many such, eager to gain the goodwill of the King of Kings and profit from his largess—of this we can be sure. We also know that Xerxes paid close attention to logistics. Depots for food were built at Persian strong-holds established at regular intervals along the coast his army would have to traverse—above all, at the White Strand in Thrace, but also at Tyrodiza to the west of Perinthus near the Thracian Chersonnesus, at Doriscus on the Hebrus, at Eion on the Strymon, and in Macedonia—and there were merchantmen in large numbers—pot-bellied galleys and Phoenician "bathtubs"—replete with ample provisions accompanying his fleet. We can, moreover, be confident that the Great King was sensitive to the value of amphibious operations. The marines on board his triremes were available for deployment on the shore, and it is telling that his fleet included horse transports—perhaps as many as the eight hundred fifty such ships mentioned by Diodorus.[5] In a pinch, if the progress of his army was blocked at a strategic choke point, thousands upon thousands of archers, infantrymen, and cavalrymen could be landed in the enemy's rear.

On the Road to Doriscus

In the second half of 481, the soldiers of the King of Kings mustered at Critalla in Cappadocia, crossed the Halys River into Phrygia, paused at Cel-aenae and Colossae, and made their way past Cydara and Callatebus to Sardis, whence he sent heralds to the cities of Hellas to ask for earth and water and to command the subject polities on his proposed route to prepare feasts for the King of Kings and his soldiers. It was, Herodotus tell us, his hope and expec-tation that those who had refused to pay homage and become his *bandaka* in the past would do so on this occasion out of trepidation and fear.[6]

Figure 14. Shieldless Persian guards armed with bows and spears, depicted in a frieze on tiles in the palace of Darius at Susa (Berlin, Pergamon Museum/ Vorderasiatisches Museum; Photograph: Mohammed Shamma [http://www.flickr.com/photos/mshamma/111901098/], Wikimedia Commons; Published November 2015 under the following license: Creative Commons Attribution 2.0 Generic).

There is reason to suspect that Herodotus' description of Xerxes' expectations and modus operandi might be on the mark. We are told that, in seeking to assemble a great army, the Great King of Persia advertised his prospective march into Greece as an unparalleled opportunity for looting, while intimating to those tempted to volunteer that he had every reason to suppose that Hellas would be betrayed by its principal men.[7] Treachery had always been a central feature of the Persian way of war.

When the Spartans, the Athenians, and those inclined to join with them in resisting the Mede learned that the Great King was at Sardis with an enormous army, they dispatched three spies to the Lydian capital to learn precisely what it was they were up against. When these were apprehended, they were examined by Xerxes' generals and condemned to death, and they were on the verge of being executed when Xerxes himself got wind of their presence and intervened to reproach his generals, summon the men into his presence, and ask them why they had been sent. After listening to their explanation, he ordered his bodyguards to show the spies his footsoldiers and his cavalry, to answer any questions they might ask, and to send them back whence they came when they had fully satisfied their curiosity. When, he said, the Hellenes learn that "his *prágmata*—his deeds, his affairs, his powers—are greater than words can describe," they will submit, become his bondsmen, and proffer water and earth.[8]

This helps explain Herodotus' ability to describe in great detail the forces fielded by Xerxes, their raiment and armament, the commanders of each unit, the course of the Great King's march, and his conduct thereon. The historian is said to have been a boy of four in Halicarnassus when the expedition took place.[9] In the three decades that passed before he appears to have begun writing his account, he had a great many opportunities to speak with eyewitnesses and their heirs. What he did not glean from his conversations with the descendants of Demaratus and Hippias; with Zopyrus, the son of Xerxes' general Megabyzos; with Dikaios the Athenian Medizer; with Artemisia the tyrant of his native Halicarnassus; with those among his compatriots who had accompanied her to Salamis; and with aging Aeolians, Ionians, and Dorians from Lesbos, Chios, Samos, Miletus, Rhodes, and the like who had also served in the expedition when they were young, he may well have learned from the detailed reports compiled by these three Greek spies.

When the winter had passed and spring came, the navy gathered in the harbors at Cumae and Phocaea on the Anatolian coast, and the army set out for Abydos from Sardis. First, we are told, went the baggage carriers, then a motley force of many nationalities, then a thousand Persian cavalrymen, and another thousand Persian spear-bearers. After them came the sacred chariot of Ahura Mazda and another chariot bearing the King of Kings, and behind him there followed another thousand spear-bearers, another thousand horsemen, ten thousand Persian spear-bearers, another ten thousand cavalrymen, and a mixed multitude of indeterminate size.[10]

The Persians were culturally sensitive. They paid attention to those of their advisors with local knowledge, and they tried to present themselves to those whom they attacked in the best light. Thus, as we have seen, when Cyrus set out to invade the Babylonian realm, he did what he could to propitiate the gods and heroes of the land, to win over their devotees, and to legitimize his conquest in the eyes of the ordinary Babylonians and of the Jews in their midst. To the same end, Datis the Mede had dedicated a chariot and rich Persian robes at the temple of Athena when he paused at Lindos on Rhodes in 494; and four years later when he stopped at Delos while en route to Naxos, Eretria, and Attica, he had burned three hundred talents of incense and left a gold necklace as a votive offering at the temple of Apollo. Xerxes was cut from similar cloth. When he came to the river Scamander in the Troad, he paused to climb up to the acropolis of Ilium, and there, we are told, he had one thousand cattle sacrificed to Athena while the Magi poured libations in honor of the heroes of the land. With this gesture and with others of a similar character, the Great King and his minions presented himself to the Hellenes as men sent by the goddess to avenge the crimes committed against Priam and his kindred.[11]

At Abydos, Xerxes had a throne of marble set upon a hill so that he could look down on the force then gathering and take satisfaction in its magnificence. When they were ready to cross the bridges over the Hellespont, the King of Kings poured a libation from a golden cup into the sea as he faced the sun and prayed for success. Then, he threw the cup, a Persian sword, and a golden mixing bowl into the Hellespont. It took, Herodotus reports, a week for the footsoldiers, the cavalry, the beasts of burden, and the train of servants, marching day and night, to get across the two bridges.[12]

Then, the army marched east-northeast up the long peninsula of the Chersonnesus toward Thrace and turned abruptly westward toward Doriscus, while the fleet sailed directly west by the much shorter maritime route toward Cape Sarpedon, the mouth of the Hebrus River, and Cape Serreion beyond. There, just short of the latter cape, between Zone and the Samothracian settlement on the mainland at Sale, Xerxes had his trierarchs beach their ships, haul them out of the water to dry out, and careen them so that they could be scraped, recaulked, and recoated with pitch as everyone waited for the army to make its way from the Hellespont. In due course, when his footsoldiers and cavalry reached the great plain to the west of the Hebrus, Xerxes reportedly paused for a time to review his forces and count the numbers in his host.[13]

We are not told that Xerxes conducted this review in the presence of Greek spies, but it makes good sense to suppose as much. They would certainly have been welcome, and their presence would have afforded the King of Kings yet another opportunity to impress upon the Hellenes the breathtaking scope of the power he wielded. We are told that he counted his troops in the most ostentatious manner possible—by setting up an enclosure of a size capable of accommodating ten thousand men and then by having each unit, after

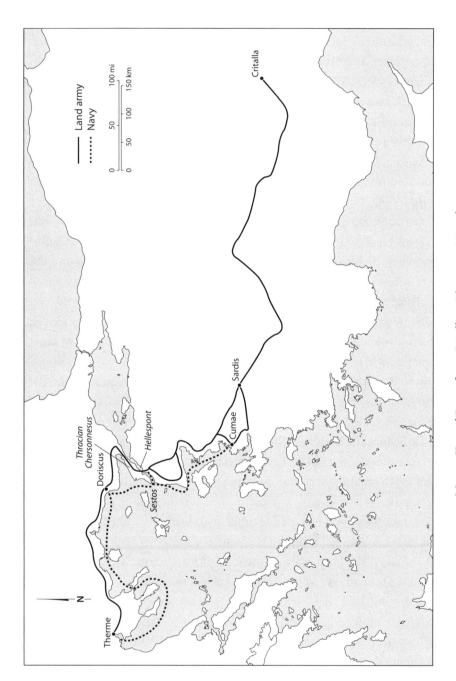

Map 12. Xerxes' Route from Critalla to Therme in Macedon

Critalla

Sardis

Cumae

Thracian
Chersonnesus

Doriscus

Hellespont

Sestos

Therme

N

Land army
Navy

0   50   100 mi
0   50   100   150 km

it marched by, enter the enclosure so that their numbers could be estimated, and we are also told that he had his scribes produce what we would today call an order of battle: a written record of the character—and no doubt the size—of each national unit. In the aftermath, Xerxes may even have arranged for a go-between present at the review to pass to the Greeks a translation of this written record of the number and character of the soldiers and ships in his expedition. In their endeavor to make manifest the grandeur of their king, the Persians were not inclined to leave anything to chance.[14]

Alexander son of Amyntas, who was his father's heir both as king of Macedon and as native satrap in the Persian province constituted by his kingdom, was on excellent terms with the Athenians, who had voted at some point in the recent past to name him their "benefactor" and *próxenos.* As we have seen, there is reason to suspect that he may have smoothed the way for the audience that their embassy garnered with Artaphernes in Sardis on the eve of the Peloponnesian, Theban, and Chalcidian invasion of Attica in 506; and, as we shall soon have occasion to observe, he may well have seized upon a more recent opportunity in which to demonstrate his affection for the Athenians. Be this as it may, Alexander was also on excellent terms with Xerxes, who was so pleased with the Macedonian king's hospitality that, on the occasion of his visit, he extended the man's authority, at the expense of the neighboring Molossian realm, to encompass "the entire district lying between the mountains Olympus and Haemus."[15]

Alexander no doubt welcomed the visit, but he can hardly have been eager to host the Great King and his immense army for an extended period— which helps explain why, in the spring of 480, he sent messengers to convey to the Greeks intent on resistance "the size of the army and the number of ships" they were up against, warning them that any force attempting to obstruct the Achaemenid monarch's march into Hellas at one of the mountain passes through which he had to proceed would be "trampled underfoot."[16] It is perfectly conceivable that Alexander later provided the Greeks with a copy of the order of battle produced for Xerxes at Doriscus and that this forms the basis for Herodotus' astonishingly precise description of his forces.

Herodotus tells us that Xerxes brought with him from Asia one million seven hundred thousand footsoldiers, eighty thousand cavalrymen, and twenty thousand camel drivers and charioteers; and in a description modeled on the catalogue of ships in the second book of Homer's *Iliad* he describes each of the forty-six ethnic contingents, specifying its garb and weaponry. The list is long and amounts to a survey of the nations within the Achaemenid empire. He tells us as well that, accompanying the Persian armada, there were three thousand triaconters, penteconters, light boats, and horse transports. The fleet proper, he asserts, consisted of twelve hundred seven triremes (a figure, lifted from Aeschylus' *Persians,* which exceeds by seven the number of ships in Homer's catalogue), and he specifies the size of each region's contribution to the fleet of triremes and describes the outfit and arms of the men who manned them. With regard to both the army and the navy, moreover, he names the Persian commanders and specifies the lineage of each.[17]

Xerxes' captains constituted an all-star cast. It is in these pages that we are told that the six marshals placed in charge of his army were Mardonius son of Darius' co-conspirator and spear-bearer Gobryas, Tritanaichmes son of Xerxes' uncle Artabanus, Smerdomenes son of Darius' brother Otanes, Masistes son of Darius and Atossa and full brother of Xerxes, Gergis son of Ariazos, and Megabyzos son of Zopyrus and grandson of the conspirator from whom he took his name. It is here that we learn not only that Harmamithres and Tithaeus, the sons of Datis the Mede, commanded Great King's cavalry but also that the navy was entrusted to Prexaspes son of Darius' quiver-bearer Aspathines, Megabazos son of Darius' cousin Megabates, Ariabignes son of Darius by the daughter of Gobryas, and Achaemenes son of Darius and Atossa and full brother to Xerxes himself—with Ariabignes keeping a watchful eye on the untrustworthy Carians and Ionians, and Achaemenes, their new satrap, doing the same for recently rebellious Egyptians.[18]

Herodotus' catalogue is a bravura literary performance, well worthy of Homer himself—for, among other things, the historian from Halicarnassus is clearly guilty of epic exaggeration, as he no doubt was perfectly aware. It is, after all, one thing to assert that an army drank rivers dry and another to believe that it actually did so. Moreover, as Herodotus clearly understood, the numbers that he provides in describing the army deployed by the Great King bear no relation to the numbers for which provision could actually have been made—especially when the army, marching by land and lugging its own provisions, parted company with the fleet and the merchantmen accompanying it.

General Sir Frederick Maurice, who had firsthand experience during World War I of what it meant to move British army units in the eastern Mediterranean with the help of animal transport, traveled on foot along the road taken by Xerxes from the river Scamander on the Asian side of the Hellespont to Abydos and then from Sestos to Doriscus not long after the Great

War. With an eye to the provision of fresh water, he estimated that the Great King's army could not have exceeded two hundred ten thousand in number and that it would have had to be accompanied by seventy-five thousand pack animals, including fifteen thousand camels. It is perfectly possible that Xerxes collected another one hundred twenty triremes as he made his way from Doriscus through Thrace and Macedonia to Thessaly, but Herodotus' claim that along this route he also recruited an additional three hundred thousand infantrymen renders his tale even less plausible.[19]

General Maurice suggested that, in reporting the number of footsoldiers, cavalrymen, charioteers, and camel drivers at Doriscus, Herodotus—or those on whose testimony he relied—mistook a chiliad, consisting of one thousand men, for a myriad, consisting of ten times that number, and it is no less possible that he or his informants deliberately misrepresented the former as the latter, as Xerxes may well have instructed Alexander son of Amyntas to do. Reducing the size of his army by a factor of ten would certainly bring the numbers much, much closer to the range of plausibility. But even these numbers are high. It is hard to see how, in Greece, the Persians could have found water every day and provided food for one hundred seventy thousand footsoldiers and eight thousand cavalrymen—much less for their horses, pack animals, and the men needed to drive them—leaving aside their servants, concubines, and the camp followers as well as the men in the fleet (some two hundred thirty per trireme). The merchantmen accompanying the fleet were no doubt a great help, but there were times when the terrain forced the army to part company with the fleet and march inland for ten days or even two weeks at a time, and there was a limit to its capacity to bring along provisions adequate for its needs. It is by no means an accident that the greatest army deployed by any Hellenistic king numbered eighty thousand and that the largest cavalry force we hear of numbered ten thousand five hundred. The larger of the two armies at Waterloo amounted to something like ninety-three thousand men. The Union army at Gettysburg numbered only ninety thousand. The landing in Normandy on D-Day was effected by one hundred thousand infantrymen.[20] Additional reductions of Herodotus' figures are clearly required, and for this there would appear to be two expedients.

First, it would not have been hard for the Great King to arrange at Doriscus to have chiliads that had passed by once return by a route unseen to parade by again and again, crowd into the enclosure he had set up, and be counted on each occasion anew. Deception of this very sort, aimed at instilling fear in one's adversaries, has always been part and parcel of psychological dimension of the art of war; and three decades after the event, when the author of the *Historíai* is thought to have begun composing his account, he may have fallen prey to tricks that Xerxes played on Alexander son of Amyntas and on the observers from Hellas that he had every reason to suppose would be present. Second, one might also presume that, when Xerxes resumed his march through Thrace and the territory of Macedon to Thessaly, he took with him few apart from his most reliable troops—the units of Iranian stock armed and trained in much the same fashion as the Persians and the Medes. As every soldier knows, there is all the difference in the world between an army on parade and an army on the march; and, when Herodotus describes the clash of forces that took place later at Thermopylae and Plataea, he makes no mention of any of the more exotic contingents in the Great King's army.

None of these arguments rules out the possibility that Xerxes' navy was as large, at the outset, as Aeschylus and Herodotus report. Its provisioning would have required an enormous effort on the part of the Achaemenid dominion, but the resources of the Great King were more than sufficient, and the armada at sea could have been supplied with food and even fresh water by a steady stream of merchantmen making their way to Hellas from the Black Sea, Asia Minor, Phoenicia, Cyprus, and Egypt.[21]

Nor do these logistical arguments prove that the army fielded by Achaemenid Persia on this occasion was not by ancient standards immense. Nor do they demonstrate that Xerxes did not bring with him, at least as far as Doriscus, colorful contingents from every corner of his empire. His purpose, after all, was not just to conquer. It was to dazzle and overawe. Like Darius' construction of magnificent palaces at Susa and Persepolis, a public display of the grandeur and diversity of the empire, of its astonishing wealth, and the enormous army it could put into the field served a purpose—if only to bolster Persian prestige and bring home to the notables in the contingents included and to those with whom they would speak when they returned home the degree to which resisting the King of Kings was apt to be suicidal.[22] The building of the canal at Athos and the bridging of the Hellespont were achievements on a scale that beggars the imagination.

It would be a mistake to belittle the size of Xerxes' armada. This was, after all, a crusade, a *jihad,* a holy war. With his father's throne, the son of Darius had inherited his father's mission. He it was who was now "King on this great earth far and wide." He it was who was now "the man in all the earth" and "King in all the earth." He it now was who was chosen by the Wise Lord Ahura Mazda, when the god "saw" parts of Europe "in commotion," to restore order, "put" everything there "in its proper place," and bring "happiness" to the peoples of Europe as yet unpacified—and, as we have seen, he appears to have regarded his *jīhad* against the Greeks as the final battle foretold by Zarathustra—as the holy war that would end all wars.

Of course, the magnitude of this effort may have been counterproductive. As Hermocrates son of Hermon, one of the most formidable statesmen to appear in Thucydides' account of the Peloponnesian War, points out in a speech said to have been delivered to his fellow Syracusans on the eve of Athens' invasion of Sicily, "In truth, few great expeditions, whether of Greeks or barbarians, have ventured far from their own land and emerged with a success. For the invaders cannot be more numerous than the land's inhabitants and neighbors, who will all be united by fear"; and, "in the land of another," interlopers are apt to "be tripped up by a dearth of necessities."[23]

Herodotus caps off his account of the review of forces that took place at Doriscus by reporting a conversation that purportedly took place at this time between Xerxes and Demaratus, in which the former expressed his doubts as to whether anyone in Hellas would resist his advance, and the erstwhile Spartan king attempted to explain to him the manner in which the Greeks of his time managed to turn "poverty," which he called "the foster brother" of Greece, to advantage by treating it as a challenge to be met by "a virtue acquired—fabricated from wisdom and from law that is strong." It is, he explained, "by constantly making use of this virtue" that "Hellas wards off poverty and despotism." And he went on to predict that, even if all of the other Greeks were to come to think as Xerxes did, the Spartans would stand and fight. Then, when Xerxes laughed and suggested that men are most apt to resist their natural instincts and fight when they are ruled by one man, skilled in the employment of the lash, whom they greatly fear, Demaratus responded that, although he had no reason to be fond of his former compatriots, he could not bring himself to deny what he knew to be true. "As for the Spartans," he observed,

> fighting each alone, they are as good as any, but fighting as a unit, they are the best of all men. They are free, but not completely free—for the law is placed over them as a master, and they fear that law far more than your subjects fear you. And they do whatever it orders—and it orders the same thing always: never to flee in battle, however many the enemy may be, but to remain in the ranks and to conquer or die.

The dialogue between Xerxes and Demaratus recounted by Herodotus serves a real dramatic purpose. It describes with great precision from a Greek perspective the character of the struggle that would soon at Thermopylae begin in earnest between the impoverished, self-governing cities of Hellas and the fabulously wealthy, universal empire in the east established by Cyrus, extended by Cambyses, and restored, reinvigorated, and further expanded by Xerxes' father Darius.[24]

The only real question is whether the Great King of Persia would ever have allowed himself the luxury of a frank exchange with a foreigner such as the one described. As Herodotus himself makes clear in his account of the origins of the empire of the Medes, oriental despotism is a species of sacral kingship, which relies for its success on rituals reinforcing through forms and formalities the profound distance that must be maintained between a ruler thought to be godlike and the subjects over whom his authority, at least in principle, knows no bounds.[25]

There is, however, another side to the story. Oriental despots are human beings, and more often than not they are desperately in need of company and counsel. If the forms and formalities are rigorously and systematically sustained on all occasions, they can never have either. It may, moreover, have been safer for such a despot to remove his mask in the presence of a foreigner of known inferiority than for him to display weakness before a potential rival of his own stock.

Preparing for the Onslaught

In the decade that passed between the battle of Marathon and the arrival of Xerxes at Doriscus, the Athenians and the Spartans got their respective houses in order. Had the Persians left them less time, it is by no means certain that either would have been able to do so. By 480, however, the Athenians had settled the political dispute that had racked the city in the years since 506, when their ambassadors first gave earth and water in Sardis; and by that time Sparta had to a considerable degree restored its position within the Peloponnesus.

The Athenians' problems were largely internal. In the wake of Marathon, Athens remained a deeply divided city. At first, to be sure, the Athenians were elated; and Miltiades, who had led them to victory, moved quickly to capitalize on his success. If we had only Herodotus, whose account derives from the Alcmaeonid heirs of Miltiades' enemies, it would be difficult to figure out what Miltiades was up to. Fortunately, however, we also have a biography by the first-century Roman writer Cornelius Nepos, which reflects the work of the fourth-century Atthidographer Demon, and we possess fragments of the fourth-century historian Ephorus of Cumae as well. Nearly all that Herodotus tells us actually makes good sense if we fit it into the narrative provided by Nepos.[26]

After his victory, when he was riding high, Miltiades turned to the Athenian assembly once again—this time to ask that he be allowed to undertake an expedition with seventy ships, a small army, and money to pay the costs—promising that the enterprise would both profit the city and be in its interest. His personal prestige at that moment was such that he secured the authorization required with no questions asked. The fleet Miltiades gathered presumably included the four triremes with which he had successfully fled the Thracian Chersonnesus and no doubt some others as well. But for the most part, if the testimony of Thucydides is to be trusted, it consisted of penteconters. Even if, as I have suggested, Themistocles in his year as archon persuaded the Athenians to begin building a fleet of triremes, the numbers in service in 489 will still have been modest. When the campaigning season came around in the spring of that year, with the ships available and the infantrymen conveyed on them, the victor of Marathon toured the islands, ousted the Medizers from power, and attempted to put these polities on a footing to resist the Persians when they returned. In most respects, Miltiades appears to have been successful in this endeavor.[27]

Paros was, however, an exception to the rule. There, Datis and Artaphernes had installed in power a local Medizer of some influence named Lysagoras son of Teisias—who had earlier made trouble for Miltiades in the east, probably at the time of the Scythian expedition, by speaking ill of him to an influential Persian named Hydarnes, quite likely the distinguished man of that name who had been Darius' co-conspirator in 522 or his like-named son. Apart from Naxos—which had once in the recent past successfully fended off the Persians, which claimed to have put up more of a resistance to Datis and Artaphernes than Herodotus reports, and which was apt in any case to have been open to persuasion on the part of Miltiades as soon as the Persians left the scene—Paros was, because of its marble quarries, the wealthiest and most important island in the Cyclades; and, no doubt at the insistence of Lysagoras, it had actually sent a trireme to join the Persians at Marathon.[28]

Knowing that, if he could succeed at Paros, all of the other island communities would fall in line, Miltiades demanded that the Parians pay an indemnity of one hundred talents (2.85 tons) of silver for what they had done against Athens. When they refused, in the fashion of the free-booting raiders depicted in Homer, he initiated a siege and began a systematic attempt to undermine the walls of the town. This he did in the manner pioneered by the Assyrians, Babylonians, and Persians—using mantlets and tortoise sheds, in a fashion unprecedented in Greek warfare, to protect the men working at the base of the wall from the arrows, lances, and other objects directed at them from above. The Parians attempted at the same time to double the height of their walls. After twenty-six days, however, they were reportedly on the point of negotiating terms and paying the requisite ransom when a forest fire on nearby Mykonos was taken by both sides as a signal indicating Datis' imminent return. The Parians then broke off negotiations. Miltiades panicked; and, at his instigation, the Athenians withdrew in disarray.[29]

In temperament, Miltiades was not a democrat. He had come of age under the old political dispensation, and, in his days as ruler in the Thracian Chersonnesus, he had grown accustomed to giving commands. When he returned to Athens after the Ionian Revolt, as we have seen, his enemies had put him on trial for having been a tyrant. They did not succeed, but they would not have made the attempt had the Philaid married to a Thracian princess not already been an object of resentment in some quarters. When he took the lead in the assembly in 490 and again on the battlefield at Marathon, Miltiades earned and elicited the admiration of his compatriots. But, as Nepos points out, he also stoked the envy that democratic peoples are inclined to direct at those in their midst who seem too imperious and loom too large.[30]

It is surely telling that, after Marathon—when the Athenian assembly voted to bury the Athenian dead in a mound on the battlefield, to inter the Plataeans and the slave volunteers in another mound nearby, and set up inscriptions listing the one hundred ninety-two Athenians who had died by both tribe and name—its members also voted to construct in Miltiades' honor the monument at Marathon described by Pausanias the geographer. But it is no less revealing that, when Miltiades requested that the city also confer on him a crown of olive, Sophanes of Deceleia—a man of great courage and prowess who would later repeatedly win renown himself—intervened to object that so signal an honor should be reserved for someone who had defeated the barbarian in single combat, and Miltiades was denied the recognition that he sought.[31]

After the debacle on Paros, at Athens, envy and resentment trumped admiration. The situation for Miltiades was complicated by the fact that he had been wounded by an arrow while on the island and the wound had become seriously infected. When he returned to Athens, his enemies brought him to trial for treason, arguing that he had misled the Athenians and charging that he must have been bribed to withdraw from Paros by agents of the King of Kings. Miltiades, who was too ill to be able even to speak in his own defense, lost the case. He was fined fifty talents (1.425 tons) of silver, which may have been the estimated cost of the expedition and which was an enormous sum for an individual. When he was unable to come up with the money on short notice, he was jailed; and there, after gangrene set in, he died, leaving it to his son Cimon, a young man still in his early twenties, to pay off what remained of the fine. Had it not been, we are told, for the marriage of his younger sister Elpinike to Callias son of Hipponicus, the richest man in Athens, Cimon might never have been able to pay the debt.[32]

In this little post-Marathon drama, more was involved than the fate of one great man. Miltiades stood for a policy—resistance to the Persians at all costs. He had started down this path at the time of the Scythian expedition, and he never deviated from it thereafter. Moreover, the man who brought him to trial was a close associate of the Alcmaeonid advocates of appeasement and accommodation. His name was Xanthippus son of Ariphron. His father appears to have been a friend of Peisistratus. He was himself married to the tyrant's granddaughter, the offspring of Cleisthenes' younger brother Hippocrates and his Peisistratid bride Koisyra; and in his attack on Miltiades he is said to have been acting on behalf of the Alcmaeonid clan.[33]

In time, events would vindicate the policy of Miltiades and even, in some measure, his execution of that policy. Nine years after his trial, Herodotus tells us, the Carystians, Andrians, Tenians, "and all the rest of the islanders" joined the Persian fleet after the battle of Artemisium. But it is hard to discern which other islanders from the Cyclades the historian can have had in mind—for he also reports that the citizens of the *póleis* on the islands of Ceos, Seriphos, Siphnos, and Melos defied the Persians and sent ships to Salamis to support the Hellenes, and he notes that the contingent dispatched from the island of Naxos, though ordered by those in charge to support the Mede, rebelled under the leadership of the trierarch Democritus and sided with the Hellenes. Moreover, even with regard to Paros, Miltiades' abortive venture appears to have yielded gratifying results. The Parians deployed a fleet in 480, but it did not proceed to Salamis to fight on either side. Instead, it remained on the sidelines at Cythnus and awaited the battle's outcome. By means of his foray into the Cyclades, Miltiades had given encouragement to the friends of liberty in that corner of Hellas; and, at the same time, he had brought home to those inclined to medize the fact that Persia might not, in the event, be the power that they most had to fear.[34]

In the aftermath of Miltiades' death, Themistocles son of Neocles came into his own. As we have seen, in his days as archon, he had begun fortifying the Peiraeus, and he may have sponsored Phrynichus' presentation of *The Sack of Miletus*. Now he revived an old law, never before fully implemented, and he made use of it to eliminate the advocates of appeasement and accommodation from the body politic for a time.

The law had been proposed by Cleisthenes and passed by the assembly in or soon after 508. It provided for a procedure by which the Athenians could, if circumstances merited it, opt for what came to be called an ostracism—which is to say, the temporary banishment from Attica for a ten-year period of a public figure, presumably someone of great prominence, thought by many to be a danger to the city, who was not as yet known to have committed any crime. At the outset, this measure was reportedly aimed at Hipparchus son of Charmos, but it was left unused for twenty years—perhaps because its Alcmaeonid author and his associates soon found themselves in an awkward and uneasy alliance with Hipparchus and the other former adherents of the Peisistratids grounded in an eagerness on the part of both factions to avoid conflict with Persia at almost any cost.[35]

The law proposed by Cleisthenes may have conferred the right to ostracize on the probouleutic Council of 500 set up by his tribal reform.[36] If so, however, by 488/87, another set of procedures was in place. Tellingly, this was the very year in which another populist reform was enacted in which, with regard to the archonship, the principle of equality was allowed to trump that of merit and a board once filled by election came to be filled by lot from a sizable elected pool.

Under the procedures in place by the first half of 487, once a year—a bit more than halfway through the term of that year's archons—the assembly at Athens was asked to vote whether to hold an ostracism. If it did so, about two and a half months later, on a specified day, any Athenian who wanted to participate could show up at the designated place to leave an *óstrakon*—which is to say, a potsherd—inscribed with the name of the man he wanted to banish. If a quorum of six thousand citizens voted in this fashion,[37] the individual who received the most votes was required to absent himself from Athens for a decade.

Early in 487, a bit more than a year after Miltiades' trial, the assembly voted for the first time to hold an ostracism, and two and a half months later Hipparchus son of Charmos was sent abroad. A year later, it was the turn of Megacles, son of Cleisthenes' younger brother Hippocrates and Peisistratus' daughter Koisyra. Aristotle identifies both Hipparchus and Megacles as "friends of the tyrants," and he says the same about the unnamed public figure, almost certainly another Alcmaeonid or a close associate of the clan, who was ostracized the following year. A year after that, it was the turn of Megacles' brother-in-law and Miltiades' prosecutor Xanthippus son of Ariphron. And, two years later, Aristeides son of Lysimachus was singled out in the same fashion. This last figure was a fellow demesman of the Alcmaeonids. In his youth, Plutarch tells us, he had been a "member of the political club [*hetaîros*]" to which Cleisthenes belonged. At Marathon, he served as his tribe's general; and a year later, a few months before Miltiades was tried, he assumed office as archon eponymous.[38]

More than ten thousand potsherds survive from the fifth century with names scratched upon them. It is highly likely—given the sheer number of these sporting Themistocles' name—that in each of these years an unsuccessful attempt was made to ostracize him. Some of the *óstraka* include epithets suggesting treason or medizing on the part of a member or associate of the Alcmaeonid clan—one of these may even have described Aristeides as "the brother of Datis the Mede"—and Herodotus indicates that there was a story making the rounds that, in the course of the confrontation at Marathon, someone in the Alcmaeonid family used a shield to send a signal to the Persians.[39] It is clear what was happening. One by one, Themistocles was purging his political opponents—the advocates of appeasement.

There was more to this than a vendetta. In 483, the year in which Aristeides was ostracized, a great deal was at stake. There had been a silver strike in the mines at Laurium. In ordinary circumstances, it was the practice in Greek cities to make an equal distribution of at least part of the proceeds to each and every citizen. Themistocles proposed, instead, that the entire sum be allocated

Figure 15. (*Top to bottom*) *Óstrakon* naming Megacles son of Hippocrates, 486 (Ancient Agora Museum at the Stoa of Attalus, Athens: Photographer: Giovanni Dall'Orto, Wikimedia Commons, Published November 2015 under the following license: "The copyright holder of this file allows anyone to use it for any purpose, provided that the copyright holder is properly attributed. Redistribution, derivative work, commercial use, and all other use is permitted."); *óstrakon* naming Themistocles son of Neocles, 480s; and *óstrakon* naming Aristeides son of Lysimachus, 483/2 (Ancient Agora Museum at the Stoa of Attalus, Athens: Photographer: Marsyas, Wikimedia Commons; Published November 2015 under the following license: Creative Commons Attribution-ShareAlike 3.0 Unported).

for the construction of triremes in large numbers. Herodotus has him propose that two hundred be built. These were the ships, he adds, with which the Athenians subsequently defended Hellas against Xerxes. In the same context, however, Aristotle mentions only one hundred.

This discrepancy should give us pause. Triremes were, as we have seen, large, complicated ships, requiring a great deal of seasoned timber and precision carpentry. It is hard to believe that, in a span of only three years, with a more or less nonexistent trireme-building industry, the Athenians could have constructed as many as two hundred triremes. If, however, as I have already suggested, the Athenians in the time of Hippias, Cleisthenes, and Melanthios already possessed a small number of triremes and if at Themistocles' instigation they launched a trireme-building campaign in the wake of the Ionian defeat at Lade, they might already have had by 483 a fleet of fifty or more triremes—with another fifty or so in the works; and, if they could lay their hands on a sufficient stock of seasoned wood, their trireme-building capacity might well have become sufficient to enable them to finish the fifty and construct the additional one hundred mentioned by Aristotle in relatively short order. It is also conceivable that some of these vessels were built in shipyards, always at work, nearer the sources of timber. Either way, however, what Themistocles had in mind in 483 was a program that would give Athens a fleet larger than that of any city in or near mainland Greece. At the time, we are told, Themistocles laid emphasis on Athens' ongoing difficulties with Aegina.[40] Herein lies a tale.

Sometime not too long after Marathon, the long and colorful life of Cleomenes came to an abrupt and ugly end. Herodotus was told that, after his return from Arcadia, the Agiad king lost his mind and that he was apt to attack with his staff anyone who approached him. The Spartans relegated him to the care of his family—to his daughter Gorgo, no doubt; and surely also to her husband, his half-brother and heir Leonidas. Cleomenes they confined to the stocks, and they left a helot, armed with only a knife, to guard him. The Agiad king reportedly pressed the man to give him the knife; and, with it, he purportedly sliced the skin from his shins, thighs, hips, and, finally, his abdomen before bleeding to death. The Spartans blamed his madness on the practice of drinking wine unmixed with water that he had learned from the Scythians. Other Greeks tended to believe that it was a punishment for impiety—for bribing the Delphic oracle, invading the precinct of Demeter and Persephone at Eleusis, or burning down the grove of Apollo at Argos. Herodotus regarded it as payback for what he had done to Demaratus. Many modern scholars suspect foul play. Others note, however, that the symptoms described by Herodotus fit perfectly a diagnosis of paranoid schizophrenia.[41] The mystery remains and will forever remain unsolved.

When news of Cleomenes' death reached the Aeginetans, they sent an embassy to Lacedaemon to denounce Leotychidas son of Menares for having joined Cleomenes in delivering ten of their leading citizens to the Athenians as hostages. The Spartans, who must by this time have regretted the deposition of Demaratus, offered to surrender the Eurypontid king to the Aeginetans in recompense. When, however, the latter came to collect him, they were persuaded by a leading Spartan to think again regarding the long-term consequences for their relations with Lacedaemon of what they were on the verge of doing, and an agreement was thrashed out. Leotychidas was released by the Aeginetans, and he consented to accompany an embassy from Aegina to Athens to ask for the return of the hostages—and this he did. But the Athenians, probably at the instigation of Themistocles, refused to comply with his request, observing puckishly that two kings had deposited the ten hostages with them while only one had come to ask for their release.[42]

This refusal on the part of the Athenians led to a renewal of the conflict between the two cities. Initially, the Aeginetans kidnapped some of the leading men of Athens as they were making their way to Cape Sunium to conduct a festival, and the Athenians responded by colluding with a faction intent on overthrowing the oligarchy on Aegina and substituting for it a democracy. When this revolutionary enterprise failed, the Athenians settled the survivors at Cape Sunium and allowed them to conduct raids from there against Aegina. Step by step, in the early to mid-480s, the struggle escalated. There were battles at sea. The Aeginetans were able to field a fleet of seventy galleys—no more than forty or fifty of them triremes. The Athenians had only fifty ships—many of them pentec6nters. Finding themselves short of what Herodotus pointedly describes as "battle-worthy ships," the Athenians then turned to the Corinthians, who sold them twenty galleys, presumably superannuated triremes, for a pittance; and, though with these the Athenians won one battle, in the end they got the worst of it.

The first rule of strategic thinking is that one should regard every disappointment as an opportunity, and this is precisely what Themistocles did in this situation. Had the Athenians constructed a substantial squadron of triremes in the time of Hippias, Cleisthenes, and Melanthios, as some suppose, and, more to the point, had they possessed seventy such galleys in 483, as some scholars contend, Themistocles would not have been able to advance the argument he made—for such a force would have been more than adequate to handle the fleet of triremes and the additional pentecónters that the Aeginetans were able to deploy. As things stood, however, Athens' fleet was demonstrably inferior to the one fielded by her neighbor.[43] In the assembly therefore, after news had spread concerning the silver strike at Laurium, Themistocles emphasized the inadequacy of Athens' naval defenses vis-à-vis the Aeginetans. We can be confident, however—and men such as the fifth-century Greek historian Thucydides were—that, while playing up the threat near at hand, he and others in his camp had their eyes on the Persians who had that very year begun cutting a canal through the Acte peninsula in the Chalcidice.[44]

We are not expressly told that Aristeides argued against building triremes on this occasion, but Aristotle links his ostracism chronologically with the assembly's decision in this particular in such a way as to suggest that the two were somehow connected, and there is every reason to suppose that Aristeides vigorously opposed the aggressive posture with regard to Aegina championed by Themistocles. It would otherwise be difficult to explain why, after being ostracized, he chose to reside on that island—where, there is reason to suspect, Megacles son of Hippocrates, Xanthippus son of Ariphron, and perhaps even Hipparchus son of Charmos had already found refuge.[45] By securing in the course of this struggle the ostracism of the last and most formidable of his rivals and by setting Athens firmly on the path to becoming a major maritime power, Themistocles made it possible for the city to resist the onslaught to come.

It is a reasonable guess that, for the lumber required for the conduct of their war with Aegina, the Athenians turned to their "benefactor" and *próxenos* Alexander son of Amyntas. Macedon was not far away; it was well wooded; and its king controlled the export of timber. Xerxes was not inclined to interfere with commerce, and his native satrap in Macedonia did somehow manage to sustain his credit with the Athenians in these years. Had he refused them the delivery of timber in their time of greatest need, they surely would have turned on the man.[46]

As always, we are less well-informed about Sparta. In the course of his career, Cleomenes had done great harm to the system of alliances that sustained Lacedaemon. His mismanagement of relations with Athens in the last few years of the sixth century had driven a wedge between Sparta and Corinth and had sown distrust of Lacedaemon throughout the Peloponnesus. His flight to Thessaly or Sellasia and his subsequent attempt to unite the Arcadians against the city had endangered it and appear to have occasioned a helot revolt. Few at Sparta can have mourned his passing. The willingness of the Lacedaemonians to hand over to the Aeginetans Leotychidas, the man whom Cleomenes had installed as the Eurypontid king, tells the tale.[47]

Except vis-à-vis Aegina itself, we do not know how the Spartans conducted themselves with regard to the Messenians and their own allies during the decade following 490. But we do know the result. When Xerxes led
his great army and navy to Greece, the helots of Laconia and Messenia did
not revolt, and with rare exceptions, apart from Argos, the cities in the Peloponnesus rallied to the Spartan standard. The helot revolt of 490 must have
been crushed with great ruthlessness, and thereafter the Lacedaemonians
must have devoted considerable care to the management of the coalition they
led. In 481, when Xerxes once again sent out heralds demanding earth and
water, the Spartans were as fully prepared as they had been unready nine years
before.

By this time they were superbly prepared in one other crucial regard. We
do not know who persuaded the magistrates at Sparta or the assembly to break
with a practice sanctioned by religion and time out of mind and hurl into a well
the heralds dispatched in 491 by Darius. But it is not hard to guess. As Demaratus'
fate makes clear, Cleomenes was at the time in charge, and he was an impulsive
man quite capable of so shocking a deed. Moreover, at the time, he appears
to have been more hostile to the Mede than any other figure of importance
at Lacedaemon. In any case, what we do know without a doubt is that in the
aftermath, when the Spartans sacrificed victims, the omens were consistently
bad.[48]

It would be a mistake to underestimate the seriousness with which the
Spartans regarded such matters. In a passage pertaining to Apollo, Herodotus
tells us that the Spartans "made the things of the god take precedence over
[*presbútera*] those of men." In another similar passage, he later claims that "at-
tending to the affairs of the god was something that the Spartans took with the
greatest seriousness." His narrative and those of Thucydides and Xenophon
bear out these assertions. In this case, we are told, the situation persisted for a
considerable period of time, and the Spartans became vexed and even fearful.
In due course, after holding assembly after assembly in which their plight in
this particular was repeatedly discussed, they concluded that their treatment
of the heralds must be the cause of divine disfavor; that Talthybius, the herald
of Agamemnon, was the demigod offended; and that the only way to propitiate him and turn away his wrath was to offer proper recompense. So, they
issued a proclamation asking whether any of the Lacedaemonians was willing
to die for his city; and, when two wealthy, well-born Spartiates volunteered,
they sent them off to the Medes for execution.[49]

We cannot be certain what happened when Sperthias son of Aneristes and Boulis son of Nikolaus reached Susa. We know that, by this time, Xerxes had succeeded his father. We are told that the two Spartiates refused to prostrate themselves in the customary fashion before one whom they regarded as a mere man like themselves. And we know that, in a display of magnanimity, Xerxes spared them both, saying that he was not about to do to them what he had reason to reproach the Lacedaemonians for doing to his father's heralds. What is not mentioned, however, is whether, during the sojourn in Susa of Sperthias and Boulis, any negotiations took place. It stands to reason, however, that Xerxes would seize on the opportunity, and there is evidence suggesting that a guest-friendship was established between the two men and their Persian benefactor—for, a bit more than a half-century thereafter, when the Spartans resolved to make a diplomatic approach to the King of Kings, they included in their embassy to Susa the sons of Sperthias and Boulis.[50]

If Xerxes made any attempt at this time to persuade the Spartans to medize, it came to nothing, and it is easy to see why. En route, we are told, the two Spartans had spent some time with a certain Hydarnes son of Hydarnes. This man was a figure of note. As his patronymic suggests, he may have been the son of Darius' like-named co-conspirator. At the time of their visit, he commanded the soldiers of the Great King stationed along the coast in Asia Minor. Later, he would lead the Ten Thousand Immortals on Xerxes' epic march into Greece. When this Hydarnes asked his Lacedaemonian guests why they fled from friendship with the Great King, when he drew their attention to the fact that the King of Kings knew how "to honor good men," and when he suggested that, if the Spartans were to pay homage to Xerxes, he would give to each of them a territory in Hellas to rule, they reportedly responded that their host's limited experience of life made of him a poor counselor. He knew, they explained, what it meant to be a slave, but he had never tasted liberty, and he was in no position to judge whether it was sweet or not. "If," they concluded, "you were to experience liberty, you would advise us to fight for it not just with spears but with battle-axes as well."[51] If Xerxes had any of his minions at court make overtures to the two, we can be confident that they responded to his agent in Susa much as they had in Anatolia to Hydarnes. If, in their hour of need, the Greeks managed to rally against the Mede, it was first and foremost because the Spartans were stalwart in defense of the liberty exemplified by their regime.

More to the point, the gesture—by which the two Spartiates were dispatched to Susa in compensation for the heralds thrown in the well—was
thought to have propitiated the wrath of Talthybius, at least for a time. At
Lacedaemon, to which the two men in due course returned, when sacrifices
were made, the omens were no longer consistently unfavorable,[52] and morale
was restored. It was, as it turned out, none too soon. For within a few years of
the return of Sperthias and Boulis, Xerxes' invasion was under way.

Taking Up the Gauntlet

We do not know precisely when the Hellenes became cognizant of the
Persian plan. They must, however, have had a pretty good idea well in advance of Xerxes' march. They can hardly have failed to hear that Darius, then
Xerxes, had ordered the building of ships. The construction of triremes took
time, and the merchants plying the sea in the eastern Mediterranean and carrying information, as well as goods, were numerous.[53] In 484 or 483, when
the Great King began cutting a canal through the Acte peninsula in the Chalcidice, they surely became alarmed. When he began building up vast stores
of food at depots along the road from the Hellespont to Thessaly, they can
hardly have ignored the logic unfolding. Well before Xerxes' agents began the
construction of two bridges across the Hellespont, it must have been obvious
what he had in mind.[54]

We do not know whether, in Susa, Sperthias and Boulis ever met with
Demaratus, but the odds are good that they did. Indeed, if Xerxes wanted to
make an overture to the Lacedaemonians through these two, there was no
better go-between. If there was such a meeting, one can imagine that the three
men made an arrangement—that Demaratus would tip off his countrymen at
the first indication that Xerxes or one of his generals was about to set out for
Hellas. It is even conceivable that Xerxes himself suggested such a ploy to his
once-royal guest. The Great King of Persia was a despot. Like his father and
like Cyrus and Cambyses before them, he had an excellent understanding of
the interplay between greed and abject fear. In this venture, as we have already
seen, he was inclined to broadcast his intentions in the hope that his prospective adversaries would take note, calculate the slim chances of their surviving
and prospering should they resist, and surrender in advance.

Whatever the circumstances and whether his motive was goodwill toward his erstwhile compatriots or, as Herodotus suspected, spiteful exulta-

tion, Demaratus reportedly did send just such a message and he did so in apparent secrecy. Taking a pair of tablets, he scraped off the wax, wrote his message on the wood, covered them with wax again, and passed them on to his emissary. At Sparta, when the two apparently blank tablets were delivered, Gorgo—the daughter of Cleomenes and wife of the Agiad king Leonidas—is said to have solved the riddle. When, at her urging, the wax was scraped off and Demaratus' message was read, word was sent to Athens and the other cities of Greece, and the Spartans reportedly did forthwith what god-fearing Greeks nearly always did on the eve of a crisis clearly foreseen: they sent an embassy to Delphi to consult the oracle of Apollo.[55]

We can be confident that, as the Persians made ostentatious preparations for Xerxes' invasion, the authorities at Delphi gave thought to the questions likely to be posed. They had long experience in balancing interests that were sometimes at odds. On the one hand, if the reputation of the Pythia was to be sustained, the oracles she issued could not be demonstrably false. To this end, they were often cryptic—even obscure—and easily interpreted in ways opposed, as Croesus had learned to his great regret. On the other hand, Delphi had to please. In the past, when the oracle had taken sides, there had been wars fought over its control. In this case, the Great King had sent a signal. When Datis the Mede visited Lindos in 494 and Delos in 490, he had displayed just how generous his royal master could be. Herodotus makes no claim regarding Persian gold. In fact, there is no credible evidence suggesting that there was, on this occasion, bribery.[56] But this does not mean that Xerxes made no attempt to use the oracle to undermine Greek morale. The Great King of Persia was certainly capable of doing such a thing. But he may not in this instance have done it. We know only that the authorities at Delphi were loath to bet on a loser and that they were cautious. If they ostentatiously took sides and bet wrong, the consequences could be most unpleasant.

So, naturally enough, the Pythia couched her responses in such a fashion as to welcome the likely victor while hinting vaguely at the possibility that the likely victor might in some unlikely fashion encounter defeat:

> As for you who locate your households in Sparta, wide in territory,
>> Either your town, great and glorious, will be sacked
> By Perseus' manly descendants, or not—if from Heracles' stock
> A king is killed whom those within Lacedaemon's limits shall bewail.
>> For neither the might of bulls nor that of lions can stand as a
>> counter-force,

> Since he is in possession of the might of Zeus. And he, say I, will not
>   be contained
>   Until one of the two, town or king, is wholly torn apart.

Perhaps the most telling detail is the oracle's repetition of the Persian claim that the Achaemenid kings were descended from Perseus,[57] the legendary king of Tiryns, founder of Mycenae, and great-great-grandfather of Heracles—with its implication that the Peloponnesus might well by right be theirs.

The Argives also appear to have had advance warning, for Herodotus uses language to describe their situation in this regard which is virtually identical to that which he deploys in describing that of their rivals to the south. In this case, however, their being so well-informed is almost certainly a sign of collusion with the Mede on their part. For even if, as a consequence of their hatred for the Lacedaemonians, the Argives did not, in fact, send earth and water to Darius and become his *bandaka* in 491 when their Aeginetan neighbors medized, we can be confident that Demaratus tipped off his Achaemenid hosts to the antipathy setting Argos and Lacedaemon at odds and told them a great deal more concerning the Argives and their legendary origins and that his hosts took advantage of these tidbits of intelligence.

Something of the sort was certainly supposed at the time, for Herodotus cites testimony, circulating in his own day, that, before he even set out from Susa for Sardis, Xerxes sent a herald to Argos, claiming that as Perseids he and his kindred were of Argive stock and intimating that they were natural allies, and he reports that Argives promised help to Mardonius in 479 and went out of their way to perform for him a service. Moreover, the historian also mentions a putative attempt on the part of the Argives in later years to renew a friendship with Xerxes' son Artaxerxes that had, they claimed, existed between Argos and that Great King's father. This was a time when one had to take sides, and there is considerable justice to Herodotus' claim that the Peloponnesian communities which purported to be neutral were, in effect, Medizers all.[58]

When the Argives got advance word of Xerxes' intentions, they, too, are said to have sent a delegation to Delphi, and the oracle reportedly issued a response to them hardly less favorable to the cause of the Mede than the one issued to the Lacedaemonians:

> Hostile to those who dwell nearby, dear to the immortal gods,
>   Sit still holding your spear withdrawn and be on your guard,
> And guard especially well your head. For the head shall save the body.[59]

In the circumstances, this was not bad advice. But it certainly ruled out Argos' entry into the conflict on the side of Sparta and Athens.

In time, the Athenians also learned that Xerxes had set out, and they, too, approached the oracle of Apollo at Delphi. When, however, their delegates entered the inner shrine and sat down, before they could even pose a question, the Pythia, a woman named Aristonice, issued a warning far harsher than the one directed at the Lacedaemonians:

> O pitiable men, why do you sit here? Flee to the very ends of the earth
> And leave your homes and the lofty heights encircled by your city.
> For neither the head nor the body will remain firm-set.
> Neither the feet below nor the hands nor anything in-between
> Will be left in place, but all is unenviable. Fire hurls it all down
> And so does harsh Ares, driving a Syrian chariot.
> Many other strongholds he will destroy, and not just yours.
> Many sanctuaries of the deathless ones he will give over to raging fire.
> Even now these temples stand dripping in sweat,
> Quivering in fear. Dark blood pours down
> From the rooftops, forecasting evil necessities.
> But, you, leave this shrine and fortify your spirit for ills to come.

This was not, however, the end of the matter, for we are told that a citizen of Delphi, named Timon son of Androboulos, urged the Athenians to consult Apollo once again. This time, he suggested, they should approach the sanctuary as suppliants with olive branches in hand, asking for an oracle more favorable to their city—which is what they did. And, in answer to their plea, Aristonice responded:

> Unable is Pallas [Athena] to propitiate Olympian Zeus,
> Entreating him with arguments many and counsel sage.
> To you again I say this word, rendering it as firm as adamant:
> Although all else will be taken—whatever lies within
> The boundaries of Cecrops and the hollows of sacred Cithaeron—
> The wooden wall, alone unravaged, far-seeing Zeus
> To Tritogenes gives to be of benefit to you and your offspring.
> Do not stay in wait at rest for the horsemen and footsoldiers,
> The host multitudinous coming by land, but withdraw,
> Turning your backs. The time will come for you to meet him face to face.
> O Salamis divine! You will destroy the children of women
> Either when Demeter's seed is scattered or when her fruit is gathered in.

It was, needless to say, the second of the two oracles that provided the basis for subsequent debates within the Athenian assembly. So we learn from Herodotus.[60]

Some scholars are inclined to reject Herodotus' testimony outright. The oracles he attributes to Delphi are, they say, a pious fraud propagated after the event for the purpose of making Apollo seem prescient. In the circumstances, however, there can be little doubt that these were the oracles actually pronounced and that the Spartans, the Argives, and the Athenians sent delegations to Delphi late in 481 as soon as they learned that the King of Kings had resolved to conquer Hellas. All of this was surely a matter of public knowledge at the time. Herodotus was closely attentive to everything said to have been spoken by Apollo, and he was assiduous in gathering information. Moreover, it was his practice to recite his *Historíai* in public performances in places such as Athens and Olympia. Had he erred in reporting the context within which these oracles were delivered or their content, those among his listeners who had been present at the time would have set him straight.[61]

Of course, none of this rules out the possibility that at the time, by one means or another, the Pythia had been persuaded to say what the delegates wanted to hear. The second of the two oracles delivered to the Athenians is especially suspect. We know that the Athenians were unhappy with its predecessor. We even know the name of the citizen of Delphi who arranged for them to entreat the Pythia to speak again, and it certainly would not have been beyond Themistocles son of Neocles—who was supreme in Athenian counsels at the time,[62] who was almost certainly a member of the delegation, and who was not known for being overly scrupulous—to discreetly indicate to Timon son of Androboulos what it was that he and his compatriots wanted to hear, to hint at what Delphi might suffer should the Pythia fail to please, and to reward those at Delphi who accommodated his wishes.

Themistocles was a man with a plan. He had been prominent in opposing the appeasers in the 490s. He had seen to the ostracism of their leaders in the 480s. He had promoted the building of a proper harbor at Peiraeus when he was archon eponymous in 493/92; and, when the silver strike at Laurium took place, he had seized upon the Athenians' fecklessness in the ongoing war with Aegina to persuade them to bring their fleet up to a complement of two hundred triremes. He knew that the Persians would return, he had worked out in his own mind a precise strategy for the invaders' defeat, and he did everything within his power to ensure that the Athenians would be ready to meet them on this occasion.

The second of the two oracles delivered to the Athenians by the Pythia was tailor-made for his purposes. It called for the Athenians to withdraw from Attica. It suggested that they would find protection behind a wall of wood. It promised that they would someday confront the Mede; and, in this last context, it mentioned Salamis. It is in no way surprising that Themistocles emerged in the public assembly to persuade his fellow citizens that the "wooden wall" mentioned in the oracle was Athens' fleet, that they would in due course fight at Salamis, and that the children of women, destined for destruction, were not for the most part his compatriots but those rowing and serving as marines in the vast armada about to set out for Attica with Xerxes.[63] If Themistocles did not draft the second oracle himself, he surely dictated its contents.

It was at this time, thanks in large part to the machinations of Themistocles, that, "in obedience to the god," the Athenians summoned the requisite courage and resolved to evacuate Attica if the invader made it that far; to take to the sea; and to confront the Mede on that element, displaying in the process a measure of foresight and determination that commanded admiration in antiquity and still commands it today. To this end, early in the fall of 481, they started making preparations to take their movable property, their wives, and children from Attica, and they began the arduous task of transforming a community largely made up of landlubbers into masters of the sea.[64]

Herodotus tells us that, in 500, the adult male population of Athens was approximately thirty thousand. To this number, we can presumably add the four thousand Athenian cleruchs who farmed the Lelantine plain in the territory of Chalcis on the island of Euboea.[65] These totals were probably no larger twenty years thereafter. To fully man two hundred triremes required a force of forty thousand; and, if the vessels were to be as effective in battle as they could be, each required its full complement of two hundred men. We must presume that every able-bodied citizen of Athens was pressed into service, that slaves were offered their freedom if they agreed to row, that metics resident at Athens were drafted, and that other foreigners willing to lend a hand were welcomed with open arms.

We must also presume that, whenever the weather was favorable, the Athenians were out on the water, learning not only how to maneuver the ships that Themistocles had persuaded them to build but also how to coordinate the operations of each trireme in concert with the rest of the fleet. It is this effort that explains why, in the course of this stage of their conflict with Persia, the Athenians lost not just one harvest, in 479, but two. As Pericles would later remark, one cannot acquire the skills of seamanship in a short time.[66] In the winter of 481/80, the men of Athens had next to no time in which to sow and, when harvesting time came around the following May, they were for the most part too busy to reap. If, in the crisis, they ultimately proved equal to the monumental challenge they faced, it was because, in anticipation of the horrors to come, long before the event, they had resolved not only on evacuating their families and salvageable property from their homeland but also on dedicating themselves wholeheartedly to what the Ionians at Lade had shirked: an acquisition of the requisite nautical skills.

We may have a snapshot of the initial stages in this process in the inscription that scholars call the Themistocles Decree. Discovered just over sixty years ago near ancient Troezen—where most of the women and children evacuated from Athens in anticipation of the Persian onslaught found refuge—it purports to be the measure passed by the Athenian assembly in response to the oracles. It appears, in fact, to be a slightly edited, updated version of the original, newly inscribed in the early third century and set up, almost certainly at a time when Athens and Troezen were once again closely allied, as a commemoration of their earlier collaboration.

Although it is certain that the Themistocles Decree was edited and many scholars are inclined to suppose it a forgery, it seems to me to be far more likely that it is for the most part authentic. That the pertinent issues were debated in and after 481 we know. That the assembly passed a decree or a series of decrees in response to the crisis is a given. That there was at the time a written record of some sort, kept as a guide for those charged with implementation, goes without saying. That this decree or set of decrees is not quoted or mentioned in any of our sources from the fifth or early fourth century merely reflects the scantiness of what survives. That, at a later time of crisis, Athenian orators should allude to and read from the decrees proposed on similar occasions by the likes of Miltiades and Themistocles, as Aeschines reportedly did in 348 when Philip of Macedon first posed a threat—this is precisely what one would expect, and the same can be said for the decision to commemorate the Themistocles Decree at the time it was inscribed on stone at Troezen. The odds are, in fact, good that the decrees proposed by Miltiades and Themistocles were mentioned with some frequency in orations no longer extant which were delivered in Athens in the late fifth and early fourth centuries on the occasion of earlier crises. What we have is clearly not a verbatim transcription of a decree proposed by Themistocles and passed by the Athenian assembly.

But it is not plausible to suppose it is simply a later invention. In matters rhetorical, verisimilitude is essential, and rough accuracy is the best guarantee of verisimilitude.[67]

The decree specifies that the women and children of Athens be lodged in Troezen, that the elderly and the movable property of the citizens be sent to Salamis, that the treasurers and priestesses remain on the acropolis to guard the things belonging to the gods, and that everyone else—including the resident aliens—man Athens' two hundred ships and drive off the barbarian in cooperation with the Lacedaemonians, the Corinthians, and any others willing to share in the danger. In this last regard, it mentions as well—in a place on the stone that would accommodate eight or nine letters but is too weathered to be readable—another Greek community already committed to the cause, perhaps the Eretrians, the Chalcidians, the Sicyonians, or the Plataeans.

The decree then directs the generals to appoint trierarchs from among those blessed with legitimate children who own homes and land in Attica and to assign to each by lot a ship to command and the requisite nautical specialists. It calls for the enlistment of ten marines, drawn from among the young men aged twenty to thirty, and four archers per ship. It arranges for the allotment of one hundred men, drawn from among the citizens and resident aliens, to each ship as rowers, and it orders that one hundred of the ships be dispatched in due course to Artemisium on the northern coast of Euboea and that one hundred lie at anchor around Salamis and along the coast of Attica to guard the territory of the Athenians. The last sentence on the part of the stone that is still readable alludes to the need for civic solidarity, provides for the recall of those who had been ostracized for a ten-year span, and orders them to go to Salamis and to remain there until the people of Athens decide what they wish to do about them.

Apart from the fact that it gibes with Herodotus' account of the decisions made in 481; confirms Aristotle's report that Aristeides, Xanthippus, and the others ostracized in the 480s were recalled from exile in the archonship of Hypsichides in 481/80;[68] and shows the Athenian democracy efficiently at work, using the lot to rule out the possibility of favoritism, the Themistocles Decree is of interest in three particulars. It points up the difficulties that Athens initially had in fully manning the triremes the assembly had ordered built. It suggests that, at this point, the Athenians still feared that their enemies on Aegina might side with Mede as they had threatened to do in 491

and that, in consequence, they thought it necessary to keep one hundred triremes in their home waters to deter attack from that quarter. And it highlights
Themistocles' foresight in a variety of ways.

It makes it clear, for example, that Themistocles had persuaded his compatriots to construct far more ships than they could themselves ever hope to
man in a war against Aegina. It suggests that he was contemplating combined
operations, that he had already held discussions with the authorities at Lacedaemon, and that he had reason to suppose that he could rely on the Spartans
and their Peloponnesian allies for infantrymen. It shows that he had already
identified as a strategic choke point—where the Persian armada might be
headed off, stopped, and possibly even destroyed—the Oreus channel lying
between the waters off the eastern coast of Magnesia and the Euboean Gulf.
This, in turn, suggests that he and the leaders of Lacedaemon were already
contemplating the possibility that, if reinforced by an Athenian fleet stationed
near the entrance to this channel at Artemisium, a comparatively small but
intrepid force of Peloponnesian hoplites, deployed at Tempe in Thessaly or,
more likely, at Thermopylae on the Gulf of Malia, might delay or even block
the advance of Xerxes' army. The Athenian statesman really was what Thucydides claimed he was: "the best predictor of things to come across the broad-
est expanse of time," who, "in a future as yet obscure, could in a preeminent
fashion foresee both better and worse."[69]

Once the Athenians had settled on a policy of armed resistance at sea,
they responded to an invitation from the Spartans and sent a delegation to
Lacedaemon to work out a common strategy with their hosts, the Corinthians, and their other prospective allies. There, as Herodotus tells us, pledges
were exchanged, and a formal alliance was forged. Then, at the suggestion of
Themistocles and with the help of a prominent Arcadian named Chileos, the
hostilities and wars that divided the Hellenes were brought to an end; and,
no doubt to the relief of all concerned, Athens and Aegina were reconciled so
that the ships of both could all be redeployed against the common enemy. It
was probably also at this time that a decision was made to conduct all such deliberations in the future in the precinct of Poseidon at the Isthmus of Corinth,
a place centrally located and much more convenient for most of the league's
members, which was to serve as the headquarters of the alliance from this
time on.

It was obvious to nearly everyone that Sparta should take the lead on
land. The Athenians, who were prepared to commit many more ships than

any other power to the league's navy, staked a claim for the leadership at sea. But the members of the league were not prepared to accept their claim, and Themistocles was not about to risk the unity of the alliance over such a matter. It is a sign of their stature and of the confidence reposed in them that, by default, the Spartans ended up at least nominally in charge on an element which they had little knowledge of or familiarity with.[70]

CHAPTER 6

Thermopylae and Artemisium

As for the Spartans, fighting each alone, they are as good as any, but fighting as a unit, they are the best of all men. They are free, but not completely free—for the law is placed over them as a master, and they fear that law far more than your subjects fear you. And they do whatever it orders—and it orders the same thing always: never to flee in battle, however many the enemy may be, but to remain in the ranks and to conquer or die.

—DEMARATUS OF SPARTA

WHEN word reached Hellas regarding Xerxes' arrival in Lydia, and the Hellenes (those then already united against the Persians) sent to Sardis spies charged with discovering the size and character of the Great King's army, they also dispatched emissaries far and wide within Hellas in search of aid. To Argos in the Peloponnesus, they sent envoys to invite the citizens of that *pólis* to join in their alliance against the Mede, and they dispatched embassies in search of aid to Corcyra in the Adriatic, to Crete well to the south of the Cyclades, and to Gelon son of Deinomenes, the tyrant of Syracuse in Sicily—whose resources were known to be considerable.[1]

These overtures made sense. Thanks to the damage done by Cleomenes and the additional losses suffered when one thousand Argive hoplites journeyed as volunteers to help defend Aegina against Athens, Argos had little at this time to offer the Hellenes in the way of soldiers or ships. But that great city was strategically important, nonetheless. As everyone realized, if the Persians were to make it as far as the Peloponnesus, the Argives could offer them a harbor and a base. The Corcyraeans were important in another fashion. They were a major maritime power, able to spare a fleet of sixty triremes. Crete was a large island, populous and replete with small cities, famous for its archers. And Syracuse was a truly great power, dominant in eastern Sicily and able, Gelon claimed, to contribute to the common Hellenic cause two hundred triremes, twenty thousand hoplites, two thousand cavalrymen, two thousand archers, two thousand slingers, and two thousand light-armed troops trained to operate in cooperation with the cavalry.[2] Had these powers been willing to rally to the cause, it would have made a considerable difference.

Three of these overtures came to naught. Of those approached, only the Corcyraeans were forthcoming. They promised help without further ado, declaring in ringing tones that their fate was inseparable from that of the rest of Greece.[3]

The Cretans were wary. They consulted the Delphic oracle, which is said to have reminded them that, hundreds of years before, in the aftermath of the Trojan War, the Greeks of the mainland had refused to help them avenge the death of Minos. On these specious grounds they justified their refusal to aid their fellow Hellenes against the Mede. The Argives, who were no less attentive to Delphi's advice, were more devious in their response. They pretended to be willing to join the coalition but only on condition that they be accorded a peace of thirty years' duration with Lacedaemon and that they be given a leadership role which, they knew perfectly well, no one—least of all, the Spartans—would find acceptable. One must wonder whether, had the Lacedaemonians called their bluff by offering them on the spot a peace of the requisite length instead of announcing merely that they were prepared to refer the matter to the assembly at Lacedaemon, the Argives might not have joined the Hellenes.[4]

Gelon—who had much, much more in the way of resources to offer than Argos—made an even more extravagant demand along the same lines. But, as he surely understood from the outset, neither the Spartans nor the Athenians were willing to accept the hegemony of a power that was not itself directly and immediately threatened by Xerxes' advance. His offer of ships, men, and horses on a magnificent scale is likely, in any case, to have been no more than a show of bravado on his part, and the ambassadors sent by the Hellenic League may have known as much. There was a reason why he had so large and up-to-date an armada. He had formidable enemies close to home, and he was not in a position to send a large fleet and army far afield. Indeed, if he made it a practice to keep tabs on his potential enemies, as he surely did, he is very likely to have been aware that the Carthaginians had for some time been making preparations for war. Moreover, if he had well-placed spies in their stronghold in North Africa, he may even have learned what the fourth-century historian Ephorus of Cumae would later report: that Xerxes and the Phoenicians had sent an embassy to Carthage more than three years before, urging that there be a Punic attack on the Hellenes in Sicily to coincide with the Persian advance into mainland Greece. There is certainly no reason to dismiss Ephorus' assertion out of hand. His report dovetails with everything that we know concerning the painstaking preparations that the Persians always made before initiating a major war; the Great King's Phoenician allies maintained cordial relations with their kindred in North Africa—and, of course, the conflict in the west that the Persians are said to have proposed to the Carthaginians did, in fact, take place at a time exceedingly convenient for the Mede.[5]

This was not all that the wily Syracusan tyrant did, and his handling of the situation deserves attention, for it was, in fact, indicative of the careful calculations in which many in Hellas were engaged at this time. When word came that Xerxes had crossed the Hellespont, Gelon dispatched to Delphi a trusted agent—a Dorian notable from the isle of Kos, just off the Asia Minor coast, who was thoroughly familiar with the protocols of the Persian court. This emissary he instructed to present to the Great King, should the Persians prove victorious, a large sum of money; and he authorized him as well to pay homage, give him earth and water, and make of his master a bondsman of this King of Kings.[6] Gelon recognized what some modern scholars resolutely refuse to concede: that the ambitions inspired by the regime imperative animating Xerxes' great venture extended well beyond the Balkan peninsula.

On the Greek mainland, outside the Peloponnesus, the Spartans, the Athenians, and their allies were also engaged in diplomacy. When they formed the Hellenic League, to discourage medizing on the part of their fellow Greeks, they took a solemn oath that they would confiscate the land of those communities which joined the Persians without being compelled to do so, sell their populations into slavery, and pay from the proceeds a tithe to the god at Delphi. This may have influenced some of the Thessalians, who had medized at the outset under pressure from the Aleuads of Larissa. In the spring of 480, when Xerxes set out for the Hellespont, those in Thessaly hostile to the Aleuads and wary of the Mede dispatched messengers to the Hellenes at the Isthmus of Corinth to ask that they send hoplites to help them prevent the Persians from entering Thessaly from Macedon, warning that otherwise they really would have to come to terms with the Great King.[7]

At Athens, news of the Thessalian overture appears to have struck a nerve. The strategy outlined by Themistocles in response to the advice given by the Delphic oracle had been grudgingly accepted, but it was—for understandable reasons—unwelcome. The Athenians of this time were farmers, not seamen, and they were attached to the land. They were prepared to evacuate Attica and had already made preliminary preparations, but they did not relish the prospect of abandoning their farms and homes to the Mede, even temporarily. Nor did they look forward with bated breath to a battle at sea near Salamis in the triremes Themistocles had thrust upon them. They were landlubbers, most of them. It was not yet the case, as it soon would be, that the Athenians were as apt to be able to swim as to read; and initially, at least, before they found themselves forced to think about taking to the sea, very few of those from the interior of Attica will have even known how to dog-paddle. If there was any way to obviate the need for an evacuation and warfare at sea by stopping the Persians on land before they even entered Greece, the Athenians were keen to give it a try.[8]

Themistocles had anticipated the need for such a venture. The fact that the Themistocles Decree presupposes an initial strategy of attempting to block the advance of the Persian fleet at Artemisium suggests that, in the 480s, its author had done a bit of traveling, that he had examined the lay of the land between Attica and Macedonia, and that he had carefully studied the most obvious of the various alternative routes that an invading army and its attendant fleet might take. There is no shortage of mountainous terrain along the way, and there are a number of choke points where one could imagine a determined hoplite force interrupting the progress of the Persian army. But, as Themistocles realized, no such effort on the part of his fellow Hellenes would be sustainable if they failed to post a fleet at or near Artemisium to prevent the Persian navy from rounding Cape Magnesia and landing thousands of marines and cavalrymen behind the Greek lines.

The odds are good that Leonidas—Cleomenes' half-brother, son-in-law, and successor as the Agiad king at Sparta—was no less well-informed than Themistocles with regard to this crucial particular. The Lacedaemonians were astute and had long been aware of the Persian threat. Their kings were charged with the homeland's defense, and they paid close attention to its approaches. We can be confident that Themistocles had held conversations regarding possible strategies of resistance with leading Spartans and Corinthians well before Demaratus tipped off his erstwhile compatriots that the Great King was about to undertake a massive invasion of Greece.[9]

The Spartans were homebodies. As we have seen, the size and character of their helot population tied them to Laconia and Messenia. They were never enthusiastic about venturing forth en masse from their fastness in the southern Peloponnesus. The prospect of making a journey to distant Thessaly cannot have fired their imaginations. Apart from the Corinthians and the islanders on Aegina, who had numerous traders in their midst, Sparta's allies in or near the Peloponnesus were farmers. As such, they were no less and, in all likelihood, even more parochial than the Lacedaemonians in their outlook. So it is no surprise that, when the Thessalians made their plea, and Themistocles, a democratic statesmen quite sensitive to the sentiments of his compatriots, urged the representatives of the Hellenes, as he must have done, to respond positively to their overtures, to test their resolve, and encourage them not to medize, the Lacedaemonians and their Peloponnesian allies did so halfheartedly. It can hardly be an accident that the Spartans sent neither Leonidas nor his Eurypontid colleague Leotychidas nor even Leonidas' younger brother Cleombrotus to lead this expedition but a polemarch, instead—a man named Euainetos son of Karenos who was, Herodotus pointedly tells us, not of royal blood.[10]

Nor is it a surprise that Themistocles himself led the Athenian contingent. The odds are, in fact, good that Athens supplied a disproportionate number of hoplites to the force of ten thousand—which rowed up through the Euboean Gulf past the narrows at Euripus to the territory of Halos in Achaea Phthiotis on the Gulf of Magnesia, joined the cavalry supplied by their Thessalian allies, and then made its way on to the Vale of Tempe, the pass that runs up from the coast into Thesssaly along the Peneus River between Mount Olympus and Mount Ossa, whence they may have sent a probe forward as far as Heracleum on the coast.[11]

The Peloponnesians might suppose that the Persians could be stopped at the Isthmus of Corinth. For the Athenians, who lived on the other side of that narrow strip of land, such dreams were not a comfort. For Themistocles, it was of paramount importance that as many of his countrymen as possible see for themselves just how many routes there were by which the Persians could make their way from Macedon into Thessaly and that they consider whether the Hellenic League could muster the manpower needed to defend all of the passes. If, as Herodotus indicates, this expeditionary force was dispatched to Thessaly months before its deployment there was necessary or even appropriate, at a time when Xerxes was still at Abydos in Asia Minor shepherding his troops across the Hellespont, it was because some thought it crucial to buck up those in and around Thessaly hostile to the Mede while others recognized

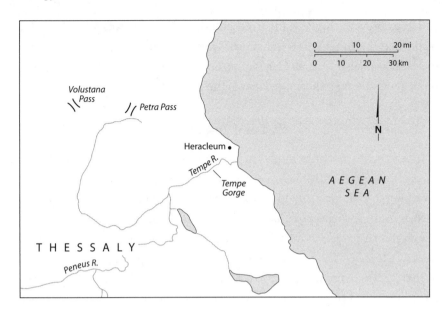

Map 13. The Passes at Tempe, Petra, and Volustana

that it was essential to Athenian morale that the defects of this particular line of defense be explored and be made manifest to all.

The expedition was short-lived, Herodotus tells us, not because the Hellenes panicked when messengers arrived from the Macedonian king Alexander son of Amyntas to tell them just how many troops and ships Xerxes had brought with him and to warn them that they would be trampled underfoot, but because they saw for themselves that there was nearby another path by which the Great King and his soldiers could conduct his army from Pieria over the shoulder of Mount Olympus and through Perrhaibia to Gonnus, upstream from the Vale of Tempe. Although Herodotus does not mention the fact, the Athenians on this expedition were probably also made aware that there were two other routes over the mountains from Macedonia into Thessaly as well—the pass at Petra between the hills of Pieria and the western reaches of Mount Olympus, and the pass at Volustana further inland. Nor does Herodotus observe, as Diodorus Siculus does, that the generals sent to Thessaly discovered shortly after their arrival that the Ainianians, Dolopians, Malians, Perrhaibians, and Magnesians really were on the side of the Mede and that only a few of the Thessalians were actually willing to put their lives on the line—but this, too, must have become evident. As Plutarch intimates, it was the recognition that the Hellenes simply did not have the means with which to prevent the Persians from entering Thessaly that, in the end, fully reconciled the Athenians to the naval strategy originally outlined by Themistocles. It was also this, as Herodotus suggests, that persuaded the Hellenes more generally that Thermopylae was the place at which to take a stand.[12]

By Land and by Sea

Xerxes was not in a hurry. According to Herodotus, after wintering in Sardis, he set out with his forces for Abydos in the spring. We are not told how long it took his army to traverse the two hundred fifty miles separating Sardis from the Hellespont, but, given that its progress was less like a forced march than a parade, it must have taken at least a month—if not, in fact, six weeks or longer—for it to make the journey. In one passage, Herodotus tells us that Xerxes' army spent seven days and seven nights working its way across the suspension bridges linking Abydos with Sestos on the European shore. In another, he asserts that the crossing occupied a month. The two passages need not be at odds—for it is perfectly possible that Xerxes and his men had to cool their heels for three weeks on the Asian shore while the Phoenicians were putting the finishing touches on the bridge for which they bore responsibility and their Egyptian rivals were doing the like. We know that their first attempt had fallen prey to a storm and that the functionaries judged responsible for the inadequacy of the two bridges were made to pay for their failure with their heads. Mindful of the dangers they now faced, their successors will have taken the greatest possible care. In any case, the Persians will have needed some time in which to marshal their army for a trek that they would have to make across each of the two bridges in something like single file. Cornelius Nepos' claim that the journey from Sardis to Athens took six months may be close to the mark.[13]

The march from Sestos to Doriscus, where Xerxes' fleet awaited his army, and, then, after an extended pause in which the Great King reviewed his forces, the trek across Thrace to the Macedonian capital at Therme (modern Thessalonica) covered a distance of three hundred miles all in all—and traversing it may have taken two months or more.[14] In their march from Sestos up the Chersonnesus to Thrace, Xerxes and his men had to squeeze through a narrow defile; and by all accounts, as we have seen, the Persian army was immense. It moved, as armies generally do, at the pace of its slowest elements; and the King of Kings was inclined to pause frequently to build roads, see the sights, make sacrifices appropriate to the occasion, and engage in the ritual feasting dictated by court protocol.[15]

There were also obstacles. One indication of their seriousness was Xerxes' decision to divide his army into three columns following different routes in the march from Doriscus to Acanthus.[16] This was no doubt done in part because it was apt to speed up the pace somewhat, but it was probably also a necessity. In high summer, even in Thrace, fresh water is in short supply; and where it is accessible, given the size of the Great King's forces, crowding could have been a problem.

Thessaly is a great garden ringed by mountains and irrigated by rivers fed by the snows on the nearby peaks. To get to it from Therme on the Macedonian coast, one must either march around the Thermaic Gulf along the shore and then leave the coast by the Vale of Tempe or journey inland within Macedonia and make one's approach from the north by one of the three routes mentioned above. The Persian army paused for a time at Therme, where Xerxes and his army could enjoy the hospitality of Alexander son of Amyntas. During this time, the Great King once again indulged his appetite for touring. One day, for example, he went on shipboard to the delta of the Peneus River to make a reconnaissance of the Vale of Tempe—not, however, because he was seriously thinking of taking this route into Thessaly. He had, we are told, already settled on another purportedly safer road. He sailed to the Peneus simply because he wanted to see the gorge.[17]

Thereafter, if the indications provided by Herodotus are correct, Xerxes journeyed up the eastern shoulder of Mount Olympus and "spent many days in Pieria while one-third of his army cleared the mountain" of debris and made the road passable for his soldiers and cavalrymen and for the carts in the baggage train bearing their provisions. It must have been at this point, when the road was fully ready, that the remainder of the army at Therme parted company with the Persian fleet and made its way toward Thessaly. Herodotus claims that the fleet was scheduled to set out from that same location eleven days after this parting of the ways. He implies that the two arms of the Great King's forces were expected to rendezvous at the Gulf of Malia, roughly one hundred forty miles over land from Therme, in something like two weeks, and he makes it clear that the advance guard of the army arrived at the appointed place three days before the fleet, which was delayed by a storm.[18] All of this makes sense—for the path over the shoulder of Olympus was much shorter than the roads running to and over the passes at Petra and Volustana.

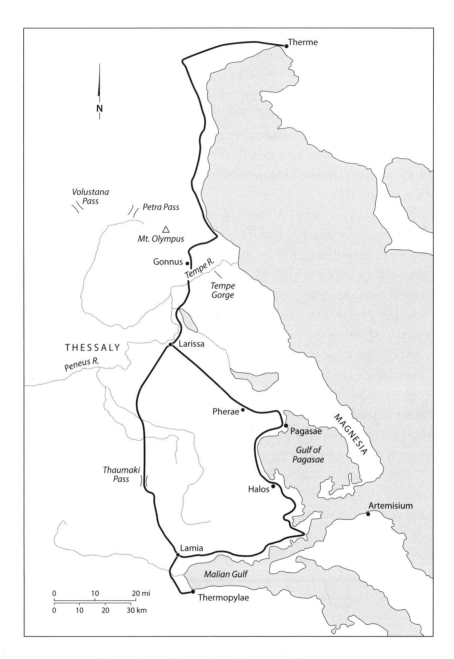

Map 14. Xerxes' Route from Therme to Thermopylae

The plains of Thessaly could far more easily and quickly be traversed than the rough road over Mount Olympus. But, in Thessaly, we can be confident, there was feasting. The Aleuads had purportedly been the first of the Greeks to medize. Regarding their enthusiasm for the Achaemenid cause there can be no doubt. Moreover, they were, by Hellenic standards, extremely wealthy and powerful; and, on the occasion of a visit by the King of Kings, never likely to be repeated, they had to be afforded an opportunity to make a memorable display of their opulence and generosity. Of this Herodotus has little to say. But he does tell one revealing anecdote confirming such a suspicion. While sojourning in Thessaly, he says, the Great King staged horse races in which the steeds of Persia demonstrated their decisive superiority over those of the Thessalians.[19] We are left with the impression that Xerxes had a certain amount of time to kill—which, we will in due course discover, he did.

On this trek away from the sea, Xerxes had no use for his fleet. To get, however, from the plains of Thessaly to those of Boeotia, one of the few places in Hellas where a large army equipped with first-rate cavalry could be deployed to full advantage, one had to make one's way back to the coast either on the road over the pass at Thaumaki down to the Gulf of Malia, which part of Xerxes' army may have taken, or by the much easier road running to that same body of water from the Aleuad stronghold at Larissa by way of Pherae, Pagasae, and the environs of Halos near the Gulf of Magnesia, which Xerxes, his bodyguard, and baggage train took.[20] Either way, one must then march around the Gulf of Malia and, then, traverse parts of eastern Locris and Phocis before entering Boeotia. There was at this time, however, a choke point on this route—a narrow shelf of land lying between the slopes of Mount Kallidromos and the waters of the Malian Gulf. Those who lived in its vicinity called it "the Gates." Because of the sulfurous springs still to be found nearby, those in Greece from more distant parts (many of them graced with "gates" of their own) referred to it as Thermopylae: "the Hot Gates."

From the territory of Trachis, just short of the western entrance to the narrows at Thermopylae, there were, to be sure, at least two other routes south. One of these ran from the Gulf of Malia up the Asopus ravine and over the Pournaraki pass. The other ran from the coast west of the Asopus over the foothills of Mount Oetae to the modern village of Duo Vhouna and, then, over the Dhema pass. Both would land a unit of soldiers in Doris, from which they could descend via the Cephisus River valley into Phocis. And, from there, they could then march on east southeast to Boeotia. Or, if they wished to out-

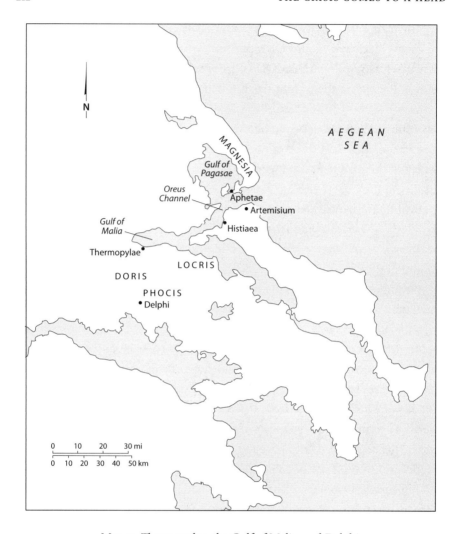

Map 15. Thermopylae, the Gulf of Malia, and Delphi

flank a force blocking the Hot Gates, they could turn north; cross into eastern
Locris via the Kleisoura pass, the Fontana pass, or the more distant pass near
Hyampolis; and make their way back to the coastal road along the Gulf of
Malia to the east of Thermopylae.

There were, however, obstacles. The entrance to the Asopus gorge is controlled by the acropolis of Trachis on cliffs immediately to the west. In the
spring, the defile is filled with rushing water. In high summer, when the flow
greatly diminishes, there are still places where one must ford the stream. Early
on, for more than three miles, the path along the ravine is rough and difficult,

littered with boulders from the cliffs above. In all seasons, it is ill suited to cavalry and impossible for a large baggage train. In places, where there are vertical walls of stone on either side, the Asopus gorge is also extremely narrow—less than five yards wide. In antiquity, it offered determined defenders ample opportunity for resistance should they dare to stand up for themselves.[21]

The road to the Dhema pass was less onerous, but it would have been difficult for cavalry and for baggage carts, and it, too, afforded defenders places in which to resist an army's advance. There is a reason why armies ordinarily made their way past Thermopylae and over one of the passes from eastern Locris into Phocis. Moreover, as it happens, the citizens of Doris and the Phocians were the only peoples in this region who had resolutely refused to medize. Of these, the latter were numerous and profoundly hostile to the Persians' Thessalian allies. When cornered, as the Thessalians had more than once learned to their great dismay, the Phocians—who had it in their power to face six thousand hoplites—could be formidable. Were a few thousand thousand of them to take a stand and fight alongside the citizens of Doris, after having occupied a position of advantage on the Asopus ravine or blocking egress from the Dhema pass, they might well prove victorious—even against a far more numerous foe.[22] As Xerxes was no doubt aware, ten years before, another group of Greeks had demonstrated that, in the absence of their cavalry, the archers of the Mede, performing their secondary function as infantrymen, could not withstand a determined effort by a phalanx of hoplites.

For the Persian army as a whole, then, there was no alternative to the route that passed through the Hot Gates. This posed a problem, which Xerxes and his commanders foresaw and attempted to forestall by way of a combined operation. If an invader intent on making his way along the main road through Thermopylae had no fleet, a comparatively small hoplite force could block his way at the narrows and with fortitude and determination stop him in his tracks. If, however, as the Persians recognized, this same invader possessed a fleet, he could easily outflank and crush those blocking his progress by landing troops on the shore to the east of the Hot Gates. But, of course, if the defenders also mounted a combined operation, if the blocking force was supported by ships of its own, capable of preventing the disembarkation of the invader's soldiers, the gates could be kept closed. Well before Xerxes even got to Sardis, his agents had learned what it was that he would need if he was successfully to invade Greece, and this is one of the reasons why the King of Kings had brought with him so many triremes and horse transports. In consequence, upon their arrival in the territory of Trachis, just short of the narrows at Thermopylae, Xerxes' advance guard built a camp for his army near the river Spercheios; and there he waited for his fleet to appear.[23]

The time of Xerxes' arrival was in one respect propitious. Ten years before, quite possibly to the day, Datis and Artaphernes had beached their ships at Marathon and had begun unloading their horses from the transports designed for their conveyance. On that occasion, as we have noted, the Persians had reached the place where they were most likely to meet resistance at a moment when the Spartans, the most formidable of their likely opponents, were otherwise occupied and temporarily unavailable while celebrating the nine-day festival of the Carneia. The same can be said with regard to Xerxes' arrival at Thermopylae. It, too, coincided with the Carneia. Moreover, this time the Persians arrived at the place where their progress was most likely to be contested at a moment when the Greeks in general were preoccupied with their quadrennial celebration over four days of the Olympic Games, which would soon be under way.[24]

It is hard to believe that this coincidence was an accident. Lightning rarely strikes the same place twice. This time, moreover, we know the name of at least one man in the Great King's entourage who will have been fully informed concerning the Spartan religious calendar and the timetable for the contests in Olympia. His name was Demaratus. He was himself an Olympic victor,[25] and, as we have had occasion to note, he had for many years been a king at Lacedaemon. If the Great King of Persia conducted his march from the Hellespont in the manner of a royal progress at an elephantine pace, if he dawdled on the road from Therme to Thermopylae, it was arguably in part because he really did have time that he needed to kill.

In another respect, however, Xerxes' time of arrival was anything but propitious. Ten years before, Datis and Artaphernes had paid a heavy price for putting off their attack on Athens until quite late in the summer. The Aegean was then no longer safe, and the weather was about to undergo a seasonal change rendering travel by sea considerably more perilous. This meant, among other things, that in Attica Darius' generals had had to press for an immediate decision and could not, when things went awry at Marathon, have tarried in the hopes that they could find an opening.

Xerxes paid a far greater price. Because he had deliberately taken so much time, his fleet, which was making its way from the Gulf of Therme south along the coast of Magnesia, was left dangerously exposed. Once his ships had passed the delta of the Peneus River, there were no safe harbors on its route. There were no protected bays of any size on which to beach those ships. In good weather, this would not matter much. In a pinch, one could anchor one's ships off shore. All that it would take, however, to drive Xerxes' vast armada of triremes and horse transports and the even larger fleet of supply ships onto Magnesia's unforgiving coast was a Hellesponter from the northeast, and late August and September, the period in which the Carneia was ordinarily celebrated, was a time of the year in which such storms were by no means rare.

Herodotus does not tell us that Xerxes or his commanders had the crews of his triremes haul their ships out of the water at Therme to dry and to careen them so that they could have the barnacles scraped off and be recaulked and recoated with pitch, as the oarsmen and their colleagues had done at Doriscus. But we can presume that they did so as they waited for the day appointed for their departure, and on both occasions they no doubt unloaded the horse transports to enable the cavalrymen accompanying the fleet to exercise their mounts. Eleven days after the main body of Xerxes' army marched out from that city,[26] this majestic fleet set out on what, everyone presumed, would be a two- or three-day journey, which would, they calculated, get them to the Gulf of Malia just as the first elements in Xerxes' army reached the western gate at Thermopylae.

According to Diodorus Siculus—who was presumably following the fourth-century historian Ephorus of Cumae, as was his wont—the commander directing the fleet's progress down the Magnesia coast and commanding it in the battle that followed was Darius' cousin Megabates, the admiral whose mishandling of the expedition against Naxos twenty years before had set off the Ionian Revolt. This possibility cannot be ruled out—for, though no longer young, this Megabates was still a presence. He shows up in the tablets found at Persepolis, where he is described as an admiral; and, in the immediate aftermath of the Persian War, he briefly becomes visible again at Dascyleium, where he had apparently been ensconced for some time as the satrap of Hellespontine Phrygia. It is also conceivable that Ephorus had in mind Megabates' son Megabazos, whom Xerxes is said by Herodotus to have placed in charge of his fleet—alongside three other members of the same generation: the Great King's own half-brother Ariabignes, his full brother Achaemenes, and Prexaspes, the son of Darius' quiver-bearer Aspathines.[27]

On the penultimate day of its journey, after the fleet had rowed the seventy-mile stretch of the Thermaic Gulf past the delta of the Peneus River and on to the coast of Magnesia, it stopped for the night (no doubt at the direction of Megabates or his son Megabazos) and sought shelter somewhere between the city of Kasthaneia and the Sepias shore—either at a single long beach large enough to accommodate one thousand three-hundred twenty-seven triremes, probably that of Ayiókambos, which is over six miles long; or at a series of small beaches further south. The first triremes to arrive their crews moored to the shore itself. Those which came thereafter had to anchor further out. In places, Herodotus tells us, they were anchored eight rows deep—almost certainly in what is now called a Mediterranean moor, with the sterns of the ships in each succeeding row lodged between and lashed to the prows of ships in the preceding row.[28]

This is how things stood, when at daybreak, a Hellesponter struck. Those who had moored their triremes close to the shore were able to pull the twenty- to twenty-five-ton vessels up on the beach. There was no room for the triremes anchored further out, which slammed against one another or broke loose entirely. Some of the latter were dashed on the rocks at the limestone caves called the Ovens of Pelion. Others were thrown on the beach or wrecked at the strand of Sepias and at the towns of Meliboia and Kasthaneia, as the storm continued to rage and the Etesian winds to blow for a total of three long days.[29]

Herodotus tells us that the Persians started out with one thousand two hundred seven triremes and picked up one hundred twenty more from Thasos and the Greek cities scattered along the Thracian shore in the Chalcidice and elsewhere. Of these, he was told, four hundred were lost in the course of this storm, and the number of merchantmen and other ships lost at the same time he describes as incalculable.[30] Even if all of these numbers are inflated, these losses must have been a terrible blow.

When the remnants of Xerxes' fleet rounded Cape Magnesia and slipped through the passage between the island of Sciathus and the mainland, a Hellenic fleet was waiting for them on the shore opposite—moored to the beach, roughly ten miles long, at Artemisium (now called Pevki Bay). This site lay in the territory of Histiaea on the island of Euboea a few miles from the entrance to the Oreus channel, which leads on to the Gulf of Malia. More than a month before, when the delegates of the Hellenes at the Isthmus of Corinth had learned that Xerxes had set out from Therme and was working his way through Pieria, they had dispatched a small holding force under the command of Leonidas, the Agiad king of Lacedaemon, to occupy the narrows at

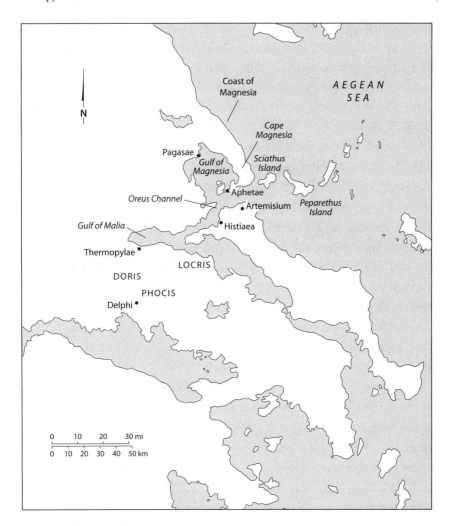

Map 16. Cape Magnesia, Artemisium, the Gulf of Magnesia, and the Gulf of Malia

Thermopylae, and they had sent a fleet under the command of the Spartan navarch Eurybiades son of Eurycleides to Artemisium to prevent the Persian fleet from landing soldiers on the south shore of the Gulf of Malia to the east of the Hot Gates. This was to be a combined operation, and it required coordination. To this end, the two commanders from Lacedaemon appear to have arranged that each should have a triaconter or the like at his disposal by which to convey messages to the other across the forty miles of water in between Artemisium and the port at Alpenus just to the east of the Hot Gates.[31]

Initially, the Greek fleet consisted of two hundred seventy-one triremes.

With the help of the Plateaeans—men "with no experience of seamanship, moved by virtue and a spirited eagerness"—the Athenians managed to man one hundred twenty-seven of these with something like twenty-five thousand four hundred men, and they supplied twenty additional triremes to be manned by the citizens of Chalcis—men, Herodotus specifies, of Ionian, not Athenian, stock.[32]

In manning ships and, even more emphatically, in providing ships, no other Greek community came even close to the Athenians. The Corinthians fielded forty triremes; the Megarians, twenty; the Aeginetans, eighteen; the Sicyonians, twelve; the Lacedaemonians, ten; the Epidaurians, eight; the Eretrians, seven; the Troezenians, five; the Styrians, two; and the Ceans, another two. In addition, the Ceans sent two penteconters, and the Locrians of Opuntia, an additional seven. It is no wonder that, in formulating the orders he issued, the Spartan navarch Eurybiades was wont to take direction from Themistocles, the Athenian commander.[33] He could not afford to ignore the wishes of the man responsible for constructing and supplying more than half of the ships under his command, and the odds are good that initially he knew next to nothing about seamanship himself.

As always, the Persians had been methodical. At some point, probably not more than a week after Xerxes' departure from Therme, Megabates or his son Megabazos had sent ten of the Great King's fastest ships down the Magnesian coast in the direction of Sciathus to reconnoiter. En route, they encountered three Greek triremes—one from Troezen, one from Aegina, and one from Attica—probably the fastest in the Hellenic fleet that had recently arrived at Artemisium. These were on patrol well to the north of their base at Sciathus; and, as the Persian triremes approached, they fled, and—no doubt to the consternation of the observers posted by the Hellenes on the peaks of Sciathus—two of the three were overrun and captured while the third fled out of sight to the mouth of the Peneus, where its crew abandoned the ship, moved inland with alacrity, and made their way overland to Attica. In the aftermath of this skirmish, three of the Persian triremes proceeded to the channel between Sciathus and Magnesia—where, on a dangerous reef called Myrmex, they erected a stone pillar as a warning signal for the fleet preparing to sail from Therme. With their prisoners and the three Hellenic triremes captured, the remaining seven returned to Therme, where, we can presume, the prisoners were interrogated, tortured, and forced to reveal everything that they knew about the Hellenic fleet.[34]

According to Herodotus, the news of this encounter, conveyed to the Hellenes at Artemisium by fire beacons lit by lookouts posted on the peaks of Sciathus, unsettled Eurybiades, who pulled the Hellenic fleet back from Artemisium to Chalcis to guard the narrows at Euripus.[35] This judgment may be correct. If so, it suggests a certain blindness on the part of the Spartan navarch. If the Persians were to achieve mastery of the seas in the vicinity of the Gulf of Malia, when Xerxes and his army appeared, Leonidas and his men would not stand a chance.

Alternatively, Herodotus may not have fully digested the evidence at his disposal. To be precise, he may not have fully grasped that Leonidas and Eurybiades were conducting a combined operation and that the ground forces at Thermopylae and the naval forces at Artemisium were interdependent. We can be confident, however, that Eurybiades and his advisors—above all, Themistocles—understood this perfectly well. For their withdrawal, they may well have had another, better motive than the one Herodotus suggests.

The commanders at Artemisium may not have had intelligence concerning the Persian fleet that they trusted. They knew what Alexander son of Amyntas had conveyed to those in charge of the expeditionary force sent to Tempe—Themistocles had been among the recipients—and subsequently the Macedonian monarch may have sent the Athenians the order of battle drawn up on Xerxes' behalf at Doriscus. But they cannot have fully reposed confidence in their informant. He had done the Athenians important favors in the past, but he was also a native satrap within the Persian empire. He had a foreign master to serve. In any case, what they had gleaned from his testimony and from other reports must have persuaded them that they might be badly outnumbered. Xerxes had not yet arrived at Thermopylae, and there was no reason to expect him to arrive there soon. In the meantime, if the sudden appearance of the ten Persian triremes was a harbinger of the arrival of the Persian fleet and if they could lure that fleet into the comparatively narrow channel between the Greek mainland and the island of Euboea, they might be able to force a fight right away in circumstances in which greater numbers would not yield an advantage. That Themistocles was already thinking along such lines seems likely.

The weather may also have been a consideration. It was already early September—the beginning of a season in which storms become more common in the Aegean. The Greeks were well aware of the danger; and, as the heat built up and the atmosphere grew heavy, they could sometimes sense a storm coming on. At Artemisium, which faced north, the Hellenes would have been exposed to the full force of a Hellesponter. This they knew. The beach there was long, to be sure; and, in such circumstances, it would have been possible for them to drag or even carry their triremes (immensely heavy though they were) further up on the sand. In the bay at Chalcis, however, they would be sheltered from the Etesian winds by the headland at Euripus, just to the north, which juts out from Euboea toward the mainland. Moreover, in the channel to the south there was ample room in which to practice maneuvers. They could hardly defeat a fleet that was larger if they were not themselves exceedingly well trained.

The Hellenes might appear to have had another option. Had the sole aim of their fleet been to prevent the Persian fleet from coming to the support of Xerxes at Thermopylae, it would, one might suppose, have made better sense for it to have established its base at Histiaea than at Artemisium. After all, Histiaea was a real city, where provisions could much more easily be obtained. Moreover, it lay inside the channel of Oreus, considerably closer than Artemisium to the Gulf of Malia and to Thermopylae itself, and the straits on which it lay were much narrower than the channel running between the peninsula of Magnesia and Artemisium. If a battle were to take place deep within the channel of Oreus, the size of the Persian armada would not have given it a decisive advantage.

This option, alluring though it might seem to the modern imagination, had one grave drawback. Had the Greeks left Artemisium unoccupied, the Mede could have used it as a base for unloading a powerful force of archers, infantrymen, and cavalry able to seize the great island on which Histiaea was to be found, and then they could have excluded the Hellenic navy from that and every other Euboean port. Moreover, the Greeks had two missions that they had to weigh against one another—protecting Leonidas and preserving their fleet for future use, if need be, further south. When viewed in this light, Artemisium was clearly for them the better spot. From it, one could escape in either of two different directions: east and out to the open sea or west down the channel of Oreus to the Gulf of Euboea and then south past Euripus to Attica and the Saronic Gulf. Moreover, if the Greeks, situated at Artemisium, were to put lookouts atop the mountains on Sciathus within sight of Artemisium— as we know they did—these lookouts could employ fire beacons, as was the practice, to issue a warning if a detachment of the Persian fleet were to row between Sciathus and Peparethus and head for the eastern coast of Euboea in order to circumnavigate the island, approach the Gulf of Malia from the south, and set a trap for anyone situated in the channel of Oreus. It is, in fact, conceivable that, before retreating to Chalcis, Eurybiades and his colleagues misinterpreted fire signals from Sciathus and presumed that the Persians were doing what they most feared and that they withdrew southward in order to intercept what they took to be a force circumnavigating Euboea.

Later, when the Hellesponter came, the Greeks who had pulled back to Chalcis must have thought their earlier withdrawal a brilliant, or at least a lucky, stroke. Moreover, on the storm's second day, we are told, lookouts posted by Eurybiades on the mountains of Euboea climbed down and sought out their commander to inform him of the violence of the storm and to report that great damage had been done the Persian armada.[36] Herodotus does not indicate to us how they could have learned this. There is no place on the island of Euboea from which one can see past the mountains along the eastern coast of Magnesia to the waters below along its shore. Perhaps, however, the Greeks still had lookouts on Sciathus, and their counterparts on Euboea had seen and this time correctly interpreted their fire signals. Or perhaps the lookouts in Euboea saw numerous wrecks driven south through the channel between Sciathus and the mainland on the current produced by that magnificent storm.

In the interim, Leonidas may also have sent Eurybiades a message by ship, informing him that Xerxes had arrived. In any case, as soon as the storm abated, the Spartan navarch conducted the Hellenic fleet back past Euripus up the Euboean Gulf and through the Oreus Channel to its former post at Artemisium, hoping and even expecting that very few of the enemy ships had escaped damage.[37] They cannot have arrived much before the time when the remnants of the Persian fleet sailed through the channel between Sciathus and the mainland, carefully avoiding the Myrmex reef.

One squadron within what remained of the Persian fleet was in for a surprise. Communications within that force of many disparate tongues were imperfect; and the fifteen ships of divers origins making up this particular unit set out later than the others. When this squadron slipped past Sciathus, rounded Cape Magnesia, and sighted the Greek fleet across the channel at Artemisium in the glare of the sun, it mistook it for the Persian armada and sailed unwittingly right into the hands of the Hellenes. As a consequence, before sending their prisoners off to the Isthmus of Corinth, the interrogators employed by Eurybiades and his subordinate commanders learned everything that they needed to know—including the fact that, despite the Persian losses, their fleet was still enormous.[38]

By this time, Xerxes had been camped below Trachis for three days. While he was in Thessaly, the Great King had heard that a small army had gathered at Thermopylae and that it was led by a Heraclid from Lacedaemon named Leonidas. Shortly after his arrival in the territory of Trachis, he had sent a scout forward to reconnoiter. When the man returned, he reported that he had been unable to get an accurate count of the enemy army but that he had seen an exceedingly strange sight. There was, he said, a wall stretching across the pass. In front of this wall, there were men unclothed, exercising and combing their long hair, and they had paid him no heed. Herodotus reports that Xerxes then consulted Demaratus, who explained that the naked men with the long hair were Spartans and that it was their custom to comb their locks when they were about to risk their lives.[39]

By this time, Leonidas had been at Thermopylae for some weeks. He had examined the ground on which he intended to fight with consummate care, and he may even have conducted exploratory raids into the territory beyond, where Xerxes would make his camp. At the defile constituting Thermopylae, there were, in fact, three gates—a narrow place to the west near the Phoenix River wide enough for a single wagon, another to the east near Alpenus of similar breadth, and a third, about fifty feet wide, in the middle. At the middle gate, where the pass was less narrow than it was at the eastern and western gates, the Kallidromos massif was sheer and there was no possibility, as there was at the other two gates, that an opposing force could send a unit to climb up the hillside and manage to outflank those in the flats below obstructing their progress. There, at the middle gate, many years before, the Phocians had built a wall to contain the Thessalians, and it was this wall that Leonidas had had his men restore.[40]

The Agiad king had with him as a royal bodyguard three hundred Spartiates—the customary number. But these *hippeîs* differed from the norm in one particular. Mindful of the words of the oracle issued at Delphi to Lacedaemon's *Púthioi,* predicting that it would take the death of a Heraclid king to save Sparta from its Perseid claimant, Leonidas had, according to Herodotus, selected this body of three hundred from among the *néoi* at Sparta with living sons. This report dovetails closely with Diodorus' claim that Leonidas took with him a total of one thousand Lacedaemonians and refused to take more because he expected them all to die, and it fits as well with Plutarch's asser-

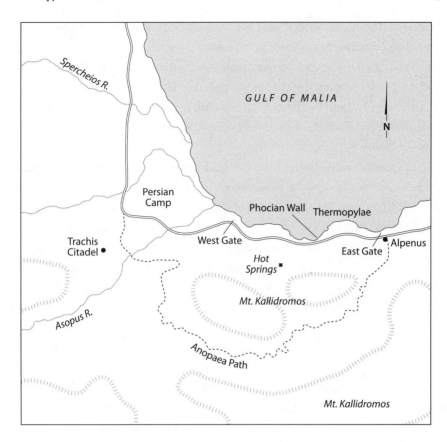

Map 17. Thermopylae and the Anopaea Path

tion that those who accompanied the Agiad king celebrated their own funeral games before departing.[41]

In addition, Leonidas had brought with him two thousand eight hundred hoplites from the Peloponnesus: five hundred from Tegea and a similar number from Mantineia, one hundred twenty from Orchomenos, another thousand from the rest of Arcadia, four hundred from Corinth, two hundred from Phlius, and eighty from Mycenae. Of the Boeotians, the Thespians, who had resolutely refused to medize, sent seven hundred hoplites, as many heavy infantrymen as they had; and the Thebans—who appear to have taken the Persian side at the time of Marathon, to have quickly given earth and water once again in 481, and to have come under pressure from Lacedaemon in 480—dispatched a token force of four hundred hoplites. This body of men was drawn, we are told, from among the minority in the ruling order at Thebes

hostile to the Mede; and it was led by a distinguished Theban named Leontiades, who, like his offspring, may have been closely associated with the
Spartans. The Opuntian Locrians, who had medized, and the Phocians, who
had not, also responded to Leonidas' call. The latter sent one thousand men
to Thermopylae, and the former came in full force—almost certainly with the
same number, although one source credits them with sending five or even six
times as many.[42]

   In comparison with the force fielded by Xerxes, the Hellenes at Thermopylae were few. They were, however, an advance guard. They saw their task
as a holding operation, and they had every reason to believe that, as soon as
the Carneia and the Olympic Games were over, ample reinforcements would
arrive to spell them and, from a base in Boeotia, prevent them from being
outflanked. When the Persians descended upon them while the first of these
festivals was already under way and the second was about to begin, there was
consternation in the ranks. But the Phocians and the Locrians, who had the
most to lose, insisted that they attempt to hold the Hot Gates until the reinforcements arrived, and Leonidas, who dispatched messengers immediately
to ask the cities to the south for help, stood firm.[43]

   By this time, to be sure, one of the citizens of Trachis had made the Spartan king aware of the so-called Anopaea path—which begins a mile or so east
of the Asopus River, running initially into the high country between Mount
Oeta and Mount Kallidromos, then turns east up one of the two ridges of the
latter mountain and through a well-watered upland plateau, then northeast
and finally north by a circuitous route that winds down to the ancient village
of Alpenus. But it was by no means certain that the Persians would discover
it, and Leonidas took precautions against this possibility by posting one thousand Phocian hoplites to guard it.

   That should have been sufficient. The path was broad, as mountain paths
go, and not especially steep. But, by determined Greek hoplites ranged in
phalanx against footsoldiers on the Persian model, it could easily have been
defended. Moreover, apart from the Locrians of Opuntia—who had medized,
promised to secure Thermopylae for the King of Kings, and then, no doubt to
the consternation and fury of the Persians, turned coat—none of the Greeks
present had a greater stake in stopping the Persians than the Phocians—who
had no doubt dispatched a much larger force to join the citizens of Doris in
blocking the road over the Dhema pass.[44] Entrusting the Anopaea path to the
Phocians and the Phocians alone was nonetheless a mistake. Had Leonidas

dispatched ten of the Spartiates in his bodyguard to supervise the Phocian militia, impose a measure of discipline upon them, and put steel into their spines, the outcome of the struggle at Thermopylae might well have been different.

The strategy of the Hellenes at Thermopylae and Artemisium was sensible. The two locations were, as we have seen, roughly forty miles apart, and provision, in the form of vessels capable of carrying messages back and forth, had been made to sustain communications between them. If the Greek navy could prevent the Persians from becoming masters of the sea in those parts, and if Leonidas' little army could prevent them from breaking through, the war could be won at this choke point.

Xerxes' weakness lay in his strength. The army that had overawed everyone it encountered prior to Thermopylae was its own worst enemy. It was immense. Just how immense it was we do not know with any precision—but this does not matter, for it certainly was large enough that the logistics involved posed problems almost insuperable.[45] When Xerxes left Macedon for Thessaly, he left behind the food that he had stored in massive amounts at various points along the way in anticipation of the difficulties he would face, and he departed from his fleet and the merchantmen, who were his other source of supply. In Thessaly—which was well watered, fertile, and exceedingly productive—he had no doubt been able to rely for provision on his hosts. But when he departed Thessaly for Achaea Phthiotis and Malia, he left all that behind, and he entered a region in which, as Herodotus points out, fresh water was not abundant in high summer. Until he was able once again to make contact with his fleet, his army had to subsist on the food its members could transport on pack animals, on wagons, and on their own backs. Until that army passed through the Hot Gates—though the river Spercheios, where Xerxes must have established his main camp, never ran fully dry even in high summer—water was apt to be in short supply. How long the Great King's soldiers could hold out is a matter for conjecture, but it is certain that they could not manage for very long. Delay might well mean defeat.[46]

That was one problem. There was another. On the eighteenth of September in this particular year, the moon would be full and the Carneia and the Olympic Games would come to an end.[47] Soon thereafter, reinforcements would be on their way from the Peloponnesus to the Greeks at Thermopylae. If Eurybiades could somehow keep the Persian fleet at bay and if Leonidas could hold out until the reinforcements arrived, Xerxes would have to turn back, and the onset of fall, which was fast approaching, would force his fleet to do so as well. In the face of mass dehydration and starvation, magnificence and grandeur quickly lose their luster.

Three Days in September

Initially, the Greek fleet did well. After the great storm, when the remnants of the Persian armada finally straggled around Cape Magnesia, Herodotus tells us that this multinational force went directly to "the gulf leading to Pagasae," which he also calls the Gulf of Magnesia. There they anchored at a place called Aphetae, the embarkation point from which Jason and the Argonauts are said to have set out. Elsewhere, however, he indicates that the rowers in the fleets at Aphetae and Artemisium could see the ships of their opponents anchored across the water.[48] For this to be the case, however, Aphetae would have to have been located outside the Gulf of Magnesia on the south coast of the peninsula of Magnesia at the Bay of Plataniá, roughly ten miles across the channel from Artemisium.

Herodotus' confusion in this regard may have arisen from the fact that the surviving triremes, penteconters, triaconters, horse transports, and the supply ships supporting them were simply too many to be accommodated at Plataniá. Initially, one can imagine that the trierarchs in charge of the triremes were eager to find shelter from storms, which would explain their eagerness to reach the Gulf of Magnesia. Soon, however, Xerxes' admirals will have insisted that as many of their warships as could safely be moored to the strand at Plataniá Bay should be posted there, where they could keep an eye on the Greek fleet. But, unless these men were once again willing to resort to the Mediterranean moor, Plataniá could accommodate no more than one hundred triremes. There is no reason to dismiss out of hand the later report that the Persian fleet was divided among a number of anchorages.[49] It was a necessity dictated by the lay of the land.

Herodotus tells us that the Persian fleet arrived early in the afternoon on the day after the storm ended. He then crowds into the remainder of that day a series of events for which there cannot have been time. This was surely the day when the squadron of fifteen fell into the hands of the Athenians. But one must doubt whether the men manning the Persian fleet were in any shape at this point to do much more than to begin refitting the ships that had been damaged, to lick their wounds, and ponder their options.[50]

On the other side of the channel, there were, the Athenians noticed, not only a multitude of ships but a great many footsoldiers as well. Strictly speaking, there was no Persian navy. It consisted of a host of independent units. In most cases, the ships were furnished and manned by subject maritime peoples—such as the Egyptians, Cypriots, Phoenicians, Cilicians, Pamphylians, and Carians as well as the Greeks of the Chalcidice, the Thracian coast, and perhaps the Black Sea. In other cases, the Persians had triremes built; and, when needed, subject peoples with a record of infidelity—such as the Greeks of Asia Minor and the Aegean islands—were called on to provide the crews. In truth, the loyalty of all these peoples was uncertain, and Xerxes was not a trusting soul. So he arranged for there to be thirty marines of Iranian descent on each and every trireme in addition to the fourteen or so ordinarily supplied by the peoples manning the oars.[51]

The sheer size of the opposing force gave the Hellenes a start; and, late that afternoon and into the evening, they debated whether once again to pull back from Artemisium. Needless to say, the prospect upset the Euboeans in their midst, who pressed Eurybiades to delay so that they could evacuate from their cities their children and the elderly. When this did not work, Herodotus tells us, they offered Themistocles thirty talents (.855 tons) of silver in return for his persuading the Greeks to remain and fight. He then reportedly bribed the Spartan navarch with five talents and Adeimantus son of Ocytus, the Corinthian commander, with an additional three and kept the change. They all then resolved to stay and see what they could accomplish in a fight at sea.[52]

Some scholars doubt the veracity of Herodotus' tale, and they suggest that he was sold a bill of goods by his Alcmaeonid friends and by Athenians of a later time who were hostile to the Spartans. Herodotus did not, they argue, fully appreciate the relationship between what was going on at Thermopylae and what was taking place at Artemisium. As long as Leonidas was holding the Persians back, it was incumbent on the Hellenic fleet to deny its Persian counterpart free access to the Gulf of Malia, and everyone associated with the venture understood as much.

On this last point, Herodotus' critics are, of course, right. But it is important to remember that the commanders of the fleet were not expected to attempt the impossible. Indeed, if they were not in a position to put the Persian fleet out of commission, it was their duty to avoid unnecessary risks and keep their own fleet intact and available for later use. The proper subject for discussion that afternoon and evening was the question whether there was any hope at all that the Hellenes could defeat the Persians in the channel running between the peninsula of Magnesia and the island of Euboea, and this is no doubt precisely what they discussed. We must also keep in mind Themistocles' reputation for wiliness. It is hard to believe, given what we know of the man, that he would have spurned the Euboeans' offer—especially if he was already inclined to stay and fight. One could do a great deal with twenty-two talents (five-eighths of a ton) of silver, and Themistocles knew it.

The next day, when they had a better idea where they stood, Megabates or his son Megabazos is said to have devised a plan to catch the Greeks at Artemisium in a trap. To this end, he sent two hundred triremes back in the direction of Sciathus, with orders to slip behind the island and row out to sea where they could not be observed, then to turn south along the eastern coast of Euboea, circumnavigate the island, and come up the Gulf of Euboea to the Euripus and beyond. There, he supposed, the Greek fleet could be finished off should it be defeated in the vicinity of the channel of Oreus and flee down the long passage separating Euboea from the Greek mainland.[53]

This was an audacious enterprise. The eastern coast of Magnesia is fifty miles long—twice the length of the lee shore at Mount Athos that had done so much damage to the fleet of Mardonius in 492. The eastern coast of Euboea is no less forbidding, and it is more than one hundred miles in length. Given the season, the risk that there would be another mishap was high—so high, in fact, that some scholars are incredulous.[54]

What one can say in defense of Herodotus and Diodorus Siculus, however, is that the circumnavigation made good strategic sense and that the vast size of the Persian armada was an invitation to take what would otherwise be considered unreasonable risks. If the ships were lost, it did little to alter the military balance. But, if they actually made it to Euripus, Xerxes' admirals had good reason to believe that they themselves could carry out the Great King's instructions to the letter. Not one Greek trireme was to be allowed to get away. Such were their orders. "No one," Herodotus tells us, paraphrasing in Greek the Persian original, "not even, as they put it, a fire-bearer—was to be allowed to escape alive."[55]

In this situation, it made sense for those serving in the Persian fleet to bide their time, continue work on refitting those of their ships that had sustained damage during the storm, and wait for word that the two hundred

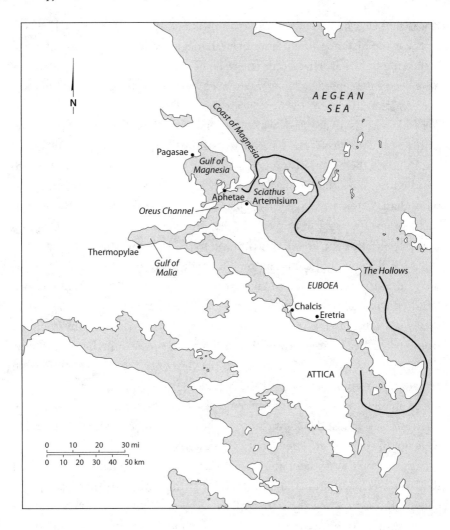

Map 18. The Persian Circumnavigation of Euboea

triremes had reached Euripus. In the meantime, we are told, the Great King's commanders counted their ships and took stock of their losses.[56]

The Greeks at Artemisium had expected the Persian fleet to attack. When it failed to do so, they were puzzled. Soon, however, a defector made his way across the channel from Aphetae. His name was Scyllias, and he hailed from Scione in the Chalcidice. He was famous as a diver; and, after the storm, he had reportedly helped the Persians recover some of their lost property from the seabed. It is not clear how he crossed the channel from Plataniá, however.

It was said that he had swum the ten miles, and this story may well be cor-rect. For the distance would have been manageable for such a man, and had he taken a boat—as, Herodotus suggests, he did—he would almost certainly have been intercepted. Scyllias might even have made the swim for the most part under water, as was claimed. For the Greeks had snorkels of a sort, as Aristotle reports. In any case, while the Persian commanders were conducting a muster and counting ships, this native of the Chalcidice was spelling out to the Hellenes the extent of the Persian losses and telling them about the two hundred triremes making their way around Euboea. This information was more than merely welcome. It was precious, and the Greeks recognized it as such. When the wars were over, the Amphictyons would erect at Delphi a statue celebrating this man's contribution to the Hellenic cause.[57]

After discussing the matter, the Greeks decided to withdraw in the mid-dle of the night and situate themselves where they could confront the two hundred triremes when they came in sight. They feared being attacked while they were withdrawing, and they were not in a hurry. The circumnavigation would take at least three days. This they knew. In the interim, however—now that they knew how much damage the Hellesponter had done the Persian armada and were informed that the surviving fleet had been temporarily re-duced in size by two hundred triremes—they decided, at the insistence of Themistocles, to test the competence of the crews who remained. The Greeks were not likely to be afforded a better occasion.

They waited until late afternoon to draw their opponents out. Mindful that they were outnumbered and fearful that they might be outclassed, they chose a moment when the Persian fleet, dispersed at various anchorages as it was, would not have time to muster as a whole and when there would not be occasion for more than a skirmish. Their aim was to engage the triremes ranged along the beach at Aphetae and those nearby and to inflict on them an unexpected defeat before the triremes lodged within the Gulf of Magnesia could rally and make an appearance.[58]

As it turned out, both fleets were well prepared. The Athenians had been working on their seamanship without respite for almost a year, and the Greek fleet as a whole had been practicing joint maneuvers for some weeks. The Per-sian crews had had ample opportunity to do the like in the spring when the fleet gathered at Phocaea and Cumae and later during their extended sojourns in the vicinity of Doriscus and Therme.

The tactical approaches of the two fleets differed. The triremes of the Persian fleet were fully decked, and the ships were manned by something on the order of forty-four marines, as we have seen. Their principal *modus operandi* was to fight land battles at sea by pulling alongside an enemy trireme, grappling the two boats together, bombarding and boarding the other craft, and seizing it by force. In contrast, most, if not all, of the triremes in the Greek fleet were only partially decked, which suggests that Themistocles' triremes may already at this time have been equipped with outriggers in the manner of the Athenian triremes of the late fifth and fourth centuries. On their decks, the Greek ships carried ten to fourteen hoplites and a handful of archers, and they had been practicing maneuvers and wanted to confront the barbarian and see whether they could defend themselves against the *diékplous*.[59]

The barbarian fleet fell into the trap. When the Hellenes rowed toward them, Megabates or his son Megabazos had the enemy crews row out, thinking their outnumbered opponents daft. Initially, there was skirmishing, and the Greeks, who had the jump on their opponents, did quite well. In time, however, the Persians managed to gather a sizable force. Taking advantage of their superiority in numbers, their triremes swarmed around the Greek ships and carried out a maneuver which appears to have been called the *períplous*—in which they surrounded the Greek fleet and rowed one behind another around it in a circle, gradually reducing the circumference so that the enemy triremes would be forced back into a smaller and smaller space and eventually run afoul of one another in such a manner that their helmsmen would lose control over their craft. The Greeks responded by forming, when a prearranged signal was given, what was called a *kúklos*—engaging in an exceedingly difficult maneuver that they must have frequently practiced in advance. Each trireme backed water so that their sterns formed a circle. Then, as the Persian fleet tightened the *períplous* and drew nearer, the Greek ships, when a second prearranged signal was given, suddenly shot forward en masse and attempted to hull the ships of their opponents. When the skirmish was over, the Persians had lost to the Hellenes thirty triremes, and they were no longer contemptuous. It was at this point that Antidorus of Lemnos defected with his trireme to the Greeks. He was the first of the Greek trierarchs in the Persian fleet to switch sides.[60]

While the Persian commanders at Aphetae were lamenting the loss of a skirmish, Xerxes was doing the same at Thermopylae. For four days after his arrival at Trachinian Malis, he and his men had endured winds and heavy rain; and there, temporarily incapacitated, they had waited for the fleet and the rest of his army to arrive. In the course of these days, he is said to have sent a herald to invite the Greeks at the middle gate to lay down their arms, go home, and become allies of the Persians, promising them what the Great King nearly always promised: that, if they did all of this, they would be given territories larger and better than the ones they already possessed. Leonidas reportedly rejected the offer. In fact, if Plutarch is to be believed, when the herald conveyed the Persian monarch's request that the Greeks hand over their arms, the Spartan king responded with a challenge. If you want our weapons, he calmly replied, "Come take them!"[61] And so on the fourth day—probably the morning after one of the fastest boats in his fleet had come from Aphetae to announce its arrival—that is what Xerxes tried to do.

Herodotus tells us that he ordered the Medes and Cissians out against the Greeks and that he instructed them to bring the enemy hoplites back alive and conduct them into his presence. We are also told that the Great King sent into battle the brothers and sons of those who had fallen at Marathon. When the Medes failed to budge the Hellenes and there was a great loss of life on their side, Xerxes is said to have summoned the Immortals under the command of Hydarnes son of Hydarnes, who were no more successful.[62]

Herodotus does not describe in full detail how the Cissians, Medes, and the Persians fought. He does, however, provide one indication, mentioning that, before the fighting began, a citizen of Trachis had reported to the Hellenes that there were so many barbarians in Xerxes' army that, when they shot their arrows, it would block the sun, and adding that the Spartiate who would most distinguish himself in the struggle to come, a man named Dienekes, had responded that this was excellent news since it would mean that he and his colleagues would fight in the shade.[63] This suggests that, on this occasion, the peoples of Iran fought in their accustomed fashion, launching a massive barrage of arrows meant to break up the enemy formation, and then advancing to finish them off.

In this case, as at Marathon, the artillery barrage appears to have been ineffectual—perhaps this time, in part, because, in the narrow confines past Thermopylae's western gate, not enough archers could get within range to be of much use. Moreover, in the hand-to-hand combat, which took place at the middle gate, the soldiers of the Great King could not take advantage of their superior numbers, and they made no progress. This was due in part, Herodotus suggests, to the fact that the spears of the Cissians, Medes, and Persians were shorter than those of the Hellenes. But it also owed a great deal to the size and solidity of the hollow shields borne by the Greeks as well as to the Hellenic practice of fighting in phalanx, shoulder to shoulder, eight men deep, behind a wall of *aspídes.*

In telling fashion, Herodotus underlines the discipline and tactical skill of the Spartans. First, he says, they would boldly advance and then feign flight. Thereby, as we can easily imagine, they would lure the Iranian footsoldiers from behind the protective wall afforded by their barricade of *gérra* or wicker shields. Then, Herodotus tells us, the Lacedaemonians would suddenly reverse course, form up, and mow down the hapless spearmen of the King of Kings. In these circumstances, the splendid body armor that the latter wore afforded them little in the way of protection—for they were either shieldless altogether and virtually naked, as Herodotus implies; or, as Diodorus Siculus claims, some wore bucklers on their left arms while others bore small round shields inadequate to the task.[64]

The Spartans were by no means the only ones who fought. All of the contingents—apart from the Phocians posted on the Anopaea path and probably also on the Dhema road—took a turn, spelling one another, and none gave way in the face of the barbarian onslaught. Such was the superiority of the weaponry possessed and the tactics employed by the hoplite Greeks, and this went on for two days straight—as Xerxes tried every expedient, including, we are told, the deployment of those within each of the national contingents of his army who were thought to be the bravest and most daring.[65]

On the night between the first and the second day, another storm struck, delaying for at least a day the Greek withdrawal from Artemisium. The thunder echoed off Mount Pelion; the rain fell hard throughout the night; and the wind, almost certainly once again from the northeast, drove corpses and debris further down the Magnesia coast to Aphetae, where, we are told, they collected around the prows of the Persian ships at Aphetae and became tangled up in the blades of their oars. The triremes which Megabates or his son Megabazos had dispatched down the eastern coast of the Euboean shore the day before fared far, far worse. They were caught off the "hollows of Euboea," and the wind, which here also can only have been blowing from the northeast, drove them mercilessly on the rocks along that dread coast.[66]

On the second morning, the rowers at Aphetae made no move to man their ships. The storm may have left them rattled, and they no doubt needed time to clear the debris from around their ships. It was, moreover, too early to expect that the two hundred triremes circumnavigating Euboea had reached

Euripus, and the Persian commanders, the trierarchs, and the crews were no doubt wondering what damage the second Hellesponter had done that squadron.[67]

The Greeks at Artemisium were no doubt similarly curious. In the course of the day, they received reinforcements. Fifty-three Athenian ships—manned, we must suppose, by an additional ten thousand six hundred men—arrived, and they brought good tidings. Whether these triremes had come directly from Athens itself or had been posted at Chalcis to guard the southern approaches to Euripus we do not know. What we can say, however, is that, at this point, there were more men at Artemisium manning the one hundred eighty ships sent by Athens than there appear to have been adult male Athenians. Even more to the point, the newcomers confirmed that the hopes that the Hellenes had entertained the night before when the second Hellesponter struck had been fulfilled and that the Persian fleet circumnavigating Euboea had been destroyed. Toward the end of the day, the Greeks rowed out again, hoping to engage a part (and only a part) of the Persian fleet, and there was once again a skirmish—in which some of the opposing triremes from Cilicia were destroyed.[68]

Meanwhile at Thermopylae, toward the end of the second day of fighting —probably on the seventeenth of September, just before the night when the harvest moon would appear, as the Carneia and the Olympic Games were coming to an end—Xerxes got a break. A man from Anticyra in Malis named Ephialtes son of Eurydemos approached the Great King in hopes of gaining a great reward; told him about the Anopaea path around Thermopylae, up and over the upland plateau on Mount Kallidromos; and offered to serve as a guide.[69]

All in all, it was not a bad time for an all-night trek. The storms had for the time being passed, the moon would be full, and it would rise shortly after sunset and last until daybreak. For the entire night, the rough path through the mountains would be lit up by a ghostly light. That evening, we are told, at the time when the lamps were being lit, the Great King dispatched, under the guidance of this Ephialtes, his personal bodyguard—the Ten Thousand Immortals—under the leadership of their commander Hydarnes son of Hydarnes; and they reached the high point on the lower of the two ridges of Mount Kallidromos at dawn on the third day of the struggle.[70]

We do not know when the admirals at Aphetae learned that the two hundred triremes they had sent around Euboea had been destroyed by the second storm. It is possible that they discovered that their worst fears were justified by dawn on the day when Hydarnes son of Hydarnes and the Ten Thousand Immortals began their descent from the high point along the Anopaea trail toward Alpenus and the east gate of Thermopylae. It is also possible that they had no certain knowledge at this stage and, having allowed those circumnavigating the island the three days thought to be requisite for their getting into position at Euripus, they acted according to plan. Whichever the case may be, it was on this day that Megabates or his son Megabazos ordered the trierarchs of the barbarian fleet to proceed out in search of battle with the Greeks.[71]

We also do not know precisely when Leonidas learned that the Immortals had taken the Anopaea path and how he responded. Herodotus tells us that the first to issue a warning was the seer Megistias, who examined the sacrificial victims the evening before the battle and predicted that the Greeks would encounter death at dawn. Thereafter, he adds, deserters made their way under cover of darkness from the Persian camp to report that the Immortals were making their way around the mountain and, at daybreak, the lookouts climbed down from the heights to confirm their claims.[72]

Diodorus Siculus—again almost certainly following the fourth-century writer Ephorus—tells us that among these deserters was a man named Tyrrhastiadas, who came from Cumae in Asia Minor. According to this account, parts of which Plutarch and Justin repeat, Leonidas had those of the Greeks willing to remain at their posts take a very early breakfast, observing that they would dine in Hades. Then he led them by night on a suicide mission into the Persian camp to assassinate the Great King. It was there, we are told, that he, his fellow Spartans, and those who remained with them died.[73]

There is no reason to suppose that Ephorus invented this story out of whole cloth. He was a careful historian. His normal procedure as a writer about times before his own appears to have been to correct or supplement the accounts supplied by his most authoritative predecessors. This he ordinarily did on the basis of testimony—preserved in the poets, in local histories, and in family lore—which may have been unknown to or deliberately ignored by them. Recognizing this, modern scholars look to those known to have drawn on his work for details additional to what they find in Herodotus, Thucydides, Xenophon, and the like. In this case, it may well be significant that, like Tyrrhastiadas, Ephorus was a native of Cumae, for he may be repeating a story handed down at Cumae within the man's family. It may equally well have been the case that Ephorus was following a lost prose writer such as the physician Ctesias of Cnidus, Charon of Lampsacus, or Damastes of Sigeum or that his source was the poet Simonides, whose long choral song regarding Thermopylae Diodorus quotes.[74]

Be this as it may, the story supplied by Ephorus makes no sense. To believe it, one must ignore (as Diodorus, Plutarch, and Justin do) or dismiss as fraudulent Herodotus' claim that Leonidas had been forewarned about the Anopaea path and that he had sent the Phocians to block the way. Had he been warned early that night that the Persians were on their way, he would certainly have sent a messenger to alert the Phocians; and, if he had full confidence in the veracity of these reports, he might have sent reinforcements as well. Even if one were to read the Phocians out of the story, one would have to ask why Leonidas dismissed a part of the holding force and led the rest against the Persian camp when he could have sent the ones dismissed to block the Anopaea path.

The story told by Herodotus is much more plausible, if incomplete. He neglects to canvass the possibility that the deserters had been dispatched by Xerxes shortly before dawn to sow fear and confusion in the Greek ranks, but he does report that the Phocians were situated on the trail below its high point; he implies that they had posted no sentries on the ridge above their camp; and he claims that the Persians, in their descent from the high plateau, were on them before they could fully arm themselves. When Hydarnes learned that he had come upon Phocians and not Lacedaemonians, he drew up his battle line. When hit with a dense barrage of arrows unleashed by the Persian bowmen, the Phocians, who should have charged the foe, panicked instead and scrambled up the slope, expecting to be killed; and the Persians ignored them and marched on toward Alpenus and the east gate of Thermopylae.[75]

All of this makes sense. But what Herodotus has to say about the report made by the lookouts at dawn does not—for it is hard to fathom where, on the high peak directly above his camp, Leonidas could have posted lookouts who would have been able to see what was going on behind the mountain on the Anopaea path and still have time to make their way down the long and dangerously steep slope and reach him soon after daybreak.[76] If, however, these lookouts employed fire beacons or were equipped with flags of the sort used by the Greeks and the Persians in their navies,[77] they would have been able, by way of a predetermined code, to signal to Leonidas what a general in his situation most wanted to know—that, for example, the Great King's fleet was on its way unimpeded to the Malian Gulf or that a unit of Persian footsoldiers was marching around Mount Kallidromos and had routed the Phocians guarding the Anopaea path.

If we assume something along these lines, the rest of Herodotus' story would then make sense—that, in the morning, when the information conveyed by the deserters was confirmed and not before, Leonidas and the other Greek commanders had a few moments in which to deliberate as to how they should respond; that their counsel was then divided; that most decided to withdraw and resist the Persian advance elsewhere on another day; and that the latter still had sufficient time in which to make their escape—while the Spartans and the Thespians chose to stay on, intending to fight a rearguard action and fully expecting to die. With them, Pausanias tells us, were the Mycenaeans; and Herodotus claims that Leonidas retained the Thebans as hostages. If Ephorus is right in claiming that the latter were volunteers, drawn from the Theban party hostile to the Mede, then Plutarch is surely correct in rejecting as slander Herodotus' denial that they, too, voluntarily remained.[78]

It is likely that the battle at sea and that on the land began on the third day at about the same time. At sunrise, Herodotus tells us, Xerxes poured libations, and at mid-morning, "the hour when the market is apt to be full," he ordered the attack, as Ephialtes had urged. By this time, we may presume, the fleet at Aphetae and the ships anchored within the Gulf of Magnesia had made their way out into the channel separating the southern coast of Magnesia from Euboea, and they had formed a crescent with an eye to encircling the Greek fleet and hemming it in.[79]

We know very little about the battle between the two fleets. Herodotus tells us that the Hellenes rowed out and entered the fray. He says nothing about the tactics employed. He tells us only that the two fleets were an even match. If the armada of Xerxes failed to crush the Greeks, he intimates, it was in part because the sheer size of the barbarian fleet produced crowding and caused the Great King's ships to collide with one another repeatedly and do one another damage in the process.[80]

More can perhaps be said. For it is highly likely that the Phoenicians were intent on using the *diékplous* in this battle, as was apparently their wont; and it is possible that—under the guidance of the Heracleides of Mylasa who had commanded the Carians in ambushing the Persian army on the road to Pidasa in the time of the Ionian Revolt—the Hellenes deployed their fleet in line abreast in two distinct squadrons, one placed some distance behind the other, in such a manner as to render any triremes attempting to "row through" the first line "and out" vulnerable to being rammed by triremes in the line behind. According to Sosylus of Lacedaemon—a well-informed historian who, centuries thereafter, tutored the great Carthaginian general Hannibal in Greek—a citizen of the pertinent Carian town named Heracleides was, in fact, responsible in this very fashion for a defeat of the Phoenicians at a place called Artemisium.[81]

In the conflict that did take place, Herodotus acknowledges, many Greek triremes were captured, destroyed, or incapacitated—but not as many as the barbarian ships they engaged. Technically, at least as the Greeks understood it, the Hellenes were victorious—for, when it was all over, they controlled the sea-lanes in which the battle was fought, and they and they alone were in a position to collect and bury the corpses and to haul off the ships that had been wrecked. But theirs must have been a Pyrrhic victory, for we are told that fully half of the Athenian triremes were damaged and at least temporarily disabled. Moreover, in confronting the Greeks, the Egyptian squadron, under the command of Xerxes' full brother Achaemenes, had been notably successful.[82]

At Thermopylae, as Xerxes' men advanced, so did the remaining Greeks—who marched on this occasion well to the west of the Phocian wall. "There was no way," Herodotus says, "to make an assessment of the dead." The Persian commanders drove their troops into the breach, and the Greeks massacred them, fighting "with all their strength recklessly and without regard for their own lives." In time, all of the spears of the Greeks were broken, and they turned to their swords. At this point, Leonidas fell; and as his fellow Spartans, the Thespians, and perhaps also the Mycenaeans fought for possession of his corpse, they killed Xerxes' half-brothers Abrokomes and Hyperanthes, the sons of Darius and his niece Phratagoune, daughter of his brother Artanes. When Ephialtes arrived with Hydarnes and the Immortals, the Thebans reportedly drew apart and offered to surrender. Some of these men were slaughtered as they laid down their arms. Others, who sought the help of the Thessalians and were taken captive, were branded by Xerxes' men and lived to tell the tale. The remainder of the Hellenes retreated to and past the Phocian wall, where they occupied a small hill. And there on this hill where the Spartans, the Thespians, and perhaps also the Mycenaeans would eventually be buried, these hoplites died, fighting to the bitter end with daggers and with their teeth and hands as the barbarians pelted them with missiles from all sides.[83]

The epitaph posted alongside the lion erected in honor of Leonidas on the mound where the Spartans were buried captures the spirit underpinning their accomplishment on this momentous occasion:

> Stranger! Convey to the men of Lacedaemon this message:
> That in this place we lie—obedient to their commands.

Never in human history has a political community gained as dramatically in prestige by losing a battle as the Spartans did on this particular occasion.[84]

The Lacedaemonians understood better than anyone what Leonidas and the three hundred had achieved on their behalf, and this had a profound impact on their conduct with regard to one another. Of the three hundred Spartiates dispatched to Thermopylae, there appear to have been three who were in no position to contribute in any substantial way to the struggle against the Mede. Eurytus and Aristodemos were purportedly laid up in Alpenus—both with diseases of the eye. In the crisis, if Herodotus has the story right, the first of the two armed himself and asked the helot assigned to him to lead him into the fighting; and there, as anticipated, he lost his life. The latter was too feeble to follow his example, and he survived the final battle and eventually made his way back to Lacedaemon. There, however, he was shunned: no one would speak to him or even share fire with him, and behind his back they referred to him as a "trembler." His was, he discovered, a life not worth living, and at the battle of Plataea he put an end to that life by charging the Persians in such a fashion as to guarantee that he would be impaled upon their spears. There was also a third Spartan named Pantites, who had been sent away to Thessaly as a messenger and, in consequence, missed the final battle. When he returned to Sparta, he was treated with such contempt that he hanged himself.[85] Henceforth the standard that Leonidas had set was going to be applied to everyone at Lacedaemon.

In the meantime, once it was clear that, at Thermopylae, the game was up and that Leonidas would no longer be able to hold the pass, Themistocles' friend Abronichus son of Lysicles rowed off in his triaconter from Alpenus on the Gulf of Malia to report to Eurybiades and the Greeks at Artemisium that Leonidas was or soon would be dead, that the combined operation was at an end, and that the army of the Persians would soon be in Boeotia on its way to Attica. Even before his arrival, however, the Greeks at Artemisium were contemplating a withdrawal. Given their limited numbers and the damage done their ships, what counted technically as a victory was strategically a defeat, and it was time to reposition themselves and reconsider their tactics in light

of what they had learned from their encounter with the Mede. The news conveyed by Abronichus removed any remaining doubts there might have been
and settled the question. There was nothing to be gained or even salvaged
from their remaining at Artemisium.[86]

In the limited time available, many of the wrecks that the Greek crews
had collected after the battle were beyond their capacity to repair; and, given
their need for a speedy withdrawal and the considerable distance they had to
row, these could not safely be towed to the Saronic Gulf. So, fearful that the
Persians might find a way to refit them, the Hellenes dragged the damaged triremes up on the beach, placed upon them the corpses that they had recovered
from the sea, and set the boats aflame.

Half a millennium thereafter, when Plutarch journeyed from his native
Chaeronea in Boeotia some miles to the south to look over the scene of the
famous battle, he visited the temple of Artemis set back on a hillock just east
of the bay, and he admired the pillars of white marble erected by the Athenians around the sacred enclosure. When rubbed, he tells us, this wondrous
stone assumed the color and gave off the odor of saffron. Inscribed on one
of the pillars, Plutarch found elegiac verses commemorating (and greatly ex-
aggerating) the actual Athenian achievement in the bloody encounter. After
copying these, he wandered down to the beach nearby, and there he came to
a place where, deep below the surface of the sand, there was a layer of ashes
thought to mark the spot where Eurybiades and those who had served under
him had in good Homeric fashion turned disabled triremes into funeral pyres
to honor those of their comrades who had lost their lives while defending at
sea the liberty of their fellow Hellenes.[87]

CHAPTER 7

Salamis

A man, a Greek, coming from the Athenian host,
Told your son Xerxes these things:
That when dusk arrives and, then, black night,
The Hellenes would not remain, but spring to the rowing benches
Of their ships—scattering in every direction,
Each seeking by clandestine flight to preserve himself alive.

—AESCHYLUS

A T Themistocles' urging, the Greeks delayed their retreat from Artemisium until well into the night, when their departure would be less apt to attract notice and interference was exceedingly unlikely. In the meantime, mindful that the herds tended by the citizens of Histiaea who found pasture in those parts would soon in all likelihood fall into the hands of the enemy, they seized and slaughtered the animals, roasted the meat over roaring fires meant to be seen on the other side of the straits, and feasted. Then, further to mask their withdrawal, they presumably piled even more wood on the fires, engaging in a subterfuge others would subsequently imitate. When all was ready, they slipped off as unobtrusively as possible by the light of the harvest moon and made their way west, then west-southwest along the northern coast of Euboea past Histiaea toward the channel separating that island from the mainland—with the Corinthians in the lead and the much larger Athenian contingent bringing up the rear.[1]

That the Greek fleet moved with alacrity we can be confident. The Plataeans were eager to get home and to evacuate their families from Boeotia before the Persians descended upon them, and the same was surely true of the Chalcidians and the Eretrians as well, for the peoples of Euboea had not anticipated the worst and taken precautions.[2] The Athenians were, as we have seen, better prepared. Long before, they had planned for just such an eventuality, and there is every reason to suppose that they had by this time already ferried the vast majority of their women and children to Troezen, as originally planned.

The ancient sources are, nonetheless, undoubtedly right in supposing that, at this point, the evacuation of Attica was by no means complete, that the Greek fleet initially put into Salamis for the purpose of helping the Athenians to ferry across to that island those still in Attica, that it was at this time that an evacuation was formally proclaimed, and that Themistocles and his associates enlisted superstition on their side in persuading Athenians reluctant to leave their ancestral homeland that it was imperative that they withdraw. It was probably at this moment also that Cimon son of Miltiades led a contingent of his fellow cavalrymen on a procession through the Ceramicus up to the Acropolis to dedicate to Athena, the city's patron goddess, the bridles of their horses as a sign of their recognition and acceptance of the fact that, at least for the time being, Athens had to concentrate its energies single-mindedly on the war at sea.[3]

Some Athenians hoped that the Peloponnesians would mobilize, make a stand in Boeotia, and prevent the Persians from entering Attica; and these men considered their allies' refusal to do so a betrayal.[4] But, once Thermopylae fell and the Persians in full force entered central Greece, there was no serious chance of this happening; and the Themistocles Decree and the plans for evacuating Athens' territory, drafted long before, presupposed the contrary. The terrain in Boeotia, because so much of it was suitable for cavalry maneuvers, greatly favored the Persians; and the Peloponnesians were not about to stage a fight on the enemy's terms. They had an alternative plan.

When word reached the Peloponnesus that Leonidas and his men had perished at Thermopylae, the deceased king's younger brother Cleombrotus assumed office as regent for his nephew Pleistarchus, the young son of Leonidas and Gorgo; and the Spartans immediately dispatched him to the Isthmus of Corinth. There not only the Lacedaemonians but also the Arcadians, Eleans, Corinthians, Sicyonians, Epidaurians, Phleiasians, Troezenians, and Hermionaeans gathered, took council, and resolved to treat the Peloponnesus as the acropolis of Hellas and build a protective wall across the isthmus— probably, as Diodorus claims, along the five-mile stretch between Cenchreae on the Saronic Gulf and Lechaeum on the Corinthian Gulf, or possibly, as some scholars suppose, at a narrower point nearer the *díolkos* linking the two bodies of water. And build with a will they did—with tens of thousands of

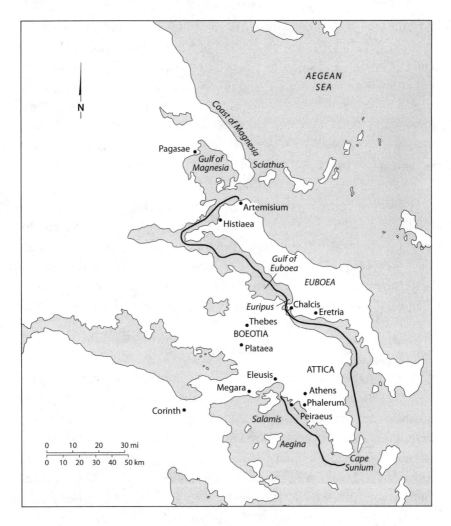

Map 19. From Artemisium to Salamis

men steadily laboring around the clock on the project, throwing together a ramshackle barrier made of wood, stones, brick, and baskets filled with sand, of which there remains today not a single identifiable trace.[5]

Herodotus tells us that, at this time, the Peloponnesians had next to no faith in the Hellenic fleet. Themistocles had more respect than they did for the capabilities of the Greeks. At Artemisium, on the eve of their departure, he had announced to the other commanders that he had concocted a scheme for encouraging the Ionian and the Carian contingents within the Persian armada to revolt. On a voyage requiring continuous rowing, as he no doubt knew, the crew of a trireme consumed something on the order of two tons of water per day. This dictated on the part of a fleet frequent stops for replenishing its stocks—and so, as the Greek fleet gradually made its way down the Gulf of Euboea toward Euripus and the Saronic Gulf, the wily Athenian put his plan into operation, assembling an elite squadron of the fastest Athenian triremes and seeing to it that one of them paused at each place where the Persians were likely to put in for fresh water and left a message appealing to the Ionians and the Carians to switch sides, adopt a posture of neutrality, or, if constrained, turn tail at the onset of battle. The archaeological record belies Herodotus' claim that the Athenians scratched Themistocles' exhortation onto the rocks at these watering places, but it does not rule out their employment of chalk—which, given the limited time available, would have far better suited their needs. The Greeks were certainly familiar with its use, and they knew that, even if such a maneuver failed to stir a rebellion on the part of the Ionians and Carians, it would sow distrust within the Persian fleet.[6]

The Persian Advance

Thanks in part to the cultural hegemony exercised by Homer, the ethos of classical Hellas was agonistic, and the rivalries that grew up within its various constitutive communities tended to be so intense that, as Herodotus has Xerxes point out, the Greeks were often more generous and forthcoming in their dealings with their guest-friends from abroad than with their fellow citizens at home. In antiquity, there certainly was never any shortage of Greeks willing to betray their fellow Hellenes in return for remuneration and political advantage. So it was that, shortly before dawn on the morning after the Greeks had abandoned Artemisium, a citizen of the nearby Euboean city of Histiaea rowed across the channel to Aphetae to report the news to the Persians.[7]

Xerxes' commanders were not quick to trust the man. This might, they thought, be a trick. So they put their informant under guard while they dispatched some of their faster ships to reconnoiter. When these returned and their trierarchs confirmed his report, he was no doubt duly rewarded and enrolled on the list of the Great King's benefactors; and that very morning the fleet crossed over to the friendlier anchorage along the bay at Artemisium. We must wonder whether this Medizer looked on with Schadenfreude that afternoon when the Persians stormed his fatherland a few miles to the west of the bay at Artemisium and overran, looted, and ravaged the coastal villages located in its territory.[8] In Hellas, such things were wont to happen, and those who, by such a stratagem, escaped a calamity reserved for their erstwhile friends and neighbors were apt to congratulate themselves on their cleverness and, sadly, sometimes even gloat.

It was after they stormed Histiaea that those serving in Persia's fleet first learned of the defeat of the Greeks at Thermopylae, and the next day, at the invitation of the Great King, many of them crowded into boats and crossed over from Euboea to the Greek mainland to tour the battlefield and view the dead. For the purpose of concealing the extent of his losses, Xerxes had reportedly interred all but one thousand of his own dead soldiers. The Spartans, Thespians, and their allies he had left unburied. No one, we are told, was fooled by his attempt to hide the extent of the losses inflicted on his army.[9]

After visiting the Hot Gates, those in the Persian fleet returned to Histiaea and paused there for three days. We are not told why they tarried, but it is easy to guess. Many of their triremes had been damaged and disabled during the final battle at Artemisium. At Aphetae and in the Gulf of Magnesia, they had no doubt been able to replace the oars broken in that melee, but there had not been time to carry out more serious repairs. That on the day that Histiaea was overrun—along the shore in the Gulf of Magnesia, at Aphetae and Artemisium, and in the harbor at Histiaea itself—the carpenters accompanying the fleet went to work with a will: this we may take as a given.

Herodotus does not tell us which of the Persian admirals was in charge at this point, but the geographer Strabo does. Like Diodorus Siculus, he sometimes relied on Ephorus, and, like Diodorus, he identifies Megabates as the Persian commander when he should, perhaps, have specified the man's son Megabazos. By the time that the repairs were done, he adds, this admiral had secured the assistance of a pilot named Salgoneus, a Boeotian closely familiar with the waters they were about to traverse. It was, we are told, under the latter's guidance, that, on the fourth morning after their tour of Thermopylae, the Persians and their fleet set out from Histiaea and made their way at a stately pace east-southeast down the Gulf of Euboea, dispatching units from time to time to ravage and burn the settlements along the Euboean coast.[10]

A bit more than halfway down this body of water, the Persian armada came to Euripus—a remarkable spot where the gulf narrows dramatically and Euboea and the mainland come to be just a bit more than forty yards apart. In these fearsome straits, a powerful tide violently reverses its course at irregular intervals in the course of each day. At first, as the triremes approached the narrows, the admiral in charge appears not to have been able to discern that there was a gap between the mainland and Euboea. Supposing that he and his men had been tricked and were sailing into a cul-de-sac where they might be ambushed, he fell into a fury and had Salgoneus executed on the spot, only to regret his impulsiveness almost immediately. Through Euripus, without its pilot, the fleet then made its way; and not long thereafter, when the triremes had left the Boeotian coast in their wake, the marines on board these ships turned their attention to plundering and setting on fire the coastal settlements on both sides of the gulf—in Attica as well as Euboea.[11]

While the Persian admiral was having his triremes repaired and later while his fleet was wending its way along the Gulf of Euboea, Xerxes and his soldiers were busy. When Leonidas fell, most of those within the barbarian host were, in fact, well rested. Very few can have managed to force their way into the narrows at Thermopylae to engage the enemy at any one time—and for some of those not in need of recuperation, the Aleuads of Larissa had an immediate use.

The Thessalians, who had medized, had for generations been at odds with the Phocians, who had firmly refused to do so. The quarrel between these two peoples was bitter—so bitter, Herodotus asserts, that, had the Thessalians taken the side of the Hellenes, the Phocians would have joined the Mede. The Persian victory at Thermopylae opened the way for the former to exact a vengeance long contemplated, and the Aleuads were not behindhand in seizing the opportunity.[12]

In the immediate aftermath of the battle, the Thessalians sent a herald to their ancestral enemy to gloat but also to make the Phocians what they represented as a magnanimous offer. It was in their power, the Thessalians observed, to determine whether or not the Phocians would be deprived of their land and enslaved. For a pretty penny, they offered to set aside their ancient grudge, forgive their former foe, and direct the Persians elsewhere. All that the Phocians had to do was to fork over the princely sum of fifty talents (1.425 tons) in silver.[13]

This, as the Thessalians no doubt expected, the Phocians proudly refused to do;[14] and so, perhaps as early as the morning after the Persian victory at Thermopylae, Thessalian guides led a column of Persian footsoldiers south and inland from their camp along the Gulf of Malia to the west of Thermopylae—either up the Asopus gorge and over the Pournaraki pass or more

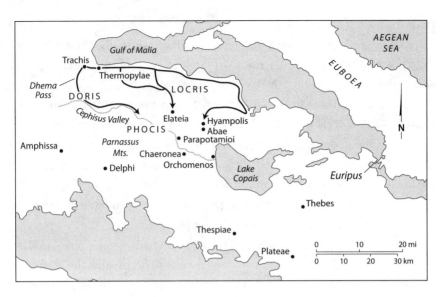

Map 20. Routes from Thermopylae to Phocis

likely, as most scholars suppose, along a route further to the west which ran through the foothills of Mount Oetae past the Trachinian cliffs and over the Dhema pass. In this march, they were unopposed—for, no doubt at the suggestion of the Thessalians, the citizens of Doris, who controlled both roads, nimbly shifted allegiances, welcomed the Medes with open arms, and were spared punishment. From Doris, the Persians pushed on into the heartland of Phocis in the upper Cephisus valley, whence the Phocians fled in divers directions—some westward with their families and their belongings to Amphissa in Ozolian Locris, others to the heights of Mount Parnassus, and some also to the isolated peak of Tithorea, which hovered over the city of Neon.

As the Persians advanced down the Cephisus valley, they plundered and burned everything in their path: the farms of the Phocians, their cities, and even the sanctuary of Apollo at Abae. Whether the men and children the barbarians captured they enslaved or slaughtered we do not know, but Herodotus does report that they gang-raped the Phocian women they came across, and he tells us that at least some of these women died as a consequence of the number of men who piled on.[15] Such was to be the fate reserved for all who resolutely resisted the Mede. This was the message that Xerxes wanted to convey to prospective Medizers from within the Hellenic League.

Although Herodotus does not say so, the bulk of the Persian army must have set out not long thereafter on another route—far easier to traverse and, throughout antiquity, much more often employed. Initially, they must have marched east through the narrows at the Hot Gates. From there, roads ran across the Kleisoura and the Fontana passes to the Cephisus valley east of Elateia; and another path, longer but for the most part gentler, followed the coast through Locris Epiknemidia and Locris Opuntia and ran inland from there via Opous over the pass near Hyampolis and Abae to Parapotamioi. It would have been exceedingly difficult for Xerxes' cavalry and impossible for his baggage train with its multitude of carts to pass through the Asopus ravine, and, had the road over the Dhema pass been as suitable for transport as some scholars imagine, there would have been no need in the first place for the Persians to have forced their way through the narrows at Thermopylae.[16]

It is also possible that Xerxes sent some units of his cavalry ahead through the Hot Gates and over the Kleisoura or the Fontana pass to support the column of footsoldiers descending on the Cephisus valley from Doris. Although they had farther to go, the valiant horsemen of Iran could move at a much more rapid pace than their comrades traveling on foot.

When his forces rendezvoused at Panopeos, roughly two miles northwest of the Boeotian city of Chaeronea, Xerxes divided his army again, dispatching along the road that went around Mount Parnassus in the direction of Delphi a unit largely made up, one must suspect, of the men who had marched from Doris down the Cephisus valley. West they went via Daulis, then over the Arachova pass—or southwest through Ambryssus, west again past Antikyra, and, finally northwest—toward the sacred site. The principal Phocian settlements in those parts they were instructed to plunder and set on fire, and this command they fulfilled.[17]

The Hellenes doubted that ravaging southern Phocis was the chief object of this expedition. They were persuaded that Xerxes was intent on seizing the rich offerings in the treasuries built by the various Greek cities near the temple of Apollo at Delphi and even on destroying the various temples in and around the sacred site.[18] Persia's monarchs were known to have a liking for objects of beauty and a powerful craving for silver and gold, and Darius had done the like at Didyma in the territory of Miletus (and elsewhere as well) when he crushed the great Ionian revolt.

In anticipation of just such an attack, Herodotus tells us, the citizens of Delphi evacuated their women and children and sent them across the Corinthian Gulf to Achaea. The men followed the example set by the Phocians.

Some withdrew to Amphissa in Ozolian Locris. Most climbed Mount Parnassus. Their valuables they lugged up to the Corycian cave some five hundred feet above the sacred site. Sixty of the citizens gamely remained in Delphi, as did a prophet named Aceratus. But the Persians appear never to have reached the treasuries and the sacred enclosure. So we are told, and the archaeological record confirms that, at this time, no destruction took place and no damage was done.

According to the citizens of Delphi, as the barbarians approached the sanctuary of Athena Pronaia about a mile short of the temple of Apollo, a miracle took place. Thunderbolts came hurtling down, an avalanche from the upper slopes of Parnassus fell upon the barbarians, some of the citizens armed themselves and charged down the mountain against the Persians, and the latter fled in panic—chased by two hoplites more than human in stature: heroes, demigods, of the land.[19]

Here, needless to say, a measure of skepticism is in order. It is perfectly possible that Xerxes' men had been ordered to stop their march short of Delphi. In the past, except when provoked, Persia's Great Kings had consistently treated the religious predilections of their subjects and prospective subjects with a prudent and exaggerated respect. Ostentation in the pursuit of piety, as this was variously understood in each locality, was, Persia's rulers believed, a powerful tool for pacification and a political virtue of surpassing importance.

The authorities at Delphi were canny. The city prospered because those in control of Apollo's oracle were well informed and disinclined to make waves or back losers. These men understood what Datis was signaling in the 490s, and they knew which way the political winds were blowing. With good but not, as it turned out, sufficient reason, they concluded that the Greeks would be unable to withstand Xerxes' onslaught; and, by means of the oracles issued to the Spartans, Argives, Cretans, and Athenians, they did what they could to please their prospective sovereign and undermine Greek morale. If the column dispatched by the Great King against southern Phocis stopped short of Delphi in an ostentatious and respectful fashion, as it may well have done, it was in the interest of the authorities there—especially, when their calculations were proven wrong and the Persians were driven from Greece—to misrepresent the approach of the barbarian as an attack fended off by the god.

This is precisely what the ruling order at Delphi did. As Diodorus Siculus tells us, those in authority set up a trophy at the temple of Athena, and on it they inscribed an elegy of great elegance just four lines long:

As a memorial of a battle fought to ward off men and as a witness
   to victory
The Delphians placed me here to gratify Zeus,
Who with Phoebus Apollo drove off the city-sacking ranks of Medes,
Delivering from danger the sacred precinct crowned with bronze.

The marble slab bearing this quatrain is no longer anywhere in evidence. But for its existence we have incontrovertible proof. Some two millennia after the supposed miracle it commemorated, an itinerant Englishman, who just happened to be passing through, found the trophy near what was left of the temple of Athena Pronaia and copied into his diary the elegy inscribed thereon.[20]

Xerxes in Attica

While one column of his army was working its way through southern Phocis, Xerxes crossed with the great bulk of his forces into Boeotia, heading through the territory of Orchomenos in the direction of Attica. Ahead of him, to smooth the way and clarify for the Great King and his commanders just who had medized and who had not, went a number of Macedonians operating on behalf of their king, Alexander. It was at this time that the Spartan Demaratus arranged for his guest-friend Attaginus, the leader of the narrow oligarchy then in charge at Thebes, to become a guest-friend of the King of Kings, and it was at the instigation of this Attaginus and his comrades within the ruling clique at Thebes that units of Persians were briefly detached to plunder and burn Thespiae and Plataea.[21]

According to Plutarch—who, as a native of Chaeronea on the Boeotian border with Phocis, knew the terrain—it took a day and a half to journey from Thermopylae to Thebes.[22] In principle, then, a determined traveler—who did not delay, who journeyed via one of the shorter routes from eastern Locris to Phocis over the Kleisoura or the Fontana pass, and who bypassed Thebes and headed straight for Thespiae, Plataea, and the Dryoscephalae pass into Attica—could make the trek, one hundred ten miles in length, from the Hot Gates to Athens within three days.

This rapid a pace the Persians did not keep up. But if Herodotus is to be trusted, Xerxes covered the distance in something like twice this time—no doubt in company with his cavalry, his bodyguard of Ten Thousand Immortals, and at least some of his other footsoldiers. It might well be impossible for an army burdened with what the Romans aptly termed *impedimenta* to complete such a journey within seven or eight days; and even for the vanguard of such an army, if it left its baggage train to bring up the rear, a march of this sort would have been an accomplishment. But it was by no means impossible.[23]

Xerxes had no time to waste. As we have had occasion to note, on the march from Sardis to Thermopylae, he had advanced at a leisurely pace, almost certainly with an eye to arriving at the Hot Gates in mid-September—during the window of opportunity when the Spartans were busy celebrating the Carneia and the Olympic Games were also under way. Now, however, it was incumbent on the Great King to move with alacrity, for it was late in the year. *Cheîmōn*—the word in classical Greek for winter—meant storm as well, and winter with its attendant storms loomed on the horizon. The campaigning season would soon be over. The fleet and the supply ships accompanying it would have to repair to winter quarters. In need of provisions, Xerxes' foot-soldiers would have to follow suit, and his victory over the Hellenes was as yet incomplete.

When Xerxes reached Attica, he found it almost deserted. His soldiers captured five hundred Athenians who had foolishly remained behind, thinking, perhaps, that they could evade detection. The city of Athens resembled a ghost town. The only Athenians to be found there were holed up on the Acropolis, barricaded behind a "wooden wall" of planks and doors. Persian archers occupied the Areopagus—a hill nearby—and from there they shot arrows at the barricade, which they first wrapped in hemp and set afire. Although their wooden wall went up in smoke, the men occupying the Acropolis nonetheless held out. When the Peisistratids came near to offer them terms of surrender, they refused to parley. When the Persians approached the gates of the Acropolis, they rolled great stones down upon them. In time, however, a number of Persians managed to scale a steep cliff left unguarded on the Acropolis' seemingly inaccessible eastern end, and soon they reached the sanctuary of Aglaurus the daughter of Cecrops. From there, they ascended to the summit and opened the gates. Those of the suppliants who did not immediately hurl themselves from the precipice were slaughtered. The Acropolis itself was set on fire and the temples, torn down. As the archaeological evidence makes clear, the damage done was extensive.[24]

Punishing the Athenians for their participation in the raid on Sardis mounted by the rebellious Ionians eighteen years before had been one of the invasion's stated aims. It was no doubt with a sense of great satisfaction that Xerxes, at this time, dispatched a mounted courier to announce to his uncle

Artabanus in Susa that he had accomplished his mission by conquering Athens, plundering its territory, and burning the sanctuaries therein. It is telling, however, that on the very next day the Great King of Persia instructed the Peisistratids and the other Athenian exiles in his entourage to climb up to the Acropolis and conduct the sacrifices in the Athenian fashion.[25] It was one thing to take vengeance on the Athenians. It was another, as Xerxes knew only too well, to cross the gods and heroes of the land. Propitiation was the order of the day.

While Xerxes' cavalry and his crack troops were scouring the Athenian countryside, pillaging and burning the sanctuaries and villages they came across, the remainder of his army and its baggage train were ponderously making their way through Boeotia and over one or more of the passes that run through Cithaeron-Parnes mountain range separating that territory from Attica; and his fleet, under the command of Megabates or his son Megabazos, was completing its journey down the Gulf of Euboea. On the evening of the eighth day after the final battle at Artemisium, Xerxes' triremes rounded the cape at Sunium, rowed up the western coast of Attica, and came to rest in Phalerum Bay.[26] The armada was not as large as it once had been.

In the beginning, as we have seen, Xerxes' fleet is said to have consisted of twelve hundred seven triremes. Along the way, another one hundred twenty—from Thasos, Abdera, and the other Greek cities along the Thracian coast—had reportedly been added. But something on the order of four hundred of these triremes had foundered along the coast of Magnesia when the Hellesponter had struck; something like another two hundred had been destroyed in a storm while circumnavigating Euboea; and the Persians had suffered further attrition at Artemisium. Herodotus asserts that Xerxes' losses were made up by the support he had gathered while passing through Malia, Doris, Locris, and Boeotia and by the forces dispatched by the Carystians, Andrians, Tenians, and the other islanders. This claim, insofar as it pertains to his army, may well be accurate. But it cannot be true for the Persian navy. The Malians, Dorians, Locrians, and Boeotians had an ample supply of hoplites and cavalrymen to contribute but few, if any, triremes. The islanders from the Cyclades and beyond had ships but not in great numbers. Moreover, many of the communities on these islands—the Chalcidians, Eretrians, Ceans, Naxians, Styrians, Cythnians, Seriphians, Siphnians, and Melians—had escaped or rejected the blandishments of the Mede or had rebelled, and these had sent ships to join the fleet of the Hellenic League, while the Parians, remembering the attack mounted by Miltiades nine years before, had refused to commit their forces, waiting to see who would emerge victorious.[27] When, on the day after the arrival of his fleet, Xerxes made his way down to Phalerum to consult with the commanders of its various contingents, he cannot have had more than seven hundred triremes to deploy, and he probably had six hundred fifty or fewer.

Earlier, in the immediate aftermath of the Persian victory at Thermopylae, Xerxes is said to have consulted Demaratus with regard to the strategy that he should follow in the remainder of the war. In response, Demaratus had reportedly told him that, at the Isthmus of Corinth, the Peloponnesians were likely to mount a resistance to the Persian advance far fiercer than that which the Great King's footsoldiers had encountered at Thermopylae. If, however, he then added, the Great King could find the means with which to divide the Peloponnesians, he could easily overcome them on land.

Off the coast of Laconia, Demaratus explained, lay an island called Cythera. Chilon, the savviest of the Spartans, had once observed that it would be greatly to the advantage of his people if this island were to sink beneath the waves. Demaratus may not have fully explained why this was so. We are not told that he mentioned the grave threat that their helot population posed to the Lacedaemonians. But he did predict that, if the Great King were to divide his fleet and send a squadron of three hundred triremes south along the eastern coast of the Peloponnesus to Cythera, the Spartans would have to abandon the isthmus and return home to defend their fatherland. And if they did this, he told the Great King, the other Peloponnesians would surrender without a fight.[28]

Xerxes is said to have taken Demaratus' counsel seriously and to have firmly dismissed as unjust his brother Achaemenes' accusation that the advice proffered to him by the erstwhile Spartan king was treacherous in intent. In the end, however, he was persuaded by his brother's argument that it would be dangerous to divide his fleet—that, if he dispatched three hundred triremes to Cythera, the navy deployed in the Saronic Gulf by the Greeks would be a match for the force that remained at his disposal.[29]

At Phalerum Xerxes faced a similar dilemma. There he summoned the commanders of the various contingents and seated them in order of precedence—first, the king of Sidon in Phoenicia; then, the monarch of that city's neighbor Tyre; and, after those two, the others—and he instructed Mardonius to circulate among them and ask whether they would advise that he seek a decision at sea. According to Herodotus, all but one of those whom Mardonius consulted gave the same answer—and their answer was that the Great King should wage battle at the first opportunity. The exception to the rule was Artemisia, the ruler of Halicarnassus.

This should give us pause. As we have already noted, if the ancient reports can be trusted, Herodotus was born into a prominent family at Halicarnassus a few years before Xerxes' invasion and was reared there. The odds are good that in his youth he was acquainted with Artemisia; it is certain that he knew her offspring. If he did not hear this story from Artemisia herself, he heard it from one of her children or from others who had heard her tell it. If it is not entirely accurate, it is because, like many another tale, it grew more dramatic in the telling.

There is one false note in the story Herodotus relates. It is perfectly plausible that, at Doriscus, Demaratus praised his fellow Spartans in the manner suggested by the Halicarnassian. After all, what he has Demaratus say to Xerxes is what, we know, the Spartans thought. But when Herodotus has Artemisia tell Mardonius that the men in the Greek fleet "surpass in strength at sea" the men in his fleet "to the same degree that men surpass women" and when he has her denounce the Egyptians, Cypriots, Cilicians, and Pamphylians as being "of no use," he is attributing to her extravagant claims unjustified by any prior experience. At Lade and Artemisium, the men serving in the Persian fleet had proven to be formidable, and at the latter battle the Egyptians had won the prize for valor.[30] It is only in retrospect, after Salamis, that such claims could have been entertained—and, even then, they would arguably have been unjust.

In contrast—when Herodotus has Artemisia suggest that, if he really wishes to win, all that Xerxes needs to do is wait patiently or advance directly against the Peloponnesus at the isthmus, and when he has her add that there is or soon will be a shortage of food on Salamis and that his opponents are likely to scatter to their own cities if given time and allowed to follow their inclinations—he is attributing to her a plausible calculation that anyone closely familiar with the circumstances of the Greeks on Salamis and with the propensities of the Hellenes more generally would have entertained. Had Xerxes chosen the path outlined by Demaratus or had he followed the advice Mardonius elicited from Artemisia, he would in all likelihood have succeeded in his quest. But, no doubt mindful that it was late in the campaigning season, he chose instead to press what he took to be his advantage and force a decision at sea—persuaded, Herodotus tells us, that those who had fallen short off the

Euboean coast, when he had been elsewhere, would distinguish themselves if they were made to fight under the unrelenting gaze of the King of Kings. If, on the eve of the battle, Xerxes made his half-brother Ariabignes the fleet's principal admiral and relegated the admiral hitherto in charge to a subordinate position, as he appears to have done, it was presumably because the latter had failed to meet expectations and achieve a decisive victory at Artemisium.[31]

What Herodotus does not say that no doubt also exercised a powerful influence on Xerxes' calculations was that time was running out. He could not afford to tarry in Attica long. September was drawing to an end. If he did not achieve a final victory quite soon, he would have to reposition his forces for the winter where they could be adequately provisioned, and this would allow the Greeks time in which to build more ships, seek out allies, and regroup. At his command, we are told, late on the very day that the council took place and in preparation for the battle expected the following day, the Persian fleet set out from Phalerum in the direction of Salamis, presumably with an eye to examining the entrances to the channel running between the island of Salamis and the mainland and the southernmost reaches of that narrow body of water; and then, in a fashion evidently meant as a challenge to the Greeks, it briefly deployed for battle.[32]

The Greeks on Salamis

A part of the Greek fleet had not gone to Artemisium but had remained behind—in part, no doubt, to perform guard duty in the Saronic Gulf. It had been ordered to assemble at Pogon, the harbor of Troezen, on the Peloponnesian coast; and there it had been joined by a number of ships from Leucas and Ambracia, Corinthian colonies on the Ionian Sea, and by one such ship—manned largely if not wholly by exiles—representing Croton in distant Italy.[33] Notably absent were the sixty triremes promised by the Corcyraeans, which had, indeed, left the island; rowed south past the entrance to the Corinthian Gulf along the western shore of the Peloponnesus; and then stopped abruptly, at an inviting beach near Pylos in Messenia and at another further east near Cape Taenarum. Later, when called to account by those who had actually fought on Hellas' behalf, they put forward a seemingly plausible excuse, claiming that the Etesian winds had prevented them from rounding Cape Malea. But, mindful that these winds had not stopped the ships from Ambracia and Leucas, no one credited their claim, and it was supposed that the Corcyraeans had paused short of Malea to await the outcome of the great contest under way at Artemisium and Salamis.[34]

When the news reached Pogon that the fleet from Artemisium had arrived at Salamis, the triremes gathered there rowed across the Saronic Gulf to join their brethren in the bays on the eastern coast of the island. When the entire coalition fleet had come together, the ships assembled are said to have outnumbered those which had fought at Artemisium—with contingents from Hermione, Ambracia, Leucas, Naxos, Cythnus, Seriphos, Siphnos, Melos, and Croton joining those already deployed by Lacedaemon, Corinth, Sicyon, Epidaurus, Troezen, Athens, Megara, Aegina, Chalcis, Eretria, Ceos, and Styra. The only communities represented at Artemisium but absent from Salamis were the Opuntian Locrians, who had gone over to the Mede, and the Plataeans, who were busy conveying their families to the Peloponnesus. The numbers that Herodotus provides do not, however, add up. He specifies the contribution of each community—sixteen triremes from Lacedaemon, forty from Corinth, fifteen from Sicyon, ten from Epidaurus, five from Troezen, three from Hermione, one hundred eighty from Athens, twenty from Megara, seven from Ambracia, three from Leucas, thirty from Aegina, twenty from Chalcis, seven from Eretria, two from Ceos, four from Naxos, two from Styra, one from Cythnus, and one from Croton—and then gives us a total for the whole fleet of three hundred seventy-eight triremes, which exceeds by twelve the sum of its parts. Even if one includes the penteconters said to have been provided by Cythnus, Seriphos, Siphnos, and Melos and the trireme from Lemnos that had defected from the Persian fleet at Artemisium, one comes up short.[35]

That is one problem. There is another that bears in a more serious fashion on our assessment of the strategy of the two sides and on the battle itself. In a tragedy produced eight years after the battle, Aeschylus—who had fought at Marathon and was almost certainly present in one capacity or another at Salamis—gives us another figure, claiming that the Greeks fielded a fleet of three hundred ten triremes.[36] The disparity between the figure he provides and the numbers supplied by Herodotus has nothing to do, insofar as anyone can tell, with a dramatic imperative restricting the playwright. Nor is it dictated by metrical constraints. It is arguably a function of the Greek losses at Artemisium, which Aeschylus seems to have taken into account and Herodotus almost certainly ignored. The fact that the Corinthians, Megarians, Chalcidians, Eretrians, Ceans, and Styrians are said by Herodotus to have manned precisely the same number of ships at the two great naval battles does not inspire confidence, and the same can be said for his claim that the Athenians, without any help from the Plataeans, manned exactly the same number of ships at Salamis as they had manned, with their help, at Artemisium.

Even if it were not difficult to square Herodotus' testimony in this particular with the account he gives of the battle and of the damage done the Greek fleet at Artemisium, however, it would be reasonable to prefer the testimony of an eyewitness to hearsay collected decades after the event. Stories often grow with the telling. A little less than fifty years after the battle, Athenian envoys are said to have boasted in a speech delivered before the Spartan assembly that the Hellenes at Salamis had fielded four hundred triremes and that the Athenians had supplied nearly two-thirds of these. We should probably suppose, as Achaemenes reportedly did, that the Persian fleet was a bit more than twice the size of its Greek counterpart.[37]

Once the evacuation of Attica was complete, Eurybiades, who remained the allied commander, came face to face with a genuine dilemma. On Salamis, as Herodotus' Artemisia had the wit to divine, the Greeks were deeply divided; and it was the task of the Spartan navarch, the overall commander at sea designated by the Hellenic League, to manage the coalition and hold the alliance together. The Corinthians and the citizens of the communities intent on stopping the Mede at the Isthmus of Corinth thought it prudent that the fleet withdraw to the Corinthiad and operate in close coordination with the army gathering there. Those from communities situated on islands in the Saronic Gulf or on the mainland outside of the Peloponnesus saw things differently. The Athenians, the Megarians, and the Aeginetans thought it far better to confront the Persians nearer the entrance to the Saronic Gulf and to prevent them from even approaching the isthmus.

According to Herodotus, when the leaders of the various civic contingents met with the Eurybiades to consider where they should seek a naval engagement, a majority of those who spoke up favored abandoning the posture of forward defense. With the exception of the Corinthians, almost all of those living within the Peloponnesus were landlubbers at heart, and they had little confidence in the capacity of the Hellenes to achieve victory at sea. Instead, they anticipated defeat; and, as was only natural in such circumstances, they favored making contingency plans based on this assumption. If they were trounced on the sea at the isthmus, they observed, they could go ashore and join their own people. If, however, they were defeated at sea near Salamis, they would find themselves trapped on an island under siege.[38] If Herodotus' report is both accurate and complete, no one at this particular conference made the case that the Hellenes could actually win and explained how this might be accomplished.

In the midst of their meeting, an Athenian arrived with word that the barbarians had reached Attica and were setting everything aflame. Some of the commanders panicked and left the meeting immediately to ready their ships for flight. Those remaining voted to fight at the isthmus, and at night-fall they dispersed to their ships to make preparations. When the Athenian commander Themistocles returned to his trireme, he encountered an older compatriot, named Mnesiphilus, a man of sufficient political prominence to have once been a target for ostracism, whom Plutarch identifies as having been a mentor to Themistocles in the days of his youth. According to Hero-dotus, when Themistocles reported what those at the meeting had resolved to do, his old friend warned that, when the contingents left Salamis, disaster would ensue: each man would succumb to a desperate longing to return to his own home, Eurybiades would not be able to prevent the fleet from breaking up, and the coalition army assembled at the isthmus would in due course follow suit. Thinking his friend's admonition sound, Themistocles sought out Eurybiades on the trireme that the latter commanded, restated Mnesiphilus' warning, and persuaded him to call the commanders of the civic contingents together for another meeting.[39]

When they again assembled, the Athenian spoke up with great fervor be-fore Eurybiades could even explain why he had called them together, and he reportedly ran into fierce opposition from the Corinthian commander Adei-mantus son of Ocytus, who appears to have been the spokesman for those who wished to withdraw to the isthmus. According to Herodotus, Themisto-cles was circumspect. Thinking that, if he spoke his mind fully, he would be apt to offend, he chose not to repeat the argument that Mnesiphilus had made to him and that he in turn had pitched in private to Eurybiades. Instead of calling into question the staying power of his fellow commanders and raising their hackles by warning that, once the fleet left Salamis, its contingents would disperse and each return to its home, he pointed out that, in abandoning their post near the entrance to the Saronic Gulf, they would in effect be conceding to the enemy not just Salamis but Megara and Aegina as well; and he cannily suggested that, in withdrawing to the isthmus, they would not be defending the Peloponnesus at all. They would be leading the enemy there.

Themistocles appears also to have given considerable thought to what could be learned from the Hellenic experience at Artemisium. Prior to the two skirmishes and the great battle that had so recently taken place in the straits separating Magnesia from Euboea, some of the Greeks from the mainland, Aegina, Euboea, and the islands nearby had had a bit of experience with trireme warfare. The Eretrians had dispatched triremes to support the Ionian revolt in 499. The Athenians would not have chosen to build so large a fleet of triremes in the late 480s had their Aeginetan enemies not outclassed them in this particular, and the Corinthians, who had long been the preeminent naval power in the region, are not apt to have been behindhand in this regard. But the experience that these powers possessed cannot have been extensive; and, prior to the engagements at Artemisium, few of them had witnessed a major fleet action. How well the Hellenic navy would stand up if matched against the Persian fleet they had no notion.

Themistocles was now sanguine. He had emerged from these initial encounters with his confidence enhanced. He did not believe, as did most of the Peloponnesians, that, at sea, the Hellenic cause was doomed; and he recognized that, if the Greeks failed on that element, they would fail also on land. If at sea, he knew, the Persians had a fully free hand, they could land marines and even cavalrymen in substantial numbers behind the Greek lines almost anywhere they pleased in the Peloponnesus and outflank the forces assembling at the isthmus. A recognition on the part of the Hellenes that the barbarians could do this would be sufficient to induce each of the cities to withdraw its forces from the Corinthiad and focus its attention narrowly on homeland defense while attempting to negotiate a separate and favorable deal with the Mede. In this regard, Themistocles' calculations closely resembled those of Miltiades at Marathon. Both men were acutely sensitive to the difficulty that their fellow Greeks had in sustaining solidarity in the face of a looming foreign threat.

In his remarks to his fellow commanders, Themistocles argued with great passion that, if the two fleets fought in the channel between Salamis and Attica, the Greeks could defeat the Persians but that, if the two came to blows in the open sea near the isthmus or anywhere else, the Hellenes would lose. The Greeks would be at a grave disadvantage in open water, he explained, as they had been the third day at Artemisium, and for this there were a number of reasons.[40]

The Greek ships had been in continuous service for some time. There had, we must suspect, been little or no opportunity to haul them out of the water and careen them so that they could dry out, have the barnacles scraped off, and be recaulked and recoated with pitch to protect them against shipworms. In consequence, though designed for speed and agility, they were heavier and more sluggish than the well-maintained triremes in Xerxes' fleet. They were also far fewer in number and their rowers, less well drilled. Even more to the point, their officers had considerably less experience than their counterparts on the Persian side, and they were less skillful in complex maneuvers—shortcomings that mattered a great deal, as Pericles in later years would emphasize to his fellow Athenians.[41]

In the open seas, Themistocles feared, the Greeks would be outclassed, and the barbarians could quite effectively exploit their decisive numerical superiority. In the narrow straits between Salamis and Attica, however, he implied, the weight of their ships would actually give the Hellenes an advantage—for there was little maneuvering to be done and, when it came to bringing brute force to bear in ramming the ships of the other side, the heavier, slower triremes were apt to suffer less and do more damage than those which were lighter and more agile. Moreover, he pointed out, in the straits the Persians would not only be unable to profit from their superiority in numbers. That superiority might, in fact, prove to be their undoing. For, if the triremes collected by the Mede tried to crowd into the narrows, they would be apt to run afoul of one another.[42]

In the past, as we have seen, the Athenians and the Corinthians had enjoyed cordial relations. At this point, however, their interests—at least, as they perceived them—were at odds; and, as was only natural, Themistocles' vehemence elicited a like vehemence from his Corinthian counterpart. When Adeimantus responded sharply and angrily that a man without a city should remain silent and urged the Spartan navarch not to put the motion of such a man to a vote, Themistocles played his trump card, responding that the number of ships that he commanded constituted a city and territory greater than that of any community represented there. Then, turning to Eurybiades, he issued a threat. If the Hellenes abandoned Salamis, the Athenians would take to their ships, sail to Siris on the boot in Italy, and establish a colony there. "You will remember my words," he said, "when you find yourself alone and bereft of allies like us." If Eurybiades needed swaying—and the odds are good that he shared Themistocles' perspective from the outset—this was more than sufficient. He asserted his authority as commander of the coalition forces and announced that they would remain and fight at Salamis, and the others acquiesced—but not for long.[43]

The next morning, at the break of day, there was an earthquake, which was felt both on the land and at sea—a common occurrence in Hellas, then and now. The Greeks, regarding this as a portent, prayed to the gods; and they called on the heroes of the land—Aeacus, the son of Zeus and Aegina; his sons Peleus and Telamon; and their offspring Ajax, Achilles, and Neoptolemos— to come to their aid. Then, they dispatched a boat, probably a triaconter or pentaconter, to Aegina fifteen miles to the south to bring to Salamis as divine protectors the images of Aeacus and the Aeacidae.[44]

The Greeks on Salamis had reason to be nervous. Things were coming to a head. The Persian fleet had reached Phalerum the day before. This the Hellenes can hardly have failed to notice. They may not have been aware of Xerxes' journey down to consult the commanders of his fleet's various contingents the next day, and they may not have learned that he had resolved to force a decision at sea. But they were aware that, late that afternoon, the Persian fleet had put out to sea and approached Salamis from the south arrayed for battle, and they comprehended the significance of this event. "Fear and terror gripped the Hellenes," Herodotus tells us, "and not least the Peloponnesians," who worried that, if they were defeated at sea, "they would be trapped on the island and besieged while leaving their own land unguarded."[45]

If at this time—as Ctesias, Aristodemos, and Strabo all assert—Xerxes' engineers began constructing a mole of sorts at the narrows between Mount Aegaleos on the mainland and Salamis, this, too, will have stoked Greek fears. Hellas is a place of seismic shifts, and these can have a dramatic effect on waterways. In the fifth century, if we are to judge by the structures in or near the Salamis channel now submerged, the water level was five to ten feet lower than it is today. The channel to the south of the little island of Aghios Georgios, separating it from Salamis, was then too shallow for navigation; and the reef lying something like six hundred yards east of Aghios Georgios near the mainland was almost certainly then an islet. It was in the vicinity of these two islands—the Pharmakoussae isles, as they were then called—that, Strabo tells us, Xerxes' engineers began their work. They appear to have attempted, initially, to build a causeway from the mainland to the islet. Then, by lashing together Phoenician merchantmen towed up the Attic shore, they apparently planned to block the deep but narrow channel between the islet and Aghios Georgios to the west and construct a bridge of boats by which, if they could build a second causeway between Aghios Georgios and Salamis, they might introduce footsoldiers onto the island. Against this effort, Ctesias tells us, the Athenians deployed a corps of archers hired from Crete, who made life miserable for Xerxes' engineers.[46]

The Greeks on Salamis may also have had another ground for concern. An Athenian Medizer named Dikaios son of Theokydes, who was part of Xerxes' entourage, later told Herodotus that, on this very day, he happened to be on the Thriasian plain outside Eleusis in the company of Demaratus; and there the two men had witnessed a cloud of dust arising from the cult site the likes of which, in ordinary times, was to be seen only on that very day— the nineteenth day of the lunar month of Boedromion when thousands of Athenians and other Greeks marched en masse in procession to celebrate the Eleusinian Mysteries. This semblance of a ghostly procession at the very time appointed for this festival he interpreted not as an indication that the cavalry and footsoldiers of Xerxes were ostentatiously working their way around the Bay of Eleusis in the direction of Megara and the Isthmus of Corinth, as we have reason to think they were, but as a sign that the gods had not abandoned the Athenian cause.[47] If the Greeks on Salamis knew better, if they got wind of these Persian maneuvers, as they may well have, it will surely have magnified their fears.

According to Herodotus, that same day, when the Hellenes on Salamis learned that a wall was being built at the Isthmus of Corinth, those within their number who hailed from the Peloponnesus again grew restive. "Eurybiades' folly" they reportedly regarded as "a wonder." That afternoon, when an assembly was called, the proponents of withdrawal and those favoring a fight in the channel nearby are said to have squared off again, repeating the same arguments. Athens, Aegina, and Megara provided something like two-thirds of the triremes making up the allied fleet, and this surely mattered. But, when things came to a head, each city, whether large or small, had an equal vote. There were twenty such cities represented; and the Peloponnesian communities and their colonies farther afield were more numerous than the cities that sympathized with the Athenians, Aeginetans, and Megarians. Soon enough it became clear that Themistocles and the Aeginetan and Megarian commanders who were seconding his argument were not going to carry the day.[48]

We are not told whether the commanders from the Peloponnesus and those who lent them support supposed that this great peninsula could be defended at sea in the absence of the Athenian contribution to the Hellenic fleet. It is possible that, in the heat of the moment, they could think of nothing but their families and friends at home. It is also possible that they regarded the ultimatum that Themistocles had issued the previous evening as an idle threat. Whether, in the circumstances, he could have persuaded his compatriots to follow his lead and relocate their city to Italy is by no means clear. All that we really know is that, at this time, the Athenian commander sized up the situation and, in desperation, took matters into his own hands.

He slipped from the meeting and put into operation a plan that he must have devised well before the meeting even began. Among his household slaves was a *paidagōgós*—a fellow assigned to look after his children. He was called Sicinnus, and Themistocles was fully confident that he could rely on the man. On this occasion, he dispatched him in a small boat to the Persian camp at Phalerum with a message for the commanders of the Persian fleet. Aeschylus reports that Sicinnus was a Greek and that he delivered Themistocles' message to Xerxes himself. Herodotus says nothing about his nationality and implies that he met with Xerxes' admirals but not with the Great King. Plutarch asserts that Sicinnus was of Persian extraction, and he and Diodorus presume that he met with the King of Kings. Athenaeus reports a claim that he hailed from Crete. We are left to guess at the details, and guess we will.[49]

Aeschylus was personally acquainted with Themistocles. He is likely to have known whether Sicinnus was a Greek or a Persian in origin, and about this, in his play, he had no reason to lie. It is, moreover, highly unlikely that, at this time, many, if any, Persians had made their way into the slave markets in Greece. Most of them lived upcountry, far from the coastal regions to which the Hellenes had access; and, in the regions in which they did reside, they were, after all, the master race. Of course, Sicinnus is not a Greek name. It was ordinarily reserved for slaves of barbarian origin from Phrygia in northwestern Anatolia. But there were Greek cities in that region, and one could easily imagine a slaveholder conferring such a moniker on a Phrygian Greek. If there was anything to the claim that Sicinnus was a Persian, it will have stemmed from the fact that Phrygia had long been under Persian control and that a young person reared there might have picked up a smattering of the Persian tongue and learned something of Persian ways. It is perfectly conceivable that Themistocles chose Sicinnus for this mission because the pedagogue was able, at least in a limited fashion, to make himself understood in the Persian tongue.

In judging Aeschylus' testimony, one must always keep in mind that he was a poet—apt to take license when his art demanded it—and not an historian. In this case, the protagonist of his play was Xerxes, and it made dramatic sense for him to posit a meeting between Themistocles' slave and the Great King. In such circumstances, precision and accuracy may well have been a secondary consideration.

Herodotus, who was an historian, cared about accuracy a great deal, but he was also a storyteller—not at all averse to staging dramatic confrontations. Had he not been informed that on this occasion no direct exchange took place between Sicinnus and the King of Kings, he would undoubtedly have regaled his readers with the tale told by Aeschylus.

Most of what Sicinnus is said to have related to the Persian commanders was true or a slight but telling and convenient exaggeration of the truth. He explained that he had come from the Athenian commander without the knowledge of the other Greeks, and he had. He announced that he had been instructed to report that his master and the Athenians had come to favor the Persian cause, and these were, indeed, his instructions. He reported that, in terror, the Hellenes were about to flee from Salamis, which they were. He claimed that they were bitterly divided, and divided they were. He contended that they were on the verge of engaging in combat against one another, which they were not, and he suggested that they were unlikely to withstand a determined assault, which was a matter for conjecture. If the Persians were to attack and prevent the escape of the Hellenes, he told them, their achievement would be glorious.[50] The most effective lies are those which closely resemble the truth.

Whether Sicinnus also told Xerxes' admirals that the Greeks were intent on slipping off that very night, as Aeschylus asserts and Plutarch implies, neither Herodotus nor Thucydides nor Diodorus indicates.[51] It is, nonetheless, highly likely that this was the case—for such an assertion would have suited Themistocles' purpose perfectly, and it helps explain the alacrity of the Persian response. It is also possible—even likely—that Themistocles had Sicinnus ask for terms. The Persian commanders, who were skilled in eliciting betrayal, would have expected something of the sort. Had the pedagogue explicitly asked what was on offer, had he intimated mercenary inclinations on the part of his master and the Athenians more generally, it would have made his testimony seem more credible—and it would explain why his barbarian interlocutors allowed him to return to Salamis.

Sicinnus' report was precisely what Achaemenes, Ariabignes, Prexaspes, and Megabazos wanted and expected to hear. From the outset of the expedition, as we have seen, they had been under strict instructions to allow no one, "not even a fire-bearer," to escape retribution at the hands of the King of Kings. Moreover, that very day, they had been ordered to seek a decision at sea.

When Xerxes learned of the message sent by Themistocles, he was no doubt similarly pleased. Fourteen years before, at Lade, as the admirals and their master knew only too well, when the Ionian Greeks had come under pressure of the very sort being brought to bear on the Hellenes at Salamis, they had found it impossible to remain loyal to one another. Moreover, time and again in the previous seventy years, the Persians had inflicted defeat on their enemies with the help of Medizers more than willing to sell out their compatriots for the rich rewards that the King of Kings was known to confer on his benefactors.

The message sent by Themistocles was, from all perspectives, a masterstroke. It cannily played upon the expectations of the Great King and his advisors, and it left Athens' Odysseus—for this was the nickname he would be in due course be awarded[52]—perfectly situated to profit whichever way the upcoming battle went. If the Greeks collapsed and fled in the face of the barbarian onslaught, Themistocles would emerge as a friend and benefactor of the King of Kings and perhaps even as his quisling at Athens and in Hellas more generally. If, on the other hand, the Hellenes defeated the Persians, as he no doubt fervently hoped they would, he could take credit for a brilliant stratagem, and his entire strategy—from the moment he persuaded the Athenians to devote the proceeds of the silver strike at Laurium to the building of a fleet of triremes on—would be vindicated.

Prelude to Battle

Not long after Sicinnus left the camp at Phalerum, Xerxes and his commanders set things in motion. They had been urged by Themistocles' slave to cut off every exit from the channel between Salamis and the mainland, and this they did. Aeschylus tells us that the Great King warned that, if any of the Greeks were allowed to escape, those responsible would pay with their heads; and he informs us that he then instructed his commanders to split the main body of their fleet into three distinct files and "to arrange the rest in a circle around Ajax' isle." Diodorus' report puts flesh on these poetic bones. At the outset, he tells us, Xerxes dispatched the triremes of the Egyptian contingent—once two hundred but now presumably somewhat depleted in number—west into the Saronic Gulf and, then, north to circumnavigate Salamis and block the narrow channel (modern Troupika) that separates both the island from the Megarid and the confined waters of the Gulf of Eleusis from the open waters of the Saronic Gulf.[53] It would, as he surely knew, take some time for this squadron to reach its post. But this mattered not one whit. For, should any Greeks flee up the Salamis channel to the Gulf of Eleusis and then west to Troupika, it would take them no less time. On these Egyptians and on their admiral and satrap, his own brother Achaemenes, Xerxes no doubt thought that he could depend. After all, at Artemisium, they had won the prize for valor.

Some scholars are reluctant to believe the testimony of Diodorus in this regard. Aeschylus lists the Egyptians among those who suffered losses in the battle of Salamis, and a speech that Herodotus puts in the mouth of Mardonius seems to presume that they were among those there put to flight.[54] So these scholars observe. But, on close inspection, neither of the passages they cite appears to have much heft as evidence. The commanders named by Aeschylus in the pertinent lines of his play are figures of his own invention, and the rest of what he says in this passage is likely to be an entertaining mixture of fact and fiction. Aeschylus means to convey an impression; he is not in this passage providing a precise factual report of the actual losses on the Persian side.

The same can be said for Mardonius' speech. It is an example of special pleading. He wants to be left behind with the army to finish the job of conquering the Greeks. So he denounces as cowards all of the maritime peoples who field triremes for the Great King while singling out for praise the Iranian peoples who will make up the bulk of the army he hopes to lead. It is especially telling that later, when he has achieved his aim, he insists on retaining for his use in Greece the Egyptian marines.[55]

Plutarch confirms that a contingent the size of the original Egyptian squadron was sent to undertake the task mentioned by Diodorus, and Herodotus uses language suggesting that a wing of the Persian fleet was sent westward to circle about Salamis.[56] Such a maneuver made good military sense. Given the narrowness of the Salamis channel, the Great King had on hand more ships than he could profitably deploy. If his aim was to annihilate the

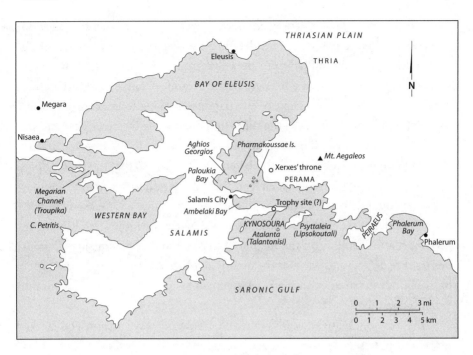

Map 21. Phalerum, Salamis, the Bay of Eleusis, and Troupika

Hellenic fleet and bring the war to a swift end, it made sense to bar every possible avenue of escape.

From the south, there are two entrances to the Salamis channel—on either side of the rocky little island of Psyttaleia (the modern Lipsokoutali). On that island, Aeschylus and Herodotus inform us, Xerxes' commanders landed a contingent of footsoldiers. These were, Aeschylus writes, "Persians in the prime of life, and they were exceptionally courageous of soul and distinguished in birth, always among the first in their lord's trust." Pausanias tells us that they were four hundred in number, and both Aeschylus and Herodotus indicate that they were deployed on Psyttaleia in the expectation that it would be in the path of the battle; that shipwrecks, rowers, and marines would drift onto its shores; and that the crack troops of the Great King placed there would be in a position to protect their own men and slaughter their opponents.[57] We are not told when this landing took place, but the odds are good that it was effected before the darkness of the night fully obscured the approaches to the island and made it impossible for the men managing the landing craft to pick out and avoid the reefs.

After dispatching Achaemenes and the Egyptians to Troupika and making the other preliminary arrangements that were necessary, Xerxes is said to have readied the remainder of his fleet in a more leisurely fashion, directing it to make its way out of Phalerum after dark, round Peiraeus, and row up the Attic coast to the southern entrances of the Salamis channel, and instructing it to intercept and sink or capture any triremes seeking to escape from Salamis. Before the fleet set out in the three files mentioned by Aeschylus, Xerxes is said to have arranged it in discrete ethnic groups—with the Phoenicians on the right and his Greek-speaking subjects on the left—so that the sharing of a common tongue within each squadron and their familiarity with one another would encourage them to come with enthusiasm to one another's assistance. In the middle of the night, then, south of Psyttaleia, in a line stretching from Mounychia in Peiraeus on the mainland to the island of Salamis itself, Ariabignes, Prexaspes, and Megabazos quietly deployed something on the order of five hundred triremes with an eye to blocking egress to the south from the Salamis channel.[58]

There is no way for rowers to move a trireme sideways. In consequence—no doubt, precisely as Themistocles had intended—while their Greek counterparts slept soundly on the shore at Salamis, the rowers, marines, helmsmen, subordinate officers, trierarchs, and admirals in the Persian fleet spent an anxious, restless, sleepless night at sea, exhausting their strength by rowing forward, then backing water in a never-ending struggle to remain in formation.[59] Some of the triremes belonging to the Hellenes were situated within the confines of what we now call Ambelaki Bay—the best anchorage at Salamis, then and now. This body of calm water—narrower then, when the sea level was lower than it is today—is sandwiched between the Kamateró peninsula to its north and Cape Varvari to the south, a promontory which stretches out from Salamis toward the Attic shore north of Peiraeus on a line running a bit to the north of Psyttaleia in the manner of a dog's tail (whence its ancient Greek name, Kynosoura). The remaining Greek triremes, given the considerable size of the Hellenic fleet, must have been lodged in what we now call Paloukia Bay, which lies to the north of the Kamateró peninsula and is sheltered from the east by the little island of Aghios Georgios. It is, crucially, in this region of Salamis, near the Kamateró peninsula where the island's principal town was located, that fresh water in abundance was and is to be found. If there were also ships in the Bay of Arapis a few miles further north, where the modern Greek navy now has a base, their crews were at a disadvantage in this particular.

On the night before the great battle, while the rowers, marines, and helmsmen of Hellas were taking their rest and the Persian fleet was positioning and incessantly repositioning itself, the commanders of the individual Greek contingents were once again trying to thrash out a common policy; and, as the night wore on, the wrangling between them reportedly became intense. In the midst of this heated debate, we are told, an Athenian appeared at the doorway and asked to speak with Themistocles, who responded by stepping outside. The new arrival was Aristeides son of Lysimachus, a man whose relations with the Athenian commander had long been fraught. Among other things, he had been ostracized in 483 and then recalled from exile two years thereafter, on both occasions at the instigation of the political rival with whom he was about to converse. Plutarch tells us that, in recalling Aristeides, Themistocles was moved by the fact that his compatriots wanted the man back and by the fear that his rival might otherwise take the side of the Mede—who had, we are told by another source, offered the exile a handsome bribe of six thousand darics—more than one hundred eleven pounds in gold. Themistocles' aim was to promote civic solidarity, and Aristeides' conduct on this occasion suggests that he achieved this end.

Aristeides had just arrived on Salamis from Aegina to the south—where, as we have seen, he was well connected. Why he had come and why at this particular time we do not know. He may have been returning from a trip in which he helped conduct evacuees from Attica to that island; he may have been on some other mission. What we do know is that he had just with some difficulty run the Persian blockade and that, upon his arrival on Salamis, he had learned that the Greeks were contemplating an immediate withdrawal from the island. It seemed to him essential that Eurybiades and the subordinate commanders be informed with regard to the disposition of the Persian fleet, and he suggested that Themistocles break the news to those inside.[60]

These tidings no doubt left Themistocles overjoyed. It meant that his stratagem had worked. The Greeks were trapped, the oarsmen in the Persian fleet were busy wearing themselves out, and a battle on terms highly favorable to the Hellenes was in the offing. The Athenian knew better, however, than to suppose that, if he were to inform his fellow commanders about the disposition of the Persian fleet, he would be believed. He was, after all, a fierce and notorious partisan of a particular strategy, and he had provoked fury from its opponents. This news would be seen as providing grist to his mill, and it would be dismissed as a trick. So, instead, Themistocles brought in Aristeides, a man known to be personally hostile to him. But first he divulged to his Athenian rival the role that he had himself played in bringing on the Persian blockade, and the two men shook hands, pledging to set aside their enmity and rivalry until after the defeat of the Mede.[61]

When Aristeides broke the news, a majority of the commanders refused to credit his testimony. They knew what the Athenians wanted, and these tidings were simply too convenient to be believed. But shortly thereafter a trireme from the Persian fleet defected, and its commander—Panaetius son of Sosimenes, a man from Tenos—confirmed everything that Aristeides had related. Because of Panaetius' contribution at Salamis—at this moment and in the battle that followed—the Tenians would be listed among the Hellenes who had successfully fought the Mede.[62]

If the testimony of Diodorus can be trusted, the Hellenes were rewarded with one additional source of information. The commanders of the Ionian squadrons, he reports, sent a Samian to swim across the straits and warn the Greeks of what was afoot.[63] Whether this last tale is true or not, one thing is clear. From Salamis, the Greeks now knew, there was no escape. They would have a fight on their hands at the break of dawn; and, as Themistocles had intended, they planned accordingly.

A Clash of Arms

At some point not long before first light on the twentieth day of the Athenian month of Boedromion—which is to say, on the twenty-eighth day of our own September—Xerxes situated himself on the lower slopes of Mount Aegaleos, a promontory which thrusts out dramatically from the Attic coast toward the Pharmakoussae isles, Paloukia Bay, and the shores of Salamis. His golden stool he set down above the sanctuary of Heracles, which lay on the southwest corner of the mountain spur above the modern port of Perama, whence the ferry to Salamis ran then and still runs now.[64]

One could hardly imagine a better vantage point. From this high hill, he could see not only the Pharmakoussae isles and the Paloukia and Ambelaki inlets—where most, if not all of the Greek fleet was harbored—but also the Kynosoura peninsula, the Salamis straits, and the island of Psyttaleia. On a clear day, he could even make out ships at sea on either side of the island, where the Persian fleet had established itself the night before.

With effort, Xerxes, his companions, assistants, and scribes could pick out individual ships in the channel below and identify them by the painted plaque on the prow of each, advertising its name. He could observe and assess the conduct of his captains and their men, precisely as he had intended; and he could ask his scribes to write down on the list of his benefactors the names, patronymics, and communities of origin of those who distinguished themselves in the fight. His *bandaka* were no longer out of sight and out of mind, as they had been at Artemisium. They operated under the discriminating gaze of the King of Kings, and they all knew as much—for they could see their master with as much clarity as he could see them. Moreover, if Polyaenus is right in supposing that, at sea, the Greeks and the Persians employed flags to convey orders and other information, he may even in some measure have been able to direct their movements in the battle about to take place.[65]

In the early morning hours, while Xerxes was making his way to his station, the commanders of the Greek fleet were rousing their men, dispatching them to their triremes, and preparing for battle. When all was ready and daybreak neared, the Athenian commanders and marines gathered, and Themistocles gave a speech exhorting them to overcome the weakness to which human nature is prone and do their best. As these men made their way to their triremes, a ship from Aegina arrived with the images of Aeacus and his offspring. The Hellenes could take comfort in the fact that the heroes of the land would be fighting close by their side.[66]

We do not know for certain the disposition of the Persian fleet at this moment. Some scholars think that, in the course of the last few hours of darkness preceding the dawn, when the Greeks failed to appear, some of the contingents in the Persian fleet, perhaps as many as one hundred or even two hundred ships, were ordered to leave the post they had occupied earlier in the night, enter the channel to the north and east of Psyttaleia, and make their way quietly along the friendly shore of Attica toward the position that would soon be occupied by the Great King. In support of their opinion, they cite Herodotus' claim that, in the battle that actually did take place, "the Phoenicians were ranged against the Athenians, who held the wing off toward Eleusis and the west, while the Ionians were ranged opposite the Lacedaemonians, who held the wing off toward the east and Peiraeus."[67]

Others think that the Persian triremes remained at the post they were originally assigned and advanced past Psyttaleia into the channel only when the Hellenes put out to sea. They argue that rowing up the coast in the dark would have been an unattractive and counterproductive maneuver. In their wildest dreams, say they, the Persians could not have had any confidence that their progress would pass unremarked. The noise produced by thousands of oarsmen rowing in unison, the stench given off by the sweat and urine and excrement of tens of thousands of desperately anxious men, and the sight of triremes in motion on a night lit in the last five hours before dawn by a waning crescent moon would be apt to betray them. By such a maneuver, the Persians would have risked sacrificing what they took to be their greatest advantage: the crucial element of surprise—and to no obvious purpose.

These scholars also point to the testimony of Aeschylus, an eyewitness writing eight years after the event for a hypercritical audience filled with his fellow eyewitnesses. He, they note, makes no mention of a repositioning of the Persian fleet in the early morning hours. Instead, he reports that the Persians were themselves caught by surprise at dawn when they first heard singing—then recognized the paean, the voice of a trumpet [sálpınx], pipers keeping time, the sound of oars striking the water in unison all echoing from the hills round about—as the Greeks rowed out from Ambelaki and Paloukia Bay. And he asserts that the barbarians heard the Hellenes well before the latter were made manifest [ekphaneîs] and they laid eyes on them—which can only mean that to discern and to be discerned, to see the triremes of the enemy and to be seen by the trierarchs, helmsmen, and marines on their decks, the Hellenes similarly positioned had to emerge into the channel from behind Kynosoura.[68]

Fortunately, we do not have to choose between Aeschylus and Herodotus. After all, the former is describing the situation at dawn, and the other is describing the battle as it was subsequently fought. It is perfectly possible that— on impulse or at the command of Xerxes or of Ariabignes, the admiral he put at their head—the Phoenicians on the Persian right, when they first heard the Greeks singing the paean, raced in one or more columns north-northwest up the Attica coast the three nautical miles separating the waters about Psyttaleia from the Heracleum with a speed that none but the sea dogs of Sidon and Tyre, with all of their experience and skill, could have achieved. And it is no less plausible that the Cypriots, Cilicians, Pamphylians, Lycians, Carians, and Ionians, who had been in the formation in that order on the Phoenicians' left, then smoothly moved in behind them. At the same time, if this scenario is correct, the Athenians will have rowed out from Paloukia Bay in line ahead, skipping past the shallow water directly south of Aghios Georgios and moving north, then east around that island before then wheeling suddenly south

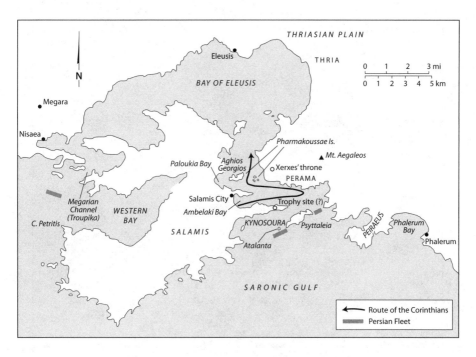

Map 22. The Battle of Salamis: The Corinthian Flight

to approach in disciplined units ordered in line abreast the narrow channel, then roughly six hundred yards across, that separated the larger of the two Pharmakoussae isles from its companion, the tiny island just off shore from the Heracleum. Later, the Lacedaemonians, Aeginetans, and Megarians must have slipped in single file out of Ambelaki Bay to ambush the Carians and Ionians at the tail end of the long line pursuing the Phoenicians up the Attica coast.[69]

On this reconstruction, the aim of Eurybiades and his fellow commanders was to lure the Persians from their position in the open sea to the south of Psyttaleia not just into the Salamis channel but up to its narrowest navigable point—where, as Plutarch would later put it, the Hellenes would "by the confined space be made equal in number to the barbarians, who would be forced to attack in detachments and made to run afoul of one another." To this end, at the outset, Eurybiades offered the barbarians tempting bait of a familiar kind. When the Spartan navarch had the Greeks strike up the paean, he instructed the Corinthians to take the lead, row up Ambelaki Bay past the tip of Kynosoura, and—when they became visible to those in charge of the enemy fleet— to wheel, hoist their sails, reapply their oars, and simulate a flight west-north-

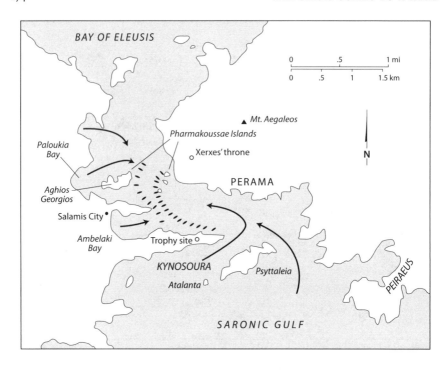

Map 23. The Battle of Salamis: The Conflict

west past the island of Aghios Georgios, then north toward the Bay of Eleusis beyond. The Athenians, who made up something on the order of half of the coalition fleet, and the others quartered in Paloukia Bay he ordered to move north and east initially as if they were going to follow the Corinthians—and this feint appears to have worked. For the Persian fleet racing up the Salamis channel soon found itself in a position in which all of its strengths—above all, its size and the lightness and agility of the triremes belonging to it—weighed against it.[70]

The Athenians were fully familiar with the Salamis channel. They knew where the water was deep. They knew where there were reefs and shoals, and their fellow Hellenes—quartered as they had been for some days in the bays along this channel—had become familiar with its features. The Phoenicians and the other contingents in the Persian fleet enjoyed no such advantage. They were operating in waters unknown. When the Phoenicians and Cypriots reached the Heracleum and approached the treacherously narrow channel between the Pharmakoussae isles—Aghios Georgios and the tiny island just off the Attic coast—they found suddenly and unexpectedly, no doubt to their great dismay, that they had to reduce radically the width of their column and, to this end, pull many of their triremes aside. This endeavor produced in the Persian formation an unwonted confusion—which made it difficult, if not impossible, to deftly maneuver the triremes in that fleet and rendered them vulnerable to assault.

Leading the Phoenicians unwittingly into this trap was Ariabignes son of Darius, admiral of the fleet, grandson of Gobryas, nephew of Mardonius, and half-brother of Xerxes himself. When he entered that narrow channel, an enterprising Athenian from Pallene named Ameinias darted forward in his ship and rammed the trireme of the admiral head-on. The two ships then became inextricably entangled. And, when Ariabignes tried with the Iranian marines assigned his trireme to board the Athenian boat, Ameinias and his comrade Socles of Paeania speared and killed him, and the Achaemenid admiral fell into the sea. In the aftermath of this brief but dramatic struggle, which decapitated the Persian fleet and threw the commanders of the individual squadrons back on their own devices, the Athenians, taking advantage of the confusion besetting their foe, drove forward, rammed some ships, and sheared off banks of oars from others, leaving the latter helpless, like birds with broken wings, unable to maneuver and incapable of defending themselves against oncoming triremes intent on using their rams to crack open their hulls.[71]

Everything worked to the advantage of the Hellenes—even the weather. Although the triremes in the Persian fleet were comparatively light and agile, they were top-heavy. As we have noted, all of them had full decks. Those of the Ionians may have had outriggers for the *thranítai,* as seems to have been the case with those of their Athenian opponents. But the Phoenician triremes were equipped, instead, with high bulwarks decorated with shields. More to the point, on deck, each of the triremes in the Persian fleet carried thirty marines of Iranian stock in addition to the ship's officers, the men who managed its sails, and its ordinary complement of four archers and ten marines, This much extra weight on the deck of a vessel with a draft of only three and a half feet substantially raised its center of gravity and rendered it not just unstable but exceedingly hard to handle if the sea was in any way rough;[72] and, at Artemisium, Themistocles had noticed that the Phoenician triremes in particular were vulnerable in precisely this fashion.

At some point within the first two hours after dawn—as, in late summer, Athenian fishermen familiar with the local microclimate had reason to expect —a stiff breeze came up, fresh from the Saronic Gulf to the south, and the hills on Salamis and the Attic coast channeled it into the straits. There it produced a swell in the water and caught the Phoenician triremes off guard, swinging them around and briefly exposing their long, fragile hulls to being rammed by the comparatively stable and sluggish, low-lying triremes of the expectant Greeks, who, on Themistocles' signal, were quick to take advantage of the opening not only anticipated but actually, in this instance, afforded them.[73]

Some of the Phoenician and Cypriot triremes the Athenians drove ashore near where Xerxes watched from his golden stool. Others, in a panic, fled in the direction of Phalerum; and when they did so, they ran afoul of the Cilician, Pamphylian, and Lycian ships lined up to their east, and these in turn took to flight, leaving the Athenians free to turn their attention to the wing held by the Carians and Ionians, whom they pressed hard.[74]

In these circumstances, the Aeginetans, who were lined up with the Megarians and Lacedaemonians on the right wing of the Hellenic line, had a field day, picking off the triremes of the Persian fleet as they fled, heedless, down the channel from the Athenian assault. Their success was so magnificent that, when the battle was over, they, and not the Athenians, were awarded the prize for valor. Among the individuals subsequently singled out for conspicuous courage was Polycritus of Aegina, son of that Crius who had defied the Spartan king Cleomenes in 491 and who had subsequently been arrested by Cleomenes and Leotychidas and confined in Athens as a Medizer. As he rammed a Sidonian ship, this Polycritus is said to have spied Themistocles nearby, aboard his own trireme, and to have taunted him, asking him to consider what sort of Medizers the Aeginetans were now.[75]

According to Herodotus, the presence of Xerxes had its intended effect, and his subordinates entered the fray with much greater vigor and élan than they had displayed at Artemisium. In these circumstances, however, their enthusiasm may not have worked fully to his or their advantage—for, when the Phoenician ships in the lead turned to take flight, they frequently collided head-on with other triremes deployed further down the channel, whose captains were eager to sail past them and perform noteworthy feats under the gaze of that paragon of generosity: the King of Kings.[76]

Among those overly ambitious in this regard were the Ionians—who, perhaps encouraged by the Iranian footsoldiers on board their triremes, appear to have been far more interested in pleasing their master than in honoring Themistocles' request that they defect. Herodotus, who had ample opportunity in later years to interview the survivors, mentions by name two of their captains—Theomestor son of Androdamas and Phylakon son of Histiaeus, both from Samos—who were recognized as benefactors of the king. But he tells us that he could list many other Ionian trierarchs who captured Greek ships.[77]

Against the Ionians, certain Phoenicians, who had apparently lost their own ships as a consequence of these head-on collisions, brought a charge of treason. But when Xerxes, to whose redoubt on Mount Aegaleos they had climbed, witnessed the prowess of a Greek crew from Samothrace, which in short order sank one Hellenic trireme and took control of another, he turned on those accusing the Ionian cousins of these Samothracians, blamed them for the way the battle was going, and on impulse ordered that their heads be cut off.[78] Someone had to be made to pay for the disaster under way.

There is much that we do not know about this great event. Plutarch quotes a passage from Simonides' narrative account of the battle, in which Democritus of Naxos—the trierarch who had persuaded the crews of the four ships dispatched from that island in support of the Mede to defect to the Hellenes—is singled out as the third Hellenic trierarch to lead his trireme into the fray, and in which he is credited with capturing five Persian ships and with saving a Dorian vessel from being seized by the barbarian. We know as well that the Corinthians distinguished themselves, but we do not know precisely how,[79] and there is every reason to suppose that the Spartans, Megarians, Chalcidians, Eretrians, Sicyonians, Epidaurians, Troezenians, Ceans, Styrians, Ambraciots, and Leucadians had a good day as well and were proud of what they had accomplished. But of their exploits we know nothing at all.

A number of things stand out. The battle took place at the time of the fall equinox. We are told by Plutarch that the Persian assault persisted until nightfall, and Aeschylus intimates that the struggle lasted the full twelve hours separating dawn from dusk at that time of the year.[80] This suggests that contingent after contingent sailed up the channel to be slaughtered in turn by the Greeks, and it leaves one wondering just how long the rowers in the Persian fleet—who had been active, as Themistocles had intended, the entire night before the battle—had the stamina to man the oars in their triremes with any effectiveness.

Moreover, Herodotus indicates that, after the Phoenician line broke, the battle became a melee [*thórubos*]. As the day wore on and it became clear that the Greeks were succeeding on the sea, he adds, confusion [*thórubos*] reigned and, when the wind shifted and came in from the west, as it often does in the afternoon, wrecks and men began drifting down the channel toward Psyttaleia, where the Persians had landed their footsoldiers. On the shore of Salamis at Kynosoura stood Aristeides son of Lysimachus, watching these Persian soldiers in action, as they rescued the survivors from their own fleet and killed off the Hellenes who swam to that shore. On impulse, we are told, he collected some of the hoplites lined up along the strand and found boats to ferry them across to the little island, where they massacred the Persian footsoldiers and began saving Greeks and slaughtering those of the foe who drifted to its shores. If, from his perch on Mount Aegaleos, Xerxes was able to discern what was happening on Psyttaleia, he may, in lamentation, have torn his robes, just as Aeschylus claims.[81]

But if Persia's Great King could not fully make out what was happening at that distance, as seems possible, there was plenty going on in the waters nearer his perch that was more than sufficient to justify on his part an eloquent gesture of grief. Here is what Aeschylus has the messenger, dispatched by Xerxes to Susa at the end of the battle, tell the queen mother Atossa:

> The ramming a Greek boat initiated,
>   Breaking off in its entirety the high-pointed stern
> of a Phoenician ship, and against one another both sides were
>   hurling spears.
>   At first the stream of Persian vessels maintained itself in formation;
>   But when the multitude of ships congregated in the narrows,
>   Not a one could be of assistance to another,
> for they were smiting one another with their bronze-mouthed rams,
>   Shattering all the oars with which they had been equipped,
>   And the ships of the Hellenes, not in a reckless, thoughtless manner,
>   Were circling and striking, upending
>   the hulls of ships; so that the sea was no longer to be seen,
>   Chock-full as it was with wrecks and mortals slain,
>   The headlands also and the shoals round about were stuffed with
>   bodies dead.
>   Then, in flight without order was every ship rowed
>   Which belonged to the barbarian armada.
>   And with broken fragments of oars and wrecks
> They kept clubbing us, deboning us, as if we were tunny
>   Or a net-load of fish. Close at hand, wailing
>   And shrieking encompassed the salt sea,
>   Until black night's visage got in the way.
>   Not even if I related the multitude of ills
> For ten long days could I finish them off for you.
>   Learn, then, this well: that never in a single day
> Did so great a number of men meet up with death.[82]

Of course, the full story was lost on the vast majority of the participants, who did not have so panoramic a view—as is in battle, Thucydides reminds us, ordinarily the case. When the day was done, Herodotus tells us, the Greeks, who controlled the channel, hauled up on the Salamis shore the wrecks that were still afloat and made preparations for another battle at sea, expecting that, on the morrow, the Great King would make use of those of his ships still intact. They had lost forty triremes, and most of the oarsmen in these had managed to swim to the Salamis shore.[83] This their commanders were in a position to discover. They may well have had a vague notion of the destruction and slaughter that they had inflicted on the enemy, but they had no clear idea.

The Aftermath

Xerxes knew far more than did any of the Hellenes—except, perhaps, for the handful of Athenians who watched the battle from the heights of the Kynosoura peninsula. From his perch on Mount Aegaleos, he had taken in what almost no observer on the Greek side was in a position to see: the battle on all sides as it progressed. His admirals—those who survived—were in a position to count the triremes at Phalerum and report to their master; and all concerned probably recognized that, when a trireme in their fleet was holed, the Iranian marines on board—few of whom could swim at all—were doomed. The Egyptian squadron, dispatched toward Troupika under Achaemenes' command, was intact. On this they could depend. But, of those ships which had fought in the Salamis channel, some two hundred, if we can trust Diodorus, had been destroyed, and many more had been captured. Moreover, after the Great King had ordered the beheading of some of the Phoenician trierarchs, he had threatened to inflict on the rest the punishment he thought they deserved, and at least some of the ships from Sidon and Tyre had fled in search of temporary refuge on the Athenian coast to the south of Phalerum; and then, at nightfall, we are told, they had hoisted sails and headed home.[84]

In sum, the fleet of the King of Kings was but a shadow of what it had been. Its morale was shattered, and its commanders had lost Xerxes' trust and respect. In the wake of the battle, with the supposed achievements of Artemisia in mind, he was heard to say, "My men have become women and my women, men." To her, he reportedly awarded a suit of Greek armor, and to the admiral who took charge after Ariabignes' death—either Prexaspes or Megabazos or the latter's father—he sent a distaff and spindle as an indication that he was fit solely for women's work. There was, the Great King knew, no way to continue the war at sea.[85]

To confuse the Greeks, however, and instill a measure of confidence in his own men, Xerxes ordered that, on the next day, ostentatious preparations be made for a renewal of the fight. At the same time, he instructed his engineers to renew their attempt to build a mole from the mainland to Salamis, which they did. Almost everyone, we are told, was fooled.[86]

In the meantime, at the suggestion of Mardonius and on the advice of Artemisia, the Great King decided to return to Asia Minor. That night, his admirals surreptitiously put out to sea, leading what remained of his fleet back to the Hellespont to protect the two bridges there. Aeschylus reports that these remained intact, but Herodotus, writing much later, claims that they had in the interim been swept away by a storm.[87]

At about this time, Artemisia was given the signal honor of ferrying Xerxes' bastards to Ephesus, and within a few days of the battle Xerxes found himself on his way through Boeotia. On the first stage of his journey, he was escorted by Mardonius, who—like the elder Megabazos in Thrace after Darius' Scythian expedition—would be left behind with the core of the Persian army to finish the job begun by his master but left unfinished.[88]

Xerxes staged his departure and that of his army from Attica on the second of October. We know the precise day because it coincided with an eclipse that astronomers can easily date—which deterred Cleombrotus son of Anaxandridas, the Lacedaemonians, and their Peloponnesian allies at the Isthmus of Corinth from attempting to capitalize on the maritime victory at Salamis by marching forth in an attempt to turn the Persian retreat into a rout, as they were hoping to do.[89]

In Thessaly, where Mardonius intended to spend the winter and make preparations to renew in the spring the struggle to conquer Hellas, Xerxes and his marshal parted company. The former managed to make the journey from Thessaly to the Hellespont, a trek of some five hundred fifty miles, in forty-five days—half the time his army had spent while actually on the march between the Hellespont and Athens. Along the way, he paused at Abdera, where in the past he had stationed his fleet; and there he contracted a guest-friendship with the citizens of that community, leaving, as a sign of his regard, a tiara encrusted with gold and a golden sword. When he and his bodyguard reached the Hellespont, they found that a storm had destroyed the bridges of boats, and so he and they crossed back into Asia by ship.[90]

   Scholars tend to deny that the troops who accompanied the Great King on this journey suffered from famine and cold on the route through Boeotia, Phocis, Thessaly, Macedonia, and Thrace—as Aeschylus, Herodotus, and Justin assert[91]—and they are no doubt right in suggesting that the tragedian and the two historians exaggerate for dramatic effect. Had the food shortages been severe, we can be confident that Xerxes would have proceeded at an even faster pace. But we should not reject outright their claims that provisions were hard to come by. This journey took place in the second half of October, in November, and perhaps also in early December through lands which the Persians had already stripped bare, and Xerxes in defeat may not have been able to elicit support as readily as when victory on his part had seemed a foregone conclusion. In this season, moreover, merchantmen bearing foodstuffs were reluctant to sail.[92] We must never forget that the army fielded by Xerxes for his Greek expedition was, by all accounts, the largest known in human history up to this time. From the outset, logistics was its Achilles heel.

CHAPTER 8

Plataea and Mycale

From Salamis I shall gain the Athenians' gratitude as my reward,
And I shall sing of the struggles before Cithaeron,
In which conflict the curve-bowed Medes went down to defeat.

—PINDAR

THE departure of the Persian navy from Phalerum caught the Greeks on Salamis flat-footed. It was only when they became aware of the fleet's disappearance that it began to cross their minds that the defeat they had inflicted on the Mede at sea had been decisive, at least on that element, and that it might have broken the enemy's morale. It did not take Eurybiades and the commanders of the various contingents long to size up their new situation and to act. With an eye to capitalizing on their victory, they quickly set out in pursuit of the remnants of Xerxes' maritime armada. They rounded Cape Sunium, rowed east toward Ceos, then raced northeast toward the gap between Euboea and Andros. But they were too late. The enemy following that same route had a considerable head start and had made good time, and the Greeks never even caught sight of their foe.[1]

At Andros, the Hellenic commanders paused to parley. According to Herodotus, Themistocles suggested that they continue their pursuit of Xerxes' fleet, make their way through the islands, and tear down the bridges spanning the Hellespont. Eurybiades reportedly countered that it would be an error to bottle up the Great King in Europe and make him desperate. If trapped, he would not sit still and watch his army starve. For provisions, he would confiscate the crops grown by the Hellenes. Moreover, if he remained in Europe and worked at it, the Spartan navarch warned, Xerxes might well win over the Hellenic cities, as well as the various Greek peoples lacking urban centers, one community at a time—reaching agreements with some, and violently laying hold of others. In the circumstances, he urged, it would be better to allow

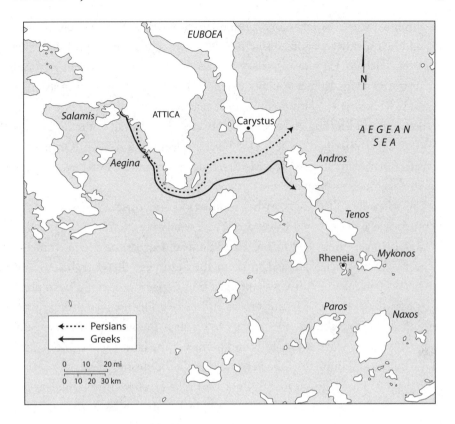

Map 24. From Phalerum and Salamis to the Andros-Euboea Gap

Xerxes to flee to his own land and then, the following year, renew the contest outside Hellas on the other side of the Aegean in territory hitherto ruled by the Achaemenid monarch.[2]

It seems not to have crossed Eurybiades' mind that the only way to guarantee a full Persian withdrawal from Europe at this time might be for the Greeks to strike directly and immediately at the Great King's realm and stir up a rebellion along the coast of Asia Minor and in the Hellespontine region. The Spartan navarch and the Peloponnesians who rallied in defense of his stand wanted, above all else, to avoid a battle on land against the Mede— which, for understandable reasons, they feared they might lose. Later, they were no doubt surprised and deeply dismayed to learn that—while Xerxes had, indeed, departed from Europe, as they had hoped—the core of his army had remained behind under the command of his cousin and brother-in-law Mardonius son of Gobryas.

Themistocles was a man of supreme self-confidence. But he knew his limits, and he quickly recognized that he was not in a position to prevail in this particular debate. He may also have had second thoughts about the wisdom of his initial suggestion, especially when, in private conversation, Aristeides seconded Eurybiades' argument against tearing down the bridges over the Hellespont and bottling Xerxes up in Europe. The Spartan commander was no fool. September had passed. October had begun—and, with it, came the prospect of violent storms. The Mediterranean in winter can be exceedingly cruel. This much everyone knew.

So when he called together his compatriots—who were furious that the Persians had been allowed to get away, and who were even more eager than he was to make their way to the Hellespont and drive the Mede from the Aegean—Themistocles pitched to them the argument that Eurybiades and Aristeides had made to him, warning just how dangerous it could be to press one's advantage in such circumstances and force a formidable adversary, intent on flight, to fight. In any case, he told them, the victory was not really theirs. It was the work of the gods and heroes of the land and a consequence of the hubris and impiety of the Persian king. In the spring, they could gather again, sail to the Hellespont and Ionia, and take revenge. In the interim, he urged, they should rejoice in the fact that they had driven the barbarian from Hellas, and they should return home, rebuild their houses, and turn to sowing so that there would be a harvest in the spring.[3] Underpinning Themistocles' advice was a false presumption, entertained also by Eurybiades and the Peloponnesians. He, too, for all of his foresight, seems never to have imagined that, when Xerxes withdrew to Asia Minor, he would leave much of his army behind in Greece and that, come harvest time, Attica would once again be occupied by the enemy.

At some point after he learned of the departure of the Persian fleet, Themistocles is said to have dispatched to the Achaemenid monarch a messenger once again. About this gesture, there is, however, considerable confusion. Whether, for example, Themistocles sent Sicinnus on this second mission, as Herodotus and Diodorus claim, or Arsaces, a royal eunuch captured at Artemisium or Salamis, as Plutarch reports—we do not know.[4]

Even more to the point, there is disagreement in the sources regarding the content of the message conveyed. Herodotus tells us that the Athenian statesman dispatched an emissary after the decision of the Hellenes to give up their pursuit of the Persian fleet and that he instructed the man to announce that Themistocles son of Neocles, the commander of the Athenians, had conferred on Xerxes a great benefit by persuading the Greeks to refrain from pursuing his fleet and destroying the bridges over the Hellespont. Diodorus Siculus and Cornelius Nepos, both presumably following Ephorus, have a different tale to tell—that, with an eye to hastening the Great King's departure, Themistocles warned him, perhaps before the Hellenic fleet left Salamis, that the Greeks intended to tear down the bridges and obstruct his retreat.

In his brief lives of Themistocles and Aristeides, Plutarch—who wrote in a much later time and was thoroughly familiar with nearly all of the earlier reports—compounds the confusion. In the first of these two accounts, Plutarch claims that Themistocles warned Xerxes that the Greeks intended to destroy the bridges in the Hellespont and promised to do everything within his power to delay the endeavor—while, in the second, he restates Herodotus' claim that, in his message, the Athenian commander took credit for having already put an end to the Greek enterprise.[5]

Ordinarily, it would make sense to prefer Herodotus' testimony. He was, after all, closer to the events. But there are reasons for hesitation. First, no one—apart from Themistocles, his emissary, and those who witnessed the latter's delivery of the former's message to the Great King—was in a position to know what actually took place. Second, Themistocles was an exceedingly controversial figure, about whom there was much malicious gossip; and, to make matters even more perplexing, he was not himself overly given to telling the truth. Moreover, a decade and a half subsequent to these events, Themistocles was charged with medizing; and he fled to the court of Xerxes' son Artaxerxes, representing himself, so Thucydides tells us, as having benefited the royal house in precisely the fashion indicated by Herodotus. Whether earlier, at Athens, he told the story in the manner in which it is related by Diodorus and Nepos we do not know, but it is certainly possible. All that we can be sure of is that, in 480, Athens' Odysseus was at the top of his game. As Herodotus contends, he may already have been aware that eventually he might run afoul of the Athenians and need to find refuge beyond their reach.[6] And, as Herodotus should have added, Themistocles found a way of doing his compatriots good and of making provision for himself at the same time—for, whichever story we choose to believe, the import of the message he dispatched was that Xerxes would do well to absent himself from Greece at the first opportunity. From the perspective of the Athenians and every other community associated with the Hellenic League, this was a consummation devoutly to be wished.

After deciding to abandon their pursuit of the Persian fleet, the Hellenes did not immediately suspend operations and return home. Instead, they paused for a time at Andros in a halfhearted and short-lived attempt to mount and sustain a siege of the city located on that island. This community was, we are told, the first of a series of medizing Cycladic *póleis* solicited by Themistocles which flatly refused to pay the indemnity he asked. From the Carystians and the Parians, he had reportedly collected large sums, but the Andrians had dug in their heels, and his aim was to make an example of them. In relating this information, Herodotus makes the same error that he committed when discussing Miltiades' expedition to Paros in 489. He ignores the strategic significance of bringing the Cyclades under Hellenic control, he pays no attention to the fiscal difficulties faced by the Hellenes, and he traces the allied endeavor to motives purely personal and mercenary on Themistocles' part.[7]

It was, in fact, quite expensive to keep a single trireme at sea and to provide adequately for the needs of two hundred men. To do so for hundreds of triremes and their crews was a challenge breathtaking in its difficulty, and none found the task as burdensome as did the Athenians. Their contribution to the coalition effort dwarfed that of all of the other allies. They had, moreover, suffered grievously. They had lost one harvest. Their farms had been ravaged and their city and its sanctuaries, pillaged and burned. To sustain for another campaigning season the effort that they had begun they needed every ounce of silver that they could extort from those in the Cyclades who had sided with the Mede. When it comes to armed conflict at sea, money was then, as it is now, the sinews of war.[8]

While the Hellenes in the fleet were busy extracting resources in this fashion, Xerxes was making his way to Thessaly in the company of Mardonius. When the Great King and his entourage paused in that well-watered and agriculturally rich land, Mardonius, as they had agreed at Athens, picked out the troops he wished to retain—nearly all of them Iranians. Prior to the departure of the fleet from Phalerum, he had requested the Egyptian marines, who had so distinguished themselves at Artemisium. Now, as the Great King prepared to depart, Mardonius asked as well for the Ten Thousand Immortals, the elite brigade of Persian footsoldiers issued breastplates, and a thousand Persian cavalrymen. Then, he named the infantry, archers, and cavalry fielded by the Medes, the Sacae, the Bactrians, and the Aryans of the Indus valley, and he is said to have selected from the other national contingents those who were the most impressive in appearance or who had distinguished themselves by the services they had performed.[9]

Before Xerxes left Thessaly for the Hellespont, Herodotus tells us, a curious event took place. A herald arrived from the Spartans, who had been urged by the oracle at Delphi to demand satisfaction for the killing of Leonidas and to accept whatever the Great King offered. When confronted with this unanticipated demand, Xerxes is said to have laughed heartily and to have pondered the matter in silence for a time. Then, he pointed to Mardonius, who was standing nearby, and said—no doubt with a sly and knowing grin on his face—that his bondsman would in due course give them their just deserts.[10] It may have been in this oblique fashion that the Greeks were first informed that the war in Hellas was by no means at an end and that, at least in the short run, there was no way in which those who had sided with Ahriman and embraced the Lie could work out a modus vivendi with the man whom Ahura Mazda had chosen as his instrument and made the King of Kings.

A Winter of Discontent

When the Greeks at Andros abandoned the siege, they returned to their base and set up trophies on Psyttaleia, at Salamis town, and on the heights of the Kynosoura peninsula, the only point on the island from which one could have had a panoramic view of the battle. Then, they set aside, from the spoils that they had collected, rich votive offerings for the gods—among them three Phoenician triremes, which they agreed to dedicate to Poseidon at the Isthmus of Corinth, to Poseidon and Athena at Cape Sunium in Attica, and to Ajax on Salamis itself. From the spoils, they also dispatched celebratory offerings to Delphi—and from these they later constructed a statue eighteen feet in height, holding aloft the model of a ship. At a still later date, on the recommendation of the oracle, the Aeginetans, who had won the prize for valor in the battle, dedicated in thanks three golden stars on a bronze mast.[11]

At the isthmus, the commanders then solemnly gathered to name the individual from within their number who had most distinguished himself for bravery. It says a great deal about the ethos of intense rivalry dominant within classical Greece that, when the time came for them to cast their ballots at the altar of Poseidon, each commander reportedly voted first for himself, and it says something about their sense of justice that a majority of them are said to have cast their second vote for Themistocles. His wisdom was, we are told, the talk of Greece, and the poet Simonides, in his famous narrative of the battle of Salamis, celebrated not only the valor and eagerness of those who had fought there in common but also "the judgment and astuteness of Themistocles."[12]

In Lacedaemon, soon thereafter, the Athenian statesman would be honored as no one had been or ever would be again. On Themistocles, as well as on Eurybiades, the Lacedaemonians conferred an olive wreath, celebrating their compatriot for his courage and no doubt also for his achievement in holding the coalition together, and honoring the Athenian for his wisdom and cunning. To Athens' Odysseus they also awarded the most splendid chariot in Sparta. Moreover, when Themistocles departed for home, as a token of honor, they had the royal bodyguard of three hundred *hippeîs* accompany him in triumph to the northern borders of Lacedaemon.[13]

The Athenians did not take this at all well. Like Miltiades in the wake of Marathon, Themistocles basked in glory after Salamis. And like the elder man, he quickly became an object of envy and resentment. Moreover, when he touted his own accomplishments, as Greeks were apt to do—especially when he built near his ancestral home a small temple dedicated to Artemis the Best Counsellor and set up in the sacred precinct a statue of himself—he made himself insufferable.[14] Human beings tend to find gratitude a heavy burden. But for the Hellenes, nourished as they were on Homer, living in the shadow of another's grandeur and being constantly reminded of the debt of gratitude one owed the man was impossible to bear. It is far easier to elicit from human beings a just and generous assessment of a statesman's achievements years later when he has passed from the scene.

Moreover, while Themistocles was dining out and being lionized at the Isthmus of Corinth and in Lacedaemon, his compatriots were finding their way back to an Attica which was a shambles. Their temples had been burned. Many homes had been destroyed. And that year there had been no harvest. Absent the kindness of strangers—a humiliation in itself—it would be impossible to make it through the winter. Themistocles had devised the strategy that had produced this result. He was the man responsible for leading them into a measure of hardship hitherto hardly imaginable.

It did not help at all that the Spartans and the Peloponnesians more generally had gotten off so easily. Their sanctuaries were intact. Their homes were as they had left them, and they had managed to sow and reap. They had lost some men at Thermopylae, to be sure. But this was not to be compared with the Athenian sacrifice at Artemisium and Salamis. The losses suffered by Themistocles' compatriots had been comparable to their contributions to the allied fleet, which had exceeded that of all the cities in the Peloponnesus put together.

It was not surprising, the Athenians could tell themselves, that the Lacedaemonians had so honored Themistocles. He had served these foreigners very well, indeed. He had persuaded his compatriots to acquiesce in their leadership at sea. He had gone along with their refusal to march out to Boeotia and stop the Mede before he crossed into Attica. If the Spartans were free riders, it was because this insolent man had given them permission.

Themistocles was eloquent, and he had a powerful and, one might even argue, compelling counter-argument to make. In other circumstances, he might have been able to weather the resentment, envy, frustration, and anger felt by his fellow Athenians. He had explained everything in advance. There was no other way to defeat the Great King; and, when they paused to reflect, his compatriots had recognized as much. They had gone into this war with their eyes open, not only knowing precisely what they had to do and why, but also recognizing that the price they would have to pay would be high. Themistocles had promised them blood, toil, tears, and sweat; and, in a magnificent manner that would earn the Athenians admiration for millennia to come, he had delivered fully on his pledge.

There was, however, one ground of complaint against the son of Neocles that really was unanswerable. At Andros, when he had persuaded his compatriots to suspend operations for the winter, he had offered them hope. He had urged them to go home, rebuild, and sow so that they could reap in the spring. He had encouraged them to envisage a postwar world in which they would no longer be on the defensive—in which they would be safe at home and could, at their leisure, take the war to the Mede.

All of this made sense if one supposed, as everyone apparently did, that Salamis had brought armed conflict within Hellas to an end and that the Great King, when he retraced his path to Sardis, would take his archers, infantry, and cavalry back with him. But by early November, if not before, the Athenians learned that Xerxes had left the bulk of his army in Thessaly under the command of Gobryas' son.

There was no point in rebuilding. It contradicted everything that the Athenians had learned about their allies to suppose that the Lacedaemonians and Peloponnesians would in the spring venture boldly forth from the isthmus to confront Mardonius on the broad plains of Boeotia. There was every reason to suppose that the Persians would reoccupy Attica when the campaigning season began. There was no point in sowing if the Mede would be there in the late spring to reap. It was, we must suppose, at the moment when all of this became clear that the dam burst and that the resentment that had grown up in the course of this time of unspeakable suffering suddenly poured forth on the remarkable man whose clairvoyance had finally failed.

We know very little about the procedures by which the Athenian assembly conducted itself in the early fifth century, but it is a reasonable bet that it followed something like the procedures known to have been in place in the fourth century. At that time, the political year was divided into ten prytanies of thirty-five or thirty-six days, the assembly met four times a prytany, and, at one of these four meetings, this body was charged with reviewing the conduct of the generals and the other magistrates and with considering whether to cashier or retain them in office.[15] Some such event appears to have taken place in the fall of 480 not long after the campaigning season had come to an end.

It was at this moment that Themistocles' compatriots learned of the manner in which the Lacedaemonians and the Hellenes more generally had showered gifts and honors on the Athenian statesman. It was at this time that they were told of the fashion in which he had accepted this adulation, and the anger that the Athenians had long felt with regard to their allies they now redirected at the man who had led them into and through the great crisis. In reaction to what they heard on this occasion, if Diodorus is to be trusted, the Athenians inflicted on Themistocles a political repudiation even more dramatic and unjust than the one which the British would deal out to Winston Churchill in the immediate aftermath of World War II. In their fury, they voted to strip from the architect of victory his generalship and to bestow the office on his former rival Xanthippus son of Ariphron.[16]

The ire felt by the Athenians did not quickly abate. In 479, we hear from Herodotus and from our other sources not one word about the victor of Salamis. Themistocles disappears from the narrative altogether. In the sixth prytany—if, at this early date, the Athenians elected their ten generals near the end of winter as they later would[17]—they appear to have passed over him altogether. In the campaigning season of 479, Xanthippus would lead the Athenian forces at sea, and Aristeides son of Lysimachus would command the city's army.

This was an astonishing development. As we have seen, Xanthippus and Aristeides had in the past been closely associated with the Alcmaeonid clan. The odds are good that like their Alcmaeonid associates, in the 490s and perhaps later as well, both had favored reaching an accommodation with the Persians. In the wake of the debacle at Paros, Xanthippus had successfully prosecuted Miltiades, and we have reason to suspect that Aristeides, in a graffito, had later been described as "the brother of Datis the Mede." In the late 480s, when Themistocles pressed his compatriots to build a much larger fleet of triremes than they had hitherto possessed, he had found it necessary to effect the ostracism of both of these men. If, in 481 or 480, figures as suspect as were these two were actually allowed to return to Athens, it was chiefly because their erstwhile rival had, in a magnanimous gesture, arranged for their recall. Now, in a manner typifying the rivalry fostered by republican government, they repaid him for this generosity of spirit by capitalizing on the resentment directed at their benefactor, and they pushed out the mastermind of war and assumed command in his stead. It was perhaps at this time that Themistocles said of his compatriots that it was their wont to treat him "like a plane tree—running in under his branches in search of safety when there was a storm, and plucking at them and pruning them when the weather grew fair."[18]

Coalition Management

It cannot have taken long for word to spread regarding Themistocles' precipitous fall and its causes. He had been the talk of Hellas before his compatriots had turned on him. Now, we can be sure, his trajectory provided his fellow Greeks with even more of an occasion for rumination, reflection, and animated conversation of the sort in which they took delight. Not all of the last was idle gossip, however. As everyone understood, new men bring new measures. The Spartans and their allies in the Peloponnesus had reason to fear that this turn of events might endanger them; and when the news reached Mardonius in Thessaly—as, of course, it did—it had a powerful impact on his calculations as well. There is, in fact, reason to suppose that he informed Xerxes at Sardis and received instructions as to how he should proceed.[19]

Themistocles was a wily man, who had raised Persian hopes on at least one occasion. But, for the most part, he was a known quantity. He had long been hostile to the Achaemenid realm, and the Lacedaemonians had found him a reliable ally. He had understood their needs and their concerns. He had been sensitive to the difficulties that they had in managing relations with their allies in the Peloponnesus, and he had been accommodating. Had it not been for Sparta and its alliance within the Peloponnesus, it would not have been possible to mount a resistance against the expeditionary force led to Greece by Xerxes. This the Athenian statesman had recognized, and he had bent over backward in his efforts to contain the resentment of his compatriots and smooth relations. Moreover, when Themistocles had been assertive and even when he had acted unilaterally, taking matters into his own hands, his judgment had nearly always proved to be impeccable.

Xanthippus and Aristeides were figures less familiar to the Spartans and their Peloponnesian allies. That, in the past, they had had suspect connections —about this there were no doubt stories told. Of this, moreover, we can be confident: the Peisistratids and the other Athenian Medizers in the Persian camp were fully aware of the political trajectory followed by both. It was, as we can see, a foregone conclusion that Mardonius would test the mettle of Athens' new leaders at the start of the campaigning season. No one really knew where they stood.

Before doing so, Herodotus tells us, the son of Gobryas took all of the proper precautions, dispatching a man named Mys, who appears to have been of mixed Greek and Carian lineage, to consult a variety of oracles in Phocis and Boeotia and record their advice. Notably absent from the list of the sanctuaries that he visited was that of the oracle of Apollo at Delphi—which appears, after Salamis, to have shifted allegiances and to have come down firmly on the side of the Hellenes.[20] When he had considered the responses collected by Mys and pondered whatever intelligence his servant had gathered along the way, Mardonius sent Alexander son of Amyntas, king of Macedon, to Athens with an offer.

There is reason, as we have seen, to suspect that Alexander may have been an important source of information for Herodotus, and the speech that the historian has this *próxenos* and erstwhile benefactor of Athens deliver to the Athenians has a peculiar character suggestive of authenticity. In it, initially, Alexander purported to be repeating word for word what Mardonius asked him to say—to wit, that a messenger has come from the Great King informing his general of his willingness to forget the wrongs done him by the Athenians, to restore to them their land, to respect their autonomy, and allow them to choose another territory in addition to their own. If they were willing to come to an agreement with the King, the latter's general was also to rebuild the sanctuaries Xerxes had burned. Such were the instructions brought by the messenger of the King.

Mardonius himself intimated that he would regret having to carry out these orders, but he conceded that he was bound to do so if the Athenians agreed to cooperate. He merely added his own opinion that it would be insane for them to wage war against the King given the extent of the latter's resources and the size of his army. Even if they were to defeat the forces of the King now in Hellas, he warned, they would soon thereafter have to face another expedition even larger than its predecessor. "Be free," he concluded, "and form a league with us devoid of trickery or deceit." To this, Alexander added a personal plea, urging the Athenians in all sobriety to weigh the alternative, which was, he argued, exceedingly grim.[21]

When the Macedonian king arrived, the authorities at Athens did not immediately give him a hearing. Instead, they made him cool his heels, knowing that, when the Spartans learned of his presence, they would immediately dispatch an embassy to respond. Only when it had arrived and they were in a position to exert maximum leverage on all concerned did they give Alexander leave to make his pitch.[22]

The Lacedaemonians had reason to be nervous. They were aware of the reasons for Themistocles' fall. They knew that the Athenians were not only unhappy with the conduct of their Peloponnesian allies but angry,[23] and quite recently they had come to be much more appreciative than in the past of the contribution that sea power had made and might still make to the defense of Hellas. Salamis had been a revelation. It had profoundly altered their strategic understanding.

Prior to that epic encounter and to its chief consequence, Xerxes' sudden withdrawal from Hellas, the Spartans had taken for granted that it was the army and the army alone that really mattered, and they had regarded the fleet as an ancillary arm—necessary to prevent the Persians from outflanking the Greek army, to be sure, but otherwise of no great significance. It was, as Herodotus intimates, quite telling that Eurybiades, the navarch the Lacedaemonians had sent out in 480, was a commoner who belonged to neither of the two royal houses.

It was even more revealing that, in 479, the Spartans chose to reverse course and send out as their admiral Leotychidas son of Menares, the Eurypontid king, and that he had called the Hellenic fleet together at Aegina that spring before the army had even assembled.[24] It suggested, in fact, a change in strategy. The Spartans and the Peloponnesians more generally were, as we have seen, reluctant to fight a pitched battle against the Persians in the plains of Boeotia, and they had come to recognize that building a wall at the Isthmus of Corinth was merely a stopgap measure. It might, for a time, keep the Mede at bay, but it would not in and of itself compel him to retreat from Greece. Once, however, they had fully digested the significance of the battle of Salamis, they came to believe what they had refused to countenance before: that, by stirring up a rebellion in Ionia, they could force Xerxes to recall his army from Europe. Short of that, they would have to roll the dice in a battle against Mardonius and his army in Hellas itself.

There was one obstacle to implementing the aggressive naval strategy that the Spartans had in mind. The fleet that gathered at Aegina in the spring of 479 was inadequate to the task. It consisted of no more than one hundred ten ships—nine fewer than the Aeginetans and the Peloponnesians are said to have provided the previous year at Salamis. When some notables from Chios—who had conspired unsuccessfully to assassinate Strattis, the tyrant imposed on the island by Darius long before—sought the help of the Hellenes in raising Ionia, Leotychidas shifted this flotilla to Delos. But he dared go no further. From the perspective of this landlubber, Herodotus explains, Samos was as far off as were the Pillars of Heracles at Gibraltar, and he feared, we can surmise, that the triremes he commanded would be outnumbered—and outclassed as well.[25]

Herodotus does not highlight the fact that Leotychidas' fleet was less than half the size of the Hellenic fleet at Salamis the previous year, and he says not a word of explanation, but it is not hard to see how this came to pass. The Spartans and their Peloponnesian allies wanted to pursue the war at sea, and they were happy to let the Athenians do most of the fighting for them—while the Athenians, for their part, wanted to prevent Mardonius from returning to Attica. Neither could achieve its end without the cooperation of the other, and the Athenians were not about to dispatch their fleet to Leotychidas until the Spartans and the Peloponnesians committed their land forces against Mardonius. That the Athenians were withholding their fleet was known to the Spartan ambassadors who rushed to Athens on getting the news that Alexander son of Amyntas had arrived there to make an approach to the Athenians on Mardonius' behalf. Moreover, they knew, as did the son of Gobryas, that, if the Athenians were to switch sides, the fortifications at the isthmus would be worthless—for the Athenian navy could ferry Mardonius' forces anywhere in the Peloponnesus they pleased.[26]

The Lacedaemonians were, however, stubborn and petulant. They were not willing to bargain. So they called the Athenians' bluff instead. They are said to have urged the Athenians to remain faithful, to have pointedly reminded them that it was Athens' participation in the Ionian attack on Sardis in 498 that had provoked the war and brought this calamity down on all of the Hellenes, and to have undiplomatically intimated that the suffering inflicted on Hellas by the Mede was all their fault. They acknowledged that the Athenians had lost two harvests, and they offered to provide shelter and food for their dependents for as long as the war continued.[27] This offer, generous though it may have been, was a blow not only to the pride of the Athenians but also to their most fervent hopes—for it hinted at, even if it was not tantamount to, a refusal on the part of the Lacedaemonians to march out of the Peloponnesus against the Mede.

Aristeides, who appears to have been the Athenian in charge and who is said to have framed his compatriots' response, opted for a display of magnanimity. He rejected the blandishments of Alexander, swore never to reach such an agreement with Xerxes, warned Alexander never to approach Athens with proposals of this sort again, and introduced a motion that the priests be directed to curse all who negotiated with the Mede or abandoned the alliance made by the Hellenes. The Spartans he reportedly chided for underestimating his compatriots, and he ostentatiously told them that no amount of gold would lure them into such an agreement with the Mede. His compatriots, he explained, had the gods, whose images and sacred precincts the Persians had burned, to avenge; and they were not about to betray "that which made them all Greek"—the blood and tongue they shared, the shrines held in common and the sacrifices, as well as the customary practices and ways that were so much alike. Gently but firmly and proudly, he rejected the Lacedaemonian offer of maintenance, and he urged the Spartans, instead, to rise to the occasion and send out an army to do battle in Boeotia before Mardonius reached Attica.[28] What he did not do, however, was promise to send out the Athenian fleet forthwith, and there is excellent reason to believe that the Athenians did not then send it out.

Instead, the Athenians made preparations to use their fleet to effect a second evacuation from Attica. For it was their expectation that Mardonius would set out from Thessaly for Attica as soon as Alexander returned with the news that the citizens of Athens were not prepared to switch sides, and this is precisely what the Persian commander did, gathering hoplites and cavalrymen from each of the communities he passed as he advanced toward Boeotia and Attica beyond.[29]

When Mardonius reached the border of Boeotia, the Thebans reportedly urged him to establish an encampment there and settle down—arguing that it would be difficult to subdue the Hellenes by the force of arms if they remained of the same mind, and suggesting that, if he was patient, he might be able to achieve their subjugation without a battle. All that he had to do, they explained, was to send money to the men exercising power in the cities opposed to him. Divide, they intimated, and conquer you will. With the help of the partisans that you acquire by hook or by crook, you can easily overcome those who think as you do not. According to Herodotus, the son of Gobryas rejected the advice proffered to him by the Thebans. Instead, he supposedly fell prey to an irresistible longing to take Athens a second time, guided, at least in part, by a senseless pride and a desire to inform the Great King at Sardis by way of fire beacons on the islands that he had Athens in his grasp.[30]

Herodotus does not specify where these fire beacons were placed. Nor could he have done so—for, at this point, the Cyclades were for the most part in Greek hands. Nor does he give us any reason why Mardonius should not have combined an invasion of Attica with an attempt at bribing the leaders of some of the cities in the Peloponnesus, which is the policy attributed to him by Diodorus Siculus.[31]

The son of Gobryas was by no means as foolish as Herodotus makes him seem. The Persian commander harbored doubts as to whether he could force his way past the fortifications at the Isthmus of Corinth into the Peloponnesus. To bring this war to a successful conclusion in the campaigning season under way, he had to do one of two things—induce the Athenians to switch sides and ferry his troops across to the Peloponnesus, or lure the hoplites of the Hellenes onto the plains of Boeotia where the cavalry brought by the Great King from Asia and provided by his Thessalian and the Theban allies could outflank them, break up their phalanx, and then hunt them down. By returning to Attica, he could make the Athenians desperate and thereby pursue both alternatives at the same time. Those who had ousted Themistocles from his generalship and assumed command in his place knew that, one way or another, they had to succeed where the great statesman had failed: they had to recover Attica for their compatriots. Mardonius knew precisely what he was doing. By offering the Athenians a separate peace and then, when they rejected the offer, by bringing home to them the terrible price associated with refusal, he believed that he could force a decision. He knew that they were fed up with doing the Spartans' fighting for them and that they would turn once more for aid to the Lacedaemonians and the other Peloponnesians, and he suspected that, if Athens' allies repeatedly rejected their pleas for help in their time of utmost need, the Athenians would grow furious and rethink their allegiance. In the meantime, he recognized that bribery would do no harm and might yield valuable fruit. Even Herodotus entertained the possibility that the Persians might at this time have been cannily disbursing gold.[32]

When the Persian forces reached the northern border of Boeotia, the Athenians, finally and reluctantly acknowledging to themselves that the Peloponnesians really would not be coming to their rescue, began the evacuation they had planned. In consequence, when the son of Gobryas finally reached Attica near the end of June, he found it, as Xerxes had fully nine months before, largely deserted and bereft of men. Most of the Athenians were, Herodotus reports, at Salamis with their ships—and to them Mardonius sent a second messenger to renew the offer Alexander son of Amyntas had made on his behalf. This emissary's name was Mourychides. He hailed from the Hellespont, and it is conceivable that he was of Athenian stock. There were Athenians of this name. One such served as archon in 440/39, and another proposed a decree in honor of Sigeum in 451/50. Mardonius' emissary may well have been a henchman of the Peisistratid tyrant who governed the colony of that name which Athens had established long before in the Troad.[33]

In any case, when this Mourychides restated to the Council of Five Hundred the Great King's offer, one member of that deliberative body, a man named Lycidas, urged that Xerxes' proposal be placed before the Athenian assembly. In response, we are told, his fellow councilors and those nearby fell into a rage and in tandem stoned the man to death; and, when word spread, the women of Athens did the same to his children and wife. Mourychides returned to his master unharmed but no doubt shaken—and with empty hands.[34]

Herodotus tells us that Mardonius had dispatched Mourychides to Salamis in the hope that, now that all of the Athenians' territory had been taken by the spear and was under his control, they would give up their foolish pride. That the Persian commander entertained the thought that this might be possible seems perfectly plausible. But, given what had happened on the occasion of Alexander's earlier visit to Athens, he probably expected that the Athenians would do precisely what they did—which was to dispatch an embassy to Sparta, demanding help and conveying a threat.[35]

The evidence available to Plutarch suggests that, on this occasion, Aristeides once again took the lead, proposing, by way of a decree, that Cimon, Xanthippus, and Myronides be sent to Lacedaemon forthwith. It is hard to believe that the Xanthippus mentioned in the decree was the eponymous archon of that name chosen for 479/8 by lot from an elected pool. The man had not yet taken up his office, and, in any case, it was not the practice of the Athenians to send nonentities on important embassies. Myronides was a general for 479, and Cimon was the son of the celebrated Miltiades and may have held the office that year, as he certainly would in 478.[36] The presence of Xanthippus son of Ariphron alongside a son of the man whom he had successfully prosecuted in 489 would have been read as a signal that, divided as they might be over some questions, the Athenians were as one in demanding that the Lacedaemonians act, and the inclusion of the commander of the Athenian fleet would have confirmed what common sense would, in any case, have indicated—that Athens' navy, which had been needed for the evacuation of Attica, had not yet been sent to join Leotychidas at Delos. The Athenian admiral's presence was intended, moreover, to give the delegation particular weight and to convey by indirection an important message. If the Spartans really wanted Athens' help in the battle they wished to stage at sea just off the coast of Asia Minor, they would have to give the Athenians the support that, for understandable reasons, this long-suffering people so desperately craved.

Herodotus reports that these ambassadors were told to remind the Spartans of the generosity of the offer that the Great King had made them, and they were instructed to make it clear that, if the Lacedaemonians and their Peloponnesian allies did not come to Athens' defense, the Athenians would "find for themselves a means of escape, shelter, or defense" (the word *aleōrḗ*, which Herodotus uses, can denote any one of these). The arrival of these ambassadors coincided with a three-day religious festival called the Hyacinthia, which was celebrated at Amyclae in Laconia, primarily by the residents of the southernmost of the five Spartan villages. En route to Lacedaemon, the three Athenians saw that the finishing touches were being put on the fortifications at the Isthmus of Corinth, and they were joined by ambassadors from Megara and Plataea, who seconded their plea that the Peloponnesians sally forth to battle the Mede in Attica on the Thriasian plain outside Eleusis. It was presumably at this time that Aristeides sent an embassy to Delphi seeking an oracle promising the Hellenes victory if they fought on this plain.[37]

The ephors, we are told, pledged that they would reply the next day but then postponed responding while the ambassadors cooled their heels—not just overnight, but day after day for ten days in all. There was confusion in the sources available to Plutarch. At least one of these, a figure named Idomeneus of Lampsacus, mentioned an embassy led by Aristeides himself. This may well have been an error on the part of the Lampsacene, as Plutarch suspected. But it is also conceivable that, during this time of delay, Aristeides journeyed from Salamis to reinforce the demands made at Sparta by Cimon, Xanthippus, and Myronides.[38]

We are also told that a Tegean named Chileos—who exercised great influence at Lacedaemon, and who was presumably the Arcadian of that name who had played a prominent role at the time of the founding of the Hellenic League in bringing to an end the internecine struggles then dividing Greece—approached the ephors to remind them that the wall being completed across the Isthmus of Corinth would be worthless if they alienated the Athenians. Whether it was his intervention that swayed the Lacedaemonians we cannot say. All that we know is that, without informing the Athenian ambassadors in advance, the Spartans suddenly dispatched in the direction of the Isthmus of Corinth and Attica five thousand Spartiates under the command of Pausanias son of the recently deceased Cleombrotus, regent for Pleistarchus son of Leonidas; that this Pausanias selected, to share in the command, his cousin Euryanax son of Dorieus, the ill-fated older brother of Leonidas and Cleombrotus; that five thousand *períoikoi* were sent after them the next day; and that the ambassadors of the Athenians, Megarians, and Plataeans were told of this just in time to join the *períoikoi* on their march.[39]

It was, we can surmise, not long after the Peloponnesians gathered at the isthmus and marched through the Megarid into Attica that Xanthippus appeared at Delos with a complement of one hundred forty Athenian triremes—enough to bring Leotychidas' fleet up to the respectable number of two hundred fifty ships mentioned by Diodorus Siculus.[40] The impasse was broken. The Spartans had come to recognize that, short of a battle on land, Mardonius was not going to be expelled from Hellas; and the Athenians were now ready to join the Aeginetans and the Peloponnesians in prosecuting the war at sea in the waters off Asia Minor. By this time, it was late July or early August.

The Road to Plataea

When it came to political matters, the Spartans were, as we have often had occasion to note, a secretive lot. The five thousand Spartiates under Pausanias' command left for the Isthmus of Corinth, Herodotus tells us, not just abruptly but in a stealthy fashion under cover of night; and, when they had marched up the Eurotas, they traveled not by the most direct route north-northeast via Sellasia, but turned, instead, north-northwest to the town of Oresthasion in Maenalia, a few miles southeast of the district where, more than a century thereafter, the great Arcadian city of Megalopolis would be founded. They may have had in mind the fact that this was a less onerous road for the carts bearing provisions that accompanied them on their journey, as they reportedly did some sixty years thereafter. They may well have been informed that the Argives had promised the Persians, with whom they were secretly allied, that they would interrupt such an advance.[41] They may have feared that their ancestral enemies, on whom they had inflicted so severe a defeat at Sepeia fifteen years before, would actually summon up the nerve to make the attempt, and they may, for this reason, have chosen a route as distant from the Argolid as was feasible.

But, as always, there was something else, much closer to home, that loomed larger than such concerns in Spartan calculations; and, apart from these other considerations, this alone would have been sufficient to dictate that the Spartiates set off secretly at night for a point not far from the upland Arcadian plateau just to the north of Messenia. There was, after all, one reason and one reason only why the Lacedaemonians had been so reluctant to leave their Peloponnesian fastness; and, if they were to set this reluctance aside, they had to confront head-on its foundations. In 490, the news that the Persians were on the doorstep of Greece had occasioned a helot revolt, and the Spartans were not about to countenance the possibility of a repeat. And so, when they finally came to terms with the necessity that they march into central Greece and drive Mardonius and the Great King's army from Hellas, the authorities at Sparta concluded that they could not risk dispatching two-thirds of their army to the Isthmus of Corinth and beyond unless they were to send a large proportion of the helots of military age along with them. Some of the thirty-five thousand helots who, according to Herodotus and Plutarch, were summoned to accompany the five thousand Spartiates no doubt hailed from Laconia. But the vast majority—and those who were most dangerous—

must have come from Messenia; and, as a glance at the map will indicate, the strategically important town of Oresthasion in Arcadia northeast of this Spartan province was the perfect place for them to muster.[42]

As the Lacedaemonians and the ambassadors from Athens, Megara, and Plataea made their way north toward the Corinthiad, the Argives got wind of what was going on and dispatched a long-distance runner in the guise of a herald to warn the son of Gobryas of what was in store and to apologize for their own inability to stop the Spartan advance. We are told that Mardonius had genuinely hoped that the Athenians would turn coat. When, however, he learned that, to head off this possibility, the Spartans were on the march, he elected to wreak havoc in Attica and withdraw to Boeotia. He might have staged a battle in the Thriasian plain along the Bay of Eleusis or even in the plain immediately outside Athens, but he reportedly judged Attica unsuitable for cavalry—presumably because neither plain was large enough for him to deploy the Great King's horsemen to maximum advantage—and he is said to have been persuaded that, if his troops were defeated in Attica, there was only one route of escape and that it was a narrow road which a small force could block.[43] There were, to be sure, a number of passes leading from Attica to Boeotia, but one's options in retreating from any given battlefield were more limited; and, as later became evident, Mardonius was right to worry that a rout might be followed by a massacre.

Before he set out, Mardonius is said to have received a message mistakenly reporting the presence in the Megarid of a force of one thousand Lacedaemonians. Seeing an opportunity to strike at Spartan morale by wiping out this force, he led at least part of his army toward Megara and sent his cavalry deeper into Megarian territory, but they found no Lacedaemonians, and this ineffectual foray marked the high tide of the Persian advance.[44] For, when he learned that the Peloponnesians were gathering at the Isthmus of Corinth, Mardonius shifted his forces far, far away from the Megarid and ordered a Persian withdrawal to Boeotia by way of Deceleia in northeastern Attica, whence his retreat was most likely to be uninterrupted.

On the other side of the mountains, Mardonius was met by guides from Asopia, whom the Boetarchs in command of the Boeotian forces had dispatched to assist him; and these men conducted him, first, to Tanagra in eastern Boeotia and then, the next day, westward to Scolus in the territory of Thebes to the south of the latter city, where (presumably, over a period of two

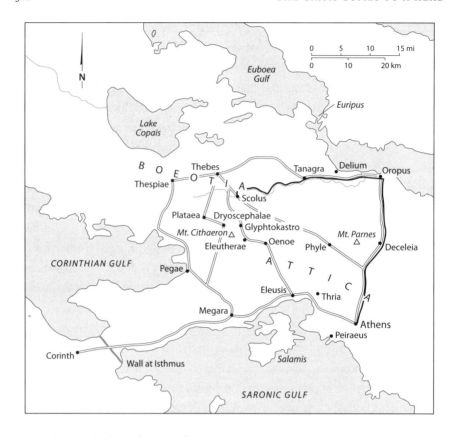

Map 25. Mardonius' Retreat from Attica via Deceleia and Tanagra to Scolus

or more weeks) he built an immense stockade, encompassing an area of nine hundred acres, which was still more or less intact a century thereafter. This fort was intended either, as Herodotus claims, to serve as a refuge for his army should it be defeated or, as Plutarch suggests, to protect the Persians' headquarters and their baggage train or, in fact, for both purposes. When it had been constructed and a trench had been dug around it, Mardonius deployed his army nearby, along the north bank of the easily forded Asopus River opposite the Boeotian cities of Erythrae, Hysiae, and Plataea—all three of which sat in the foothills extending from the Cithaeron massif in the direction of the river's south bank.[45]

No one knows how many footsoldiers and cavalrymen there were in Mardonius' army. Herodotus tells us that they numbered three hundred thousand; Ctesias gives us a figure of one hundred twenty thousand. But if we suppose that Mardonius built the fort for his army and not just for his headquarters and baggage train and if we are to judge its capacity by the size of the camps later built by the Roman legions, as some scholars quite plausibly suggest we should, the nine hundred acres said to have been encompassed by Mardonius' fort was sufficient for an army of, at most, seventy thousand men—of whom no more than ten thousand were cavalrymen.[46]

There was, we must note, a second Persian army present. Commanded at this time by Artabazus, son of Darius' uncle and treasurer Pharnaces, it is said to have been composed, initially at least, of some sixty thousand men, to have conducted Xerxes to Sestos, and then to have wintered in Thrace. While there, it reportedly seized Olynthus from the Bottiaeans and besieged, without success and at a considerable cost in manpower, the rebellious Potidae-ans on Pallene, the westernmost prong of the Chalcidice. In the spring, with the forty thousand men that remained to him—apparently, for the most part, Medes—Artabazus reportedly joined the son of Gobryas in Thessaly. He is said, however, to have entertained grave doubts about the strategy adopted by Mardonius. He was an Achaemenid by birth, not an in-law. He was more than willing to speak his mind; and, on the battlefield, as we shall soon see, he operated with a modicum of independence.[47] It is perfectly possible that Mar-donius made provision with the fort at Scolus solely for his own army and not for the troops of Artabazus, who were left to make their own arrangements. If so, it is conceivable that Ctesias' report concerning the size of Mardonius' army is close to the mark and that the Great King left behind to fight for the control of Greece a force of more than one hundred thousand footsoldiers and up to twenty thousand cavalrymen.

To this force, before occupying Attica, Mardonius had added substantial contingents from Thessaly, Malis, Locris, and Boeotia. They were joined at the Asopus by one thousand Phocian hoplites under the command of a local notable named Harmodyces. Before deploying these suspect and reluctant re-inforcements, Mardonius, on the advice of the Thessalians, sent the Persian cavalry to test their mettle and overawe them. We are not told how many men the Thessalians, Malians, Locrians, and Boeotians mustered on Mar-donius' behalf. Herodotus hazards a guess—that the infantrymen provided may have numbered as many as fifty thousand. This number seems large. The Thessalians, who had for some time now been fully committed to the Persian cause, no doubt contributed a substantial cavalry force, but one may wonder whether they had more than two or three thousand hoplites at their disposal. The Malians and Locrians are not likely to have been able to top this. For hoplites, the son of Gobryas had to rely primarily on the Boeotian confederation and on the Thebans in particular. The battle to come was to be fought on their territory, and we can be confident that their cavalrymen and their hoplites turned out in full force. Attaginus, the leader of the narrow oligarchy then governing Thebes, was an enthusiastic Medizer. With the help of Demaratus the Spartan, as we have seen, he managed to form a guest friendship with the Great King; and in 480, when the army of Xerxes pulled back from Attica to Boeotia, he did everything he could to solidify and strengthen the Persian connection by staging a magnificent dinner at Thebes for Mardonius and fifty of his officers in which he had each of the Persians invited share a couch with a notable from Thebes or from one of the other Boeotian towns. All in all, Mardonius' Greek allies may have been able to field a force of eighteen thousand hoplite soldiers and an additional two thousand cavalrymen.[48]

The son of Gobryas and his men were the first to arrive on the field of battle, and they profited from the advice of the Thebans and the other Boeotians who resided nearby. As one would expect, they situated themselves in an advantageous position on a broad, undulating plain where they could deploy their cavalry to maximum advantage. Moreover, they made sure that they had easy access to fresh water—no mean expedient in July and August, when the sun can be fierce, and streams less well-fed than the Asopus at that time are apt to run dry.

In only one particular was Mardonius' army vulnerable. The great superiority in numbers that made it so formidable also made it exceedingly hard to provision. The Boeotians were well off. Their land was fertile, and nearly all of it could be farmed. In ordinary circumstances, they could feed themselves. But they could contribute only in modest ways to meeting the needs of their allies. In consequence, the supply lines for the Persian army stretched a considerable distance—one hundred miles back to Thessaly and perhaps beyond. It is possible that supplies were being carted down from as far away as Macedonia. It is even conceivable that supply ships were making their way from the Hellespont to the Gulf of Malia or even to harbors along the northern reaches of the Boeotian coast. We know of no effort on the part of the Hellenes to interdict maritime trade. But, even if a transport network existed on this scale, the son of Gobryas must have been hard pressed to feed so many men, and it cannot have helped that many of the Phocians had resolutely refused to medize and had holed up, instead, on Mount Parnassus, from which they regularly attacked and plundered the supply trains on which Mardonius' army relied.[49]

While Mardonius was making his withdrawal from Attica and his dispositions in Boeotia, Pausanias remained at the Isthmus of Corinth, slowly and steadily gathering infantrymen from the communities that belonged to the Peloponnesian League. When a sufficient number of hoplites had come together, the Spartans made the usual sacrifices at the border and, when they were favorable, led the Peloponnesians across into the Megarid and then presumably repeated this elaborate ritual before entering Attica. In the meantime, the Athenians on Salamis had divided their manpower, emptying out forty triremes and equipping with the full hoplite panoply the eight thousand men reassigned, then using the one hundred forty Athenian triremes still in service to ferry these hoplites across to the mainland to join their commander Aristeides and the Peloponnesian army at Eleusis before sending Xanthippus and these triremes off to rendezvous with Leotychidas son of Menares and the Peloponnesian fleet at Delos.[50]

By this time, the embassy dispatched by Aristeides to Delphi had almost certainly returned with an oracle promising victory if the battle were fought on the Thriasian plain. In consequence, as the army of the Hellenes and the wagons loaded with its provisions journeyed from Eleusis across Mount Cithaeron to Boeotia by way of the carriage road running past Oenoe and Eleutherae through the Glyphtokastro pass, Aristeides and Athens' Plataean allies must have begun considering the fancy rhetorical footwork in which they would have to engage if they were to reinterpret the oracle to fit a battle well to the north of Attica.[51]

After clearing the pass, Pausanias and the forces under his command moved eastward and took up a strong position on the heights above Erythrae with an eye to exploring the lay of the land and considering their options. From this perch, they could easily see the Persians and their stockade at a distance down below to the north of the river Asopus, and there, for a time, they paused to await the arrival of further reinforcements.[52]

Pausanias was a neophyte in his mid-twenties who may never before have commanded troops.[53] The death of Leonidas at Thermopylae the previous September and that of Pausanias' father Cleombrotus later in the fall had suddenly thrust him into the limelight. As a Spartiate reared within the *agōgḗ* and deployed in the recent past within Laconia and Messenia and perhaps also at the isthmus, he was familiar with the Spartan way of war. But, in all likelihood, he had never been outside the Peloponnesus, and he needed time in which to size up the situation he now faced. With him were men famil-

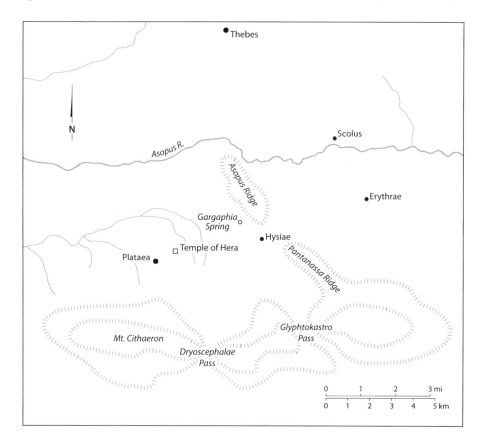

Map 26. Plataea, Hysiae, Erythrae, and the Passes from Attica into Boeotia

iar with the terrain—Plataeans, who knew southern Boeotia well; Athenians, who had traveled in the region; Megarians and Corinthians of a similar stripe; and, perhaps, a handful of Spartans who had functioned as diplomats or traveled on special missions as *agathoergoí* after having distinguished themselves for years as *hippeîs*. With their help, in these first few days, he and his older cousin Euryanax weighed the dangers now facing the Hellenes and the opportunities southern Boeotia afforded.

Pausanias, Euryanax, the Athenian commander Aristeides, and Mardonius had this in common: they all understood the lessons of Marathon. If the battle that loomed was fought in the relatively flat, gently rolling plains to the north of the river Asopus, the Persians would be able to deploy their cavalry and their superior numbers to advantage; and the Greeks would almost certainly be massacred. If, on the other hand, the Persians were drawn onto the rougher ground in the foothills to the south of the river Asopus, where their horsemen could not so easily operate, the odds would favor their defeat and slaughter even if they greatly outnumbered the Hellenes. This much the commanders on both sides knew from the start. The battle to come was going to be a lot like the battle of Salamis. The Greek David could defeat the Persian Goliath—but only, as everyone recognized at the outset, if he could dictate the terms on which the contest took place. As is often the case in war, everything turned on maneuvering one's opponent into fighting on unfavorable ground.

When the Greeks fanned out along the foothills of Mount Cithaeron and displayed no immediate inclination to descend to the plain, the son of Gobryas decided take the initiative and test their mettle. For the most part, the hoplites on the heights were beyond the reach of his cavalry, but the Megarians had been assigned a position on lower ground—probably on the road that led down from the Glyphtokastro pass and ran on by a bridge across the Asopus in the direction of Thebes—and this rendered them vulnerable to assault. Mardonius turned to his cavalry commander Masistius—a tall, broad-shouldered, handsome man in the good graces of the Great King, who was mounted on a noble steed from the Nisaean plain in Media, itself equipped with a bit of gold and other ornamentation—and he ordered him to slip cross the Asopus, ride up into the foothills of Cithaeron, and see how much damage he could do with his cavalry in a surprise attack staged at night, perhaps shortly before dawn. Masistius failed to catch the Greeks off guard. He soon discovered that taunting them as women would not cause them to break ranks and descend onto more level ground, and he found that none but the Megarians were vulnerable to assault. Deployed as they were in a phalanx protected on either flank by the spurs of Mount Cithaeron, the Megarians were impervious to a cavalry charge. But they were not, however, well equipped to defend themselves against regiment after regiment of horse archers wheeling past, hurling javelins or firing arrows from horseback, and returning time and again to repeat this deadly maneuver. The Megarians were hard pressed, we are told, and they sent a herald to Pausanias asking to be relieved.

In response to a request from Pausanias for volunteers, Aristeides dispatched to the assistance of the Megarians three hundred members of an elite corps—commanded by Olympiodorus son of Lampon and almost certainly made up either of agile light-armed troops or of cavalry—which functioned, we learn, as the Athenian general's bodyguard. With them he also sent a unit of archers, which had accompanied his hoplites. We are told next to nothing

Figure 16. Greek hoplites confronting Persian horse-archers; side B of an Athenian red-figure cup by the Triptolemos Painter, c. 490–480 (National Museums of Scotland, Edinburgh, 1887.213; from Paul Hartwig, *Die Griechischen Meisterschalen der Blüthezeit des Strengen Rothfigurigen Stiles* [Stuttgart: Spemann, 1893], pl. 55).

about the tactics these two units employed, but we can guess that Olympiodorus' men resorted to hurling javelins, and we know that the corps of archers the Athenians had earlier brought in from Crete played a highly significant role—for one of the arrows that they dispatched penetrated the ribs of Masistius' great steed, and the animal, in pain, reared and hurled its master to the ground—where, burdened with heavy gilt armor as he was, he could not get up, and there he was soon attacked and killed by Olympiodorus' men, one of whom drove the spike at the end of his spear through one of the eyeholes in the cavalry commander's helmet. Moreover, when the Persian cavalry wheeled around and, in an attempt to retrieve the body of their chief, charged the three hundred Athenians, the Greek hoplites on the hillsides nearby descended to come to their defense, formed up in a phalanx, and drove off the men on mounts.

This dramatic skirmish—worthy though it was of Homer—decided nothing. But it was a blow to the morale of the Persians, who ostentatiously mourned the commander of their cavalry, shaving their hair and cutting off the manes of their horses and mules; and it buoyed the hopes of the Greeks, who put Masistius' corpse on a wagon so that he could be paraded past the entire army[54]—presumably along a road through the foothills linking Erythrae, Hysiae, and Plataea. The Persians, those with no prior experience of the Mede now came to recognize, were men, just as they were; and, where the terrain limited their ability to maneuver, even their cavalry could be fended off.

Between Cithaeron and the Asopus

Herodotus and the other ancient sources were aristocratic in temper. They were high-minded. They knew of such low-minded concerns as the provisioning of armies, just as we are aware of the location of sanitary facilities. But, in practice, they never pause to discourse at length on matters so mundane, so obvious, so coarse. When, however, they touch on base concerns of this sort, even if only in passing, we should be especially attentive—for it is frequently the need for provisions that gives one army leverage over another. In this case, the facts were straightforward. There was not a great deal of water to be found at this season high in the foothills of Mount Cithaeron—which meant that Pausanias and those under his command had to descend from their perch and resituate themselves along the southern shore of the Asopus.

By this time, Pausanias' army constituted the largest hoplite force ever assembled. From the outset, there had been eight thousand Athenian hoplites, five thousand Spartiates, and five thousand *períoikoi* from Lacedaemon. In time, there came to be an additional fifteen hundred Tegean hoplites, five thousand Corinthians, three hundred Potidaeans dispatched (no doubt by ship) from Pallene in the Chalcidice, six hundred Orchomenians from Arcadia, three thousand Sicyonians, eight hundred Epidaurians, one thousand Troezenians, two hundred Lepreates, four hundred Mycenaeans and Tirynians, one thousand Phleiasians, three thousand Hermionaeans, six hundred Eretrians and Styrians, four hundred Chalcidians, five hundred Ambraciots, eight hundred Leucadians and Anactorians, two hundred Cephallenians, five hundred Aeginetans, three thousand Megarians, and six hundred Plataeans. All in all, Cleombrotus' son had thirty-eight thousand seven hundred hoplites to deploy, and he had thirty-five thousand helots at his disposal and another thirty-four thousand light-armed troops from outside Lacedaemon.[55]

Notably missing from the mix were not only the Medizers of Argos, but also the hoplites of Mantineia and Elis, two of the more populous cities within Sparta's Peloponnesian alliance—communities capable in a pinch, then as they would be later, of fielding something on the order of six thousand hoplites. In the case of these two polities, the gold disbursed by Mardonius' agents appears to have had the predicted effect.[56]

The Plataeans, who knew the lay of the land and the sources of water, persuaded Pausanias to march westward across the foothills of Cithaeron past Hysiae and descend in the vicinity of their town. There, at a bend in the river

Asopus, he situated the Lacedaemonians and Tegeans on the high ground above the spring of Gargaphia (now called Rhetsi). The Athenians and Plataeans he placed well to his left, almost certainly on Pyrgos hill quite near the Asopus; and the other Greeks he then arranged, in the order in which the contingents are mentioned above, from right to left on the low hills and level ground in between the two wings, with the Peloponnesians nearer the Spartans and the islanders and Megarians next to the Athenians.[57]

The ridge running along the south bank of the Asopus may have obscured Pausanias' advance until his men appeared on top of it, off to the west of Mardonius' headquarters. When the Persian commander finally did learn of the Greeks' redeployment, he followed suit in a fashion utterly predictable, shifting the forces under his command westward along the north bank of the Asopus with the Persians ordered in much greater depth than usual opposite the Lacedaemonians and Tegeans; with the Medes facing the Corinthians, Potidaeans, Orchomenians, and Sicyonians; with the Bactrians confronting the Epidaurians, Troezenians, Lepreates, Mycenaeans, and Phleiasians; with the Aryans from the Indus valley opposite the Hermionaeans, Eretrians, Styrians, and Chalcidians; with the Sacae facing the Ambraciots, the Anactorians, the Leucadians, the Cephallenians, and the Aeginetans; and with the Boeotians, Locrians, Malians, Thessalians, and the one thousand Phocians confronting the Athenians.[58]

There they all hunkered down—for Pausanias was not eager to expose his hoplites to Mardonius' cavalry on the relatively flat, undulating land north of the Asopus River, and Mardonius was reluctant to leave his cavalry behind and abandon the plains for the rougher terrain to the south of the Asopus. Moreover, Teisamenus son of Antiochus of the Iamid clan, Hegesistratus of Elis from the Telliad clan, and Hippomachus of Leucas—the seers assisting at the sacrifices and examining and interpreting the entrails for Pausanias, Mardonius, and the Thebans, respectively—confirmed the opinions entertained by their generals and reinforced their authority, as seers usually did, telling them in this case that, if they took the offensive. they would lose and that, if they remained on the defensive, they would win.[59]

In the days of seemingly endless tedium interspersed with moments of high anxiety that followed, discontent may have grown among some of the well-to-do in Athenian ranks. But if there was conspiratorial talk, Aristeides quickly quelled it, as Plutarch reports.[60] The allied commanders may also have seized upon this as an occasion to impose on their troops an oath, modeled on the one taken by the Athenians in 490 as they were about to march to Marathon and on the oath imposed in 481 on members of the Hellenic League. In it, the Hellenes in alliance against the Persians are said to have pledged not only to prefer freedom to life, to follow their leaders, and bury those of their allies who fell in battle but also to refrain forever, if victorious, from destroying any of the cities participant in their struggle against the Mede, to seize the cities that had medized and pay a tithe from the booty to Apollo at Delphi, and to leave in ruins the sanctuaries destroyed by Xerxes and Mardonius so that future generations would have a memorial of the impiety of the barbarians.

About the imposition of this oath, there was some confusion in antiquity. Diodorus Siculus reports that the oath was sworn at the Isthmus of Corinth; the Athenian orator Lycurgus contends, more plausibly, that it was sworn after the Hellenes reached Plataea. In either case, its imposition reflected a felt need on the part of the allies to abjure the bitterness that had so recently characterized their relations, to formally set their differences aside, and to reassure one another of their common commitment.

Theopompus of Chios, who was no friend to Athens and its pretensions, contended that the oath was falsified somehow, and some scholars today regard it as an outright forgery. No fifth-century author mentions the oath, and both Diodorus' source Ephorus of Cumae and the orator Lycurgus wrote in the fourth century—the former at a moment when Athens and Sparta were once again allies and it served the purpose of the orators to remind everyone of the unity these two cities had once achieved in mounting a defense of the freedom of the Greeks, and the latter after Athens' defeat in the battle of Chaeronea when he and his fellow Athenians needed the encouragement provided by a reminder of past glory. But, as in the case of the Themistocles Decree, the silence of the fifth-century writers means considerably less than one might initially be inclined to suppose: for, apart from Herodotus himself, there are no surviving fifth-century authors whose failure to mention the oath is in the slightest surprising; and the historian from Halicarnassus—who, in his narrative more generally, leaves out many a passing detail—was less than fully informed concerning what the Hellenes were up to at Plataea, as we shall soon see.

There is, moreover, archaeological evidence strongly suggesting the oath's authenticity. For more than three decades after the battle of Plataea, the Athenians left in ruins the temples and shrines destroyed by the Persians. Had they not pledged to do so in the manner indicated in the oath, it is hard to see why they would not have rebuilt those temples and shrines soon after their return to Attica.

In any case, it is far more likely that those who appealed to the so-called Oath of Plataea in speeches delivered over a century after the Persian Wars drew and perhaps embroidered on something well-known and ready to hand than that they invented so solemn and memorable an event out of whole cloth. Ockham's razor is a noble instrument. The least complex and ornate account is usually the one that is the most plausible. The most economical explanation for the claim propagated by Ephorus, Lycurgus, and others in the fourth century that such an oath was sworn by the Hellenes not long before the battle of Plataea is that an oath of this sort really was sworn at this time.[61]

At Plataea in the end, as is frequently the case in war both ancient and modern, everything turned on logistics. If we are to give any credence at all to the ancient sources—as, I think, we must—the army left Mardonius by the Great King was exceedingly large: too large, as Thucydides intimates, for its own good. Provisioning an army in the field was difficult in the best of circumstances; and thanks, perhaps in part, to the raids mounted against the Persians' supply line by the Phocians holed up on Mount Parnassus, the time came when Mardonius could foresee that his forces would soon be short of food.[62]

For eight days, the Great King's general sacrificed to no avail, sat patiently, and watched with growing concern as further hoplites arrived in a steady stream to reinforce the infantry of Pausanias. Then, finally, when a well-informed and sympathetic Theban named Timagenides son of Herpys suggested that, in a surprise attack, he might be able to intercept these reinforcements as they emerged from Mount Cithaeron, Mardonius once again seized the initiative. This time, he ordered a contingent of his cavalry to ride at night upstream or down, cross the Asopus, and circle around behind the Greek lines to the relatively flat land between the Asopus ridge and the foothills of Mount Cithaeron. Their principal purpose was not, however, to intercept the Greek reinforcements in the manner suggested by Timagenides— and this says much about the chief difficulty facing the Persian forces.

Mardonius' army must at this point have been dangerously short of supplies, for he ordered his cavalrymen to intercept the supply train emerging from the carriage road running from the Peloponnesus and Megara via the Dryoscephalae pass through Cithaeron. This they did to startling effect, capturing a host of wagons and something on the order of five hundred oxen, which were conveying food from the Peloponnesus to the Greek camp. The light-armed troops guarding this supply train and the men in charge of the wagons they slaughtered, and in their frenzy they even killed some of the oxen. The remaining provisions they then brought to the Persian camp, where they were without a doubt most welcome; and, by threatening to repeat this maneuver, they closed off at a crucial juncture a route of supply vital to the Hellenes.[63] The shoe was now on the other foot. It was suddenly the Greeks who were in danger of running short on food.

Thereafter, we are told, with strong support from the Thebans, the Persian cavalry harried the Greeks on the south side of the Asopus as best they could.[64] We do not know how they accomplished this, but they probably did so in the manner of Masistius' cavalry just over a week before—by fording the Asopus; by approaching, from the narrow plain lying between the foothills of Cithaeron and the Asopus ridge, those of the Greeks deployed between the Spartans and the Athenians on the lower slopes of that ridge; and, then, by raining down on them a steady stream of javelins and arrows.

Mardonius' aim was to dislodge the Spartans and the Athenians from the high ground that they had occupied and to force them to fight on his terms. But Pausanias and his forces nonetheless stubbornly remained precisely where they were; and two days later Mardonius is said to have taken counsel with Artabazus, who reportedly repeated the advice said to have been proffered to Mardonius himself by the Thebans some weeks before—that he pull back to a place where his army could be more easily provisioned and that he make maximum use of the gold and silver in his possession to bribe the most important of the leaders in the various Greek cities. Mardonius did not take any such advice, for he reportedly believed his army superior, and he is said to have feared that, if he did not force a battle soon, the army of the Hellenes would grow further in size in such a fashion as to render it more formidable.[65]

It does not matter much whether Herodotus—who seems to have been especially well-informed concerning the councils of the Thebans, Macedonians, and Persians opposed to the Hellenes[66]—invented this particular exchange or not. The option purportedly proposed by Artabazus was available, and Mardonius knew it. Moreover, the argument in its favor was strong. In Hellas, the bitter rivalries between individuals and those between cities virtually guaranteed that bribery on a large scale would do the trick. If Mardonius pressed ahead, nonetheless, it may have been because he had gotten word—

perhaps through his Argive allies—that the notables whom he had bribed at Elis and Mantineia were no longer in a position further to delay the arrival of the hoplites from these two sizable cities.[67] Given what he presumably knew of what had happened at Marathon, the prospect that Pausanias might soon have something on the order of six thousand additional hoplites to deploy must have been most unwelcome.

In the middle of the night following Mardonius' supposed parley with Artabazus, a solitary horseman is said to have ridden up to an Athenian guard post and to have asked to speak to Aristeides or to Athens' generals as a group. When Aristeides and, perhaps, his colleagues arrived, this horseman reportedly revealed himself as Alexander son of Amyntas, king of Macedon, and he firmly asserted his identity as a Hellene. Then, he is said to have revealed that the son of Gobryas had not been able to get from the sacrifices that he had conducted the omens that he desired; and he informed them that Mardonius was about to launch an attack at dawn anyway, out of desperation, because of his fear that the numbers in Pausanias' hoplite force would soon grow in a dramatic and decisive fashion. If Mardonius did not attack, he urged the Athenians and their allies to persevere, telling them that the Persian army was running short of supplies; and he begged that, if they were victorious, they remember his contribution to their quest for liberation.[68]

Scholars are wont to reject Herodotus' testimony in this particular, and there is this to be said for their stance. Alexander appears to have been one of Herodotus' sources; and, in the postwar atmosphere, this story would have served his interests all too well. If widely propagated, it would have put his conduct toward the Hellenes in a positive light. This Alexander surely knew.

Skepticism of this sort always deserves consideration. But it is unlikely that Herodotus would have taken such claims at face value and that he did not in due course question surviving Athenians in the know. Moreover, the tale is consistent with what we can determine concerning the canniness of the Macedonian king—for, given the war of nerves under way, his mission was just the sort of venture that could easily be pitched in one fashion to Mardonius, who was eager to dislodge Pausanias' army and force them to fight on unfavorable ground, and presented in another to the Hellenes, who would have welcomed an immediate attack on what they rightly regarded as a strong position. Like many another weakling, Alexander was exceptionally adept at straddling fences.[69]

The next morning, however, Mardonius did not launch a general attack.

Instead, he unleashed his cavalry in a fashion suggestive of tactical brilliance. The Greeks to the south of the Asopus were still deployed along a line stretching from the high ground above the springs of Gargaphia to Pyrgos hill. The Athenians, Plataeans, the Megarians, and the others on or near the army's left wing could, in principle, draw water from the Asopus, which was nearby. In practice, however, the Persian archers on the river's north bank rendered their approach to the river hazardous, if not impossible; and this had as its consequence a dependence of the entire army on the springs of Gargaphia. Recognizing this fact, Mardonius sent his cavalry across the river to the low country lying between the Asopus ridge and the foothills of Mount Cithaeron and ordered them to render the springs undrinkable, which, in short order, they did.[70]

This left the Greeks in a quandary. They were increasingly short of provisions. Now they had no access to fresh water. When their commanders met with Pausanias, they agreed on two things: they had to move somewhere where abundant fresh water could be found, and they had to reopen the route by which they received their supplies. They resolved that, if Mardonius did not attack that day, a part of the army would advance to the Dryoscephalae pass and serve as a convoy for the wagons backed up there—while the bulk of the army shifted to a tract of land, called "the island," that lay "in front of," which may well mean to the east of, Plataea. This tract cannot today be precisely located—for "the island" was apparently a strip of land, roughly two thousand yards in width, that lay between two streams, no longer there, which, in those days, ran down from Mount Cithaeron to the plain below and joined together as the Oëroë before flowing into the Asopus.[71]

In the meantime, Mardonius stepped up the cavalry attacks on those in the center of the Greek line.[72] His purpose in harassing those of the Greeks who were more vulnerable, in attacking the supply lines of the Hellenic force, and in depriving his foe of access to fresh water had been to compel the Athenians, the Spartans, and those deployed alongside them on the Asopus ridge to descend to the plain that lay between the foothills of Cithaeron and the ridge. There, as they attempted to effect a redeployment, he hoped to use his cavalry and archers to throw the Greek hoplites into disorder and then to finish them off with his infantry.

Mardonius' aim was apparent, and Pausanias and the other Greek commanders understood it only too well. So, we are told, they resolved to redeploy under cover of night at the second watch when they would be less vulnerable to assault and then to dispatch a part of their army later in the night to convoy their provisions down from Cithaeron. Herodotus' account of the Greeks' attempt to do this is confused and confusing—in part, one must suspect, because the redeployment that took place that night and early the next morning was anything but orderly. Pausanias' army was made up of nearly forty thousand hoplites and their attendants, along with tens of thousands of light-armed troops, and it represented a multitude of disparate polities in which different dialects of Greek were spoken. By light of day, it would be hard enough to shift such a force in a smooth and untroubled fashion from one location to another a few miles away. At night, it would be virtually impossible to pull off anything of the sort; and on this particular night, if Plutarch is correct in dating the battle the next day to the third or fourth of the Athenian month of Boedromion (27 or 28 August), there was only a sliver of a moon to light their way.[73]

If Herodotus is to be trusted, however, disorder and confusion were the least of the Greeks' problems. The Hellenes in the center of the line were assigned to take the lead; and at the appointed time, during the second watch, they pulled out as instructed. But they did not proceed to "the island," for they were purportedly so rattled by what they had suffered at the hands of Mardonius' cavalry that, once they were in motion, they fled in panic to the outskirts of Plataea itself and camped around the sanctuary of Hera.[74]

The Spartans, who were to follow suit, appear to have had troubles even more serious. Pausanias the son of Cleombrotus was a regent and not a king, and he was exceedingly young. He lacked the sacerdotal authority that came with regality, and most of the men he commanded were older and more experienced than he was. Moreover, if Herodotus is to be trusted, his initial response to the news, conveyed by Alexander son of Amyntas the previous night, that Mardonius was planning an attack at dawn had been to switch places with the Athenians and leave the Persians to them—a maneuver that had earned the Lacedaemonians public mockery on the part of the son of Gobryas, who had also issued on this occasion a challenge, to which Pausanias had failed to respond, calling for the dispute between the Hellenes and the Great King be decided by a new battle of the champions, pitting an equal number of Spartans and Persians against one another.[75]

There may be something to this charge, which has, for obvious reasons, frequently been dismissed as outlandish and highly improbable.[76] If true, it would help explain why, when Pausanias and Euryanax gave the order to move out at the second watch that night, one of the subordinate commanders within the Lacedaemonian army—a Spartiate from an ancient aristocratic family named Amompharetus son of Poliades, who led a *lóchos* from the Spartan village Pitana—had the effrontery to challenge their authority and dug in his heels and refused to budge: arguing, in such a manner as to accuse his commanders, that it was a disgrace for Spartans to flee in the face of a foreign threat. His obstinacy paralyzed the Lacedaemonian force—for Pausanias and Euryanax were reluctant to leave behind one fifth of the Spartiates present to be slaughtered, and they found it impossible to persuade the man.[77]

The conduct of the Spartans caused the Athenians in turn to hesitate, for the Spartans had a well-earned reputation for saying one thing while intending another, and the herald sent by the Athenians, when the Spartans failed to leave their post, reportedly found them quarreling angrily.[78] When told to follow the Spartan lead, however, the Athenians did just that.

At dawn, in desperation, Pausanias and Euryanax gave up the quarrel and led out the Lacedaemonians, hoping that Amompharetus and his men would follow, as in time they did. Pausanias and his men headed, however, not in the direction of "the island" but in the opposite direction—for it was either too late for this or Herodotus is confused and it had been Pausanias' intention all along to use this force to open up for the supply wagons the carriage road running from Attica via Eleusis, Oenoe, and Eleutherae through the Glyphtokastro pass. In an attempt to avoid the Persian cavalry, this force crossed to the foothills of Cithaeron and marched toward the sanctuary of Eleusinian Demeter, while the Athenians moved down into the plain between the Asopus ridge and those foothills and followed as best they could.[79]

The son of Gobryas had more than achieved his aim. So it certainly appeared. He had dislodged the Hellenes, as he had hoped; and, to boot, as he must eventually have realized, the Greek army was now divided into three contingents at a distance one from another. The degree to which these three contingents were isolated from each other deserves attention. Plutarch, a Boeotian from Chaeronea familiar with this part of the world, tells us that the sanctuary of Eleusinian Demeter, where the Spartans and Tegeans ended up, was to the east on the outskirts of Hysiae, and inscriptions and fragmentary architectural remains found near the Pantanassa ridge strongly support his claim. The Athenians and Plataeans were, Herodotus tells us, in the plain below en route to the same destination, while the remainder of the army was on the outskirts of Plataea. All were far more vulnerable than they had been when deployed close to one another between the springs of Gargaphia and Pyrgos hill.[80]

When dawn came, the Persian cavalry were quick to follow the Lacedaemonians and Tegeans and do what they could to harass them with javelins and arrows. Pausanias responded by sending a messenger to the Athenians to ask that they come to the aid of their allies. Indicative of the character of his predicament was the fact that he specifically requested that, if the Athenians were unable to come, they send the archers who had earlier been of so much use to the beleaguered Megarians. But this the Athenians were unable to do. For they soon had their hands full—as the Boeotian, Malian, Phocian, Locrian, and Thessalian hoplites wheeled into place and launched a furious assault.[81]

When Mardonius realized that his stratagem had succeeded and that he had forced the Spartans and the other Hellenes to descend from the Asopus ridge and retreat, he gloated. He appears to have presumed that the Greeks visible in the foothills near Hysiae were in full flight—making for the Glyphtokastro pass above the town, whence they had first entered Boeotia on their march from Eleusis—for, at this point, he rolled the dice, ordering the Persian footsoldiers under his command to ford the Asopus and pursue at a run these retreating Hellenes, and Herodotus tells us that the rest of his barbarian troops followed after in considerable disorder, intent on storming what turned out to be the position occupied by the Spartans and the Tegeans.[82]

We should perhaps treat this last claim regarding the remainder of the barbarian troops under Mardonius' command as an exaggeration, for Herodotus' account leaves something to be desired. What he offers us is a series of snapshots focused almost solely on the conduct of the Spartans and the Athenians and based on the testimony of ordinary soldiers who may not have been fully in the know. Moreover, the little that he tells us regarding the conduct of the other Greeks, those originally arrayed on the lower slopes of the Asopus ridge between the two wings of the Hellenic force, is, in at least one crucial particular, inconsistent with the testimony of the poet Simonides—who, in his narrative account of the battle, which was written long before Herodotus composed his *Inquiries*—reported that the Corinthians played a prominent role in the conflict that followed.[83]

Some of the Medes, Bactrians, Indians, and Sacae that had been lined up opposite the Greek center in days then past may well have followed in the wake of Mardonius and his Persians, as Herodotus claims. But others

must have engaged the Greek hoplites located near the temple of Hera outside Plataea, and these hoplites may have been situated where they were quite
deliberately—with an eye to covering the road leading to the logistically vital
Dryoscephalae pass. In any case, it says much about the advantages to be had
from occupying high ground of this sort that, when the Megarians and Phleiasians descended into the plain to come to the aid of the Lacedaemonians, a
contingent of Theban horsemen under the command of Asopodorus son of
Timandrus ran them down, slaughtered six hundred of them, and drove the
rest back to Cithaeron.[84]

Incomplete though his account may be, Herodotus was nonetheless right
to focus on the Spartans and the Tegeans. It was, after all, the reputation of the
Lacedaemonians and their alliance within the Peloponnesus that had made
the Hellenic coalition possible, and the Spartan mystique had been powerfully enhanced by Thermopylae. It was no doubt vital that the Athenians and
Plataeans defeat the hoplites fielded by Persia's Greek allies. But if Mardonius
could slaughter the soldiers of Lacedaemon, the entire Hellenic effort would
collapse. On that fateful day, the future of Hellas and of republicanism as a
form of government lay in the hands of young Pausanias.

The Spartans were situated on high ground at the end of what is now
called the Pantanassa ridge. The javelins thrown and the arrows shot by the
Persian cavalry were for them an irritation. But, thanks to the terrain, Persia's
horsemen could neither draw near nor approach them from the rear, and they
were not at this point in any other respect a grave and immediate threat to the
survival of the Lacedaemonians and the Tegeans.[85] The footsoldiers amassed
by Mardonius were another matter. Down below, within range of the Greeks,
the *gerrophóroi* in the front ranks of the Persian army set up, in the customary
manner, a barricade made up of the wicker shields they bore; and, from behind it, the ordinary infantrymen—who were, as Herodotus tells us, "lacking
the hoplite shield [*ánoploi*]" and bore only bow and spear—shot volleys of
arrows at the Lacedaemonians and the Tegeans on a scale that threatened over
time to do real damage. While this was happening, the Lacedaemonian and
Teagean hoplites sat down and sheltered themselves behind their capacious
hoplite shields, while Pausanias, with the assistance of Teisamenus, gamely
conducted the sacrifices, hoping for favorable omens. But none, we are told,
were to be had.

Pausanias possessed a formidable force—something on the order of thirteen thousand hoplites and thirty to forty thousand light-armed troops. As

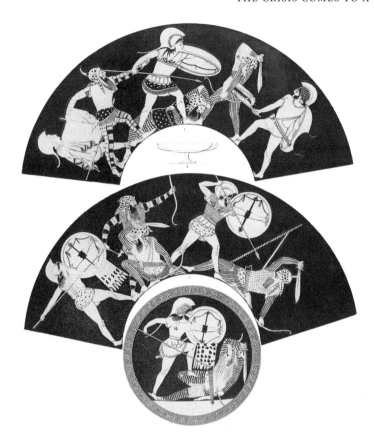

Figure 17. Greek hoplites fighting shieldless Persians, Athenian red-figure cup by the Painter of the Paris Gigantomachy, c. 490–480 (Metropolitan Museum of Art, New York, 1980.11.21; from Eduard Gerhard, *Auserlesene Griechische Vasenbilder: Hauptsächlich Etruskischen Fundorts* [Berlin: G. Reimer, 1840–58], III, pl. 166).

he looked westward toward the sanctuary of Hera at Plataea and prayed to the goddess for support, the Tegeans, no longer able patiently to tolerate the artillery assault, stood up and edged forward toward the barricade of wicker shields. At this moment, Herodotus tells us, the omens suddenly became favorable (as they were apt to do on such occasions), and Pausanias unleashed the Lacedaemonians. In the face of their attack, the Persians and the Medes and Cissians who had followed Mardonius—all or nearly all of them similarly armed—cast down their bows and took up their spears, as they were wont to do. For a long time, we are told, the struggle went on about the wicker barricade. But eventually push came "to shove [*es ōthısmón*]," as happened often enough in ordinary hoplite battles; and the barricade collapsed.

At this point, the Great King's footsoldiers found themselves, as they had eleven years before at Marathon, at a distinct and serious disadvantage. They were, Herodotus observes, "unfamiliar" with hoplite warfare. Their spears were shorter than those borne by the Greeks; and though at least some of them wore body armor, as individuals, they were *ánoploi*. They were, as he puts it later, by way of repetition, wholly "bereft of hoplite shields." If there were any dedicated infantrymen among them, they bore at best small *aspídes* or bucklers—with the latter situated on their left arms or carried by a handle. From Herodotus' perspective, however, they were all "naked [*gumnêtes*]," light-armed troops.

Nonetheless, in desperation—with great courage and determination and with tactics ill-suited to their situation—these Persians and their allies fought on as best they could. Eventually, however, a figure named Arimnestus or, more likely, Aeimnestus—who is said by Herodotus to have been "a man of note [*lógimos*] at Sparta"—managed to hurl a great stone at Mardonius and bring him down. Then, when the Lacedaemonians overwhelmed the picked men in the commander's bodyguard, all resistance collapsed, and the soldiers whom the son of Gobryas had commanded fled in disorder to the great stockade their general had built at Scolus on the northern shore of the Asopus.[86]

Mardonius lost for one simple reason. He crossed the Asopus, abandoned the broad plains to the north of that river, and sent his footsoldiers onto terrain on which his cavalry could not operate to full advantage. If we are to judge solely by the story told in Herodotus, as many scholars think we should, Mardonius was hoist on his own petard. He was tempted to risk everything and cross the Asopus because his attack on the supply lines of the Hellenes, his attempt to deny them fresh water, and his cavalry's harassment of the Greeks in the center on lower ground had succeeded so brilliantly and had managed to throw the army of the Hellenes into disarray. Or so it appears—for there is another possibility.

In the Hellenic imagination, Odysseus loomed almost as large as Achilles. The Greeks took pride in their capacity for trickery, and they were exceedingly well-practiced in the art of deception. At Thermopylae, the Spartans had repeatedly lured the Persians and their allies to their own destruction by feigning flight. At Salamis, the Hellenes had done the like. With the help of Sicinnus, Themistocles had persuaded the Persian commanders to approach the narrows between Salamis and the Greek mainland; and the Corinthians, almost certainly on the orders of Eurybiades, had helped draw them into these narrows by simulating flight. Herodotus' account suggests that, in Boeotia, the Greek withdrawal from the Asopus ridge near Plataea was a genuine—one might even say, an utterly desperate—retreat. But Herodotus was, as we have seen, ill-informed concerning the strategy pursued in Asopia by the Hellenes; and it is conceivable that cunning played a much larger role than he imagined.

Among the Plataeans, there was a man of some distinction named Arimnestus or Aeimnestus. At Marathon, he had served as their commander, and he is said to have been in charge of their forces at the battle of Plataea as well. On the day of the latter battle, however, he is known to have been with the Lacedaemonians, and it is a reasonable guess that he was there because, in staging a retreat, Pausanias wanted someone close at hand who was intimately familiar with the terrain.

This figure is worthy of mention here not so much because it is conceivable (as it is, in fact) that the warrior, *lógimos* at Sparta, who brought down Mardonius on that fateful day was not a prominent Spartiate, as is generally assumed, but a Plataean, who was also at Lacedaemon a man of note. This Plataean is worthy of close attention here chiefly because, in passing, Plutarch tells us two things about the man which may help explain why Pausanias made a bee line for Hysiae in the wee hours on that fateful day: first, he observes that this Plataean commander had joined with Aristeides of Athens in carefully scouting out the Pantassa ridge *before* the army of the Hellenes made its descent from Cithaeron to the river Asopus; and, second, he remarks that the two commanders had paid particular attention on this occasion to the advantages the ridge would afford an infantry force deployed against an enemy superior in cavalry.

In short, it is perfectly possible that Pausanias knew what he was doing. To be precise, it is perfectly possible that his ostentatious reluctance to have the Lacedaemonians situated opposite the Persians when they were reported to be about to launch an attack was a ploy designed to suggest that the Spartans had lost their nerve, and his subsequent refusal to countenance Mardonius' call for a new Battle of the Champions may have been intended to foster the same impression. It is no less likely that, in staging his army's awkward withdrawal from the Asopus ridge and in heading shortly before dawn for the temple of Eleusinian Demeter on the Pantassa ridge, Pausanias deliberately baited a trap and that Mardonius fell into it. As we learn from Plato's *Laches*, in later times, there were Greeks who suspected something of the sort. There was a reason why the Spartans were notorious for thinking one thing and saying another. They regarded it as far more glorious to achieve victory by a ruse than in a pitched battle. On this occasion, with assistance from a certain Plataean *lógimos,* they may have duped Mardonius and deceived posterity as well.[87]

If so, however, they did not fool the canny son of Pharnaces, who doubted Mardonius' wisdom—for, when the son of Gobryas ordered his Persians to cross the Asopus and many of the other Iranians under his command followed their example, Artabazus reined in the forty thousand men under his command and deployed them in close formation. Initially, he led them cautiously in the direction of the sanctuary of Eleusinian Demeter. But when he saw Mardonius' Persians take flight, he immediately reversed course and led his men, in as rapid a manner as possible, neither to Mardonius' stockade nor to Thebes, but toward Phocis, then Thessaly, Macedonia, Thrace, and Byzantium. A year or two after he reached Asia Minor with most of his army intact, Xerxes rewarded him with the satrapy of Hellespontine Phrygia, hitherto held by his father's cousin Megabates.[88]

Whether Xerxes was right to do so is contested. One can argue that, had Artabazus committed his troops, the Spartans would have been overwhelmed.[89] One can also argue that his judgment was sound—for the Iranians who fled to Mardonius' stockade did not fare at all well. At first, they held their own—for most of the Hellenes were preoccupied, especially the Athenians. When the latter engaged Mardonius' Greek allies, they did not find the Malians, Locrians, Phocians, and Thessalians arrayed against them at all formidable. But the Boeotian hoplites, especially the Thebans at their head, fought long and hard; and eventually, when they fled to Thebes, their cavalry prevented the Athenian hoplites from running down and slaughtering what was left of their infantry.[90] It was not until after the Boeotian retreat that the Athenians and the other Hellenes joined the Lacedaemonians in focusing their attention on Mardonius' stockade.

The Athenians, who would come to have a reputation for skill in siege warfare, in time mounted the wall and tore a section down. Then, the Tegeans and the others streamed in, and, in that confined space, the slaughtering began. Tens of thousands were killed before the fury of the Hellenes was slaked, and no more than three thousand survived to be ransomed as prisoners of war.[91] Xerxes' invasion of Hellas had come to a disastrous and bloody end.

The War at Sea

If Greek tradition can be trusted, in the late afternoon on the late August day in which the Persians went down to defeat at Plataea, Leotychidas and the Hellenic forces at sea finished off what remained of the Persian fleet in the Aegean. After Salamis, the surviving ships in Xerxes' fleet had sailed to the Hellespont, ferried the Great King and the soldiers in his entourage from Sestos to Abydos, and wintered along the Asia Minor coast—for the most part at Cumae with the overflow relegated to the harbor built by Polycrates on Samos. In the spring, the triremes at Cumae shifted to Samos; and Mardontes son of Bagaios and Artayntes son of Artachaias, with the help of the latter's nephew Ithamitras, took over the command. With the three or four hundred ships they possessed, they were expected to guard against a revolt in Ionia. In the beginning, at least, it apparently crossed no one's mind that the Hellenes, who had not pursued Xerxes' fleet very far when it fled Salamis, would seize the initiative and prosecute the war at sea in Ionia.[92]

We do not know when the commanders at Samos first learned of the presence of Leotychidas and his fleet at Delos. We are only told that they were as reluctant to sail west of Samos as the son of Menares and the Hellenes were to sail east of Delos. "Fear," Herodotus tells us, "stood sentry over the space in between."[93] The Persian fleet had been savaged the previous year, and its commanders were now extremely risk-averse. At one hundred ten triremes, the Hellenic fleet was, Leotychidas evidently believed, unequal to the task of raising Ionia in revolt.

The arrival of Xanthippus and the Athenian fleet appears to have changed everything. Leotychidas now had, according to Diodorus, two hundred fifty ships under his command—enough with which to take on Persia's Aegean fleet. Some time after Xanthippus' arrival, three messengers arrived from Samos—Lampon son of Thrasycles, Athenagoras son of Archestratides, and Hegesistratus son of Aristagoras. All were hostile to Theomestor son of Androdamas, the trierarch at Salamis whom Xerxes had recently installed as tyrant on the island; and, acting on behalf of their fellow citizens, they invited the Hellenes to help them instigate a revolt against the Persians in Ionia. Leotychidas they told that the Persian fleet was in poor sailing condition and that the barbarian soldiers would be no match in battle for the Greek marines.[94]

After sacrificing and securing favorable omens, Leotychidas directed the fleet to sail to Samos; and the Persians, in fear, rowed across from the island

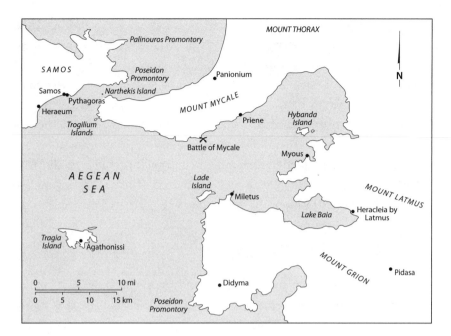

Map 27. Samos, Mycale, and the Battle of Mycale

to the Mycale peninsula on the mainland. If there were any Phoenician ships left in the Aegean fleet, which Diodorus firmly denies, Mardontes, Artayntes, and Ithamitras sent them away, and the triremes that remained they lugged up on the shore and safeguarded there within a stockade they built so that Tigranes—an Achaemenid who had led the Medes during Xerxes' invasion and who now commanded the Persian army in that district—could use his soldiers to protect the fleet, their admirals, and the crews of the ships.[95]

Herodotus' account speaks eloquently about the consequences of the battle of Salamis. It may have been true that Persia's Aegean fleet had seen better days. But something on the order of ten months had passed since it had suffered a mauling at the hands of the Hellenes off Salamis. There had been plenty of time for refitting and repairs, for drying out, for recaulking and recoating with pitch. Moreover, by all accounts, the fleet at Samos greatly outnumbered Leotychidas' armada. If its commanders chose to haul the ships up on the Mycale peninsula rather than to risk a fight at sea, it suggests either that, at Salamis, the morale of that fleet's captains was broken or that the fleet's Persian commanders feared that, in a battle, its Ionian and Aeolian officers and crews would stage a rebellion and switch sides—or both.

The Greeks paused at Samos to prepare gangways for boarding. Then they sailed to Mycale and learned that the ships in the Persian fleet had been beached and that there was a sizable army deployed near the shore to defend it. Leotychidas sailed close to the shore and had a herald exhort the Ionians to recall to mind liberty first of all and to remember the password, which he stated. The Hellenes then beached their ships at an undefended place not far away, and the marines on board disembarked on shore. Tigranes and his fellow commanders responded by stripping their arms from the Samians, who had earlier connived in the release of five hundred Athenians taken captive by Xerxes. In similar fashion, the Milesians, who had also earned Persian distrust, were dispatched to guard the passes leading up and over Mount Mycale. Then, the Persian *gerrophóroi* set up their wicker shields, as was their wont, to form a barricade.[96]

The Athenians, Corinthians, Sicyonians, and Troezenians advanced quickly along the shore. The Lacedaemonians approached the stockade at a slower pace across the higher ground inland; and, by the time that they arrived, the Athenians and those with them had pushed through the barricade and rushed within the stockade; and here, as in the stockade at Plataea, a massacre took place—for, as we have seen, ordinary Persian footsoldiers, those who doubled as archers and spearmen, were armed with relatively short spears and bore no shields, while the few who were dedicated infantrymen bore only small *aspídes* or bucklers—either on their arms or in their hands. Of the Persian commanders, Artayntes and Ithamitras escaped; Mardontes and Tigranes died in the fight. Many of the Persians who fled were either led back to the foe or done in by the Milesians guarding the passes; and, before departing, the Hellenes set fire to the stockade and the Persian ships.[97]

Epilogue
The Aftermath

IN 479, as events unfolded in mainland Greece and Ionia, Xerxes waited patiently in Sardis, providing guidance insofar as communications allowed. It was he who decided that an offer should be made to Athens, and it was no doubt he who, come spring, had the fleet shifted from Cumae to Samos to keep watch over the Ionians. It was he who had earlier ordered Tigranes with his army to stand guard over Ionia, and he it must have been who arranged for that commander's troops to be reinforced in 479 by military colonists from Sardis and its environs. It may even have been Xerxes who decided to forgo another battle at sea and to have the surviving triremes lugged ashore at Mycale where, everyone supposed, his soldiers could protect them.[1]

In Sardis, Xerxes tarried, anxiously awaiting news—at least until, one must suspect, the arrival of Artabazus son of Pharnaces with his report. In the spring of 478, after weighing the consequences of Plataea and Mycale for his realm, he made dispositions for the defense of Anatolia. Then he departed from Lydia. We do not know where he headed—whether toward Susa, as Herodotus reports, or Ecbatana, as Diodorus claims. But before setting off, he installed as the new ruler of Cilicia a henchman from Halicarnassus who had demonstrated a fierce loyalty to the royal house, and he appears to have taken revenge on the Milesians for the support they lent the Hellenes at Mycale by sacking the temple of Apollo at Didyma and carrying off the bronze statue of the god. Along the way, Xerxes paused for a considerable period of time to fortify the citadel at the strategic city of Celaenae in southern Phrygia on the border with Lydia and to construct a royal palace and no doubt a *parádeisos* at the foot of the acropolis there.² If Xerxes was dismayed at what had happened, he certainly did not let on.

There is, in fact, reason to suspect that the Great King and his minions may have represented the Greek campaign to the larger public within the empire as an unmitigated success. Half a millennium after these events—after purportedly hearing a Mede dismiss Marathon as a minor skirmish and sum up the results of Xerxes' invasion with the observation that the Great King had vanquished the Lacedaemonians at Thermopylae and killed Leonidas, then sacked Athens and sold into slavery those of its citizens who had not fled, and returned to Asia after imposing tribute on the Greeks—the Bithynian orator and philosopher Dio Chrysostom openly wondered whether this is the tale that Xerxes had spread.³

It would not have been especially hard for Xerxes and his minions to spin events in this fashion. After all, he bore with him—on his initial journey to Sardis and on his later travels between Babylon, Pasargadae, Susa, and no doubt Ecbatana and Persepolis as well—proof positive of his glorious victory in the form of statues, images, and votive offerings (including the famous bronze of the tyrant-slayers Harmodius and Aristogeiton), which he had looted from Athens and the other cities he had sacked. Indeed, were we to judge the outcome of the war solely on the basis of the inscriptions that Xerxes himself put up, almost certainly thereafter, at Persepolis, Pasargadae, and presumably elsewhere as well, we would know nothing of his failures at Salamis, Plataea, and Mycale; and we would suppose that, after the war, he ruled over and collected tribute from not only the "Ionians who dwell by the Sea" but also the Ionians "who dwell beyond the Sea" as well as the peoples of "Thrace."⁴

Of course, none of this would have fooled the courtiers who accompanied the Great King on his seasonal peregrinations between Persepolis, Susa, Ecbatana, and Babylon. Nor would it have bamboozled the great families of Persia. They must have recognized his failure; they must have known that very little tribute was coming in from Ionia, that none was coming in from the islanders and the Greeks who lived in the Balkans, and that Thrace with its gold and silver mines was lost as well. In Xerxes' attempts to mislead the public they must have discerned nothing other than weakness. No one from the high aristocracy who remembered Darius can have harbored much respect for his feckless son, and no one in their number who worshipped the Wise Lord Ahura Mazda and embraced the political theology of the Achaemenid kings can have thought the son of Darius worthy of the office he held. Of course, had Xerxes seized control of the seas once more, had he mounted a second and successful invasion of Hellas, his initial failures would have been forgotten. But this he did not do, and over time the Persian defense posture along the coast of Anatolia deteriorated further. In a realm that has expansion as its raison d'être, in a polity that has the unification of the world as its god-given aim, such a development is apt to have profound consequences—not only abroad, but even more emphatically at home.

Contemporary students of Achaemenid history are quick to denounce Plato's contention that the moral formation [*paideía*] afforded Cambyses, Xerxes, and their successors was defective and his suggestion that the spectacular achievements of Cyrus and Darius were made possible by the fact that neither was reared in luxury by women and eunuchs at the court and that both knew little but the hardships of the campaign.[5] There is this to be said for their argument. The Persian empire did not collapse after Salamis, Plataea, and Mycale. It survived for another century and a half. It was resilient, and Achaemenid administration appears to have been competent, efficient, and effective throughout.

There is, however, more to be said for Plato's analysis than these scholars are currently willing to admit. The survival of the Achaemenid empire may be a reflection of Darius' genius and of his success in thoroughly cowing its subjects and in setting up institutions more than adequate to insure continued submissiveness on their part. As Machiavelli understood, it takes moxie for a "new prince" to establish an empire and to defend it in its infancy, and it takes very little to sustain it once it is firmly in place.[6] A well-oiled machine can compensate for weakness and self-indulgence on the part of those at the very top. The Roman empire instituted by Augustus not only survived Tiberius, Caligula, Claudius, Nero, Domitian, Commodus, and the sons of Septimius Severus. For the most part, it flourished under their rule.

To deny that Xerxes was weak, self-indulgent, and more than a bit of a fool, we would have to reject the only real evidence that we have about the man as a man. It would be unwise to do so if we really want to understand. Thanks to the yeoman's work done over the last twenty-five years by the scholars from a great variety of disciplines who regularly attended the annual meetings of the Achaemenid History Workshop, no one now doubts that Herodotus, Xenophon, and even Ctesias, not to mention the others in Hellas who wrote about Achaemenid Persia, knew a great deal. What they have to say about Persian institutions and practices dovetails exceedingly well with the evidence we have from the Jewish Bible; from Achaemenid Egypt and Babylon; from the surviving Old Persian, Akkadian, Elamite, and Aramaic tablets and royal inscriptions; and from the pictorial representations found at Persepolis, Susa, and elsewhere.

The lurid tale that Herodotus tells us concerning Xerxes, his son Darius, his wife Amestris, his brother Masistes, and Masistes' wife and daughter is bizarre, to be sure. But this does not mean that it is wholly or even largely false. Similar tales are known to be true regarding dynasty after dynasty under the Roman principate, and Plato's analysis of the reasons why Cyrus and Darius were so much more impressive than Cambyses, Xerxes, and most of the latter's successors can be applied to the Roman *principes* with no less interpretive force. That a despot's son—reared at court with the expectation that, if he pleases his father, he might inherit the throne—should come, when king, to entertain a sordid passion for his brother's wife; that he should contrive a marriage between that woman's daughter and his own first-born son; that he should subsequently debauch the daughter; that his attempts to please the young woman should in time enrage his wife and eventuate in a fatal breach with his brother: this tawdry little domestic drama is shocking in the extreme but it is in no way incredible.[7] It does not top what Tacitus and Suetonius have to report regarding the successors of Augustus and their womenfolk at Rome. Where a monarch's word is law, the only discipline to which he will be subject is self-discipline; and those who have not become inured to this species of discipline while young are not apt to acquire it later in life.

It is no surprise that Xerxes was eventually assassinated. Many a self-indulgent Roman *princeps* suffered the like in similar circumstances. Moreover, Justin is surely right when he claims that, after the catastrophe in Greece, Xerxes came to be held in contempt by his own people; and it makes perfect sense that the commander of the royal bodyguard—the Persian equivalent of the Roman principate's praetorian prefect—should play a prominent role in such a conspiracy. No one could be better placed to witness and reflect on what Justin rightly calls "the decline day-by-day-by-day in the majesty of the kingship."[8] For the Persian empire, Salamis, Plataea, and Mycale may well have been a mere bump on the road. For the self-indulgent, out-of-control son and heir of Darius the Great, however, these battles, the failure to mount a successful expedition soon thereafter, and the further setbacks in the Levant that took place in later years were arguably fatal—especially when matched with the man's propensity for egregious and imprudent personal misconduct.

The results that eventually brought Xerxes down left his Greek opponents elated, as one would expect. The Athenians could now rebuild their cities and homes and sow their land. The Megarians and the Peloponnesians could return to their farms, and the Aeginetans and Corinthians could turn their minds once more to commerce. The danger had receded.

In the wake of the battles at Plataea and Mycale, the Spartans faced a quandary, nonetheless. The Persians were gone, and they were not likely to return. They had been annihilated on both land and sea, and they no longer, in any obvious way, posed a threat to Lacedaemon, its form of government, and way of life. What were the Spartans to do next? What was to become of the grand alliance that they had created?

Prior to 481, the Spartans had entertained the hope that the Persian challenge would be evanescent and that their hegemony within the Peloponnesus might be more or less sufficient. The skein of alliances constituting this hegemony had enabled them to keep the Messenians down, the Arcadians close, and the Argives out—which left them free to live in splendid isolation in the discreetly opulent manner to which they had grown accustomed. Xerxes' invasion had shown the Lacedaemonians, however, that the grand strategy which they had gradually articulated in the first half of the sixth century was not entirely adequate to their needs. In the crisis, at least, this strategy required a supplement—which the Spartans supplied by bringing their Peloponnesian allies into a league with Athens and by inviting others, further afield, to join.

This had proved a brilliant stroke. The Hellenic League had managed to field a fleet capable of countering and, in the end, defeating the naval armada dispatched by the King of Kings. It had, then, managed to field an army of nearly forty thousand hoplites capable of countering and, in the end, defeating the core of Xerxes' army. In both cases, to be sure, the struggle had been close-run. In both cases, the Hellenes had profited from egregious errors committed by the Great King and his marshal Mardonius. In both cases, they had enjoyed good fortune. In both cases, moreover, canniness had been required on their part. But they had won—that they had done—and they had won decisively. The victory had bolstered their prestige; and, should the Mede return in force, as everyone understood, the Hellenic League organized against him would be much, much larger, and the Greeks would win again.

This victory was no small thing. In amassing footsoldiers, cavalrymen, and triremes, the King of Kings had stinted not one whit. He had put his own prestige and that of the Achaemenid regime on the line by leading the invasion himself, and he appears to have rallied the peoples of Iran behind his banner by representing the campaign in Zoroastrian terms as a crusade, a *jihad*, a holy war to unite mankind, end all wars, and bring on the end times. The realm that the Spartans and their allies had so decisively defeated drew strength from religious fervor in a manner hitherto in human history unprecedented, and it was the wealthiest and the most powerful empire that mankind had, up to that time, ever known.

Even by much later standards, as we have already had occasion to observe, the Achaemenid empire was exceedingly grand. It stretched from the Indus well past the Nile, from the Sudan to Bulgaria and Romania, from the Indian Ocean, the Persian Gulf, and the Red Sea in the south to the Aral Sea, the Caspian Sea, the Black Sea, and the eastern Mediterranean in the north. It encompassed Libya, Egypt, Palestine, Phoenicia, Syria, Jordan, Anatolia, Thrace, and Macedonia as well as Mesopotamia, Armenia, Georgia, Azerbaijan, Iran, Afghanistan, parts of Uzbekistan, and no small proportion of the territory constituting modern Pakistan. The Achaemenid realm was one of the largest contiguous land empires in human history, and it included among its subjects something on the order of 40 percent of the human race—a greater proportion than any empire before or since. That an alliance of small cities—none of them, on its own, able to field an army of more than ten thousand hoplites and most much, much less populous—should stand up to and annihilate what was arguably the largest army and the most formidable fleet ever assembled—this was and still is a wonder well worthy of extended contemplation.

In the aftermath, the Spartans had a choice. They could declare victory, retreat to their fastness in the Peloponnesus, and return to their time-honored ways, grateful that they had weathered the storm, confident that no such threat would reappear, and satisfied with their diminutive realm and the disciplined way of life it made both possible and necessary. Alternatively, they could try to sustain their extended hegemony on both land and sea by continuing the war; by incorporating central Greece, the Aegean islands, and the Hellenic cities on the coast of Asia Minor within the Hellenic League; and perhaps also by seeing just how far they could project power into Anatolia and Egypt and along the Mediterranean coast of Syria, Phoenicia, and Palestine in between. After Plataea and Mycale, as was only natural, many Spartiates breathed a sigh of relief and hankered for home. Others, as was no less natural, were tempted by what the larger world had to offer.

In the short run, however, there was no need for a decision, and none was made. The task at hand was obvious. After Mycale, the son of Menares and the commanders of the civic contingents within the Hellenic navy gathered at Samos to consider what to do with the Ionians, who were clamoring for admission to the Hellenic League. The Peloponnesians were reluctant to assume ongoing responsibilities so far afield; and they were mindful of the fact that, when the league was founded, its members had taken an oath to confiscate the land of the communities which sided with the Persians without being compelled to do so, to sell their populations into slavery, and to pay from the proceeds a tithe to Apollo at Delphi. With this prospect in mind, they proposed that the eastern Greeks be evacuated and given the lands of those who had medized in mainland Greece.[9]

The Athenians had another opinion. They imported grain—much of it from the Crimea on the Black Sea—and they wanted to insure that the trade route running through the Hellespont, the Sea of Marmara, and the Bosporus remained open. With this in mind, they insisted that their Ionian kin retain their homelands and that the Hellenic League pledge to defend them—which is what the allies decided to do, at least with regard to the islanders. According to Herodotus, the Samians, the Chians, the Lesbians, and the other islanders were admitted into the alliance, and the Hellenic fleet then sailed toward the Hellespont—with an eye to tearing down the bridges, which the Greek commanders still supposed intact. When the Peloponnesians learned that the bridges no longer existed, they sailed home. But Xanthippus and the Athenians stayed on to recover for Athens the fine farmland on the Thracian Chersonnesus once controlled by Miltiades and his predecessors in the Philaid clan and to besiege and seize Sestos, which would come to be known proverbially as "the dinner table of the Peiraeus." Then, the following year the Hellenic League liberated the Greek cities on the island of Cyprus garrisoned by the Persians, captured Byzantium on the Bosporus, and opened up the route to the Black Sea.[10]

At Plataea, there were also things to do. Initially, Pausanias saw to it that the Hellenes in his command buried their dead, collected the booty strewn about the Persian camp,[11] and provided for the prisoners of war. We do not know how many Greeks were killed. But, as in the case of the Athenians and Plataeans at Marathon, their losses appear to have been modest.

Herodotus tells us that, in the final encounter, ninety-one Lacedaemonians from Sparta, sixteen Tegeans, and fifty-two Athenians were killed. To these, we can add the six hundred Megarians and Phleiasians who were mowed down by the Theban cavalry that day. But there must have been more. Diodorus' claim that the Greek losses amounted to ten thousand may well be implausible, but Plutarch, who was a Boeotian, may be on the mark when he puts the number of hoplites killed at something like one thousand three hundred sixty. We can almost certainly dismiss Herodotus' contention that the burial mounds built by the Aeginetans and the other peoples not mentioned above were empty. The losses suffered by the Orchomenians from Arcadia and by the Corinthians, Potidaeans, Sicyonians, Epidaurians, Troezenians, Lepreates, Mycenaeans, Tirynians, Hermionaeans, Eretrians, Styrians, Chalcidians, Ambraciots, Leucadians and Anactorians, Cephallenians, Aeginetans, and Plataeans may have been modest. But, located as they were on the lower ground along the Asopus ridge in the days preceding the final battle, they had been vulnerable to assault by the Persian cavalry, and they were surely involved in the attack on the stockade.[12]

A tenth of the booty collected on Pausanias' orders was set aside for Olympian Zeus, and from it, in time, Pausanias and the Hellenes dedicated a bronze statue of the god at Olympia some fifteen feet tall, and on the base of the statue a list of those participant in the war was inscribed. A tenth was also reserved for the forging of a statue of Poseidon some seven feet tall to be set up at the Isthmus of Corinth. And another tenth was set aside for Apollo at Delphi, and, in time, Pausanias would set up next to the altar there a golden tripod mounted on an eighteen-foot column of bronze constituted by three serpents intertwined. On the coils of the column—which, centuries later, the Emperor Constantine would move to the Hippodrome in his new capital at Constantinople, where, in the city now known as Istanbul, it can still be found today—the son of Cleombrotus had a couplet inscribed celebrating his leadership of the Hellenes and memorializing his destruction of the army of the Medes. Not long thereafter, his fellow Lacedaemonians would have the couplet erased and another substituted honoring all of those within Hellas who had helped "save their cities from a hateful subjection," and at that time they would have inscribed a list of thirty-one communities that had fought in the war.[13]

Pausanias' handling of other particulars is also worthy of note. When the concubine of one of Xerxes' cousins, a woman from Kos, approached him as a suppliant, claiming to be the daughter of one of his guest-friends, he treated the woman honorably, sending her to Aegina, as she wished. When an Aeginetan notable urged him to mutilate the corpse of Mardonius in the fashion in which Xerxes had treated the remains of Leonidas, he scorned to do so. And when the Mantineians and Eleans finally showed up, weeks after the other Peloponnesians and too late to be of any use, he sent them home in disgrace, and they voted to exile the leaders responsible for their having missed the battle.[14]

Once these pressing matters were settled, the son of Cleombrotus called a conference of the Hellenes to consider what was to be done with the Thebans. It was September, and the campaigning season was over. Everyone involved no doubt wanted to go home. But something had to be done, nonetheless. They could not very well leave the Plataeans and the surviving Thespians undefended and at the mercy of their neighbor; and there may have been some within the Hellenic League who were intent on revenge and eager that its members honor their oaths and seize the territory of these Medizers, sell their women and children into slavery, and pay a tenth of the proceeds to Apollo at Delphi.

In this case, however, there were reasons for hesitation. At that time, Thebes was not a democracy or even a broad-based oligarchy. It was governed by a narrow clique; and it was, moreover, an open question whether the city had medized willingly or only when compelled. After all, four hundred Thebans had volunteered to fight at Thermopylae; and, whatever its predilections may have been, the city's ruling order had not prevented them from showing up. The leading members of the Hellenic League were also, as it happened, members of the Amphictyonic League—as was Thebes. As such, they were pledged never to destroy another member or cut it off from fresh water, even in time of war.[15]

In the event, in 479, the conferees decided to demand that Thebes turn over to the Hellenes Attaginus, Timagenides, and the other leading proponents of Medism in the city. If the authorities refused, they resolved to seize the city and destroy it. To this end, on the eleventh day after the great battle, the Hellenes marched on Thebes and presented their demand. When it was refused, they began ravaging the city's territory, and they initiated a siege. Twenty days later, after it became clear that they were not going to back off, Timagenides suggested that his compatriots offer the Hellenes as compensation a sum of money from the public treasury. If the latter refused this as a settlement, he indicated a willingness to turn himself over for judgment, and he suggested that his colleagues do the same.

It was the latter course that was followed. All of the leading Medizers— apart from Attaginus, who managed to slip out of Thebes and effect an escape —handed themselves over to the Hellenes. When it was learned that Attaginus had fled, his sons were seized and brought before Pausanias, but he generously refused to hold the man's offspring responsible for the misdeeds of their father.

The Theban Medizers were, we are told, confident that, if there was a trial, they could evade punishment by a resort to bribery. Pausanias anticipated this danger; and, after dismissing the allied army and sending everyone home, he carted his Theban captives off to Corinth and saw to their execution himself.[16]

All in all, in the wake of the battle of Plataea, Pausanias appears to have handled himself with dignity, grace, magnanimity, and good sense. There was only one thing that the Spartan commander did that might have seemed to anyone odd. In the immediate aftermath of the struggle, when he came upon the tent of Xerxes, which had been left behind for Mardonius' use, he is said to have seized upon the occasion to highlight in a memorable fashion the difference between the two political regimes and ways of life that had been at odds in the conflict so recently concluded. According to the reports heard by Herodotus, the son of Cleombrotus asked Mardonius' cooks to produce a meal like the ones they ordinarily prepared for their master, and when they set out the couches of gold and silver with their expensive coverings and the gold and silver tables on which they placed a sumptuous feast, he was, we are told, "struck dumbfounded as he gazed upon the good things lying before him." As a joke, he then ordered his own servants to prepare a meal of the sort that one could expect in Laconia; and, when they did so, he dissolved in laughter and summoned the commanders of the various contingents within his army. "Men of Hellas," he reportedly said, pointing to the two meals, "I have assembled you for this purpose—to show you the mindlessness of the Persian leader Mardonius, who, having a mode of living like this, came against us to deprive us of the dreary mode of living that we possess."[17]

Abbreviations and Short Titles

In the notes, I have adopted the standard abbreviations for texts and inscriptions, for books of the Bible, and for modern journals and books provided in *The Oxford Classical Dictionary,* fourth edition revised, ed. Simon Hornblower, Antony Spawforth, and Esther Eidinow (Oxford: Oxford University Press, 2012); *The Chicago Manual of Style,* fifteenth edition (Chicago: University of Chicago Press, 2003), 15.50–53; the bibliographical annual *L'Année philologique;* Roland G. Kent, *Old Persian: Grammar, Texts, Lexicon,* second edition, revised (New Haven, CT: American Oriental Society, 1953), 107–63; Pierre Lecoq, *Les Inscriptions de la Perse achéménide: Traduit du vieux perse, de l'élamite, du babylonien et de l'araméen* (Paris: Gallimard, 1997), 177–277; *The Persian Empire: A Corpus of Sources from the Achaemenid Period,* ed. Amélie Kuhrt (London: Routledge, 2007), 910–18; and http://www.livius.org/aa-ac/achaemenians/inscriptions.html. Where possible, the ancient texts are cited by the divisions and subdivisions employed by the author or introduced by subsequent editors (that is, by book, part, chapter, section number, paragraph, act, scene, line, Stephanus page, or by page and line number).

Unless otherwise indicated, all of the translations are my own. I transliterate the Greek, using undotted i's where no accent is required, adding macrons, accents, circumflexes, and so on. When others—in titles or statements quoted—transliterate in a different manner, I leave their transliterations as they had them.

For other works frequently cited, the following abbreviations and short titles have been employed:

AT	John S. Morrison, John F. Coates, and N. Boris Rankov, *The Athenian Trireme: The History and Reconstruction of an Ancient Greek Warship,* second edition (New York: Cambridge University Press, 2000).
Balcer, *PCG*	Jack Martin Balcer, *The Persian Conquest of the Greeks, 545–450 B.C.* (Konstanz: Universitätsverlag Konstanz, 1995).
Briant, *CA*	Pierre Briant, *From Cyrus to Alexander: A History of the Persian Empire,* tr. Peter T. Daniels (Winona Lake, IN: Eisenbrauns, 2002).

Burn, *PG*   Andrew Robert Burn, *Persia and the Greeks: The Defense of the West,*
                      546–478 B.C., second edition (Stanford, CA: Stanford University Press,
                      1984).

Cawkwell, *GW*   George L. Cawkwell, *The Greek Wars: The Failure of Persia* (Oxford:
                      Oxford University Press, 2005).

CH   David Asheri, Alan Lloyd, and Aldo Corcella, *A Commentary on Her-*
                      odotus Books I–IV, tr. Barbara Graziosi, Matteo Rossetti, Carlotta Dus,
                      and Vanesa Cazzato, ed. Oswyn Murray and Alfonso Moreno (Oxford:
                      Oxford University Press, 2007–).

Evans, *BH*   James Allan Stewart Evans, *The Beginnings of History: Herodotus and the*
                      Persian Wars (Toronto: University of Toronto Press, 2006).

Figueira, *AE*   Thomas J. Figueira, *Excursions in Epichoric History: Aeginetan Essays*
                      (Lanham, MD: Rowman & Littlefield, 1993).

Green, *XS*   Peter Green, *Xerxes at Salamis* (New York: Praeger, 1970).

Hignett, *XIG*   Charles Hignett, *Xerxes' Invasion of Greece* (Oxford: Clarendon Press,
                      1963).

Krentz, *BoM*   Peter Krentz, *The Battle of Marathon* (New Haven, CT: Yale University
                      Press, 2010).

Lazenby, *DG*   John F. Lazenby, *The Defence of Greece, 490–479 B.C.* (Oxford: Aris &
                      Phillips, 1993).

Lewis, *SP*   David M. Lewis, *Sparta and Persia* (Leiden: Brill, 1977).

Lewis, *SPGNEH*   David M. Lewis, *Selected Papers in Greek and Near Eastern History,* ed.
                      Peter J. Rhodes (Cambridge: Cambridge University Press, 1997).

Lincoln, *HfM*   Bruce Lincoln, *"Happiness for Mankind": Achaemenian Religion and the*
                      Imperial Project (Leuven: Peeters, 2012).

Llewellyn-Jones,   Lloyd Llewellyn-Jones, *King and Court in Ancient Persia, 559 to 331 BCE*
KCAP   (Edinburgh: University of Edinburgh Press, 2013).

MBAD   *Marathon: The Battle and the Ancient Deme,* ed. Kostas Buraselis and
                      Katerina Meidani (Athens: Institute of the Book, 2010).

MM   *The Mariner's Mirror.*

PE   *The Persian Empire: A Corpus of Sources from the Achaemenid Period,*
                      ed. Amélie Kuhrt (London: Routledge, 2007), cited by page or by chap-
                      ter, item, and line or paragraph.

Rahe, *RAM*   Paul A. Rahe, *Republics Ancient and Modern: Classical Republicanism*
                      and the American Revolution (Chapel Hill: University of North Carolina
                      Press, 1992), cited by book, chapter, and section, which correspond with
                      volume, chapter, and section in the three-volume paperback edition
                      published in 1994.

Rahe, *SR*   Paul A. Rahe, *The Spartan Regime* (New Haven, CT: Yale University Press, 2016).

Roobaert, *II*   Arlette Roobaert, *Isolationnisme et imperialism: Spartiates de 520 à 469 avant J.C.* (Louvain: Peeters, 1985).

Root, *KKAA*   Margaret Cool Root, *The King and Kingship in Achaemenid Art: Essays on the Creation of an Iconography of Empire* (Leiden: Brill, 1979).

SA   *The Sea in Antiquity,* ed. Graham J. Oliver, R. Brock, Tim J. Cornell, Stephen Hodkinson (Oxford: British Archaeological Reports, 2000).

SAGT   W. Kendrick Pritchett, *Studies in Ancient Greek Topography* (Berkeley: University of California Press, 1965–89; Amsterdam: J. C. Gieben, 1991–92).

Schachermeyr, *MPP*   Fritz Schachermeyr, "Marathon und die Persische Politik," *HZ* 172:1 (1951): 1–35.

Scott, *HCH*   Lionel Scott, *Historical Commentary on Herodotus, Book 6* (Leiden: Brill, 2005).

Vasilev, *PDXTM*   Miroslav Ivanov Vasilev, *The Policy of Darius and Xerxes towards Thrace and Macedonia* (Leiden: Brill, 2015).

Wallinga, *SSP*   Herman T. Wallinga, *Ships and Sea-Power before the Great Persian War: The Ancestry of the Ancient Trireme* (Leiden: Brill, 1993).

Wallinga, *XGA*   Herman T. Wallinga, *Xerxes' Greek Adventure: The Naval Perspective* (Leiden: Brill, 2005).

Waters, *AP*   Matt Waters, *Ancient Persia: A Concise History of the Achaemenid Empire, 550–330 BCE* (New York: Cambridge University Press, 2014).

Wees, *SSTT*   Hans van Wees, *Ships and Silver, Taxes and Tribute: A Fiscal History of Archaic Athens* (London: I. B. Tauris, 2013).

Notes

Prologue

Epigraph: Jean-Jacques Rousseau, "[Histoire de Lacédémone]," in Œuvres complètes de Rousseau, ed. Bernard Gagnebin and Marcel Raymond (Paris: Bibliothèque de Pléiade, 1959–1969), III 545–46.

1. This prologue is a summary and restatement of the argument and conclusions presented with a full citation of the evidence and secondary literature in Rahe, SR. Here I will keep the annotation to a minimum. The first two chapters of that work and much of the material in this prologue had its origins in my dissertation and was first presented in Rahe, RAM, I.ii.2, v–vi.

2. Kósmos: Hdt. 1.65.4. From kakonomía to eunomía: 1.65, Thuc. 1.18.1, read in light of Tyrtaeus F2 (West). See Xen. Lac. Pol. 1.2; Pl. Phdr. 258b–c, Leg. 1.624a, 632d.

3. See Schol. Pl. Leg. 1.625b and Isoc. 7.14.

4. Cf. Arist. Pol. 1263b36–37 with 1276a8–b15.

5. The term "grand strategy" was introduced in 1906 by Julian Stafford Corbett in the so-called Green Pamphlet, which was many decades later published as an appendix to the 1988 reprint of the book Some Principles of Maritime Strategy (London: Longmans, Green, 1911), wherein he had elaborated on the idea without resorting to the term. The notion was taken up and first fully developed after World War I by J. F. C. Fuller, The Reformation of War (London: Hutchinson, 1923), 211–28. For a recent discussion of its application to the study of ancient history, see Kimberly Kagan, "Redefining Roman Grand Strategy," Journal of Military History 70:2 (April 2006): 333–62 (esp. 348–50).

6. Pure democracy: Alexander Hamilton, James Madison, and John Jay, The Federalist, ed. Jacob E. Cook (Middletown, CT: Wesleyan University Press, 1961), no. 10. Pólis the men: the references are collected by Charles Forster Smith, "What Constitutes a State," CJ 2:7 (May 1907): 299–302. Alcaeus: F112.10 and F426 (Lobel-Page).

7. See Thomas Babington Macaulay, The History of England (Philadelphia: E. H. Butler, 1861), I 273.

8. For an extended meditation on the pólis as a species of political community, see Rahe, RAM, I.i–vii.

9. See Rahe, SR, Appendix I, for a defense of this now fiercely contested claim.

10. Arist. Pol. 1269b36–39.

11. Plut. Cleom. 9.1–2.

12. Marriage for procreation only: Plut. Comp. Lyc. et Num. 4.1. Apatheía with regard to wife: 3.4. Matrimony slighted: Joseph. Ap. 2.273.

13. Plut. *Lyc.* 21.2.

14. Tyrtaeus F10 (West). Good for stirring up the *néoi:* Plut. *Cleom.* 2.4.

15. Cf. Tyrtaeus F12 (West) with Hom. *Il.* 11.784 (cf. 6.208–9) and *Od.* 1.1–3.

16. Tyrtaeus F12.1–9 (West).

17. Cf. John F. Lazenby and David Whitehead, "The Myth of the Hoplite's *Hoplon*," *CQ* n.s. 46:1 (1996): 27–33, with Adam Schwartz, *Reinstating the Hoplite: Arms, Armour and Phalanx Fighting in Archaic and Classical Greece* (Stuttgart: Franz Steiner Verlag, 2009), 25–27.

18. Arist. *Pol.* 1297b19–20.

19. Eur. *HF* 190.

20. Thuc. 5.71.1, Plut. *Mor.* 220a. Note also Diod. 12.62.5; Plut. *Pel.* 1.10. For an in-depth discussion of this species of warfare with extensive citations from the secondary literature, see Rahe, *SR,* Chapter 3.

21. Tyrtaeus F11–12, 19 (West). For a defense of reading these passages as a description of hoplite warfare, see Rahe, *SR,* Chapter 3.

22. Tyrtaeus F12.10–22 (West).

23. Tyrtaeus F12.23–34 (West).

24. Tyrtaeus F12.35–44 (West).

25. Plut. *Lyc.* 21.7, *Mor.* 238b.

26. Isoc. 12.177–79, Dem. 20.107–8, Polyb. 6.48.2–5.

27. Arist. *Pol.* 1270b17–25, 1294b13–41.

28. Hdt. 8.114.2.

29. Cic. *Rep.* 2.33.57–58, *Leg.* 3.7.15–16.

30. Xen. *Hell.* 2.4.38, 3.2.23, 4.6.3; Arist. *Pol.* 1322b12–16.

31. Arist. F538–39, 611.10 (Rose) = F543, 545, Tit. 143.1.2.10 (Gigon); Plut. *Lyc.* 28, *Cleom.* 9.3.

32. Ruled by laws and ephors: Plut. *Mor.* 211c. Royal oath to maintain *nómoi:* Nicholas of Damascus F114.16 (*FHG* Müller III 459). Monthly exchange of oaths with kings: Xen. *Lac. Pol.* 15.7.

33. Plut. *Dion* 53.4, Dem. 20.10, Dion. Hal. *Ant. Rom.* 2.14.2.

34. Dem. 20.107, Arist. *Pol.* 1270b23–25, Plut. *Lyc.* 26.

35. Ephraim David, "The Trial of Spartan Kings," *RIDA,* third ser., 32 (1985): 131–40.

36. Isoc. 12.154.

37. Alexander Hamilton: *The Records of the Federal Convention of 1787,* ed. Max Farrand (New Haven, CT: Yale University Press, 1911–37), I 288–89, 309–10: 18 June 1787.

38. Arist. *Pol.* 1329a2–17.

39. Xen. *Hell.* 4.2.11–12.

Part I. The Crisis of Sparta's Grand Strategy

Epigraph: Xenophanes *Vorsokr.*[6] 21 B22.

1. Assyrians and Babylonians: J. A. Brinkman, "Babylonia in the Shadow of Assyria (747–726 B.C.)"; A. K. Grayson, "Assyria: Tiglath-pileser III to Sargon II (744–705 B.C.)," "Assyria: Sennacherib and Esarhaddon (704–669 B.C.)," and "Assyria 668–635 B.C.: The Reign of Ashurbanipal"; Joan Oates, "The Fall of Assyria (631–609 B.C.)"; and D. J. Wiseman, "Babylonia 605–539 B.C.," in *CAH,* III:2[2] 1–193, 229–51, and T. F. R. G. Braun, "The Greeks in the Near East," in *CAH,* III:3[2] 1–31 (at 23).

2. Pl. *Phd.* 109a–b.

3. Greeks in Cilicia, Pamphylia, and Cyprus: Abydenos *FGrH* 685 F5; Hdt. 2.182.2; T. F. R. G. Braun, "The Greeks in the Near East," and V. Karageorghis, "Cyprus," in *CAH,* III:3[2] 1–31, 57–70, with Christopher J. Tuplin, "Cyprus before and under the Achaemenids: Problems in Chronology, Strategy, Assimilation and Ethnicity," in Tuplin, *Achaemenid Studies* (Stuttgart: Franz Steiner Verlag, 1996), 15–79. Mermnadae: Machteld Mellink, "The Native Kingdoms of Anatolia: II. The Lydian Kingdom," in *CAH,* III:2[2] 643–54. Assaults prior to time of Croesus: Hdt. 1.14.4–22.3. Miletus' accommodation: 1.21–22. Croesus' conquests: 1.26. Maritime ambitions: 1.27. In weighing what Herodotus has to say and in considering the Near Eastern evidence, I have found the first volume of *CH* invaluable. For a hyperskeptical, dismissive posture with regard to his testimony, see Reinhold Bichler, *Herodots Welt: Der Aufbau der Historie am Bild der fremden Länder und Völker, ihrer*

Zivilisation and ihrere Geschichte (Berlin: Akademie Verlag, 2000), and Josef Wiesehöfer, "Greeks and Persians," in *A Companion to Archaic Greece*, ed. Kurt A. Raaflaub and Hans van Wees (Oxford: Wiley-Blackwell, 2009), 162–85.

4. Mermnadae and Greek religious concerns: Hdt. 1.14, 19–22, 25, 46–55, 69.3–4, 90–92, 5.36.3–4. Spartan alliance with Croesus: 1.56, 65–70.

5. Persians as Medes: J. L. Myres, "'Μηδιζειν: Μηδισμός,'" in *Greek Poetry and Life: Essays Presented to Gilbert Murray* (Oxford: Clarendon Press, 1936), 97–105. Cf. David J. Graf, "Medism: The Origin and Significance of a Term," *JHS* 104 (1984): 15–30, with Christopher J. Tuplin, "Persians as Medes," *AchHist* 8 (1994): 235–66. The fact that the Jews followed the same linguistic convention as the Greeks suggests that the latter's use of this terminology cannot be explained solely with reference to Cyrus' employment of the Medes Mazares and Harpagus to pacify Ionia: cf. Waters, *AP*, 122–23. Herodotus (1.96–107) was persuaded that the kingdom of Deioces and his earlier successors was much grander than, the Near Eastern evidence strongly suggests, any early Median principality can have been, and some now actually doubt that there was ever a Median empire on the Near Eastern model at all: Heleen Sancisi-Weerdenburg, "Was There Ever a Median Empire?" *AchHist* 3 (1988): 197–212; "The Orality of Herodotus' *Medikos Logos* or: The Median Empire Revisited," *AchHist* 8 (1994): 39–55; and "Medes and Persians in Early States?" in *The Dynamics of the Early State Paradigm*, ed. Martin A. van Bakel and Jarich G. Oosten (Utrecht: ISOR, 1996), 87–104, as well as Robert Rollinger, "Das Phantom des medischen 'Grossreiches' und die Behistun-Inschrift," *Electrum* 10 (2005): 11–29. In the circumstances, the dearth of Near Eastern evidence corroborating the magnitude Herodotus and Xenophon attribute to the kingdom of Cyaxares and Astyages after the fall of Nineveh does not seem to me to justify dismissing in its entirety their testimony. The question is discussed in detail with great intelligence by a variety of scholars in *Continuity of Empire(?): Assyria, Media, Persia*, ed. Giovanni B. Lanfranchi, Michael Roaf, and Robert Rollinger (Padua: S.a.r.g.o.n., 2003). See also the judicious discussion in Christopher J. Tuplin, "Medes in Media, Mesopotamia and Anatolia: Empire, Hegemony, Domination or Illusion?" *AWE* 3:2 (2004): 223–51. This vexed question is also bound up with the forays of the Scythians into the Near East: see Chapter 2, note 21, below.

6. Battle, eclipse, and aftermath: Hdt. 1.73–74 with T. Cuyler Young, Jr., "The Early History of the Medes and the Persians and the Achaemenid Empire to the Death of Cambyses," in *CAH*, IV^2 1–52 (at 6–23). Whether Thales or anyone else at the time could have predicted an eclipse is doubted. In my judgment, this does not bear on the question whether there was a battle and it was interrupted by the eclipse known to have taken place shortly before sundown on 28 May 585. Cf., however, Robert Rollinger, "The Western Expansion of the Median 'Empire': A Re-Examination" in *Continuity of Empire(?)*, 289–319.

7. Cyrus' rebellion: Hdt. 1.46.1, 95–130; Young, "Early History," 1–33. I am not inclined to doubt Herodotus' contention that Anshan was at the time tributary to Media. See, however, Robert Rollinger, "Zur Lokalisation von Parsu(m)a(š) in der Fārs und zu einigen Fragen der frühen persischen Geschichte," *ZA* 89 (1999): 115–39. Croesus' alliance with Amasis and Nabonidus: Hdt. 1.77.2. That Cyrus and his successors owed an immense debt culturally and politically to the example of Elam is now clear: see Wouter F. M. Henkelman, "Persians, Medes, and Elamites: Acculturation in the Neo-Elamite Period," in *Continuity of Empire(?)*, 181–231, and *The Other Gods Who Are: Studies in Elamite-Iranian Acculturation Based on the Persepolis Fortification Texts* (Leiden: Nederlands Instituut voor het Nabije Oosten, 2008), along with *Elam and Persia*, ed. Javier Álvarez-Mon and Mark B. Garrison (Winona Lake, IN: Eisenbrauns, 2011).

8. Cf. David T. Potts, "Cyrus the Great and the Kingdom of Anshan," in *Birth of the Persian Empire*, ed. Vesta Sarkhosch Curtis and Sarah Stewart (London: I. B. Tauris, 2005), 7–28, who denies the identity of Anshan and Parsumaš and makes of Cyrus and his predecessors Elamites, with Henkelman, *The Other Gods Who Are*, 55–57, as well as Matt Waters, "Parsumaš, Anšan, and Cyrus," and Mark B. Garrison, "The Seal of 'Kuraš the Anzanite, Son of Šešpeš' (Teispes), PFS 93*: Susa—Anšan—Persepolis," in *Elam and Persia*, 285–95, 375–405, who are more cautious.

9. For an up-to-date and thorough discussion of the Near Eastern, as well as the classical Greek and Latin, evidence concerning the Medes and the Persians in the period discussed in this preface to Part I, see Briant, *CA*, 5–511. Nearly all of the pertinent evidence can be found in English

translation in a volume with helpful introductions and detailed explanatory notes: *PE.* Unfortunately, the most recent overview—Waters, *AP*—is marred by its author's frequent dismissal of the ancient Greek and Jewish testimony concerning the Persian monarchy as distorted by "stereotypes" and "literary tropes." In fact, when judged in light of what we know about despotisms of a similar sort in other places and times, this testimony stands up rather well: see Lewis, *SP,* 21–22, and Llewellyn-Jones, *KCAP,* 96–148.

10. A reexamination of the Nabonidus Chronicle has shown that the invasion mounted by Cyrus in 547 was directed at Urartu and not at Lydia, as once was thought: see Robert Rollinger, "The Median 'Empire,' the End of Urartu and Cyrus the Great's Campaign in 547 BC (Nabonidus Chronicle II 16)," *AWE* 7 (2008): 51–65. Delphic oracle: Hdt. 1.46.1–56.1. Egyptian contingent: Xen. *Cyr.* 7.1.32–45 with *Hell.* 3.1.7. Stalemate in Cappadocia: Hdt. 1.71.1–73.1, 75.1–76.4.

11. Allies summoned for spring campaign: Hdt. 1.77.

12. Cyrus' seizure of Sardis: Hdt. 1.78–84; Young, "Early History," 33–35. Croesus a captive and client: Hdt. 1.85–91, Ctesias *FGrH* 688 F9.5, Xen. *Cyr.* 7.2.9–14, Castor *FGrH* 250 F11. Croesus dead: Bacchylides F3 (Maehler), Nicolaus of Damascus *FGrH* 90 F68. See Mellink, "The Native Kingdoms of Anatolia: II. The Lydian Kingdom," 653.

13. Thales' dissuasion: Diog. Laert. 1.25. Other cities loyal to Croesus: Hdt. 1.76.3. Cyrus' handling of Miletus and the other Ionian cities: Hdt. 1.141, 143. It is, of course, possible that Miletus sided with Cyrus only after the rebellion of Pactyes: cf. Gerold Walser, *Hellas und Iran: Studien zu den griechisch-perschischen Beziehungen vor Alexander* (Darmstadt: Wissenschaftliche Buchgesellschaft, 1984), 14–15. But this is not what Herodotus implies.

14. Pactyes, Mazares, and Harpagus: Hdt. 1.153.3–165.3, 168–70.

15. Cyrus conquers Babylon: Hdt. 1.153.3, 178–91. Meant to conquer Egypt: Hdt. 1.153.4. Cambyses does so in his stead: 2.1, 3.1–29. See Young, "Early History," 35–52.

16. Croesus appeals to allies: Hdt. 1.81.1–82.1. Peloponnesian mercenaries sought: Ephorus *FGrH* 70 F 58a–d.

17. Battle of Champions: Hdt. 1.82, Sosibius *FGrH* 595 F5, Paus. 2.38.5, 10.9.12; Plut. *Mor.* 306 with Thuc. 5.41. Cf. Noel Robertson, *Festivals and Legends: The Formation of Greek Cities in the Light of Public Ritual* (Toronto: University of Toronto Press, 1992), 179–207, who denies the historicity of the battle (and much else besides), with W. Kendrick Pritchett, "Aetiology sans Topography: 2. Thyreatis and Battle of Champions," in Pritchett, *Thucydides' Pentekontaetia and Other Essays* (Amsterdam: J. C. Gieben, 1995), 228–62.

18. Cyrus soon master in Sardis: Hdt. 1.83.

19. Ionians prepare defense, seek Spartan aid: Hdt. 1.141. For an earlier account of the interaction that took place between the Persians, the Greeks of the eastern Aegean, and their brethren to the West at this time and in the course of the seven decades following, see Burn, *PG.* Apart from David M. Lewis, "Postscript 1984," in ibid., 587–612, the second edition of Burn's great work is a corrected version of the first edition published in 1962. Although it is less judicious in its treatment of the sources and, on the whole, less reliable than Burn's account, an occasional insight can be gleaned from Balcer, *PCG,* which is an attempt to look at the same period from a Persian perspective.

20. The sentiment said to have been expressed by Aristeides in 479, shortly before the battle of Plataea (Hdt. 8.144.1–3), was not a product of Greek resistance against the Persians. It was a prerequisite for that resistance. Cf. Jonathan M. Hall, *Hellenicity: Between Ethnicity and Culture* (Chicago: University of Chicago Press, 2002), and *A History of the Archaic Greek World* (Oxford: Blackwell, 2007), 255–75, with Lynette G. Mitchell, "Ethnic Identity and the Community of the Hellenes: A Review," *AWE* 4:2 (2005): 409–20; and see Christopher Tuplin, "Greek Racism? Observations on the Character and Limits of Greek Ethnic Prejudice," in *Ancient Greeks West and East,* ed. Gocha R. Tsetskhladze (Leiden: Brill, 1999), 48–75, and Lynette G. Mitchell, *Panhellenism and the Barbarian in Archaic and Classical Greece* (Swansea: Classical Press of Wales, 2007), esp. 39–75.

21. Pythermos at Lacedaemon, Lakrines at Sardis: Hdt. 1.152. For an overview of intelligence operations, see Frank S. Russell, *Information Gathering in Ancient Greece* (Ann Arbor: University of Michigan Press, 1999).

22. Persian conquest of coastal Asia Minor: Hdt. 1.153.3–165.3, 168–76.

23. Cf. Roobaert, *II,* 1–80, who makes no mention of Lakrines and never even canvasses the

possibility that Lacedaemon formulated its foreign policy during the reign of Cleomenes with an eye to the Persian threat.

Chapter 1. A Shadow Growing in the East

Epigraph: Is. 41, tr. Ronald Knox.

1. Longinus on Herodotus: *Subl.* 13.3. Herodotus on own aim: Pref. Hostility to Tyranny: 5.78.

2. See Alexis de Tocqueville, *De la Démocratie en Amérique,* ed. Eduardo Nolla (Paris: Librairie Philosophique J. Vrin, 1990), II.i.3, 20.

3. *Historíai:* Hdt. Pref.

4. Herodotus as truth-teller: W. Kendrick Pritchett, *The Liar School of Herodotus* (Amsterdam: J. C. Gieben, 1993). Asides: Ernst Badian, "Herodotus on Alexander I of Macedon: A Study in Some Subtle Silences," in *Greek Historiography,* ed. Simon Hornblower (Oxford: Clarendon Press, 1994), 107–30. Word of warning: Hdt. 7.152.3. For a study casting light on Herodotus' modus operandi, see Thomas J. Figueira, "Herodotus on the Early Hostilities between Aegina and Athens," *AJPh* 106:1 (Spring 1985): 49–74, reprinted with revisions in Figueira, *AE,* 35–60. See Rosalind Thomas, *Herodotus in Context: Ethnography, Science and the Art of Persuasion* (Cambridge: Cambridge University Press, 2000), and *The Historian's Craft in the Age of Herodotus,* ed. Nino Luraghi (Oxford: Oxford University Press, 2001).

5. On medizing as such, see Christopher J. Tuplin, "Medism and Its Causes," *Transeuphatrène* 13 (1997): 155–85.

6. Cyrus' self-representation as universal monarch: *PE* 3:21, 23. Perceived as such: Is. 41:1–5, 25, 42:1–7, 44:28–45:7.

7. Missions of exploration: Hdt. 3.135–38, 4.44; Ctesias *FGrH* 688 F13.20.

8. That Harpagus settled in Lycia, as was once supposed, is most unlikely. But a daughter, son, or other kinsman may have married into the local dynasty, for the name of the conqueror does reappear in the pertinent family: see Anthony G. Keen, *Dynastic Lycia: A Political History of the Lycians and Their Relations with Foreign Powers, c. 545–362 BC* (Leiden: Brill, 1998), 61–66, 75–82, 112–18.

9. Harpagus defects to Cyrus: Hdt. 1.107–29. Babylonian evidence: *PE* 3:1. Cyrus lures Babylonians and Jews: consider 3:21–27 in light of Morton Smith, "II Isaiah and the Persians," *JAOS* 83:4 (September–December 1963): 415–21, and see *The Cyrus Cylinder: The King of Persia's Proclamation from Ancient Babylon,* ed. Irving Finkel (London: I. B. Tauris, 2013), and John Curtis, *The Cyrus Cylinder and Ancient Persia: A New Beginning for the Middle East* (London: British Museum Press, 2013).

10. Phanes' aid: Hdt. 3.4–9, 11.2, 88.1.

11. Psammetichus at Pelusium: Polyaen. *Strat.* 7.9 with Diod. 1.33.8. Supposed betrayal by Combaphis: Ctesias *FGrH* 688 F13.10. Career of Udjahorresnet: *PE* 4:11 with Joel P. Weinberg, "The International Elite of the Achaemenid Empire: Reality and Fiction," *ZATW* 111:4 (January 1999): 538–608.

12. Herodotus on Samian appeal, airing of grievances: 1.70, 3.47–53. Greek propensity to cite legendary events in diplomatic negotiations: 7.158–61, 169–71, 9.26–27; Xen. *Hell.* 6.3.2–6.

13. Enduring Corinthian hostility to Corcyra: Thuc. 1.13.4, 25.3–4. Cf. Plut. *Mor.* 859f.

14. Syloson son of Calliteles founds tyranny in late 590s: Polyaen. *Strat.* 6.45. Geōmóroi overthrown: Plut. *Mor.* 303e–304c. Priene defeats Samos on mainland: 296a. Aeaces son of Brychon: ML no. 16. Sons Polycrates, Pantagnotos, Syloson: Hdt. 3.39.1–2. Anacreon tutors Polycrates: *PMG* 491, Himerius *Orat.* 29.22 (Colonna). Ibycus visits and praises beauty of Polycrates: *PMG* 282, *Suda* s.v. *Íbukos.* For a discussion of the evidence, see Mary White, "The Duration of the Samian Tyranny," *JHS* 74 (1954): 36–43; John P. Barron, "The Sixth-Century Tyranny at Samos," *CQ* n.s. 14:2 (November 1964): 210–29; M. L. West, "Melica," *CQ* n.s. 20:2 (November 1970): 205–15 (at 206–9), whose emendations of the *Suda* and of Himerius I accept; B. M. Mitchell, "Herodotus and Samos," *JHS* 95 (1975): 75–91; and Graham Shipley, *A History of Samos, 800–188 B.C.* (Oxford: Clarendon Press, 1987), 49–80. Cf. Alastar Jackson, "Sea-Raiding in Archaic Greece with Special Attention to Samos," in *SA,* 133–49, and Aideen Carty, *Polycrates, Tyrant of Samos: New Light on*

Archaic Greece (Stuttgart: Franz Steiner, 2015), whose reconstruction of developments is quite frequently a stretch.

15. See Lilian H. Jeffery and Paul Cartledge, "Sparta and Samos: A Special Relationship?" *CQ* n.s. 32:2 (1982): 243–65. Note Ernst Baltrusch, "Polis und Gastfreundschaft: Die Grundlagen der spartanischen Aussenpolitik," in *Das Frühe Sparta,* ed. Andreas Luther, Mischa Meier, and Lukas Thommen (Stuttgart: Franz Steiner Verlag, 2006), 165–91. See Thuc. 8.21.

16. Herodotus on response of Ionian islanders to Cyrus' conquest of Anatolia: cf. 1.169.2 with 1.143, 151.3.

17. Evidence for Mytilenian and Chian collaboration with Persians: Hdt. 1.156.2–160.5, Charon of Lampsacus *FGH* 262 F9, Plut. *Mor.* 859a-b. Note Xen. *Hell.* 3.2.11. Mytilenians faithful: Hdt. 3.13.1, 14.5.

18. Republican interregnum on Samos; Pythagoras, back from Egypt and Babylon, plays prominent role: Strabo 14.1.16; Iambl. *De vita Pyth.* 5.20, 6.28. Persians burn Heraeum ca. 540: Paus. 7.5.4 with John Boardman, "Chian and Early Ionic Architecture," *Antiquaries Journal* 39:3–4 (July–October 1959): 173–217 (at 199–203). Polycrates' seizure of power, help from Lygdamis of Naxos: Hdt. 3.39.1–2, 120.3; Polyaen. *Strat.* 1.23.2. The *terminus post quem* for this event can be inferred from the fact that Lygdamis' accession to power in Naxos followed upon that of Peisistratus in Athens: Hdt. 1.61.4, 64.2; Arist. *Ath. Pol.* 15.2–3. Though frequently mentioned in Herodotus, the giving of earth and water as a token of submission to the Great King does not appear in any eastern source apart from the book of Judith, and it is not mentioned in the Greek sources with regard to Cyrus, Cambyses, or any of Xerxes' successors: Amélie Kuhrt, "Earth and Water," *AchHist* 3 (1988): 87–99, and Aldo Corcella, "Dare terra e acqua: Da Herodoto a Giuditta," *Annali della Facoltà di Lettere e Filosofia dell'Università degli studi della Basilicata, 1993–1994* (1996): 41–56. As a ritual of submission, it may have been inspired by Zoroastrian doctrine: see Louis L. Orlin, "Athens and Persia ca. 507 B.C.: A Neglected Perspective," in *Michigan Oriental Studies in Honor of George G. Cameron,* ed. Louis L. Orlin (Ann Arbor: Department of Near Eastern Studies, University of Michigan, 1976), 255–66 (esp. 265–66).

19. Thalassocracy list: W. G. G. Forrest, "Two Chronographic Notes," *CQ* n.s. 19:1 (May 1969): 95–110 (at 95–106), and Molly Miller, *The Thalassocracies* (Albany: State University of New York Press, 1971), esp. 25–43. Thucydides on Ionian thalassocracy and Polycrates' maritime supremacy: 1.13.6. Late Roman sources on Samian defeat of Persians at sea: Johannes Malalas, *Chronographia* 6.200–220 (Migne, *PG* 97, col. 260), and Georgius Cedrenus, *Historiarum compendium* 138 (Migne, *PG* 121, col. 277). Both derive their report from the early third-century A.D. chronographer Julius Africanus.

20. Polycrates tries to lure Milesians: Schol. Ar. *Plut.* 1005. Victory over Mytilenians supporting Milesians: Hdt. 3.39.4.

21. Penteconters, mercenaries, archers, and seizure of islands and mainland towns: Hdt. 3.39.3–4. First thalassocracy since Minos: 3.122.2. Empire in eastern Aegean, dedication of Rheneia to Delian Apollo: Thuc. 1.13.6, 3.104.2. Polycrates and Delian festival: Thuc. 3.104 in light of H. W. Parke, "Polycrates and Delos," *CQ* 40:3–4 (July–October 1946): 105–8; Walter Burkert, "Kynaithos, Polycrates, and the Homeric Hymn to Apollo," in *Arktouros: Hellenic Studies Presented to Bernard M. W. Knox on the Occasion of His 65th Birthday* (Berlin: Walter de Gruyter, 1979), 53–62; and Richard Janko, *Homer, Hesiod and the Hymns* (Cambridge: Cambridge University Press, 1982), 109–15.

22. Polycrates' penteconters: Hdt. 3.39.3.

23. Penteconters, *gaúloi,* and the like: Lionel Casson, *Ships and Seamanship in the Ancient World* (Princeton, NJ: Princeton University Press, 1971), 43–76, 157–200, and *Ships and Seafaring in Ancient Times* (Austin: University of Texas Press, 1994), 36–77.

24. Polycrates' Samos craft: Lysimachos *FGrH* 382 F7, Plut. *Per.* 26.3–4, *Suidas* s.v. *Samíōn ho dēmos,* Hesychius s.v. *Samiakòs trópos.*

25. Amasis' guest-friendship with Polycrates: Hdt. 2.182, 3.39.2. Saite monarchs reliant on mercenaries from Ionia and Caria: 2.151–54, 163. Amasis no exception: 3.4–11. On excellent terms with Samos' Ionian, Aeolian, Dorian neighbors: 2.178–79. Polycrates as possible mercenary recruiter: Herman T. Wallinga, "Polycrates and Egypt: The Testimony of the Samaina," *AchHist* 6 (1991): 179–97. Cf. Carty, *Polycrates,* 129–220.

26. The archaeological evidence is consistent with Aristotle's assertion (*Pol.* 1313b24) that "the

great works of construction" singled out by Herodotus (3.39.4, 60) and others for high praise were "Polycratean": see Shipley, *A History of Samos,* 74–80, 95, and Hermann J. Kienast, "Topography and Architecture of the Archaic Heraion at Samos," in *Excavating Classical Culture: Recent Archaeological Discoveries in Greece,* ed. Maria Stamatopoulou and Marina Yeroulanou (Oxford: Beazley Archive and Archaeopress, 2002), 317–25.

27. Breach between Polycrates and Amasis: Hdt. 3.40–43.

28. Phoenicia absorbed by Persians: Hdt. 3.19.3. Xenophon claims Cypriot kings shift allegiance at same time: *Cyr.* 1.1.4, 7.4.1–2, 8.6.8, 21. Falsely attributes conquest of Egypt to Cyrus: 1.1.4, 8.6.20–21. Cyprus perhaps the work of Cambyses: Henry Jay Watkin, "The Cypriote Surrender to Persia," *JHS* 107 (1987): 154–63. Cambyses takes control of the sea with Phoenician and Cypriot help: Hdt. 3.19.2–3, 34.4.

29. Polycrates turns on Lydian fugitives: Diod. 10.16.4. Offers triremes to Cambyses: Hdt. 3.44. Amasis' triremes: 3.4.2.

30. Thucydides' puzzling observations on early naval developments: 1.13.2–3.

31. Pentecontors in 535 defeat Etruscan-Carthaginian fleet: Hdt. 1.162–67.

32. See Fik Meijer, "Thucydides 1.13.2–4 and the Changes in Greek Shipbuilding," *Historia* 37:4 (4th Quarter 1988): 461–63.

33. Nechos' triremes: Hdt. 2.159.1. Earliest mention among Greeks: Hipponax of Ephesus F28 (West).

34. Amasis' conquest of Cyprus: Abydenos *FGrH* 685 F5, Hdt. 2.182.2. Invention attributed to Sidon: Clement of Alexandria *Strom.* 1.16.76. Origins of trireme: Wallinga, *SSP,* 1–129. See also Alan B. Lloyd, "The Saite Navy," in *SA,* 81–91. That many disabled triremes did sink is now, however, clear: cf. Barry Strauss, *The Battle of Salamis: The Naval Encounter That Saved Greece—and Western Civilization* (New York: Simon and Schuster, 2004), 198–208, with Sebastiano Tusa and Jeffrey Royal, "The Landscape of the Naval Battle at the Egadi Islands (241 B.C.)," *JRA* 25 (2012): 7–48 (at 36–39).

35. See *AT,* with Lucien Basch, "Roman Triremes and the Outriggerless Phoenician Trireme," *MM* 65:3 (November 1979): 289–326, and *Le Musée imaginaire de la marine antique* (Athens: Institut Hellénique sur la Préservation de la Tradition Nautique, 1987), 303–36; *The Athlit Ram,* ed. Lionel Casson and J. Richard Steffy (College Station: Texas A&M Press, 1995); William M. Murray, *The Age of Titans: The Rise and Fall of the Great Hellenistic Navies* (Oxford: Oxford University Press, 2012), 3–68; and Boris Rankov, "The Dimensions of the Ancient Trireme: A Reconsideration of the Evidence," in *Trireme Olympias: The Final Report,* ed. Boris Rankov (Oxford: Oxbow Books, 2012), 225–30. If the multitude of relatively small three-pronged Roman and Punic bronze warship rams recently recovered from the seas off the Aegates Islands near Sicily, where there was a great naval battle between Rome and Carthage in 241, really are from triremes—as Sebastiano Tusa and Jeff Royal, "The Landscape of the Naval Battle at the Egadi Islands (241 B.C.)," 7–48 (esp. 39–42), and "Battle of the Egadi Islands: Where the First Punic War Was Won," *Current World Archaeology* 65 (19 May 2014): 18–24, suspect—a case can be made that these third-century galleys were considerably smaller than those of the sixth and fifth centuries and measured between 82 and 92 feet in length. Cf. Alec Tilley, *Seafaring on the Ancient Mediterranean: New Thoughts on Triremes and Other Ancient Ships* (Oxford: Hedges, 2004), and see John R. Hale, "The Lost Technology of Ancient Greek Rowing," *Scientific American* 274:6 (May 1996): 82–85; and Alec Tilley, "Rowing Ancient Warships: Evidence from a Newly-Published Ship-Model," *IJNA* 36:2 (September 2007): 293–99.

36. Cf. Wallinga, "The Ancient Persian Navy and Its Predecessors," *AchHist* 1 (1987): 47–78; *SSP,* 171–85; and *XGA,* 32–46, who insists that triremes were habitually undermanned, with Cawkwell, *GW,* 117–18, 228–29, 271, who shows that this claim is unproven and argues on the grounds mentioned in my text that it is improbable in the extreme.

37. Warships for Cambyses from Aeolis and Ionia (Hdt. 3.1.1, 13.1, 14.5), Phoenicia and Cyprus (3.19.2–3).

38. Anacreon at Polycrates' court: *PMG* 483, Strabo 14.1.16, Himerius *Orat.* 28.2 (Colonna). Anacreon on *muthētaí: PMG* 353. Note Ath. 13.602a–d.

39. Polycrates asks Cambyses to deal with dissidents on triremes: Hdt. 3.44.2. Dissidents deploy triremes against Polycrates, seek Spartan and Corinthian aid: 3.45–49, Arist. *Oec.* 2.2.9.

40. Spartans never before near Asia Minor: Hdt. 3.56.2. Spartans and Corinthians defeat or overawe Polycrates' fleet and mercenaries, initiate siege: 3.54–55.

41. Fifth-century Spartans notoriously inept at sieges: Hdt. 9.70.2, Thuc. 1.102.1–2.

42. Herodotus' exile on Samos: *Suda* s.v. *Heródotos, Panúassis.* Samian family lore in narrative: Mitchell, "Herodotus and Samos," 75–91. Interview at Sparta with grandson of warrior killed on Samos: Hdt. 3.55. Spartans, Corinthians return home after forty-day siege: 3.56.1. Fortifications: 3.60.

43. Story groundless: Hdt. 3.56.2. Lead coins covered with electrum: John P. Barron, *The Silver Coins of Samos* (London: Athlone, 1966), 14–18. Cf. Colin M. Kraay, *Archaic and Classical Greek Coins* (Berkeley: University of California Press, 1976), 29–30. Spartans vulnerable to bribery: K. L. Noethlichs, "Bestechung, Bestechlichkeit und die Rolle des Geldes in der spartanischen Aussen- und Innenpolitik vom 7. bis 2. Jh. v. Chr.," *Historia* 36:2 (2nd Quarter 1987): 129–70.

44. Lygdamis at odds with wealthier Naxians: Arist. *Oec.* 1326b7–13. Dodges Spartan embassy: Plut. *Mor.* 236c. Spartans oust: 859c–d, Schol. Aeschin. 2.77 with D. M. Leahy, "The Spartan Embassy to Lygdamis," *JHS* 77:2 (1957): 272–75. Naxians later resist the Mede: Hdt. 5.30–34.

45. Polycrates treats Oroites' emissaries with contempt: Hdt. 3.120.2–121.2.

46. Oroites tricks, impales Polycrates: Hdt. 3.120–25. Extravagance: Ath. 12.540c–541a.

47. Maeandrius possibly party to Oroites' plot: Hdt. 3.123, Lucian *Charon* 14. Calls for *isonomía*, consolidates control of island: Hdt. 3.142–43. See Joseph Roisman, "Maiandrios of Samos," *Historia* 34:3 (3rd Quarter 1985): 257–77.

48. From Cambyses to Darius: T. Cuyler Young, Jr., "The Consolidation of the Empire and Its Limits of Growth under Darius and Xerxes," in *CAH,* IV^2 53–63; Stefan Zawadzki, "Bardiya, Darius and Babylonian Usurpers in the Light of the Bisitun Inscription and Babylonian Sources," *AMIT* 27 (1994): 127–45; and Briant, *CA,* 97–114.

49. Bisitun inscription and relief: DB (*PE* 5:1) with Root, *KKAA,* 182–226. Posted elsewhere: Young, "Consolidation of the Empire," 53. See Jonas C. Greenfield and Bezalal Porten, *The Bisitun Inscription of Darius the Great: Aramaic Version* (London: Lund Humphries, 1982). Translation of Persian proclamations: Esther 1:22, 3:12, 8:9. Herodotus repeats: 3.30, 61–88. The Achaemenid inscriptions can most easily be accessed at Roland G. Kent, *Old Persian: Grammar, Texts, Lexicon,* second edition, revised (New Haven, CT: American Oriental Society, 1953), 107–63, and http://www.livius.org/aa-ac/achaemenians/inscriptions.html. They can also be found in English translation scattered throughout *PE.* For an index listing their locations in that work, see ibid., 902–3.

50. Official account of the succession crisis, putative lineage of Darius: DB, CMa–c = DMa–c (*PE* 5:1, 19). See also *PE* 5:2–10, Hdt. 3.75.1.

51. Cassandane's lineage and marriage: Hdt. 3.2.2. Mother of Cambyses: 2.1.1, 3.2.2 with *PE* 3:1 col. iii 23–25; cf. Ctesias *FGrH* 688 F13.11. Hystaspes satrap of Parthia: cf. Hdt. 3.70 with DB §§ 1–2, 35–36, XPf § 3 (*PE* 5:1, 7:1). Darius Cyrus' quiver-bearer: Aelian *VH* 12.43. Cambyses' spear-bearer: Hdt. 3.139.2. See Matt Waters, "Cyrus and the Achaemenids," *Iran* 42 (2004): 91–102.

52. Succession story regarded as suspect: see, for example, A. T. Olmstead, *History of the Persian Empire* (Chicago: University of Chicago Press, 1948), 107–13; Jack Martin Balcer, *Herodotus and Bisitun: Problems in Ancient Persian Historiography* (Wiesbaden: Frank Steiner, 1987); Briant, *CA,* 97–109; and Lincoln, *HfM,* 375–92.

53. A likely Persian source for Herodotus: Hdt. 3.153–60 and Ctesias FGrH 688 F14.34–45 with Joseph Wells, "The Persian Friends of Herodotus," *JHS* 27 (1907): 34–47.

54. It is revealing that Herodotus (3.72) represents Darius as a man more than willing to lie. Note Lincoln, *HfM,* 30–40, who cannily interprets an apparent contradiction in the Bisitun inscription as a tacit confession on Darius' part that he is unwilling to swear to the truth of this part of the tale he tells. Also revealing is the report that property had been seized: DB § 14 (*PE* 5:1).

55. Dissension among Cyrus' sons: Xen. *Cyr.* 8.8.2. Cambyses' successor lawful monarch, Artaphernes heads conspiracy: Aesch. *Pers.* 774 (where I follow the manuscript reading). For an ingenious, if fanciful, defense of Darius' veracity, cf. Stephanie West, "'Falsehood Grew Greatly in the Land': Persian Intrigue and Greek Misconception," in *Getrennte Wege? Kommunikation, Raum und Wahrnehmung in der alten Welt,* ed. Robert Rollinger, Andreas Luther, and Josef Wiesehöfer (Frankfurt am Main: Verlag Antike, 2007), 404–24. The skepticism expressed by Waters, *AP,* 58–80, seems justified.

56. Genealogy claimed by Darius: cf. *PE* 3:21.20–21 with DB §§ 1–10, CMa–c = DMa–c (*PE* 5:1, 19), and see Robert Rollinger, "Der Stammbaum des achaimenidischen Königshauses oder die Frage der Legitimtät der Herrschaft des Dareios," *AMIT* 30 (1998): 155–209. Father and grandfather alive: DSf (*PE* 11:13). Note XPf (*PE* 7:1). Rebellions in Parsā: DB §§ 21–22, 40–48, 52 (*PE* 5:1).

57. Uprisings on death of Cyrus: Xen. *Cyr.* 8.8.2. Rebels aim at local autonomy under traditional kings: DB §§ 16, 19, 22, 24, 31, 33, 49, 52 (*PE* 5:1). There is material in the Bisitun inscription suggesting on Darius' part a fleeting and tacit admission of the legitimacy of some of these kings: Lincoln, *HfM*, 34–37, 393–405.

58. The ethnic stakes: Hdt. 3.65.6. Massacre of the Magi: 3.79. All seven conspirators identified as Persian in the Bisitun inscription: DB §68 (*PE* 5:1). Otanes identifies himself as a Persian: Abolala Soudavar, "The Formation of Achaemenid Imperial Ideology and Its Impact on the *Avesta*," in *The World of Achaemenid Persia: History and Society in Iran and the Ancient Near East*, ed. John Curtis and St. John Simpson (London: I. B. Tauris, 2010), 111–38 (at 126–27). Darius does the same: DSab §2, DZc §3, DPe §§ 2–3, DSe § 2, DNa §§2, 4 (*PE* 11:2, 6–7, 12, 16). Xerxes also: XPh §2 (*PE* 7:88). Plato (*Ep.* VII 331d-332d) rightly emphasizes Darius' reliance on his co-conspirators.

59. Persians and Elamites: see the secondary literature cited in the preface to Part I, notes 7 and 8, above.

60. Cyrus' mother a Mede: Hdt. 1.108, Xen. *Cyr.* 1.2.1–5.2. Bactrian submission: Ctesias *FGrH* 688 F9.1–3. Adoption of Median garb: Hdt. 1.135, 7.62.1; Xen. *Cyr.* 1.3.2–3, 8.1.40, 3.1. Debt to Medes perhaps more considerable: Strabo 11.13.9. Telling reference to Mede in Bisitun inscription: DB § 13 (*PE* 5:1), emphasis added. See Matt Waters, "Cyrus and the Medes," and Nicholas V. Sekunda, "Changes in Achaemenid Royal Dress," in *The World of Achaemenid Persia*, 63–71, 255–72.

61. Cf. Mary Boyce, "The Religion of Cyrus the Great," *AchHst* 3 (1988): 15–31, who thinks Cyrus a Zoroastrian, with Miltiades Papotheophanes, "Heraclitus of Ephesus, the Magi, and the Achaemenids," *IA* 20 (1985): 101–61. Note, in this connection, Elias J. Bickerman and Hayim Tadmor, "Darius I, Pseudo-Smerdis, and the Magi," *Athenaeum* 56 (1978): 239–61. Cult sites destroyed by Gaumata restored: DB §14 (*PE* 5:1).

62. Preeminence of Ahura Mazda. In Bisitun inscription: DB (*PE* 5:1). Otanes' expression of gratitude: Soudavar, "The Formation of Achaemenid Imperial Ideology and Its Impact on the *Avesta*," 126–27. In other inscriptions of Darius: DPh, DH, DSab, DPg, DZc, DPe, DPd, DPf, DSe, DSf, DSz, DSaa, DNa, DNb, DSk (*PE* 11:1–3, 6–8, 10, 12–13, 16–17, 38). In pertinent inscriptions of Xerxes: XSa, XSd, XPg, XV, XE, XPh, XPl, XPa (*PE* 7:84–88, 11:17, 12:4). Denunciation of "demon-worshipers": XPh § 4b (*PE* 7:88). Note DB § 71–72 (*PE* 5:1). Greatest of the gods: DPg, DPd, DSz (*PE* 11:3, 8, 13) and XV (*PE* 7:86). God of the Aryans: Elamite version of DB § 62 (*PE* 5:1), emphasis added. The iconography provides a vivid illustration of the intimate relationship between the Great King and his god: Root, *KKAA*, 169–226. Ammianus Marcellinus links Darius' father Hystaspes with Zarathustra: 23.6.32.

63. Zoroastrian influence on Pherecydes, Anaximander, and Heraclitus: Martin L. West, *Early Greek Philosophy and the Orient* (Oxford: Clarendon Press, 1971). Note, in this connection, Papatheophanes, "Heraclitus of Ephesus, the Magi, and the Achaemenids," 101–61. Learned, literate Zoroastrian in Xerxes' army: Pliny *NH* 30.2.8. Allusion to Zoroaster and its import: consider Xanthus of Lydia *FGrH* 765 F32 in light of the secondary literature cited in the preface to Part II, note 12, below. It is in light of Xanthus' testimony regarding the Zoroastrianism of the Magi that we should read the testimony of Herodotus (1.140.1–2) and others (Strabo 15.3.20, Cic. *Tusc. Disp.* 1.108) regarding their practice of exposing corpses so that the birds and dogs can eat their flesh—for this is a practice associated with Zoroastrianism in later times. Herodotus' testimony regarding the Persian rejection of anthropomorphism is also pertinent: 1.131; Strabo 15.3.13; Cic. *Rep.* 3.14, *Leg.* 2.26.

64. Reports on the education of young Persians and on the centrality of truth-telling: Hdt. 1.136.2, 138.1; Pl. *Alc.* I 121e-122a with Lincoln, *HfM*, 335–54, who cites Xen. *An.* 1.9.7, *Cyr.* 1.2.6–7, and Strabo 15.3.18 as well, and with Peter Kingsley, "Meetings with Magi: Iranian Themes among the Greeks, from Xanthus of Lydia to Plato's Academy," *JRAS*, third ser., 5:2 (July 1995): 173–209 (esp. 195–207), who draws attention to evidence for the presence of Zoroastrian Magi at the Academy in Plato's day. Cf. Hdt. 3.72.4–5; Xen. *Cyr.* 1.2.3–16, 6.27–46. Zoroastrians at the Achaemenid court: Rüdiger Schmitt, "Onomastica Iranica Symmicta," in *Scríbthair a ainm n-ogaim: Scritti in*

memoria di Enrico Campanile (Pisa: Picini Editore, 1997), 922–24. Achaemenid abhorrence of *Drauga:* DB §§ 10–64, DNb § 2b, XPl § 2b (*PE* 5:1, 11:17). Otanes' promise: Soudavar, "The Formation of Achaemenid Imperial Ideology and its Impact on the *Avesta*," 126–27.

65. Dualism embraced by Magi of Persia: Eudoxus of Cnidus F341 (Lassere), Aristotle F6 (Rose) = F23 (Gigon), and Theopompus of Chios *FGrH* 115 F64–65. Artaxerxes and the evil spirit Ahriman: Plut. *Them.* 28.6.

66. I find the argument advanced by Boyce, "The Religion of Cyrus the Great," 20–26, and the case made by Prods Oktor Skarjærvø, "Avestan Quotations in Old Persian? Literary Sources of the Old Persian Inscriptions," *Irano-Judaica* 4 (1999): 1–64, and "The Achaemenids and the *Avesta*," in *Birth of the Persian Empire*, 52–84, that the early Achaemenids were Zoroastrian, fully persuasive. The religious question continues, nonetheless, to generate debate. For a discussion of the secondary literature prior to 1980, see Clarisse Herrenschmidt, "La Religion des achéménides: État de la question," *StIr* 9:2 (1980): 325–39, and Muhammad A. Dandamaev and Vladimir G. Lukonin, *The Culture and Social Institutions of Ancient Iran,* tr. Philip L. Kohl with D. J. Dadson (Cambridge: Cambridge University Press, 1989), 320–60. For citations of the more recent literature, see Albert de Jong, "Religion at the Achaemenid Court," in *Der Achämenidenhof/The Achaemenid Court,* ed. Bruno Jacobs and Robert Rollinger (Wiesbaden: Harrassowitz, 2010), 533–58. For the evidence, see William W. Malandra, *An Introduction to Ancient Iranian Religion: Readings from the Avesta and Achaemenid Inscriptions* (Minneapolis: University of Minnesota Press, 1983). For an overview based on Zoroastrian practices as well as on the surviving holy books of the Zoroastrians and the commentaries written on them in and after the Sassanian period, see Mary Boyce, *A History of Zoroastrianism* (Leiden: Brill, 1975–91). That the practices of the Achaemenid kings should not conform in all respects with the imperatives of Zoroastrianism as it was practiced in later times is what one would expect. Nor, given the absence of any mention of Zarathustra in the Sassanian royal inscriptions, should we be surprised at his absence from the Achaemenid texts. The worship at Persepolis and elsewhere accorded the "other gods" created by Ahura Mazda may have resembled the veneration that Roman Catholics and the eastern Orthodox accord the angels and saints: see Wouter F. M. Henkelman, *The Other Gods Who Are: Studies in Elamite-Iranian Acculturation Based on the Persepolis Fortification Texts* (Leiden: Nederlands Instituut voor het Nabije Oosten, 2008), 65–454. One of the few defects of *PE* lies in its omission of the Greek texts testifying to the Zoroastrianism of the Achaemenids. Consider *PE* 11:1–68 in light of ibid., 473–75 (with notes 4–7). Briant, *CA,* who is usually meticulous, also fails to properly address this evidence and weigh its significance.

67. Judgment in the afterlife: XPh § 4c (*PE* 7:88). Note DB § 73 (*PE* 5:1), and see Briant, *CA,* 550–54. Political focus of Persian prayer: Hdt. 1.132.2.

68. See Tom Holland, *Persian Fire: The First World Empire and the Battle for the West* (London: Little, Brown, 2005), who rightly accords central importance to the Achaemenids' adherence to a species of Zoroastrianism. Note also Burn, *PG,* 80.

69. Darius' dynastic marriages and offspring: Hdt. 3.88.2–3, 7.2–4. Cyrus turned into an Achaemenid: CMa–c = DMa–c (*PE* 5:19) with Matthew W. Waters, "Darius and the Achaemenid Line," *AHB* 10:1 (1996): 11–18, and David Stronach, "Darius at Pasargadae: A Neglected Source for the History of Early Persia," in *Actes du séminaire international autour de l'ouvrage de P. Briant, Histoire de l'empire perse: De Cyrus à Alexandre (1996),* ed. M.-F. Boussac (Lyon: Topoi, 1997), 351–63. Darius may also have followed Cyrus' lead in his iconography of the Great King in state: Root, *KKAA,* 285–99.

70. Empire reorganized by shopkeeper: Hdt. 3.89–97, 5.52–53; Pl. *Leg.* 3.695c–d; Polyaen. *Strat.* 7.11.3; Plut. *Mor.* 172f; T. Cuyler Young, Jr., "The Early History of the Medes and the Persians and the Achaemenid Empire to the Death of Cambyses," in *CAH,* IV⁷ 1–33 (at 6–23). Tribute in silver from maritime communities, in kind from those in the interior: Polycleitus of Larissa *FGrH* 128 F3a with DB §§ 6–7, DSe, DSf, DSz, DSaa, DNa (*PE* 5:1, 11:12–13, 16) and *PE* 11:11, 15, 20, 25, 30, 12:25–27, 39–40, 14:1–44, 16:1–12, 16, 18–26. Consider *Le Tribut dans l'empire perse,* ed. Pierre Briant and Clarisse Herrenschmidt (Paris: Peeters, 1989), in conjunction with Root, *KKAA,* 227–84, and see Briant, *CA,* 388–471. Note, in this connection, Dandamaev and Lukonin, *The Culture and Social Institutions of Ancient Iran,* 177–209, 360–66, and Caroline Waerzeggers, "Babylonians in Susa: The Travels of Babylonian Businessmen to Susa Reconsidered," in *Der Achämenidenhof/*

The Achaemenid Court, 777–813. Balcer, *PCG,* 159–98, may be right in suggesting that the Persian demand for silver as tribute goes a long way toward accounting for the active role played by the mints in the Greek cities under Achaemenid control.

71. See Christopher J. Tuplin, "The Administration of the Achaemenid Empire," in *Coinage and Administration in the Athenian and Persian Empires,* ed. Ian Carradice (Oxford: British Archaeological Reports, 1987), 109–66, and "The Seasonal Migration of Achaemenid Kings," *AchHist* 11 (1998): 63–114, as well as Kenneth G. Hoglund, *Imperial Administration in Syria-Palestine and the Missions of Ezra and Nehemiah* (Atlanta: Scholars Press, 1992); W. J. Vogelsang, *The Rise and Organisation of the Achaemenid Persian Empire: The Eastern Iranian Evidence* (Leiden: Brill, 1992); Briant, *CA,* 114–38, 165–511; and Llewellyn-Jones, *KCAP,* passim (esp. 74–95). On the system of royal roads, see the preface to Part II, note 3, below.

72. Crimes and fall of Oroites: Hdt. 3.126–28.

73. Otanes installs Polycrates' brother Syloson as tyrant on Samos: Hdt. 3.139–49. Within a few years, we find his son in charge: 4.138.2.

74. Maeandrius flees Samos for Lacedaemon: Hdt. 3.144.1–48.1. Cleomenes witnesses earlier appeal of Samian exiles: Plut. *Mor.* 223d. Refuses bribe of Maeandrius, effects expulsion from Peloponnesus: Hdt. 3.148–49.

75. For varying scholarly assessments of Cleomenes' statesmanship, see Pierre Carlier, "La Vie politique à Sparte à l'époque de Cléomène 1er: Essai d'interprétation," *Ktèma* 2 (1977): 65–84, reprinted with revisions as Carlier, "Cleomene I, re di Sparta," in *Contro le 'legge immutabili': Gli Spartani fra tradizione e innovazione,* ed. Cinzia Bearzot and Franca Landucci (Milan: Vita e Pensiero, 2004), 33–52; W. G. G. Forrest, *A History of Sparta, 950–192 B.C.,* second edition (London: Hutchinson University Library, 1980), 85–93; Roobaert, *II,* 1–80; George L. Cawkwell, "Cleomenes," *Mnemosyne,* fourth ser. 46:4 (November 1993): 506–27, reprinted in Cawkwell, *Cyrene to Chaeronea: Selected Essays on Ancient Greek History* (Oxford: Oxford University Press, 2011), 74–94; Mischa Meier, "Kleomenes I, Damaratos und das spartanische Ephorat," *GFA* 2 (1999): 89–108; and G. E. M. de Ste. Croix, "Herodotus and King Cleomenes I of Sparta," in Ste. Croix, *Athenian Democratic Origins and Other Essays,* ed. David Harvey and Robert Parker (Oxford: Oxford University Press, 2004), 421–40. For Agesilaus, see Paul Cartledge, *Agesilaos and the Crisis of Sparta* (Baltimore: Johns Hopkins University Press, 1987). There is more to the story of Cleomenes' commitments with regard to foreign affairs than can be discussed here: see Rahe, *SR,* Chapter 4.

76. Cleomenes rejects Scythian appeal for help against Darius: Hdt. 6.84 read in light of 4.1–4, 83–93, 97–98, 102, 118–19. Learns from them to drink wine neat: 6.84.

77. Aristagoras and Ionian revolt: Hdt. 5.28–38. For further details, see Chapter 3, below. Persian arms: Hdt. 5.49.3, 97.1 with Chapter 4, note 50, below. Aristagoras fails to lure Cleomenes and the Spartans into supporting the revolt: Hdt. 5.38.2, 48–54. Map devised by Anaximander, corrected by Hecataeus: Strabo 1.1.11, Agathermos *GGM* 2.471.

Chapter 2. Mainland Defense

Epigraph: David Hume, "Of Commerce," in *Essays Moral, Political, and Literary,* revised edition, ed. Eugene F. Miller (Indianapolis: Liberty Fund, 1987), 259.

1. Cleomenes, Athens, and Plataea: Hdt. 6.108.1–4 and Thuc. 3.68.4 with Joseph Wells, "Of the Reign of Cleomenes I," in *Studies in Herodotus* (Oxford: Basil Blackwell, 1923), 81–86. The fact that Thucydides' dating of this event sits ill with what some ancient historians take to be the circumstances of Athens and Sparta in 519 I regard as an indication that this understanding of their circumstances needs adjustment. Cf. Gordon S. Shrimpton, "When Did Plataea Join Athens?" *CPh* 79:4 (October 1984): 295–304 (esp. 295–99), with Hornblower, *CT,* I 464–65. Thucydides characterizes the relationship between Athens and Plataea as an alliance; Herodotus uses language suggesting something like what the Romans called a *deditio in fidem.* In effect, the Plataeans placed themselves under the protection of the Athenians. I doubt that either party thought of the Plataeans as *doûloi:* cf., however, Shrimpton, "When Did Plataea Join Athens?" 300–303, and Ernst Badian, "Plataea between Athens and Sparta: In Search of Lost History," in Badian, *From Plataea to Potidaea: Studies in the History and Historiography of the Pentecontaetia* (Baltimore: Johns Hopkins University Press, 1993), 109–23.

2. Corinthian intervention on behalf of Athens and Plataea: Hdt. 6.108.5–6.

3. Guest-friendships linking Peisistratids with Spartan kings: Hdt. 5.63.2, 90.1. For what follows, I have found the philological and historical commentary in Herodotus, *Histories: Book V,* ed. Simon Hornblower (Cambridge: Cambridge University Press, 2013), quite valuable.

4. The recent work on Peisistratus' career includes: Brian M. Lavelle, *The Sorrow and the Pity: A Prolegomenon to a History of Athens under the Peisistratids, c. 560–510 B.C.* (Stuttgart: Franz Steiner Verlag, 1993), and *Fame, Money, and Power: The Rise of Peisistratos and "Democratic" Tyranny at Athens* (Ann Arbor: University of Michigan Press, 2005), as well as *Peisistratos and the Tyranny: A Reappraisal of the Evidence,* ed. Heleen Sancisi-Weerdenburg (Amsterdam: J. C. Gieben, 2000).

5. Peisistratus from Brauron: Pl. *Hipp.* 228b, Plut. *Sol.* 10.3. Eupatrids: Henry Theodore Wade-Gery, "Eupatridai, Archons, and Areopagus," *CQ* 25:1–2 (January and April 1931): 1–11, 77–89, reprinted in Wade-Gery, *Essays in Greek History* (Oxford: Basil Blackwell, 1958), 86–115. Cf. Thomas J. Figueira, "The Ten Archontes of 579/8 at Athens," *Hesperia* 53:4 (October–December 1984): 447–73, and Alain Duplouy, "Les Eupatrides d'Athènes: 'Nobles défenseurs de leur patrie,'" *CCG* 14 (2003): 7–22, who believe that the term *eupatrid* is indicative of partisan approval and political aspiration and does not, as Wade-Gery argues, denote a caste or juridical order analogous to the Roman patricians. Note also Louis Gernet, "Les dix archontes de 581," *RPh,* third ser. 12:2 (July 1938): 216–27.

6. Regionalism in Athens, Peisistratus ousted from tyranny: Hdt. 1.59.1–60.1, Arist. *Ath. Pol.* 13.3–14.3. Abortive dynastic marriage to Megacles' daughter: Hdt. 1.60.2–61.2, Arist. *Ath. Pol.* 14.41–5.1 with Davies, *APF* nos. 9688 §§ IV–V and 11793 §§ I–VI. Megacles gives younger son Peisistratus' father's name: Hdt. 6.131.2 with Davies, *APF* no. 9688 § X. I see no reason to reject the testimony of Herodotus and Aristotle concerning the regional divisions at Athens and their political significance. Cf., however, Lavelle, *Fame, Money, and Power,* 67–68, 219–21; and Greg Anderson, *The Athenian Experiment: Building an Imagined Political Community in Ancient Attica, 508–490 B.C.* (Ann Arbor: University of Michigan Press, 2003), 13–84.

7. Alcmaeon and First Sacred War: Plut. *Sol.* 11.2. Benefactor of Mermnad king: Hdt. 6.125. Alyattes and Delphi: 1.19.2–3, 25.2. Megacles and Agariste: 6.126–30. Alcmaeonids thought accursed: 5.70.2–71.2, Thuc. 1.126.2–12. See Davies, *APF* no. 9688 §§ I–IV. Megacles breaks off marriage alliance with Peisistratus: Hdt. 1.60.2–61.2, 6.121.2; Arist. *Ath. Pol.* 15.1.

8. Peisistratus withdraws to Eretria, Hippias encourages renewed effort: Hdt. 1.61.2–3. Probable link to Macedonian royal house: 5.94.1. Settles at Rhaecelus, mines gold and silver at Mt. Pangaeum: Arist. *Ath. Pol.* 15.2, Hdt. 1.64.1 with Davies, *APF* no. 11793 § XI.

9. Peisistratus' return, guest-friends contribute: Hdt. 1.61.3. *Hippeis* of Eretria prominent: Arist. *Ath. Pol.* 15.2. Dynastic marriage to Koisyra: Schol. Ar. *Nub.* 46, 48. See also Schol. Ar. *Ach.* 614 and Schol. Ar. *Nub.* 64, 800. Cf. T. Leslie Shear, Jr., "Koisyra: Three Women of Athens," *Phoenix* 17:2 (Summer 1963): 99–112, with Davies, *APF* no. 9688 § X, and see Brian M. Lavelle, "Koisyra and Megakles, the Son of Hippokrates," *GRBS* 30:4 (Winter 1989): 503–13, whose reconstruction seems to me sound. Connection with the horse barons of Thessaly: Hdt. 5.63.2–4, 94.1 with what can be inferred from the name Peisistratus gave the youngest of his legitimate sons: Thuc. 1.20.2, 6.55.1. Thebans surpass others in the giving of gifts: Hdt. 1.61.3.

10. Hippias, Hipparchus, Thettalus sons of Peisistratus by first wife: Thuc. 1.20.2, 6.55; Diod. 10.17. Second wife Argive Timonassa and Cypselid connection: Plut. *Mor.* 859c–d. Sons Iophon and Hegisistratus, thousand men from Argos, Lygdamis from Naxos: Hdt. 1.61.4; Arist. *Ath. Pol.* 15.2, 17.3–4.

11. Dates of first two attempts at tyranny disputed: Antony Andrewes, "The Tyranny of Pisistratus," in *CAH,* III:3² 392–416; Rhodes, *CAAP,* 189–99; and *CH,* I 119–26.

12. Third attempt at tyranny follows not long after Cyrus' overthrow of Astyages: Hdt. 1.61.2–65.1. Peisistratus' landing at Marathon, march on Athens: 1.62–63.

13. Lygdamis seeks tyranny on Naxos: Arist. *Pol.* 1305a37–41, F558 (Rose) = F566 (Gigon). Peisistratus sends mercenaries, lodges hostages there: Hdt. 1.64.1–2.

14. Peisistratus seizes Sigeum in Troad: Hdt. 5.94. Awarded Athens long before by Periander: 5.95. Active honoring Apollo on Delos: 1.64.2, Thuc. 3.104.1–2. Anacreon later flees Samos to join Hipparchus at Athens: Arist. *Ath. Pol.* 18.1. Earlier praise for the beauty of the son of one of Pei-

sistratus' adherents: Thomas J. Figueira, "Xanthippos, Father of Perikles, and the 'Prytaneis' of the 'Naukraroi,'" *Historia* 35:3 (3rd Quarter 1986): 257–79 (at 277), reprinted with revisions in Figueira, *AE*, 151–72.

15. Twenty-year reign of Peisistratus: Arist. *Ath. Pol.* 17.1. Installs Argive son Hegisistratus as tyrant in Sigeum: Hdt. 5.94.

16. Universal creator god, Darius universal monarch: DSab, DPg, DZc, DSe, DSf, DSz, DNa, DNb (*PE* 11:2–3, 6, 12–13, 16–17). Chosen to end turmoil and commotion: DSe § 4, DNa § 4 (*PE* 11:12, 16). *Bandaka*: DB § 7, DNb § 2e (*PE* 5:1; 11:17). The lie: DB §§ 10–64, DNb § 2b (*PE* 5:1, 11:17). Rewards for cooperation: DB § 8, DNb §§ 2c, 2e (*PE* 5:1, 11:17). Achaemenid art and architecture as a program of imperial propaganda: Root, *KKAA*, passim. For a series of extended meditations on the implications of the regime imperatives implicit in the political theology articulated by Darius and the Achaemenids more generally, see Marijan Molé, *Culte, mythe, et cosmologie dans l'Iran ancien: Le Problème zoroastrien et la tradition mazdéenne* (Paris: Presses Universitaires de France, 1963); Clarisse Herrenschmidt, "Désignation de l'empire et concepts politiques de Darius Ier d'après ses inscriptions en Vieux Perse," *StIr* 5 :1 (1976): 33–65, "Les Créations d'Ahuramazda," *StIr* 6 :1 (1977): 17–58, and "Aspects universalistes de la religion et de l'idéologie de Darius 1er," in *Orientalia Josephi Tucci memoriae dicata*, ed. Gherardo Gnoli, Lionello Lancioti, and Giuseppe Tucci (Rome: Instituto Italiano per il Medio ed Estremo Oriente, 1987), 617–25; Gregor Ahn, *Religiöse Herrscherlegitimation im Achaemenidischen Iran: Voraussetzungen und die Struktur ihrer Argumentation* (Leiden: Brill, 1992); as well as Bruce Lincoln, *Religion, Empire and Torture: The Case of Achaemenian Persia* (Chicago: University of Chicago Press, 2007), 3–96, and *HfM*, 1–79, 107–49, 171–268, 357–424, 446–61.

17. Missions of exploration: Hdt. 3.135–38, 4.44. Example of Ariaramnes: Ctesias *FGrH* 688 F13.20, who is presumably an Achaemenid, for he bears the name of Darius' great-grandfather (Hdt. 7.11.2), and he reappears at Xerxes' side at Salamis: 8.90.4. For examples of hyperskepticism, cf. Alan Griffiths, "Democedes of Croton: A Greek Doctor at Darius' Court," *AchHist* 2 (1987): 37–51, and Malcolm Davies, "From Rags to Riches: Democedes of Croton and the Credibility of Herodotus," *BICS* 53:2 (December 2010): 19–44, who think the Democedes story an invention.

18. Conquest of Scythians ruled by Skunkha: DB §§ 74–75 (*PE* 5:1). Indus valley: Hdt. 4.44. Completion of Suez canal: 2.158, 4.39.1; cf. Diod. 1.33.8–12. See Georges Posener, *La Première domination perse en Égypte: Recueil d'inscriptions hiéroglyphiques* (Cairo: Institut Français d'Archéologie Orientale du Caire, 1936), 76–77, 180–81, and Alan B. Lloyd, "Darius I in Egypt: Suez and Hibis," in *Persian Responses: Political and Cultural Interaction with(in) the Achaemenid Empire*, ed. Christopher J. Tuplin (Swansea: Classical Press of Wales, 2007), 99–115. On the chronology of Darius' conquest of the Indus valley and of the canal's construction, see *CH*, I 358–59, 613–14. Some scholars doubt that Darius could ever have even contemplated opening up communications by sea between the Indus, the Tigris and Euphrates, and the Nile: see Jean-François Salles, "La Circumnavigation de l'Arabie dans l'antiquité classique," in *L'Arabie et ses mers bordières: Itinéraires et voisinages* (Lyon: Travaux de la Maison de l'Orient, 1988), 75–102. But the evidence powerfully suggests the contrary: see Christopher J. Tuplin, "Darius' Suez Canal and Persian Imperialism," *AchHist* 6 (1991): 237–83.

19. Danube, forts, Scythians: Hdt. 4.1.1, 89–93, 124; Plut. *Alex.* 36.4. Bosporus and Danube bridged with boats: Hdt. 4.83.1–89.2. For the date, see *Chronikon Romanum FGrH* 252 F8 with A. Shapur Shahbazi, "Darius in Scythia and Scythians in Persepolis," *AMIT* 15 (1982): 189–235. Herodotus, who lived for a time on Samos, had no doubt seen the picture of Darius' army crossing the Bosporus bridge that Mandrocles dedicated at the Samian Heraeum, and he may have been acquainted with Mandrocles himself.

20. See Christopher J. Tuplin, "Revisiting Dareios' Scythian Expedition," in *Achaemenid Impact in the Black Sea: Communication of Power*, ed. Jens Nieling and Ellen Rehm (Aarhus: Aarhus University Press, 2010), 281–312, and Vasilev, *PDXTM*, 40–123.

21. Scythian incursion: Hdt. 1.103–6, 130, 4.1–12 with Askold Ivantchik, "The Scythian 'Rule over Asia': The Classical Tradition and the Historical Reality," in *Ancient Greeks West and East*, ed. Gocha R. Tsetskhladze (Leiden: Brill, 1999), 497–520.

22. Gold-wearing Agathyrsi: Hdt. 4.48.4, 104. Gold mines of the Siebenbürgen: J. B. Bury, "The European Expedition of Darius," *CR* 11:6 (July 1897): 277–82, and Pericles B. Georges, "Dar-

ius in Scythia: The Formation of Herodotus' Sources and the Nature of Darius' Campaign," *AJAH* 12 (1987): 97–147. Inscribed brick found at Gherla: DG with Jan Harmatta, "A Recently Discovered Old Persian Inscription," *AAntHung* 2:1–2 (1954): 1–14; Manfred Mayrhofer, *Supplement zur Sammlung der Altpersischer Inschriften* (Vienna: Verlag der Österreichischen Akademie der Wissenschaften, 1978), 16; and Pierre Lecoq, *Les Inscriptions de la Perse achéménide: Traduit du vieux perse, de l'élamite, du babylonien et de l'araméen* (Paris: Gallimard, 1997), 128, 228. Forgery: Balcer, *PCG*, 150, n. 14. Parks, gardens, palaces: Christopher J. Tuplin, "The Parks and Gardens of the Achaemenid Empire," in Tuplin, *Achaemenid Studies* (Stuttgart: Franz Steiner Verlag, 1996), 80–131 with Wouter F. M. Henkelman, "The Achaemenid Heartland: An Archaeological-Historical Perspective," and Loria Khatchadourian, "The Achaemenid Provinces in Archaeological Perspective," in *A Companion to the Archaeology of the Ancient Near East*, ed. David T. Potts (Malden, MA: Wiley-Blackwell, 2012), 931–83, and the preface to Part II, note 16, below.

23. Black Sea to be made a Persian lake: Ellis H. Minns, *Scythians and Greeks: A Survey of Ancient History and Archaeology on the North Coast of the Euxine from the Danube to the Caucasus* (Cambridge: Cambridge University Press, 1913), 116–17, and John R. Gardiner-Garden, "Dareios' Scythian Expedition and Its Aftermath," *Klio* 69:2 (December 1987): 326–50. Human tribute from Colchis: Hdt. 3.97.4. Elaborate administrative apparatus in Caucasus: Florian Knauss, "Ancient Persia and the Caucasus," *IA* 41 (2006): 79–118. Palaces in Georgia and Azerbaijan: Florian Knauss, "Persian Rule in the North: Achaemenid Palaces on the Periphery of the Empire," in *The Royal Palace Institution in the First Millennium BC: Regional Development and Cultural Exchange between East and West*, ed. Inge Nielsen (Aarhus: Aarhus University Press, 2001), 125–43, and Florian Knauss, Iulon Gagoschidze, and Ilias Babaev, "A Persian Propyleion in Azerbaijan: Excavations at Karacamirli," in *Achaemenid Impact in the Black Sea*, 111–22.

24. Danube bridge to be kept intact for sixty days: Hdt. 4.89.2–98.3.

25. Herodotean anthropology largely accurate: Askold Ivantchik, "Une Légende sur l'origine des Scythes (Hdt. IV, 5–7) et le problème des sources du *Scythicos Logos* d'Hérodote," *REG* 112:1 (January–June 1999): 141–92, and "La Légende 'grecque' sur l'origine des Scythes," in *Origines Gentium*, ed. Valérie Fromentin and Sophie Gotteland (Bordeaux: Editions Ausonius, 2001), 207–20; *CH*, I 545–71, 623–41, and Hyun Jin Kim, "Herodotus' Scythians Viewed from a Central Asian Perspective: Its Historicity and Significance," *AWE* 9 (2010): 115–35. Confused account of foray across the Danube: Hdt. 4.47–58, 99–136. Scythia flat, grassy, well-watered: 4.47. Long march through land dry and barren: 4.123. Strabo on desert of the Getae: 7.3.13–15.

26. Scythian tactics: Hdt. 4.46.2–47.1, 120–32.

27. Scythians approach Ionians and Aeolians holding bridge: Hdt. 4.133–36. Miltiades favors collusion and return to liberty: 4.137.1, 6.41.3. Lineage and family fiefdom on Thracian Chersonnesus: 6.34–39 with Davies, *APF* no. 8429 §§ I–X.

28. Histiaeus advises waiting for Darius; Hippoklos, Strattis, Aeaces, and other quislings support: Hdt. 4.137.2–142.1, 6.41.2–3; Nep. *Milt.* 3.

29. Rebellion of Byzantium and Chalcedon: cf. Hdt. 4.85 and 138 with 5.26, and note Ctesias *FGrH* 688 F13.21 (*PE* 6:13), Polyaen. *Strat.* 7.11.5. Scythian pursuit of Darius to Hellespont: Hdt. 6.40, Strabo 13.1.22 with Ctesias *FGrH* 688 F13.21 (*PE* 6:13). Darius crosses Hellespont from Sestos: Hdt. 4.143.1. Scythian foray into Thrace, attack on Istria: John Boardman, "Greek Archaeology on the Shores of the Black Sea," *AR* 9 (1962–63): 34–51 (at 36–37), and Dionis M. Pippidi, *I Greci nel basso Danubio: Dall'età arcaica alla conquista romana* (Milan: Il Saggiatore, 1971), 49–50. Time of troubles and widespread destruction north of the Black Sea: Alfonso Moreno, *Feeding the Democracy: The Athenian Grain Supply in the Fifth and Fourth Centuries BC* (Oxford: Oxford University Press, 2007), 146–62.

30. Megabazos sent to subjugate Hellespont and western Thrace: Hdt. 4.143–44, 5.2. Takes Perinthus, then Aegean coast of Thrace: 5.1.1–10. Megabazos, Amyntas, Alexander, Bourbares, and Macedon: 5.17–22, 98, 8.136.1; Justin 7.3.9, 4.1. Ernst Badian, "Herodotus on Alexander I of Macedon: A Study in Some Subtle Silences," in *Greek Historiography*, ed. Simon Hornblower (Oxford: Clarendon Press, 1994), 107–30, rightly thinks that Herodotus is politely trying to conceal the extent of Temenid collaboration with the Persians and wants his more careful readers to know as much.

31. Paeonia and gold mines: Strabo 7 F34. Paeonians deported to Phrygia: Hdt. 5.12–15, 23. Oebares son of Megabazos soon satrap there: 6.33.3.

32. Oebares, Darius' squire: Hdt. 3.85–87. This story, which seems on the face of it preposterous, may reflect the Persian practice of horse divination instanced at Agathias 4.25. See Mohammed A. Dandamayev, *Persien unter den ersten Achämeniden: 6 Jahrhundert v. Chr.* (Wiesbaden: L. Reichert, 1976), 166 n. 714.

33. Histiaeus granted Myrcinus on the Strymon: Hdt. 5.11.2. Location at Ennea Hodoi: Thuc. 4.102.2. Megabazos' warning, Histiaeus taken to Susa: Hdt. 5.23–24. Aristagoras left in charge at Miletus: 5.30.2. Interest in Myrcinus: 5.124–26. Gold mines nearby: Strabo 7 F34. Timber: Thuc. 4.108.1 with Russell Meiggs, *Trees and Timber in the Ancient Mediterranean World* (Oxford: Clarendon Press, 1982), 123, 126–27.

34. Otanes son of Sisamnes succeeds Megabazos, takes Byzantium, Chalcedon, Antandrus, Lamponia, Lemnos, Imbros: Hdt. 5.25–27. In other sources, this campaign is attributed to Darius himself: Ctesias *FGrH* 688 F13.21, Polyaen. *Strat.* 7.11.5, Strabo 13.1.22. Fort with garrison at Doriscus: Hdt. 7.59.1, 105; Livy 31.16.4. Capacity: Pliny *NH* 4.11.43. Another at Eion, perhaps at this time: Hdt. 7.107. Dominion to borders of Thessaly: 7.108.1.

35. Hippoklos: Hdt. 4.138. Conflict between Philaids in Thracian Chersonnesus and Lampsacus: 6.37–38.

36. Political import of Hippias' daughter's marriage to Aeantides: Thuc. 6.59. Mines near Mt. Pangaeum: Davies, *APF* no. 11793 § XI. At about this time Athens' exploitation of the mines at Laurium seems to have greatly intensified: Olivier Picard, "La Découverte des gisements du Laurion et les débuts de la chouette," *RBN* 147 (2001): 1–10, and Gil Davis, "Mining Money in Late Archaic Athens," *Historia* 63:2 (2014):257–77. Susa's significance: Persepolis is mentioned in no Greek source prior to the time of Alexander the Great.

37. Character and foundations of Peisistratus' rule: Hdt. 1.59.5, 64.1; Arist. *Ath. Pol.* 16, *Pol.* 1313b23; Vitruv. *De arch.* Pref.7.15 with Davies, *APF* no. 11793 §§ III–VI, XI.

38. Rule of Hippias, conduct of the younger Peisistratus and Hipparchus: Hdt. 7.6.3–4; Thuc. 6.54–57; Pl. *Hipparch.* 228c; Arist. *Ath. Pol.* 18.1, *Oec.* 1347a4–17 with David M. Lewis, "The Tyranny of the Pisistratidae," in *CAH*, IV² 287–302. Hippias first to coin owls: Wees, *SSTT*, 124–33.

39. Archons eponymous: ML no. 6, Dion. Hal. *Ant. Rom.* 7.3.1, Thuc. 6.54.6–7 with Davies, *APF* nos. 8429 § VIII, 9688 § VI, and 11793 § VIII. The marriage of Hippocrates and the younger Koisyra can be inferred from reading Schol. Ar. *Nub.* 46, 48 and Schol. *Ach.* 614 in light of Arist. *Ath. Pol.* 22.4 and Isoc. 16.25 in the manner suggested by Lavelle, "Koisyra and Megakles," 503–13.

40. Harmodius and Aristogeiton: Hdt. 5.55.1–62.1, 6.123.2; Thuc. 6.54.1–59.2; Pl. *Hipparch.* 229b; Arist. *Ath. Pol.* 18.2–19.1, *Pol.* 1311a36–39; Plut. *Mor.* 628d with Davies, *APF* no. 12267 §§ I–III.

41. Leipsydrion venture and later deployment of Delphic oracle: Hdt. 5.62.2–63.1, 6.123.2; Arist. *Ath. Pol.* 19.2–4.

42. Spartan concern with Peisistratid ties to Argos: Arist. *Ath. Pol.* 19.4.

43. Cf. Helmut Castritius, "Die Okkupation Thrakiens durch die Perser and der Sturz des athenischen Tyrannen Hippias," *Chiron* 2 (1972): 1–15, who doubts that Persia's advance played any role in Spartan calculations, with Burn, *PG*, 174–76.

44. Anchimolios defeated by Kineas of Thessaly: Hdt. 5.63.2–4, Arist. *Ath. Pol.* 19.5. Cleomenes captures Peisistratid children and forces withdrawal: Hdt. 5.64.1–65.3, Thuc. 6.59.4, Arist. *Ath. Pol.* 19.5–6.

45. Tyrants, supporters, descendants placed outside protection of law: Arist. *Ath. Pol.* 16.10. Peisistratids listed by name and banished: Thuc. 6.55.1–2. Statues of Harmodius and Aristogeiton: Pliny *NH* 34.9.17, Paus. 1.8.5. Citizen rolls purged of non-Athenians: Arist. *Ath. Pol.* 13.5. Solon and artisan immigrants: Plut. *Sol.* 24.4.

46. Isagoras son of Teisandros: Hdt. 5.66.1 with 6.127.4, 128.2. Guest-friend of Cleomenes: 5.70.1. Struggle by means of the *hetaıríaı*: Arist. *Ath. Pol.* 20.1. See Davies, *APF* no. 8429 §§ I–IV.

47. Cleisthenes' appeal to *dêmos*, tribal reform: Hdt. 5.66, 69; Arist. *Ath. Pol.* 20.1, 21, *Pol.* 1275b37, 1319b. Much has been written on this subject: see, for example, Charles Hignett, *A History of the Athenian Constitution to the End of the Fifth Century B.C.* (Oxford: Clarendon Press, 1952), 86–173; Martin Ostwald, *Nomos and the Beginnings of the Athenian Democracy* (Oxford: Clarendon Press, 1969), *From Popular Sovereignty to the Sovereignty of Law: Law, Society, and Politics in Fifth-Century Athens* (Berkeley: University of California Press, 1986), 3–28, and "The Reform of the Athenian State by Kleisthenes," in *CAH*, IV² 303–34; Rhodes, *CAAP*, 240–60; Phillip Brook

Manville, *The Origins of Citizenship in Ancient Athens* (Princeton, NJ: Princeton University Press, 1990); Josiah Ober, "The Athenian Revolution of 508/7 B.C.: Violence, Authority, and the Origins of Democracy," in Ober, *The Athenian Revolution: Essays on Greek Democracy and Political Theory* (Princeton, NJ: Princeton University Press, 1996), 32–52; Kurt A. Raaflaub, "Kleisthenes, Ephialtes, und die Begründung der Demokratie," in *Demokratia: Der Weg zur Demokratie bei den Griechen,* ed. Konrad H. Kinzl (Darmstadt: Wissenschaftliche Buchgesellschaft: 1995), 1–54; and Anderson, *The Athenian Experiment,* passim. I think Manville's volume the best study of the subject. Eponymous archon of 507/6 Alcmaeon: Poll. *Onom.* 8.110.

48. Cleomenes expels Alcmaeonids, tries to set up narrow oligarchy at Athens: Hdt. 5.70.1–72.1, Thuc. 1.26.12, Arist. *Ath. Pol.* 20.2–5.

49. Council of 500 organizes resistance, drives out Isagoras and Cleomenes, recalls Cleisthenes: Hdt. 5.72.2–73.1, which should be read in light of Manville, *The Origins of Citizenship in Ancient Athens,* 157–209. See Josiah Ober, "'I Besieged That Man': Democracy's Revolutionary Start," in *Origins of Democracy in Ancient Greece,* ed. Kurt A. Raaflaub, Josiah Ober, and Robert W. Wallace (Berkeley: University of California Press, 2007), 83–104.

50. Cleomenes' attempt to restore Isagoras thwarted: Hdt. 5.74.1–75.1, 76.

51. Authority of two kings to wage war: Hdt. 6.56.1–57.1. Demaratus' withdrawal sparks decision only one king to lead any given expedition: 5.75.2.

52. Athenians defeat Thebans and Chalcidians, ransom former, take land of Chalcidian *Hippobótai:* Hdt. 5.77–78, 6.100.1. Simonides' epigram: F2 (Page) with Anderson, *The Athenian Experiment,* 151–57. Against the Chalcidians, it is conceivable that the Athenians had Eretrian help—as Thomas J. Figueira, "Khalkis and Marathon," in *MBAD,* 185–202, suggests.

53. Evidence Amyntas guest-friend of Hippias: Hdt. 5.94.1. Alexander benefactor of and *próxenos* for Athenians: 8.136–43. May have smoothed approach to Artaphernes: Badian, "Herodotus on Alexander I of Macedon," 107–30.

54. Earth and water given, envoys charged: Hdt. 5.73 with Chapter 1, note 18, above. Consider Theopompos *FGrH* 115 F153, as interpreted by Peter Krentz, "The Athenian Treaty in Theopompos F153," *Phoenix* 63:3–4 (Fall–Winter 2009): 231–38. If, as Fritz Schachermeyr, "Athen als Stadt des Grosskönigs," *GB* 1 (1973): 211–20; Michael Zahrnt, "Der Mardonioszug des Jahres 492 v. Chr. und Seine Historische Einordnung," *Chiron* 22 (1992): 237–80 (at 274–76); and Krentz, *BoM,* 40–43, all argue, it had been the Persian alliance that had caused the Spartans to back off, no such charges would have been lodged.

55. Alcmaeonids regarded as Medizers: Hdt. 6.115, 121.1, 123–24. Public funeral and monument for Cleisthenes: Paus. 1.29.6.

56. Corinthian ties to Potidaean colonists: Thuc. 1.56.2.

57. Corinthians block attempt to restore Hippias: Hdt. 5.90–93.

58. Hippias to Sigeum (Hdt. 5.94.1); then, perhaps via Lampsacus (Thuc. 6.59), to Sardis. Artaphernes orders Athenians to restore: Hdt. 5.96.

59. See Schachermeyr, "Athen als Stadt des Grosskönigs," 211–14, and Louis L. Orlin, "Athens and Persia ca. 507 B.C.: A Neglected Perspective," in *Michigan Oriental Studies in Honor of George G. Cameron,* ed. Louis L. Orlin (Ann Arbor: Department of Near Eastern Studies, University of Michigan, 1976), 255–66. Cf. Norbert Kramer, "Athen: Keine Stadt des Grosskönigs!" *Hermes* 132:3 (2004): 257–70.

Chapter 3. The Ionian Revolt

Epigraph: Hdt. 6.11.2.

1. Aristagoras, Naxos expedition, and Ionian revolt: Hdt. 5.28–38.

2. See Carl Roebuck, "Tribal Organization in Ionia," *TAPhA* 92 (1961): 495–507, and Irene S. Lemos, "The Migrations to the West Coast of Asia Minor: Tradition and Archaeology," in *Frühes Ionien: Eine Bestandsaufnahme,* ed. Justus Cobet, Volkmar von Graeve, Wolf-Dietrich Niemeier, and Konrad Zimmerman (Mainz am Rhein: Von Zabern, 2007), 713–27. Note John Alty, "Dorians and Ionians," *JHS* 102 (1982): 1–14.

3. Grain from the Black Sea ca. 481: Hdt. 7.147.2–3 There is sixth-century evidence demonstrating that the Crimea was already then fully integrated within the trading networks of the Mediterranean world: see M. M. Austin and Pierre Vidal-Naquet, *Economic and Social History*

of Ancient Greece: An Introduction (Berkeley: University of California Press, 1977), 220–23. Note also Hdt. 4.17–18, 6.2.1–2, 5.3, 26.1. Cf. Peter D. A. Garnsey, *Famine and Food Supply in the Graeco-Roman World: Responses to Risk and Crisis* (Cambridge: Cambridge University Press, 1988), 107–33, and David Braund, "Black Sea Grain for Athens? From Herodotus to Demosthenes," in *The Black Sea in Antiquity: Regional and Interregional Economic Exchanges,* ed. Vincent Gabrielsen and John Lund (Copenhagen: Aarhus University Press, 2007), 39–68, with Michael Whitby, "The Grain Trade of Athens in the Fourth Century BC," in *Trade, Traders and the Ancient City,* ed. Helen Parkins and Christopher Smith (London: Routledge, 1998), 102–28; Antony G. Keen, "'Grain for Athens': The Importance of the Hellespontine Route in Athenian Foreign Policy before the Peloponnesian War," in *SA,* 63–73; and Alfonso Moreno, "Athenian Wheat-Tsars: Black Sea Grain and Elite Culture," in *The Black Sea in Antiquity,* 69–84, and *Feeding the Democracy: The Athenian Grain Supply in the Fifth and Fourth Centuries BC* (Oxford: Oxford University Press, 2007), esp. 144–208. Archaeological and palaeobotanical studies suggest that the great majority of the Scythian tribes in this period may still have been nomadic, as Herodotus himself contends: see Gocha R. Tsetskhladze, "The Black Sea," in *A Companion to Archaic Greece,* ed. Kurt A. Raaflaub and Hans van Wees (Malden, MA: Wiley-Blackwell, 2009), 330–46, who cites N. A. Gavrilyuk, *Istoriya ekonomiki Stepnoi Skifii VI–III vv. do n.e.* (Kiev: n.p., 1999), 25–28, 292–300 (which I have been unable to find). This need not mean, however, that there were no Scythians with grain to trade.

4. Melanthios' twenty ships: Hdt. 5.97, 99.1. Athens' fifty ships: 6.89. Thucydides asserts Greek reliance on penteconters: 1.14. Charon claims triremes dispatched: *FGrH* 262 F10. Sons of Peisistratus send Miltiades to Chersonnesus on trireme: Hdt. 6.39.1. Aeginetan fleet defeats triremes of Samian exiles: 3.44.1–2, 57–59 with Thomas J. Figueira, "The Athenian *Naukraroi* and Archaic Naval Warfare," *Cadmo* 21 (2011): 183–210 (at 191). Evidence that the sons of Peisistratus could have built, manned, and maintained a fleet of triremes and that they did so on a modest scale, suggestion that they did so on a larger scale: Arist. *Oec.* 1347a with Wees, *SSTT,* 30–143 (esp., 64–66, 97–100, 124–33, 138–40). Evidence that the Peisistratid trireme fleet cannot have been large: Hdt. 5.63.2–4, Arist. *Ath. Pol.* 19.5. Evidence for claim that, in the aftermath of 508, Athens' new democracy under Cleisthenes made arrangements pointing to the construction of a fifty-ship fleet, unsubstantiated contention that they had triremes solely or chiefly in mind: Wees, *SSTT,* 60–61, 66–68, 92–97, 128–29, 140–41, 144. Later events cast considerable doubt on this contention: Chapter 5, below.

5. Five Eretrian triremes dispatched: Hdt. 5.99.1. Eretrian hoplites and cavalry early on: Strabo 10.1.10. Delphic Amphictyony: Aeschin. 2.116. For an overview, see Keith G. Walker, *Archaic Eretria: A Political and Social History from the Earliest Times to 490 BC* (London: Routledge, 2004), 73–206.

6. Lelantine War and aftermath: consider Thuc. 1.15.3; then, Hdt. 5.99.1 with 1.18.3, Strabo 10.1.12, Plut. *Mor.* 760, and Archilochus F3 (West) in light of W. G. G. Forrest, "Colonisation and the Rise of Delphi," *Historia* 6:2 (April 1957): 160–75. For more recent attempts to come to grips with the evidence, see John Boardman, "The Islands: I. Euboea," in *CAH,* III: 1^2 754–65, and Victor Parker, *Untersuchungen zum Lelantischen Krieg und verwandten Problemen der frühgriechischen Geschichte* (Stuttgart: Franz Steiner Verlag, 1997). For an example of hyperskepticism, cf. Jonathan Hall, *A History of the Archaic Greek World, ca. 1200–479 BCE* (Oxford: Wiley-Blackwell, 2007), 1–16. It is symptomatic of the central role that Chalcis and Eretria played in overseas trade in the early archaic period that, outside of Ionia and East Greece more generally, they set the standards for weights and measures and did so early on: Wees, *SSTT,* 110–12. *Hippeîs:* Arist. *Pol.* 1289b35–40, 1306a31–36. Installation of Lygdamis: Hdt. 1.61.2–4, 64.1–2; Arist. *Ath. Pol.* 15.2–3.

7. Coinage and pay for rowers: Consider Francis Cairns, "*Chrémata dókima: IG* XII, 9, 1273 and 1274 and the Early Coinage of Eretria," *ZPE* 54 (1984): 145–55, in light of Cairns, "The 'Laws of Eretria' (*IG* XII. 9 1273 and 1274): Epigraphic, Legal, Historical, and Political Aspects," *Phoenix* 45:4 (Winter 1991): 296–313. Leverage in Cyclades: Strabo 10.1.10. Inclusion on thalassocracy list: Diod. 7.11, Euseb. *Chron.* 1.225 (Schoene-Petermann). Military prowess: Pl. *Menex.* 240a4–c1. Consider Hans van Wees, "'Those Who Sail Are to Receive a Wage': Naval Warfare and Finance in Archaic Eretria," in *New Perspectives in Ancient Warfare,* ed. Garret G. Fagan and Matthew Trundle (Leiden: Brill, 2010), 205–25, in light of the context described by Walker, *Archaic Eretria,* 207–87. If van Wees is correct, scholars will have to reconsider the conviction, still widely held, that the cities of

archaic Greece did not themselves maintain fleets: cf., for example, Christopher J. Haas, "Athenian Naval Power before Themistocles," *Historia* 34:1 (1st Quarter 1985): 29–46, and Lionel Scott, "Were There Polis Navies in Archaic Greece?" in *SA*, 93–115, with Wees, *SSTT*, passim.

8. Debt of honor: Hdt. 5.99.1. Possible Persian landing in Euboea at Eretria: Ath. 12.536f–537a. Naxos' fall a danger to Euboea: Hdt. 5.31.2–3.

9. Beginning of evils: Hdt. 5.97.3.

10. Aristagoras stages the Ionian revolt: Hdt. 5.28–38. As my choice of words should make clear, I do not believe Herman T. Wallinga's contention that the Achaemenids maintained a standing navy and summoned, in time of need, their subjects to man it: see Chapter 6, note 51, below.

11. Coës' fate: Hdt. 5.38.1.

12. In assessing the evidence, I have profited from Pierluigi Tozzi, *La Rivolta ionica* (Pisa: Giardinia Editoriali e Poligrafici, 1978); Oswyn Murray, "The Ionian Revolt," in *CAH*, IV^2 461–90; Herman T. Wallinga, "The Ionian Revolt," *Mnemosyne*, fourth ser. 37:3–4 (1984): 401–37; Balcer, *PCG*, 169–91; Pericles B. Georges, "Persian Ionia under Darius: The Revolt Reconsidered," *Historia* 49:1 (1st Quarter 2000): 1–39; Cawkwell, *GW*, 61–86; and Simon Hornblower, "Introduction," in Herodotus, *Histories: Book V*, ed. Simon Hornblower (Cambridge: Cambridge University Press, 2013), 15–18.

13. Milesian defenses: Hdt. 1.17.3. Ornament of Ionia: 5.28–29. Histiaeus awarded Myrcinus: 5.11, 23–24. Histiaeus summoned to Susa, Aristagoras left as *epítropos:* 5.24, 30.2.

14. Consider Xen. *An.* 7.8.7–15 in light of *Cyr.* 8.6.1–10 and *Oec.* 4.5–11, and see Christopher J. Tuplin, "Xenophon and the Garrisons of the Achaemenid Empire," *AMI* 20 (1987): 167–245, and Margaret C. Miller, *Athens and Persia in the Fifth Century BC: A Study in Cultural Receptivity* (Cambridge: Cambridge University Press, 1997), 91–97. More can now be gleaned from İsmail Gezgin, "Defensive Systems in the Aiolis and Ionia Regions in the Achaemenid Period," in *Achaemenid Anatolia: Proceedings of the First International Symposium on Anatolia in the Achaemenid Period, Bandirma, 15–18 August 1997,* ed. Tomris Bakır, Heleen Sancisi-Weerdenburg, Gül Gürtekin, Pierre Briant, and Wouter F. M. Henkelman (Leiden: Nederlands Instituut Voor Het Nabije Oosten, 2001), 181–88; *L'Archéologie de l'empire achéménide: Nouvelles recherches,* ed. Pierre Briant and Rémy Boucharlat (Paris: De Boccard, 2005); and Lori Khatchadourian, "The Achaemenid Provinces in Archaeological Perspective," in *A Companion to the Archaeology of the Ancient Near East,* ed. D. T. Potts (Malden, MA: Wiley-Blackwell, 2012), II 963–83 (esp. 966–69).

15. Paeonia and gold mines: Strabo 7 F34. Paeonian return to the Strymon: Hdt. 5.98. Aristagoras' eventual flight to Myrcinus: 5.124–26, Thuc. 4.102.2. See Vasilev, *PDXTM,* 86–109, 127–33.

16. Miletus under assault on landward side: Plut. *Mor.* 861a–c. Sneak attack on Sardis and damage inflicted by Persians on retreating Greeks near Ephesus: Hdt. 5.99–102, 116. Cf. Charon of Lampsacus *FGrH* 262 F10 ap. Plut. *Mor.* 861c–d. Route attackers follow: Clive Foss, "Explorations in Mount Tmolus," *CSCA* 11 (1978): 21–60 (esp. 27–34). Temple of Artemis at Ephesus left unburned: Strabo 14.1.5. Ephesians slaughter Chian survivors after Lade: Hdt. 6.16.2. For another view of these events, which invests them with considerable religious significance, see Mark H. Munn, *The Mother of the Gods, Athens, and the Tyranny of Asia: A Study of Sovereignty in Ancient Religion* (Berkeley: University of California Press, 2006).

17. Athenian withdrawal of support from the Ionians: Hdt. 5.103.1. Hipparchus son of Charmos elected archon eponymous: Dion. Hal. *Ant. Rom.* 6.1.1.

18. Charmos *paıdıká* of Peisistratus: Plut. *Sol.* 1.7. *Erastēs* and father-in-law of Hippias: Kleidemos *FGrH* 323 F15 ap. Ath. 13.609c–d with Paus. 1.30.1 Charmos' son Hipparchus linked by marital alliance with sons of Peisistratus: Arist. *Ath. Pol.* 22.3–4, Androtion *FGrH* 324 F6. Statue on acropolis: Lycurg. 1.117. See Davies, *APF* No. 11793 § IX and Harvey A. Shapiro, *Art and Cult under the Tyrants in Athens* (Mainz am Rhein: Verlag Philipp von Zabern, 1989), 119–20. Possible that younger Peisistratus returned to Athens from exile: see Michael F. Arnush, "The Career of Peisistratos Son of Hippias," *Hesperia* 64:2 (April–June 1995): 135–62, whose argument rests in the end, however, on a single *óstrakon.*

19. See Paul A. Rahe, "The Military Situation in Western Asia on the Eve of Cunaxa," *AJPh* 101:1 (Spring 1980): 79–96.

20. Greeks of Asia Minor and the islands, Carians, and Caunians rally to revolt: Hdt. 5.103.2. Cypriot Greeks also: 5.104–5.

21. Persian operations in Asia Minor: Hdt. 5.116–23. With regard to Pidasa, which was located near Miletus, see Simon Hornblower, "Commentary," in Herodotus, *Histories, Book V,* 304–5.

22. At Cyprus, Greeks victorious at sea, defeated on land: Hdt. 5.108–14. Horse transports built for Marathon expedition: 6.48.

23. Siege of Soloi: Hdt. 5.115. Paphos: Burn, *PG,* 202–5; Murray, "The Ionian Revolt," 484–85 with F. G. Maier, "History from the Earth: The Kingdom of Paphos in the Achaemenid Period (XI–XX)." *Transeuphratène* 12 (1996): 121–37. Pacification complete: Hdt. 5.116.

24. Datis naval commander on the Black Sea: Ctesias *FGrH* 688 F13.22. Ctesias as court physician and historical source: Christopher J. Tuplin, "Doctoring the Persians: Ctesias of Cnidus, Physician and Historian," *Klio* 86:2 (February 2004): 305–47, and "Ctesias as Military Historian," in *Die Welt des Ktesias—Ctesias' World,* ed. Josef Wiesehöfer, Robert Rollinger, and Giovanni B. Lanfranchi (Wiesbaden: Harrassowitz Verlag, 2011), 449–88. Datis a Mede: Hdt. 6.94.2. Sons command cavalry on Xerxes' march: Hdt. 7.88.1. Prominence of family and likely role at Persepolis: David M. Lewis, "Datis the Mede," *JHS* 100 (1980): 194–95, and "Persians in Herodotus," in Lewis, *SPGNEH,* 345–61 (at 357–58).

25. Datis at Sardis and Susa in 494: *PE* 6:41. Mardonius marries daughter of the King: Hdt. 6.43.1 with Michael Heltzer, "The Persepolis Documents, the Lindos Chronicle, and the Book of Judith," *PP* 44 (1989): 81–101. Datis and Mardonius together on expedition: *FGrH* 532 F1 (*PE* 6:42) with Carolyn Higbie, *The Lindian Chronicle and the Greek Creation of Their Past* (Oxford: Oxford University Press, 2003), passim (esp. 42–47, 141–47), who supplies a critical edition of the inscription, a translation of it, and a commentary on it. To believe, as Higbie does, that Datis descended on Rhodes in 490, one must suppose that the Persians failed to recover the island when they crushed the Ionian Revolt. Given its location on the route leading from Phoenicia, Cyprus, and the Aleion plain to Miletus and Ionia more generally, this scenario seems highly unlikely. Nor can I follow Heltzer in supposing that the Persian navy was in a position to secure Rhodes in the immediate aftermath of its defeat at the hands of the Ionians in the battle off Cyprus in or soon after 498. It is more plausible to suppose, as Burn, *PG,* 210–11, 218, does, that the fleet en route from Phoenicia, Cyprus, and the plain of Aleion to Lade in 494 paused at Rhodes to do the job. It is, of course, conceivable that the Persians bypassed Rhodes that year and returned the following summer to settle accounts before or after dealing with Chios, Lesbos, and the other islands to the north. But that seems unlikely given the fact that none of the cities on Rhodes was represented by a naval squadron at Lade. Herodotus' choice of words at 6.43.1 could be interpreted as an indication that Mardonius had already done service as a commander in putting down the Ionian revolt and mopping up thereafter.

26. Ionians prepare fleet: Hdt. 6.6–8. With regard to the sixth book of Herodotus' *Histories,* I have made ample use of Scott, *HCH.*

27. Size of rival fleets: Hdt. 6.9.1. Triremes likely to be fully manned: Chapter 1, note 36, above.

28. Phocaean achievements in Adriatic and western Mediterranean: Hdt. 1.163, Thuc. 1.13.6. Foundations of archaic walls recently discovered: Ömer Ozyğit, "The City Walls of Phokaia," *REA* 96:1–2 (1994): 77–109.

29. Phocaean withdrawal from Asia Minor, Pyrrhic victory against Etruscans and Carthaginians: Hdt. 1.162–67. The objections that Samuel Mark, "The Earliest Naval Ram," *IJNA* 37:2 (September 2008): 253–72, raises regarding the iconographic evidence cited in favor of an earlier introduction of the ram seem to me sound. He provides us, however, with no good reason for accepting his dismissal of Herodotus' testimony concerning the use of the ram by the Phocaeans at Alalia, and the supposition that the Phocaeans were the first to employ this weapon really would help explain their remarkable victory.

30. Advice of Dionysius: Hdt. 6.11. Some Phocaeans repopulate native city: 1.165.2–3. Less well-off remain: Antiochus *FrGH* 555 F8.

31. See *AT* along with *An Athenian Trireme Reconstructed: The British Sea Trials of Olympias, 1987,* ed. John S. Morrison and John F. Coates (Osney Nead: British Archaeological Reports, 1989); *The Trireme Project: Operational Experience, 1987–90: Lessons Learnt,* ed. Timothy Shaw (Oxford: Oxbow Books, 1993); and *Trireme Olympias: The Final Report,* ed. N. Boris Rankov (Oxford: Oxbow Books, 2012), as well as Lucien Basch, "Roman Triremes and the Outriggerless Phoenician Tri-

reme," *MM* 65:4 (November 1979): 289–326; N. Boris Rankov, "Reconstructing the Past: The Operation of the Trireme Reconstruction, *Olympias,* in the Light of the Historical Sources," *MM* 80:2 (May 1994): 131–46; and Alec Tilley, *Seafaring on the Ancient Mediterranean: New Thoughts on Triremes and Other Ancient Ships* (Oxford: British Archaeological Reports, 2004), 1–10. Note also Borimir Jordan, *The Athenian Navy in the Classical Period: A Study of Athenian Naval Administration and Military Organization in the Fifth and Fourth Centuries B.C.* (Berkeley: University of California Press, 1975); Barry Strauss, "Naval Battle and Sieges," in *CHGRW,* I 223–47 (at 224–36); and David Blackman and Boris Rankov, *Shipsheds of the Ancient Mediterranean* (Cambridge: Cambridge University Press, 2013). *Interscalmium:* Vitruv. *De arch.* 1.2.4.

32. Practicing the *diékplous:* Hdt. 6.12.1. Aimed at shearing off oars: A. J. Holladay, "Further Thoughts on Trireme Tactics," *G&R,* second ser. 35:2 (October 1988): 149–51. Lazenby, *DG,* 193, to the contrary notwithstanding, that this was sometimes done is attested: Diod. 11.18.6, 13.78.1. Aimed at ramming stern: John F. Lazenby, "The Diekplous," *G&R,* second ser. 34:2 (October 1987): 169–77. Cf. John S. Morrison, "The Greek Ships at Salamis and the Diekplous," *JHS* 111 (1991): 196–200. Phoenician practice: Sosylus *FGrH* 176 F1.2. Aimed at positioning at stern for boarding: Cawkwell, *GW,* 221–32. See, in this connection, Robin Oldfield, "Collision Damage in Triremes," and Andrew Taylor, "Battle Manoeuvres for Fast Triremes," in *Trireme Olympias,* 214–24, 231–43. For another view, cf. *AT,* 43.

33. Ionians refuse further exertion: Hdt. 6.12. Samian generals opt for betrayal: 6.13.1.

34. Otanes turns troops loose on Samians, deports, then restores them: Hdt. 3.147, 149. There is reason to think that the Samians blamed the ambitions of the younger Syloson for the massacres and their suffering: Arist. F574–575 (Rose) = F591–592 (Gigon), Strabo 14.1.17, Zenob. 3.90 (Leutsch-Schneidewin), Eustathius, *Comm. Dion. Perieg.* 533.

35. Battle of Lade: Hdt. 6.9–10, 13–17. Blandishments of Aeaces son of Syloson: 6:13.1. Already tyrant at time of Scythian expedition: 4.138.2.

36. Fate of Miletus and citizens: Hdt. 6.18.1–22.1. Didyma: 6.19.3, 32. The sanctuaries on Naxos and at Eretria were later treated in a similar fashion: 6.96, 101.3.

37. Postrevolt fate of Chians, Lesbians, Tenedians, Byzantines, and Chalcedonians: Hdt. 6.31–33. Human harvest to provide eunuchs and concubines a long-standing Persian practice: Briant, *CA,* 255–301, and Llewellyn-Jones, *KCAP,* 38–40, 116–19.

38. Samians spared; Carians subdued or turn coat: Hdt. 6.20, 25. Help friends, harm enemies: cf. Pl. *Resp.* 1.332a–d with Thuc. 2.41.4–5, and consider the material collected in Rahe, *RAM,* I.iv.2, note 37.

39. Hecataeus' plea: Diod. 10.25. Arbitration, land survey, democracies: Hdt. 6.42.1–43.3. Democracies not established everywhere: 6.25. In this connection, see James Allan Stewart Evans, "The Settlement of Artaphrenes," *CPh* 71:4 (October 1976): 344–48, reprinted in Evans, *BH,* 153–59.

40. Thasos threatened, improves walls, builds triremes, Mardonius to Thrace, Thasos submits: Hdt. 6.28, 43.4–44.2, 46.1–48.1 with Vasilev, *PDXTM,* 142–61. Mines on Thasos and length of walls: Robin Osborne, *Classical Landscape with Figures: The Ancient City and Its Countryside* (London: G. Phillip, 1987), 75–81 (esp. 79–81). Mines on the mainland: note Strabo 7 F34, and cf. Paul Perdrizet, "Skaptésylé," *Klio* 10:10 (December 1910): 1–27, with Meiggs, *AE,* 570–72. Note Lucia Nixon and Simon Price, "The Size and Resources of Greek Cities," in *The Greek City from Homer to Alexander,* ed. Oswyn Murray and Simon Price (Oxford: Oxford University Press, 1990), 137–70 (esp. 152–53).

41. Mardonius' losses off Athos and at hands of Byrgoi: Hdt. 6.44.2–45.1. Withdrawal: 6.45.2. In 411, a similar maritime disaster overtook a fleet of fifty triremes, all were lost, and only twelve of the ten thousand crewmen survived: Diod. 13.41.1–3.

42. Boubares at court of Amyntas: Justin 7.4.1–2. To suppose that Amyntas had broken his pledge, one would have to reject Justin's testimony, as Michael Zahrnt, "Der Mardonioszug des Jahres 492 v. Chr. und Seine Historische Einordnung," *Chiron* 22 (1992): 237–80, is quick to do. Note also Vasilev, *PDXTM,* 109–17, 124–27.

43. Herodotus on reason for Mardonius' withdrawal from Europe: 6.45.2. To get around this possibility, one must resort to special pleading: see, for example, Zahrnt, "Der Mardonioszug des Jahres 492 v. Chr. und Seine Historische Einordnung," 237–80, and Vasilev, *PDXTM,* 142–61.

Chapter 4. The First Round

Epigraph: Dio Chrys. 11.148–49.

1. Darius: DB § 63, DSf, DSz, DSaa, DNb (*PE* 5:1, 11:13, 17).

2. See Schachermeyr, *MPP.* On the subjects treated in the remainder of this chapter and in the chapters that follow, I have profited as well from Burn, *PG*, 227–546; Green, *XS;* Lazenby, *DG;* and Cawkwell, *GW,* 87–125. If, in this chapter, my conclusions tend to echo those of Schachermeyr, Burn, and Green and, if in the chapters that follow, they coincide more frequently with those of Burn and Green than with those of Lazenby or Cawkwell, it is because I share the respect that Schachermeyr, Burn, and Green accord Herodotus; their suspicion that information preserved in later sources, such as Diodorus Siculus, Plutarch, and the *Suda,* may well be accurate; and the conviction of Burn and, even more emphatically, Green that later reports concerning oracles, decrees, and oaths are far less likely to be pure inventions than to be genuine traditions mildly muddled and confused. The introduction Green added to the second edition of his book should be more widely read than it has been: Peter Green, *The Greco-Persian Wars* (Berkeley: University of California Press, 1996), xiii–xxiv. For a useful survey of the scholarship in English on Persian and Greek armaments and on the battle itself, see Dennis L. Fink, *The Battle of Marathon in Scholarship: Research, Theories, and Controversies since 1850* (Jefferson, NC: McFarland, 2014), 3–61, 116–87.

3. Darius asks earth and water, prepares expeditionary force: Hdt. 6.48 with Schachermeyr, *MPP,* 30–35, and Raphael Sealey, "The Pit and the Well: The Persian Heralds of 491 B.C.," *CJ* 72:1 (October–November 1976): 13–20, who recognize the unfolding logic of Persian expansionism. Cf. Michael Zahrnt, "Der Mardonioszug des Jahres 492 v. Chr. und Seine Historische Einordnung," *Chiron* 22 (1992): 237–80, who is incredulous.

4. Aeginetans and Sicyonians ferry Cleomenes' army to Argive coast: Hdt. 6.76, 92.1–2.

5. Battle of Sepeia: Hdt. 6.19.1–2, 77–78 with Richard A. Tomlinson, *Argos and the Argolid: From the End of the Bronze Age to the Roman Occupation* (Ithaca, NY: Cornell University Press, 1972), 93–97.

6. Cleomenes and the Argives trapped in the grove sacred to Apollo: Hdt. 6.77–80. Six thousand Argives killed: 7.148.2.

7. Cleomenes at Argive Heraeum: Hdt. 6.81. Contingent said to approach city walls: Socrates FGrH 310 F6. Demaratus involved, Telesilla organizes defense: Plut. *Mor.* 245c–f. See also 223b–c, Paus. 2.20.8–10, Polyaen. *Strat.* 8.33, Clem. Al. *Strom.* 4.19.120.3–4. Oracle and achievement of Argive women: Hdt. 6.77.2.

8. Argive *doûloi* take over: Hdt. 6.83.1. *Períoikoi* admitted to ruling order: Arist. *Pol.* 1303a6–8 with Detlef Lotze, *Metaxu Eleutherôn kai Doulôn: Studien zur Rechtsstellung unfreier Landbevölkerung in Griechenland bis zum 4. Jahrhundert v. Chr.* (Berlin: Akademie Verlag, 1959), 8–9, 53–54, 79. Plutarch, following Socrates of Argos FGrH 310 F6, resolves difference—widows and girls marry *períoikoi: Mor.* 245f. See Detlef Lotze, "Zur Verfassung von Argos nach der Schlacht bein Sepeia," *Chiron* 1 (1971): 95–109. For other views on the character of the outsiders admitted to the ruling order: see R. F. Willetts, "The Servile Interregnum at Argos," *Hermes* 87:4 (December 1959): 495–506; W. G. G. Forrest, "Themistokles and Argos," *CQ* n.s. 10:2 (November 1960): 221–41 (at 222–26); Tomlinson, *Argos and the Argolid,* 97–100; and Antony Andrewes, "Argive *Perioikoi,*" in *"Owls to Athens": Essays on Classical Subjects Presented to Sir Kenneth Dover,* ed. E. M. Craik (Oxford: Clarendon Press, 1990), 171–78. In 481, Argives still eager for thirty-year peace with Sparta: Hdt. 7.148.4–149.1.

9. Cleomenes tried, acquitted: Hdt. 6.78.2, 82.

10. In 480 and 479, Argos too weak to help the Mede: Hdt. 7.148–52. Tiryns and Mycenae rally to Panhellenic cause: cf. 9.28.4, 31.3, with 6.83, and see ML no. 27, Paus. 5.23.2.

11. Thucydides on Themistocles: 1.138.3. Archonship and date: 1.93.3 and Dion. Hal. *Ant. Rom.* 6.34.1 with T. J. Cadoux, "The Athenian Archons from Kreon to Hypsichides," *JHS* 68 (1948): 70–123 (at 116, with note 252), and David M. Lewis, "Themistocles' Archonship," *Historia* 22:4 (4th Quarter 1973): 757–58. For at least some of the events that Thucydides has in mind, see Hdt. 7.143–44, 8.22, 56–64, 74–83, 108–10, 123–25; Thuc. 1.137.3–138.2. On the man, his career, and family, see Davies, *APF* no. 6669 §§ I–VI. If, in assessing Themistocles' conduct as a statesman in the chapters that follow, I do not cite Wolfgang Blösel, *Themistokles bei Herodot: Spiegel Athens im*

fünften Jahrhundert. Studien zur Geschichte und historiographischen Konstruktion des griechischen Freiheitskampfes 480 v. Chr. (Stuttgart: Franz Steiner, 2004), it is because I do not think that there is any evidence justifying Blösel's supposition that Herodotus was a fabulist.

12. Phalerum vulnerable to attack: Hdt. 5.63, 81. Themistocles as archon and fortification of Peiraeus: Thuc. 1.93.3–6. Thasians strengthen fortifications, build triremes: Hdt. 6.46–47. Stesimbrotus of Thasos implies that, at Themistocles' instigation, the Athenians set out to build one hundred triremes at about the same time: *FGrH* 107 F2. Note the reference to Darius (not Xerxes) at Plut. *Them.* 4.1–3.

13. Themistocles *chorēgós* for Phrynichus' *Phoenician Women* in 476: Plut. *Them.* 5.5. Athenian public moved and angered by *Sack of Miletus* in his archon year: Hdt. 6.21.2. Some think message defeatism: Schol. Ar. *Vesp.* 1490, Aelian *VH* 13.17. Ammianus Marcellinus regards as reproach: 28.1.3–4.

14. Evidence for Miltiades' withdrawal from Thracian Chersonnesus: Hdt. 4.143.1, 6.40. Married to daughter of Thracian prince: 6.39.2. Sojourn in Athens: Nep. *Milt.* 3.6. Corrupt passage in Herodotus on return to Chersonnesus: 6.40. Seizure of Lemnos: 6.137–40 with Vasilev, *PDXTM,* 133–41. Perhaps with the help of a hoplite force supplied from Athens: *IG* I³ 1477. Flight to Athens after fall of Miletus: Hdt. 6.41. Trial for conduct as tyrant, acquittal: 6.104. See Henry Theodore Wade-Gery, "Miltiades," *JHS* 71 (1951): 212–21, reprinted in Wade-Gery, *Essays in Greek History* (Oxford: Basil Blackwell, 1958), 155–70.

15. Islanders and mainland towns give earth and water: Hdt. 6.48.1–49.1. Athenians toss Persian heralds into pit: 7.133. Miltiades proposes: Paus. 3.12.7. Themistocles backs proposal, has Ionian interpreter executed: Plut. *Them.* Hdt. 6.3–4; Ael. Aristid. 1.99–100, 3.184.

16. Spartans toss Persian heralds into well: Hdt. 7.133, Paus. 3.12.7. Aeginetans give earth and water, Athenians ask Spartan intervention: Hdt. 6.49.

17. Aegina once a dependency of Epidaurus: Hdt. 5.82–84, 8.46.1; Paus. 2.29.5 with Thomas J. Figueira, "Aeginetan Independence," *CJ* 79:1 (October–November 1983): 8–29, reprinted with revisions in Figueira, *AE,* 9–33. Later association with Argos: Hdt. 5.86. Asked to pay fine for ferrying Lacedaemonian hoplites: 6.92.1–2. Argive volunteers: 6.92. Relations with Sparta: Thomas J. Figueira, "Aeginetan Membership in the Peloponnesian League," *CPh* 76:1 (January 1981): 1–24, reprinted with revisions in Figueira, *AE,* 87–112.

18. Crius refuses cooperation, other king said to be opposed: Hdt. 6.50.1–2.

19. Letter from Demaratus, Cleomenes' warning: Hdt. 6.50.3.

20. Cleomenes ousts Demaratus, bribing Delphi; latter flees to Susa; Cleomenes and new king Leotychidas arrest Aeginetan Medizers: Hdt. 6.61–70, 73.

21. For the view that the rivalry between the two kings was purely personal and had no larger policy significance, see Roobaert, *II,* 63–70, who also cites the secondary literature arguing the contrary. When he arrived at the Persian court, Demaratus was honored as a benefactor of the King of Kings: see Michael Heltzer, "Mordekhai and Demaratos and the Question of Historicity," *AMIT* 27 (1994): 119–21.

22. Long ships and horse transports built: Hdt. 6.48.2–49.1. Datis and Artaphernes son of Artaphernes muster forces at Aleion: 6.94.1–95.1. Role of Eretrians in Cyprus campaign: Lysanias of Mallos *FGrH* 426 F1.

23. Plato on size of Persian force: *Menex.* 240a7.

24. Persian fleet sails from Samos to Euboea through Cyclades: Hdt. 6.95.

25. Naxos falls: Hdt. 6.96. Naxians acknowledge sanctuaries burned, claim Persians driven off: Plut. *Mor.* 869b.

26. Datis at Delos: Hdt. 6.97–98; *IG* XI ii 154A.51–52, 153.7, 161B.96, 164A.34, 199B.24. Cycladic tour, hostages, Carystus: Hdt. 6.99.

27. Eretrian leader fears betrayal, urges Athenian cleruchs to cross to Attica: Hdt. 6.100.1–101.1. Possible Theban restoration of Chalcidian *Hippobótai* to Lelantine lands: Vassilis L. Aravantinos, "A New Inscribed *Kioniskos* from Thebes," *BSA* 101 (2006): 369–77, with Thomas J. Figueira, "Khalkis and Marathon," in *MBAD,* 185–202.

28. Eretria betrayed, sacked; dragnet imposed; citizens shipped to Darius: Hdt. 6.101; Pl. *Menex.* 240a–c, *Leg.* 3.698c–d; Strabo 10.1.10. Rich rewards for Medizers: Paus. 7.10.2, Plut. *Mor.* 510b.

29. Eretrian prisoners left on Aegilia: Hdt. 6.107.2.

30. Battle commemorated at festival of Artemis Agrotera: Plut. *Mor.* 862a. Later thought to have taken place on that day: 861e, *Cam.* 19.5. Herodotus puts shortly after full moon: 6.106.1–107.1, 120. The dating turns on the likelihood that the arrival of the Persians in Attica coincided with the beginning of the celebration of the Carneia in Sparta: note 38, below. *Contra* Krentz, *BoM,* 180–82, I am persuaded that this nine-day festival ordinarily began in the second half of August or the first half of September. As we shall see in Chapter 6—if the Herodotean chronology for the battle of Thermopylae in 480, which took place at the time of the full moon on the last day of the same festival, and that for the battle of Salamis, which he has take place ten days later at the end of September, shortly before the eclipse of 2 October, is correct—then, that year, the Carneia ended on 18 September. In 490, the full moon marking the festival's conclusion came on 9 September: note 38, below.

31. Plain well-suited to cavalry: Hdt. 6.102. Marshland for foraging: Paus. 1.15.3, 32.7. Horses watered, men mustered: Hdt. 6.102, 107. On the location and topography, see Nicholas G. L. Hammond, "The Campaign and Battle of Marathon," in Hammond, *Studies in Greek History* (Oxford: Clarendon Press, 1973), 170–250; J. A. G. Van der Veer, "The Battle of Marathon: A Topographical Survey," *Mnemosyne,* fourth ser. 35:3 (1982): 290–321; Scott, *HCH,* 597–629; and Krentz, *BoM,* 111–36, who is especially thorough. Note also Norman Whately, "On the Possibility of Reconstructing Marathon and Other Ancient Battles," *JHS* 84 (1964): 119–39; Schachermeyr, *MPP;* James Allan Stewart Evans, "Herodotus and the Battle of Marathon," *Historia* 42:3 (3rd Quarter 1993): 279–307, and "Cavalry about the Time of the Persian Wars: A Speculative Essay," *CJ* 82:2 (December 1986–January 1987): 97–106, revised and reprinted in Evans, *BH,* 161–214; Richard Billows, *Marathon: How One Battle Changed Western Civilization* (New York: Overlook Duckworth, 2010); and James Lacey, *The First Clash: The Miraculous Greek Victory at Marathon and Its Impact on Western Civilization* (New York: Random House, 2011). For reconstructions based upon the presumption that Herodotus cannot be trusted, cf. Johan Henrik Schreiner, *Two Battles and Two Bills: Marathon and the Athenian Fleet* (Athens: Norwegian Institute, 2004), and Everett L. Wheeler, "Present but Absent: Marathon in the Tradition of Western Military Thought," in *Marathon the Day After: Symposium Proceedings, Delphi 2–4 July 2010,* ed. Kostas Buraselis and Elias Koulakiotis (Athens: European Cultural Center of Delphi, 2013), 241–68. As the testimony of both Herodotus and Pausanias suggest, Christopher J. Tuplin, "Marathon: In Search of a Persian Dimension," in *MBAD,* 251–74, underestimates the significance of the role that the cavalry contingents played in the calculations of Datis and Artaphernes.

32. Simonides on Persian numbers: F90 (Bergk). Number of marines per ship: Hdt. 7.184.2. Athenian custom regarding troop transports: Thuc. 6.43, 7.42.1, 8.25.1. Men-of-war apt to be fully manned: Chapter 1, note 36, above. Cf. Norman A. Doenges, "The Campaign and Battle of Marathon," *Historia* 47:1 (1st Quarter 1998): 1–17 (at 4–6), who underestimates the Persian capacity and willingness to project power.

33. See Richard M. Berthold, "Which Way to Marathon?" *REA* 78–79 (1976–77): 84–95 (at 84–87); Josiah Ober, "Edward Clarke's Ancient Road to Marathon, A.D. 1801," *Hesperia* 51:4 (October–December 1982): 453–58; and J. A. G. Van der Veer, "Clarke's Road," *Mnemosyne,* fourth ser. 39:3 (1986): 417–18.

34. Dispatch of Philippides: Hdt. 6.105, Nep. *Milt.* 4.3. Decree: Arist. *Rhet.* 1411a9–10, Schol. Dem. 19.303, Nep. *Milt.* 4.4–5, Paus. 7.15.7, Plut *Mor.* 628e, Schol. Ael. Aristid. 2.219.

35. Blood oath: *RO* no. 88.21–51 with Peter Krentz, "The Oath of Marathon, not Plataia?" *Hesperia* 76:4 (October–December 2007): 731–42. Thebans among the first in Greece to Medize: Hdt. 7.233.1. Modeled on oath of *enōmatía:* Hans van Wees, "'The Oath of the Sworn Bands': The Acharnae Stela, the Oath of Plataea and Archaic Spartan Warfare," in *Das Frühe Sparta,* ed. Andreas Luther, Mischa Meier, and Lukas Thommen (Stuttgart: Franz Steiner Verlag, 2006), 125–64 with Rahe, *SR,* Chapter 1, note 26. For the relationship between the Marathon oath and the so-called oath of Plataea and for informed speculation regarding the occasion for the former's inscription at Acharnae, see Chapter 8, note 61, below. The curse may owe something to the Amphictyonic oath: Aeschin. 3.109–11.

36. Greek position: *IG* I³ 2/3; *IG* I³ 1015bis with Eugene V. Vanderpool, "The Deme of Marathon and the Herakleion," *AJA* 70:4 (October 1966): 319–23, and "Regulations for the Herakleian Games at Marathon," in *Studies Presented to Sterling Dow on His Eightieth Birthday,* ed. Alan L.

Boegehold (Durham, NC: Duke University Press, 1984), 295–96. Gates of Marathon: *IG* I³ 1015bis and *IG* I³ 503/4 with Angelos P. Matthaiou, "Athenaioisi tetagmenoisi en temenei Herakleos (Hdt. 6.108.7)," in *Herodotus and His World: Essays from a Conference in Memory of George Forrest*, ed. Peter Derow and Robert Parker (Oxford: Oxford University Press, 2003), 190–202. I see no reason to ignore the available evidence: cf., however, Doenges, "The Campaign and Battle of Marathon," 6–8. Marathon's nook: Pind. *Pyth.* 8.79. Plataeans: Hdt. 6.103.1, 108.1; Nep. *Milt.* 4.2–5. No more than ten thousand hoplites: 5.1; Justin 2.9; Plut. *Mor.* 305b; Paus. 4.25.5, 10.20.2; *Suda* s.v. *Hippías*. Light-armed troops at Plataea: Hdt. 9.28.6, 29.2.

37. Awaiting the Spartans: *Suda* s.v. *Hippías* II. A day and a half for Philippides to make the journey: Hdt. 6.106.1 with "The Lunacy of the Long-Distance Runner," *Economist* 405:8816 (22 December 2012): 85–87. He may, in fact, have taken a route—through the Argive plain—shorter than the one followed in the Spartathlon: Pamela-Jane Shaw, "Message to Sparta: The Route of Pheidippides before Marathon," *GeorgAnt* 6 (1997): 53–78.

38. Carneia under way: Hdt. 6.106.2–3 read in light of Eur. *Alc.* 449–51; Hdt. 7.206; Thuc. 5.54, 75. For the timing of the festival, see Nicolas Richer, *La Religion des Spartiates: Croyances et cultes dans l'Antiquité* (Paris: Les Belles Lettres, 2012), 383–456 (esp. 413–19, 447–54), 547–59. Moon full in Boedromion, 490 on 9 September: http://www.skyviewcafe.com/skyview.php, where one can find precise information concerning the phase of the moon on any given date and the rising and setting of both the sun and moon at any particular location in the world on that date. I am not persuaded by the suggestion of Andreas Luther, "Die verspätete Ankunft des spartanischen Heeres bei Marathon (490 v. Chr.)," in *Getrennte Wege? Kommunikation, Raum und Wahrnehmung in der alten Welt,* ed. Robert Rollinger, Andreas Luther, and Josef Wiesehöfer (Frankfurt am Main: Verlag Antike, 2007), 381–403, that the passage in Herodotus should be read, instead, in light of Lucian *De astrologia* 25 and that the law forbade the Spartans marching anywhere in any month prior to the meeting of their assembly at the time of the full moon. I find it far easier to suppose what we know to be true—that the Lacedaemonians were occasionally hobbled by religious prohibitions—than that they stubbornly adhered to a law that in every month prevented their responding to emergencies in a timely fashion. In any case, the passage in Lucian need be nothing more than an inference from Herodotus' claim that, on this occasion, the law forbade their marching out before the full moon, and the same can be said for Paus. 1.28.4.

39. Carneia prohibition applies to Dorians in general: Hdt. 7.206; Eur. *Alc.* 449–51; Thuc. 5.54.2–3, 75.2, 76.1; Xen. *Hell.* 4.7.2–3. The younger Artaphernes knew Anatolia well. In due course, he was to command the Lydian and Mysian contingents in Xerxes' expeditionary force (Hdt. 7.74). It is unlikely that he was ignorant of Dorian customs.

40. Cf. Lazenby, *DG,* 40, 61–62, who recognizes the degree to which the Persians had made a science of war (ibid., 29–31) but cannot bring himself to believe that they had the sense to pay attention to the Spartans, the danger they posed, and the manner in which the calendar they employed could affect Greek warfare, with Schachermeyr, *MPP,* 10–11, who is not so incredulous.

41. Spartan timetable, Persian calculations: Nep. *Milt.* 5.4. Just how much time such a march would take is disputed: see note 60, below.

42. Generals at odds over fight: Hdt. 6.109.

43. Callimachus sides with Miltiades, latter delays: Hdt. 6.110.

44. Trees nearby, perhaps a grove: Nep. *Milt.* 5.3–4. Stockade an option: Frontin. *Strat.* 2.2.9.

45. June, July, August, and Port Mahon: William Ledyard Rodgers, *Greek and Roman Naval Warfare: A Study of Strategy, Tactics, and Ship Design from Salamis (480 B.C.) to Actium (31 B.C.)* (Annapolis, MD: U.S. Naval Institute Press, 1964), 85. Hesiod on safe season for sailing: *Op.* 663–77 with G. L. Snider, "Hesiod's Sailing Season (*W&D* 663–65)," *AJAH* 3 (1978): 129–35. See also Veg. *Mil.* 4.39, *Cod. Theod.* 13.9.3. Note Heliod. *Aeth.* 5.18. Cf. Dem. 56.30. Weather and season: Jamie Morton, *The Role of the Physical Environment in Ancient Greek Seafaring* (Leiden: Brill, 2001), 46–51, 255–61. Cf. Oded Tammuz, "*Mare clausum?* Sailing Seasons in the Mediterranean in Early Antiquity," *MHR* 20:2 (December 2005): 145–62, and James Beresford, *The Ancient Sailing Season* (Leiden: Brill, 2013), 1–212 (esp. 134–57, 248–57), who rightly caution against the presumption that there was no seafaring at all in the winter months and who draw attention to the variability in local conditions. As they point out, however, the winter storms were far more dangerous for galleys of shallow draft, such as triremes, than they were for sailing ships.

46. Athenians well-positioned: Nep. *Milt.* 5.3–4. Ravaging expeditions for Persian cavalry: Dem. 59.94, Plut. *Arist.* 5.1. Note Hdt. 6.118.

47. Persian cavalry landed at Marathon: Hdt. 6.102. Athenians bereft: 6.112.2.

48. Athenians convert triremes into horse transports: Thuc. 2.56.2, Ar. *Eq.* 595–610. Cram thirty mounts onto a single vessel: Thuc. 6.43, *IG* II² 1628. At 6.48, when he first mentions horse transports, Herodotus does not say anything about their size. With regard to the horse transports employed in 480, the manuscripts of Herodotus at 7.97 are at odds with one another in one important particular: according to most of them, the horse transports employed in 480 were "small ships [*ploîa smikrà*]" of some sort, which, in context, makes good sense. According to one, however, and the best of the lot, they were "long ships [*ploîa mikrà*]." Either could be correct.

49. In this connection, see Robert Drews, *Early Riders: The Beginnings of Mounted Warfare in Asia and Europe* (New York: Routledge, 2004), esp. 123–48. Persian cavalry equipped with bows, arrows, spears, and iron clubs: J. M. Cook, *The Persian Empire* (New York: Schocken Books, 1983), 102. The conduct of Datis and Artaphernes at Marathon and of Mardonius at Athens and Plataea in 479 suggests that, in his admirable review of the available evidence, Christopher J. Tuplin, "All the King's Horse: In Search of Achaemenid Persian Cavalry," in *New Perspectives on Ancient Warfare*, ed. Garret G. Fagan and Matthew Trundle (Leiden: Brill, 2010), 101–82, errs in downplaying the tactical importance of cavalry for the Persians. For the Persian way of war, see Paul A. Rahe, "The Military Situation in Western Asia on the Eve of Cunaxa," *AJPh* 101:1 (Spring 1980): 79–96.

50. Division of responsibilities between the *gerrophóroi* identified as specialists by Xenophon (*An.* 1.8.9, 2.1.6, 4.6.25–26; *Oec.* 4.5), Plato (*Laches* 191c), and Strabo (7.3.17, 15.3.18–19) and the foot-soldiers armed only with bows and relatively short spears (Hdt. 5.49.3, 97.1, 7.61–62): see Peter R. Barkworth, "The Organization of Xerxes' Army," *IA* 27 (1992): 149–67 (at 154, n. 28), who rightly points out that, in contrast to what Herodotus seems to imply at 7.61, the Persian reliefs at Persepolis and elsewhere show some soldiers carrying large wicker shields and other soldiers armed with bow and spear but no Persian infantrymen burdened with the *gérron* and also with both bow and spear. His observations are confirmed not only by the surviving Hellenic depictions of combat between Greek hoplites and Persian infantrymen—Anne Bovon, "La Représentation des guerriers perses et la notion de Barbare dans la première moitié du Vᵉ siècle," *BCH* 87:2 (1963): 579–602— but also by the *gérra* from later times: Nicholas V. Sekunda, *Marathon, 490 BC: The First Persian Invasion of Greece* (Oxford: Osprey, 2002), 22. The fact that only the *gerrophóroi* have any sizable shields at all explains why Herodotus speaks of the Persian bowmen and spearmen at Plataea as being *ánoploi* and *gumnêtes*: 9.61–63. The Persians, Medes, and Cissians who later accompanied Xerxes (and perhaps the other Iranians as well) wore body armor. Some carried *gérra*. None bore *aspídes*: 7.61.1, 62 with 5.97.1. See also Plut. *Arist.* 18. In this connection, note *Suidas* s.v. *Gérron, Gérra*; consider Xen. *Cyr.* 7.1.33–34, 8.5.10–11, in light of *An.* 1.8.9; and see Stefan Bittner, *Tracht und Bewaffnung des persischen Heeres zur Zeit der Achaimeniden*, second edition (Munich: Verlag Klaus Friedrich, 1985), passim (esp. 134–79), and Nicholas V. Sekunda, "Achaemenid Military Technology," *AMIT* 21 (1988): 69–77 with Chapter 6, note 64, below. Cf. Lincoln, *HfM*, 335–54, with ibid., 271–88, who is far too quick in the first of the two essays cited to dismiss the testimony of Herodotus as a reflection of cultural bias. If, as Lincoln documents, Aeschylus, Herodotus, Xenophon, and Strabo persistently depict the Persians first and foremost as archers, it is in keeping with the fact—pointed out by Root, *KKAA*, 164–69—that, in monumental Achaemenid art and on the coins of the realm, the Great King is represented as a bowman, never a spearman. Note also Diod. 19.21.3.

51. Difficult for Persians to ready horses before daybreak: Xen. *An.* 3.4.35. Hypothesis that Athenians attack before horses ready: Hammond, "The Campaign and Battle of Marathon," 214–15, and Krentz, *BoM*, 137–60. Note also Gordon Shrimpton, "The Persian Cavalry at Marathon," *Phoenix* 34:1 (Spring 1980): 20–37.

52. Quality of Persian steeds: Hdt. 7.196. Function of cavalry on battlefield: 9.57.3, 68. Unlikelihood battle lasted more than two or three hours: Adam Schwartz, *Reinstating the Hoplite: Arms, Armour and Phalanx Fighting in Archaic and Classical Greece* (Stuttgart: Franz Steiner Verlag, 2009), 201–25.

53. Ionian warning: *Suda* s.v. *Chōrís hippeîs* with Schachermeyr, *MPP*, 15–26.

54. Battle of Marathon: Hdt. 6.111–13; Paus. 1.15.3, 32.7 with Schachermeyr, *MPP*, 15–35; Burn,

PG, 246–52; Green, *XS*, 33–38; Evelyn B. Harrison, "The South Frieze of the Nike Temple and the Marathon Painting in the Painted Stoa," *AJA* 76:4 (October 1972): 353–78; and Lazenby, *DG*, 58–75. The simplest explanation for the fact that Herodotus' account of the battle dovetails well with what we can surmise regarding its depiction in the tripartite painting in the Stoa Poikile is that the painter and the historian accurately reported the course of events as remembered by those who had participated in the battle and as retold by their offspring: cf., however, Vin Massaro, "Herodotos' Account of the Battle of Marathon and the Picture in the Stoa Poikile," *AC* 47:2 (1978): 458–75. Range of Persian artillery and its ineffectiveness against Greek armor: Wallace McLeod, "The Range of the Ancient Bow," *Phoenix* 19:1 (Spring 1965): 1–14, and the unpublished dissertation of P. Henry Blyth, "The Effectiveness of Greek Armour against Arrows in the Persian War (490–479 B.C.): An Interdisciplinary Enquiry" (Diss. University of Reading, 1977), with Christopher A. Bergman, E. McEwen, and Rebecca Miller, "Experimental Archery: Projectile Velocities and Comparison of Bow Performances," *Antiquity* 62:237 (December 1988): 658–70; Richard A. Gabriel and Karen S. Metz, *From Sumer to Rome: The Military Capabilities of Ancient Armies* (New York: Greenwood Press, 1991), 70–73; Christophe Zutterman, "The Bow in the Ancient Near East: A Reevaluation of Archery from the Late 2nd Millennium to the End of the Achaemenid Empire," *IA* 38 (2003): 119–65; and Christopher A. Matthew, "Testing Herodotus: Using Re-Creation to Understand the Battle of Marathon," *Ancient Warfare* 5:4 (May 2011): 41–46. The fact that Herodotus does not explicitly indicate that the Athenians and Plataeans were intent on limiting the period in which the Persian archers could target them can hardly be taken as proof that this was not a concern: cf., however, Rudolph H. Storch, "The Silence Is Deafening: Persian Arrows Did Not Inspire the Greek Charge at Marathon," *AArchHung* 41 (2001): 381–94. Hoplite's capacity for jogging: Krentz, *BoM*, 143–51, and Lacey, *The First Clash*, 181–84. Cf. Lazenby, *DG*, 38, 64, 68–72, 77–79, who is unwilling to acknowledge that the envelopment of the Persian army that Herodotus credited Miltiades with engineering was deliberate, with Green, *XS*, 31–38. See also Pliny *NH* 35.34.57, 59.

55. A few horses captured: Ael. Aristid, 1.107–8. Seven ships: Hdt. 6.114–15. Horses make racket: Paus. 1.32.4. Fleet sails for Phalerum: Hdt. 6.115.

56. Tribe left to guard battlefield: Plut. *Arist.* 5.6. Forced march back to Athens, Persians sail home: Hdt. 6.115–16, Plut. *Arist.* 5.5, Frontin. *Strat.* 2.9.8. Cf. James P. Holoka, "Marathon and the Myth of the Same-Day March," *GRBS* 38:4 (Winter 1997): 329–53 (at 349–48), and Krentz, *BoM*, 165–66, who doubt that the Athenian combatants could have had the energy to make the march back to Athens in the battle's immediate aftermath, with Billows, *Marathon*, 228–33, who has a higher estimate of the endurance of these hoplites. Time requisite for the Persians to reach Phalerum: note A. Trevor Hodge, "Marathon: The Persians' Voyage," *TAPhA* 105 (1975): 155–73, and "Marathon to Phalerum," *JHS* 95 (1975): 169–71, and see Krentz, *BoM*, 164–65, who draws on *AT*, 102–6.

57. Burial on battlefield, names of dead listed by tribe: Thuc. 2.34.3–5; Paus. 1.29.4, 32.3. Epigram on inscription for tribe Erechtheis: *SEG* LVI 430.

58. *Tropaîon*: Plut. *Them.* 3.4–5. Persian losses: Hdt. 6.117.1. Vow to sacrifice goats by Callimachus (Schol. Ar. *Eq.* 660) or Miltiades (Aelian *VH* 2.25). Eventually number sacrificed limited to five hundred: Xen. *An.* 3.2.12, Plut. *Mor.* 8.

59. Booty and dedications: Plut. *Arist.* 5.6–8 with Michael Jung, *Marathon und Plataia: Zwei Perserschlachten als "Lieux de Mémoire" im Antiken Griechenland* (Göttingen: Vandenhoeck and Ruprecht, 2006), 27–224.

60. Two thousand Spartans, three-day march: Hdt. 6.120. Holoka, "Marathon and the Myth of the Same-Day March," 329–53, thinks the claim they made the journey in three days preposterous. To reject the claim that Athens sought Sparta's support and that, in due course, the Lacedaemonians belatedly marched to Attica, one must suppose, as does Michael Jung, "Spartans at Marathon? On the Origin and Function of an Athenian Legend," in *Marathon the Day After*, 16–37, that the Athenians bamboozled Herodotus and that he did not have the wit to check their tale with the Spartans with whom he was acquainted—which I find hard to believe.

61. Five times as many Lacedaemonians at Plataea: Hdt. 9.28.2.

62. Secretiveness: Thuc. 5.68.2.

63. Cleomenes' bribery of oracle discovered, flight, instigation of Arcadian rebellion, recall: Hdt. 6.74.1–75.1. Tegeans not on good terms with the Lacedaemonians: 9.37.4.

64. Helot revolt: Pl. *Leg.* 3.692d, 698c–e.

65. Thucydides' difficulties: 5.68.2. Four Messenian wars: Strabo 8.4.10. Dedication at Olympia: ML no. 22. Testimony of Pausanias: 5.24.3. Spartan-Messenian conflict in time of Leotychidas (Paus. 4.15.1–2) and Anaxilaus: 4.23.5–10, Hdt. 6.23, Thuc. 6.4.5–6 with W. P. Wallace, "Kleomenes, Marathon, the Helots and Arcadia," *JHS* 74 (1954): 32–35. Note also Jean Ducat, *Les Hilotes* (Athens and Paris: École Française d'Athènes/De Boccard, 1990), 141–43, and Peter Hunt, *Slaves, Warfare, and Ideology in the Greek Historians* (Cambridge: Cambridge University Press, 1998), 28–31. Skepticism: cf. Slobodan Dušanić, "Platon, la question messénienne et les guerres contre les Barbares," in *Esclavage, guerre, économie en Grèce ancienne: Hommage à Yvon Garlan*, ed. Pierre Brulé and Jacques Oulhen (Rennes: Presses Universitaires de Rennes, 1997), 75–86; Matthew P. J. Dillon, "The Lakedaimonian Dedication to Olympian Zeus: The Date of 'Meiggs & Lewis' 22 (*SEG* 11,1203a)," *ZPE* 107 (1995): 60–68; and Nino Luraghi, *The Ancient Messenians: Construction of Ethnicity and Memory* (Cambridge: Cambridge University Press, 2008), 173–82. If I do not mention the so-called Rhianus hypothesis, it is because Daniel Ogden, *Aristomenes of Messene: Legends of Sparta's Nemesis* (Swansea: Classical Press of Wales, 2004), 155–75, has demolished it.

66. Cf. Greg Anderson, *The Athenian Experiment: Building an Imagined Community in Ancient Attica, 508–490 B.C.* (Ann Arbor: University of Michigan Press, 2003), who overstates the significance of these years by wrongly disparaging the evidence that the Athenians had a strong sense of their own identity in the century prior to 508, with Phillip Brook Manville, *The Origins of Citizenship in Ancient Athens* (Princeton, NJ: Princeton University Press, 1990), and Wees, *SSTT*, who, from different perspectives, do justice to the earlier development of Athens as a proper political community.

Part II. The Crisis Comes to a Head

Epigraph: Xerxes XPl (*PE* 11:17).

1. Cyclades Persia's: Dio Chrys. *Or.* 11.148.

2. Apollo statue from Delium: Hdt. 6.118. Eretrians on royal road near Susa: 6.119, Philostr. 1.21–24.

3. Road system and pony express: Hdt. 5.52–54, 8.98; Xen. *Cyr.* 8.6.17–18 with David F. Graf, "The Persian Royal Road System," *AchHist* 8 (1994): 167–89, and Briant, *CA*, 364–87. The precise route is disputed: David H. French, "Pre- and Early-Roman Roads of Asia Minor: The Persian Royal Road," *Iran* 36: (1998): 15–43. Darius' response to news of Marathon: Hdt. 7.1.1–3.

4. Egypt revolts, second expedition delayed, Darius dies: Hdt. 7.1.3, 4.1.

5. Heir customarily named before departure for war: Hdt. 7.2.1.

6. Plausible claimants: Hdt. 7.2–3.

7. Artaphernes family judge: Justin 2.10.1–10. Xerxes celebrates choice as crown prince and succession: XPf (*PE* 7:1).

8. Harem intrigues played down: cf., for example, Heleen Sancisi-Weerdenburg, "Exit Atossa: Images of Women in Greek Historiography of Persia," in *Images of Women in Antiquity*, ed. Averil Cameron and Amélie Kuhrt (London: Routledge, 1983), 20–33; Pierre Briant, "Histoire et idéologie: Les Grecs et la 'décadence perse,'" in *Mélanges Pierre Lévêque*, ed. Marie Madeleine Macroux and Evelyne Geny (Besançon: Université de Besançon, 1989), II 33–47; Balcer, *PCG*; and Maria Brosius, *Women in Ancient Persia, 539–331 BC* (Oxford: Oxford University Press, 1996), passim (esp. 1–3), with the more sensible assessments of Lewis, *SP*, 21–22, and Llewellyn-Jones, *KCAP*, 96–148.

9. Egyptian revolt quelled, Achaemenes made satrap: Hdt. 7.7. Babylonian rebellions: cf. 3.153–58 with Ctesias *FGrH* 688 F13.26, and see Caroline Waerzeggers, "The Babylonian Revolts against Xerxes and the 'End of Archives,'" *AOF* 50 (2003–4): 150–78.

10. Xerxes vs. the Lie: XPl (*PE* 11:17).

11. Xerxes universal monarch hostile to commotion: XPf, XV, XE, XPh, XPa (*PE* 7:1, 86–88, 12:4). Herodotus on aspiration: 7.8γ. See the evidence concerning Darius' aspirations collected in Chapter 2, note 16, above.

12. Eschatological import of Xerxes' crossing into Europe: consider Xanthus of Lydia *FGrH* 765 F32 in light of Lincoln, *HfM*, 5–268, 357–92, 406–24, and see Peter Kingsley, "Meetings with Magi: Iranian Themes among the Greeks, from Xanthus of Lydia to Plato's Academy," *JRAS*, third

ser., 5:2 (July 1995): 173–209 (esp. 173–95). Cf. Gerold Walser, *Hellas und Iran: Studien zu den griechisch-perschischen Beziehungen vor Alexander* (Darmstadt: Wissenschaftliche Buchge-sellschaft, 1984), and Josef Wiesehöfer, "Greeks and Persians," in *A Companion to Archaic Greece*, ed. Kurt A. Raaflaub and Hans van Wees (Oxford: Wiley-Blackwell, 2009), 162–85, who resolutely deny that the two Achaemenid monarchs had unfulfilled imperial ambitions, and the work cited in Chapter 5, note 44, below.

13. Advice given Xerxes: Hdt. 7.5–6, 8–19.

14. Possible conversation with descendants of Demaratus in Troad: cf. Xen. *Hell.* 3.1.6; *An.* 2.1.3, 7.8.17, with Hdt. 2.10.1. Five sons of Hippias: Thuc. 6.55.1. Some with Xerxes in Greece: Hdt. 7.6.2–3, 8.52.2. Descendants on Chios: W. G. G. Forrest, "A Lost Peisistratid Name," *JHS* 101 (1981): 134. Dikaios son of Theodykes: Hdt. 8.65. Zopyrus in Athens: 3.160. Great grandson of co-conspirator of Darius: 3.70.2, 81, 153.1. Son of Xerxes' general: 7.82, 121.3. Greek informer from within the Persian civil service: David M. Lewis, "Postscript 1984," in Burn, *PG*, 587–612, and "Persians in Herodotus," in Lewis, *SPGNEH*, 345–61.

15. Consider Hdt. 7.12–19 in light of Simo Parpola, "Excursus: The Substitute King Ritual," in Parpola, *Letters from Assyrian Scholars to the Kings Esarhaddon and Assurpanipal, Part II: Commentary and Appendices* (Vluyn-Neukirchen: Butzon & Bercker Kevelaer, 1983), xii–xxxii (esp. xxii–xxxii), and see Karen Radner, "The Trials of Esarhaddon: The Conspiracy of 670 BC," *Isimu* 6 (2003): 165–83 (at 171–72).

16. Mardonius tempts Xerxes: Hdt. 7.5.3. Great King as gardener, horticulturist, promoter of irrigation, admirer of beautiful river valleys, builder of palaces: consider Wolfgang Fauth, "Der königliche Gärtner und Jäger im Paradeisos: Beobachtungen zur Rolle des Herrschers in der vorderasiatischen Hortikultur," *Persica* 8 (1979): 1–53; Christopher J. Tuplin, "The Parks and Gardens of the Achaemenid Empire," in Tuplin, *Achaemenid Studies* (Stuttgart: Franz Steiner Verlag, 1996), 80–131; Anders Hultgård, "Das Paradies: Vom Park des Perserkönigs zum Ort der Seligen," in *La Cité de dieu/Die Stadt Gottes*, ed. Martin Hengel, Siegfried Mittmann, and Anna Maria Schwemer (Tübingen: Mohr Siebeck, 2000), 1–43; and Lincoln, *HfM* 5–104 (esp. 59–85), 202–12, with an eye to Hdt. 3.117, 7.27, 128; Xen. *An.* 1.2.7–9, *Cyr.* 8.6.12, *Oec.* 4.13–17, 20–24; Polyb. 10.28.1–5; Strabo 15.3.3, 18; Arrian *An.* 6.24.1; DPf, DSe, DSf, DSz, A²HB (*PE* 11:10, 12–14); *PE* 11:11, 15, 21, 12:3, 46, 16:43–47, 17:46; and Alexander Uchitel, "Persian Paradise: Agricultural Texts in the Fortification Tablets," *IA* 32 (1997): 137–44. Even if the letter Darius is said to have sent Gadatas in western Asia Minor (ML no. 12) is a forgery, as some scholars suppose, it is evidence that the Achaemenid kings were long remembered for their deep-seated interest in promoting horticulture and gardening. Praise, devotion, exotic gifts, items of surpassing beauty, and generous material support from subjects: Root, *KKAA*, 131–61, 227–84.

Chapter 5. The Formation of the Hellenic League

Epigraph: Aesch. *Pers.* 15–28.

1. Time for preparations: Hdt. 7.20.1. Less for Darius: 7.1.2–3. Xerxes sets out: 7.20–21.

2. Xerxes' forces outnumber those of Agamemnon: Hdt. 7.20–12. For scholarly accounts of the expedition as such, see Hignett, *XIG*, and Wallinga, *XGA*.

3. Athos canal: Hdt. 7.22–24, 37, 122. Functions for a time: Thuc. 4.109.2. Cf. Strabo 7 F35. The site has recently received close attention: see B. S. J. Isserlin, "The Canal of Xerxes: Facts and Problems," *ABSA* 86 (1991): 83–91; B. S. J. Isserlin, R. E. Jones, S. Papamarinopoulos, and J. Uren, "The Canal of Xerxes on the Mount Athos Peninsula: Preliminary Observations," *ABSA* 89 (1994): 277–84; and B. S. J. Isserlin, R. E. Jones, V. Karastathis, S. Papamarinopoulos, G. E. Syrides, and J. Uren, "The Canal of Xerxes on the Mount Athos Peninsula: Summary of Investigations, 1991–2001," *ABSA* 98 (2003): 369–85.

4. Mandrocles' bridge over the Bosporus: Hdt. 4.85.1, 87.1, 88. Harpalus' bridges over the Hellespont: Aesch. *Pers.* 65–72, 104; Hdt. 7.25.1, 33–37, 9.121; Strabo 7 F55; Arr. *An.* 5.7 with Nicholas G. L. Hammond and L. J. Roseman, "The Construction of Xerxes' Bridge over the Hellespont," *JHS* 116 (1996): 88–107.

5. Peisistratids, Demaratus, Aleuads advise Xerxes: Hdt. 7.3.1–2, 6.2–3, 102–4, 130.3, 209, 234–35, 237. Depots for food and other supplies: 7.25 with Burn, *PG*, 318–19. Horse transports: Hdt. 7.97, Diod. 11.3.9.

6. Critalla to Sardis: Hdt. 7.26–31. Heralds: 7.32.

7. Medizing, opportunity for looting expected: Polyaen. *Strat.* 7.15.1.

8. Greek spies: Hdt. 7.145.2. Freed by Xerxes, intelligence expected to elicit surrender: 7.146–47.

9. Date Herodotus born: *Suda* s.v. *Heródotos* and *Panúassıs,* Dion. Hal. *Thuc.* 5, Aul. Gell. 15.23.

10. Navy at Cumae and Phocaea: Diod. 11.2.3. Army marches from Sardis to Abydos: Hdt. 7.37–43.

11. Xerxes at Troy: Hdt. 7.43, to be read with Hom. *Od.* 1.327, 4.499–511, and Proclus *Chrestomathia* p. 108 (Allen). See Johannes Haubold, "Xerxes' Homer," in *Cultural Responses to the Persian Wars: Antiquity to the Third Millennium,* ed. Emma Bridges, Edith Hall, and Peter J. Rhodes (Oxford: Oxford University Press, 2007), 47–63, who draws attention to the Persian desecration of the sanctuary at Elaious of Protesilaus (Hdt. 7.33, 9.116), the first of the Achaeans to set foot on the Trojan shore (Hom. *Il.* 2.701–2), and to the sacrifices to Thetis they later conducted on the site where she was said to have been raped by Peleus (Hdt. 7.191.2). In this connection, see also Pericles B. Georges, *Barbarian Asia and the Greek Experience: From the Archaic Period to the Age of Xenophon* (Baltimore: Johns Hopkins University Press, 1994).

12. Review at Abydos: Hdt. 7.44–52. Libation, cup, sword, mixing bowl thrown into Hellespont: 7.54. Crossing of bridges takes a week: 7.55–57. In scourging the Hellespont after the bridges had been swept away and in hurling fetters into it (7.35), Xerxes may have been guided by Zoroastrian doctrine, which drew a sharp distinction between salt and sweet water, regarding the former as tainted by the destructive spirit Ahriman: see Mary Boyce, *A History of Zoroastrianism* (Leiden: Brill, 1975–91), II 166.

13. Journey to Doriscus, pause, ships dried and careened: Hdt. 7.58–59, which should be read in light of Paul Lipke, with John Coates, "Trireme Life Span and Leakage: A Wood Technologist's Perspective," and Paul Lipke, "Triremes and Shipworm," in *Trireme Olympias: The Final Report,* ed. N. Boris Rankov (Oxford: Oxbow Books, 2012), 185–206.

14. Review at Doriscus: Hdt. 7.60–100. Order of battle: 7.100.1.

15. Xerxes rewards Alexander I of Macedon: Justin 7.4.1 with Thuc. 2.99.2, 4.83.1.

16. Alexander warns Greeks of size of expedition: Hdt. 7.173.3 with Burn, *PG,* 344.

17. Herodotus' catalogue of the Persian army and navy: 7.60–100, 184. Aeschylus on size of fleet: *Pers.* 342–45.

18. Xerxes' marshals: Hdt. 7.82. Cavalry commanders: 7.88.1. Admirals: 7.97. See Burn, *PG,* 333–36.

19. Limits posed by need for fresh water: General Sir Frederick Maurice, "The Size of the Army of Xerxes in the Invasion of Greece, 480 B.C.," *JHS* 50:2 (1930): 210–35. Supposed recruitment of 300,000 infantrymen in Thrace and Macedonia: Hdt. 7.185.

20. Chiliad mistaken for myriad: Maurice, "The Size of the Army of Xerxes in the Invasion of Greece, 480 B.C.," 226. Size of other armies: Cawkwell, *GW,* 237–54, and Michael A. Flower, "The Size of Xerxes' Expeditionary Force," in *The Landmark Herodotus,* tr. Andrea L. Purvis, ed. Robert B. Strassler (New York: Pantheon Books, 2007), 819–23. See also Burn, *PG,* 326–30.

21. Here, I believe, Cawkwell, *GW,* 260–67 (with notes), underestimates the administrative capacity of the Achaemenid realm and the revolutionary consequences of the invention of the *gaúlos.* The fact that previous fleets were half this size is explicable on the grounds that these smaller fleets were more than adequate for the purpose contemplated. The fact that later fleets were even smaller is explicable on the grounds that Persia no longer possessed Ionia and the income from the mines in Thrace. In 480, Xerxes' aim was to overawe and win without a fight. To do so, he needed to impress the Greeks. Given the massive trireme-building campaign mounted by Athens, of which he surely had knowledge, he needed a great many ships. Note, in this connection, Lazenby, *DG,* 92–96; Wallinga, *XGA,* 32–46; and Dennis L. Fink, *The Battle of Marathon in Scholarship: Research, Theories, and Controversies since 1850* (Jefferson, NC: McFarland, 2014), 22–26. Cf. Burn, *PG,* 330–32.

22. The best recent discussion of the logistical challenges faced by the Persians and of their ability to surmount them can be found in Christopher J. Tuplin, "Achaemenid Arithmetic: Numerical Problems in Persian History," in *Recherches récentes sur l'Empire achéménide,* ed. Pierre Briant (Lyon: Topoi, 1997), I 365–421 (at 366–73). Cf. T. Cuyler Young, "480/79—A Persian Per-

spective," *IA* 15 (1980): 213–39, who errs in adopting uncritically the minimum calorie-intake calculations of Donald W. Engels, *Alexander the Great and the Logistics of the Macedonian Army* (Berkeley: University of California Press, 1978), 1–24, 123–30. Effort to overawe: Thomas Kelly, "Persian Propaganda—A Neglected Factor in Xerxes' Invasion of Greece and Herodotus," *IA* 38 (2003): 173–219.

23. Judgment of Hermocrates: Thuc. 6.33.5–6.

24. Demaratus on the Greeks and Spartans: Hdt. 7.101–4. The literary dimension of Herodotus' use of the Demaratus saga deserves and has received attention: Deborah Boedeker, "The Two Faces of Demaratus," *Arethusa* 20:1–2 (Spring 1987): 185–201.

25. Herodotus on oriental despotism: 1.96–101.

26. Biased Herodotean account of Miltiades' intentions after Marathon: Hdt. 6.132–36. Nepos corrects: Nicholas G. L. Hammond, "The Expedition of Xerxes," in *CAH*, IV² 518–91 (at 518–21).

27. Miltiades' Cycladic venture: Hdt. 6.132 and Schol. Ael. Aristid. 3.571 (Dindorf) with Konrad H. Kinzl, "Miltiades' Parosexpedition in der Geschichtsschreibung," *Hermes* 104:3 (1976): 280–307; Robert Develin, "Miltiades and the Parian Expedition," *AC* 46:2 (1977): 571–77; and Katerina Meidani, "*Miltiádeia*: Remarks on Miltiades' Activities before and after Marathon," in *MBAD*, 167–83 (at 176–79). His four triremes: Hdt. 6.41. Penteconters predominate: Thuc. 1.14. Successes: Nep. *Milt.* 7.1.

28. Lysagoras of Paros: Hdt. 6.133.1. Darius' co-conspirator Hydarnes: 3.70.2. Homonymous son: 7.83.1, 135. Putative resistance of Naxos: Plut. *Mor.* 869b.

29. Siege and Parian resistance: Hdt. 6.133–34, Nep. *Milt.* 7.2–3. Negotiations begun, Mykonos fire, negotiations broken off, Athenian withdrawal: Hdt. 6.135.1, Ephorus *FGrH* 70 F63, Nep. *Milt.* 7.4; Stephanus of Byzantium s.v. *Anapariázein*. Modeled on free-booting raiders in Homer: *Il.* 18.509–12, 22.111–28, with Stefan Link, "Das Paros-Abenteuer des Miltiades (Hdt. 6, 132–36)," *Klio* 82:1 (January 2000): 40–53.

30. Democratic envy: Nep. *Milt.* 8.

31. Monument at Marathon in Miltiades' honor: Paus. 1.32.3–4. Sophanes objects to crown of olive: Hdt. 6.92.3, 9.73–75; Paus. 1.29.5. Miltiades denied: Plut. *Cim.* 8.1.

32. Miltiades wounded, tried, fined, jailed, dead: Hdt. 6.135–36; Pl. *Grg.* 516d; Nep. *Milt.* 7.5–8.4; Schol. Ael. Arist. 3.572, 677–78, 691 (Dindorf) with Edwin M. Carawan, "*Eisangelia* and *Euthyna*: The Trials of Miltiades, Themistocles, and Cimon," *GRBS* 28:2 (Summer 1987): 167–208. Callias, Cimon, Elpinike, and the fine: Nep. *Cim.* 1, Plut. *Cim.* 4.4–8, Dio Chrys. 73.6 with Davies, *APF* nos. 7826 §§ V–VIII and 8429 §§ VIII–XII.

33. Ariphron and Peisistratus: *POxy* 4.664 with Thomas J. Figueira, "Xanthippos, Father of Perikles, and the 'Prytaneis' of the 'Naukraroi,'" *Historia* 35:3 (3rd Quarter 1986): 257–79 (at 277). Role of Xanthippus and Alcmaeonid marital tie: Hdt. 6.131, 136.1. Said to have acted for Alcmaeonids: Schol. Ael. Arist. 3.531–32. See Davies, *APF* nos. 9688 § X and 11793 §§ I–II.

34. Some islanders later with Xerxes: Hdt. 8.66.2. Others back Hellenes: 8.46, Hellanicus *FGrH* 323a F28, Ephorus *FGrH* 70 F187, Simonides F65 (Diehl), Plut. *Mor.* 869a–c. Paros on the sidelines: Hdt. 8.67.1.

35. Early history of ostracism at Athens: Arist. *Ath. Pol.* 22.1, 3–4, 8; Androtion *FGrH* 324 F6; Philochorus *FGrH* 328 F30. For an overview, see Rudi Thomsen, *The Origins of Ostracism: A Synthesis* (Copenhagen: Gyldendal, 1972), and Stefan Brenne, *Ostrakismos und Prominenz in Athen: Attische Bürger des 5. Jhs. v. Chr. auf den Ostraka* (Vienna: A. Holzhausens, 2001).

36. Power to ostracize once lodged with Council of 500: MS Vat. Gr. 1144.

37. Decision to hold ostracism: Arist. *Ath. Pol.* 43.5. Quorum for ostracism itself: Plut. *Arist.* 7.5–6, Poll. *Onom.* 8.20, Schol. Ar. *Eq.* 855, Philochorus *FGrH* 328 F30.

38. Ostracism of Hipparchus, Megacles, and Xanthippus: Arist. *Ath. Pol.* 22.4–6 with Davies, *APF* nos. 9688 § X, 11793 § IX, and 11811 § I. Tyrant Peisistratus the maternal grandfather of this Megacles: Chapter 2, note 39, above. There is an *óstrakon* associating Xanthippus with the Alcmaeonids and including him among the accursed: Anthony E. Raubitschek, "The Ostracism of Xanthipppos," *AJA* 51:3 (July–September 1947): 257–62. Aristeides: Arist. *Ath. Pol.* 22.7; Plut. *Arist.* 1.1–2.1, 5.1–7.7, with Davies, *APF* no. 1695 §§ I–II. With regard to Aristeides' archonship, cf. Ernst Badian, "Archons and Strategoi," *Antichthon* 5 (1971): 1–34 (at 11–14), and Peter J. Bicknell, "The Archon of 489/8 and the Archonship of Aristeides Lysimachou Alopekethen," *RFIC* 100 (1972):

164–72, with Robert Develin, *Athenian Officials, 684–321 B.C.* (Cambridge: Cambridge University Press, 2003), 57.

39. Epithets on *óstraka:* ML no. 21. Shield signal: Hdt. 6.115, 121–24.

40. Two hundred triremes: Hdt. 7.144. One hundred: Arist. *Ath. Pol.* 22.7, Justin 7.144.1, Polyaen. *Strat.* 1.30.5, Liban. *Or.* 9.38. Earlier campaign aimed at constructing one hundred: Plut. *Them.* 4.1–3. Note Stesimbrotus of Thasos *FGrH* 107 F2. Practice of equally dividing civic income from mines: Hdt. 3.57.2. Silver strike, Themistocles, Aegina, construction of fleet: Hdt. 7.144, Thuc. 1.14.3, Arist. *Ath. Pol.* 22.7, Plut. *Them.* 4.1–3, Polyaen. *Strat.* 1.30.5. Significance of Athenian mines: Robin Osborne, *Classical Landscape with Figures: The Ancient City and Its Countryside* (London: G. Phillip, 1987), 75–81. Note Errietta M. A. Bissa, *Governmental Intervention in Foreign Trade in Archaic and Classical Greece* (Leiden: Brill, 2009), 39–42, 49–65. Probable resort to shipyards nearer timber sources: ibid., 107–40. For Athens in the time of Hippias, Cleisthenes, and Melanthios, see Chapter 3, notes 4 and 7, above.

41. Last days of Cleomenes: Hdt. 6.75, 84. Schizophrenia: Georges Devereux, W. G. G. Forrest, and Jacquy Chemouni, *Cléomène le roi fou: Étude d'histoire ethnopsychanalytique* (Paris: Aubier Montaigne, 1998). It may have been at the time when Cleomenes was incapacitated and left to the care of his family that the Sicilian Greeks, fearing Carthage, made an appeal to Leonidas in his capacity as "brother of the king of the Spartans": Justin 19.1.9.

42. Leotychidas' plight: Hdt. 6.85–86. If Themistocles was behind Athens' refusal to release Crius and the other Aeginetan Medizers originally delivered by Cleomenes and Leotychides, it would explain the anger later directed at him by Crius' son Polycritus: Hdt. 8.92. With regard to the chronology, see Scott, *HCH,* 546–52. See also Thomas J. Figueira, "The Chronology of the Conflict between Athens and Aegina in Herodotus Bk. 6," *QUCC* 28 (1988): 49–90, reprinted with revisions in Figueira, *AE,* 113–49. Cf. Peter J. Rhodes, "Herodotean Chronology Revisited," in *Herodotus and His World: Essays from a Conference in Memory of George Forrest,* ed. Peter Derow and Robert Parker (Oxford: Oxford University Press, 2003), 58–72.

43. Aeginetan-Athenian Wars: Hdt. 6.87–93. From the fact that Aeginetans were unable to field more than forty or fifty triremes in 480 and 479, if that, we can infer that, in 483, they had no more than this number: 8.1, 46.1. Earlier Athenian acquisition of a substantial fleet of triremes: cf. Wees, *SSTT,* 3–5, 60–61, 64–68, 92–104, 124–33, 138–42, 144, with Chapter 3, at note 4, above.

44. Cf. Wallinga, *XGA,* 21–31, who argues unpersuasively that Themistocles had Aegina in mind and not Persia at all and that his ship-building program provoked Xerxes' invasion.

45. Themistocles, Aegina, and the building of the fleet: Hdt. 7.144. Calculations regarding the Mede: Thuc. 1.14.3, Plut. *Them.* 3.4–4.3. Timing of Aristeides' ostracism: Arist. *Ath. Pol.* 22.7. Resides on Aegina while in exile: Dem. 26.6; *Suda* s.v. *Arısteídes, Dareıkoús;* Aristodemos *FGrH* 104 F1.1.4. There is an *óstrakon* charging Aristeides with the mistreatment of suppliants—possibly the exiled Aeginetan revolutionaries settled at Sunium (Hdt. 6.88, 90.1–91.2): see Anthony E. Raubitschek, "Das Datislied," in *Charites: Studien zur Altertumswissenschaft,* ed. Konrad Schauenburg (Bonn: Atheneum, 1957), 234–42 (esp. 240–42). Others from among the ostracized also on Aegina: Thomas J. Figueira, "Residential Restrictions on the Athenian Ostracized," *GRBS* 28:3 (Autumn 1987): 281–305, reprinted with revisions in Figueira, *AE,* 173–96.

46. See M. B. Wallace, "Early Greek *Proxenoi,*" *Phoenix* 24:3 (Autumn 1970): 189–208 (at 199–200, n. 13). Royal monopoly in Macedonia over timber exports: Andoc. 2.11. Xerxes and the freedom of commerce: Hdt. 7.147.2. Cf., however, Russell Meiggs, *Trees and Timber in the Ancient Mediterranean World* (Oxford: Clarendon Press, 1982), 122–24, and Bissa, *Governmental Intervention in Foreign Trade in Archaic and Classical Greece,* 107–20, who cannot imagine that either Amyntas or Alexander would have risked crossing the Great King in this fashion.

47. See Roobaert, *II,* 112–18.

48. Omens at Lacedaemon bad, tied to murder of Persian heralds: Hdt. 7.134.1–2.

49. Spartan piety with regard to Apollo: Hdt. 5.63.2, 9.7. Dispatch of two Spartiates to the Great King for execution: 7.134.

50. Xerxes spares Sperthias and Boulis: Hdt. 7.136. Sons later sent as ambassadors to Susa: 7.137, Thuc. 2.67.1.

51. Hydarnes the co-conspirator: Hdt. 3.70.2. Career of Hydarnes son of Hydarnes: 7.83.1, 135.1. Conversation with Sperthias and Boulis: 7.135.

52. After Sperthias and Boulis return, omens favorable: Hdt. 7.137.1.

53. Merchants bear intelligence: see, for example, Xen. *Hell.* 3.4.1. Note also Diod. 16.22.2: Rumor traveled fast. In his fourteenth oration, which was delivered in 354/3, Demosthenes evidenced knowledge concerning the Great King's preparations for an invasion of Egypt that did not take place until 351/50: George L. Cawkwell, "The Fall of Themistocles," in *Auckland Classical Essays Presented to E. M. Blaiklock,* ed. B. F. Harris (Oxford: Oxford University Press, 1970), 39–58 (at 47–48), reprinted in Cawkwell, *Cyrene to Chaeronea: Selected Essays on Ancient Greek History* (Oxford: Oxford University Press, 2011), 95–113 (at 106–7).

54. Preparations alarm Athenians: Pl. *Leg.* 3.698e–699b.

55. Demaratus' message: Hdt. 7.239. Word sent to Athens and elsewhere, Sparta consults Apollo at Delphi: 7.220.3, 239. The fact that Gorgo is mentioned strongly suggests that this tale is not just a self-serving story offered up to Herodotus by Demaratus' descendants in western Anatolia.

56. In asserting that Arthmius of Zelea was caught at this time on just such a mission to the Peloponnesus, Plutarch and Aelius Aristides appear to have gotten the timing and the occasion wrong: cf. Plut. *Them.* 6.4 and Ael. Aristid. 1.310, 2.287, 392, 676 with Dem. 9.41–45, 19.271–72; Aeschin. 3.258; Deinarchus 2.24–25; and Craterus *FGrH* 342 F14, in particular. Then, see Meiggs, *AE,* 508–12.

57. Oracle: Hdt. 7.220.3–4. Xerxes claims descent from Perseus: 7.150.2.

58. Argives alerted: Hdt. 7.148.2. Xerxes' appeal to the Argives: 7.150 with Lincoln, *HfM,* 304–23. Promise to help Mardonius: Hdt. 9.12. Renewal of friendship with Artaxerxes: 7.151 with Matthew W. Waters, "Earth, Water, and Friendship with the King: Argos and Persia in the Mid-fifth Century," in *Extraction and Control: Studies in Honor of Matthew W. Stolper,* ed. Michael Kozuh (Chicago: Oriental Institute of the University of Chicago, 2014), 331–36. Neutrals said to be Medizers all: Hdt. 8.72–73.

59. Apollo's advice to the Argives: Hdt. 7.148.3.

60. Apollo's advice to the Athenians debated: Hdt. 7.140–42.

61. Skepticism about oracles: cf., for example, *A Commentary on Herodotus,* ed. Walter Wyberg How and Joseph Wells (Oxford: Clarendon Press, 1912), II 212; Hignett, *XIG,* 439–47; and John F. Lazenby, *The Spartan Army* (Warminster: Aris & Phillips, 1985), 91–92, 94–96, with Burn, *PG,* 346–49, and Nicholas G. L. Hammond, "Sparta at Thermopylae," *Historia* 45:1 (1st Quarter 1996): 1–20 (at 6–7). Public recitation of *Historíai* by Herodotus: Diyllus *FGrH* 73 F3, Lucian *Herod.* 1.

62. Themistocles guides Athenians: Hdt. 7.143.1.

63. Themistocles' exploitation of the second oracle: Hdt. 7.142–44.

64. Preliminary decision to evacuate Attica and confront Xerxes at sea: Hdt. 7.144.3; Thuc. 1.18.2, 91.5; Nep. *Them.* 2.7–8. Foresight and determination admired in antiquity: Polyb. 38.2.1–4. From landlubbers to masters of the sea: Thuc. 1.18.2; Plut. *Them.* 4.1–6, *Cim.* 5.1–3.

65. Population of Attica: Hdt. 5.97.2. See also 8.65.1, Ar. *Eccl.* 1132–33, Pl. *Symp.* 175e. Cleruchs at Chalcis: Hdt. 5.77.2, 6.100.1.

66. Athenian loss of two harvests: Hdt. 8.142.3. Pericles on time required for a mastery of seamanship: Thuc. 1.142.5–9.

67. Troezen harbors Athenian women and children: Hdt. 8.41.1, Plut *Them.* 10.5. Themistocles Decree: Dem. 19.303–4 and ML no. 23 with Michael H. Jameson, "Waiting for the Barbarian: New Light on the Persian Wars," *Greece and Rome,* second ser. 8:1 (March 1961): 5–18; Anthony J. Podlecki, *The Life of Themistocles: A Critical Survey of the Literary and Archaeological Evidence* (Montreal: McGill–Queens University Press, 1975), 247–67; and Nicholas G. L. Hammond, "The Narrative of Herodotus VII and the Decree of Themistocles at Troezen," *JHS* 102 (1982): 75–93, and "The Manning of the Fleet in the Decree of Themistocles," *Phoenix* 40:2 (Summer 1986): 143–48, whose conclusions seem to me on the whole sound. Cf., however, Christian Habicht, "Falsche Urkunde zur Geschichte Athens im Zeitalter der Perserkriege," *Hermes* 89:1 (1961): 1–35; Noel Robertson, "The Decree of Themistocles in Its Contemporary Setting," *Phoenix* 36:1 (Spring 1982): 1–44; and Mikael Johansson, "The Inscription from Troizen: A Decree of Themistocles?" *ZPE* 137 (2001): 69–92, and "Plutarch, Aelius Aristides and the Inscription from Troizen," *RhM* n. f. 147:3–4 (2004): 343–51.

68. Recall of those ostracized: Arist. *Ath. Pol.* 22.8; Plut. *Them.* 11.1, *Arist.* 8.1. All but one of the ostracized appear to have returned. Hipparchus son of Charmos was later accused of treason and condemned in absentia (Lycurg. 1.117–18, Harpocration s.v. *Hípparchos*), which suggests that he may have joined the Peisistratids accompanying Xerxes.

69. Thucydides on Themistocles: 1.138.3.

70. Athenian delegation to Lacedaemon: Paus. 3.12.6. Formal alliance: Hdt. 7.145.1. Themistocles proposes end to hostilities, Chileos supports: Plut. *Them.* 6.5. Athens and Aegina reconciled: Hdt. 7.145.1. Themistocles and Athens acquiesce in Spartan leadership: 7.161, 8.2–3; Plut. *Them.* 7.3–4. For an overview, see Peter A. Brunt, "The Hellenic League against Persia," *Historia* 2:2 (1953–54): 135–63.

Chapter 6. Thermopylae and Artemisium

Epigraph: Hdt. 7.104.4–5.

1. Hellenic League's envoys: Hdt. 7.145.2.

2. Resources of Corcyra: Hdt. 7.168.2. Those of Syracuse: 7.158.4.

3. Corcyraeans promise help: Hdt. 7.168.1.

4. Cretan cities refuse alliance: Hdt. 7.169–71. Argives demand peace treaty and leadership role: 7.148–52. Most who have written regarding Argos' demands stress their request for a share in the leadership but are entirely silent with regard to the Argives' keen interest in negotiating a peace of extended duration: cf., for example, Burn, *PG*, 349–50; Hignett, *XIG*, 99–101; and Green, *XS*, 66–70, 81–82. Lazenby, *DG*, 87, 106–7, who is an exception to the rule, nonetheless places little emphasis on the latter request.

5. Gelon of Syracuse demands hegemony: Hdt. 7.153.1–163.1, Polyb. 12.26b. Carthage prepares war: Diod. 11.1.4–2.1. Xerxes makes overtures to Carthage: Ephorus of Cumae *FGrH* 70 F186, Diod. 11.1.4–2.1. Carthaginian attack takes place at the appointed time: Hdt. 7.165–67.

6. Gelon prepares to give earth and water: Hdt. 7.163.2–164.2 with Burn, *PG*, 308–10. Scholars who deny Achaemenid Persia expansionist: preface to Part II, note 12, and Chapter 5, note 44, above.

7. Oath of Hellenic League vs. Medizers: Hdt. 7.132.2, Diod. 11.3.1–5, as interpreted in *A Commentary on Herodotus,* ed. Walter Wyberg How and Joseph Wells (Oxford: Clarendon Press, 1912), II 177–78. Thessalian appeal: Hdt. 7.130.3, 172. There is evidence suggesting that the Aleuads medized not long after Lade: see H. D. Westlake, "The Medism of Thessaly," *JHS* 56:1 (1936): 12–24, and Thomas R. Martin, *Sovereignty and Coinage in Classical Greece* (Princeton, NJ: Princeton University Press, 1985), 34–36.

8. Athenians (and other Greeks) become mariners: Hdt. 8.89.1. Athenians later as apt to swim as to read: Pl. *Leg.* 3.689d. Keen to avoid evacuation: Plut. *Them.* 7.1–2.

9. For a survey of the evidence concerning Leonidas and tentative suggestions as to its import, see Roobaert, *II,* 83–111.

10. Euainetos sent to Tempe: Hdt. 7.173.2.

11. Expedition to Tempe: Hdt. 7.173.1–2. Possible probe to Heracleum: Damastes *FGrH* 5 F4.3.

12. Alexander of Macedon warns the Greeks they will be trampled underfoot, they become aware of route around Tempe: Hdt. 7.173.3–174.1. It was via the route from Pieria over the shoulder of Olympus that the Germans outflanked the New Zealanders guarding the pass at Tempe in 1941: see W. Kendrick Pritchett, "Xerxes' Route over Mount Olympus," *AJA* 65:4 (October 1961): 369–75. Hellenes discover Ainianians, Dolopians, Malians, Perrhaibians, and Magnesians with the Mede: Diod. 11.2.5–3.3. Knowledge that Persians cannot be stopped from entering Thessaly reconciles Athenians to naval strategy: Plut. *Them.* 7.1–2. Turn to Thermopylae: Hdt. 7.175.1.

13. Xerxes sets out from Sardis for Abydos in the spring: Hdt. 7.37.1. Progress like a parade: 7.37.2–43.2. Seven days, seven nights crossing Hellespont: 7.56.1. A month spent: 8.51.1. Troubles with bridges occasion caution: 7.25.1, 33.1–37.1. Journey from Sardis to Athens takes six months: Nep. *Them.* 5.2.

14. With regard to the chronology of events thereafter, I have followed Kenneth S. Sacks, "Herodotus and the Dating of the Battle at Thermopylae," *CQ* n.s. 26:2 (1976): 232–48, who anchors his chronology on the eclipse that took place on 2 October 480 (Hdt. 9.10.3), a few days after

the battle of Salamis (8.113.1). Some scholars have adopted another chronology: see, for example, Chapter 7, note 23, below.

15. With regard to Achaemenid feasting, there is Near Eastern evidence to confirm the picture presented by Polyaen. *Strat.* 4.3.32 and by Heracleides of Cumae *FGrH* 689 F2; Ctesias *FGrH* 688 F39, 53; and Deinon *FGrH* 690 F24: see David M. Lewis, "The King's Dinner," in Lewis, *SPGNEH,* 332–41; Wouter F. M. Henkelman, "Consumed before the King: The Table of Darius, Irdabama and Irašuna and That of His Satrap, Karkiš," in *Der Achämenidenhof/The Achaemenid Court,* ed. Bruno Jacobs and Robert Rollinger (Wiesbaden: Harrassowitz, 2010), 667–775, and "Parnakka's Feast: Šip in Pārsa and Elam," in *Elam and Persia,* ed. Javier Álvarez-Mon and Mark B. Garrison (Winona Lake, IN: Eisenbrauns, 2011), 89–166; and Llewellyn-Jones, *KCAP,* 90–92.

16. Doriscus to Acanthus: Hdt. 7.121.2–3 with Dietram Müller, "Von Doriskos nach Therme: Der Weg des Xerxes-Heeres durch Thrakien und Ostmakedonien," *Chiron* 5 (1975): 1–12, and Christopher J. Tuplin, "Xerxes' March from Doriscus to Therme," *Historia* 52:4 (2003): 385–409.

17. Thessaly a well-irrigated garden: Hdt. 7.129.1–130.1. Xerxes journeys to the Peneus to see the Vale of Tempe: 7.128–30.

18. Xerxes' army builds road over eastern shoulder of Olympus: Hdt. 7.131.1 with Pritchett, "Xerxes' Route over Mount Olympus," 369–75. Cf. Vasilev, *PDXTM,* 190–94. Fleet follows army after eleven days: Hdt. 7.183.2. Storm delays arrival of fleet at rendezvous: 7.188–96 with Burn, *PG,* 388–90.

19. Aleuads the first to medize: Hdt. 7.130.3. Xerxes stages horse races in Thessaly: 7.196. Quality of Persian steeds: Ahmed Afshar and Judith Lerner, "The Horses of the Ancient Persian Empire at Persepolis," *Antiquity* 53:207 (March 1979): 44–47.

20. Xerxes takes road from Larissa via Pherae, Pagasae, and Halos: Hdt. 7.196–97.

21. See W. Kendrick Pritchett, "New Light on Thermopylai," *AJA* 62:2 (April 1958): 203–13.

22. On the Dhema pass, cf. the arguments advanced by those who think it a more viable route than Thermopylae itself—Edward W. Kase and George J. Szemler, "Xerxes' March through Phokis (Her. 8, 31–35)," *Klio* 64:2 (February 1982): 353–66; Edward W. Kase, "The Isthmus Corridor Road System from the Valley of the Spercheios to Kirrha on the Krisaian Gulf," and George J. Szemler, "Some Problem of the Late Archaic Age," in *The Great Isthmus Corridor Route: Explorations of the Phokis-Doris Expedition,* ed. Edward W. Kase, George J. Szemler, Nancy C. Wilkie, and Paul W. Wallace (Dubuque, IA: Kendall/Hunt Publishing, 1991), I 21–45 (esp. 22–31), 105–15; and George J. Szemler, William J. Cherf, and John C. Kraft, *Thermopylai: Myth and Reality in 480 B.C.* (Chicago: Ares Publishers, 1996)—with those advanced by W. Kendrick Pritchett, "Passes from Thermopylai to Elateia" and "Route of the Persians after Thermopylai," in *SAGT,* IV 123–75, 211–33, and restated by John F. Lazenby in his review of *Thermopylai: Myth and Reality in 480 B.C.* in *CR* n.s. 48:2 (1998): 521–22. Then consider W. Kendrick Pritchett, "In Defense of the Thermopylai Pass," in *SAGT,* V 190–216, and "Thermopylai and Its Geomorphology," in *SAGT,* VII 190–205, as well as Denis Rousset, "Les Doriens de la Métropole: Étude de topographie et de géographie historique," *BCH* 113:1 (1989): 199–239; Jeremy McInerney, *The Folds of Parnassos: Land and Ethnicity in Ancient Phokis* (Austin: University of Texas Press, 1999), 333–39; Cawkwell, *GW,* 274–76; Paul Cartledge, *Thermopylae: The Battle That Changed the World* (New York: Vintage Books, 2006), 123–24; Rupert Matthews, *The Battle of Thermopylae: A Campaign in Context* (Stroud, Gloucestershire: Spellmount, 2006), 100–103; and *Topography and History of Ancient Epicnemidian Locris,* ed. José Pascual and Maria-Foteini Papakonstantinou (Leiden: Brill, 2013), which is invaluable. See in particular, Eduardo Sánchez-Moreno, "Communication Routes in and around Epicnemidian Locris," and "Mountain Passes in Epicnemidian Locris," as well as Adolfo J. Dominguez Monedero, "The Late Archaic Period," ibid., 279–359, 445–70. Phocians hostile to Thessalians: Hdt. 7.176.4, 8.30. Able to take on six thousand hoplites: Diod. 14.82.7–9. In 457, the Spartans had to field a force of more than ten thousand hoplites to counter their later assault on Doris: Thuc. 1.107.2. When cornered by Thessalians, Phocians effective at defense: Hdt. 8.27–28, Paus. 10.1.3–11, Plut. *Mor.* 244, with W. Kendrick Pritchett, "Hyampolis: Cults and the Early Thessalo-Phokian War," in *Greek Archives, Cults, and Topography* (Amsterdam: J. C. Gieben, 1996), 96–147.

23. Xerxes pauses short of Thermopylae to await fleet: Hdt. 7.196–201.

24. Arrival at Thermopylae coincides with Carneia and Olympic Games: Hdt. 7.206.

25. Demaratus Olympic victor: Hdt. 6.70.3.

26. Xerxes' fleet sets out eleven days after army: Hdt. 7.183.2.

27. Diodorus names Megabates as fleet commander: 11.12.2–3. Led attack on Naxos twenty years before: Hdt. 5.32.1–35.1. Described as admiral in Persepolis tablets: David M. Lewis, "Persians in Herodotus," in Lewis, *SPGNEH*, 345–61. Satrap of Hellespontine Phrygia after Persian Wars: Hdt. 5.32, Thuc. 1.129.1. Son Megabazos may have been the fleet commander: Hdt. 7.97.

28. Size of fleet: Hdt. 7.184.1–3, 185.1. Ayiókambos and other anchorages along the coast of Magnesia: Anthony M. Bowen, "The Place That Beached a Thousand Ships," *CQ* n.s. 48:2 (1998): 345–64. Small beaches: Diod. 11.12.5–6. Mediterranean moor: Ian Whitehead, "Xerxes' Fleet in Magnesia: The Anchorage at Sepias," *MM* 74:3 (August 1988): 283–87, and "Mooring," in *The Trireme Project: Operational Experience, 1987–90, Lessons Learnt,* ed. Timothy Shaw (Oxford: Oxbow Books, 1993), 95–98.

29. Impact of Hellesponter: Hdt. 7.188–91, with W. Kendrick Pritchett, "Xerxes' Fleet at the 'Ovens,'" *AJA* 67:1 (January 1963): 1–6 (with plates 1–2).

30. Persian losses in the storm: Hdt. 7.184.1–3, 185.1, 190–91; Diod. 11.12.3.

31. Hellenes waiting at Artemisium when remnants of Persian fleet reach Oreus channel: Hdt. 7.192.2–193.1. Leonidas at Thermopylae, Eurybiades at Artemisium: 7.177, 204–6, 8.2, 4–5, 42.2. Triaconter and another vessel deployed to maintain communications: 7.175.2, 8.21 with Manuel Arjona, "*Thallatta Lokrōn:* Plying the Sea of the Locrians," in *Topography and History of Ancient Epicnemidian Locris,* 361–92. Port at Alpenus: Hdt. 7.176, Demetrius of Callatis *FGrH* 85 F6. For three recent studies of the struggle that followed, see Cartledge, *Thermopylae;* Matthews, *The Battle of Thermopylae;* and Christopher A. Matthew, "Towards the Hot Gates: Events Leading to the Battle of Thermopylae" and "Was the Greek Defence of Thermopylae in 480 BC a Suicide Mission?" in *Beyond the Gates of Fire: New Perspectives on the Battle of Thermopylae,* ed. Christopher A. Matthew and Matthew Trundle (Barnsley, South Yorkshire: Pen & Sword, 2013), 1–26, 60–99. Note also Nicholas G. L. Hammond, "Sparta at Thermopylae," *Historia* 45:1 (1st Quarter 1996): 1–20.

32. Size of Greek fleet: Hdt. 8.2.1 with Burn, *PG,* 381–85. Contribution of Athenians, Plataeans, and native Chalcidians: 8.1, 46.2. Need to fully man ships: Chapter 1, note 36, above. With regard to the eighth book of Herodotus' *Inquiries,* I have found Herodotus, *Histories: Book VIII,* ed. A. M. Bowie (Cambridge: Cambridge University Press, 2007), quite valuable.

33. Size of contingents in Hellenic fleet, Athenian predominance: Hdt. 8.1. Eurybiades takes guidance from Themistocles: Diod. 11.12.4–6.

34. Skirmish between Persian triremes scouting and Greeks triremes on guard: Hdt. 7.179–82. Three Hellenic triremes captured: 7.180–82.

35. Eurybiades said to have pulled back to Chalcis: Hdt. 7.183.1. Some scholars doubt the historicity of the story: cf., e. g., Burn, *PG,* 387–88, 390–91, and Hignett, *XIG,* 161–67, with Green, *XS,* 123–24, and Lazenby, *DG,* 123–27.

36. Lookouts on Euboean mountains said to report damage done Persian armada: Hdt. 7.192.1.

37. Hellenes return to Artemisium: Hdt. 7.192.2.

38. Capture of Persian squadron: Hdt. 7.194–95.

39. Report of Xerxes' scout: Hdt. 7.208. Demaratus explains Spartan customs: 7.209.

40. Leonidas explores lay of the land and raids Malia: Polyaen. *Strat.* 1.32.3. Gates and Phocian wall: Hdt. 7.176.

41. Three hundred selected from among men with surviving sons: Hdt. 7.202, 205.2. One thousand Lacedaemonians: Diod. 11.4.2–5. Funeral games celebrated before departure: Plut. *Mor.* 866b–d.

42. Size of infantry contingents at Thermopylae: Hdt. 7.132.1, 202–3, 205.2–3, 233.1. Thebans drawn from minority hostile to the Mede: Diod. 11.4.7. Leontiades leads: Hdt. 7.205.2, 233. Offspring pro-Spartan: 7.233.2; Thuc. 2.2–6; Xen. *Hell.* 5.2.25–36, 4.7. Opuntian Locrians and Phocians: Hdt. 7.132.1, 203; Diod. 4.6–7. Number of former disputed: Diod. 11.4.7, Paus. 10.20.2.

43. Hellenic reinforcements expected: Hdt. 7.203, 206. Base in Boeotia to prevent outflanking: 8.40.2. Phocians and Locrians insist on holding the Hot Gates: 7.207.

44. Spartans become aware of Anopaea path: Hdt. 7.175.2 with Andrew Robert Burn, "Ther-

mopylai Revisited and Some Topographical Notes on Marathon and Plataiai," in *Greece and the Eastern Mediterranean in Ancient History and Prehistory: Studies Presented to Fritz Schachermeyr on His Eightieth Birthday*, ed. K. H. Kinzl (Berlin: Walter de Gruyter, 1977), 89–105 (at 98–103), and Paul W. Wallace, "The Anopaia Path at Thermopylai," *AJA* 84:1 (January 1980): 15–23. Also of value is W. Kendrick Pritchett, "New Light on Thermopylai," 203–13; "Herodotos and His Critics on Thermopylai," in Pritchett, *SAGT*, IV 176–210; and *The Liar School of Herodotus* (Amsterdam: J. C. Gieben, 1993), 298–328. Phocians guard: Hdt. 7.212.2. Locrians had betrayed Xerxes: 7.132.1, 203; Diod. 11.4.6–7.

45. See Balcer, *PCG*, 225–98.

46. Water in high summer not abundant in Achaea Phthiotis and Malia: Hdt. 7.196. River Spercheios and the region nearby: 7.198.2 with Yves Béquignon, *La Vallée du Spercheios des origines au IVe siècle: Études d'archéologie et de topographie* (Paris: E. de Boccard, 1937). Likely logistical problems: Matthews, *The Battle of Thermopylae*, 100–103, and Matthew, "Was the Greek Defence of Thermopylae in 480 BC a Suicide Mission?" 76–83. Delay as defeat: James Allan Stewart Evans, "Notes on Thermopylae and Artemisium," *Historia* 18:4 (August 1969): 389–406, reprinted in Evans, *BH*, 235–60. I visited the Thermopylae region in high summer in 1973 and again on 8 August 2014, examined the river Spercheios, and found its flow sufficient for most purposes, but not for the needs of a great army.

47. For the timing of the Carneia and the Olympic Games in 480, see Nicolas Richer, *La Religion des Spartiates: Croyances et cultes dans l'Antiquité* (Paris: Les Belles Lettres, 2012), 383–456 (esp. 413–19, 447–54), 547–59. For a different argument leading to a similar conclusion, see Gloria Ferrari, *Alcman and the Cosmos of Sparta* (Chicago: University of Chicago Press, 2008), 128–35. For precise information concerning the phase of the moon on any given date and the rising and setting of both the sun and moon at any particular location in the world on that particular date, see http://www.skyviewcafe.com/skyview.php.

48. Puzzle over location of Aphetae—within Gulf of Magnesia (Hdt. 7.193) or opposite Artemisium (8.4.1, 6.1).

49. Size of strand at Platanía: Bowen, "The Place That Beached a Thousand Ships," 358–61. Fleet divided among a number of anchorages: Diod. 11.12.5–6.

50. Arrival of Persian fleet: Hdt. 7.193.1–96.1, 8.4–6. Timetable too compressed: Burn, *PG*, 394–98; Hignett, *XIG*, 379 –85; and Lazenby, *DG*, 118–24.

51. Numerous footsoldiers with Persian fleet: Hdt. 8.4.1. Thirty Iranian marines on every trireme: 7.96.1, 184.2 with Muhammad A. Dandamayev, "Saka Soldiers on Ships," *IA* 17 (1982): 101–3. Cf. Plut. *Them.* 14.1–3. Greeks of Asia Minor and the Aegean islands provide crews for ships built and maintained by Great King: Diod. 11.3.7. This last passage will not bear the weight that Herman T. Wallinga puts on it. As Cawkwell, *GW*, 254–59 (with notes), makes abundantly clear, the evidence rules out the contention—first advanced in Wallinga, "The Ancient Persian Navy and Its Predecessors," *AchHist* 1 (1987): 47–78, and restated in *SSP*, 118–29, and *XGA*, 12–20, 39–40, 145–46—that Achaemenid Persia maintained a standing navy manned by subjects who were summoned from time to time for particular tasks.

52. Euboeans give Themistocles thirty talents to bribe Eurybiades and Adeimantus to stay: Hdt. 8.4.2–5.3.

53. Persian commander dispatches two hundred triremes to circumnavigate Euboea: Hdt. 8.6–7, Diod. 11.12.3.

54. Cf. Hignett, *XIG*, 386–92, and Cawkwell, *GW*, 93, who doubt that an attempt was made to circumnavigate Euboea, with Burn, *PG*, 394–99; Green, *XS*, 128–29: and Lazenby, *DG*, 120–23.

55. Xerxes' orders—no one to be allowed to escape: Hdt. 8.6.2. For the significance of this proverb, consider Xen. *Lac. Pol.* 13.2, Dio 39.45.4, and *Suda* s.v. *Purphóros* in light of Curt 3.3.9, Xen. *Cyr.* 8.3.11–12, Schol. Eur. *Phoen.* 1377, Zenob. *Paroem.* 5.34.

56. Persian admirals pause to take stock of losses: Hdt. 8.7.2.

57. Defection of Scyllias: Hdt. 8.8. Ancient Greek snorkel: Arist. *Part. An.* 659a8–13. Statue erected by Amphictyons at Delphi: Paus. 10.19.1–2.

58. At Themistocles' urging, Greeks issue late-afternoon challenge to Persians: Hdt. 8.9, Diod. 11.12.4–6. For the encounters that followed, see *AT*, 50–55.

59. Most of the Greek triremes partially decked: Thuc. 1.14.3, Plut. *Cim.* 12.2. Carry ten to

fourteen marines and a handful of archers: cf. ML no. 23 with Hdt. 7.96.1, 184.2; Plut. *Them.* 14.2. Had practiced defense against *diékplous:* Hdt. 8.9.

60. Function of *períplous:* cf. Ian Whitehead, "The Periplous," *Greece & Rome,* second ser. 34:2 (October 1987): 178–85. Greek defense effective, thirty Persian triremes lost, Antidorus defects: Hdt. 8.10–11, Diod. 11.12.4–6.

61. Xerxes' herald conveys offer: Diod. 11.5.5. Leonidas responds with challenge: Plut. *Mor.* 225c–d.

62. Medes and Kissians ordered to attack and bring enemy hoplites back alive: Hdt. 7.210.1. Brothers and sons of Marathon dead: Diod. 11.6.3–4. Hydarnes son of Hydarnes sent in with Immortals: Hdt. 7.210.2–211.2.

63. Dienekes' quip: Hdt. 7.226.

64. Persian spears shorter: Hdt. 7.61.1, 211.2. Effectiveness of hoplite shield wall: Diod. 11.7.1–3. Spartans feign flight: Hdt. 7.211.3. Persians, Medes, Cissians with Xerxes (and perhaps the other Iranians as well) wear body armor; some carry *gérra;* none bear *aspídes:* Hdt. 7.61.1, 62 read alongside 5.49.3, 97.1, in light of Chapter 4, note 50, above. Use of *gérra* to form barricade, Persians at Plataea *gumnêtes* and *ánoploi:* 9.61–63. See Scott Rusch, *Sparta at War: Strategy, Tactics, and Campaigns, 550–362 BC* (London: Frontline Books, 2011), 48. At Doriscus, the Assyrians and Egyptians are said to have borne *aspídes* of some sort: Hdt. 7.63.1. Note, in this connection, Xen. *An.* 1.8.9, *Cyr.* 7.1.33–34. The Paphlagonians, Phrygians, Mysians, and some other peoples are said to have borne "small *aspídes*": Hdt. 7.72.1, 73, 74.1, 76.1, 78.1, 79.1. The Thracians are said to have borne *péltai:* 7.75.1. Only the Lydians appear to have been armed in the Greek fashion: 7.74.1. Not one of these peoples, however, is mentioned with regard to the actual fighting at Thermopylae and Plataea. It is, of course, perfectly possible that the Medes and Cissians at Thermopylae were armed with *péltai* and "small *aspídes,*" as Diodorus Siculus (11.7.1–3), who is no doubt following Ephorus, asserts. There is iconographic evidence confirming that there were Iranian infantrymen who were equipped in this fashion: Stefan Bittner, *Tracht und Bewaffnung des persischen Heeres zur Zeit der Achaimeniden,* second edition (Munich: Verlag Klaus Friedrich, 1985), 158–66. Moreover, at *Cyr.* 2.1.9, 21, Xenophon employs the term *gérra* to denote *péltai;* and at 8.5.11 he distinguishes the shields borne by Cyrus' *gerrophóroi* as *mégala gérra.* Diodorus' testimony regarding the armament of the Great King's footsoldiers on this expedition receives no support from Herodotus or any other fifth-century source, but it may nonetheless be correct.

65. Greeks spell one another for two days straight: Hdt. 7.212. Xerxes deploys those thought bravest and most daring: Diod. 11.8.1–3.

66. Second Hellesponter: Hdt. 8.12, Diod. 13.1. Loss of fleet circumnaviating Euboea: Hdt. 8.13 with Hugh J. Mason and Malcolm B. Wallace, "Appius Claudius Pulcher and the Hollows of Euboia," *Hesperia* 41:1 (January–March 1972): 128–40.

67. Persians make no move second morning: Hdt. 8.14.1.

68. Fifty-three more Athenian triremes arrive with news circumnavigating fleet destroyed, skirmish near end of day: Hdt. 8.14.

69. Ephialtes tells Xerxes of Anopaea path, offers himself as a guide: Hdt. 7.213–14, Diod. 8.4.

70. Immortals take Anopaea path: Hdt. 7.215.1–217.1.

71. Persian admiral orders full-scale attack: Hdt. 8.15.

72. Leonidas told Immortals on Anopaea path: Hdt. 7.219.1.

73. Ephorus' tale of desertion of Tyrrhastiadas of Cumae: Diod. 11.8.4–5. Early breakfast and supposed suicide mission: Diod. 11.9.1–11.6, Plut. *Mor.* 866a, Justin 2.11.12–18.

74. See Michael A. Flower, "Simonides, Ephorus, and the Battle of Thermopylae," *CQ* n.s. 48:2 (1998): 365–79.

75. Phocians on Anopaea path panic and flee: Hdt. 7.217.2–218.3.

76. I visited the site in 1973 and again on 8 August 2014 and confirmed my initial impression that descent from atop Mount Kallidromos would have taken a number of hours.

77. See Chapter 7, note 65, below.

78. Spartans and Thespians elect to stay and die, Thebans supposedly retained as hostages: Hdt. 7.219–22. Mycenaeans said to have stayed as well: Paus. 10.20.2. Plutarch claims Thebans volunteer to stay: *Mor.* 865d.

79. Xerxes orders mid-morning attack: Hdt. 7.223.1. Persian triremes form crescent to envelop Greeks: 8.16.1.

80. Even match at Artemisium, size of Persian fleet produces collisions: Hdt. 8.15–16.

81. Historian Sosylus of Lacedaemon tutors Hannibal in Greek: Nep. *Hann.* 13.3. Tale told regarding Heracleides of Mylasa and defense against *diékplous* at Artemisium: Sosylus of Lacedaemon *FGrH* 176 F1.3 with Hignett, *XIG*, 393–96. The Athenians employed the same tactics as a defense against the *diékplous* three-quarters of a century later at Arginousae: Xen. *Hell.* 1.6.29–30.

82. Pyrrhic victory for Greeks at Artemisium: Hdt. 8.15–18. Success of Egyptian squadron under Achaemenes: 7.97, 8.17. On the importance of the Egyptians in this war, see Albert Deman, "Présence des Égyptiens dans la seconde guerre médique (480–79 av. J.-Chr.)," *CE* 60:119–20 (1985): 56–74.

83. All but Thebans fight to the death at Thermopylae: Hdt. 7.223.2–227.1, 233.

84. Lion and Thermopylae epitaph: Hdt. 7.225.2, 228 with John Dillery, "Reconfiguring the Past: Thyrea, Thermopylae and Narrative Patterns in Herodotus," *AJPh* 117:2 (Summer 1996): 217–54.

85. Fate of those in Leonidas' bodyguard who miss the battle: Hdt. 7.229–32, 9.71.2–4.

86. News from Abronichus spurs withdrawal from Artemisium already planned: Hdt. 8.18, 21.

87. Plutarch visits Artemisium: *Them.* 8.3–6.

Chapter 7. Salamis

Epigraph: Aesch. *Pers.* 355–60.

1. Roaring fires as subterfuge: Polyaen. *Strat.* 4.18.2; Frontin. *Strat.* 1.5.24, 2.5.17. Nighttime withdrawal of the Greeks from Artemisium: Hdt. 8.19–21.

2. Plataeans eager to evacuate their families: Hdt. 8.44.1. Chalcidians and Eretrians probably also eager: 8.1. Failure to take precautions: 8.4.2, 20.

3. Greek fleet at Salamis for final evacuation of Attica: Hdt. 8.40–41, Diod. 11.13.3–4, Paus. 2.31.7, Frontin. *Strat.* 1.3.6. See Plut. *Them.* 10. Cavalrymen dedicate bridles on acropolis: *Cim.* 5.1–3.

4. Some Athenians hope for stand in Boeotia: Hdt. 8.40.2, Thuc. 1.74.2, Plut. *Them.* 9.3–5.

5. Peloponnesus as acropolis of Greece: Strabo 8.1.3. Isthmus wall: Hdt. 8.71–72, 74.1; Aen. Tact. 32.3; Isoc. 4.93. Likely trajectory: Diod. 11.16.3. Archaeology: James Wiseman, *The Land of the Ancient Corinthians* (Göteborg: P. Åström, 1978), 59–64.

6. Peloponnesians doubt effectiveness of fleet: Hdt. 8.74.1. Themistocles has messages left for Ionians and Carians at watering places urging defection: 8.19, 22.1–2; Plut. *Them.* 9.1–2. Supposedly scratched on rocks: Hdt. 8.22.1. Chalk as option: 8.27.2–4. Attempt to sow distrust in Persian fleet: 8.22.3.

7. Xerxes on Greek propensity for valuing guest-friends over fellow citizens: Hdt. 7.237.2–3. Citizen of Histiaea tells Persians of Greek withdrawal: 8.23.1.

8. Persians check Artemisium, storm Histiaea, loot coastal villages: Hdt. 8.23, Diod. 11.13.5. List of benefactors: Esther 6:1–2, Thuc. 1.129.3.

9. Tour of Thermopylae battlefield, Persian losses concealed: Hdt. 8.24–25.

10. Megabates commands Persian fleet, Boeotian Salgoneus pilots fleet down channel between Euboea and the mainland: Hdt. 8.66.1, Diod. 11.14.5, Strabo 1.1.17, 9.2.8–9.

11. Euripus and surroundings: Pericles B. Georges, "Saving Herodotus' Phenomena: The Oracles and the Events of 480 B.C.," *ClAnt* 5:1 (April 1986): 14–59 (at 46–49). Salgoneus executed: Strabo 1.1.17, 9.2.8–9. South of Euripus, Attica and Euboea ravaged: Hdt. 8.66.1, Diod. 11.14.5.

12. Thessalian-Phocian quarrel: Hdt. 7.176.4, 8.27–28; Paus. 10.1.3–11; Plut. *Mor.* 244b–d. Degree of bitterness: Hdt. 8.29–30.

13. Thessalians offer Phocians protection at a price: Hdt. 8.27.1, 29.

14. Phocians defiant: Hdt. 8.30.

15. Persians in Phocis: Hdt. 8.31–33, Diod. 11.14.1–2.

16. The various possible routes, see W. Kendrick Pritchett, "Passes from Thermopylai to Elateia" and "Route of the Persians after Thermopylai," in *SAGT*, IV 123–75, 211–33. With regard to the suitability of the Dhema pass, see, in context, Chapter 6, note 22, above.

17. Persian unit dispatched toward Delphi: Hdt. 8.34.1–35.1.

18. Greeks suspect treasures at Delphi the aim: Hdt. 8.35.2, Diod. 11.14.2.

19. Demigods defend Delphi: Hdt. 8.34–39, Diod. 11.14.2–3.

20. Elegy on trophy at temple of Athena: Diod. 11.14.4 with Benjamin D. Merritt, "The Persians at Delphi," *Hesperia* 16:2 (April–June 1947): 58–62.

21. Macedonian envoys smooth Xerxes' way into Boeotia: Hdt. 8.34. Attaginus leader of narrow oligarchy at Thebes: Hdt. 9.15.4–16.5, 86.1, 88; Thuc. 3.62.2–3; Paus. 7.10.2. Demaratus makes him a *xénos* of Xerxes: Plut. *Mor.* 864f. Thebans direct Persian units to plunder and burn Thespiae and Plataea: Hdt. 8.50.2.

22. Thermopylae to Thebes in a day and a half: Plut. *Mor.* 864f.

23. Rapid Persian pace: Hdt. 8.66.1–67.1 with Hignett, *XIG*, 193–96. As Frank J. Frost, *Plutarch's Themistocles: A Historical Commentary* (Princeton, NJ: Princeton University Press, 1980), 123–26, points out, Herodotus' account has the battle of Salamis following quickly after the collapse of Greek resistance at Thermopylae. He finds this implausible and therefore dates the Carneia, the Olympic Games, and the crisis at Thermopylae to August 480. For reasons indicated in my narrative, I see no reason to jettison the sources.

24. Xerxes in Attica: Hdt. 8.50–55. Five hundred Athenians captured: 9.99.2. Location of Aglaurus sanctuary: George S. Dontas, "The True Aglaurion," *Hesperia* 52:1 (January–March 1983): 48–63. Damage done the acropolis: Ione Mylonas Shear, "The Western Approach to the Athenian Akropolis," *JHS* 119 (1999): 86–127 (at 119–20), and Jeffrey M. Hurwit, *The Athenian Acropolis: History, Mythology, and Archaeology from the Neolithic to the Present* (Cambridge: Cambridge University Press, 1999), 135–36.

25. Stated aim of invasion: cf. Hdt. 8.102.3 with 5.105.2. Peisistratids and other exiles conduct traditional sacrifices: 8.54–55.

26. Persian fleet reaches Phalerum Bay: Hdt. 8.66.1.

27. Xerxes' losses made up by forces gathered on the way: Hdt. 8.66.2–67.1. Many islanders refuse support or join Hellenic League: 8.46, 48. Parians wait to see who is victorious: 8.67.1.

28. Demaratus quotes Chilon on Cythera: Hdt. 7.234–35.

29. Achaemenes warns Xerxes not to divide his fleet: Hdt. 7.236–37.

30. Herodotus' Artemisia defames Egyptians, Cypriots, Cilicians, and Pamphylians: 8.68α–γ. Egyptians win prize for valor at Artemisium: 8.17.

31. Artemisia recommends patient waiting or advance on Peloponnesus: Hdt. 8.68γ. Xerxes trusts in effect of his own gaze: 8.69. Brother Ariabignes made chief admiral: cf. 8.89.1 with Diod. 11.18.3–5.

32. Persians approach Salamis channel, deploy for battle: Hdt. 8.70.1.

33. Reserve fleet at Pogon, joined by ships from Leucas, Ambracia, Croton: Hdt. 8.47, Paus. 10.9.2.

34. Corcyraeans cite Etesian winds as excuse: Hdt. 7.168. Ships from Ambracia and Leucas round Malea: 8.45.

35. Catalogue of ships gathered at Salamis: Hdt. 8.4, 43–48. Numbers do not add up: 7.168, 8.1, 11.3, 42–48, 82; Diod. 11.15.1.

36. Aeschylus at Salamis: Ion of Chios *FGrH* 392 F7, Paus. 1.14.5. Size of Greek fleet: Aesch. *Pers.* 338–40.

37. Story that grew in the telling: Thuc. 1.74.1. Achaemenes' estimate: Hdt. 7.236.2.

38. Peloponnesians favor withdrawal of fleet to Isthmus: Hdt. 8.49, Diod. 11.15.2–3.

39. News that Attica aflame: Hdt. 8.50.1. Panic and preparation for withdrawal from Salamis: 8.56. Mnesiphilus once a candidate for ostracism: Rudi Thomsen, *The Origins of Ostracism: A Synthesis* (Copenhagen: Gyldendal, 1972), 93–94, and Stefan Brenne, *Ostrakismos und Prominenz in Athen: Attische Bürger des 5. Jhs. v. Chr. auf den Ostraka* (Vienna: A. Holzhausens, 2001), 243–45. Mentor to Themistocles: Plut. *Them.* 2.6–7. Warns withdrawal to isthmus will lead to breakup of fleet: Hdt. 8.57. Themistocles repeats to Eurybiades: 8.58.

40. Themistocles argues for staging battle in Salamis channel: Hdt. 8.59–60.

41. Athenian triremes designed for speed and agility: Plut. *Cim.* 12.2. Heavier and more sluggish than Persian triremes: Hdt. 8.60α with John S. Morrison and Roderick T. Williams, *Greek Oared Ships, 900–322 B.C.* (Cambridge: Cambridge University Press, 1968), 134–35 and the secondary literature cited in Chapter 5, note 13, above. Relative inexperience of officers important: Thuc. 1.142.5–143.2.

42. Themistocles argues narrows more favorable to Greeks than open sea: Hdt. 8.59–60.

43. Threat of Athenian departure for Italy prevents immediate withdrawal from Salamis: Hdt. 8.62–63, Diod. 11.15.2–4, Plut. *Them.* 11.2–6. I see no reason to doubt that Adeimantus and his compatriots took the stand that they reportedly took. In the circumstances, its propriety could easily have seemed obvious.

44. Earthquake and dispatch of triaconter to Aegina for images of Aeacus and Aeacidae: Hdt. 8.64.

45. Persian fleet's deployment rekindles Greek fears: Hdt. 8.70.

46. Xerxes' mole, Greek response: Ctesias *FGrH* 688 F13.30, Aristodemos *FGrH* 104 F1.1.2, Strabo 9.1.13–14 with Burn, *PG,* 436–40. Water level: W. Kendrick Pritchett, "Towards a Restudy of the Battle of Salamis," *AJA* 63:3 (July 1959): 251–62, and "Salamis Revisited," in *SAGT,* I 94–102. Aim to introduce footsoldiers onto Salamis: Hdt. 8.97.1.

47. Dikaios son of Theokydes sees cloud of dust near Eleusis: Hdt. 8.65. Possible Persian cavalry and footsoldiers on road to Megara and Isthmus of Corinth: 8.71.1.

48. News of construction of isthmus wall: Hdt. 8.71, 74.1. Evident commanders will vote to withdraw from Salamis: 8.74, Diod. 11.16.1, Plut. *Them.* 12.1–2.

49. Various stories told concerning identity of Sicinnus and his mission to Phalerum: Aesch. *Pers.* 353–73, Hdt. 8.75, Plut. *Them.* 12.3–4, Diod. 11.17.1–2, Ath. 14.630b. Note also Polyaen. *Strat.* 1.30.2.. Cf. Hignett, *XIG,* 403–8, and Green, *XS,* 177–83, who evidence in quite different ways greater skepticism concerning the story told by Herodotus than I can countenance, with Lazenby, *DG,* 167–70, and Wallinga, *XGA,* 47–86. For a dramatic and largely persuasive reconstruction of Themistocles' stratagem and of the battle that followed, see Barry Strauss, *The Battle of Salamis: The Naval Encounter That Saved Greece—and Western Civilization* (New York: Simon and Schuster, 2004). Note Victor Parker, "Herodotus' Use of Aeschylus' *Persae* as a Source for the Battle of Salamis," *SO* 82 (2007): 2–29, and see Georges Roux, "Éschyle, Hérodote, Diodore, Plutarque raconte la bataille de Salamine," *BCH* 98:1 (1974): 51–94. See also *AT,* 55–61.

50. Sicinnus' message to the Persians: Hdt. 8.75.2–3.

51. Sicinnus tells Persians Greeks intent on slipping off that night: Aesch. *Pers.* 353–60, Plut. *Them.* 12.3–5. Other sources silent on question: Thuc. 1.74.1, 137.4; Diod. 11.17.1.

52. Themistocles the Athenian Odysseus: Plut. *Mor.* 869f.

53. Xerxes' preliminary orders for battle of Salamis: Aesch. *Pers.* 361–73. Egyptian contingent sent to block egress from Gulf of Eleusis: Diod. 11.17.2. Note Plut. *Them.* 12.5–7, *Arist.* 8.2–6. Once two hundred triremes: Hdt. 7.89.2, Diod. 11.3.7.

54. Aeschylus on Egyptian casualties: *Pers.* 311–13. Mardonius seems to imply Egyptian flight at Salamis: Hdt. 8.100.4.

55. Mardonius wants Egyptian marines left in Greece for own use: Hdt. 9.32.

56. Plutarch on contingent tasked with blocking egress from Gulf of Eleusis: *Them.* 12.5–8, *Arist.* 8.2–6. Herodotus on wing sent westward to circle about Salamis: Hdt. 8.76.1.

57. Psyttaleia the modern Lipsokoutali: Paul W. Wallace, "Psyttaleia and the Trophies of the Battle of Salamis," *AJA* 73:3 (July 1969): 293–303. Persian troops landed on the island: Aesch. *Pers.* 441–53, Hdt. 8.76.1–2. Four hundred in number: Paus. 1.36.2.

58. Persian fleet deployed in discrete ethnic groups at southern entrances to Salamis channel: Hdt. 8.76; Diod. 11.17.2; Plut. *Them.* 12.5–6.

59. Anxious, restless, exhausting night for Persian forces at sea: Aesch. *Pers.* 374–85, Hdt. 8.76.3.

60. Aristeides tells Themistocles of Persian blockade: Hdt. 8.78–79; Plut. *Them.* 12.6, *Arist.* 8.2–6. Themistocles' aim in recall of Aristeides: *Arist.* 8.1, *Them.* 11.1. Persians offer bribe: *Suda* s.v. *Aristeídes, Dareikoús.* Some think the story concerning Aristeides apocryphal: cf. Hignett, *XIG,* 408–11, and Green, *XS,* 183–85, who do, with Lazenby, *DG,* 175–83.

61. Themistocles reveals to Aristeides own role in bringing on Persian blockade: Hdt. 8.80; Plut. *Them.* 12.6–8, *Arist.* 8.5. The two shake hands, pledge to set aside rivalry until Mede defeated: Polyaen. *Strat.* 1.31.

62. Defector from Tenos confirms Aristeides' testimony: Hdt. 8.81–82, Plut. *Them.* 12.8. Tenos treated as member of Hellenic League after the war: Hdt. 8.82.1, ML no. 27, Paus. 5.23.1–2.

63. Diodorus reports Ionians send Samian swimmer to warn: 11.17.3–4.

64. Date of Salamis: Plut. *Cam.* 19.6, Polyaen. *Strat.* 3.11.2. Xerxes' perch: Hdt. 8.69.2, 86, 88.2, 89.2, 90.4; Phanodemus *FGrH* 325 F24; Diod. 11.18.2–3; Plut. *Them.* 13.1.

65. Xerxes able to see and be seen: Aesch. *Pers.* 466–67; Hdt. 8.69.2, 85.2–86, 88.2, 89.2, 90.4; Diod. 11.18.3; Plut. *Them.* 13.1. Use of flags to convey orders: Polyaen. *Strat.* 8.53.1, 3. See, for example, Diod. 13.46.3, 50.3, 67, 77.4.

66. Themistocles' speech, images of Aeacus and offspring arrive from Aegina: Hdt. 8.83.

67. Phoenicians ranged against Athenians, Ionians opposite Lacedaemonians: Hdt. 8.85.1. Persians row up the channel at night: Lazenby, *DG,* 180–90, and Strauss, *The Battle of Salamis,* 137–39.

68. Aeschylus' testimony on the beginning of the battle: *Pers.* 386–98 with Burn, *PG,* 456–57, and Wallinga, *XGA,* 120–22, who suggest that, if the Persians had fully penetrated the narrows, they would have mounted a surprise attack on the Athenian fleet while it was still drawn up on the shore. Note also *AT,* 59–60, and Anthony Podlecki, *The Political Background of Aeschylean Tragedy* (Ann Arbor: University of Michigan Press, 1966), 8–9. Cf. Christopher Pelling, "Aeschylus' *Persae* and History," in *Greek Tragedy and the Historian,* ed. Christopher Pelling (Oxford: Clarendon Press, 1997), 1–19, who is surely right in supposing that Aeschylus' audience would have allowed him considerable poetic license, but who also acknowledges that verisimilitude was expected of him. I would suggest that, when it came to the battle itself as it was experienced by those in his audience, verisimilitude required accuracy.

69. Early stages of the battle of Salamis: cf. Diod. 11.18.1–19.2, with Hdt. 8.83.2–84.2, 89.1.

70. Plight of Persians in the narrows: Plut. *Them.* 15.4. Corinthians simulate flight: Hdt. 8.94. For a different hypothesis, see Burn, *PG,* 457–58. For the hoisting of sails as a sign of flight, see Hdt. 6.14.2. Cf. Thuc. 7.24.2, 8.28.1; Xen. *Hell.* 2.1.29. Persian advantages become disadvantages: John S. Morrison, "The Greek Ships at Salamis and the Diekplous," *JHS* 111 (1991): 196–200.

71. Ameinias takes out Ariabignes, Persian forces decapitated, confusion reigns: Hdt. 8.84–92, Diod. 11.18.3–6, Plut. *Them.* 14.3–4.

72. Persian triremes top-heavy: Hdt. 8.118.1–4, Plut. *Them.* 14.1–3 with Lucien Basch, "Phoenician Oared Ships," *MM* 55:2 (May 1969): 139–62 and 55:3 (August 1969): 227–45. In this connection, see James Beresford, *The Ancient Sailing Season* (Leiden: Brill, 2013), passim (esp. 134–57).

73. Themistocles takes advantage of stiff breeze up channel: Plut. *Them.* 14.3 with Jamie Morton, *The Role of the Physical Environment in Ancient Greek Seafaring* (Leiden: Brill, 2001), 51–53, 56–61, 90–99. For a comparable example, see Thuc. 2.84.2–3.

74. Fleeing Phoenicians and Cypriots run afoul of Cilician, Pamphylian, and Lycian ships coming up the channel: Diod. 11.19.1–2.

75. Aeginetans pick off enemy triremes in flight: Hdt. 8.91. Awarded prize for valor: 8.93.1. Polycritus, son of the Aeginetan Crius who had defied Cleomenes, singled out: 6.50, 73, 8.93.1. Taunts Themistocles: 8.92.

76. Xerxes' presence spurs subordinates on: Hdt. 8.86. Zeal results in head-on collisions with own ships: 8.89.2.

77. Samians Theomestor and Phylakon named benefactors of the King: Hdt. 8.85.2.

78. Xerxes turns in fury on Phoenician captains: Hdt. 8.90.1–4, Diod. 11.19.4.

79. Plutarch quotes Simonides on exploits of Democritus of Naxos: *Mor.* 869c. Had persuaded Naxian crews to defect with triremes to the Hellenes: Hdt. 8.46.3. Corinthians distinguish themselves: consider 8.94 in light of ML no. 24, Plut. *Mor.* 870b–71b.

80. Battle from dawn to dusk: Plut. *Them.* 15.4 with Aesch. *Pers.* 386–91, 428.

81. Battle becomes melee: Hdt. 8.90.1, 91. Confusion reigns: 8.95. Aristeides ferries hoplites to Psyttaleia, Xerxes tears robes: Aesch. *Pers.* 454–69 with Hdt. 8.95 and Plut. *Arist.* 9.1. If, like Burn, *PG,* 466–67, 474–75, and Lazenby, *DG,* 195, I do not share the skepticism voiced by Charles W. Fornara, "The Hoplite Achievement at Psyttaleia," *JHS* 86 (1966): 51–54, and Green, *XS,* 196–97, concerning the role attributed by Herodotus and Plutarch to Aristeides and the hoplites with him on Salamis, it is in part because I do not think Aeschylus' dramatic description of the Greeks' seizure of Psyttaleia incompatible with the tale told by Herodotus and Plutarch and in part because the argument these two scholars articulate presupposes that the distinction between hoplites and seamen at this time or quite soon thereafter possessed a political charge that it is not likely to have acquired until considerably later.

82. Messenger dispatched by Xerxes to Susa at end of battle: Hdt. 8.98. Report put by Aeschylus in messenger's mouth: *Pers.* 409–32.

83. Majority of participants in battle apt to know little: Thuc. 7.44.1. Greeks haul wrecks up on Salamis, prepare for renewal of battle: Hdt. 8.96. Forty Greek triremes lost: Diod. 11.19.3. Greek oarsmen swim to Salamis: Hdt. 8.89.1.

84. Iranian marines unable to swim: Hdt. 8.89.1. Two hundred ships destroyed, more captured, some Phoenician ships flee Xerxes' anger: Diod. 11.19.3–4.

85. Xerxes' comment to Artemisia: Hdt. 8.87–88. Suit of Greek armor to her, distaff and spindle to Persian admiral: Polyaen. *Strat.* 8.53.2, *Excerpta* 53.4. See Rosaria Vignolo Munson, "Artemisia in Herodotus," *ClAnt* 7:1 (April 1988): 91–106.

86. Ostentatious preparations for renewing fight, building of mole fool nearly everyone: Hdt. 8.97.

87. Decision of Xerxes to return to Asia Minor: Hdt. 8.100–103. Admirals lead fleet out at night toward Hellespont: 8.107. Bridges intact: Aesch. *Pers.* 734–36. Swept away by storm: Hdt. 8.117.1.

88. Artemisia ferries bastards of the King to Ephesus: Hdt. 8.103–4. Mardonius escorts Xerxes to Boeotia: 8.113.1.

89. Withdrawal from Attica marked by eclipse: Hdt. 9.10.3.

90. Xerxes and Mardonius part company in Boeotia: Hdt. 8.113. Trek of 550 miles in 45 days: 8.115.1. Half the time allotted for the march from the Hellespont to Athens: 8.51.1. Gifts to city of Abdera: 8.120. Crosses to Asia by ship: 8.117.1.

91. Retreating troops suffer from famine and cold: Aesch. *Pers.* 482–514; Hdt. 8.115, 117; Justin 2.13.12.

92. See Beresford, *The Ancient Sailing Season,* 1–212. This was especially true for galleys and less so for sailing ships.

Chapter 8. Plataea and Mycale

Epigraph: Pind. *Pyth.* 1.76.

1. Greeks fail to catch Achaemenid fleet: Hdt. 8.108.1.

2. Eurybiades chooses not to pursue Persians past Andros-Euboea gap: Hdt. 8.108.2–4.

3. Themistocles restates Eurybiades' argument against pursuit: Hdt. 8.109.2–4. Aristeides' advice: Plut. *Them.* 16.2–4, *Arist.* 9.5–6, *Mor.* 185b. In this connection, see Jenifer Neils, "Salpinx, Snake, and Salamis: The Political Geography of the Pella Hydria," *Hesperia* 82:4 (October–December 2013): 595–613.

4. Identity of messenger Themistocles sends on second occasion to Xerxes disputed: Hdt. 8.110.2; Diod. 11.19.5; Plut. *Them.* 16.5, *Arist.* 9.5–6.

5. Content of Themistocles' second message to Xerxes disputed: Hdt. 8.109.5–110.3; Diod. 11.19.5–6; Nep. *Them.* 5.1–2; Plut. *Them.* 16.5, *Arist.* 9.5–6.

6. Themistocles' later flight to the court of Artaxerxes: Thuc. 1.135.2–138.2. Had long desired refuge: Hdt. 8.109.5.

7. Attempts to extort money from Carystians, Parians, and Andrians: Hdt. 8.111–12.

8. Cost of sustaining a fleet: Vincent Gabrielsen, "Naval Warfare: Its Economic and Social Impact on Ancient Greek Cities," in *War as a Cultural and Social Force: Essays on Warfare in Antiquity,* ed. Tønnes Bekker-Nielsen and Lise Hannestad (Copenhagen: Det kongelige Danske Videnskabernes Selskab, 2001), 72–89.

9. As agreed at Athens (Hdt. 8.100–104, 107.1), Mardonius selects footsoldiers (largely Iranian) for following year's campaign: 7.61–62, 8.113.2–3; Diod. 11.19.6. Egyptian marines already chosen: Hdt. 8.17, 9.32.

10. Xerxes' response to Spartan herald demanding satisfaction for killing of Leonidas: Hdt. 8.114.

11. Greek votive offerings in wake of Salamis: Hdt. 8.121–22; Paus. 2.1.7, 5.11.5, 10.14.5–6.

12. Themistocles honored at isthmus with everyone's second vote: Hdt. 8.123. His wisdom the talk of Greece: 8.124.1. Simonides celebrates Themistocles' judgment and astuteness: Plut. *Them.* 15.4.

13. Themistocles honored at Sparta: Hdt. 8.124.2–3, Thuc. 1.74.1, Plut. *Them.* 17.3, Ael. Aristid. 46.289 with Borimir Jordan, "The Honors for Themistocles after Salamis," *AJPh* 109:4 (Winter 1988): 547–71.

14. Themistocles resented, thought insufferable: Hdt. 8.125, Plut. *Them.* 22.1–3. Temple of Artemis the Best Counsellor found: Johannis Threpsiades and Eugene Vanderpool, "Themistokles' Sanctuary of Artemis Aristoboule," *AD* 19 (1964): 26–36, and Frank J. Frost, *Plutarch's Themistocles: A Historical Commentary* (Princeton, NJ: Princeton University Press, 1980), 184–85.

15. Monthly review of magisterial conduct in fourth-century Athens: Arist. *Ath. Pol.* 43.2–4.

16. Themistocles stripped of generalship, replaced with Xanthippus: Diod. 11.27.3.

17. Athenian practice of holding elections in sixth prytany: Arist. *Ath. Pol.* 44.4.

18. Compatriots treat Themistocles like a plane tree: Plut. *Them.* 18.4. Cf. Anthony J. Podlecki, *The Life of Themistocles: A Critical Survey of the Literary and Archaeological Evidence* (Montreal: McGill-Queen's University Press, 1975), 30, who finds it hard to believe that the Athenians would have turned on the victor at Salamis, with Hignett, *XIG*, 16, 275–78; Green, *XS*, 211–16; and Lazenby, *DG*, 204, 208–10, who are less inclined to incredulity. Note Burn, *PG*, 490–92, and Frost, *Plutarch's Themistocles*, 166–68.

19. Calculations of Mardonius and Xerxes: Diod. 11.27.3–28.1, Hdt. 8.140α–β.

20. Mys sent to consult Phocian and Boeotian oracles: Hdt. 8.133–35. After Salamis, Delphi with the Hellenes: 8.114.

21. Mardonius sends Alexander son of Amyntas with offer for Athenians: Hdt. 8.140α–β.

22. Alexander allowed to make pitch only after Spartan embassy arrives: Hdt. 8.141.

23. Spartans aware of anger Athenians direct at them: Diod. 11.27.3–28.1.

24. Eurybiades commoner: Hdt. 8.42.2. Leotychidas naval commander for 479: 8.131.

25. Hellenic fleet initially smaller than Peloponnesian and Aeginetan contingents at Salamis: cf. Hdt. 8.131.1 with 8.43, 46.1. Strattis longtime tyrant of Chios: 4.138.2. Chiot appeal brings Leotychidas to Delos, fears to go further: 8.132.

26. Athenian fleet as bargaining chip: cf. Hignett, *XIG*, 249–54, who is skeptical, with Green, *XS*, 227–29; John P. Barron, "The Liberation of Greece," in *CAH*, IV^2 592–622 (at 592–97); and Lazenby, *DG*, 208–9.

27. Spartans call Athenian bluff: Hdt. 8.142.

28. Aristeides frames Athenian response to Alexander son of Amyntas: Plut. *Arist.* 10.1–6. Warning not to return: Hdt. 8.143. Motion that priests curse Medizers: Plut. *Arist.* 10.6. Statement of Panhellenic loyalty, call for Spartans to confront Mardonius in Boeotia: Hdt. 8.144 with the preface to Part I, note 20, above.

29. Athenian fleet used to evacuate Attica: Hdt. 9.3, 6. Mardonius' advance: 9.1.

30. Thebans urge patience, bribery: Hdt. 9.2. Mardonius desires to retake Athens: Hdt. 9.3.1. For what follows, I have found the philological and historical commentary in Herodotus, *Histories: Book IX,* ed. Michael A. Flower and John Marincola (Cambridge: Cambridge University Press, 2002), quite valuable.

31. Mardonius combines invasion of Attica with bribery: Diod. 11.28.3.

32. Herodotus suspects gold disbursed: 9.5.2.

33. Attica evacuated: Hdt. 9.6. Most at Salamis with ships: 9.3.2. Mardonius' emissary Mourychides from the Hellespont: 9.4. Possibly from Sigeum since there were Athenians of that name: Russell Meiggs, "The Dating of Fifth-Century Attic Inscriptions," *JHS* 86 (1966): 86–98 (at 95).

34. Mourychides' offer spurned, fate of Lycidas and family: Hdt. 9.5.

35. Mardonius hopes Athenians sober about prospects: Hdt. 9.4.2. Embassy to Sparta demanding help: 9.6.

36. Aristeides sends Cimon, Xanthippus, and Myronides to Sparta: Plut. *Arist.* 10.7–9. A Xanthippus archon for 479/8: Arist. *Ath. Pol.* 22.5. Myronides a general for 479: Plut. *Arist.* 20.1. Cimon a general in 478: 23.1–2, *Cim.* 6 with Davies, *APF* no. 8429 §§ X–XII.

37. Embassy to Spartan conveys threat: Hdt. 9.6. Megarian and Plataean ambassadors join in plea for battle on Thriasian plain: 9.7. Embassy to Delphi concerning battle in that location: Plut. *Arist.* 11.3–6.

38. Ephors promise reply, then repeatedly postpone: Hdt. 9.8.1. Idomeneus of Lampsacus mentions embassy by Aristeides: Plut. *Arist.* 10.7–9 with Hignett, *XIG*, 283–84; Green, *XS*, 230–31; and Barron, "The Liberation of Greece," 596–97. Cf. Lazenby, *DG*, 213–14.

39. Advice of Chileos; sudden, secret dispatch of Pausanias the regent with five thousand

Spartiates, an equal number of *períoikoi* sent a day later: Hdt. 9.8–11. Chileos at the founding of the Hellenic League: Plut. *Them.* 6.5. With regard to Dorieus, see Rahe, *SR,* Chapter 4.

40. Xanthippus and Athenian fleet appear at Delos: Diod. 11.34.2.

41. Spartans secretive: Thuc. 5.68.2. March by night toward isthmus via Oresthasion in Maenalia: Hdt. 9.10.1, 11.2. Better road for carts: Thuc. 5.64.1–3, 72.3 with Hdt. 9.25.1 and Lazenby, *DG,* 217. Later uses of this route: Xen. *Hell.* 6.5.10–11, 7.5.9. Argive promise to obstruct Spartan advance: Hdt. 9.12.1. Location of Oresthasion and its strategic importance: Rahe, *SR,* Chapter 4 (esp. note 29).

42. Thirty-five thousand helots accompany the Spartans: Hdt. 9.10.1, Plut. *Arist.* 10.8.

43. Argives alert Mardonius to Spartan march: Hdt. 9.12. He redeploys to Boeotia: 9.13.

44. Part of Persian army dispatched to Megarid: Hdt. 9.14.

45. Boeotian guides lead Mardonius to Tanagra, then Scolus in territory of Thebes: Hdt. 9.15.1–2. Stockade built, intact a century thereafter: Xen. *Hell.* 5.4.49, *Ages.* 22. Note Paus. 9.4.4. Meant as refuge: Hdt. 9.15.2–3. Meant to protect Persian headquarters and baggage train: Plut. *Arist.* 11.2. Army deployed on north bank of Asopus opposite Erythrae, Hysiae, and Plataea: Hdt. 9.15.3.

46. Size of Mardonius' army disputed: Hdt. 9.32, Ctesias *FGrH* 688 F13.28. Stockade adequate for seventy thousand footsoldiers and ten thousand cavalrymen: Burn, *PG,* 511.

47. Size and accomplishments of army of Artabazus: Hdt. 8.126–29, 9.66, 77.2. He harbors doubts about Mardonius' strategy: 9.41. Operates independently on battlefield: 9.66.

48. Experience of Phocian contingent in Persian army: Hdt. 9.17–18. Herodotus guesses infantry from Thessaly, Malia, Locris, and Boeotia number fifty thousand: 9.32.2. Attaginus of Thebes holds dinner for Mardonius and officers: 9.15.4–16.5.

49. Phocian irregulars raid supply trains of Mardonius: Hdt. 9.31.5.

50. Peloponnesians and Athenians gather at Eleusis, Xanthippus and triremes head to Delos: Hdt. 9.19.1–2.

51. Interpretation of oracle describing Thriasian plain: Plut. *Arist.* 11.3–8. Roads crossing Cithaeron: Eugene Vanderpool, "Roads and Forts in Northeastern Attica," *CSCA* 11 (1978): 227–45.

52. Pausanias reconnoiters from heights above Erythrae: Hdt. 9.19.3–25.1. For the topography, see W. Kendrick Pritchett, "New Light on Plataia," *AJA* 61:1 (January 1957): 9–28; "Plataia Revisited," in Pritchett, *SAGT,* I 103–21; "The Roads of Plataiai," in Pritchett, *SAGT,* IV 88–102; and "The Strategy of the Plataiai Campaign," in Pritchett, *SAGT,* V 92–137, as well as John M. Fossey, *Topography and Population of Ancient Boiotia* (Chicago: Ares, 1988), I 101–32, and Emeri Farinetti, *Boeotian Landscapes: A GIS-Based Study for the Reconstruction and Interpretation of the Archaeological Datasets of Ancient Boeotia* (Oxford: Archaeopress, 2011), 179–90. For intelligent recent discussions of the battle itself, see Jean-Nicolas Corvisier, *La Bataille de Platées, 479 av. J.-C.* (Clermont-Ferrand: Lemme, 2010), 50–68, and Scott Rusch, *Sparta at War: Strategy, Tactics, and Campaigns, 550–362 BC* (London: Frontline Books, 2011), 55–66.

53. Age of Pausanias: Mary White, "Some Agiad Dates: Pausanias and His Sons," *JHS* 84 (1964): 140–52.

54. Fate of Masistius: Hdt. 9.20.1–25.1, Diod. 11.30.1–4, Plut. *Arist.* 14.

55. Size of Pausanias' army: Hdt. 9.28–30. Given the security risk involved, I find it hard to imagine that the Spartans would have deployed armed helots in large numbers in the ranks of the phalanx behind the Spartans serving as hoplites: cf., however, Peter Hunt, "Helots at the Battle of Plataea," *Historia* 46:2 (2nd Quarter 1997): 129 44, and *Slaves, Warfare, and Ideology in the Greek Historians* (Cambridge: Cambridge University Press, 1998), 32–39. At home, they took great care to keep the helots disarmed: Critias F37 (Diels-Kranz), Xen. *Hell.* 3.3.7. When abroad with them, the Spartans were always on their guard: *Lac. Pol.* 12.2.

56. Capacity of Mantineia and Elis: Thuc. 5.58.1, 65–74, 75.5; Diod. 12.78.4; Lys. 34.3. Failure to appear in a timely fashion: Hdt. 9.77.

57. Pausanias' deployment of army near Plataea: Hdt. 9.25.2–3, 28.1–30.1.

58. Mardonius redeploys opposite the Greeks: Hdt. 9.31–32.

59. Seers on both sides predict victory if on defense: Hdt. 9.33–38, Plut. *Arist.* 15.1. For an overview, see Michael A. Flower, *The Seer in Ancient Greece* (Berkeley: University of California Press, 2008).

60. Aristeides quells conspiratorial talk: Plut. *Arist.* 13.

61. Dispute about locus for oath of Plataea: Diod. 11.29.2–3, Lycurg. 1.81. If Peter Krentz is

right, as I think he may well be, *RO* no. 88.21–51 records not the oath said to have been sworn at Plataea, but an oath sworn before Marathon—which, in fact, provides a model for the later oath: see Chapter 4, at note 35, above. Oath somehow falsified or even an outright forgery: Theopompus of Chios *FGrH* 115 F153 with Hignett, *XIG,* 460–61; Michael A. Flower and John Marincola, "Appendix C: The 'Oath of Plataea.'" in Herodotus, *Histories: Book IX,* 323–25; and, more recently, Paul Cartledge, *After Thermopylae: The Oath of Plataea and the End of the Graeco-Persian Wars* (Oxford: Oxford University Press, 2013), who alludes to Michael Jung, *Marathon und Plataia: Zwei Perserschlachten als "Lieux de Mémoire" im Antiken Griechenland* (Göttingen: Vandenhoeck and Ruprecht, 2006), 282–95 (esp. 294, n. 242). Cf., however, Burn, *PG,* 512–15; Green, *XS,* 239–41; Meiggs, *AE,* 504–7; Peter Siewert, *Der Eid von Plataiai* (Munich: Beck, 1972); Barron, "The Liberation of Greece," 604; and Ira S. Mark, *The Sanctuary of Athena Nike in Athens: Architectural Stages and Chronology* (Princeton, NJ: American School of Classical Studies at Athens, 1993), 98–104, who believe the oath authentic. Herodotus less than fully informed concerning the Hellenes at Plataea: Ray Nyland, "Herodotos' Sources for the Plataea Campaign," *AC* 61 (1992): 80–97. For an ingenious attempt to make sense of the decision in the fourth century to record on an inscription the oath found at *RO* no. 88.21–51, see Giustina Monti, "Alessandro e il giuramento di Platea," *IncidAntico* 10 (2012): 195–207.

62. Mardonius' army too large for own good: Thuc. 6.33.5–6. Provisioning armies difficult: Hdt. 9.41.2. Shortages a threat: 9.45.2, Plut. *Arist.* 15.2–6.

63. Mardonius successfully attacks Greek supply train: Hdt. 9.38.2–39.2, 50, 51.4.

64. Persian cavalry harries Greeks on south side of Asopus: Hdt. 9.40.

65. Artabazus presses for pullback and bribery, Mardonius thinks own army superior: Hdt. 9.41.

66. See Nyland, "Herodotos' Sources for the Plataea Campaign," 80–97.

67. Elean and Mantineian troops on the way: Hdt. 9.77.

68. Alexander visits Greek camp: Hdt. 9.45, Plut. *Arist.* 15.2–6.

69. Cf. Burn, *PG,* 528 (to be read with ibid., 134, 342); Hignett, *XIG,* 316–17; and Lazenby, *DG,* 230–31, who are skeptical, with Green, *XS,* 259–60, who finds the tale told concerning Alexander's nocturnal visit plausible.

70. Mardonius has cavalry render springs of Gargaphia undrinkable: Hdt. 9.49.2–50.1.

71. Greek repositioning planned: Hdt. 9.50.1–51.4.

72. Renewed cavalry attacks on Greek center: Hdt. 9.52.

73. Decision to redeploy at night: Hdt. 9.51.3–4. Herodotus' narrative suggests disorder: 9.52–57. Battle dated to third or fourth of Boedromion: Plut. *Arist.* 19.8, *Cam.* 19.5, *Mor.* 349f. Mere sliver of a moon on 27–28 August: http://www.skyviewcafe.com/skyview.php.

74. Flight to sanctuary of Hera on outskirts of Plataea: Hdt. 9.52.

75. Report that Pausanias wants to leave Persians to Athenians, refuses duel with Mardonius: Hdt. 9.46–48.

76. Scholarly incredulity: cf. Hignett, *XIG,* 316–18, and Lazenby, *DG,* 231–32, with Burn, *PG,* 528–29, who is inclined to believe the tale. Green, *XS,* 260n, treats the question as academic.

77. Obstinacy of Amompharetus: Hdt. 9.53. Army made up of five *lóchoi:* Rahe, *SR,* Chapter 4.

78. Spartans quarreling, reputation for saying one thing and doing another: Hdt. 9.54–55.

79. Spartans march toward sanctuary of Eleusinian Demeter, Athenians in plain between Cithaeron foothills and Asopus ridge: Hdt. 9.56–57.

80. Spartans and Tegeans at sanctuary of Eleusinian Demeter: Hdt. 9.57.2–3. Location: Plut. *Arist.* 11.6–8 and *IG* VII 1670–71 with Pritchett, "Plataea Revisited," 103–10, and pl. 96–97. Athenians and Plataeans below in plain: Hdt. 9.56.2. Remainder of army on outskirts of Plataea: 9.52.1–53.1.

81. Persian cavalry pursues Lacedaemonians and Tegeans: Hdt. 9.57.3. Pausanias asks Athenian help, especially archers; Athenians in hoplite battle: 9.60.1–61.1.

82. Mardonius orders Persian footsoldiers to attack Lacedaemonians and Tegeans: Hdt. 9.58.1–59.1. Rest of barbarian troops follow in disorder: 9.59.2.

83. Simonides asserts Corinthians play prominent role: Plut. *Mor.* 872b–d, *POxy* 3965 F5 with Michael A. Flower and John Marincola, "Appendix A: Simonides' Poem on Plataea," in Herodotus, *Histories: Book IX,* 315–19. Defects of Herodotus' account: Nyland, "Herodotos' Sources for the Plataea Campaign," 80–97. In general, as Nyland points out, Herodotus appears to have relied on Theban, Macedonian, and perhaps Persian sources. He seems to have known very little about

the plans pondered by Pausanias and Aristeides and even less about the rest of the Hellenes. We now know a bit more about Simonides' treatment of the battle: see Simonides F1–22 (West²) with Deborah Boedeker, "Heroic Historiography: Simonides and Herodotus on Plataea," and Simon Hornblower, "Epic and Epiphanies: Herodotus and the 'New Simonides,'" in *The New Simonides: Contexts of Praise and Desire,* ed. Deborah Boedeker and David Sider (Oxford: Oxford University Press, 2001), 120–47.

84. Theban cavalry slaughter Megarians and Phleiasians: Hdt. 9.69.2.

85. Terrain near temple of Eleusinian Demeter unsuited to cavalry: Plut. *Arist.* 11.6–8.

86. Size of force commanded by Pausanias: Hdt. 9.61.2. Tegeans edge forward, omens become favorable: 9.62.1. Character and course of decisive battle: Aesch. *Pers.* 239–40, Hdt. 9.62.2–65.1, Plut. *Arist.* 18.1–19.2 read in light of Chapter 4, note 50, and Chapter 6, note 64, above; my discussion of the battle of Marathon in Chapter Four; and my brief defense of the traditional understanding of hoplite warfare in the Prologue, above. Persians, Medes, Cissians (and perhaps the other Iranians as well) wear body armor, carry *gérra* but not capacious *aspídes:* Hdt. 7.61.1, 62 with 5.49.3, 97.1. What Herodotus has in mind when he (9.62–63) calls the Persians *ánoploi* and *gumnêtes* is widely misunderstood: cf. Burn, *PG,* 538–39; Green, *XS,* 268–69; and Lazenby, *DG,* 242–43, with Hignett, *XIG,* 334–35; Barron, "The Liberation of Greece," 608; and Rusch, *Sparta at War,* 48, 62–63, who get it right.

87. Arimnestus or Aeimnestus, the leader of the Plataeans (Paus. 9.4.1–2), and Aristeides scout out Pantassa ridge: Plut. *Arist.* 11.5–8. Plataean bearing this name present with the Spartans at the actual battle: Hdt. 9.72.2. If this Arimnestus or Aeimnestus was, in fact, the worthy who brought down Mardonius, this was not his last service to Lacedaemon: 9.64.2. It is hardly likely to be an accident that, half a century after the battle at Plataea, there was in that *pólis* a man named Lakon son of Aeimnestus who served as *próxenos* of the Lacedaemonians: Thuc. 3.52.5 with George L. Huxley, Two Notes on Herodotos," *GRBS* 4:1 (1963): 5–8 (at 5–7). It is, of course, possible that in 479 there were two men at the battle named Aeimnestus—one, a Spartan and the other, a Plataean—and that they shared a name because they were hereditary guest-friends, as Gabriel Herman, "Epimenides and the Question of Omissions in Thucydides," *CQ* 39:1 (1989): 83–93 (at 92–93), suggests. But with William of Ockham I think it imprudent to multiply entities. At Lacedaemon, more glorious to win by trickery than in a pitched battle: Rahe, *SR,* Chapter 1, note 24. Spartans lure Mardonius into attack: Pl. *Laches* 191c with Burn, *PG,* 530–39; Green, *XS,* 260–65; and Barron, "The Liberation of Greece," 605–8. Lazenby, *DG,* 231–32, cannot imagine that any general at this time could have been so cunning.

88. Artabazus holds his troops back, flees toward Phocis when things go wrong: Hdt. 9.66, 89. Xerxes makes him satrap of Hellespontine Phrygia: Thuc. 1.129.1.

89. See Balcer, *PCG,* 283–89.

90. Thebans fight hard versus Athenians: Hdt. 9.67–68.

91. Athenians scale stockade wall; no more than three thousand Persian survivors: Hdt. 9.70.

92. Deployment of Persian fleet in Ionia: Hdt. 8.130, Diod. 11.27.1.

93. Fear as sentry: Hdt. 8.131–32.

94. Size of Leotychidas' fleet: Diod. 11.34.2. Samians summon help, claim Persian fleet in poor condition and Persian footsoldiers no match for Greek marines: Hdt. 9.90 read in light of 8.85.2–3.

95. Diodorus denies Phoenician ships in Aegean fleet: 11.19.4, 27.1. Persians build stockade, Tigranes and footsoldiers defend: Hdt. 9.96 read in light of 9.15.2–3, 70.

96. Leotychidas appeals to Ionians in Persian service to rebel: Hdt. 9.98. Marines land, Persians set up shields as barricade: 9.99–101.

97. Greek victory at Mycale: Hdt. 9.102.1–106.1 with Iain McDougall, "The Persian Ships at Mycale," in *"Owls to Athens": Essays on Classical Subjects Presented to Sir Kenneth Dover,* ed. E. M. Craik (Oxford: Clarendon Press, 1990), 143–49.

Epilogue

1. Xerxes at Sardis: Hdt. 8.117–19, 130, 9.96.2–3, 107.3. Fleet shifted from Cumae to Samos in the spring: Diod. 11.27.1. Tigranes ordered to stand guard over Ionia: Hdt. 9.96.2. Military colonists reinforce: Diod. 11.34.3. Triremes lugged ashore at Mycale: Hdt. 9.96.2–97.1.

2. Xerxes awaits news at Sardis: Hdt. 9.107.3. Artabazus makes report: 9.89.1–90.1. Xerxes

makes dispositions for defense of Anatolia: Diod. 11.36.7. Dispute whether heads for Susa or Ecbatana: Hdt. 9.108.2, Diod. 11.36.7. Installs new ruler of Cilicia: Hdt. 9.107.3. Sacks Didyma: Ctesias *FGrH* 688 F13.31, Strabo 14.1.5, Paus. 8.46.3. Fortifies citadel of Celaenae: Xen. *An.* 1.2.7–9.

3. Mede's statement to Dio Chrysostom: 11.148–49. Students of Achaemenid history are similarly inclined to underestimate the significance for Persia of Xerxes' defeat: see, for example, Waters, *AP,* 132.

4. Xerxes' loot: Plut. *Them.* 31.1; Arr. *An.* 3.16.7–8, 7.19.2; Paus. 1.8.5, 8.46.3. Xerxes' inscriptions: XPh (*PE* 7:88). The Achaemenid kings do not give up their claim to Ionia: Thuc. 8.5.5.

5. Plato on defective moral formation of Cambyses, Xerxes, and those of their successors reared by the women at court: *Leg.* 3.694c–696a. Scholars dismiss: for example, Briant, *CA,* 515–68. The pertinent passage from Plato's *Laws* is notably absent from *PE,* and the same can be said for the passage from Herodotus that I am about to discuss. With regard to the Greek testimony concerning the court, see the sensible observations of Lewis, *SP,* 21–22, and Llewellyn-Jones, *KCAP,* 96–148.

6. See Niccolò Machiavelli, *Il principe* 2–9, in Machiavelli, *Tutte le opere,* ed. Mario Martelli (Florence: Sansone Editore, 1971), 258–72.

7. Herodotus on Xerxes and his brother's wife and daughter: 9.108–12.

8. Xerxes assassinated: *PE* 7:90–91, Ctesias *FGrH* 688 F13.33–F14.34, Diod. 11.69. Justin attributes assassination to decline in majesty of his kingship: 3.1. Assassination in August 465: Matthew W. Stolper, "Some Ghost Facts from Achaemenid Babylonian Texts," *JHS* 108 (1988): 196–98.

9. Peloponnesian reaction to Ionian appeal: Hdt. 9.106.2–3. Cf. Diod. 11.37.1–2. Pledge to punish Medizers: Chapter 6, note 7, above.

10. At Athenian insistence, islanders taken into the alliance, bridges gone, Peloponnesians sail home: Hdt. 9.106.2–4, 114.1–2. For a somewhat confused account, see Diod. 11.37.1–4. Xanthippus and Athenians besiege and seize Sestos: Hdt. 9.114.2–121.1, Thuc. 1.89.2, Diod. 11.37.4–5. Dinner table of the Peiraeus: Arist. *Rhet.* 1411a14. See also Schol. Ar. *Eq.* 262. In 478, Hellenic League liberates Cyprus, captures Byzantium: Thuc. 1.94, Diod. 11.44.1–3.

11. Dead buried at Plataea, booty collected: Hdt. 9.80–81, 85. On the latter, see Margaret C. Miller, *Athens and Persia in the Fifth Century BC: A Study in Cultural Receptivity* (Cambridge: Cambridge University Press, 1997), 29–62.

12. Lacedaemonian, Tegean, Athenian dead: Hdt. 9.70.5. Megarians and Phleiasians mowed down by Theban cavalry: 9.69.2. Dispute over extent of Greek losses: Diod. 11.33.1, Plut. *Arist.* 19.5–7. Herodotus on empty burial mounds: 9.85.3. On the inadequacy of Herodotus' account with regard to the role played by those other than the Spartans, Tegeans, Athenians, Phleiasians, and Megarians, see Ray Nyland, "Herodotos' Sources for the Plataeai Campaign," *AC* 61 (1992): 80–97.

13. Bronze statue of Zeus at Olympia with list of cities participant: Hdt. 9.81.1, Paus. 5.23.1–3. Statue of Poseidon at isthmus, dedications at Delphi: Hdt. 9.81.1, Paus. 10.13.9. Couplet celebrating Pausanias' leadership erased, another inscribed honoring cities of Hellas with participant list: ML no. 27, Thuc. 1.132.2–3, Diod. 11.33.2.

14. Treatment of woman from Kos: Hdt. 9.76. Concubine of one of Xerxes' cousins: 4.43.1–2, 7.79. Refusal to mistreat corpse of Mardonius: 9.78–79. Mantineians and Eleans late, sent home, exile leaders: 9.77.

15. Oath of the Amphictyonic League: Aeschin. 2.115 with François Lefèvre, *L'Amphictionie pyléo-delphique: Histoire et institutions* (Athens: École française d'Athènes, 1998), passim (esp. 147–51). Note also Aeschin. 3.109–11.

16. Actual handling of Thebes in 479: Hdt. 9.86–88.

17. Juxtaposition of Spartan and Persian meals: Hdt. 9.82.

Author's Note and Acknowledgments

This book, intended as the first volume in a trilogy dedicated to the study of Sparta and its conduct of diplomacy and war from the archaic period down to the second battle of Mantineia, has—like its prelude *The Spartan Regime*—been a long time in gestation, and I have incurred many debts along the way. I was first introduced to ancient history by Donald Kagan when I was a freshman at Cornell University in the spring of 1968. The following year, I took with him a seminar on the ancient Greek city and another seminar on Plato's *Republic* with Allan Bloom. After graduating from Yale University in 1971, I read *Litterae Humaniores* at Wadham College, Oxford, on a Rhodes Scholarship. It was there that my ancient history tutor W. G. G. Forrest first piqued my interest in Lacedaemon.

I returned to Yale University in 1974 for graduate study, completed a dissertation three years later under the direction of Donald Kagan entitled *Lysander and the Spartan Settlement, 407–403 B.C.;* published two articles—one on Sparta, the other on the Achaemenid Persian army and the tactics it customarily employed; and then turned my attention to the history of self-government both ancient and modern. In the intervening years, I ordinarily taught a lecture course on ancient Greek history in the fall and a seminar on some aspect of that subject in the spring, and I frequently gave thought to Lacedaemon and to Persia, to questions of diplomacy and war, and to the work I had once done with George Forrest and Don Kagan. This book, like its prelude, is a belated acknowledgment of what I owe them both.

In one sphere of ancient history touched on repeatedly in this book, there has been a scholarly revolution. When I completed my dissertation more than thirty-eight years ago and made in print my one contribution to the study of Achaemenid Persia, it was already clear that those of us who studied classical antiquity knew a great deal less about that realm than could be known if we could only find a way to get adequate access to the pertinent Near Eastern evidence. In the interim, the situation has changed dramatically for the better. In the 1980s, an enterprising scholar at the University of Groningen named Heleen Sancisi-Weerdenburg began organizing an annual summer gathering that became known as the Achaemenid History Workshop. For the first time—thanks to her efforts and to those of scholars such as Amélie Kuhrt, Pierre Briant, David M. Lewis, Christopher Tuplin, Matthew Stolper, and Josef Wiesehöfer, to name only a few—those who were expert in the history of Egypt in the Achaemenid period and those who were expert in the history of Babylon in the same period joined together with archaeologists from the various lands once under Achaemenid Persian rule, with historians of ancient Greece and Israel, and with students of Egyptian hieroglyphic, Aramaic, Akkadian, Elamite, and Old Persian to compare notes.

The effect was electric. For the first time, those familiar with only some of the particulars began to get a sense of the whole, and this meant in turn that they began to reassess that which they thought they knew. Very little of the evidence that they discussed was, strictly speaking, new—but much of it was new to nearly all of those in attendance, for hitherto linguistic, geographical, and disciplinary barriers had stood in the way of their learning about it. Now, thanks to their cooperation, most of the important written evidence is available in English translation in a magnificent work edited by Amélie Kuhrt under the title *The Persian Empire: A Corpus of Sources from the Achaemenid Period.* To say that her labors, the endeavors of those who contributed to the annual *Achaemenid History,* and the achievement of David Lewis in his *Sparta and Persia* and of Pierre Briant in his monumental *Histoire de l'Empire Perse: De Cyrus à Alexandre*—have revolutionized the study of Achaemenid Persian history would be an understatement.

In these same years, another group of scholars, who were rightly more sensitive than most to the centrality of religion in ancient polities, devoted their attention to Zoroastrianism and to the relationship between that ancient Iranian religion and the political theology articulated in the inscriptions posted by Darius and the other Achaemenid kings. In the process, students of the subject such as Mary Boyce, Clarisse Herrenschmidt, Gregor Ahn, Prods Oktor Skarjærvø, and Bruce Lincoln further transformed the field.

In this book, to a degree that not even the notes can make clear, I am in the debt of these two groups of scholars. Thanks to them, I possess an advantage that A. R. Burn did not have half a century ago when he first published *Persia and the Greeks: The Defense of the West, 546–478 B.C.*, the work that my own most closely resembles. Thanks to them, a subject well-handled by Burn sorely needs revisiting.

I have also profited from the labors of J. S. Morrison, J. F. Coates, N. B. Rankov, Alec Tilley, and the others in Britain, in Greece, and elsewhere who, in the 1980s and 1990s, contributed to designing, building, launching, and to rowing and sailing in sea trials a reconstructed trireme that they named the *Olympias*. If we now have a better sense of trireme warfare than scholars did in the past, it is because of the labors and ingenuity of the practitioners of what has come to be called "experimental archaeology" who devised this project and lent a hand.

The material published in the Prologue is a restatement of the conclusions I draw in *The Spartan Regime*. The material in the prologue of that work and in its first two chapters had its origin in my dissertation and was first published in a more elaborated form in the first book of *Republics Ancient and Modern: Classical Republicanism and the American Revolution*. I am grateful to the University of North Carolina Press for giving me permission to reprint there the material that I summarize here.

I began working on this volume in the summer of 2009, when I was a visiting fellow at the Social Philosophy and Policy Center at Bowling Green State University, and I am grateful to Ellen Frankel Paul, Fred D. Miller, Jr., and Jeffrey Paul for hosting me there. On 23 November 2009, thanks to the kind invitation of Heinrich Meier, I was able to test my perceptions regarding Lacedaemon by delivering a lecture entitled "The Spartan Way of Life" to a learned audience at a *Vortragsabend* sponsored by the Carl Friedrich von Siemens Stiftung in Munich. The final revisions of this manuscript were completed while, with added assistance from the Earhart Foundation, I was a W. Glenn Campbell and Rita Ricardo-Campbell National Fellow at the Hoover Institution on the campus of Stanford University. My debts are many, and I am grateful for the support, advice, and encouragement I have received.

For the most part, this book was written in years in which I was teaching history at Hillsdale College. I am grateful to the Charles O. Lee and Louise K. Lee Foundation, which supports the chair I hold at the college; to the trustees of the college and its president, Larry Arnn; and to my colleagues and students there, who were always supportive. I owe a special debt to Dan Knoch, the director of the Hillsdale College Library; to Maurine McCourry, who arranged for the purchase of books; to Judy Leising and Pam Ryan, who handled interlibrary loan; to Henry Blyth, who gave me a copy of his dissertation almost forty years ago; and to Angela Lashaway and my colleague Patricia Bart, who helped me with the scanning of images. I am indebted as well to Michael M. Murray and Margaret C. Miller, to Matthew Stolper and the staff of the Oriental Institute at the University of Chicago, and to Andrew Ruddle and his colleagues at the Trireme Trust, who generously allowed me the use of illustrative images in their possession. I also owe a particular debt to one of my anonymous readers, who went over the manuscript with great care and made a multitude of helpful suggestions; to Bill Nelson, who made the maps; and to my copyeditor Noreen O'Connor-Abel, who read the manuscript with sympathy and care. Librarians, scholars who generously share their expertise and material in their possession, mapmakers, and those who read and edit manuscripts for academic presses are the unsung heroes of the academic world, and no one knows better than I how much we scribblers owe them.

Throughout the period in which this book was written, my four children were patient, and they and my wife kept me sane. From time to time, they brought me back to the contemporary world from classical antiquity, where, at least in my imagination, I may sometimes have seemed more at home than in the here and now.

Index